Key Terms and Concepts for Investigation

Key Terms and Concepts for Investigation provides students and practitioners with a compilation of concise, accurate articles on major topics pertaining to criminal, private, and military investigations. Each entry in this reference features a definition and then describes its function in investigation, including best practices and job characteristics. From financial crimes, digital forensics, and crime scene investigation to fraud, DNA, and workplace violence, this compilation helps students master investigation and offers seasoned investigators a resource to further their knowledge of recent developments in the field.

John J. Fay was a special agent of the U.S. Army Criminal Investigation Division (CID) and later the Director of the National Crime Prevention Institute at the University of Louisville. He has held security management positions in the petroleum industry, as well as teaching at the university level. He holds the Master of Business Administration degree from the University of Hawaii, and is a well-known and respected author of many books.

Jack Fay is an icon in the law enforcement and security management fields. He has pioneered the merger of law enforcement and security into a professional practice, eclipsing the highest ideals of both disciplines. Like his other books, this book provides a reasoned and logical process of value to investigators.

Sal DePasquale, *Criminal Justice, Texas A&M University*

Jack Fay's extensive experience and knowledge of law enforcement and criminal investigation is evident in this collection of common sense discussions and advice by him and many of the top-ranked professionals in the field.

Warren Cox, *Retired U.S. Army CID*
Special Agent and Retired Corporate Investigator

When Jack Fay and I were partnered he taught and guided me through many a difficult situation. In my experience, his knowledge of investigative practices is unmatched.

Harry Kinsella, *Former Special Agent,*
U.S. Army Criminal Investigation Division

Key Terms and Concepts for Investigation

A Reference for Criminal, Private, and Military Investigators

Edited by John J. Fay

Routledge
Taylor & Francis Group

NEW YORK AND LONDON

First published 2016
by Routledge
711 Third Avenue, New York, NY 10017

and by Routledge
2 Park Square, Milton Park, Abingdon, Oxon, OX14 4RN

Routledge is an imprint of the Taylor & Francis Group, an informa business

© 2016 Taylor & Francis

Library of Congress Cataloging in Publication Data
Key terms and concepts for investigation : a reference for criminal, private, and
   military investigators / edited by John J. Fay.
      pages cm
   Includes bibliographical references and index.
   1. Criminal investigation—Terminology.   2. Private investigators—
Terminology.   3. Investigations—Terminology.   I. Fay, John, 1934–
   HV8073.K439 2015
   363.2503—dc23
   2014049498

ISBN: 978-1-138-91465-0 (hbk)
ISBN: 978-0-323-29612-0 (pbk)

Typeset in Sabon and HelveticaNeue
by Apex CoVantage, LLC

CONTENTS

D

Workers' Compensation Fraud, 356

Workplace Violence, 357

Appendices

INTRODUCTION

The field of investigation is both wide and narrow. It is wide because investigation is a function performed in many sectors and at many levels. In the public sector are law enforcement investigators working at municipal, county, state, and government levels. Investigators in the government sector work cases that cross state borders and have national implications. Branches of the military services use investigators that enforce military law. In the sector called the "intelligence community" are investigators gathering and processing information for national defense purposes. In the private sector are investigators working alone or in agencies of varying size, or working for clients who run the gamut from individuals to international corporations.

The field of investigation can be seen as narrow because the nature of the work demands specialization. An investigator in a city police department may work burglary cases only; a sheriff's deputy may spend a career investigating crimes that occur in the county jail; a state patrol investigator may work highway-related deaths and nothing else; and an agent of a federal investigation bureau may have one job, such as an investigator of stock exchange fraud or a hostage negotiator. Specialization in the private investigation field is no exception. Private investigators tend to migrate to specialties such as background checking, surveillance, and forensic auditing.

Contributors to this book, all of whom are investigators, were asked to submit an article on a practice or concept representative of their area of expertise. A general structure was suggested. Tell the reader: What is it? How does it work? Why is it important? This structure provides a degree of uniformity and a focus on "nuts and bolts." Little will be found in this book that theorizes and postulates. A great deal will be found on how to investigate particular specialties across the board.

CONTRIBUTOR BIOGRAPHIES

JAMES F. BRODER, CPP

Mr. Broder, now retired, was a consultant to Confidential Management Services, Inc. in San Dimas, CA, and Marsh and McLennan, Inc. He is former special agent, U.S. State Department, and the former assistant and chairman of the Investigations Subcommittee, U.S. House of Representatives. He is a member of the American Society for Industrial Security International, Society of Former Special Agents of the FBI, and Association of Former Intelligence Officers, and he is a past member of the Congressional Staff Association of the U.S. House of Representatives and the International Association of Professional Security Consultants. He holds the Legion of Merit, Vietnam. Mr. Broder has a bachelor of arts degree in criminology from the University of California. He is the author of *Risk Analysis and the Security Survey* (Butterworth-Heinemann); *Investigation of Substance Abuse in the Workplace* (Butterworth-Heinemann); *Resources Control in Counter-Insurgency* (Agency for International Development, U.S. State Department); and "Case Management and Control of Undercover Operations for Business and Industry," which appeared in *Professional Protection*. He is a contributing author to the *Encyclopedia of Security Management* (Butterworth-Heinemann), and a contributing author to *Effective Security Management* (Butterworth-Heinemann).

JOSEPH P. BUCKLEY III

Joseph P. Buckley III is a forensic interviewer, detection of deception examiner, lecturer, and consultant. Mr. Buckley is president of John E. Reid and Associates in Chicago, Illinois. He has been with the firm since 1971. He is co-author of three books: *The Investigator Anthology*, *Criminal Interrogation and Confessions*, and *Essentials of The Reid Technique*, as well as numerous articles and papers. He is a contributing author to *The Encyclopedia of Police Science* and the *Encyclopedia of Security Management*. He is a member of the International Association of Chiefs of Police and the American Society for Industrial Security, as well as numerous other professional organizations. Mr. Buckley has lectured extensively to law enforcement, government, and business groups.

LEE DRESSELHAUS

Lee Dresselhaus is a retired police lieutenant who served honorably with the Slidell Police Department, a nationally accredited agency in Slidell, Louisiana. He served as a patrol officer, detective, shift supervisor, and shift commander. During and after Hurricane Katrina, he served as deputy patrol commander of operations in Slidell, a city on Lake Pontchartrain close to New Orleans.

During the Hurricane Katrina disaster period, he designed and instituted the American Red Cross "drive through" system of relief card distribution, which is now a national model. For his excellent service as a commander during this period, he received an Exceptional Service Award. In his last two years of police service, Mr. Dresselhaus worked in the Internal Affairs Office.

Mr. Dresselhaus is currently a criminal defense investigator. He has examined police investigations of several high-profile crimes and the prosecution of them by the district attorney's office. He is a court-certified expert in police procedure, operations, and investigations.

JOAN EARNSHAW

Joan Earnshaw has been a licensed private investigator since 1997; a certified hypnotherapist since 1990; a tax preparer since 1996; a registered tax return preparer since 2012; and an Internal Revenue Service agent from 1970 to 1996. Ms. Earnshaw is a trained IRS instructor and part-time adjunct instructor at San Juan College. In 1986, she was awarded a bachelor of science degree in accounting and business administration by Thomas Edison State College. For seven years, she performed volunteer services for VITA and served as a religious education teacher and program coordinator. Ms. Earnshaw has done research for the writing of *The Search for the Forgotten Thirty-Four Honored by the U.S. Marines, Unheralded by their Hometowns*.

JOHN J. FAY

Mr. Fay is a former special agent, U.S. Army Criminal Investigation Division (CID), 1965–1974; chief of Training Standards, Georgia Peace Officer Standards and Training Council (POST), 1974–1976; chief of Plans and Training, Georgia Bureau of Investigation (GBI), 1976–1979; director, National Crime Prevention Institute, University of Louisville, 1979–1980; director of Corporate Security, Charter Co, Jacksonville, FL, 1980–1984; security manager, Western Operations, British Petroleum, Houston, TX, 1984–1999; and an adjunct professor at North Florida University; University of Houston; DeKalb Technical College; and Texas A&M University. Mr. Fay is the published author of: *Approaches to Criminal Justice Training* (University of Georgia); *Police Dictionary* (Charles C. Thomas); *Handbook of Drug Abuse* (Charles C. Thomas); *Butterworth's Security Dictionary, Concepts and Practices* (Elsevier); *Encyclopedia of Security Management* (Elsevier); *Drug Testing* (Elsevier); *Model Security Policies, Plans and Procedures* (Elsevier); *Drug Free-Workplace* (Elsevier); *ASIS Dictionary* (American Society for Industrial Security); and *Contemporary Security Management* (Elsevier). Mr. Fay holds a bachelor of arts and science from the University of Nebraska at Omaha and a master of business administration from the University of Hawaii.

LARRY FENNELLY

Mr. Fennelly is an internationally recognized authority on crime prevention, security planning and analysis, physical hardware, alarms, lighting, site design, management practices, security liability and litigation, and criminal victimization. He is also an authority in crime prevention through environmental design (CPTED).

Prior to his recent retirement, Mr. Fennelly was employed by Apollo International Security where he was involved in the management and supervision of guard operations; development of security policies and procedures; and design of physical safeguards such as security fencing, lighting, and locking systems.

Early in his distinguished career, Mr. Fennelly was a deputy sheriff sergeant in the campus police department at Harvard University, Cambridge, Massachusetts. His duties included crime prevention and training of campus police officers.

He is the author and coauthor of several books published by Butterworth-Heinemann, a subsidiary of Elsevier, a global publishing house.

EUGENE FERRARO

Mr. Ferraro is the founder and chief ethics officer of Convercent, Inc. He has been a corporate investigator for over 30 years. Specializing in the investigation and prevention of workplace violence, employee dishonesty, fraud, harassment, discrimination, substance abuse, and ethical misconduct in the workplace, he has conducted thousands of investigations for employers (public and private) throughout the United States and elsewhere. His clients include some of the most successful corporations, law firms, and insurance companies in the country. His expertise includes loss prevention/asset protection and security management, negligent and inadequate investigation, negligent hiring, supervision, and retention. He is also a published author and book critic, and lectures frequently on the topics of workplace investigations, applicant screening, and employee misconduct prevention and intervention. He is board certified in both security and human resources management.

RICHARD J. HEFFERNAN, CISM

Richard J. Heffernan is the president of R.J. Heffernan and Associates, Inc. in Guilford, Connecticut. He is a member of the American Society for Industrial Security (ASIS); a member and past chairman for ASIS Information Asset Protection and Pre-Employment Screening Council; an author for ASIS Information Security Guidelines; an author for Information Assets Protection Manual; an expert witness representing ASIS concerning the Economic Espionage Act before the U.S. House Judiciary Committee; and a faculty member for ASIS Assets Protection Courses I and II. He is a recipient of the ASIS Standing Committee Chairman of the Year and ASIS President's Award. He is the chairman and principal investigator for ASIS Technology Theft Surveys and is a past member of the Advisory Board National Counterintelligence Center.

STACY JONES

Stacy Jones is the director of criminal investigations at Mission Possible Investigations. She is a published freelance writer and has close to 15 years of experience as an investigator. With master's degrees in forensic psychology and journalism, Ms. Jones specializes in crimes against persons and handles child abuse and neglect cases as well as cases of domestic violence, sexual assault, and stalking. Further, Ms. Jones has a specialty in forensic interviews with children and victims of violence and has worked nationally in the field of child abuse and child fatality.

Previous to Mission Possible Investigations, Ms. Jones was an executive director of a children's advocacy center in Kissimmee, Florida, where she trained and managed a multi-disciplinary team of providers responsible for the investigation, prosecution, and treatment of child physical and sexual abuse. She has also worked on various Department of Justice initiatives related to victims of violence in New York, Arkansas, and Florida. Ms. Jones has worked extensively within the criminal justice system and has been a team member on child fatality and elder fatality review teams nationally. In addition, Ms. Jones has been involved in investigations both for prosecution and the defense on the federal, state, and local levels.

Ms Jones has been working with Mission Possible Investigations since its inception and has been trained by the New York State Police, Arkansas State Police, Florida State Police, and Federal Bureau of Investigation in investigative and surveillance techniques. In addition, Ms. Jones is a certified law enforcement trainer related to sexual offences, domestic violence, stalking, and child abuse.

J. DAVID LEONARD

J. David Leonard is the president of Reveal Audio Services (2000–present), a company specializing in audio enhancement for legal and personal purposes, and Writeside Productions (1992–2003), which offers professional music production services including instrumentation, arranging, audio engineering, and mastering. Mr. Leonard is a member of the Audio Engineering Society (AES); associate member of Georgia Association of Professional Private Investigators (GAPPI); and a certified forensic consultant. He has earned a Forensic Audio Enhancement Certificate of Completion from Owen Forensic Services and Forensic Authentication of Digital Audio from National Center for Media Forensics, University of Colorado, Denver. He is the author of a multimedia presentation, "Understanding Audio Surveillance Issues." Mr. Leonard holds a bachelor of music degree from Florida State University.

LEON C. MATHIEU

Mr. Mathieu is an investigator consultant, Houston, TX; retired senior investigator, Corporate Security, Legal Department, Conoco, Inc., Houston, TX; former chief of investigations, The Charter Company, Jacksonville, FL; former detective, Metropolitan Dade County Police, Miami, FL; former insurance adjuster, Employer's Service Corporation, Coral Gables, FL; former instructor, Miami-Dade Community College, Miami, FL; member, American Society for Industrial Security; former chapter chairman, Jacksonville, Florida, Chapter of ASIS; member, International Society of Crime Prevention Practitioners; and member, Houston Metropolitan Criminal Investigators Association. He holds a bachelor of science degree from Florida International University and a master of science from Nova University.

VALERIE MCGILVERY

Valerie McGilvery holds a Texas property and casualty adjusters' license with government document fraud experience, insurance fraud investigation, and witness location and has performed countless complex investigations into all types of crime—from white-collar fraud to loss-of-life investigations. She has interviewed thousands of persons in matters of criminal and civil offenses.

Ms. McGilvery has worked for Nationwide Insurance and Farmers Insurance Group where she investigated insurance fraud pertaining to bodily injury, auto property damage, and homeowner property claims. She has 16 years of experience in locating people who are deliberately hiding and uncovering documentation to support facts in civil and criminal trial settings.

She has authored two books that describe the highly successful methods for locating people and conducting background searches. *Skip Trace Secrets* and *Background Check* have reached the top of the civil law book lists in the United States. She currently owns Asset Management Service, which is located in Conroe, Texas. Ms. McGilvery conducts seminars that teach the art of pretexting and skip tracing to legal professionals and recovery and investigative associations nationwide.

Ms. McGilvery has also consulted with *Psychology Today* on the topic of pseudocide and provided written training material for Allstate Insurance, Safe Auto, and numerous other automotive dealer magazines and investigative online publications.

JIMMIE N. MESIS, LPI

When the public needs help, they often call upon a private investigator. When PIs need help or specific direction, they call Jimmie Mesis. His international reputation as an experienced and talented investigator, as well as a successful businessman, and his passion for the investigative profession for more than three decades have made him a frequently requested consultant, instructor, and conference speaker.

Jimmie started his career as a private investigator after serving as a trilinguist with the United States Marine Corps, S-2 Intelligence Unit. Jimmie has been court recognized as an expert witness in the area of private investigative practices, surveillance, and covert video technology. He is also an expert in finding people and gained national recognition as a featured investigator for the History Channel television series *Operation Reunion*, on which he located and reunited soldiers who had not seen each other since the battlefields of the Korean and Vietnam Wars given nothing more than the subjects' last names. He has also been featured in the FX television series *P.I.* and as a guest on various radio and television shows, including CNN's *Larry King Live* and *ABC World News Tonight*. He is often quoted by the Associated Press, USA Today, Wall Street Journal, and many other national media outlets.

His career as a private investigator has been uniquely diverse. He and his investigator wife own and run several investigative related companies, including *PI Magazine*, the only international print trade magazine for private investigators; PI Bookstore.com, the largest single-source supplier of investigation-titled books; PI Gear.com, a supplier of surveillance equipment for PIs and law enforcement; and his latest venture, PI Directory.com, the largest free directory of private investigators in the world.

Jimmie currently serves as an advisory board member to the University of Northern Texas–Professional Development Unit. He has lectured at several colleges and universities and has provided instruction to PIs, police detectives, and U.S. postal inspectors on the subject of covert video surveillance. He has also provided instruction to more than 11,000 private investigators throughout the world at various conferences, seminars, and mentoring programs, as well as through private consulting.

Jimmie is the recipient of both a New Jersey State Senate and State Assembly Proclamation in recognition for his investigative accomplishments as well as numerous professional awards including: New Jersey Licensed Private Investigators Association, Investigator of the Year; National Association of Investigative Specialists, Speaker of the Year; the Hal Lipset Award for Investigative Excellence presented by the World Association of Detectives; and a Leadership Award, a Duffy Award, and a Wunder Award by the National Council of Investigative and Security Services, which are their highest honors. Other awards include a Special

Achievement Award from the World Investigators Network, a Person of the Year Award from the Professional Association of Wisconsin Licensed Investigators, and many other recognition awards from various investigative organizations throughout the United States.

Jimmie is a former director and past legislative chairman for NCISS and is an honorary life member of the Texas Association of Licensed Investigators, the Georgia Association of Professional Private Investigators, and the World Association of Professional Investigators based in London, England.

J. "TRIPP" MITCHELL

Mr. Mitchell's career spans many years in public law enforcement, security consulting, and private investigation. His early start in loss prevention and asset protection for two major Georgia retailers set the tone for his long-term investigative career. After graduating from the police academy, he began his career as a police officer; he served as a patrol officer, field training officer, and detective. In 1997, he became a criminal investigator with the state court prosecutor's office and was eventually promoted to chief investigator. Those duties included being the chief executive of a law enforcement agency that is recognized by the Georgia Peace Officer and Standards Council (POST) and as daily manager of the criminal investigations division. In 2003, Governor Sonny Purdue appointed him to serve on the Georgia Board of Private Detective and Security Agencies (GBPDSA). This board regulates licensed security companies as well as licensed private detectives in the state of Georgia. At 33 years of age, he was the youngest member ever to be appointed to the board, where he served as chairman and vice chairman. He was reappointed to the board by Governor Nathan Deal; he serves on the education, training, and testing committees. Mr. Mitchell is a past president of the Georgia Association of Professional Private Investigators and served that association in many areas. Other memberships include the Georgia Association of Chiefs of Police, Association of Threat Assessment Professionals (ATAP), and American Society for Industrial Security (International), in which he holds the designation of Certified Protection Professional (CPP). Mr. Mitchell is certified as a training instructor by both POST and the GBPDSA. He received his degree in Criminal Justice from Mercer University and holds a master's degree in Public Administration from Columbus State University. He is also a graduate of the Georgia Law Enforcement Command College. Throughout his career, he has earned certifications and received extensive training in investigative coursework such as homicide, psychological profiling, stalking, criminal investigation, security management, threat assessment, and private investigation training. Mr. Mitchell is an adjunct criminal justice instructor at various colleges and technical schools and a general instructor at many regional police academies. He teaches a variety of courses that relate to law enforcement, management, and subjects in the security and investigation fields. He also serves as an advisory board member for the Fulton County Police Academy in Atlanta, Georgia, and participates in many criminal justice advisory capacities.

WEEDEN ROCKWELL NICHOLS

Weeden Rockwell Nichols is a former special agent, USAF Office of Special Investigations (OSI), and special agent, Army Criminal Investigation Division (CID). His career as a military investigator included five years in the Far East and four years on the faculty of the U.S. Army Military Police School. His military investigative experience includes experience in crime prevention, including service as chief of a crime prevention section in a large investigative unit and service as a headquarters staff officer with responsibility for coordinating U.S.

Army logistics security efforts in the Republic of Korea. After retirement from the military, Mr. Nichols was employed for five years by the state of Kansas as a field auditor. He has been an administrator for two nonprofit corporations and has been part-owner and chief financial officer for three small businesses (Great Plains Bicycle Shop, Inc.; Bike Tek, Inc.; and Great Plain Bread Company, Inc.). He has been an adjunct faculty member of Jacksonville (Alabama) State University, teaching crime prevention and retail security, and of Marymount College of Kansas, teaching economics.

Mr. Nichols's education includes a BA in economics (Park College, now Park University); BS in accounting, with an additional major in business administration (Marymount College of Kansas, now defunct); and MA in public administration (University of Oklahoma). Mr. Nichols has many other interests as well. From 1975 to 1991, he was a regionally successful age-group athlete, competing as a foot racer, bike racer, dual athlete, and triathlete, before becoming physically disabled. Although no longer able to compete, he remains an active cyclist. He is a competitive bridge player and American Contract Bridge League (ACBL) Bronze Life Master. He owns a Piper Cherokee 180 and holds a commercial pilot certificate with instrument and seaplane ratings, with over 3,800 hours pilot-in-command time. Mr. Nichols is a cooperating artist (photography) in the Mesilla Valley Fine Arts Gallery, Mesilla, New Mexico (www.nicholsfinephotos.us). He is married to Rosalie S. Nichols, PhD, Professor Emeritus, Fort Hays (Kansas) State University. They have five children and 15 grandchildren. Weeden and Rosalie have retired to Las Cruces, New Mexico. He receives mail at redolaf1@gmail.com.

KELLY E. RIDDLE

Mr. Riddle is president of Kelmar Global Investigations and has more than 35 years of investigative experience. He earned a bachelor of science degree in criminal justice from the University of North Alabama. He was chosen "PI of the Year" by the National Association of Investigative Specialists, and PI Magazine named Mr. Riddle the "Number One PI in the United States." He is a designated expert in surveillance, insurance investigations, nursing home abuse, and computer investigations. He was chosen as "One of the Top 25 PIs of the 20th Century." Mr. Riddle is a Texas certified investigator and is also past president (2010–2012) of the Texas Association of Licensed Investigators (TALI) and served on TALI's Board of Directors (2007–2010). He also served on the Board of Directors of the Freedom of Information Foundation of Texas. Mr. Riddle is a member of the Public Relations committee, Council of International Investigators, and membership chair of the San Antonio Chapter of the American Society for Industrial Security International (ASIS). He is a founding board member and board advisor for the nonprofit organization "Can You Identify Me." He was the recipient of the 2013 Hudgins-Sallee award, the highest recognition presented by the Texas Association of Licensed Investigators. Mr. Riddle is the author of ten books and more than 40 articles. He has been the guest speaker at more than 400 events and has appeared on national TV and radio and in newspapers. His law enforcement experience included SWAT team member, training officer, emergency medical technician, evidence technician, arson investigator, juvenile specialist, and traffic investigator. Mr. Riddle is the founder and president of the PI Institute of Education, as well as the Association of Christian Investigators, an association having more than 1000 members in the United States and in 19 countries. He is the founder of the Coalition of Association Leaders, an association comprised of past and present board members from state, national, and international associations. Mr. Riddle is a member of AIS, TALI, ASIS, NALI, FAPI, LAPI, USAPI, ACI, NAAA, PICA, WIN, NLLI, CTIB, CLEAR, IOPIA, TIDA, CII, and ASSIST.

KEVIN J. RIPA

Kevin J. Ripa is the owner of Computer Evidence Recovery, Inc. and past president of the Alberta Association of Private Investigators. He is a former member, in various capacities, of the Department of National Defense, serving in both foreign and domestic postings. He is now providing computer forensic services to law enforcement departments, Fortune 500 companies, and the legal community. He has consulted and directly assisted in many complex cyberforensics and hacking response investigations around the world.

Mr. Ripa is a respected and sought-after individual for his expertise in information technology investigations. He is a court-certified expert witness and has testified on numerous occasions at various judicial proceedings. He has also provided training and lectures to companies and law enforcement agencies around the world. Mr. Ripa has authored numerous articles that are currently in circulation and chapters in professional manuals, books, and texts on the subjects of computer security and forensics.

GREG ROEBUCK

Greg Roebuck is a regional director of Criminal Justice Associates, a multistate licensed firm that provides investigative, security management, and lie detection services to companies and government agencies. Mr. Roebuck has 20 years of public and private investigative experience. He is a specialist in cybervetting and social media investigations. He has a computer science technical education from IBM Systems Science Institute, Armonk, NY; criminal justice technology AS degree, Seminole State College, Sanford, FL; and a bachelor of arts degree in criminal justice administration, Columbia College, Columbia MS. He is a NITV Certified CVSA Examiner. Professional memberships include the International Association of Chiefs of Police, American Society of Industrial Security, National Association of Computer Voice Stress Analysts, International Association of Crime Analysts, and Association of Certified Fraud Examiners.

KEITH ROSENTHAL, CEP

Mr. Rosenthal is and has been a certified evidence photographer, analytical forensic photographer, pre trial photographic consultant, optical micro photographer, and expert witness. He has provided services in matters involving photographic documentation, crime scene lighting reconstruction, photographic and lighting analysis, and compliance issues related to police photography standard operating procedures.

Mr. Rosenthal has more than 40 years of accreditation as a professional photographer and presently owns and operates Keith Rosenthal Photography (keithrosenthal.com and keith@keithrosenthal.com). In 2010, he earned the Certified Evidence Photographer designation from the Professional Photographer Certification Commission, which represents the highest level of technical excellence in the professional photography profession. Mr. Rosenthal is one of less than 50 photographers worldwide to earn this distinction. At various times from 1966 to the present, Mr. Rosenthal has provided training, consulting, and expert witness services to the California Attorneys for Criminal Justice, Silverado Resort, Napa Valley Show & Gallery, Robert Mondavi Winery, Inglenook Winery, Vintage 1870, Van Nuys Air National Guard, Pacific Bell, and the Transamerica Corporation. On April 15, 2013, he appeared on the Nancy Grace television show to speak on the photographic aspects of the Jodi Arias murder investigation.

Mr. Rosenthal has received instruction and training at *Look* magazine, military service with the Air National Guard, Sirchie Fingerprint Laboratories, and various professional seminars and conferences. He holds membership in the Evidence Photographers International Council (EPIC), California State Division of the International Association for Identification (CSDIAI), International Association for Identification (IAI), California Attorneys for Criminal Justice (CACJ), and Forensic Expert Witness Association (FEWA). Mr. Rosenthal has been a speaker at numerous conferences and has authored several professional articles. He has testified as an expert witness at trials held at the Placer County Superior Court, Los Angeles Superior Court, and Alameda County Superior Court.

C. JOSHUA VILLINES, MA, CPP, ICPS

After 17 years as an investigator, consultant, and trainer, C. Joshua Villines became the executive director of the Human Intelligence Group in 2011 so he could focus specifically on his areas of expertise in training, crime prevention, and the various aspects of human intelligence collection. Joshua first learned the basic skills of an investigator from his father, John C. Villines. By the time he was fifteen, Joshua was working in the office of his father's detective and security agency. He would go on to work in every role within the company, from uniformed security to executive protection—first as a junior employee and eventually as a supervisor. The army provided Joshua the opportunity to grow as an investigator and a leader. He is a graduate of the Defense Language Institute (Russian), the U.S. Army Intelligence Center and School (Interrogation), the U.S. Army Airborne School, the British Joint-Services Interrogation Course, the Primary Leadership Development Course (honor graduate), and the Basic Noncommissioned Officer's Course. Joshua held a top-secret (SSBI) clearance and earned DoD certification as a Russian (3/2+) and a Spanish (3/3) linguist. Joshua's civilian education has dovetailed and further enhanced his work. He holds a BA cum laude from Berry College, an MDiv from Mercer University, and an MA from Vanderbilt University. He has also reached the candidacy stage for a PhD from Vanderbilt University, and he shoehorns his ongoing dissertation work into his other duties as best he can. Joshua is certified in Georgia as a professional law enforcement instructor, specializing in interviews and interrogation, and he is also certified in Georgia as both a classroom instructor and a firearms instructor for private security and private detectives. Joshua holds the Certified Protection Professional (CPP) certification from ASIS International and the International Crime Prevention Specialist (ICPS) designation from the International Society of Crime Prevention Practitioners. As the executive director of the Human Intelligence Group, Joshua provides the overall vision for the organization. He sets the standards for all training curricula used by their instructors, provides general oversight for ongoing intelligence missions, provides threat assessment and crisis mitigation consultation for public agencies, and develops both qualitative and quantitative research methodologies. Joshua is deeply committed to providing the highest level of training to investigators in the public and private sectors, and he spends as much time as possible serving as an instructor in the classroom, on the range, and in the field.

JOHN C. VILLINES, MS, ICPS, CPP

Mr. Villines has dedicated his adult life to security, investigations, and crime prevention. He is the founder of John C. Villines LLC and has maintained a company license (security and investigations) in Georgia for approximately 25 years. The original business was formed in 1979 to provide crime prevention assessments, consulting services, training, and investigations for government entities, shopping centers, retail businesses, and other commercial operations. It evolved into a more comprehensive operation—providing a wider range of services, including: expert testimony; crime prevention analysis; CPTED (Crime Prevention through Environmental Design) consultations; training seminars; risk, threat, and vulnerability assessments; and other specialized investigative and consulting services. The client base has expanded to include governmental agencies at the local, state, and federal levels; Fortune 100 corporations; multinational companies; financial services institutions; educational facilities; and other businesses and individuals.

His academic background includes a bachelor of science in urban studies, with a field of concentration in criminal justice; a master of science in security management; and postgraduate course work in quantitative methods at Harvard.

His professional designations include: Certified Protection Professional, ASIS International, International Crime Prevention Specialist, International Society of Crime Prevention Practitioners, National Crime Prevention Specialist (Level II; Advanced Certification), and the National Crime Prevention Association.

His professional affiliations include the American Society of Criminology, Academy of Criminal Justice Sciences, Association of Threat Assessment Professionals, International Society of Crime Prevention Practitioners, and International Association of Crime Analysts. Appointed by Governor Sonny Perdue to serve on the Georgia Board of Private Detective and Security Agencies in 2003, Mr. Villines was elected by his colleagues as chair of that board from 2004 to 2007 and again in 2010. Mr. Villines developed the Crime Prevention Specialist training program for the State of Georgia and served as a POST-certified instructor for advanced and specialized training of police officers. He is also board certified as an instructor for security and investigations. As a consultant, Mr. Villines has been retained in hundreds of cases throughout the United States and has provided services to private industry, law firms, the United States Government, law enforcement agencies, community organizations, and others.

A

AFFIDAVIT

An affidavit is a document used to support or justify issuance of a warrant, such as a search warrant or arrest warrant, and is made under oath. The affidavit is presented by an agent of a government to a person authorized by law to issue the warrant, such as a judge, and gives details sufficient to conclude that a crime was committed and that a warrant should be issued. The details in the affidavit provide what is called probable cause.

The warrant is an order. It compels the agent to do what the warrant says to do, such as make an arrest, conduct a search, or seize property. A warrant is sought by and carried out by an agent of a government. A nongovernment investigator does not write the affidavit, request a warrant be issued, or carry out the warrant. An investigator working outside of the government can, however, provide information to an agent of government; if the agent believes the information constitutes probable cause, the agent will prepare the affidavit and submit it to the issuing authority as a request for issuance of the warrant. A nongovernment investigator cannot carry out or participate in the execution of the warrant but can be an observer.

John J. Fay, *Encyclopedia of Security Management,* second ed., Butterworth-Heinemann, Burlington, MA, 2007, pp. 239–240.

AGENCY STAFFING

The recruitment and selection of job candidates should correspond to specific and well-established criteria such as where the position sits on the chain of command, pay or salary and amount, number of subordinates, spending authority, job functions and duties, and knowledge and skills the incumbent must possess.

A candidate for a position should be told what the position entails. The agency should assess candidates to determine who does and who does not meet the requirements of the job. A tool commonly used for making an assessment is the position description form. It reflects the nature of the position and the competencies required to effectively carry out the duties of the position.

Depending on size, a private investigation agency can have several job positions:

- Person in charge
- Supervisor of investigators
- Investigators
- Secretaries/typists/clerks
- Evidence custodian
- Equipment custodian/repairman

Positions differ according to:

- Level of authority
- Pay grade
- Number of persons supervised

- Spending authority
- Duties performed
- Knowledge and skills required

The expected behavior and performance of agency employees should be stated verbally and in writing at the time of hire and periodically thereafter. In addition, an employee should acknowledge and agree to abide by agency rules, which should be presented to the employee in permanent writing of some type such an employee's handbook. Of special importance are agency policies regarding:

- Harassment and discrimination of all types
- Workplace violence
- Substance abuse
- Compliance with laws
- Ethics
- Working hours
- Safety
- Personal appearance and demeanor
- Adherence to supervisory instructions

The agency head may choose to express rules and policies in a single, overarching document that addresses the full range of issues.

John J. Fay, *Encyclopedia of Security Management*, second ed., Butterworth-Heinemann, Burlington, MA, 2007, pp. 40–47.

AGGRAVATED ASSAULT

Aggravated assault has two components. First, the defendant must commit an assault. Second, the assault must be committed with intent to murder, rape, or rob or be committed with a deadly weapon.

In some jurisdictions, intent may be general, such as "with intent to commit a felony." Another element might be added, such as "discharging a firearm from within a motor vehicle toward another person without legal justification."

Assault with a Deadly Weapon

A deadly weapon is a weapon that is deadly as a matter of law or an object that when used offensively is likely to or actually does result in serious bodily injury.

It is not necessary for the state to admit into evidence the deadly weapon used in an aggravated assault case.

Aggravated assault with intent to rob is included in armed robbery; in other words, they are merged into a single crime. However, if the assault is committed prior to the robbery, both crimes can be charged separately.

Wayne W. Bennett and Karen M. Hess, *Criminal Investigation*, Wadsworth Publishing, Belmont, CA, 1998, p. 306.

ARREST PROCEDURES

Authority

For an arrest to be lawful, it must be founded on a legal authority. Law enforcement officers, and a very few other persons who hold special status, are granted by law to make arrests. Except in very few jurisdictions and in very few circumstances, a private investigator does not possess arrest authority. Two examples of such circumstances would be present when:

- The PI has been hired to protect a certain property or premises and the arrestee has gained access to the property or premises without authority and refuses to leave
- A person is in possession of stolen property or contraband (illegal drugs, counterfeit money, prohibited firearms, etc.)

When a PI is also a law enforcement officer, arrests made by the PI are made under authority granted to law enforcement.

Under common law, a person can make an arrest when a serious crime has been committed in the person's presence. This procedure is called a "citizen's arrest." It is not an arrest made under authority of statutory law. A question arises here: what does "serious" mean? What is serious to one person may not be serious to other persons. The question can be settled when the word "serious" is replaced by "felony."

Call the Police Immediately

At the very earliest moment when a citizen's arrest is proper and needed, the investigator should call the police. The police should be on the way before an attempt is made to perform the arrest. This is both a matter of self-protection (in case the individual responds with violence) and a matter of precluding an accusation of unlawful detention. An investigator can't be held responsible if the police are slow in responding, but the investigator can be faulted for not calling the police quickly.

It is a common mistake to engage in a talking mode with an individual without first calling for police assistance. The time spent talking can be regarded as time the individual spent being detained. If time spent talking is unreasonably long, unlawful detention can be inferred. Talking is fine and is often a good way to calm an agitated individual. The best to be expected is for the investigator and the individual to be in a talking mode when the police arrive.

- When the police arrive, describe why a citizen's arrest was justified.
- Provide details of the offense that was committed.
- Give to the police all evidence of the offense committed.
- Give to the police all weapons taken from the individual's possession.
- Obtain a receipt for all items given to the police.
- Obtain copies of all reports prepared by the police at the scene.
- If possible, take photographs of the scene.

Evaluate the Situation

Before the police arrive, the investigator should avoid making an arrest if the arrest can be made by the police. The decision to arrest first and then call the police should be based on observable facts such as:

- The individual will be gone before the police can arrive.
- Stolen property will be hidden or removed before the police can arrive.
- The individual is damaging or destroying someone else's property.
- The individual is assaulting someone.

If the above circumstances (or circumstances like them) are not present, the correct course of action is to call the police, remain at the scene, observe what is continuing to happen, and—if possible—record facts as they occur. No matter what, the police should be called.

Another circumstance for the PI to consider is the probable capacity of the individual to elude or resist arrest. For example, is the individual in a motor vehicle, ready to flee? In possession of a weapon? Are accomplices nearby? Will an arrest or an attempt to arrest place anyone in danger?

The Approach

Apart from the obvious need to exercise caution and be self-protective, the PI should be prepared to state three facts to the individual:

- The individual has committed a certain crime.
- The individual is under arrest.
- The arrest is a citizen's arrest.

The use of force to make an arrest is the last-step option. Physical confrontation might be avoided by:

- Projecting an image of calmness and professionalism

- Getting into a thinking versus emotional mode
- Avoiding an appearance of intimidation
- Keeping hands visible
- Being assertive
- Stating intentions clearly
- Refusing to react to verbal abuse

Look, Listen, and Touch

- The manner of making an arrest is determined by what is seen. Is the individual holding a weapon?
- Are there indications that a weapon is hiding in the individual's clothing or in a place that is accessible nearby?
- Has the individual said he has a weapon or has a person nearby said the same?
- Has the individual made threatening statements? For example, "Don't come closer or I'll kill you."

If the individual offers no resistance to arrest, the PI can do one or two things or both. Both involve touching, touching raises tension, tension can lead to resistance, and resistance can lead to violence.

Touching is unavoidable and should be held to a minimum. It is unavoidable because searching for a weapon on the individual's person is necessary for self-protection and protection of others. Touching is also involved when handcuffing is necessary, such as when there is a chance the individual will resort to violence or attempt to run away. Excessive touching or rough touching can result in resistance.

Reasonable Force

When attempting to overcome an individual's resistance, the investigator can apply force but only if the degree of force is reasonable under the circumstances. In this context, simple refusal to follow instructions does not justify striking the individual.

Although it would be reasonable to pursue a fleeing individual, it is not always advisable to do so. A person who flees is action oriented, which suggests physical resistance if caught. Also, the chase may take the investigator away from the location that has been reported to the police.

Reasonable force is the degree of force necessary to carry out an arrest. Clear examples of excessive force are punching an unarmed and unresisting person, striking with a solid object, or applying a chokehold.

A chokehold is a hold around the neck, usually done with a rigid item. Pressure applied around the neck can cause the person to pass out and die from asphyxiation or a heart attack. It can also break the hyoid bone, which often results in death. A chokehold is considered a form of deadly force, not unlike the use of a firearm.

A person who flees after escaping immediate control should not be shot at. The reasons are:

- Innocent persons can be injured or killed.
- The individual no longer poses a threat.

A Four-Step Procedure

The objective is to make an arrest that does not use force to any degree, but avoidance of physical resistance is not always possible. This objective can be met by following a four-step approach.

Professional Bearing. A nonforceful arrest can be made when an appearance of professional bearing is projected. The impression conveyed to the individual will influence what happens next. If the individual's response is to resist, the next step should be followed.

Verbal Commands. At this level, appearance and bearing are augmented with an advisement that the individual has committed an offense and is being placed under citizen's arrest.

Physical Contact. Level three is the transition to restraint. If the individual responds with physical resistance, the investigator's response should be self-protection coupled with an attempt to subdue the individual and extend the length of confrontation in order to give the police time to arrive.

Force. At this level, the investigator's responses to violence must be strictly defensive in nature. The investigator may have no alternative except to use force—and only that degree of force needed to overcome resistance.

Search

An individual should be searched only as needed for self-protection and protection of others. For example, search would be appropriate when there is a visible indication of a weapon, such as a suspicious bulge in clothing. Another would be a declaration from a witness who says the individual has a weapon.

The purpose of a search is to discover and confiscate anything that could be used to injure or kill. A purpose is not to find evidence of the offense committed by the individual.

A search incidental to arrest is called a "frisk search" because it is a pat-down of clothing. The mechanics of making the search require that the person conducting the search:

- Stand behind the individual.
- Instruct the individual to stretch arms to the side of the body.
- Run hands over the outside of the individual's body.
- Pat the clothing, especially in areas where a weapon might be concealed, such as around the chest, waist, and above the ankles.
- Remove anything that feels like a weapon.
- If something is felt that might be illegal to possess, such as a vial of crack or a bag of marijuana, it should remain as is.

Inform the police when they take custody of the individual.
- Probe inside a pocket only if the pat-down indicates the pocket may contain a weapon.
- If the inside of a pocket is probed, the investigator should be cautious of anything that could break the skin, such as a hypodermic syringe or a razor blade.

Deadly Force

If resistance escalates to the point that the individual has an imminent capacity to injure or kill, and demonstrates intent to do so, the investigator has no choice except neutralize the individual.

- Imminent means right then, not before or later.
- Neutralize means to cancel or remove the individual's capacity to injure or kill.
- Capacity is demonstrated by brandishing a knife or firearm or other lethal weapon. A fist or a stick is not a lethal weapon.
- Intent is displayed by an overt act such as pointing a weapon or charging with a knife. Statements like, "I'm going to kick your butt" and "Get out of my way or you'll be sorry" are not convincing as to intent.

Document the Arrest

The basic facts of the arrest must be recorded:

- What happened
- Who did what
- When it happened
- Where it happened
- How it happened
- Why it happened
- The time the police were called
- The time the police arrived

- Identity of the individual arrested
- Identities of witnesses
- What was found/confiscated
- Injuries sustained
- Property damaged or stolen
- Persons notified

Arrests are problematic because they can be difficult to carry out and can result in the filing of charges, such as unlawful detention, false imprisonment, brutality, and violation of constitutional or civil rights.

Wayne W. Bennett and Karen M. Hess, *Criminal Investigation*, Wadsworth Publishing, Belmont, CA, 1998, pp. 104–105.

ARSON INVESTIGATION

Arson Defined

Arson is a crime of intention. The intention is to damage a structure, whether occupied or vacant. A structure can be a dwelling place, garage, underside of a bridge, tree house, building, railroad car, bus, aircraft, watercraft, or any other place where humans dwell, even for a short period of time.

A dwelling house can be any structure in which a person or persons reside, work, or occupy temporarily or regularly.

Insurance

A structure that has been damaged or destroyed by fire or explosion, as the result of arson, is usually insured. The insurance policy owner is usually motivated by a need or desire to convert the physical structure to money. Other motives can include intent to defeat, prejudice, or defraud the rights of another, such as a co owner, investor, friend, relative, or spouse.

Motive is not an element of a crime, but knowing the motive is a first step in solving the crime. Any person who would benefit from damage or destruction of a structure or its contents is a logical suspect.

Elements of the Crime

Arson has three elements. First is damage or destruction by fire or explosion. Second is the intent to destroy or damage with knowledge that destruction or damage will result. Third is a lack of the owner's consent.

In the absence of any one of the three elements, a charge of arson cannot be sustained. It might appear that remuneration will not be afforded to the owner of a destroyed or damaged structure, thus removing the third element, but the investigation should not stop there. The truth may be that a separate person who is not known had something to gain, had advance knowledge that arson would be committed, and gave consent, implicit or otherwise.

Premeditation

Premeditation is a reflection of intent, which is one of the three elements of the crime. Intent is demonstrated by any number of facts, and it is the investigator's job to discover them. For example, evidence that:

- A fire alarm system, which had usually been turned on, had been turned off just before the incident occurred.
- A fire control or fire suppression system did not activate.
- Material or property had been removed from the structure just before the incident had occurred. Also of interest should be removal of personal property such as family photos, trophies, golf clubs, and other items that the owner did not want to lose.
- Doors and windows had been closed or locked to delay and deter efforts to extinguish the fire or opened to facilitate air movement and migration of the fire.
- The inflow or outflow ducts of a ventilating system had been reversed so that the fire could move freely into or out of particular areas within the structure.

- A delay in notifying the fire department occurred.
- Flammable materials were in the building at the time of the fire when such was not the case prior to the fire.

Intent

Intent is essential to proving the offense of arson; when intent is malicious, the crime takes on a more serious character. Malice is shown when the arsonist harms the property of another with intent to inflict serious harm. In some cases, the harm to another has no relation to financial gain; the purpose is to satisfy a personal agenda. Revenge, hatred, jealousy, prejudice, and intimidation can be agenda items.

Intent and motive are intertwined. When the motive is known, suspects can be identified and intent discovered. A motive can be a desire to conceal something, such as a loss due to poor business practice, or to hurt a business competitor, sabotage a business, or redress a personally perceived wrong, such as abortion and damage to the environment. At the extreme, arson may be an attempt to conceal an on-the-premises homicide.

Pyromania and mental illness are often at the root of arson.

Initial Response

The first step for the investigator is rudimentary. It is a simple step, which may explain why it is so often ignored. The tasks of the investigator in this first step are as follows:

- Time that the fire was discovered
- Circumstances under which the fire was first discovered
- Name of the person who turned in the alarm
- Means by which the fire was reported
- Time interval between the discovery of the fire and the report to the fire department

Details

The initial and subsequent reports of investigation should address certain details. The investigator can be helped by placing the details into certain categories. For example,

When

- Time when the burning is believed to have first started
- Time the fire department received notification
- Arrival time of the fire department
- Time extinguishment began
- Time extinguishment concluded
- Time of notice to the arson investigator

Where

- Address of the structure
- Parts of the structure that sustained damage
- Source or origin of the fire
- Migration of the fire, from origin to ending place

What

- Shape, dimension, and age of the structure
- Construction characteristics such as concrete foundation, compositions of siding, roofing, windows and doors, etc.
- Value of structure and contents
- Inventory at time of fire
- Terrain, immediate and surrounding
- Nearby buildings
- Fire apparatus on the scene
- Major appliances/equipment in the structure
- Burglar and fire alarm systems
- Fire control and suppression systems
- Items taken from the structure immediately preceding the fire

Who

- Owner of the structure and its contents
- Investors
- Entities/persons with ownership rights

- Insurance companies
- Person in charge of fire responders
- Name of person who reported the fire
- Names of witnesses
- Occupants at time of fire
- Persons who were last to leave before the fire began
- Persons having keys to the structure

How

- Explosion, flash fire, smoldering fire, or rapidly spreading fire
- Multiple places of burning
- Color, odor, height of smoke, and intensity of flames
- Direction and quantity of air currents within the structure during the burning
- Direction of spread
- Significant noises noted before and during the burning
- Area that sustained the greatest damage
- Area that sustained the least damage

Physical Evidence

- Devices that initiated the fire, e.g., candle, matches, chemicals, or timer
- Blistered paint, charred wood, crazed and fractured glass, burned wires, etc.
- Debris of peculiarly colored ashes and clinkers, traces of paraffin, saturated cloth, waste, or other fire spreaders
- Debris containing an accelerant such as gasoline or kerosene
- Mattress, sofa, linoleum, and wallpaper
- If death is involved, autopsy report

Electrical

- Concealed and exposed electric wiring, fuses, splices, connections, terminals, etc.
- Cut wires
- Short circuits, voltage overloads
- Recent alterations or repairs to the electrical system
- Electric motors, generators, and pumps
- Portable electric heaters

Natural Gas and Heating Appliances

- Gas pipes for heating, air conditioning, fireplace; bottled propane and barbecue grill
- Stoves, ovens, countertop ovens, pilot lights, portable heaters, microwaves, and heat-resistant insulation

Documentation

- Photographs or sketches of the scene, interior and exterior, taken during the burning and after the burning was extinguished, supplemented with notes
- Photographs and impressions of forced entry
- Photos of the careless storage of flammable materials
- Copies of fire inspection reports prepared previously
- Copy of the Fire Code as it pertains to the incident under investigation
- Witness statements
- Investigator's statement

Wayne W. Bennett and Karen M. Hess, *Criminal Investigation*, Wadsworth Publishing, Belmont, CA, 1998, p. 534.

John J. Fay, *Contemporary Security Management*, second ed., Elsevier, Burlington, MA, 2011, pp. 127–130.

Learning Shop USA, Arson Investigation, www.learningshopusa.com

AUDIO RECORDINGS

A good audio recording can be the difference between going to trial and settling out of court. If the evidence that is needed can be clearly understood, many times the opposing party will decide not to contest. The good news is that there are many types of small, covert recording devices currently being manufactured. Even so, surveillance recordings made in the real world usually suffer from some kind of interference that makes intelligibility difficult. While it may not be possible to capture a perfect recording, you can at least improve the odds by employing a basic knowledge of audio in your investigative work.

Understanding Your Recording Device

The microphone of a digital voice recorder or cell phone is omnidirectional. This means that the device is picking up sounds from every direction. The recorder doesn't necessarily have to be facing a person to pick them up clearly. It also means that any sound that happens around the device will also be picked up. Since only one microphone is used, the recording is not stereo and there is no sense of left/right. There is only a sense of distance, not direction, with the closest sounds usually being the loudest.

Most digital voice recorders and cell phones have an automatic level control. This means that you don't have to worry about setting a recording level before you record a conversation. The device automatically sets the level from the loudest sound detected. If you turn on a device in an unattended room, the level will set itself to the loud handling noise it picked up as it was put in place. After a few minutes of nothing happening, it will adjust to the room itself and any quiet sound will be picked up, along with a lot of general broadband noise. With each new loud noise, it will readjust the recording volume accordingly, but until it readjusts, the noise or speech that exceeded the threshold may be distorted.

Avoid recorders with a "voice-activated" feature, which is an automatic process that starts recording when speech is detected and turns off when no speech is heard. In low speech-level situations, the recorder may stop and start several times, resulting in an audio file that is not a continuous recording. There is no way of knowing how much time went by between one segment and another. Worse, when it does automatically start, it will miss the beginning of the first sentence, making it unintelligible in many cases. Even

worse, it may cut off mid-sentence if the subject is speaking at a low volume.

All digital voice recorders and cell phones use a "lossy" algorithm in their recordings, meaning that more than 90 percent of the original sound is tossed out immediately because researchers have determined that we don't need those frequencies in order to understand what is being said. This results in a tradeoff of recording quality versus time/size. Choosing a better recording quality creates a larger file size, resulting in less total time available on the device. Choosing a longer recording time means compromising your recording quality in some way.

The first area to suffer in lower quality audio recordings is the high frequencies. In many cases, the quality can be worse than a telephone. The next thing that can occur is the appearance of audible digital artifacts from the lossy algorithm. These include sounds like warbling, talking underwater, and general garbage that make it extremely difficult to distinguish one word from another or even an external sound from a spoken word. Try to choose a compromise setting that will allow you the time and disc space you need, while preserving as much of the high end as possible.

Understanding the Telephone

Talking on a telephone is like looking at the world through glasses that only allow green light to pass through. The bottom and top end of the audio spectrum are filtered out, and only the frequencies where normal voice conversation occurs are allowed to pass. The high end is cut off at the lowest region of sibilant speech. This is the reason we have to say things like, "F as in Frank" or "S as in Sam."

Many cell phones also have a "noise reduction" feature that works by setting a minimum level that incoming sound must exceed in order to be transmitted. This is why, when you stop talking for a while, the other party must ask, "Are you still there?" They are hearing dead silence. This is fine for normal conversation, but the setting should be disabled if you are using the cell phone as a recording device in order to pick up the lowest levels of speech.

The worst way to record a telephone conversation is to hold another recorder to the mouthpiece, since the *earpiece* is where the other party's speech is heard. The second worst way is to place the telephone on the speaker setting and hold another recorder to the speaker. This results in extreme differences in volume (near party/far party) as well as a severe lack of low end frequencies, resulting in an inability to distinguish "Bs," "Ps," "Ds," and other hard consonants.

With so many cell phone conversations taking place, you would think that there would be apps for this. There are indeed, but the problem with most of these is that they only record from either the microphone or the line. Obviously, if using the "microphone" setting, the other party will not be heard unless the phone is switched to speaker. If the "line" option is chosen, only the other party's voice will be heard, not the caller's. The better solution is an external recording device that plugs into the earphone jack of the cell phone. This way, both sides of the conversation can be recorded.

If using a land line or cordless handset, there are many devices and hardware adapters that can be connected to either the phone line itself or attached by suction to the handset. Whichever solution you choose, try to minimize the near party/far party problem and the high end frequency cutoff problem by recording both sides of the conversation from the phone itself.

Understanding Sound

Simply put, anything that vibrates makes a sound. The faster the vibration, the higher the sound.

1. Low sounds (rumbles, human voice fundamental tones) act like ocean waves. They travel in all directions and can pass through physical objects like doors and walls.
2. High sounds (esses, effs) act like light rays. They are directional and are easily deflected and absorbed by the surfaces of objects.
3. Sound volume level is directly related to distance. Simply put, as the distance is doubled, the sound volume level decreases by half.

Using these three pieces of knowledge, let's apply them to some common recording situations.

Person-to-Person while Wearing the Recorder. One method is to conceal the recorder in a purse or pocket. This has a couple of drawbacks. First of all, be aware of the microphone location on the device. If the device is placed with the microphone facing the bottom of the purse or pocket, it will not pick up the necessary high end detail since those frequencies will be absorbed or blocked by the container's material. Also, any movement of the container will cause the surface of the microphone to contact and scrape the material, resulting in very loud impulse noises.

Many times, recordings are made with the investigator wearing the device in an open shirt or coat pocket. This puts the recorder maybe eight inches from the investigator's mouth. If the target is standing just two feet away (24 inches), the target's speech will be three times as soft as the investigator's. A better placement would be a midway point, such as the wrist or the waist. There are dedicated recording devices disguised as clothing accessories (wristwatches, tie clasps) that are ideal for this purpose.

Person-to-Person while Conversing in a Restaurant. This is always a challenge since there are usually simultaneous conversations going on and the software typically used to enhance an audio recording will bring these out as well. If you have only one recorder, try to place it at a midway point, maybe somewhere on the table. If you're using a cell phone for this, be sure to enable a setting where an incoming call will not disturb the recording.

Another option is to use two recorders and combine the recordings later using an audio trick known as "reverse polarity." Just like the crest and bottom of waves, digital audio has positive and negative values. If you have two recordings of the same thing and combine the two recordings, the result will be twice as loud. But if the polarity of one of the recordings is reversed so that the positive values are now negative and vice versa, the combination of the two recordings will result in silence—they cancel each other out. Keep in mind that this only happens when the waveforms are exactly of the same volume and lined up exactly opposite each other. So in this scenario, one person would record the conversation at one table, and a helper would record the sounds of the restaurant at another nearby table. When the two recordings are aligned together and the polarity is reversed on one of them, much of the room noise would disappear. Because so many things have to line up precisely for this to work, it is important that the two recorders be the same model and that their record settings are identical.

Person-to-Person while Conversing on the Street. There's no way around it; this is probably the toughest situation to make a clean recording. The noise of passing traffic, walking and clothing contact, and general unpredictability make this particularly difficult. The best suggestion would be to find a location somewhat shielded from the direct sound of passing traffic and stand as close as possible to the target with the recorder located midway between or at least facing the target (a device concealed as a hat decoration could work).

Unattended Audio Surveillance Indoors. Low sounds in rooms collect in the junctions of walls and room corners. Microphones located here will produce bass-heavy, boomy recordings. The center of the room is often the most ideal location, but concealing a recording device may be difficult. The next best place is the center point of a wall, mounted as close to the wall as possible to avoid blurring from surface sound reflections.

If possible when positioning a device in an interior room or office, put your ear where the microphone will be placed and listen to the natural room noise for a few seconds. Listen for any steady tones such as refrigerators or other electrical appliances. Be aware of the location of television, radio, and home stereo sets. Especially note the locations of air conditioning and heating vents. Remembering that sound level decreases by half for every doubling of distance; if the microphone is located a foot from an air conditioning vent and the conversation is taking place eight feet away, the noise of the air will be eight times as loud compared to the conversation.

If a recorder is placed in one room but the conversation is taking place in another room, the low sounds of speech will be heard through the wall or the door, but the high sounds will be trapped. It will be hard to tell 'fin' from 'sin' without knowing context. With this in mind, multiple recorders may be a solution.

Unattended Audio Surveillance in an Automobile. While hiding a recording device under the seat of a car may sound like a good idea, it has some very big drawbacks. Road vibrations travel from the tires to the chassis and will cause the recorder to vibrate, too. Since this noise is less than one inch from the microphone and the target's mouth is three feet away, this road noise will overpower any speech that is heard. Also, the target is facing the windshield, and any high frequencies will be reflected from the glass and absorbed by the seat and carpet before being picked up by the microphone.

A better option is the sun visor, mirror, or dome light. These locations are away from AC vents and road noise and will pick up the high-end sibilance directly. Cell phones will not work here, but something like a pen recorder clipped to the visor would work great.

I hope that the information presented in this section will guide you in avoiding some of the most common pitfalls of audio field recording and will result in clear evidence that can be used effectively.

J. David Leonard

B

BACKGROUND INVESTIGATION

The separate terms background investigation and background check mean nearly the same. Where a difference exists it is in the depth or intensity of the inquiry. Both practices start with a routine inquiry, that is to say, a check that for the most part will verify, refute, or cast doubt on an application made by a person seeking to receive something of value or importance, such as a job, a job transfer, or a loan of money.

When a background check moves to a deeper examination, the inquiry becomes a background investigation. The reason for going "deeper" may be that the applicant appears to have lied on the application and that further investigation is needed to resolve the issue one way or another. Also, going "deeper" is the rationale when a job is related to national security or a job that involves a potential for causing harm to others.

When background checking/investigating services are provided to a business, the investigator can be an employee of the business, such as a corporate investigator, a private investigator, or an investigator/agent employed by a government agency. In the private sector, the investigator's usual point of contact is the head of the human resources department. The areas of interest will vary according to the needs of the business. For example, a business that operates in a safety-sensitive environment will be interested in a job applicant's accident history, and a retail sales business will be interested in a job applicant's honesty.

The usual sources of information are:

- Records
- Databases
- Personal references
- Knowledgeable persons

Records

Public agency records reside with law enforcement agencies, criminal and civil courts, licensing bureaus, the military, the Social Security administration, and others. Private-sector sources include educational institutions, banking and finance institutions, credit bureaus, telephone and utility companies, and professional associations.

Generally available public records include:

- Criminal history
- Lawsuits and judgments
- Doing business as (DBA) files
- Divorce and marriage records
- Property tax records, deeds, and mortgages
- Uniform Commercial Code (UCC) files
- Voter registration files*
- Estate records and bankruptcy filings
- Professional license files
- Motor vehicle registration files

A voter registration record can be particularly helpful. It includes full name, current and former addresses, and other details. Information on a voter registration record may reflect data different than that provided by the applicant and can also help the investigator track the applicant's history through other records, such as those mentioned above.

Records at the state level include:

- Corporation filings
- Workers' compensation claims
- Professional licensing files
- Driver's license files

When an applicant pledges collateral on a loan, a Uniform Commercial Code (UCC) filing will reveal if others have filed a claim against the same collateral. The UCC online search can provide:

- Debtor's name and address
- Secured parties' names and addresses
- Collateral description (e.g., equipment, real estate, inventory)
- Amendments, terminations, and continuations

Where fiscal responsibility is an issue, credit information can be gathered concerning:

- Debt load
- Payment history
- Garnishments
- Liens
- Bankruptcies

Databases

A good deal of information can be found in computer databases. Some databases are easily accessible to the investigator directly or, in other cases, through a vendor. Database searches can provide extensive information at low cost and are useful when the person of interest worked or lived in numerous counties or states. A local search, such as one made at a county courthouse, will not reflect an individual's criminal conviction in another county or state. Success with a database service will depend on the quality and quantity of the identifying data provided by the employer. For each name run through a database, there may be hundreds of persons with the same name. Full and accurate information inputted at the front end can produce good information at the back end.

Not all records, however, are computerized or accessible by electronic means. For this reason, the investigator has to go to the places where the records of interest are physically stored. Examples of record-storing places are state houses, county courthouses, and driver's license offices.

Knowing the Social Security number (SSN) held by the person of interest can be very, very helpful to a background investigation. It is important to know that SSNs are not assigned consecutively or regionally. The nine-digit SSN, which has been issued in more than 400 million different sequences, is divided into three parts: area numbers, group numbers, and serial numbers.

- Area Numbers. Originally, the area numbers (the first three numbers) represented the state in which a person first applied for a Social Security card. But since 1973, the Social Security Administration has assigned numbers and issued cards based on ZIP codes.
- Group Numbers. These are the two middle digits, which range from 01 through 99. They are simply used to break area numbers into smaller blocks, which makes administration easier.
- Serial Numbers. The last four digits run consecutively from 0001 through 9999.

Personal References

In this area of inquiry, the person to be investigated provides information and written consent to verify the information. When the reference provided is a personal reference, the investigator can expect the reference to answer glowingly because, logically, a person will provide references that can be expected to be supportive.

An application form is the main administrative device for capturing personal references. Quite commonly, a dishonest person will provide some truth. For example, a job applicant might provide the correct name of a former employer and change the location or provide the correct city and state of the school but change its name. Personal references can produce recommendations that are excellent but totally false. It helps greatly when the investigator inquires with persons other than those named on the form.

Checking references by mail or e-mail is not as effective as checking in person or by phone. People tend to be candid and outgoing in face-to-face and voice-to-voice communications. Facial expressions, pregnant pauses, and voice inflections can reveal a great deal; more can be learned from the manner of response than the content of it.

Knowledgeable Persons

A first objective in this step is to identify people who are likely to know the individual and likely to be candid. Such persons can be current and former coworkers, acquaintances, neighbors, and others who may be aware of integrity issues not reflected in written and digital records.

It is important to corroborate negative information. If the individual claims an achievement but a knowledgeable person says otherwise, the investigator needs to resolve the issue one way or the other.

At the opening moment of an interview, the investigator must explain to the interviewee that the questions to be asked are intended to verify information provided by the individual.

Background Investigation Checklist

- Criminal history records
- Civil history records
- Bankruptcy records
- Credit history
- Driving record
- Education credentials
- Social Security number
- Current and former employers
- Employment dates
- Job title and duties
- Salary
- Reasons for leaving
- Eligibility for rehire
- Productivity
- Punctuality
- Relationships with others
- Notices given
- Personal references
- Personal characteristics
- Employability
- Workers' compensation
- Reports of injury
- Court-contested claims
- Medical awards
- Lost time claims
- Compensable claims
- UCC filings
- Real property ownership and transfer
- Marriage and divorce
- Registered voter

Criminal History Summary

A criminal history summary, often called a criminal history record, is a listing of certain information taken from fingerprint submissions retained by the FBI in connection with arrests and, in some instances, federal employment, naturalization, or military service.

If the fingerprints are related to an arrest, the Criminal History Summary includes the name of the agency that submitted the fingerprints to the FBI, the date of the arrest, the arrest charge, and the disposition of the arrest, if known to the FBI. All arrest data included in a Criminal History Summary are obtained from fingerprint submissions, disposition reports, and other information submitted by agencies having criminal justice responsibilities.

To obtain a job or license in the United States, the applicant may be required by state statute or federal law to submit a request through a state identification bureau, federal agency, or other authorized agency.

When a Criminal History Summary is not on file, the FBI will send to the requesting agency a response that indicates there are no prior arrest data on file at the FBI.

John J. Fay, *Contemporary Security Management*, third ed., Elsevier, Burlington, MA, 2011, pp. 238–245.

BATTERY

Battery is often broken down into simple battery, battery, and aggravated battery. Simple battery involves the offensive touching or intentional physical harming of another individual.

Battery is committed when a person intentionally causes visible bodily harm to another.

Aggravated battery is committed when a person renders a member of the victim's body useless or severely disfigures the victim. Simple battery has three elements:

1. Intent
2. Causation
3. Touching that is insulting, provoking, or harmful

"Visible bodily harm" means bodily harm capable of being perceived by a person other than the victim and may include blackened eyes, swollen lips or other facial or body parts, and substantial bruises to body parts.

A person commits aggravated battery when he maliciously does any one of three things:

- Deprives a victim of a member of his body
- Renders a member of a victim's body useless
- Seriously disfigures a victim

Wayne W. Bennett and Karen M. Hess, *Criminal Investigation*, Wadsworth Publishing, Belmont, CA, 1998, p. 307.

BILL OF RIGHTS

Personal Freedoms

The first ten amendments to the U.S. Constitution are called the Bill of Rights. These amendments guarantee the personal freedoms of citizens.

- The First Amendment guarantees freedom of speech, freedom of the press, and freedom of association (assembly). It protects the right to worship and the right not to be forced to support someone else's religion. The First Amendment also provides for the right to assemble and to demand a change in government policies.
- The Second Amendment protects the right of the people to own weapons as members of state militias.
- The Third Amendment forbids the government from quartering soldiers in private homes during peacetime without the homeowner's permission and during wartime only according to law.
- The Fourth Amendment prohibits the police from searching people or their homes or seizing their property without reasonable grounds to believe that a crime has been committed.

- The Fifth Amendment provides five important protections against arbitrary government actions: (1) a person may not be prosecuted for a federal crime without first being indicted by a grand jury; (2) a person may be prosecuted only once for each crime; (3) a person cannot be forced to testify against himself in any criminal case; (4) the Due Process Clause bars the government from arbitrarily depriving anyone of life, liberty, or property; and (5) the government may not take anyone's private property unless it is necessary for a public purpose, and the government must pay just compensation to the property owner.
- The Sixth Amendment guarantees the right to a speedy and public trial and to have an impartial jury. It prohibits the government from prosecuting an accused person without first informing him or her of the nature of the charges. The accused has the right to confront his accusers and be assisted by an attorney.
- The Seventh Amendment, which does not apply to the states, guarantees the right to a jury in federal civil trials.
- The Eighth Amendment prohibits the government from administering cruel and unusual punishments, imposing excessive fines, or requiring excessive bail.
- The Ninth Amendment declares that just because certain rights are not mentioned in the Constitution does not mean that they do not exist. Courts may not infer from the silence of the Constitution that an unlisted right is unavailable to protect individuals from the government.
- The Tenth Amendment says that if a particular power was not assigned to the federal government by the Constitution itself, then the people or the states may exercise the power, unless the Constitution also prohibits the states from exercising it.

Two of the above Amendments deserve to be highlighted because they especially limit the authority of police officers. Let's look at those two amendments in closer detail.

The Fourth Amendment

Unreasonable Searches and Seizures. This Amendment says that the police cannot conduct unreasonable searches and seizures. A search or seizure by the police is considered reasonable, and therefore permitted, when a warrant to search and seize has been issued by a court.

Probable Cause. Before issuing the warrant, the court will require the police to show probable cause as to why a warrant should be issued. Probable cause is a combination of facts and circumstances derived from credible sources that would cause a person of reasonable caution and prudence to believe that crime-related evidence may be found at the place to be searched.

Warrant. A warrant is an order by a court to the police to search a specifically named place and to seize at that place specifically named items.

Warrantless Searches. In certain situations, the police can search and seize without a warrant. These situations are:

- During an arrest and only for the purpose of discovering if the suspect possesses a lethal weapon that could be used to harm the arresting officers
- When there is no time to obtain a warrant and immediate action is required, such as when stolen goods are at risk of being removed to an unknown location
- When contraband is seen in plain view. Contraband is any item that is illegal to possess, such as an illegal weapon, illegal drugs, stolen goods, and the tools of a crime
- When a person freely and intelligently gives consent to a search

The Fifth Amendment

The most important of the protections afforded by the Fifth Amendment, as far as police operations are concerned, is the prohibition against requiring a suspect to answer questions. The U.S. Supreme Court, in a case called *Miranda v. Arizona*, emphasized the protection against self-incrimination by ruling that a person in police custody has the right to be silent and the right to have counsel present during questioning. The Court developed a set of procedures for the police to follow before questioning a person in custody. The procedures are called the Miranda Warnings.

Joseph A. Senna and Larry J. Siegel, *Introduction to Criminal Justice*, West Publishing, Minneapolis/St. Paul, MN, p. 159.

BLOOD ALCOHOL TEST

A blood alcohol test determines the relative proportion of ethyl alcohol within blood, based upon the number of grams per millimeter of blood, and is often expressed as a percent.

The Blood Alcohol Tester

A blood alcohol tester is an instrument for capturing and analyzing the alcohol content of a deep lung breath sample. A tester typically has components for collecting a blood sample, holding the sample in a chamber, sensing any hydrocarbons that may be present in the sample, emitting a readout display of the well-established relationship between the concentration of alcohol in blood and deep lung breath, calibrating controls, and an energy source.

Blood Alcohol Zones

Blood alcohol zones are the standards that are commonly employed as measures of intoxication. In this measure, the parts of alcohol per thousand parts of blood are expressed as a percentage. Three zones are typical:

Zone 1. An alcohol value between 0.00 and 0.05 percent is considered fairly good evidence that the person tested is sober.

Zone 2. An alcohol value between 0.05 and 0.15 percent is considered inconclusive as to whether or not the person tested is under the influence.

Zone 3. An alcohol value above 0.15 percent is considered evidence that the tested person is under the influence.

The amount of alcohol consumption that would cause intoxication is estimated to be 8 ounces of whiskey or eight 12-ounce bottles of beer.

John J. Fay, *Security Dictionary*, American Society for Industrial Security, Alexandria, VA, 2000, pp. 29–30.

Body Language

Body language is a combination of physical expressions that are almost entirely rooted in the subconscious. Body language can provide clues as to the state of mind of a person, such as a person being questioned by an investigator. Interpretation of body language can reveal if the person being questioned is:

- Deceptive
- Amused
- Contemptuous
- Content
- Embarrassed
- Excited
- Relieved
- Satisfied
- Shamed
- Combination of any of the above

Deception

It may be helpful to think of deception in terms of the stimulus/response concept. The interrogator provides a stimulus that produces a response from the person questioned. The stimulus might be a verbal statement, a remark, a question, the showing of a photograph or piece of evidence, or even a nonverbal message sent by the interrogator in the form of a gesture or facial expression. For every stimulus, there is a response. The response can range from entirely concealed to highly perceptible. Even when the response is small or hidden, the interrogator may see an indication of deception or nondeception. The capacity for sending deceptive signals may be present, but the capacity of the interrogator to see and interpret the signals may not be present. It is the role of the interrogator to provide the stimulus and evaluate the response.

To employ the stimulus/response mechanism, the interrogator should:

- Determine demeanors that represent a normal pattern and look for changes in the pattern, especially when a fear-provoking question has been asked.
- Look for consistency of behavioral signals. One quick change in behavior is not conclusive. Repeated changes from the normal pattern may be indicative of deception.
- Interpret deceptive signals in clusters rather than single observations.
- Compare the suspect's behavior in relation to case details and evidence.
- Look, listen, and don't be afraid to follow intuition.

The interrogation must be planned and modified during execution so that the line of questioning moves toward issues that have the greatest threat. A successful interrogation is dependent, to a very large degree, upon the ability of the interrogator to confront the person with questions that focus upon specific, self-threatening issues.

General Demeanor

General demeanor is the outward manner, attitude, or bearing of a person in relation to other persons; it is the attitudinal framework within which deceptive signals appear. For example, deceptive signals can be wringing of the hands, slurred and rapid speech, knee jerking, fidgeting, and nail biting. It is the totality of signals that convey a general demeanor.

Major Body Movements

Many of the gestures and mannerisms of a deceptive person are somewhat difficult to detect because they are of short duration. This is not the case with gross body movements in which the person shifts the entire body from one side of the chair to the other, stands up, walks in circles, or leaves without notice. A major body movement can be accompanied by a small gesture such as a blink or a tap of the finger. Particularly significant body movements are to move the chair away from the interrogator. The person derives a degree of psychological comfort by increasing distance and moving behind a physical barrier.

Gestures

A gesture indicates inner tension. A gesture can be consciously or unconsciously initiated. A consciously initiated gesture may be an attempt to mask an emotion suggestive of deception. A question that "touches home" can produce an innocent-appearing reaction such as flicking a piece of lint from a pants leg or yawning. A gesture of this type has meaning when it is delivered in the immediate aftermath of a probing question, and it reveals the person as clever, willful, and self-controlled.

Facial Expressions

Research suggests that about 90 percent of all facial expressions involve the eyes. When two people are engaged in a normal conversation, eye contact is maintained between 30 and 60 percent of the time. The implication here is that abnormal eye contact occurs below or above the 30 to 60 percent range.

Shifting the eyes back and forth and looking away are signals of deception. Prolonging eye contact can mean that the person is aware of the significance of eye movements and is overcompensating. Intense, prolonged eye contact signals defiance and arrogance.

A single facial expression by itself does not conclusively indicate deception. Greater import is derived by observing the variety and intensity of facial expressions, especially as they relate to particular questions. Noticing facial movements is relatively easy to do; accurately interpreting their meanings is very difficult to do. Distinguishing between expressions that are normal (genuine) and abnormal (false) is the main hurdle.

Facial expressions, particularly those involving movements of the eyes and mouth, are easy to misinterpret. For example, a person raised or living in an environment unfamiliar to the investigator might avert the eyes or smile when asked a sensitive question. Similarly, culture has effects. A person living in deprived circumstances might respond with slang that is beyond the interrogator's ability to understand.

Signals of the body can be likened to road signs that guide the interrogator to the desired destination, which is truth. The effective interrogator will see the road signs and follow where they lead.

Leon C. Mathieu, *Encyclopedia of Security Management*, second ed., Elsevier, Burlington, MA, 2011, pp. 161–167.

BRIBERY

Bribery is the offering, giving, receiving, or soliciting of something of value for the purpose of influencing the action of an official in the discharge of his or her public or legal duties.

The crime occurs when a corrupt employee working in a responsible position accepts a payment of some type in exchange for special consideration. Payment can be cash in advance or at a later time, discounts on personal purchases, gifts, leased automobiles, home improvement, or other rewards. The special consideration provided to the briber can include favoritism in the award of a contract, overlooking deficiencies in the performance of a contract, certifying payment for unsatisfactory work or work not performed, and agreeing to purchase supplies at inflated prices.

The expectation of a particular voluntary action in return is what makes the difference between a bribe and a private demonstration of goodwill. To offer or provide payment in order to persuade someone with a responsibility to betray that responsibility is known as seeking undue influence over that person's actions. When someone with power seeks payment in exchange for certain actions, that person is said to be peddling influence. Regardless of who initiates the deal, either party to an act of bribery can be found guilty of the crime independently of the other.

A bribe can consist of immediate cash or of personal favors, a promise of later payment, or anything else the recipient views as valuable. No written agreement is necessary to prove the crime of bribery, but usually a prosecutor must show corrupt intent. Bribery charges may involve public officials or private individuals. In the world of professional sports, for example, one boxer might offer another a payoff to "throw" (deliberately lose) an important fight. In the corporate arena, a company could bribe employees of a rival company for recruitment services or other actions at odds with their employer's interests. Even when public officials are involved, a bribe does not need to be harmful to the public interest in order to be illegal.

When a public official accepts a bribe, he or she creates a conflict of interest. That is, the official cannot accommodate the interests of another party without compromising the responsibilities of her or his position.

John J. Fay, *Security Dictionary*, American Society for Industrial Security, Alexandria, VA, 2000, p. 33.

Bruce L. Berg, *Policing in Modern Society*, Butterworth-Heinemann, Woburn, MA, 1999, pp. 365–370.

BURGLARY: LOCKS

A door lock is usually all that prevents movement into a protected area, whether commercial or residential. Occasionally, a door lock will be supplemented with a padlock. Most door locks are key operated. They consist of a cylinder or other opening for inserting a key that mechanically moves a bolt or latch. The bolt (or deadbolt) extends from the door lock into a bolt receptacle in the doorframe.

The cylinder part of a lock contains the keyway, pins, and other mechanisms. Some locks, called double-cylinder locks, have a cylinder on each side of the door and require a key for both sides. With a single-cylinder lock, a thief may be able to break glass in or nearby the door and reach inside to turn the knob to release the lock. The disadvantage is that a key to the lock on the inside of the door must be readily available for emergency escape, such as during a fire.

Key-in-Knob Lock

The key-in-knob lock works on the same principles as the cylinder lock except, as the name implies, the keyway is in the knob. In the single key-in-knob lock, the keyway is almost always on the outside door knob, and a push or turn button for locking/unlocking is on the inside knob. The double key-in-knob lock has a keyway on the outside and inside knobs, which increases security but also decreases safety.

Cylinder Lock

From the standpoint of forced entry, the cylinder lock is somewhat resistive in that it cannot be ripped easily from the door because it is seated flush or close to the surface. One model of the cylinder lock features a smooth, narrow ring around the neck of the cylinder. The ring moves freely so that even if it can be grasped by a tool, it cannot be twisted. The cylinder lock is vulnerable to a burglary tool called the slam hammer or slam puller. The device usually consists of a slender rod with a heavy sliding sleeve. One end of the rod has a screw or claw for insertion into the keyway. The other end has a retaining knob. When the sleeve is jerked away from the lock, striking the retaining knob, the lock cylinder or keyway is forcibly pulled out.

By contrast, the key-in-knob lock is somewhat more vulnerable because the knob itself can be hammered off; pried off with a crowbar; or pulled out by a grasping tool, such as channel lock pliers. Once the inner workings of the lock are exposed, the burglar can retract the bolt to open the door.

Slip-Knifing

Probably one of the simplest attack techniques is slip-knifing. A thin, flat, and flexible object, such as a credit card, is inserted between the strike and the latch bolt to depress the latch bolt and release it from the strike. Slip-knifing of sliding windows is accomplished by inserting a thin and stiff blade between the meeting rail (stile) to move the latch to the open position; slip-knifing of pivoting windows is done by inserting a thin and stiff wire through openings between the rail and the frame and manipulating the sash operator.

Springing the Door

Springing the door is a technique in which a large screwdriver or crowbar is placed between the door and the doorframe so that the bolt extending from the lock into the bolt receptacle is pried out, enabling the door to swing open. A one-inch bolt will hinder this attack.

Jamb Peeling

Jamb peeling is the prying off or peeling back of the doorframe at a point close to the bolt receptacle. When enough of the jamb is removed from the receptacle, the receptacle can be broken apart or removed, allowing the door to swing open. A metal or reinforced doorframe is the antidote.

Sawing the Bolt

Sawing the bolt is inserting a hacksaw blade between the door and the doorframe and cutting through the bolt. The countermeasure is to use a bolt made of a saw-resistant alloy or a bolt that is seated in such a way that it will freely spin on its side, thereby taking away the resistance needed for the saw blade to gain purchase.

Spreading the Frame

Spreading the frame involves the use of a jack, such as an automobile jack, in such a way that the door jambs on each side of the door are pressured apart to a point where the door will swing free from the bolt receptacle. A reinforced doorframe and a long deadbolt are countermeasures.

Kicking in the Door

Kicking in the door is a primitive but effective technique. In this case, the attack is against the door so that even the best locking hardware will have little deterrent effect. The countermeasure is a metal door or a solid wood door, at least 1–3/4 inches thick, installed in a wooden doorframe at least two inches thick, or a steel doorframe. An escutcheon plate can be used to shield the bolt receptacle.

Picking the Lock

A more sophisticated attack technique is lock picking. It is seen infrequently because of the expertise required. Lock picking is accomplished by using metal picks to align the pins in the cylinder as a key would to release the lock. The greater the number of pins, the more difficult it is to align them. A cylinder should have at least six pins to be resistive to lock picking.

The high-security form of the combination lock requires manipulation of one or several numbered dials to gain access. Combination locks usually have three or four dials that must be aligned in the correct order for entrance. Because only a limited number of people will be informed of the combination, the problems associated with compromised mechanical keys and lock picking are removed. Combination locks are used at doors and on safes, bank vaults, and high-security filing cabinets; in most cases, the combination can be changed by the owner on an as-needed basis.

With older combination locks, skillful burglars may be able, often with the aid of a stethoscope, to discern the combination by listening to the locking mechanism while the dial is being turned. Another attack method is for the burglar to take a concealed position at a distance from the lock and, with binoculars or a telescope, observe the combination sequence when the lock is opened.

Padlock

The combination padlock has mostly low security applications. It has a numbered dial and may be supplemented with a keyway. On some models, a serial number impressed on the lock by the manufacturer will allow the combination to be determined by cross-checking against a reference manual provided by the manufacturer to dealers. Although a convenience, it is a risk to security.

In a technique called padlock substitution, the thief will remove the property owner's unlocked padlock and replace it with a similar padlock. After the property owner locks up and leaves, the thief will return, open the padlock, and gain entry. The preventive measure is to keep padlocks locked even when not in use.

John J. Fay, *Contemporary Security Management*, third ed., Elsevier, Burlington, MA, 2011, pp. 172–173.

C

CASE MANAGEMENT

At all times, the head of an investigation agency needs to know the progress of every matter under investigation and does so in numerous ways:

- Staff meetings in which each investigator discusses cases in progress
- One-on-one meetings between the agency head and investigators
- Informal discussions that occur casually, such as by "walking around"
- Daily activity reports
- Reports of investigation

The daily activity report, like the name implies, is particularly important. It is filled out each day by each investigator and submitted to the agency head the following morning in a word-processed configuration. The daily activity report can be a template on the investigator's hard drive. After information is entered in the template, it is sent to the agency head as an attachment to an e-mail or simply printed out and given to the agency head. The report works best for the agency head when the content of the report is cumulative, that is to say, it states the previous day's activity as an extension of activities that started when the case was first opened. This method is labor intensive for the investigator because it means that every case worked the previous day requires a separate report. For the agency head, however,

it means he or she is relieved of the need to retrieve earlier reports in order to better understand the current report.

Daily activity reports are eventually converted to a formal narrative style and become the major content of investigation reports. Investigation reports are prepared for delivery to the end-user or client, with copies placed in secure storage for later use. Later use may be to update the full file with documents that reflect outcome of a trial, restitution, and other significant facts (such as further evidence).

Every case has its own identity number, and the number is coded in a way that makes sense. A case number is often coded to reflect the year in which the case was opened and the sequence of the opening date in that year. For example, a case opened in 2016 that was the fourteenth case of that year would be identified as case number 2016–14. Another code for that case might be 6–2016–14, which indicates the case was opened in June (the sixth month of the year). The case number should be prominently displayed on the front page of the investigation report and on each page of the report; the pages should be numbered.

A status board can be helpful to the agency head in identifying cases opened, cases in progress, and cases completed. The board is usually prominently mounted in view of the agency head and visible to investigators but not visible to outsiders. A single entry on the status board might reflect the person or group under investigation, the name of the victim, the nature of the case (such as the name of a crime), the case number, the date the case was opened, the name of the investigator, and the current status of the case.

Case management includes informing other persons or groups concerning the status of a case. Informing occurs by disseminating written documents (such as memoranda and reports of investigation that have been recently opened, cases in progress, and cases completed) or by making verbal/audio visual presentations on a person-to-person basis or to a group. Informing others can include giving a deposition and testifying at a formal proceeding.

Learning Shop USA, Business Practices, Part and Part 2, www.learningshopusa.com

CENTRAL INTELLIGENCE AGENCY (CIA)

Mission

CIA's primary mission is to collect, analyze, evaluate, and disseminate foreign intelligence to assist the president and senior U.S. government policymakers in making decisions related to national security. This is a very complex process and involves a variety of steps.

In some cases, the CIA is directed to study an intelligence issue—such as what activities terrorist organizations are planning or how countries that have biological or chemical weapons plan to use these weapons—then look for a way to collect information about the problem.

There are several ways to collect information. Translating foreign newspaper and magazine articles and radio and television broadcasts provides open-source intelligence. Imagery satellites take pictures from space, and imagery analysts write reports about what they see. For example, a report may include how many airplanes are at a foreign military base. Signals analysts work to decrypt coded messages sent by other countries. Operations officers recruit foreigners to give information about their countries.

After the information is collected, intelligence analysts pull together the relevant information from all available sources and assess what is happening, why it is happening, what might occur next, and what it means for U.S. interests. The result of this analytic effort is timely and objective assessments, free of any political bias and is provided to senior U.S. policymakers in the form of finished intelligence products that include written reports and oral briefings. One of these reports is the President's Daily Brief (PDB), an Intelligence Community product, which the U.S. president and other senior officials receive each day.

It is important to know that CIA analysts only report information and do not make policy recommendations. Making policy is left to agencies such as the State Department and Department of Defense. These policymakers use the information that the CIA provides to help them formulate U.S. policy toward other countries. It is also important to know that the CIA is not a law enforcement organization. That is the job of the FBI; however, the CIA and the FBI cooperate on a number of issues, such as counterintelligence and counterterrorism. Additionally, the CIA may also engage in covert action at the president's direction and in accordance with applicable law.

The U.S. Congress has had oversight responsibility of the CIA since the Agency was established in 1947. However, prior to the mid-1970s, oversight was less formal. The 1980 Intelligence Oversight Act charged the Senate Select Committee on Intelligence (SSCI) and the House Permanent Select Committee on Intelligence (HPSCI) with authorizing the programs of the intelligence agencies and overseeing their activities.

Organizational Structure

The **Director of the Central Intelligence Agency (D/CIA)** is nominated by the president with the advice and consent of the Senate. The D/CIA has several staffs directly subordinate to him that deal with acquisitions, communications, public affairs, human resources, protocol, congressional affairs, legal issues, information management and technology, strategic resource management, and internal oversight.

The CIA has four components:

- National Clandestine Service
- Directorate of Intelligence
- Directorate of Science & Technology
- Directorate of Support

The **National Clandestine Service (NCS)** has responsibility for the clandestine collection of foreign intelligence, primarily human-source intelligence (HUMINT). The NCS serves as the national authority for coordination, conflict prevention, and evaluation of clandestine HUMINT operations across the Intelligence Community, consistent with existing laws, executive orders, and interagency agreements. The NCS is the front-line source of clandestine intelligence on critical international developments ranging from terrorism and weapons proliferation to military and political issues. To gather this important intelligence, CIA operations officers live and work overseas to establish and maintain networks and personal relationships with foreign "assets" in the field.

The **directorate of intelligence (DI)** analyzes all sources of intelligence and produces reports, briefings, and papers on key foreign intelligence issues. This information comes from a variety of sources and methods, including U.S. personnel overseas, agent reports, satellite photography, foreign media, and sophisticated sensors.

The DI is responsible for timeliness, accuracy, and relevance of intelligence analysis that is of concern to national security policymakers and other intelligence consumers. While the CIA does not make foreign policy, the analysis of intelligence on overseas developments feeds into the informed decisions by policymakers and other senior decision makers in the national security and defense arenas.

The **directorate of science and technology (DS&T)** accesses, collects, and exploits information to facilitate the execution of the Agency's mission by applying innovative, scientific, engineering, and technical solutions to the most critical intelligence problems. The DS&T incorporates over 50 different disciplines ranging from computer programmers and engineers to scientists and analysts. The DS&T partners with many other organizations in the Intelligence Community, using best practices to foster creative thinking and working level coordination. The DS&T continually seeks to push the boundaries of the state-of-the-art, infusing cutting-edge technologies with effective targeting and tradecraft.

The **directorate of support (DS)** provides support that is critical to the Agency's intelligence mission. The DS delivers a full range of support, including facilities services, financial management, medical services, logistics and the security of Agency personnel, information, facilities, and technology. DS services are international in focus, clandestine in nature, and offered on a 24/7 basis. Its responsibilities extend well beyond the CIA, into the greater Intelligence Community.

Agency Responsibilities

The CIA is responsible for providing intelligence on a wide range of national security issues to senior U.S. policymakers. The director of the Central Intelligence Agency (D/CIA) is nominated by the president and confirmed by the Senate. The director manages the operations, personnel, and budget of the Central Intelligence Agency and acts as the National Human Source Intelligence (HUMINT) Manager.

https://www.cia.gov/index.html

CHAIN OF CUSTODY

Physical evidence that is received, recovered, discovered, or collected in any manner by an investigator must be marked for identification without delay. The purpose of identification is to prove at a later date, such as during a trial, that the evidence presented is the same evidence that was originally collected. Initials, time, date, and place of collection are the usual forms of identification. Depending on the size and nature of the evidence, the identifying information can be attached to the item or on the outside of a container suited to the evidence. For example, a crow bar can be appended with a tie-on tag, a paint chip can be placed in a plastic sandwich bag, clothing can be placed in a paper bag, a fluid can be placed in a vial, and dirt or debris can be placed in a metal can. The central concept is to prevent contamination of the evidence through contact with a contaminating substance, prevent accidental or willful substitution, and positively establish the source of the evidence and identify persons or agencies that had custody of the evidence from the moment of collection to final disposition. Every person in the chain of custody is responsible during the period of custody to provide care and safekeeping.

John J. Fay, Encyclopedia of Security Management, second ed., Butterworth-Heinemann, Burlington, MA, 2007, p. 139

CHILD CUSTODY SURVEILLANCE

Child custody surveillance cases can be lucrative work for private investigators. These cases are often very rewarding, and they allow investigators to attain satisfaction by helping ensure the safety and welfare of a child. Child custody cases can be challenging because they are notoriously messy and complicated. They also give investigators the opportunity to hone their skills, particularly skills in mobile, stationary, and covert surveillance. Skills in using surveillance equipment can be sharpened as well.

Preparation

An investigator must spend a considerable amount of time gathering as much information as possible about the client, the person who is the subject of the investigation, and the child before the case begins.

Study the Players. An investigator should know and document all biographical data about everyone involved in the case, including identification of people and relationship to the child. Knowing the custody arrangement and schedule, including stipulations in the court papers and visitation orders, will help the investigator know the acceptable and common behaviors of the parties involved.

Learn the Child's Routines. At the start of the investigation, the investigator should know the child's routines, particularly when the child attends school. This will help the investigator set up a plan that takes into consideration the best times to conduct the surveillance.

Prepare for a Lengthy Surveillance Case. Child custody surveillance cases can be particularly lengthy. The investigator must be prepared for that from the outset, even if not retained for a long period of time. Often, family courts want to see the subject's behavior over a period of time, rather than seeing one or two incidents. Courts want to see strong evidence before ordering a change to the custody agreement.

Know Your Moral Compass. It is important for an investigator to be mentally prepared to take action if the child appears to be in danger at any time during the course of the investigation. The investigator has a moral obligation to act when a child's life is in danger. There is also an obligation to notify child protective services. Notification, although not typically mandated, should be made when a child's life is at risk.

Surveillance

Know the Lay of the Land. Before beginning surveillance, an investigator should become familiar with the setting or multiple settings; know the entrances and exits of surveillance locations and do not assume there is only one way in or out of the home or building being watched. This is true of almost any surveillance case, and the same knowledge and skill should apply in child custody cases.

Identify Other Players Involved. Once in the field, an investigator needs to identify the persons coming and going from the home and interacting with the child and with the subject of the investigation. Utilizing database searches and social networking can assist in identification. If the investigator becomes overly focused on information provided by the client, the investigator could miss discovering evidence and pertinent information. The client's assessment of what's happening is valuable but not to the extent it excludes everything else.

Just the Facts. Finally, the investigator should document the facts. Assumption, speculation, and opinion have no role to play in writing a report. The investigator's personal view on parenting must be excluded also. The investigator should not judge another person's actions in light of his or her personal belief.

Conclusion

Child custody surveillance cases are a great source of income and a good challenge for investigators. The cases often go far beyond what meets the eye. Planning, surveillance, and good investigation work can help separate truth from fiction.

Stacy Jones

CIVIL LAW

Legal systems elaborate rights and responsibilities in a variety of ways. A general distinction can be made between civil law jurisdictions, which codify their laws, and common law systems.

In general, law is a system of rules, usually enforced through a set of institutions. It shapes politics, economics and society in numerous ways and serves as a primary social mediator in relations between people. Here are examples:

- Contract law regulates everything from buying a bus ticket to trading on the stock market.
- Property law defines rights and obligations related to the transfer and title of personal (often referred to as chattel) and real property.
- Trust law applies to assets held for investment and financial security, while tort law allows claims for compensation if a person's rights or property are harmed (often considered a civil case if filed under an issue of tort law vs. criminal). If the harm is criminalized in penal code, criminal law offers means by which the state can prosecute the perpetrator.
- Constitutional law provides a framework for the creation of law, the protection of human rights, and the election of political representatives.
- Administrative law is used to review the decisions of government agencies.
- International law governs affairs between sovereign nation states in activities ranging from trade to environmental regulation or military action.
- A crime is a public wrong and a tort is a private wrong. A public wrong is remedied in a criminal proceeding, and a private wrong is remedied in a civil proceeding. A single act in some instances will constitute both a crime and a tort. For example, if a person commits an assault and battery upon another, he commits a crime

(a public wrong) and a tort (a private wrong). The law will seek to remedy both wrongs, but it will do so in different ways.

The state will move on its own authority to do justice by bringing a criminal action against the offender. The victim is also entitled to bring action against the offender in a civil suit. Tort law gives the victim a cause of action for damages in order that he may obtain sufficient satisfaction. The victim, however, pursues a civil remedy at his own discretion and in his own name. Whether the victim wins his lawsuit or not, the judgment will not prevent prosecution of the offender by the state.

Criminal Law versus Civil Law

The civil injuries involved in tort cases usually arise from acts of negligence. The fact that by his own negligence the victim contributed to the harm done may afford the offender a defense in a civil action of tort, but it does not constitute a defense to the offender in a criminal prosecution.

The single characteristic that differentiates criminal law from civil law is punishment. Generally, in a civil suit the basic questions are:

- How much, if at all, has the defendant injured the plaintiff?
- What remedies, if any, are appropriate to compensate the plaintiff for his loss?

In a criminal case, the questions are:

- To what extent has the defendant injured society?
- What sentence is appropriate to punish the defendant?

Tort Law Purposes

Tort law has three main purposes:

- Compensate persons who sustain a loss as a result of another's conduct.

- Place the cost of that compensation on those responsible for the loss.
- Prevent future harms and losses.

Compensation is predicated on the idea that losses, both tangible and intangible, can be measured monetarily.

If a loss-producing event is a matter of pure chance, the fairest way to relieve the victim of the burden is insurance or governmental compensation. When a particular person can be identified as responsible for the creation of the risk, it becomes more just to impose the loss on the responsible person (tortfeasor) than to allow it to remain on the victim or the community at large.

The third major purpose of tort law is to prevent future torts by regulating human behavior. In concept, the tortfeasor held liable for damages will be more careful in the future, and the general threat of tort liability serves as an incentive to all persons to regulate their conduct appropriately. In this way, tort law supplements criminal law.

Damages: Compensatory and Punitive

When one person's tortuous act injures another's person or property, the remedy for the injured party is to collect damages. The common law rules of damages for physical harm contain three fundamental ideas:

- Justice requires that the plaintiff be restored to his preinjury condition, so far as it is possible to do so with money. He should be reimbursed not only for economic losses but also for loss of physical and mental well-being.
- Most economic losses are translatable into dollars.
- When the plaintiff sues for an injury, he must recover all of his damages arising from that injury, past and future, in a lump sum and in a single lawsuit.

If the defendant's wrongful conduct is sufficiently serious, the law permits the trier of fact to impose a civil fine as punishment to deter him and others from similar conduct in the future. Punitive damages (also called exemplary or vindictive damages) are not really damages at all since the plaintiff has been made whole by the compensatory damages awarded in the same action. Punitive damages are justified as:

- An incentive for bringing the defendant to justice
- Punishment for offenses that often escape or are beyond the reach of criminal law
- Compensation for damages not normally compensable, such as hurt feelings, attorneys' fees, and expenses of litigation

In the absence of an effective deterrent, civil law is the only effective means to force conscienceless defendants to cease practices known to be dangerous that they would otherwise continue.

The Intentional Tort of Intrusion

Interference with the right to be "left alone" can be grouped into four categories: intrusion, appropriation of one's name or likeness, giving unreasonable publicity to private facts, and placing a person in a false light in the public eye. The latter three of these are founded upon improper publicity, usually in the public press or electronic media. They are beyond the scope of this concept and will not be discussed.

Intrusion is a tort closely related to infliction of emotional distress. Both torts protect a person's interest in his peace of mind. A person has a basic right to choose when and to what extent he will permit others to know his personal affairs.

Intrusion can also be an intentional, improper, unreasonable, and offensive interference with the solitude, seclusion, or private life of another. It embraces a broad spectrum of activities. It may consist of an unauthorized entry; an illegal search or seizure; or an unauthorized eavesdropping, with or without electronic aids.

The tort is complete when the intrusion occurs. No publication or publicity of the information obtained is required. It is, of course, essential that the intrusion be into that which is, and is entitled to remain, private. Additionally, the harm must be substantial. The intrusion must be seriously objectionable, not simply bothersome or inconvenient.

John J. Fay, *Encyclopedia of Security Management*, second ed., Butterworth-Heinemann, Burlington, MA, 2007, p. 224.

CIVIL PROCESS

Civil process is the means used by a court to acquire or exercise its jurisdiction over a person or entity. Jurisdiction is exercised through the delivery of certain documents to the person or entity. The deliverer of the documents is generally known as process server or civil process server. The documents and the process include the following.

Affidavit. An affidavit is a sworn statement of facts made under oath.

Alternative Affidavit. An affidavit that provides the facts relating to the service of the process identified in it (or inability to serve it).

Certificate of Service. A statement made under penalty of perjury, but not notarized, that provides the facts relating to the service of process related to a particular case.

Conformed Copy. An exact copy of a document on which has been written explanations of things that could not be or were not copied. A written signature might be replaced on a conformed copy with a rubber stamp or notation (/s/) indicating that it was signed by the person whose signature appears on the original.

Complaint. A document submitted by a plaintiff to a court, which is filed by a court to begin a civil lawsuit.

Court. An organ of the government, belonging to the judicial department, whose function it is to apply laws to controversies brought before it.

DBA (alt D.B.A.). "Doing business as" is the abbreviation usually preceding a person's or business's assumed name: i.e., John Smith dba Smith Lock and Key or Dr. John Smith, LLC dba Generic Medical Service.

Due Diligence. The measure of activity or attention to duty as is properly expected from, and ordinarily exercised by, a reasonable and prudent man under the circumstances that exist. It is not measured by any absolute standard but depends on the relative facts of the case. This means that determining whether you have exercised "due diligence" in attempting to locate someone for service depends on each different set of facts with which you are faced in attempting to effect service, but you should take the steps that a judge believes a reasonable person would take under that set of facts.

et al. Latin abbreviation meaning "and others."

et ux. Latin abbreviation meaning "and wife."

et vir. Latin for "and husband."

Faithfully, Truthfully, Sincerely, Accurately, and without Unnecessary Delay. As used in referring to public and private officers, this term implies honesty and the careful and prompt discharge of all the duties of the office. It requires competence, diligence, and attention to duty.

Forcible Detainer. A specific type of lawsuit associated with evictions.

Found. A person is said to be "found" within a state for purposes of service of process when actually present therein. This only applies if a person is in a place voluntarily and not by reason of fraud, artifice, or trick for purposes of obtaining service.

Garnishment. A judicial proceeding in which a creditor asks the court to order a third party who is indebted to the debtor to turn over to the creditor any of the debtor's property (such as wages or bank accounts) held by that third party.

Injunction. A court order commanding or preventing an action. A legal right or interest that a creditor has in another's property, lasting usually until a debt or duty that it secures is satisfied.

Motion. A written or oral application requesting a court to make a specified ruling or order.

Order. A written direction or command delivered by a court or judge. The word "order" generally embraces final decrees as well as directions or commands.

Order to Appear/Order to Show Cause. An order from the court directing a person before the court to appear and show cause why certain relief should not be granted.

Order for Supplemental Proceedings/ Judgment Debtor Examination. An order requiring a judgment debtor to appear and disclose assets so a judgment can be satisfied.

Petition. A word used in lieu of "complaint" when beginning certain court actions.

Prima facie. A Latin term meaning at first sight; on the first appearance; on the face of it. A fact presumed to be true unless disproved by some evidence to the contrary.

Process. Process is an official document of the court that requires the person named in it to do some act in connection with the case. It is a means by which a court compels compliance with its demands.

Pro per. A Latin abbreviation meaning to act on one's own behalf without a lawyer. Also seen as: in pro peria persona.

Restraining Order. A court order that prohibits family violence, especially an order that restricts a person from harassing, threatening, and sometimes merely contacting or approaching another specified person. Also, it can be a court order entered to prevent the dissipation or loss of property.

Return of Service. The act of a sheriff, constable, marshal, or other public officer (not a private process server) in delivering back to the court a writ or other paper that he was required to serve or execute, with a brief account of his doings. It provides information about the time and mode of service or execution, or his failure to accomplish it. Also, it refers to the notation made by the officer upon the writ or other paper, stating what he has done under it, the time and mode of service, etc.

Return Day. The day named in a writ or process upon which the officer is required to return it.

Rule of Court. A rule governing the practice or procedure in a given court. Local Rule is a rule by which an individual court supplements the procedural rules applying generally to all courts within the jurisdiction. Local rules deal with a variety of matters, such as requiring extra copies of motions to be filed with the court or prohibiting the reading of newspapers in the courtroom.

Service of Process. The delivery of a writ, summons and complaint, criminal summons, notice, order, etc., by an authorized person, to a person who is thus officially notified of some action or proceeding in which he is concerned, and by which he is advised or warned of some action or step that he is commanded to take or not to take.

Service of Process Personal. Personal service is accomplished by delivering a copy of the personal process to the named party personally. When service by this method is made out of state, it is often called direct service.

Service of Process Substitute. Substituted service refers to serving another person as an alternative to serving the defendant. Thus, the process may be served by leaving copies at the defendant's dwelling or usual place of residence with a person of suitable age and discretion. The purpose of these requirements is to provide the defendant with actual notice of the lawsuit or other action of the court. An attempted Substituted Service is not effective if the defendant did not live at the place where service was made.

Service of Process Alternative. Other methods of service, such as notice and acknowledgment, that require prior approval of the court.

Skiptracing. A service that assists in locating delinquent debtors or persons who have fled to avoid prosecution. Also, such services may include the location of missing heirs, witnesses, or spouses or other family members.

Special Detainer. A forcible detainer (eviction) action that is only applicable to residential rentals where the landlord owns both the land and the dwelling unit (apartment, house, mobile home, etc.) located on it. Specific requirements relating to whether an eviction is properly a special detainer action are found in A.R.S. § 33–1368.

Statute. A law passed by a legislative body; specifically, legislation enacted by any lawmaking body, including legislatures, administrative boards, and municipal courts.

Subpoena. A document that requires a person to appear and give testimony as a witness.

Subpoena *Duces Tecum*. *Duces Tecum* is Latin for "with things in hand" and means that the person who is to appear as a witness must bring something, perhaps records, reports, or photos, along to the trial or deposition.

Summons. A document that gives notice that a lawsuit has been filed and tells the opposing party when they should respond.

Trespass. Any unauthorized intrusion or invasion of private premises or land of another.

Writ of Execution. A court order directing a sheriff or other officer to enforce a judgment, usually by seizing and selling a debtor's property.

Arizona Process Servers Training Manual, Arizona Process Servers Association, Phoenix, AZ, 2009.

CLIENT RELATIONSHIPS

A private investigation agency cannot exist without clients. Clients are obtained in a variety of ways: cold calls, advertisements in Yellow Pages, newspapers, newsletters of professional associations, and referrals from other investigators that cannot for a variety of circumstances meet the clients' particular needs. Certainly, the greatest source of clients is word-of-mouth references by former clients to prospective clients.

Without an agreement between the investigation agency and the client, the agency may not be able to perform the client's desired services properly, and the client may not understand the services to be delivered. A point of misunderstanding by the client can be an expectation that cannot be met, such as possible exposure of the agency to civil liability, can lead to ethical lapses, and could cause the agency to fall into public disrepute. For these reasons, the nature of the case has to be precisely and accurately stated by the client. When there is a suspicion that the client is not entirely truthful, such is in a criminal defense investigation, a polygraph examination may be appropriate.

Many obstacles can creep into what is expected and what is delivered. Obstacles can consist of the private investigator not performing services requested by the client because they are against the law, operating without an agreement, misinterpreting an agreement (which is sometimes deliberately done), unacceptable performance by employees of the private investigation agency, and disputes concerning payments for services.

A services agreement is negotiated between the agency head and the client. This typically involves a face-to-face meeting. The client states what he wishes, the agency head states what he is willing to do, and both parties come to agreement as to what is to be done by the agency and how much it will cost the client. Costs other than labor, such as travel and out-of-pocket expenses, are addenda to the fee.

A retainer is often negotiated and obtained up front, a schedule of payments during and after the course of the investigation is agreed, and the frequency and manner of reporting are agreed.

Learning Shop USA, Business Practices, Part 2, www.learningshopusa.com

Code of Ethics

The following standards are based on the Code of Ethics of the National Council of Investigation and Security Services (NCISS).

- Provide professional services in accordance with local, state, and federal laws.
- Observe and adhere to the precepts of honesty, integrity, and truthfulness.
- Be truthful, diligent, and honorable in the discharge of professional responsibilities.
- Honor each client contract, adhering to all responsibilities by providing ethical services within the limits of the law.
- Safeguard confidential information and exercise the utmost care to prevent unauthorized disclosure of such information.
- Refrain from improper and unethical solicitation of business, including false or misleading claims or advertising.
- Practice due diligence to ensure that employees and coworkers adhere to this same code of ethical conduct; respect all persons, perform the job diligently, and work within the limits of the law.
- Never undertake an assignment that is contrary to the Constitution of the United States of America or the security interests of this country.

www.nciss.org/about-us/nciss-code-of-ethics.php

COMPETITIVE INTELLIGENCE

Competitive intelligence is the gathering of information from overt sources; it is legal to do and is not the same as spying. Collecting information without skullduggery is both necessary and proper. Competitive intelligence becomes industrial espionage when it crosses the line between right and wrong.

The aim of competitive intelligence is not to kill or cripple the competition but to build a position of sustainable competitive advantage. It is possible to argue that every organization needs competitors, as without them there would be less incentive for creative thinking and a tendency for the organization to lessen consideration of user needs.

Perhaps the most "legitimate" source from which confidential information can be obtained is the federal government, which for regulatory and contractual purposes requires public corporations—and even many private companies—to make extensive disclosures regarding their products, finances, and operations. Hence, various agencies of the government are repositories of considerable confidential information, knowledge of which can be useful to business competitors. There is nothing in law that prohibits studying a rival's products or services; analyzing advertisements, annual reports, published articles, and public records; and conversing with knowledgeable consultants, customers, and suppliers.

Companies that regularly collect information about the competition usually assign the task to an in-house team or a private investigative agency with skills in this area. The team is typically a committee or task force made up of specialists in marketing, sales, product development, and product management as well as one or two members at the executive level.

Some companies hire outside vendors with expertise in competitive intelligence. A tacitly understood rationale for using a third party is the defense that a company can put up if the third party crosses the line separating legitimate information gathering from illicit economic spying. More and more private investigative agencies are moving into twin fields: (1) collecting competitive intelligence for clients and (2) preventing or detecting competitive intelligence and industrial espionage.

The rules of the game require the owner of the information to take reasonable steps to protect the information, e.g., by limiting its distribution and keeping it locked up when not in use. The information also has to be not known generally, not readily ascertainable, and of a nature to confer a competitive advantage upon its owner. A crime is committed when such information is obtained by improper means, such as theft or misrepresentation, and when the obtained information has been used to the disadvantage of the owner.

In the United States, competitive intelligence has been practiced by claim jumpers, cattle rustlers, and oil scouts. The modern era practitioner is the respected businessman. The importance and value of competitive intelligence has led some business leaders to mobilize their entire workforces to actively seek information from industry peers, such as with peers over lunch; on the phone; and at trade shows, professional conferences, and seminars.

In recent years, information has come to be valued on a par with equipment, materials, and capital. This utilitarian view emerges from evidence that the possession and use of information can increase profits and improve the ways that people work and think.

John J. Fay, *Encyclopedia of Security Management*, second ed., Butterworth-Heinemann, Burlington, MA, 2007, pp. 99–104 and 429.

COMPUTER FORENSIC INVESTIGATION

Computer forensics is a complex and often misunderstood practice. The examiner is presented with massive volumes of data and forced to work within the constraints of computer-processing capabilities. Contrary to prime-time television shows, there is no "magic" button, and there is no instant feedback. Proper computer investigation is a multistep, time- and labor-intensive process.

This section is a primer on the computer forensics process and generally what an examiner will go through to conduct an investigation. This section provides a basic understanding of how a computer stores, accesses, and processes data so that the user of computer forensic services will have a clear sense of the work and time that is needed to conduct a full and thorough investigation. Also, this section explains that every investigation is different and that there is no single investigatory process to deal with every eventuality. For example, a malware or network compromise examination may be far more surgical in its approach, meaning that many of the "machine–time intensive" functions do not need to be performed. This section should be viewed as a guideline only. It is written starting from the point that an examiner would come to be in receipt of the computer/hard drive/media in question, whether that be in the examiner's lab or on-site, and consists basically of three phases: acquisition, analysis, and reporting.

Acquisition Phase

In this phase, the examiner will perform an evidentiary intake of all components provided, which includes photos, cataloguing of all items, and the start of an evidence chain of custody log that will follow the evidence throughout its life in the examination process. The computer hard drive needs to be "copied" in a special way to preserve the evidentiary integrity of its contents. The proper terminology is a "bit for bit, forensically sound image," and not a "copy" or "mirror." A copy (or mirror) is not the same thing as an image; if the process is done those ways, it can damage the case before it gets started.

In every case, the examiner should be provided with the entire computer and not just the hard drive. There is very important information on a computer chip inside the computer (which does not sit on the computer hard drive) that is instrumental in the investigation. It must be captured and catalogued separately from the hard drive and is commonly done while the hard drive is removed from the computer.

Once the hard drive is removed from the computer, it is connected to specialized hardware to start the actual acquisition. This may take the form of connecting the hard drive to a specialized computer built for the purpose or connecting directly to an acquisition device that will perform the task. In either case, the process has to follow specific protocols so as not to damage or destroy the integrity of the evidence. The preferred method is through the use of an acquisition device because of its speed but, for various reasons, this may not be feasible, such as with older hard drives or with servers or network-connected devices that cannot be taken offline for the acquisition phase.

So how long does this acquisition take? This is an often-asked question because in some cases the window for acquisition is very limited, as in a case where an employee will only be gone for a few hours, or the activity will disrupt some other work product. In all cases, this is an "it depends" answer. It depends on a number of factors that the examiner cannot control. It is dictated by things such as type of formatting on subject drive, rotational speed of drive, data density and volume, drive interface and construction, and tools used. In the case of using a hardware device as mentioned above, a general rule of thumb would be four to five gigabytes of data per minute to create the forensic image. Translated, this means that a 320 GB hard drive will take roughly 70–80 minutes to image. A one-terabyte hard drive will take roughly 3.5 to 4.5 hours to image. These are just imaging times. Immediately following the imaging process, a verification process has to be performed to ensure the integrity of the evidence collected. This roughly takes as long as the initial imaging phase, and needs to be performed during the acquisition process.

In the case of an older hard drive, or a problematic hard drive with structural problems, the imaging process may only happen at a rate of one gigabyte per minute. During a live acquisition of a machine that cannot be turned off, the same rate (one GB/min) can be expected. Hard drives in external enclosures that connect via USB must be dismantled (which can be destructive in some cases) or else the acquisition timeline will be increased.

Many times an examiner has shown up at a location only to find that the computer has more than one hard drive in it or is a server with multiple drives in it. Obviously, this seriously impacts the acquisition timeline, not to mention the cost.

Finally, during the acquisition phase, if it is a live acquisition or the computer is found to be on when the examiner arrives, it is highly recommended that the computer's RAM (Random Access Memory) be acquired. This again is dependent on the amount of RAM in the computer but can take anywhere from a few minutes to more than an hour and cannot be done concurrent with the hard drive acquisition process. As you can see, from start to finish, the acquisition phase can take the better part of an entire day just by itself before any analysis is started!

Analysis Phase

This is usually the longest phase in the process, although—depending on findings—the Reporting Phase can actually take longer.

Much of the activity performed in this phase is predicated on what the case parameters are. Understand that there are also a great many tools at a skilled examiner's disposal with which to perform tasks. This paper attempts to be tool agnostic and speak merely to the process, not the specific techniques or tools.

To better understand what the examiner faces, it behooves a potential client to have a basic understanding of how an operating system works. This paper is focused on the Windows operating system but, generally speaking, the process applies to any operating system. The purpose of this paper is not to fully train the reader in the technical functionality of Windows but rather to understand some of its complexities. For that reason, it is not necessarily important to understand the terminologies or data repositories but rather be aware of the volumes of information that get parsed of which the average client may not be aware.

Windows by itself is a complicated and highly technical living beast. Add to this the fact that there are basically two types of Windows (32 bit and 64 bit, functioning in vastly different ways) and multiple versions of each type (Windows 7 Home, Windows 7 Professional, Windows 7 Ultimate, etc.), not to mention different packages of Windows (Windows 95, 98, XP, 2000, Vista, 7, 8, etc.). As if that weren't enough, consider the vagaries of all the different programs (and their types and versions) that a user may install, and it becomes easy to see why a computer forensic examination is a highly complex undertaking. And these are only the parts that an average user sees and knows about.

Generally speaking, Windows contents (system only, not considering user data) can be classified as visible and hidden. Although these two areas don't specifically contain user-created data, they DO contain a vast amount of data ABOUT a user, their activities, preferences, and habits. These areas provide as much or more data relevant to an investigation than the user files alone. For example, the fact that a user-created Word document exists is not always that important because the client usually already knows about it. It is the "under the hood" workings that tell the examiner about the file, such as the "who, what, when, where, and how" and sometimes even "why." For the most part, this data is not visible to the average user or even known to exist.

Here then, is a brief list of the types of "behind the scenes" data that may exist but are not visible to the average user. This is certainly not an exhaustive list and, if anything, is a small subset of the available data that an examiner may have to review.

- Windows Registry
- Hidden Volumes
- Temporary Internet Folders
- Browser Cache Data
- Most Recently Used Lists
- System Log Files
- Install/Uninstall Files
- Prefetch Files
- Hibernation Files
- Virtual Memory Files
- Event Logs

Although this may initially not look like a very long list, it is actually so vast that an examiner will generally spend most of his or her time in these areas. As well, on most computers, there are multiple copies of all of the above from different snapshots in time. Below is just a very small list of the types of information that may be found in the areas described above.

- Files that have been deleted
- USB devices ever connected
- Files/folders that have been exfiltrated from a computer
- Devices that have been connected
- CD/DVDS that may have been burned
- Websites visited
- Lists of recently used programs and the files they have accessed
- Programs that have been installed and uninstalled
- Evidence of attempts at data destruction/hiding
- Program settings that can show knowledge of an act
- Programs that start when the computer starts
- Number of times a program has ever been run
- Wi-Fi connection points

- Hidden e-mail and other accounts
- Geographic location of where photos were taken
- Particular user-performed tasks

The first technical step in starting the analysis phase is getting the data into a state by which it can be searched or have data extracted. This can take many forms depending on how an examiner performs the tasks. A very common first step is to perform a function variously called "recover folders." This auto "undeletes" any files on the computer that were deleted but still have the Master File Table Entry intact. Once complete, the next step commonly performed is "indexing the case." This indexing is a very complex set of functions whereby a program or programs are used to perform a number of tasks to prepare the data for examination. Just some of the steps include the extraction and parsing of compound files such as registry hives and their components for each user, not to mention the same for every instance of these that are found in system restore points, and volume shadow copies. This will also apply to log files and other system artifact repositories. Many cases involve user-created documents, and as such, clients will need search terms ran against them to see if any are responsive.

Clients typically think this is a simple search, like looking for something in Google. It couldn't be further from the truth. In fact, files such as Microsoft Office files, PDF documents, compression files such as RAR and ZIP, TIFF files, e-mail files, Internet cache files, etc. reside on the computer in proprietary encryption packages. Without first decrypting and mounting the above files, search terms will be useless and will find nothing.

The indexing portion itself goes above and beyond everything that has already been discussed. It is performed once all compound files (registry, Office documents, PDF, e-mail, etc.) have been decrypted and mounted.

This process then crawls through the hard drive from one end to the other and creates an index of every single word, phrase, or human-readable syntax contained within. Once complete, this allows the search process to be performed based on search terms. Again, this process is dependent on software and methodologies and is meant as a general guideline.

All of the above needs to be performed before an examiner can start working with the data. It should be clear by now that with the size of hard drives today, this is going to be a time-consuming task, measured typically in days or weeks, not hours. In fact, depending on the size of the dataset, the software used, and the goals of the investigation, it can take two to three days per hard drive just to get the data into a format for the examiner to start working with it. Again, specific caveats apply.

Fortunately, much of the above are automated functions that the examiner "sets and forgets." Once the functions are complete, the examination can start, but in the interim, in a best-case scenario, three to four days or more may have passed since acquisition of the data. This is suggestive of a lab that has nothing else to do. It is the norm that successful labs will have numerous cases ongoing at any given time; in most cases, the progression of a given file is not 24/7 until completion.

Once all of the above has been completed, the heavy lifting begins. This is where the examiner starts to use experience and technical expertise to answer the client's questions. Search term hit extraction is a common function in many cases and is typically not an onerous function as it pertains to resident data. However, in cases where data has been deleted and must be manually recovered, this can be cost and labor prohibitive. For example, most forms of e-mail cannot be recovered automatically once they are deleted. There is no special script or program that can recover them because they do not contain a file signature (an important component for automated recovery). As such, they need to be located, identified, extracted, and given a name and extension that will allow for identification and for the end user to be able to read the extraction simply by clicking on it.

Imagine for a moment finding 20,000 "hits" on a particular search parameter in unallocated file space. Suggesting, in the case of e-mail, that a skilled examiner can perform the extraction at a manual rate of six per minute (10 seconds per e-mail to identify, extract, convert, name, and move to the next one), the above 20,000 extractions would take over 55 hours nonstop without a break. For this reason, it is important for clients to be realistic about what they are searching for. Asking to recover all e-mails from or to joe@bloggins.com where this is the e-mail address of the user of the computer you are investigating, is an unrealistic request but one that labs get frequently.

This is by no means the end of the Analysis Phase. It is very possible that for various case-specific reasons, more automated searches need to be performed, each taking many hours to a few days to perform. It is easy to see, then, how a case that was initially quoted at seven days can turn into 14 or more. An examiner can only give an average completion time. There is simply no way to know at the onset what the examiner may face, and no one at any stage prior can assist with that determination. In fact, a very common reason for cases to take longer than anticipated is because the client had their IT department self-investigate the case first. Mostly, this just destroys or alters evidence, making it harder and far more time consuming for the examiner to determine what was happening on the computer, when, and by whom.

Reporting Phase

Usually the most important but most neglected phase, the report is an integral part of the overall engagement. A proper report will be clear and concise, free of embellishment and guessing, and understandable to any layperson. In many cases, the report cannot be submitted in written format. Take for example, a complex spreadsheet. Printing the spreadsheet that is many columns wide cannot be portrayed properly on paper, not to mention that a printed spreadsheet cannot show the underlying formulas in the data. Another example would be a case that involves the identification of 500 pictures. It is much easier to provide an electronic report, in which the user can click in the report to be taken to the photos, than printing so much data. A proper report takes time and can stretch into many hours of examiner time.

One of the most important (and often unperformed) tasks is for the client to make the necessary time to sit with the examiner in order to best determine the ultimate goal. In many cases, a client will give the examiner a one- or two-sentence goal and a list of search terms and then send them off hunting. This only creates a great deal of wasted time and client frustration at how long a case might take.

In conclusion, a client must be realistic to what is possible, sympathetic to unseen changes to work direction and timeline, and receptive to receiving information that was unexpected. A computer forensic examiner cannot fabricate data. If you trust your examiner, and they are proficient at their science, sometimes the client must accept that either there is no evidence left to put forth or that initial theories were wrong. At the end of the day, the data does not lie. It merely sits there waiting to be interpreted.

Kevin J. Ripa, Computer Forensic Identification, PI Magazine, April 2015.

COMPUTER FORENSICS

Data residing in a digital device or a digital storage medium can be the deciding factor in the outcome of an investigation. Finding and recovering the data is a task not simple or easy. Considerable knowledge and skill are required to unearth data, and in some cases, interpret their meaning.

Computer-derived data must meet certain standards for them to be admitted into evidence in a judicial proceeding. These standards ensure authenticity and are expressed in what are called Rules of Evidence that deal with legal concepts such as probable cause, search and seizure, and chain of custody. These conditions explain use of the word "forensic," i.e., "relating to or dealing with the application of scientific knowledge to legal arguments."

The examination of a computer can reveal two important circumstances: (1) use of the computer as a tool and (2) storage of the products that derive from its use. For example, the computer is a tool when it is used to circumvent the protection of a credit card information system and it is repository for the products of the crime, which in this example is the illegally acquired information. Matters such as these often fall into the categories of fraud and theft, which are criminal offenses, and are civil offenses when related to divorce, child custody, breach of contract, and tortuous acts. Other situations involve invasion of privacy, child pornography and cyberstalking.

The scope of a forensic analysis can range from retrieving simple information to reconstructing an event or a series of events. Simple information might be s sent and received by an adulterous spouse; an event might be an illegal electronic transfer of funds; and a series of events might be embezzlement occurring incrementally. In this last example, "audit trail" is the operative term.

Recovery of deleted files is a common technique in computer forensics. Most operating systems and file storage systems do not erase data, which makes it possible to extract or reconstruct data which remain on disk sectors. Some retrieval techniques can be performed on site, such as in a business office or home; other techniques, usually more complicated, have to be performed in a laboratory setting.

Learning Shop USA, Scientific Analysis of Evidence, www.learningshopusa.com

CONFIDENTIALITY

There should be no investigation in which results are open to discussion with noncleared employees and outsiders. Exception is made when an outside agency has authority under the law to obtain confidential information. In certain instances, confidential information can be withheld from authorities when it is protected by a legal concept called the attorney-client privilege. This privilege protects communications between a client and his or her attorney and keeps those communications confidential.

Confidential information not related to investigations includes:

- Proprietary (owned) business and technical information
- Personal data concerning people such as agency employees, former employees, and job applicants
- Information owned by or shared with partners
- Information protected by a confidentiality or nondisclosure agreement

Confidentiality Agreement

A confidentiality agreement is intended to prevent unauthorized disclosure of sensitive information held by the agency's current and former employees, consultants, contractors, and other parties that have or have had access to sensitive information.

Storage

Highly confidential information that is not in active use should be stored in a steel, fireproof, and water-resistant safe fitted with a combination lock. The combination should be given to persons on a "right and need-to-know" basis.

Mid-level sensitive information that is not in active use should be stored in a metal filing cabinet fitted with a locking bar and an industrial-strength padlock. The padlock key or knowledge of the padlock's combination should be limited according to persons selected by the agency manager.

Confidential information at a low level of sensitivity can be stored in locked desk drawers, credenzas, and containers resistant to forced opening. Access to files can be limited to persons who work with the files on a continuing basis.

Confidential information stored in a computer data system should be protected by passwords, gateways, and other digital procedures that prevent theft, damage, or contamination of data.

To disclose confidential information to unauthorized persons is more than betrayal of a trust; it is a risk that carries high potential for civil liability.

John J. Fay, *Encyclopedia of Security Management*, second ed., Butterworth-Heinemann, Burlington, MA, 2007, pp. 115–117.

CONSUMER REPORTING AGENCY

The Fair Credit Reporting Act (FCRA) is the source of the term "consumer reporting agency (CRA)." A CRA is any person or entity that, for monetary fees, dues, or on a cooperative nonprofit basis, regularly engages in whole or in part in the practice of assembling or evaluating consumer credit information or other information on consumers for the purpose of furnishing consumer reports to third parties and that uses any means or facility of interstate commerce for the purpose of preparing or furnishing consumer reports.

A private investigator or a private investigation agency is a CRA when it collects and reports credit and other information to clients, such as employers.

Federal Trade Commission, http://www.ftc.gov/enforcement/rules

CONTRABAND

Contraband is any item that, by itself, is a crime to possess. Bootleg whiskey is contraband because possession of it is against the law. The same holds true for certain types of firearms, explosives, illegal drugs, marijuana, and counterfeit money. A search and seize warrant is issued when it is known in advance that contraband is present at a certain place.

If contraband is seized without a warrant, the seizure is illegal; however, contraband that is discovered accidentally can be seized without a warrant. How the seizure was made will determine if the possessor can be prosecuted. Whether or not charges are brought, the contraband is not returned to the possessor.

John J. Fay, *Encyclopedia of Security Management*, second ed., Butterworth-Heinemann, Burlington, MA, 2007, p. 240.

CONTROLLED SUBSTANCES

There are five schedules of controlled substances. They are Schedules I, II, III, IV, and V.

Schedule I

- The drug or other substance has a high potential for abuse.
- The drug or other substance has no currently accepted medical use in treatment in the United States.
- There is a lack of accepted safety for use of the drug or other substance under medical supervision.

Schedule II

- The drug or other substance has a high potential for abuse.

- The drug or other substance has a currently accepted medical use in treatment in the United States or a currently accepted medical use with severe restrictions.
- Abuse of the drug or other substances may lead to severe psychological or physical dependence.

Schedule III

- The drug or other substance has less potential for abuse than the drugs or other substances in schedules I and II.
- The drug or other substance has a currently accepted medical use in treatment in the United States.
- Abuse of the drug or other substance may lead to moderate or low physical dependence or high psychological dependence.

Schedule IV

- The drug or other substance has a low potential for abuse relative to the drugs or other substances in schedule III.
- The drug or other substance has a currently accepted medical use in treatment in the United States.
- Abuse of the drug or other substance may lead to limited physical dependence or psychological dependence relative to the drugs or other substances in schedule III.

Schedule V

- The drug or other substance has a low potential for abuse relative to the drugs or other substances in schedule IV.
- The drug or other substance has a currently accepted medical use in treatment in the United States.
- Abuse of the drug or other substance may lead to limited physical dependence or

psychological dependence relative to the drugs or other substances in schedule IV.

http://www.deadiversion.usdoj.gov/21c-fr/21usc/index.html

CORPUS DELICTI

The term *corpus delicti* means "body of the crime." It is often used erroneously to describe the body of a victim. Actually, the term relates to the essence of an offense and thus implies that every offense must have a *corpus delicti*.

In proving an accused's guilt of a specific crime, the prosecution establishes three general facts:

- An injury or loss particular to the crime involved has taken place.
- The injury or loss was brought about by somebody's criminality, meaning that the injury or loss resulted from a criminal act as opposed to an accident or other cause.
- The accused, possessing the requisite state of mind (i.e., intent), was the person who caused the injury or loss.

The first two facts constitute the *corpus delicti*. The third fact simply establishes the identity of the offender. For example, the *corpus delicti* in a larceny would be (l) the loss of property (2) by an unlawful taking. In an arson offense, it would be (1) a burned house (2) that was deliberately set on fire.

John J. Fay, Encyclopedia of Security Management, second ed., Butterworth-Heinemann, Burlington, MA, 2007, p. 221.

COST MANAGEMENT

In addition to overall management of case work, the agency head is concerned with management of operating costs. A common practice is to compute costs per case worked.

For the nonprivate investigation agency, this approach allows expenses to be shown in broad categories such as crimes against persons, crimes against property, cyber crimes, intelligence gathering, or any activity falling within the agency's area of responsibility. For the private investigation agency, the rationale for assigning costs per case is to invoice clients. The total cost per case is computed according to expenses.

Operating costs are not costs for purchasing big-ticket items like land, buildings, and vehicles. Big-ticket expenditures are called capital expenses. Capital expenditures are reflected in a separate budget, although it can be possible for monthly payments to be paid out of the operating costs budget.

Operating cost categories are based on historical experience; for example, an agency that pays a monthly retainer to a forensic expert will have a cost category called "Forensic Services." A different agency may not require forensic services (at least on a monthly basis) and therefore will not reflect such a category in its monthly overhead report. The point here is that operating costs vary from one agency to another—yet all agencies have operating costs and should keep track of them monthly, no matter what they happen to be.

A common method for keeping track of monthly operating costs is to maintain a file (typically called the overhead file) containing bills that were paid in that month. The bills are of different types: utility bills, rent bills, credit card statements, purchase orders, auto and travel expense reports, and the like.

The overhead budget is both a planning tool and a tool for tracking costs. As a planning tool, the agency head uses it to estimate costs for the upcoming budget period, which is almost always a fiscal year. Based on the previous year's experience, the agency head can project future costs and in which categories.

Using an overhead budget form, the agency head can, as each month passes, look at expenditures in all of the categories. Where expenditures exceed projections, the agency head can cut back on that category's expenditure or change the budget itself by allocating more total funds or by moving funds from an "underspent" category to the "overspent" category. It helps to think of a budget as a large coat with many pockets. When one pocket is empty, money can be moved to it from a pocket that is full.

Operating Expenses

Operating expenses are usually routine but can occur out of the blue, such as unexpected case work. Routine expenses are numerous: utilities, telephone, gas and water, electricity, rent and leases, office supplies, advertising, and others. Expenses that can be volatile include expenditures for motor vehicle operation, travel, and payroll.

Motor Vehicle Expenses. Money spent to buy, operate, and maintain a vehicle can be substantial. Motor vehicle cost is a combination of purchase price less depreciation over a period of time, number of miles driven, and maintenance. This combination is used to determine the cost per mile driven. Assume, for example, that the cost per mile is set at 40 cents; that 40 cents, times the number of miles the motor vehicle is expected to be driven in its lifetime, represents the total cost of the vehicle. If a moderately priced vehicle can be expected to give 120,000 miles in its lifetime and the cost per mile is 40 cents, the overall motor vehicle cost is $48,000. How long will it take before the odometer gets to 120,000? Let's say it takes 4 years (120,000 divided by 4 is 30,000 miles per year). The cost per year is $12,000 (40 cents times 30,000 is $12,000). Since a year consists of 12 months, the cost per month is $1,000.

Now, assume that the agency head projects that the motor vehicle cost will rise relative to a rise in the costs of gasoline and maintenance. So to be on the safe side, the agency head will set the per-mile cost to 45 cents. If the agency is a private investigation agency, the motor vehicle cost is passed on to the customer; if the agency is a public or government agency or a corporation, the motor vehicle cost is approved at the finance level.

Travel Expenses. These expenses reflect incidental purchases made by employees who travel away from the office. Among these expenses are travel tickets, toll fees, taxi payments, lodging, and food/entertainment. A travel expenses report, while administrative in nature, can require confidentiality. For example, if a trip was made to follow a person of interest from one city to another, the travel expenses report needs to be treated with confidence because the details of the expense report could allow an outsider to deduce the purpose of the travel.

Payroll Expenses. Labor cost is almost always an agency's largest cost. In a business setting, and with respect to nonsalaried employees, time sheets or similar administrative devices keep track of hours worked. The employee prepares his or her time sheet and submits it to a person who keeps track of hours worked by the employee; payroll is computed for that employee. Since salaried persons are not paid on an hours-worked basis, the payroll for them is simple to compute, i.e., total salary divided by the work period (every two weeks or every month or whatever the frequency may be).

The cost of nonemployee labor, such as work performed by a consultant, is usually paid from a separate account.

Offsets to Expenses

The lifeblood of a private investigation agency is revenue. Money owed to the agency is typically collected by first sending an invoice to the client. The invoice is brief and to the point but is accompanied by documentation that supports the money owed. The documentation can consist of a statement of hours worked, copies of auto mileage reports, air tickets, hotel bills, food bills, taxi receipts, and toll tickets.

An invoice is numbered and has a payment due date. The invoice number is an accounts receivable device that allows the agency head to keep track of who was billed, what was billed, and when payment is due. When payment is not received when due, the payment is considered delinquent.

John J. Fay, *Contemporary Security Management*, third ed., Elsevier, Burlington, MA, 2011, pp. 83–95.

COURT PROCEDURES

The trial court is a cornerstone of democratic societies. It embodies the principles that distinguish the rule of law from the rule of capricious will.

Five principles guide the American trial court system. They are:

- Trials are public proceedings that are open to public view and committed to public record.
- Only under the authority of a court can punishment be delivered in the form of a sentence.
- The trial embodies fairness in the form of due process, the presumption of innocence, and the rules of evidence.
- Trials are presided over by impartial judges who receive their authority from the consent of the people.
- Trials uphold the rule of law by providing sanctions for offenders.

The procedures that are called "due process" assure the right:

- To counsel
- Of first notice of charges
- To speedy trial
- To prepare a defense
- To testify and call witnesses
- To cross examine
- Of appeal

Preparing a case for trial requires "professional presence." In the field of investigation, professional presence is demonstrated by thoroughness, honesty, and impartiality in the gathering of facts and by reports of investigation that are accurate, complete, and clearly written.

In the end, many cases will be plea-bargained and settled out of court. The reasons for doing so are:

- Relieving pressure on courts that are overburdened with heavy caseloads
- Obtaining value by trading for important information
- Reducing the possibility of acquittal when a prosecution's case is weak

Larry Fennelly

CRIME CATEGORIES

Crimes are divided into two general classes: felonies and misdemeanors. A felony is an offense more serious and calls for greater punishment than a misdemeanor. State laws vary, but in most U.S. jurisdictions and in federal statutes, felonies are tried by a jury and carry punishment by death or imprisonment for more than one year.

The seriousness of an offense is often determined by a dollar value. A theft under a certain amount is a misdemeanor; at or above the certain amount, it is a felony. Seriousness is also measured by the nature of the act, which explains why murder, aggravated assault, and kidnapping are felony crimes.

A misdemeanor can be upgraded to a felony when the act involves an exacerbating circumstance, such as the use of a weapon or an attack upon a peace officer.

A misdemeanor is less serious than a felony and, by federal and state laws, is usually punishable by fine or imprisonment for less than one year. Depending on the value of property involved, misdemeanors can be subdivided using terms like major and minor or gross and petty.

Elements of Crime

Criminal statutes define offenses in very specific terms using what are called the elements of a crime. The elements must be present for an act to be considered a crime. The job of the investigator is to identify the elements of the crime being investigated (for example, by researching the applicable criminal statute) and establishing with some form of proof that the elements were present in the act. The simple act of theft would include:

- Unlawful taking
- Of the property of another, with
- Intent to permanently deprive the owner of the property

The investigator would have to prove each element. For example, let's assume the property in question is an automobile. A sworn written statement obtained from the owner and/or the owner's initial complaint to the police could establish the unlawful taking of the automobile. The ownership element could be established with a certificate of title and/or a bill of sale. The intent to permanently deprive might be shown by a newspaper advertisement in which the suspect offered the vehicle for sale.

Proving the Case

In proving guilt of a specific crime in a court of law, the prosecution establishes three general facts:

- An injury or loss has taken place.
- The injury or loss resulted from a criminal act as opposed to an accident or other cause.
- The accused was the person who caused the injury or loss.

The first two facts are primary. The third fact establishes the identity of the offender. For example, the primary facts in a burglary would be an unlawful entry coupled with intent to commit a crime therein. In an arson offense, it would be a burned house coupled with a deliberately set fire.

Corpus Delicti

The term *corpus delicti* means "body of the crime" and is often used erroneously to describe the corpse of the victim in a homicide case. Actually, the term relates to the essence of an offense and thus implies that every offense must have a *corpus delicti*. In a theft by taking, the investigator must establish that the property taken did in fact exist and was owned by the person from whom it was taken. This is the *corpus delicti* or body of the crime.

Criminal Intent

Criminal intent is a clearly formulated state of mind to do an act that the law specifically prohibits, without regard to the motive that prompts the act and whether or not the offender knows that what he or she is doing is in violation of the law. Intent is generally regarded as falling into two categories: general criminal intent and specific criminal intent. General criminal intent is an essential element in all crimes. It means that when the offender acted, or failed to act, contrary to the law, he or she did so voluntarily with determination or foresight of the consequences. For example, general criminal intent is shown in the offense of assault and battery when the offender voluntarily applies unlawful force to another with an awareness of its result. In larceny, general criminal intent (often called larcenous intent) is shown by intent to knowingly take and carry away the goods of another without any claim or pretense of right, with intent wholly to deprive the owner of them or to convert them to personal use.

Specific criminal intent requires a particular mental state in addition to that of general criminal intent. The laws relating to certain crimes may describe an additional, specific mental purpose. For example, the crime of murder has a general criminal intent in that the offender voluntarily applies unlawful force with an awareness of its result. In addition, the crime of murder in a particular jurisdiction may require showing that the offender acted with premeditation.

Motive

Motive and intent are separate concepts in criminal law. Motive is the desire or inducement that tempts or prompts a person to do a criminal act. Intent is a person's resolve to commit the act. Motive is the reason that leads the mind to desire a certain result. Intent is the determination to achieve the result. Motive is an important investigative consideration but is not an essential element of a crime. Intent must be established for a crime to exist. A good motive (as might be represented in a mercy killing) does not keep an act from being a crime, and an evil motive will not necessarily make an act a crime. Furthermore, an accused would not be acquitted simply because a motive could not be discovered. The basic urge that led the offender's mind to want the result of the forbidden act is immaterial as to guilt. Proof of motive, however, may be relevant and admissible on behalf of either side at trial. Motive can be especially pertinent where the evidence in a case is largely circumstantial. In some statutes, proof of motive may be required.

Malice

Malice is a mental state accompanying a criminal act that is performed willfully, intentionally, and without legal justification. The term "malice aforethought" is the state of mind or attitude with which an act is carried out, i.e., the design, resolve, or determination with which a person acts to achieve a certain result. In the death of another, it means knowledge of circumstances that according to common experience would indicate a clear and strong likelihood that death will follow the contemplated act. Malice aforethought is usually coupled with an absence of justification for the act.

Overt Act

An overt act is an outward act from which criminality may be inferred. The breaking of a lock on a door may be an overt act of burglary, and the acquisition of a handgun may be an overt act of armed robbery. In the crime of conspiracy, the overt act is an essential element of proof.

Parties to Crime

Persons culpably concerned in the commission of a crime, whether they directly commit the act constituting the offense or facilitate, solicit, encourage, aid or attempt to aid, or abet its commission, are called the parties to the crime. In some jurisdictions, the concept is extended to include persons who assist another who has committed a crime in order to avoid arrest, trial, conviction, or punishment.

The parties to a felony crime fall into four categories:

- Principals in the first degree
- Principals in the second degree
- Accessories before the fact
- Accessories after the fact

Generally, a principal in the first degree is the actual offender who commits the act. If the offender uses an agent to commit the act, the offender is still a principal in the first degree. There may be more than one principal in the first degree for the same offense.

A principal in the second degree is one who, with knowledge of what is afoot, aids and abets the principal in the first degree at the very time the felony is being committed by rendering aid, assistance, or encouragement. A principal in the second degree is typically at the crime scene, nearby, or situated in such a way as to render assistance. Under the concept of "constructive presence," a principal in the second degree could be a considerable distance removed from the crime while it is being committed. An example might be a lookout monitoring police radio communications at a remote location who calls burglar accomplices at the crime scene to alert them of police patrol movements.

An accessory before the fact is a person who, before the time a crime is committed, knows of the particular offense contemplated, assents to or approves of it, and expresses a view of it in a form that operates to encourage the principal to perform the deed. There is a close resemblance between an accessory before the fact and a principal in the second degree. The difference relates to where the accessory was and the nature of the assistance rendered at the time the crime was committed. If a person advises, encourages, and gives aid prior to the act, but is not present at the act and not giving aid at the time of the act, the person would be regarded as an accessory before the fact.

An accessory after the fact is a person who, knowing that another has committed a felony, later aids the felon to escape in any way or prevents arrest and prosecution. The person may help the felon elude justice by concealing, sheltering, or comforting the felon while a fugitive; by supplying the means of escape; or by destroying evidence. An accessory after the fact must have an intention to assist the felon and must actually do so. Mere knowledge of the felon's offense and a failure to report it does not make a person an accessory after the fact.

Preliminary Offenses

There are three crimes that are preparatory in nature and serve as part of a larger purpose. Each of them is a means of reaching a criminal end. These so-called preliminary crimes are:

- Solicitation
- Attempt
- Conspiracy

Solicitation consists of the offender's oral or written efforts to activate another person to commit a criminal offense. The essence of the crime is to incite by counsel, enticement, or inducement. The offense of solicitation is complete if the offender merely urges another to violate the law and otherwise does nothing himself.

Attempt has two elements. First, there must be a specific intent to commit a particular offense; second, there must be a direct overt act toward its commission. Mere preparation, such as obtaining tools or weapons, may be insufficient to establish the crime, especially when made at a distance in time or place.

Conspiracy is the combination of two or more persons working in some concerted action to accomplish a criminal or unlawful purpose or to accomplish a purpose in a criminal or unlawful manner. If there is a common understanding among the participants to achieve a certain purpose or to act in a certain way, a conspiracy exists without regard to whether there is any formal or written statement of purpose, even though there is no actual speaking of words. There may be merely a tacit understanding without any express agreement.

Federal Offenses

There can be no federal crime unless Congress first makes an act a criminal offense by passing a statute, affixing punishment to it, and declaring what court will have jurisdiction. This means that all federal crimes are statutory. Although many of the statutes are based on common law, every federal statute is an express enactment of Congress. Nearly all crimes are defined in Title 18 of the U.S. Code.

Generally speaking, federal crimes fall into three large areas:

- Crimes affecting interstate commerce
- Crimes committed in places beyond the jurisdiction of any state
- Crimes that interfere with the activities of the federal government.

Crimes affecting interstate commerce are described in a variety of acts, e.g., the Mann Act, the Dyer Act, the Lindbergh Act, and the Fugitive Felon Act.

Crimes committed in places beyond the jurisdiction of a state might include, for example, murder on an American ship on the high seas or on a federal enclave such as a military reservation ceded to the United States by a state. It should be noted that when an offense not covered by a federal statute is committed on a federal enclave, the case can be tried in a federal court under the laws of the state where the enclave is located. The offense of murder, for example, is not defined in a federal statute. If murder occurs on a military reservation in Georgia, the federal government can prosecute the case using the Georgia statute covering murder.

Crimes that interfere with the activities of the federal government include fraudulent use of the mails, robbery of a federal bank, failure to pay income tax, espionage, and many similar offenses. Federal courts have no jurisdiction over crimes against the states and vice versa. It can happen, however, that an offense will violate both a state law and a federal law, e.g., robbery of a federally insured state bank. In such a case, both the federal and state court will have jurisdiction.

Joseph A. Senna and Larry J. Siegel, *Introduction to Criminal Justice*, West Publishing, Minneapolis/St. Paul, MN, pp. 159.

John J. Fay, *Encyclopedia of Security Management*, second ed., Butterworth-Heinemann, Burlington, MA, 2007, pp. 221–225.

CRIME PREVENTION ASSUMPTIONS

Crime prevention has never been an exact science; it rests upon a number of assumptions that in certain environments are very valid and in other environments not so valid. This section will state the assumptions, and readers are free to use them as they see fit.

Potential Crime

Potential crime victims are often unaware of their vulnerability to crime or to the consequences that follow. To reduce or eliminate the vulnerability, the potential crime victim, typically the owner of a business organization, has two choices: discover the vulnerability and take preventive actions, or acquire the services of a crime prevention specialist. Investigation agencies in the public and private sectors employ specialists. The Vulnerability Assessment is an investigator's tool. It is the methodology for identifying vulnerability and proposing corrective actions.

Environmental Control

Control of the environment where crime occurs is control exercised by the victim. The criminal, to succeed, must overcome that control. It is not possible to convert every criminal to honesty. It is possible, however, to keep the potential criminal honest. This is done by putting controls into place that prevent crime. Controls vary and are numerous:

- Access control
- Intrusion detection
- Nighttime lighting
- CCTV

- Alarms
- Fences
- Vaults, safes, locks, etc.
- Human observation

Installing controls such as those above are valuable to the extent they are operated efficiently. Potential criminals, particularly professional criminals, will critically examine the controls and attack where they are weak.

The Traditional Crime Prevention Approach

The criminal justice system (law enforcement, courts, and corrections) has never worked well in preventing crime. The police are response-oriented; they react to crime as opposed to keeping it from happening in the first place. Law enforcement has a central role in dealing with crime but is not a dominant force in crime prevention.

Plea bargaining and the leniency of courts allow criminals to remain "on the street." Correctional facilities are places where criminals learn from each other how to keep from getting caught next time.

In one small respect, the consequences of getting caught, being tried, and going to prison are deterrents. But if deterrence was even modestly successful, crime rates would drop and then plateau at a manageable level. Property crime in particular would decline. (Note: Crimes against persons, such as rape, assault, and homicide, are crimes that are resistant to deterrence.)

Interest Groups

In the context of this section, an interest group is a combination of people working together to prevent crime. A good example of an interest group is the Neighborhood Watch program. People living in neighborhoods and small communities will often be on the lookout for suspicious activities and quickly call the police. Potential criminals can be discouraged from committing crimes

in areas where residents are watchful. By and large, criminals do not like witnesses.

Revitalization

New construction and renovation of a crime-prone area can generate a sense of ownership, a natural part of which includes crime prevention. Two factors contribute: criminals will move on to the other areas, and persons who live and work in the revitalized area will be motivated to keep criminals out.

Crime Prevention Doctrine

Crime prevention is interdisciplinary. Its doctrine draws upon psychology, sociology, physical security, the technology sciences, and other disciplines. The crime prevention doctrine does not stand still; it is constantly in the mode of discovery and change.

Strategies and Techniques

In crime prevention, nothing is written in stone. What may work here may not work someplace else; what worked yesterday or today may not work tomorrow; and ideas that are still on the drawing board are ideas that, when introduced to real life, may not meet expectations. But failed expectations are lessons learned, and crime prevention has a way of benefiting from real-life experience.

Conclusion

Crime prevention is rarely a full-time vocation. People in many different fields are crime prevention practitioners, sometimes with knowing it. But there is one field where crime prevention is understood, preached, and practiced. That field is the field of investigation. It is not an accident that when a final report of investigation is submitted, there will be a recommendation as to how repetition of the crime can be avoided. Conclusions of this type are crime prevention conclusions.

Investigators are attuned to crime on the horizon. Some people claim that investigators were born to investigate, and others claim that attunement is the product of experience. Either way, crime prevention is in the stock and trade of criminal investigation.

John J. Fay, *Encyclopedia of Security Management*, second ed., Butterworth-Heinemann, Burlington, MA, 2007, pp. 481–484.

CRIME PREVENTION THROUGH ENVIRONMENTAL DESIGN

CPTED is a field of study that holds that crime can be eliminated or reduced by application of designs incorporated in schools, neighborhoods, apartment complexes, buildings, parks, transportation systems, and just about every physical part of the environment in which people live. Application of the concept can occur in many simple ways: locking doors, placing valuables out of reach, illuminating open areas, controlling access, installing fences and gates, installing alarm systems, increasing visibility, modifying terrain, and planting trees and shrubs.

The intent is to discourage crime. A criminal act is likely not to occur when the criminal is confronted with the possibility of being caught and also concludes that the risk exceeds the value that might be obtained by the act.

Three elements are recognized by the CPTED concept. For a crime to occur there must be:

- Desire or motivation on the part of the criminal
- Skill and knowledge needed to commit the crime
- Opportunity to commit the crime

CPTED postulates that a crime is reduced when opportunity is removed. For example, a person that is motivated by greed to burglarize a home and has a skill to pry open a window will not attempt the burglary because the criminal perceives that the home has an alarm system, outside lights, or even a barking dog. Another example: an employee might have a desire to steal the petty cash fund, knows where the fund is kept, but cannot access the fund because it is in a safe.

Sean A. Andrews, *Encyclopedia of Security Management*, second ed., Butterworth-Heinemann, Burlington, MA, 2007, pp. 484–487.

Glenn Kitteringham, *Encyclopedia of Security Management*, second ed., Butterworth-Heinemann, Burlington, MA, 2007, pp. 487–489.

CRIME SCENE PHOTOGRAPHY

Photography is an essential tool for the investigator. As a tool, it enables the investigator to record the evidence of a crime. Photographs made of a crime can be stored indefinitely and retrieved when needed. There is no other process that can record, retain, and recall criminal evidence as effectively as photography.

Photographs are also a means of communication. They tell something about the objects photographed or the scene of a crime that is helpful in clarifying the issues when testimony is given in court. Because photographs are meant to communicate information honestly, the investigator-photographer has a great responsibility. His photographs must portray a situation as it would be observed by anyone who stood in the same position as the camera and viewed the scene from where the photograph was made.

Photographs by themselves are not substantive evidence. Photographs accepted in court must be attested to by a person who saw the scene and can truthfully state under oath that the photographs accurately represent what the person saw at the scene. In the ordinary, nonlegal field of photography, only the finished photographic print is of interest, but in criminal investigative work, all photographic procedures are subject to review and inspection by the court. Obviously, this rigid requirement makes it imperative that investigative photography conform to high standards of quality and ethics.

Technique

The most frequently occurring contributor to inferior photographic results is overexposure of the negative. This produces soft, grainy images of low contrast and brightness. Exposure recommendations for any given film are based upon the requirement for a so-called average subject. This is a photographic subject that contains light, medium, and dark tones. If a photographic subject consists of all light tones, the subject would be very low in contrast and high in brightness. If the recommended speed for a given film for use with a so-called average subject were ASA 80, the fact that the photographic subject contained all light tones means that less exposure is required. If, on the other hand, the subject consisted of all dark tones, the subject is low in contrast and is therefore reflecting very little light. In this case, the investigator-photographer adjusts his equipment to provide more exposure. For example, less exposure would be called for when the photographic subject is a nude body of a white bleached blonde lying on white sand; or at the other extreme, highly blackened wool at the scene of arson will require greater exposure than an average subject in order to obtain shadow detail. In short, the investigator must learn to evaluate his photographic subject by contrast and brightness and make appropriate adjustments.

Another common difficulty is a dirty lens. Dirt and oxidation may form on the back surface of the lens, as well on the front. Both the outer and inner surfaces of the camera lens should be checked frequently and cleaned when necessary.

Loss of detail in photographic prints is a common problem. This is usually caused by movement of the camera at the time the shutter is released. This problem can be reduced through the use of a rigid tripod and a fast shutter speed.

Sharpness, or image definition, suffers when the diaphragm of a lens is stopped down, i.e., adjusted from its largest opening to its smallest opening. When a lens is stopped down, three things happen:

- The aperture is reduced and less light passes through during a given period of time.
- The depth of field increases.
- The image definition improves to a point (although in a few special cases, the definition softens at the smallest apertures).

To obtain good definition the following general rules apply:

- Use a tripod whenever possible.
- For outdoor photography with a hand-held camera, set the aperture as required by film and light conditions, and use a faster shutter speed.
- For flash pictures, use an electronic flash.

Photography plays a vital part in establishing points of proof for certain types of crime, particularly crimes involving physical violence. The characteristics and location of relevant objects need to be captured in accurate detail and permanently recorded until presented at trial. If a crime scene is altered through carelessness or haste, it can never be restored to its exact original condition; as a consequence, vital elements of proof may be lost forever. In addition, the significance of certain aspects of a crime scene may not be apparent, although later they may powerfully affect a guilty or innocent conclusion. The first step in the investigation of any crime is to photograph completely and accurately all aspects of the scene before any of the objects of evidence are removed or otherwise disturbed. Photographs should also be made after victims have been removed. It is much better to take too many photographs than not enough.

When taking photographs at a scene, the objective should be to record the maximum usable information in a series of photographs that will enable the viewer to understand where and how the crime was committed. The term "crime scene" refers not just to the immediate locality in which the offense occurred but relates also to adjacent areas where important acts took place immediately before or after the commission of the offense. The number and types of photographs will be determined by the total circumstances of the crime.

Photographs of the broad area of the locale of the crime scene should be supplemented by closer shots of portions of the crime scene so that important details are made apparent. Each object within an area should be photographed so that it can be located readily in the overall pictures, thus enabling the viewer to gain a clear picture of its position in relation to other objects at the scene and to the overall scene.

At an indoor crime scene location, at least four photographs are required to show the room adequately. Moving in a clockwise direction, each photograph will overlap a portion of the preceding photograph so that 360-degree coverage is made of the area. Obviously, when an area is large or contains many pieces of evidence, the number of photographs will be far in excess of the minimum four. Medium-distant, as well as close-up, photographs should be made of important objects. Two lenses are usually sufficient for crime scene photography. A wide-angle lens is useful for interior photographs, and a normal-angle lens should be used for outdoor photographs.

Indoor lighting is rarely satisfactory for photographic purposes. The investigator must take into account the need for additional illumination. Depending upon the size, shape, and location of a crime scene, the investigator may elect to provide additional illumination through photoflood, photoflash, or electronic flash equipment.

Because a court may object to the presence of rulers or similar measuring devices in a crime scene photograph, it is recommended that the photographs be taken first without the marker and then with the marker. Measuring devices that are used to show the relative size of and distances between objects should be placed in such a manner that they will not obscure any important part of the evidence.

The final determination of the admissibility of photographs is made in court and often depends upon legal points that have little to do with the investigator-photographer. The investigator's contribution to the admissibility of photographs relates mainly to their accuracy and to the custody of them prior to trial.

All evidence must be protected and accounted for from the time it is found until it is offered in evidence. The law requires that the person presenting physical evidence in court be prepared to prove such evidence could not have been altered or replaced. This means that an investigator must be able to account for negatives and prints at all times. This does not present any great problem when photographs taken by the investigator are developed, printed, and secured within in-house resources. Problems can arise, however, when film is processed or placed into the custody of an outside agency. When this occurs, chain of custody procedures must be followed.

To be admissible, a photograph must be verified by a person who viewed the scene, object, or person represented in the photograph and is able to state that it is an accurate and truthful representation. In other words, the photograph must be a fair and accurate representation of the scene of the crime. Depending on the desires of the court, this issue can be addressed through testimony given by the investigator who took the photographs or by some other competent witness present at the time the photograph was taken.

An investigator who is required to give testimony regarding photographs he or she took at a scene should be prepared to testify regarding safekeeping of negatives and prints and to explain the details of the photographic procedures followed. An understanding of the rules of evidence and an application of common sense is usually sufficient to ensure that photographs taken in connection with a crime will be admissible in court.

Learning Shop USA, Collection and Preservation of Evidence, www.learningshopusa.com

CRIME SCENE SEARCHING

Criminal investigation is a systematic process of collecting evidence and applying to it a combination of human reasoning and scientific analysis so that the nature of the crime and the identity of the criminal can be determined. In this context, evidence includes all manner of tangible objects plus testimony. Human reasoning refers specifically to inductive and deductive reasoning. Scientific procedures refer to forensic examinations of evidence.

This section addresses the collection of physical evidence at a crime scene.

In many cases, the success or failure of an investigation will depend on the investigator's ability to recognize physical evidence and derive understanding from it. This process of evaluation begins with the initial report of a crime and concludes when the case is adjudicated. Evaluation is usually carried out in concert with laboratory technicians, other investigators, prosecuting attorneys, experts in relevant fields, and other persons whose knowledge contributes to a better understanding of physical evidence items and their relationship to the case at hand.

Inductive and Deductive Reasoning

Inductive. The thinking process that brings together separate observations drawn from objects, occurrences, and pieces of information is called inductive reasoning. Considered together, the observations or facts lead to a theory. To illustrate, money was stolen from a business owner's locked desk; the lock was forced open with a bladed instrument; the employee who was seen leaving the owner's office was questioned; he denied stealing the money; a bladed instrument, specifically a screwdriver, was found in the suspect's trash basket; and the suspect's fingerprints were found on the screwdriver. Taken together, these facts are sufficient to form a theory.

Deductive. This thinking process tests facts against one another. To illustrate, a valuable ring was stolen from a home while the owner was at the doctor's office, there was no indication that force had been used to gain access to the house, and the ring was taken from a jewelry box under the owner's bed. Taken together, these facts are sufficient to deduce that the thief knew how to get into the house, knew when to act, and knew that the ring was in a jewelry box under the bed. Deductive reasoning can reduce considerably the range of possible suspects.

Prepare for the Search

If the area to be searched is a public area, such as a roadway, permission is not required. If the area to be searched is still under the protection of law enforcement, permission to search will need to be obtained from the police or prosecutor. If the area is private property, permission must be obtained from the property owner or manager/operator.

Crime Scene Kit

A crime scene processing kit can be large and comprehensive or small and specific. The minimal kit will include photographic equipment, ruler, writing and drawing materials, compass, measuring tape, latex gloves, magnifying glass, flashlight and batteries, evidence tags and labels, evidence containers for fluids and nonfluids, and forms.

A more comprehensive kit will additionally include small tools, portable lighting, protractor, dental stone, scissors, fingerprinting equipment and supplies, ultraviolet lamp, spatula, rope, string, Magic Markers, gunshot residue collection materials, thermometer, and tweezers.

A crime scene kit is often composed of other kits such as those used for collecting fingerprints and fluids, making impressions of tread marks, taking photographs, and making sketches.

A 35mm camera, video camera, digital camera, smart phone, and sound recorder are usually kept separate from the processing kit.

Search Objectives

Prior to going to the search scene, a study should be done of everything that is known about the case, e.g., newspaper reports, police and court documents in the public domain, the victim's account of the matter, and statements made by witnesses and other persons involved.

Search Methods

Spiral. The searcher begins at the center of the scene and spirals outward. A second or third searcher retraces the path and reverses direction. The spiral method is appropriate for a small- to medium-size scene such as a room, a cashier's counter, or a spot on a street or highway.

Block or Quadrant Method. The searcher or a team of searchers is assigned a block. Within the block, a searcher might search in the spiral method; when the block is large, the lane or grid methods would be appropriate.

Lane Method. In this method, several searchers move in one direction side by side. The distance between them will depend on the terrain and what is being looked for. This method is suitable for a large scene such as a field or a wooded area.

Grid Method. In the grid method, the searchers work in lanes in one direction (e.g., east to west) and then cover the same territory in another direction (e.g., south to north).

Looking for Physical Evidence

A logical and systematic process is followed when looking for evidence. The process follows these steps:

- Make note of the location, time, date, and environmental conditions such as weather, temperature, and lighting.
- Take note of potential points and paths of exit and entry of persons involved, e.g., the suspect, victim, and witnesses.
- Scan the scene and its immediate surroundings. Look for any secondary crime scenes that may have been missed.
- Look for hard-to-detect physical evidence such as hair, fibers, stains, and impressions.
- Be alert to unusual sights, sounds, and smells.
- Do not smoke, eat, drink, or take out of your pockets anything that might fall and alter or contaminate the scene.
- Wear latex gloves to keep from leaving fingerprints.
- To avoid risk to personal health, do not touch blood or other body fluids.
- Not everything you see at an incident scene deserves to be collected. For items to be qualified as evidence, they must be material, relevant, and competent.
- To determine what is evidence, consider the offense involved and then look for any objects related to the offense.
- Look for objects that are foreign to the scene such as clothing in a wooded area, items that are excessive in number, and items that have been damaged or broken.

- Do not form an opinion during the search of an incident scene. This can come later, after the collected evidence has been evaluated by you and forensic scientists.
- The importance of physical evidence is in showing the nature of the incident and the persons involved. More than anything, logic and experience play a part in determining the items to be looked for and collected.

Collecting and Preserving Physical Evidence

Despite what you see in the movies and on television, an investigator is rarely in the middle of the action when a crime occurs and is rarely the first person to arrive at the scene after a crime has been reported. In some few cases, a private sector investigator may arrive at the scene during the time it is being processed by the police but is not a participant and is an observer at best. When a private sector investigator examines a crime scene, it is usually done "after the fact," i.e., after the police have processed the scene and released it back to normal use.

Let us concentrate, then, on crime scene processing procedures particular to the private sector investigator and leave out law enforcement procedures related to aspects such as administering first aid to crime scene victims and demarcating and securing the scene.

The collecting and preserving process includes these steps:

- Document each item with notes and photographs. Photograph each item before and after markers are placed. Take photographs that are full scene, medium distance, and close-up. Supplement photographs with video.
- Take notes from start to end. A voice recorder can be helpful.
- Prepare sketches.

- Measure pertinent distances such as the distance between pieces of evidence and the distance between pieces of evidence and an immoveable or fixed object.
- Place each item in a container appropriate to its nature, e.g., a sterile glass vial for a fluid or a clear plastic envelope for a hair or fiber. Apply to the container a label or an evidence tag and mark it with your initials and the date.
- Initiate a chain of custody form for the item.
- Package the item, ensuring protection against damage and cross-contamination. Transport the item to a place for secure storage or analysis by forensic examiners.
- Place into the case file all materials related to the search such as notes, sketches, diagrams, photographs, videotapes, audiotapes, evidence receipts, and copies of chain of custody forms.

Gun Shot Residue

The presence of gunshot residue on the hands of an individual indicates that the person recently discharged a firearm, handled a firearm or an object with gunshot residue on its surface, or was in close proximity to a firearm when it was discharged. In a suspected suicide by gunshot, the presence of residue on the victim's hands has little probative value. In those cases where you suspect someone else may have been involved, the analysis of samples from other individuals present at the scene may prove helpful.

The commonly used method of collecting gunshot residue from skin is the use of a specially treated stub. It is removed from its adhesive backing and pressed against the skin on the back and palm of each hand. The stubs are analyzed at a forensic laboratory with a scanning electron microscope that has been made sensitive to the morphology and elemental composition of gunshot residue. A collection kit is commercially available for collecting gunshot residue.

The manner of collecting evidence directly influences its later value. Collecting requires common sense and care. Things like cartridge cases, spent bullets, and tools should be cushioned with a soft fabric, such as cotton, and placed in small plastic envelopes; fluids can be lifted with sterile syringes and dispensed into sterile glass vials; and trace evidence can be picked up with tweezers and placed into new, clean envelopes. Small versatile tools, such as pocket knives, pliers, and screwdrivers, can be used to extract items from other materials.

More than anything, care should be taken to prevent loss, damage, or cross-contamination of evidence. Stepping on top of a tire tread will result in loss of that evidence, digging a bullet from wood can damage striations, and combining fluids from separate locations can result in cross-contamination.

The most common mistakes in collecting evidence are:

- Not collecting enough of a material to make a thorough forensic evaluation.
- Not obtaining standards that can be compared against collected materials. An example of a comparison standard is to collect fire debris at the point of origin of the fire and at a place or places distant from the fire's origin. The objective is to determine if an accelerant was used at one place instead of multiple places.
- Failing to protect the integrity of the evidence.

Sketching and Measuring

Crime scene sketching should occur after photographs are taken. The reason for this is that photographs are two-dimensional representations of three-dimensional objects. Photographs can distort space relationships so that items at the scene can appear to be closer together or farther apart than is actually the case. Sketches are important because they:

- Portray physical facts such as distances between objects and their proximity to each other
- Help create a mental picture for those who were not present at the scene such as prosecutors, attorneys, and jurors
- Create a permanent record of the scene

Rough Sketch. The rough sketch is a pencil-drawn picture made at the scene. It is usually made on graph paper with each square representing a certain number of square feet or inches. The view is vertical from overhead, and the horizontal view is determined by using a compass. Measurements are proportionally reduced on the rough sketch and the objects are drawn in. Two measurements taken at right angles to each other or from two reference points will usually suffice in placing the objects where they belong in a sketch.

Distances are measured and entered on the sketch or in notes. More than one sketch is usually prepared. They can show the overall vicinity, such as nearby streets and buildings; the area immediately surrounding the scene, such as entry and departure routes, trees, telephone poles, and adjacent structures; the scene itself; and objects within the scene, such as weapons in the case of a crime or motor vehicles in the case of a traffic accident.

Sketching and measuring are often done at the same time, preferably by a two-person team. If the scene is a room, stand in the doorway and start sketching in a circular direction that corresponds with the direction taken when photographs were taken. When measuring, be careful not to disturb other evidence, particularly evidence that is remaining to be sketched and measured.

A steel measuring tape is preferred because it does not stretch. To get the best measurement possible, take measurements in both directions: from point A to point B and from point B to point A.

Do not measure from moveable objects to moveable objects. Measure only from fixed objects; for example, measure from a corner of a shed (a fixed object) to an object of evidence (a moveable object).

Triangulation. The exact location of an object can be determined by measuring to the object from two or more fixed objects.

Rectangular-Coordinate Method. A method for locating objects in a room is the rectangular-coordinate method. It uses two adjacent walls as fixed points from which distances are measured at right angles. To make this method work, the room must be square or rectangular.

Cross-Projection Method. The cross-projection type of sketch is made of the scene as if one is looking straight down. It can be used when it is important to show the relationship between evidence on the floor and evidence on the wall. Think of the cross-projection as a cardboard box in which the sides have been pushed out and made flat.

When all of the rough sketches have been completed, evidence collection can begin. A finished scale drawing is prepared later using better drawing tools such as a board and ruler, protractor, templates, computer graphics, and so on. The rough sketches are retained and placed in the case file.

Marking Evidence

The first thing that needs to be said is that evidence discovered at a crime scene is not touched until it has been photographed and recorded in notes and sketches. The marking of evidence for the purposes of identification occurs later in the processing of a scene.

Evidence must be marked for identification so that it can be positively identified at a later time, such as when it is presented at a legal proceeding. Identification data usually include the date, the collector's initials, and case number if known.

Marking for identification is usually done in one of two ways:

- Attaching a tag to the evidence
- Placing the evidence in a container and tagging or labeling the container

Identification data are supplemented by an evidence tag that is filled out at the time the evidence is acquired. Entries on the tag are made in ink, and the tag accompanies the evidence from the moment it is acquired until it is relinquished. An evidence tag is an administrative convenience for locating evidence while it is in custody; it is not a substitute for marking evidence, and it is not the same as a chain of custody form.

Packaging Evidence

Keep in mind that physical evidence, such as blood, body tissue, anthrax, and the like, can be hazardous to your health. Before touching and packaging evidence, wear protective items such as latex gloves, mouth masks, and other protective gear. Latex gloves can also prevent accidental placement of fingerprints on physical evidence.

Plastic, sealable envelopes are commonly used to package small items. However, when the evidence needs to "breathe," such as bloodstained cloth, the correct choice is an unused, clean brown paper bag.

The outer packages into which evidential items are placed for transport will vary according to size, nature, and fragility. Large bulky items, such as automobile tires, are placed in sturdy wooden boxes, while small fragile items are wrapped in protective materials and placed in heavy cardboard boxes. Except for wooden boxes, packages are covered on the outside with sturdy paper, sealed along the edges, and marked with the word "Evidence."

If the package is being shipped to a forensic laboratory, a transmittal letter is attached to the outside of the box. The transmittal letter needs to be specific as to:

- What the package contains so that it can be opened with care given to its contents
- Toxic or potentially harmful materials inside the package
- The forensic examinations requested
- The sender, case number, and other administrative details

Blood and Biological Evidence

When blood is found on the ground, collecting and packaging it can be a challenge.

Evidence of blood is often found on an object such as a knife or shirt. Do not package a bloodstained item while it is wet. Allow the stain to dry at room temperature away from a heating source before packaging it in an unused brown paper bag.

If the item cannot be packaged, capture as much of the stain as possible. Moisten a cotton swab with one or two drops of distilled water and mop the stain onto the swab. The idea is to get as much of the stain as possible onto the swab. You will have succeeded when the swab is dark red/brown in appearance.

Liquid blood is placed in what is called a "whole blood collection tube." This type of tube contains an inhibitor to both microbial production of ethanol and enzymatic breakdown of ethanol. There is also an anticoagulant in the tube to ensure the sample remains whole blood.

Biological samples should be packaged individually in sterile containers without a preservative and should be frozen if they cannot be taken to a forensic laboratory immediately. Containers of biological samples or of samples that have been in contact with blood or other body fluids should be labeled with biohazard stickers so that laboratory employees can be alert to HIV and similar risks.

Impressions, Toolmarks, and Fingerprints

Footprints and tire treads are items that cannot be moved without damage. They are first photographed and then reproduced with dental stone or other impression-making materials. The finished product can be packaged in paper or wood, making sure that it will not be damaged while being transported.

Toolmarks are photographed and then, if possible, the object upon which the toolmarks appear is collected as a whole. In situations where the object bearing the toolmarks is fixed or moveable only with difficulty, the alternative is to cut away the piece bearing the marks. The area bearing the toolmarks must be protected by soft cloth or cotton when packaged.

Fingerprints are developed, then photographed, and then lifted. A lifted print is placed in contact with a backing that both protects it and provides contrast for "reading" it. These items are usually placed into a plastic, sealable envelope for delivery to a fingerprint examiner.

Fibers and Hairs

To conduct an examination for the transfer of fibers between the clothing of the victim and the suspect, all items of clothing should be packaged and sent to a forensic laboratory. Samples of carpet or other fabric items at the scene should be collected for comparison with recovered fibers. Samples of this type should be submitted in clean paper or envelope with sealed corners.

Hair samples taken from the body of a suspect should consist of at least 20 to 25 hairs pulled at random from the same body area. The collected hairs should be folded in clean paper or an envelope with sealed corners. The envelope or package should be clearly marked with the individual's name and the body area sampled.

Glass and Arson Debris

It is best to package glass particles in a plastic or metal container rather than a paper envelope.

Epoxy-lined metal cans are recommended for packaging arson debris evidence. The container must be clean, previously unused, and airtight.

Chain of Custody

Chain of custody begins when an item of evidence is first taken. Because all persons who handle an item are considered links in the custody chain, the number of persons who handle the item should be kept to a minimum. During the time you are in possession of evidence, you are personally liable for its care and safekeeping.

The chain begins at the moment the item is first obtained, and it ends when the item is no longer evidential in nature. Whenever the item changes hands, such as when it is received at a forensic laboratory, an entry is made on an accompanying chain of custody form. Each entry reflects the name and title of the person receiving the item and the purpose of transfer. The chain of custody provides assurance that the item examined at a laboratory and later offered into evidence at a trial is the same item collected.

Evidence Documentation

The evidence collection process includes preparation of documentary materials that describe the incident, evidence collected, where it was found, its relevance to the matter under investigation, and what it tends to prove or disprove.

Sketches, drawings, and diagrams depict distance and position relationships between collected evidence and other objects. These hand-drawn documents also depict the scene in relation to surrounding areas, travel routes, and other physical features relevant to the crime. Because these descriptions are prepared at the scene, they are rough approximations. Later, in an office setting

with proper tools, they are converted to accurate renderings.

Notes, which are also hand-prepared at the scene or typed from an audio device, tie everything together. They describe the search method, each item found, its condition, how it was collected, name of the person who did the collecting, and so on.

Certain forms are included in documentation such as evidence receipts, evidence tags, and chain of custody.

Reports of investigation, which typically include a preliminary report, progress reports, and a final report, are formal documents that reflect everything that was done and discovered from beginning to end.

All of the relevant documents (or copies thereof) are kept in a case file of a type that prevents documents from being lost. They are arranged in a logical order such as notes and sketches in one section of the file, photographs in another, reports in another, and so on. Within each section of the file is another logical arrangement such as by date of collection. Some investigators prefer to place documentation in plastic sleeves inside a three-ring binder.

Case files are kept in containers that are locked when not in use and under human observation when open. Case files and their contents should not leave the office except under special circumstances. The loss of a case file or part of its contents can irreparably damage the investigation.

Documents that happen to be evidence, such as official records, should be kept in an evidence room along with their evidence tags and chain of custody receipts.

Learning Shop USA, Scientific Analysis of Physical Evidence, www.learningshopusa.com

Learning Shop USA, Collection and Preservation of Physical Evidence, www.learningshopusa.com

John J. Fay, *Encyclopedia of Security Management*, second ed., Elsevier, Burlington, MA, 2011, pp. 167–169.

CRIMINAL DEFENSE INVESTIGATION

Private investigators (PIs) conduct criminal defense investigations (CDIs) in concert with attorneys who are defending accused persons. The techniques of investigation used by a PI in a CDI vary little from techniques used by law enforcement investigators in building a case against the accused. In a CDI, the largest and most significant difference between a PI and a law enforcement investigator is that each works for a different side. Animosity can result, particularly when the PI is a former law enforcement officer. "Jumped ship" and "gone over to the other side" are terms often used by law enforcement investigators when speaking of former peers that work CDI cases. Competition also is a natural element of the animosity.

The big picture functions of the PI are to:

- Conduct a second investigation
- Evaluate the police investigation
- Confer with and advise the client and/or friendly counsel
- Prepare a written report
- Testify

To obtain an understanding of the case, the PI will read the warrant and refer to the applicable criminal code to determine the elements of the offense. The elements are compared against what is known about the case at that time. The PI looks for weaknesses in the police investigation that might be exploited and discusses any such matter with the defense attorney. The PI will examine all of the documentation available, especially witness statements. The PI will be alert for inconsistencies and for what a witness did not say that should have been said. The police may have avoided obtaining facts favorable to the defendant.

Generally speaking, PIs that conduct criminal defense investigations are seasoned veterans. They know the criminal law and criminal procedure, and they are proficient at collecting, preserving, analyzing, accounting for, and transporting evidence; taking photographs and notes; interviewing witnesses; comprehending the content of documents; writing reports; preparing trial exhibits; and testifying at legal proceedings.

The Defendant

The defendant is called the accused in a criminal proceeding. Unsavory as the accused may be, he/she has the right to be present at each stage of the criminal justice process, except grand jury proceedings. In many cases involving the services of a PI, the crime is complicated, such as using inside information to defraud stock market investors or looting savings and loan institutions. Some offenses cross international boundaries, such as drug trafficking and weapons smuggling.

The accused can be a first offender, a not-so-frequent offender, or a professional criminal. He/she can be young or old, rich or poor, smart or stupid, street thug or highly respected businessman, mafia figure or pillar of the community.

Irrespective of the crime or social standing, a defendant has a very important right—the right to counsel. When a defendant is indigent and cannot afford counsel, a court may assign a public defender to provide counsel. The attorney representing the accused may be proficient in practicing law but not in conducting investigations. In addition, the defendant's attorney simply may not have the time to check every detail of the opposition's case.

The Defender

The defender or defense attorney can represent an accused person from arrest to final appeal. Some private attorneys specialize in criminal cases, and many of them are perceived as "shysters" willing to sacrifice their clients' interests in pursuit of profit. This is an inaccurate and unfair view.

A criminal defense attorney is obligated to vigorously defend a client and is often able to use legal maneuvers to secure dismissal or, in advance of a trial, strike a plea bargain that reduces the charge. When a client is tried and found guilty, the defender attempts to reduce the severity of the punishment.

A defense attorney, particularly when a serious crime is alleged, will form a defense team. An important member of the defense team can be a private investigator skilled in criminal defense investigations. The tasks of the private investigator, which are assigned by the defense attorney, must be clearly spelled out. The nature of the tasks will be influenced by the facts of the case and the defense strategy mapped out by the defense attorney.

A different type of defense attorney is the public defender. The public defender can be an attorney working for a formal, state-funded agency or an attorney working for a private firm that performs pro bono services. In some circumstances, a private law firm will have a contract with a court to provide legal services for stipulated fees.

State-funded defenders are often considered "bottom feeders" in the legal profession because they represent persons of low social standing and command small to moderate fees for their work. This, too, is an unfair view.

A private firm public defender typically does not have the same level of experience as the state-funded defender and may not be highly motivated if the arrangement is pro bono. Both types of attorneys, however, are usually young and in the learning stage.

The Prosecutor

A prosecutor is an attorney working at a local, county, state, or federal level prosecuting office. Prosecutors represent the state (i.e., "the people"). For example, an assistant state's attorney general prosecutes violations of state law. He/she brings charges against offenders, engages in plea bargaining, conducts trials, and helps determine sentences.

A prosecutor brings the state's case against accused persons by charging them with a crime and eventually bringing them to trial. If the evidence against the accused is weak, the prosecutor may choose not to bring the case to trial. With a court's permission, a prosecutor is free to plea bargain with the accused person's attorney to negotiate a resolution in the interest of the state, such as reducing the charge in exchange for saving taxpayers the cost of the trial and alleviating a crowded court calendar.

While the prosecutor's main function is to determine guilt and punish offenders, he/she has a fundamental obligation to not seek prosecution when facts indicate that the accused is innocent.

A main function of the PI is to demonstrate through investigation the weakness of the prosecutor's case and/or uncover facts that indicate client innocence.

The Criminal Courts

The administration of justice for the commission of crimes takes place in a criminal court. Criminal justice is administered through a court system consisting of lower criminal courts, superior courts, and appellate courts. Each state and the federal government have their own court system. Criminal defense investigations are conducted mostly for cases tried in superior courts.

The superior courts (also called major trial courts) ordinarily house trials for felony offenses. Trials are formal and strictly respect the defendant's constitutional rights. (This fact demands that the PI understand rules of evidence and courtroom procedure and be skilled in giving testimony.)

Because of the more serious nature of crimes tried in superior courts, convictions tend to be more severe. This explains to some extent why some defendants plead guilty rather than face the possibility of losing in court and going to prison for an extended period.

Appellate courts rule on alleged procedural errors of trial courts, such as admitting into evidence items that were unlawfully obtained. A PI who is able to show that the police collected evidence illegally can be of great assistance to the defense.

Defenses to Criminal Charges

In many cases, the client will first say to his/her attorney, "I didn't do it" or "This is a case of mistaken identity." Of course, these defenses are inadequate. Friendly counsel will look instead for an alibi such as the client being out of town or being away from the scene of the offense. The PI's job would be to obtain supporting travel documents (plane ticket, gas receipts, etc.) or a witness statement that will show the client could not have committed the offense.

Consent. A person charged with a crime can represent that the alleged victim consented to the alleged crime. For example, a defendant charged with theft might claim that the owner of the property gave consent to the taking of the property. In another example, a rape is not a rape when the victim voluntarily consents.

In such cases, your role is to demonstrate through investigation that consent had been given or implied. An example of showing consent could be the taking of a statement from a friend of the victim in which the victim confided that consent had been given.

Self-Defense. A defendant can claim to be not guilty by reason of self-defense such as by resorting to violence to defend against violence. In an assault case, for example, the defendant may claim that the accuser attacked the defendant, who had no choice except to counterattack.

In this event, you would try to find an eyewitness whose testimony would support the defendant's claim.

Entrapment. In this defense, the accused might claim that the police set a trap that lured the accused into committing a crime that he/she otherwise would not have committed.

Double Jeopardy. The Fifth Amendment says, "No person shall be subject for the same offense to be twice put in jeopardy of life or limb." This protection prohibits a second prosecution for the same offense in the same jurisdiction.

Mistake. A mistake of fact, such as cashing an erroneously issued check, is a defense provided there is no showing that the accused intended to defraud the person or entity that issued the check.

Compulsion. Compulsion is a defense when the accused was placed into a position where he/she or someone else would be killed or seriously injured if the unlawful act were not committed. A bank president who takes cash from the bank and gives it to a criminal has a defense if the act was compelled by the fact the criminal had custody of the banker's daughter and threatened to kill her if the money was not delivered.

Necessity. The necessity defense is based on the concept that a crime is justified when "the harm to be avoided is greater than the offense charged." For example, the father of a seriously injured child steals a car to transport his daughter to a hospital. The harm avoided (loss of the child's life) is greater than the offense charged (auto theft).

The Defendant's Rights

The Right to Confront Witnesses. The defendant has a right to see and cross-examine witnesses. This right requires witnesses against the defendant to appear in court and testify personally. In nearly all cases, the defense attorney questions witnesses on behalf of the defendant.

The Right to a Jury Trial. The defendant in a criminal trial involving a felony can choose whether the case will be tried before a judge or a jury. The circumstances of the case and the advice of defense counsel will influence the defendant's choice.

The Right to Counsel at Trial. As discussed previously, a defendant can engage an attorney of his/her choosing at personal expense. If indigent and if incarceration is a possibility, the defendant is provided the services of defense counsel at no cost.

The Right to Self-Representation. A defendant in a criminal trial is able to waive the right of defense attorney assistance. When this occurs, the court may evaluate the defendant's competency to defend against the accusation. Competency is more a matter of mental health than knowledge of the law. The defendant is allowed to conduct the defense if found competent but is not entitled to a standby defender.

The Right to Speedy Trial. This right ensures that a person's trial cannot be unduly delayed or that the person be held in custody indefinitely. The federal government and most states have enacted laws that set deadlines for the convening of criminal trials.

Post-Conviction Relief

A convicted client will almost always ask for post-conviction relief (PCR). PCR can be granted when the client can show that his/her counsel's representation fell below an objective standard of reasonableness, and the client was prejudiced by that ineffective representation. The client has suddenly become an adversary. The defense attorney, along with the PI will be accused of poor assistance. The PI will want to defend against the allegation. Do so by comparing the PI's investigative actions against the convicted client's accusations and consult with the defense attorney. Know the law in respect to PCR. If accused of incompetence, gather proof of experience, membership in a professional association, education, and training, review investigative standards and show how the PI met those standards.

The Private Investigator's Objectives

One way to refer to a CDI is to call it a second investigation. The first investigation, i.e., the police investigation, led to arrest of the defendant. In the second investigation, the objective is to find and exploit weaknesses in police work that led them to the arrest. A weakness, for example, could be a deviation from an established police procedure, such as failure to follow an evidence collection protocol. The investigator is likely to excel in discovering weaknesses if the PI is a former police investigator familiar with standard police practices.

The general approach in the CDI is to mirror the police investigation. The police detectives' activities can't be mirrored perfectly because once something has been done, such as collect a certain piece of evidence, it can't be done a second time. However, there are some tasks that can and should be repeated.

Repeating what the police have done is good practice. It will take the PI along a route the police have traveled. If the police encountered a difficulty along the way, the PI may see it also and examine it closely for errors that could have been made by the police. The PI will be sometimes amazed by the enormity of a single error. Instead of discovering a minor, technical mistake, the PI might stumble upon a major fact that could turn the entire case around.

When the findings are inconsistent with the findings of the police, a contradiction exists that deserves increased attention. A contradiction is an investigative lead. The PI needs to chase it down to see where it goes and what it might produce.

Without going into details, some investigative actions on the part of the PI are better left out of documentation that is turned over to the defense attorney.

Reconstruction of the Scene

The CDI might begin with an examination of the crime or incident scene. Scenes vary widely. In one case it may be a wooded area where an act of violence occurred; in another it may be an office safe from which money was taken; and in another it may be a bedroom where a sexual assault occurred.

Although scenes vary, an examination of each offers the PI an opportunity to visualize what happened. Images that have been preset in the mind's eye can suddenly change: a twist in the roadway, the height of a wall, the vastness of a warehouse, or the position of a window. Why didn't the vehicle go onto the shoulder of the road at that point? How could the defendant have possibly scaled a wall that high? How could the defendant know where to look for the stolen material in a warehouse of that size? Why didn't the rape victim call out for help through the open window next to the bed? Looking at a scene can produce insights that would have been missed had the scene not been examined.

A scene, of course, will be cold when the PI gets there. Evidence will have been removed, the scene and surrounding area will have been cleaned up or put back in order, and witnesses of the event will not be there waiting to be interviewed. These are not reasons, however, to not go through the process of a search.

At an outdoor scene, the process tasks can include:

- Searching for the remnants of evidence such as a skid mark, a damaged tree, a broken hasp, or a shattered window pane; searching in places not likely to have been searched by the police
- Measuring the sizes of and distances between immoveable objects such as structures, poles, trees, sidewalks, and roadways; making sketches that show positional relationships
- Photographing the scene up close, at mid-distance, and from long distance; taking photos from the center of the scene that move along a 360-degree arc at shoulder level and overlapping one

another; taking photos of access and departure routes and of possible secondary scenes
- Making notes of everything in and around the scene, including apparently inconsequential things; making notations as to who took the photographs, the equipment used, and the sequence followed (a portable voice recorder and a personal digital assistant (PDA) can be ideal for this purpose).
- Examining the scene at a time and day that correspond to the occurrence of the event. If the incident occurred at 9 PM on a Sunday night, examine the scene at that time and date; timing should also consider weather, the season, and the ascendancy of the moon.
- Searching, measuring, sketching, photographing, and notating are performed at all scenes. The place and the objects within the scene are different, but the process is the same.

Witnesses

A witness is any person, other than a suspect, who has information concerning an incident. Victims, complainants, accusers, laboratory experts, and informants are simply types of witnesses.

A witness can be anyone possessing information about the matter under investigation. A witness can be a person who:

- Directly observed the incident
- Has facts about persons involved
- Has information concerning motive
- Is a specialist able to give expert testimony
- Is the person who made the initial report
- Was victimized by the incident
- Investigated the incident

The most consistently valuable sources of information are the people involved. Properly conducted interviews can produce investigative leads, identify additional evidence, and surface background details missed in the first investigation. Of all tasks performed in a CDI, interviewing ranks at the top.

An objective is to collect information that adds meaning and context. Questions that deserve asking include: Was the victim at fault in any way? Did outside factors contribute to the severity of the incident? Would the incident have happened anyway? Was the defendant compelled to act in a certain way? Did the defendant act because he/she had no other choice? The client will be very interested in learning details that clarify, mitigate, and exculpate.

Interviewing is essentially nonaccusatory in nature. It is done with tact and respect; however, it is not unusual for a witness to switch back and forth between cooperation and hostility. The reason behind this erratic behavior is, in all likelihood, related to human factors that can either help or hinder.

Human Factors in Interviewing

Fear, Indifference, and Privacy. Many people are unfamiliar with investigative methods and are afraid to cooperate. Others think that offenses that do not happen to them directly are not their business, or they believe that the accused person does not deserve consideration. Most people tend to be private and dislike publicity in general.

Inconvenience. No one wants his/her lifestyle disrupted. We are all pretty much animals of habit, and we dislike it when our daily routines are upset. We are also aware of witnesses being required to wait several days in courthouse hallways and then told to go home. Even when a witness is compensated for lost time, there is a residue of resentment against a process that penalizes citizens in the name of civic duty.

Perception. What a witness perceives is conditioned by:

- Differing abilities to see, hear, smell, taste, and feel

- The location of the viewer in relation to the incident at the time of occurrence; distance and geographical perspective affect vision
- The amount of time intervening between occurrence and interview
- The number and nature of events that occur during the interval between occurrence and interview

What are the implications? For one thing, the PI has to discover if the person being interviewed has physical disabilities that impair the senses. If the witness has a vision problem, the PI cannot accept the witness's statement at full value. It is far better to discover a perception problem during the investigation than to have it surfaced and exploited during the trial.

Memory Erosion. Memory not only fades; it becomes colored, either consciously or unconsciously, by what the witness was exposed to after the incident. Remarks made by other witnesses or media reporting may cause an interviewee to fill in the gaps of personal memory with details about which he/she has no direct knowledge.

Stress. A person subjected to stressful, exciting, or injurious events after observing an incident is likely to forget details. To illustrate, assume a motorist observes a hit-and-run incident and stops to render help. The motorist gets caught up in a series of actions in which he/she renders first aid and transports the victim to the hospital. The stress of the situation prevents the witness from acquiring or remembering details concerning the hit-and-run vehicle.

Prejudice. A PI can expect some witnesses to be prejudiced in some way to some degree. One method for keeping information from biased distortion is to ask for detailed, specific answers. If allowed to talk in generalities, a prejudiced person will make statements that are partially accurate and partially misleading.

Self-Interest. Although we can normally expect a victim-witness to be cooperative, we cannot expect the information to be highly reliable. A victim may be overly eager to please or, with an insurance payoff in mind, inflate the severity of the offense.

Evaluating the Witness

Knowing and analyzing details about the personality and attitude of a witness can help the PI establish rapport and select a suitable questioning technique. Details of interest include age, place of birth, nationality, address, educational level, job, habits, companions, prior arrests and convictions, and hobbies.

Accuracy of information and truthfulness of a witness can be assessed when the PI has a sense of personal relationships among the parties involved (friends, relatives, acquaintances, coworkers, etc.) and any nexus they have with the offense, place of offense, tools and fruits of the offense, etc.

A very critical step in making the evaluation is readying the mind. The best start the PI can make is to acquire a thorough grasp of case facts, know something about the person to be questioned, and know what information is needed to bring the case to a successful conclusion. The PI needs to mentally prepare for an encounter with an individual who may be friendly or hostile, communicative or reticent, full or devoid of facts, truthful or lying.

Very valuable to the defense would be the acquisition of a copy of a written statement made by a witness on a previous occasion, such as when making a police report or giving testimony at a deposition. When talking with such a witness, the PI has nothing to lose and everything to gain by asking the witness's permission to make a copy of the previously made statement. Access to the statement's content has two advantages.

First, it allows the PI and friendly counsel to craft a line of courtroom questioning based on what the witness said earlier. Discrepancies in what the witness said then and later can be chinks in the opposition's armor.

Second, in examining the earlier statement, the PI and friendly counsel will pay close attention to the nature of the questions posed to the witness. The direction these questions take can indicate the opposition's planned courtroom strategy.

Typical Tasks of the Criminal Defense Investigator

The criminal defense investigator has a responsibility to ensure all facts have been collected to ensure the defendant will receive the best defense possible. Tasks expected to be performed include:

- Study the law enforcement investigation.
- Study all available police records and reports pertaining to the case.
- Examine police evidence and the findings of forensic specialists.
- Interview and evaluate the defendant.
- If appropriate, conduct a background investigation of the defendant in order to evaluate his/her history of truthfulness.
- Study witness statements.
- Interview witnesses that have already given statements to the police.
- Try to find and interview witnesses that were not contacted by the police.
- Examine the crime scene. Take photos, both still and video; make diagrams and sketches; and write notes.
- Compare your crime scene findings against police findings.
- If injury or death is involved, interview treatment providers and/or coroner.
- Learn as much as possible about key witnesses, the prosecutor and judge, and the police officers that worked the case.
- Study discovery materials.
- Create a work book such as a three-ring binder that contains photos, notes, sketches, diagrams, mug shots, 9-1-1 transcripts, a log of telephone calls made and received, reports of investigative activities, progress reports to the defense

attorney, and any other documents pertinent to the case.

- Identify facts disclosed to the police but not mentioned in their reports, and identify physical evidence collected but not produced.
- Examine procedures used by the police to collect, document, preserve, package, transport, and store physical evidence. Pay particulate attention to chain of custody.

Interviewing Decisions

The best source of information may be the client. Details can lead to witnesses who were not interviewed by the police. This may suggest the police deliberately avoided interviewing a witness or were negligent in their investigation.

As a general rule, witnesses that appear cooperative are interviewed first and uncooperative witnesses last. Also, an interview can be put on hold, for example, until a records search can be completed or forensic laboratory reports obtained and studied.

Selecting the time, place, and order of questioning can be critical. Although it is always useful to talk to an information provider (especially an eyewitness) as soon as possible, it is sometimes more valuable to postpone questioning until key facts have been determined.

From your perspective, the best place to question a witness is at your place of business. Unfortunately, this is the exception to the rule. The place of questioning is most often where the witness can be found—at home, work, hospital, or jail cell.

If a witness shows unease at being interviewed at your office, a good alternate location is a restaurant—one that provides privacy and is not noisy. A restaurant can be nonthreatening, especially if chosen by the witness. Comfort and intimacy, which are helpful to establishing rapport, can be

obtained in a restaurant when the ambience is convivial and the seating distance reduced. And if a full interview requires an hour or longer to complete, the comfort of a restaurant can keep the witness from wanting to break off the interview before it can be finished.

Having said all of the above, you may know that the witness does not want to be interviewed by the defense. Therefore, you may decide to pay an unannounced visit to the witness.

Discourage the defense attorney from interviewing a witness. At trial, an attorney cannot serve as a witness to impeach the testimony of a witness—but a private investigator can.

Introduction to the Interview

Start with a handshake and personal identification: name, title, and the matter under investigation. Next, establish the identity of the witness. A few minutes spent in idle conversation can help you assess the witness and choose an appropriate interviewing technique.

Converse in a manner that helps the witness overcome nervousness and relate to you as a friend rather than an enemy. When you've arrived at a suitable comfort level, make a general comment about the case without disclosing specifics. Two purposes are served: the boundaries of the questioning are established, and the witness is discouraged from later claiming that the purpose of the interview was not explained.

Rapport

Right from the start, try to create harmony or agreement so that a productive dialogue can follow. Your demeanor during initial moments can greatly affect the tenor and outcome of the session. The objective is to get the witness into a talkative mood and guide the conversation toward a full and accurate disclosure. In the best of situations, the witness will tell a complete story without prodding or interruption.

The rapport period is not entirely devoted to "warming up" the witness. It is also a time to mention that there is no reason why the witness would not want to be totally forthcoming.

Recording

Taking notes or using a voice recorder or a video recorder during an interview can be uncomfortable to the witness—nonetheless, creating a factual record of the interview is important. Some people will be so distracted by note taking or the whirr of a recorder that they will have trouble concentrating on what has been asked. Reluctance can be met by telling the witness that one way or another the interview will have to be documented; that being the case, it is in the best interest of everyone concerned to record the information at the moment it is delivered instead of writing it later from memory.

When a voice recorder is used, begin with a statement of the time and date, your name, the name of the witness, place of interview, and the matter to be discussed. The witness can be asked to confirm this preliminary statement by stating his/her name, address, and occupation.

A good way of making an accurate record of an interview is to take notes and make a voice recording simultaneously. This method can be further enhanced at the end of the interview. You can read from your notes each essential fact one at time and ask the witness to confirm each fact with, "Yes, that is correct." If the witness cannot confirm the fact, clarify your notes and pose a substitute question.

When you have a choice between using notes or a quality voice recorder, the best choice is the recorder. This is because a recorder, once shown to the witness, can be placed out of the witness's sight. Further, notes cannot be taken at the same rate of speed as a witness talks. To keep pace, you'd have to use shorthand or a version of it that includes jargon, abbreviations, and scribbling. Later, the notes may be undecipherable, even to yourself. A recorder, assuming it works well and does not die from lack of batteries, captures every word, nuance, and inflection.

Conducting the Interview

A sensible practice when attempting an interview of a witness is not to make an appointment but to show up unannounced. Apologize for not making prior arrangements, be polite, fully identify yourself and show your license or official credentials, and explain your purpose for conducting the interview. Give the witness time to let the details of your introduction sink in. When the interview is over, give the witness your business card and ask for a telephone call or a visit if the witness comes across any further information.

A witness may at first decline to talk with you. Persist but not offensively. Use tact and persuasion and appeal to the witness's sense of fairness. You might be helped by saying, "You wouldn't want an innocent person to go to jail, would you?"

If you threaten or intimidate a witness, you can be charged with a crime—a circumstance that can seriously damage the client's position. Try to get the witness talking and keep it that way. Look for indications of bias or prejudice, especially in matters of ethnicity, gender, sexual orientation, politics, and religion.

Casually observe the witness's surroundings. You may see items that indicate bias, prejudice, or a predisposition to unfairly judge others. Examples would include a Confederate flag, books, posters, and bumper stickers. Details of this nature might be used to impeach the witness's testimony; if they do not appear in police documentation, they can suggest the police ignored or missed them.

Take written notes if you are confident that the witness will not object. The same holds true for electronic recordings such as those made with the use of voice and visual recorders or a personal digital assistant (PDA). Try to not spook the witness.

Be careful of what you say. Remember that your objective is to discover facts, not give them away.

In many situations, you will have no choice except to listen and, from time to time, guide the conversation in a productive direction. Considerable patience may be required until the story has been told, reviewed, and clarified. Matters not touched upon by the witness can be covered at the end with questions. Allowing a witness to talk is good practice except when the talk goes far offtrack.

Let the Witness Talk

A common mistake of the fledgling interviewer is a tendency to interrupt or dominate a conversation to such a degree that the witness is not permitted to tell the story. This tendency, while mostly the product of inexperience, can result from inadequate preparation and an impulse to demonstrate competence. The PI may feel better as a result but can cause the witness to become frustrated and clam up.

Ask the Right Questions

Knowing when to ask a question is every bit as important as knowing what to ask and how to ask. Here are some pointers:

- Be systematic. For example, ask questions in an order according to what happened first, then next, etc. When all questions have been asked, go through them one more time, and a third time if necessary.
- Ask one question at a time and stick with it until it has been answered fully.
- Phrase each question simply and directly.

- Don't use legal terms; jargon; and words that might confuse, shock, or embarrass.
- Don't ask questions that have implied answers.
- Avoid questions that produce yes or no answers. Encourage elaboration.
- Don't make side remarks, gestures, or facial expressions that are open to interpretation.
- Respond differently to answers that are deliberately misleading and answers that are mistaken but honestly given.
- Keep the discussion from drifting into irrelevant matters and excessive detail.
- Shunt as needed to bring the discussion back on track. Here is an example of a shunt: "Let's get back to the moment he reached into his jacket pocket."
- Radiate enthusiasm through positive comments and a confident demeanor.
- At the closing of the interview, express appreciation and thanks, keeping in mind that a follow-up interview may be necessary.

Expect the interviewee to ask that his or her identity not be disclosed. Your correct response should be that investigative details are always treated confidentially but that laws and rules outside of your control may require otherwise.

Asking the right questions in the right order can be helped by preparing ahead of time a list of short bullet points or single words for reference as the interview progresses. If reading from the list is done skillfully, the witness may not notice use of the list and infer from the line of questioning that you have more knowledge than is really the case.

Dealing with the Reluctant Witness

There may be moments when you will use "hard" questions, i.e., questions asked forcefully and that leave little room for evasion or silence. The move into the "hard" mode is done quickly and ends quickly. You will either get the desired answer immediately or will realize that the witness does not have the answer or is determined not to give it. Asking "hard questions" can easily transition to browbeating, which is definitely not a good practice.

When a witness is reluctant to talk or continue an interview, switch to a nonthreatening subject such as the witness's hobby, sport teams followed, or the current fad in clothing or hair styling. It may help to pose a hypothetical question, answer it incorrectly, and wait for a response. The witness may not be able to resist the temptation to point out the error. This will at least get a conversation started.

Reluctance will sometimes stem from an outside issue, such as the shortcomings of the court system. Find a way to agree but also to keep the conversation moving. For example, if the witness believes that the court system is out of control, point out that it need not be a factor at all if the matter under investigation can be ended without going to trial and that the witness can help that happen.

It may also help to point out that in not giving a statement, the witness could end up in the middle of a long and arduous legal battle.

Closing the Interview

The closing of an interview is not necessarily the termination of communication. On the contrary, an effective closing can result in the acquisition of valuable information. A person who may not have been fully forthcoming during the main body of the interview may drop his/her guard after questioning has apparently ended. Pertinent facts that may have been concealed might be disclosed as the interview is ending. Details not disclosed earlier can be brought to the surface even while making a farewell handshake.

Because witnesses sometimes need to be interviewed more than once, end the session on a friendly, positive note: give thanks, saying that the provided information is important and promising that the information will be used for the betterment of all.

Forensic Testing

Forensic testing is important to you because forensic tests serve court functions, and it is in the courtroom that the defendant has his/her last chance. When you understand what a forensic test can and cannot do, you are able to spot defects. Such defects often result from chain of custody error within the lab, contaminating physical evidence, subjecting the evidence to an improper testing method, and reaching an erroneous conclusion.

Persons that perform forensic testing are trained professionals, the tests are based on scientific principles, the testing methodologies and equipment are typically state-of-the-art, and the tests are conducted in a laboratory that operates in accordance with standards acceptable to the scientific community and the court system. What has just been described is a crime lab, a publicly funded institution that serves the investigative needs of police and prosecuting agencies.

Unfortunately, PIs do not have access to crime lab services. Physical evidence collected by PIs is submitted to commercial labs and to independent specialists. In terms of capability, some commercial labs are equal or superior to crime labs. Even the FBI's crime lab uses commercial labs to perform specialized tests.

Independent forensic specialists utilize less sophisticated equipment and are limited to testing a small range of physical evidence. The testing methodologies usually combine science and human interpretation. These include examinations of documents, blood patterns, skid marks, vehicle crash materials, tread marks, and glass fragments. It is not unusual for a PI agency or law firm to place independent specialists on retainer.

There is a variety of forensic tests. These are important to understand because conclusions reached by police investigators and prosecutors rely heavily on crime lab tests. When you know little or nothing about the tests, you are not able to challenge them.

Serology

Forensic serology involves the identification and characterization of body fluids associated with a crime. Physical evidence in murder, rape, robbery, assault, and hit-and-run cases often bear body fluid stains.

Blood examinations aid investigations by:

- Identifying locations, e.g., the place on a roadway where a pedestrian was struck by a car
- Connecting a particular object to a particular event
- Proving a defendant's alibi, e.g., determining that blood found on the victim's clothing is animal blood

A criminal defense investigator can also be aided by the examination of semen and saliva. The identification of semen by chemical and microscopic means on vaginal smears, swabs, or clothing may be of value in corroborating the defendant's claims.

DNA Analysis

DNA is the basic genetic material within each living cell that determines individual characteristics. It is used to identify individuals from small samples of body fluids or tissue.

Samples of human skin, hair follicles, blood, semen, or saliva containing cells or other tissues can be examined to identify a DNA pattern. That pattern can be compared with DNA from other persons and thus exonerate a suspect. DNA examination techniques sometimes permit the use of extraordinarily small samples such as a few hairs or a single spot of blood. Moreover, DNA is durable and is relatively resistant to adverse environmental conditions such as heat or moisture. DNA degrades slowly in a decomposing body, lasting sometimes for years, thus allowing samples to be analyzed for some time after death.

Toxicology

A toxicological examination looks for the presence of drugs and/or poison in biological tissues and fluids. Findings can show whether the victim of a crime died or became ill as the result of drug or poison ingestion or whether the involved persons were under the influence of drugs at the time of the matter under investigation.

Pharmacology

A forensic laboratory can determine if materials seized as suspected drugs are in fact controlled substances. In addition, the laboratory can examine a wide variety of items, such as boats, aircraft, automobiles, clothing, luggage, and money, for the presence of trace quantities of cocaine, heroin, phencyclidine (PCP), and other controlled substances. A pharmaceutical examination can identify products for the purpose of matching recovered products with stolen products or for proving that pharmaceuticals were switched.

Arson Examination

Debris collected from the scene of a suspected arson is analyzed to learn if a distillate was used to accelerate the fire and, if so, testing can classify the distillate by product such as gasoline, fuel oil, or paint solvent. Debris most suitable for analysis is absorbent in nature, e.g., padded furniture, carpeting, plasterboard, and flooring.

The criminal defense investigator that collects suspected accelerants at a particular location within the debris should also collect a sample not containing a suspected accelerant. Such a sample is called a reference sample and is used by the lab technician to compare the suspect sample against the reference sample.

Chemicals Analysis

Chemicals analysis is helpful in cases involving theft or contamination of products, malicious destruction, and assault. Analysis of hand printing or handwriting involves comparing one against the other by a document examiner. The examiner's report can be positive, probable, or negative.

Inks on questioned documents can be matched against known ink specimens obtained from word processors, typewriter ribbons, and stamp pads.

In consumer product tampering, analysis can determine the presence and nature of contaminants, adulterants, and alterations to containers. Chemical examinations can be useful in evaluating tear gas and dyes in bank robber packets and flash and water soluble paper in gambling and spy cases.

Chemical analysis can be made of gunshot residue taken from the hands, face, and clothing of a suspect or a suspected suicide.

Questioned Document Examinations

A questioned document examiner studies handwriting, typewriting, mechanical impressions, check-writer imprints, embossed seals, rubber stamps, printed matter, photocopies, paper, altered documents, obliterated writing, indented writing, charred documents, and similar materials and devices.

A positive outcome to a criminal defense investigator can hang on the answer to a single question: Who wrote the anonymous letter? Who signed the check? Was the official record altered? Was something typed in after the document had been signed?

Proving that a particular writing was altered or authored by a particular individual is often a central issue. A notation, an address, a phone number, or a set of figures can be the key to proving a case.

A document is questioned when, for example, the author is unknown (as in the case of an anonymous letter) or when a document (such as an official record) has been altered. The examiner's function is to compare the questioned document against known writings, called exemplars. An exemplar is a known writing because the source or author has been identified.

An examiner's analysis will take into account indicators like slant, letter proportions, spacing between letters and words, width of letters or parts of letters, adherence to a baseline, rhythm, speed and flow, and pictorial quality. These indicators, singly and in combinations, allow the examiner to make an interpretive judgment. Other analyses of a more scientific nature can be made of the ink; the paper; impressions, such as the stroke of a typewriter key or of a pen; and alterations, such as those made by erasers or correction fluid.

Great value can be obtained from a document examiner's preparation of exhibits for use at court proceedings. Exhibits typically consist of enlarged photographs of the document or parts of it, such as the telltale features of a forged signature.

Explosives Examinations

Bomb remnants, explosives, blasting accessories, and toolmarks can be forensically examined.

Forensic examination can identify switches, batteries, blasting caps, tape, wire, timing mechanisms, and explosive residues. Fabrication techniques, nondetonated explosives, and overall construction of the bomb can be determined. Examination with the use of laboratory instruments explosives and explosive residues are carried on in conjunction with bomb component examinations.

The FBI Laboratory maintains extensive reference files that contain technical data such as known standards of explosives, bomb components, water gels, blasting agents, blasting caps, safety fuses, detonating cords, batteries, tapes, switches, and radio control devices.

Firearms Examination

Firearms examination is the study by which a bullet, cartridge case, or shot-shell casing may be identified as having been fired by a particular weapon to the exclusion of all other weapons. The firearms examiner will provide one of three conclusions, i.e., that the projectile, cartridge case, or casing:

- Is definitely connected to a certain firearm
- Is definitely not connected to a certain firearm
- Bears insufficient microscopic marks to make a positive connection to a certain firearm

Marks on a bullet can be produced:

- As the bullet passes through the barrel
- By a flash suppressor attached to the weapon
- By rough handling of the bullet when it was placed into the weapon

Marks on a fired cartridge case or shot-shell casing can be produced by contact with the breech face, firing pin, chamber, extractor, and ejector.

Gunshot Residue

Gunshot residue on clothing can be located, depending on the muzzle-to-garment distance:

- Microscopic identification of gunpowder residue surrounding the hole made by the projectile
- Chemical evaluation that produces a graphic representation of lead and gunpowder residue around the hole

When a person discharges a firearm, primer residues can be deposited on the firer's hands in varying amounts. These amounts are dependent upon the type, caliber, and condition of the firearm and the environmental conditions at the time of the shooting. Residue samples can be collected from a suspect's hands and analyzed for the presence of the chemical elements antimony, barium, and lead, which are components of most primer mixtures.

Hair and Fiber

Hair and fiber examinations are valuable in cases involving person-to-person contact. They can place different people at the scene by determining the interchange of hairs or fibers. Similarly, these examinations can be helpful in connecting persons to surreptitious crimes such as burglary and auto theft. Hairs or fibers found on knives, jimmy bars, and the like can identify the weapons or instruments of crime, as well as automobiles involved in hit-and-run cases.

Examination of a fiber can identify the type of fiber such as animal (wool), vegetable (cotton), synthetic (human-made), and mineral (glass). The usual purpose of a fiber examination is to determine whether or not questioned fibers are the same type and/or color.

Teeth and Bone

Identification of body remains can be made through comparisons of teeth and bone with records on file such as dental records and bone X-rays. Examinations may be made to determine if skeletal remains are animal or human. If human, the race, sex, approximate height and stature, and approximate age at death may be determined.

Materials Analysis

These examinations identify and/or compare chemical compositions of paints, plastics, explosives, cosmetics, tapes, and related materials. It is possible to establish the year and make of an automobile from a paint chip by use of the National Automotive Paint File, which contains paint panels representing paints used on all makes of American cars and many popular imported cars.

Paint on safes, vaults, windowsills, and doorframes may be transferred to the tools used to open them. Therefore, a comparison can be made between the paint on an object and the paint on a tool. Cosmetics and/or makeup can be compared with a potential source in assault cases.

Plastics Examinations

It is not possible to identify the source, use, or manufacturer of plastic items from composition alone, but microscopic comparisons can be made of automobile trim (hit and run), insulation on wire (bombing), and plastic tape.

Mineralogy

This type of examination looks for inorganic and crystalline characteristics of minerals. Examination findings can inferentially connect a person or object to a scene, prove or disprove an alibi, and provide investigative leads. Examples of mineralogical materials include glass, building materials, soil, debris, dust, safe insulation, minerals, abrasives, and gems.

Fracture patterns of glass can provide valuable information as to direction of the breaking force. Penetration of glass panes by bullets or high-speed projectiles produces a cone pattern from which the direction and some idea of the angle of penetration can be determined. Also, a physical match of pieces of glass can prove a common source.

Metallurgy

Determinations can be made to ascertain if two metals or two metallic objects came from the same source or from each other. Findings are based on surface characteristics, microstructural characteristics, mechanical properties, and composition.

Photographic Examinations

Infrared, ultraviolet, and monochromatic photography can be utilized to assist in rendering visible, latent photographic evidence that is not otherwise visible to the unaided human eye. Examples include alterations and obliteration to documents; invisible laundry marks; altered writing; and prints of fingers, hands, and feet.

A forensic laboratory can also examine a video or film made during a crime such as a robbery at a convenience store. The examination can:

- Compare in detail the robber's clothing with clothing obtained from a suspect
- Determine the robber's height
- Compare facial features of the robber with those in a known photograph of a suspect

Tread Impressions

Shoe-print and tire-tread impressions can provide investigative leads and be used as evidence at trial. Reference materials are maintained in the laboratory so that comparisons can be made between the reference items and the questioned shoe prints or tire impressions.

Toolmarks

These examinations determine if a given mark was produced by a specific tool. For example, marks made when objects are forcibly contacted against each other or objects that were originally joined before being broken or cut apart are tool marks.

Tool mark identification is based on the principle that when two objects come in contact, the harder object (the tool) will impart a mark on the softer object. The tool mark examiner can conclude that:

- The tool produced the mark
- The tool did not produce the mark
- There are not sufficient individual characteristics remaining within the tool mark to determine if the tool did or did not produce the questioned mark

Evaluating the Police Investigation: Elements of Proof

Definitions of criminal violations vary from state to state and between states and the federal government. In one jurisdiction a larceny of any type can be a felony, and in another jurisdiction it can be a misdemeanor if the value of the property stolen is lower than a set amount. Police investigators know or should know the distinctions. They presumably also know what are called "elements of proof." For a criminal act to be proved, certain elements must be met. For example, a state statute might require that to prove burglary, the police must show that (1) a certain person entered a building or structure (2) without consent of the rightful owner (3) with intent to commit a crime therein. In another state, the law might additionally require that the entry was made by a "breaking" and occurred during the hours of darkness.

When you can show that any element of the crime was not proved, the crime did not occur, and the police investigation was faulty for that reason.

Unwarranted Conclusions

Imagine that the police investigation report says, "The suspect could not explain where he was at the time the offense was committed." The police investigator has no way of knowing what a person can or cannot do. The correct way to say this would be: "The

suspect did not explain where he was at the time the offense was committed." Although in this situation the unwarranted conclusion was minor, the concept has powerful implications. In another example, an element of proof for the crime contains intent. Intent is not shown in a police investigation when it relies on "The suspect knew that what he was doing was against the law." Again, the investigator cannot know what was going on inside a person's mind. Intent would have to be factually shown or substantiated in some other way; if not, the investigation was faulty.

Opinion versus Fact

A type of unwarranted conclusion is substitution of a fact with an opinion. "The suspect signed the check" is an opinion unless the police investigator actually saw the suspect sign the check. Even worse would be, "The check was signed Herman Jones." If Herman Jones was the suspect, the sentence should have included the little word "by." Technical mistakes such as these can sway a jury to believe that the police investigator was incompetent, thus creating reasonable doubt as to the guilt of the defendant.

Police Mistakes

Showing incompetence on the part of the police investigator can be a great advantage to the defense. Incompetence can be shown by mistakes, both small and large, that resulted from poor training, little or no experience, bad judgment, poor supervision, or poor case review. A defense attorney that attempts to attack police competency is better able to succeed when you are able to show police mistakes. This was demonstrated in the O. J. Simpson trial.

A forensic examiner will look very carefully at how evidence was collected, packaged, and transported. Evidence contamination is the main issue. Could the evidence have been altered in a way that caused a laboratory's analyst to reach an unmerited conclusion? Alteration can occur as the evidence is collected, placed in a container, and when the container is placed in a package and the package transported to a lab or evidence room. Equal or greater is an erroneous laboratory conclusion that resulted from failure of the police investigator to describe the circumstances of collection. For example, the lab analyst would need to know that the bomb debris submitted for examination was collected at a fertilizer plant. The examination might conclude that the debris contained an explosive ingredient. That ingredient, however, could have come from fertilizer and not the bomb. Had the analyst known the place of collection, he/she might have looked for a different explosive ingredient, one that would be uncommon to a fertilizer plant.

Incompetence might be found in official records such as a telephone record or a bank statement. If the records cannot be obtained directly, obtain a subpoena ordering that they be produced. Other pertinent details may reside in radio tapes, dispatch logs, and police reports made prior to the case being referred for investigation. Many such documents can be obtained on the authority of the Freedom of Information Act (FOIA).

When testifying about the police investigation, the jury may become unsure of the investigator's testimony if the investigator uses disparaging remarks. Assert that the police may have done an incomplete job as opposed to having done a bad job.

Chain of Custody

A chain of custody form identifies all persons that had custody of an evidentiary item from the time of collection to final disposition. For example, the chain of custody form for bomb debris would reflect the dates of transfer and the names of the persons that received and surrendered the evidence as it moved from the scene of collection, to the laboratory, within the laboratory, to an evidence storage room, and to the site of a trial.

Your objective is to identify anyone who had custody or control of the bomb debris whose name does not appear on the form. The purpose is to cast doubt on the integrity of the evidence, as well as the competency of the persons in charge of it.

Documentation

You will want to closely examine documents collected or prepared by the police. These can include the initial police report, affidavits, search and arrest warrants, witness statements, laboratory reports, public records, and the final report of investigation. For example, look at an affidavit prepared by a police investigator to support a search warrant. Does the affidavit meet the requirements of probable cause? Look at the search warrant. Did the police investigators go beyond the limitations of the warrant? For example, did they search at midnight when the warrant said the search was to be conducted between 8:00 AM and 8:00 PM? Did the searchers look inside a notebook when the search was for a stolen television set? If you can show deviations like these, a trial judge might conclude that the search was unreasonable and rule that evidence obtained during the search is inadmissible.

Search with a Warrant

The Fourth Amendment also says that a search and seizure is permissible when a warrant has been issued. The warrant must rest on probable cause details, which are usually reflected in a police affidavit (a sworn, written statement). A search and seizure that is made without probable cause or is supported by a false affidavit renders the search invalid, and any evidence seized cannot be used against the defendant.

A search warrant is very specific. It will give a time frame for the search to be made, identify the persons or agency to make the search, name the place to be searched, and name the evidence to be seized. The Fourth Amendment is violated if the warrant (which is an order) is not obeyed. Defects discovered in the issuance and/or performance of the warrant will provide a significant advantage to the defense. Again, the PI can be a key player in discovering defects

The Private Investigator's Right to Search

The Fourth Amendment prohibitions on search and seizure apply to persons acting on behalf of the government. A PI is not an agent of the government and is therefore not subject to those prohibitions. At the same time, however, the Fourth Amendment does not confer any search and seizure rights on private citizens, including PIs. Also, and quite apart from the US Constitution, numerous state laws protect persons against searches and seizures that involve trespass and privacy intrusion.

While a PI has no conferred right to make searches and seize property, he/she has the right of citizen's arrest. In the course of a citizen's arrest (which has many restrictions), a PI can make a search of the arrested person for a weapon.

Reasonableness underlies the whole notion of search and seizure. It is reasonable for a citizen, such as a PI, to make a search when stolen property is at risk of being removed or when the person to be searched gives consent. Seizure of stolen property is permitted when it is in plain view.

Liability for Unlawful Search

At the federal level, the United States Code provides fines and imprisonment for persons found guilty of conducting unlawful searches. Most states have modeled their search and seizure laws after the federal law. Where a difference exists between a particular state and the overall guiding federal law, the difference is likely to be a matter of semantics.

In addition to possible criminal prosecution, the offending person is likely to be charged in a civil suit. A defense is possible if it can be shown that the searcher was acting in good faith, according to an official duty. A person who uses bad judgment and conducts an illegal search has an excuse, but a person can be charged when the search is conducted illegally by intent.

Material, Relevant, and Competent Evidence

Three evidence characteristics must be present for evidence to be admissible in a criminal trial.

Material Evidence. This evidence is the substantive part of a case presented at trial or an influence that has a legitimate and effective impact on the decision of the case. In a very basic sense, evidence is material to the extent it can be seen and understood in the context of the matter in question.

Relevant Evidence. This is evidence that tends to make the existence of a fact more probable or less probable than it would be without the evidence. It tends to prove or actually proves guilt or innocence.

Competent Evidence. Competency relates to what a piece of evidence purports to show. For example, a photograph taken of a forced lock is competent when it accurately depicts the lock, particularly in its relationship to other objects in the field of view.

The Hearsay Rule and Exceptions

A statement becomes hearsay when it is made by a person other than the person making the statement. Hearsay is prohibited at a trial or hearing. However, there are some exceptions to the rule preventing other persons to testify as to what a person said or did. Here are some of them:

Former Testimony. This is testimony given as a witness in a separate but related case or in a deposition related to the case. Former testimony can be admitted if the opposing party had an opportunity to question the witness by direct, cross, or redirect examination.

Present Sense Impression. This is a statement describing or explaining an event or condition made while the person was perceiving the event or condition or immediately thereafter.

Excited Utterance. This is a statement relating to a startling event or condition made while the person was under the stress of excitement caused by the event or condition.

Dying Declaration. This is a statement made by a person while believing that his/her death was imminent. For the declaration to be admissible, the person must have died.

Pictorial Evidence Requirements

Pictorial evidence can consist of photographs, digitally produced frames and videos, charts, and to some extent hand-drawn sketches. Like all forms of evidence, pictorial evidence must be material, relevant, and competent. Pictorial evidence is:

- Material when it relates to the case or fact in question. It also must have a legitimate and effective influence on the person viewing it.
- Relevant when it assists or connects to testimonial evidence. For example, a person's claim to be incapable of walking due to an on-the-job accident is shown to be false when a photograph shows the person playing basketball.
- Competent when it represents what it purports to represent.

In addition, pictorial evidence must be accurate, free of distortion, and noninflammatory.

Evidence Presentation and Standards

Presentation. A court hearing a case is responsible for exercising reasonable control over the mode and order of interrogating witnesses and presenting evidence so as to:

- Make the interrogation and presentation effective for the ascertainment of the truth
- Avoid needless consumption of time
- Protect witnesses from harassment or undue embarrassment

The Rules of Discovery

In American law, discovery is the pretrial phase in a lawsuit in which each party through the law of civil procedure, subpoena, or through other discovery devices, such as requests for production of documents, and depositions can request documents and other evidence from other parties and can compel the production of material held by the other side.

Discovery can require the production of interrogatories, motions, or requests for production of documents, requests for admissions, and depositions.

The common or traditional forms of discoverable materials include reports, photos, medical images, drawings, reconstructed video, video and audio tapes, e-mail, fax, archives, and data drawn from a variety of sources.

However, the increased use of technology has produced many new forms of discoverable materials such as that drawn from:

- Servers
- Hard drives
- PCs
- Laptops
- USB flash sticks
- iPods and similar devices
- Any material that appears to have been deleted from a hard drive but can be captured by computer forensic specialists
- Internet sites such as YouTube, Facebook, and MySpace

Because personal information is not discoverable, a law firm or investigation agency can avoid giving up some forms of discovered materials by using two PCs, two hard-wire phones, two cell phones, and two fax machines. Discoverable material that must be disclosed can be placed on one set of equipment, and information that falls under the defendant/client privilege or is of a personal nature can be placed on the other set of devices.

Testifying

Accurate testimony requires an understanding of how a jury is selected and an appreciation of the important role played by the jury at trial. More than that, the investigator must not give the jury a negative impression. When the investigator projects an appearance displeasing to the jury, the jury may regard the investigator's testimony as unreliable.

A person who is called for jury duty must perform the service or face a penalty. In some cases, for certain reasons, jurors are excused following initial evaluation of suitability. Those persons still under consideration for selection and must answer questions posed by the judge and attorneys representing both sides of the matter. The questions are designed to establish a balance between the two sides. This process is called the *voir dire*. The judge, prosecutor, and defense may dismiss potential jurors for various reasons.

After jurors have been selected, the trial begins. When the investigator is called to the stand, jurors make an evaluation of the investigator. This first impression is important because it can affect the jury's belief of testimony provided by the investigator.

A first impression consists of three intertwined characteristics: appearance, speech, and body language. Experts say that strength of appearance is first, body language second, and speech last. This is not to believe that one without the other two is acceptable. All must be apparent in the investigator's testimony.

Appearance. A good appearance is demonstrated either positively or negatively by:

- Grooming
- Hygiene
- Piercings
- Flashy jewelry
- Tattoos
- Hair care
- Makeup
- Five o'clock shadow
- Body odor
- Too much perfume, cologne, or after-shave lotion

Clothing should be:

- Conservative
- Capable of absorbing perspiration
- Neutral in color

Clothing should not be:

- Outdated
- Worn
- Stained or faded
- Baggy or sloppy
- Brightly colored
- Faddish
- Flashy and trendy
- A double-breasted or a three-or-four-button suit (A two-button suit buttoned at the top but not at the bottom will contribute to comfort while testifying.)
- A cowboy belt, cowboy boots, or bolo tie (unless testifying in an area where such attire is normal and expected)
- A brightly colored tie or a tie with a pattern that could draw a juror's attention away from the testimony
- Handcuffs on the tie or other type of police design
- White socks
- Shoes that fail to blend with the color of the clothing
- A hat

- Moccasins, sandals, or other nonconservative shoes

Body Language

Body language is next in importance for making a good impression:

- Look at the jury when making a point.
- Don't cross your legs or slouch in the witness chair.
- Remain calm and cool, especially during cross-examination.
- Enter and depart the courtroom with a confident walk.
- Do not press your forehead or make similar gestures that suggest you can't remember a particular detail.
- When asked a critical question, ponder over it even when you know the answer.
- Do not comb your hair on the witness stand.
- Do not look at the jury when entering or leaving the courtroom.
- Don't point unless asked.
- Do not use hand movements in lieu of words.
- Restrict facial expressions.

Speech

Speech is also important in making a good impression. Following are good and bad characteristics:

- Speak loudly and clearly.
- Do not have anything in the mouth such as gum, candy, or a lozenge.
- Practice ahead of time saying words that are unfamiliar or difficult to pronounce.
- Unless forced by questioning, give testimony chronologically.
- If testifying for the defense (which will usually be the case), use euphemisms for inflammatory words such as "hurt" instead of "stabbed."

- Do not answer confusing questions. Ask for clarification.
- Be as accurate as possible concerning times and places, where evidence was found, important words spoken by witnesses, and other details that help the jury form a picture in their minds.
- Use proper pronunciation. Consult the dictionary in advance if you are unclear on a word you expect to have to say while testifying.
- Do not mumble.
- Avoid lazy speech or speech suggestive of a poor education.
- Practice testimony in front of a mirror or another person, or record it with an audio or video recorder and study it prior to appearing in court.

A Trial's Key Players

The key players in a trial are:

- The judge, whose job is to preside over the trial, rule on the admissibility of evidence, maintain order in the courtroom, and interpret the law for the jury.
- The jurors, who hear and weigh the testimony of witnesses and evaluate evidence. Jurors are typically unfamiliar with the law and courtroom procedures. As much as anything else, jurors base their decisions on the personalities and attitudes of the attorneys and witnesses, especially private investigator witnesses.
- The attorneys, who represent both sides in the case. Their conduct is regulated by established procedures and the rulings of the judge.
- The defendant (or defendants), who may or may not testify.
- Witnesses for both sides, who present facts personally known to them. In a criminal case, the prosecution often relies on police witnesses, whereas the defense often relies on private investigator witnesses.

In civil cases, private investigators can be witnesses for both sides.

Witnesses are the means by which facts are communicated to and understood by a judge and jury. Jurors come into court having no prior knowledge of what happened; the picture they get will depend largely on your testimony.

A friendly witness is a person that has given a statement helpful to your client. When the witness is scheduled to testify, help him or her by explaining courtroom procedure such as how to enter and greet the court, how direct and cross-examination works, and how to testify. Answer the witness's questions and allay fear.

Direct and Cross Examination

In a criminal defense investigation, the investigator is a witness for the defense; as such, the investigator gives testimony through questions asked by the defense attorney. This is called direct examination. Leading questions are not permitted on the direct examination except as may be necessary to develop the testimony.

When the defense attorney concludes the direct examination, the prosecutor will question the investigator in what is called cross-examination. Cross-examination is limited to the subject matter of the direct examination and matters affecting your credibility. The court may, in the exercise of discretion, permit inquiry into additional matters.

After each side has conducted direct and cross-examinations, the defense is permitted to question the investigator one more time. This is called re-direct examination. The prosecutor is then able to question the investigator in what is called re-cross examination.

Use of Notes

If the investigator uses notes or other writing to refresh his/her memory, the opposing party is entitled to inspect them, to cross-examine the investigator concerning them, and to introduce in evidence those portions which relate to the testimony.

If it can be shown that the writing contains matters not related to the subject matter of the testimony, the court can choose to examine the writing in camera (out of sight and hearing of the jury) and excise any unrelated portions. It is for this reason that the investigator must be careful in the use of notes to jog the memory.

The risks are that the investigator's competency will be called into question if the notes are sloppy; the opposing party may succeed in damaging the credibility of the testimony in all respects, and the notes themselves may be taken and made a part of the trial record.

Expert Testimony

If either side plans to use an expert witness to testify, both sides must qualify the witness as an expert on the stand. It must be established that the witness has special knowledge that persons of moderate experience and education in the same field do not possess.

A person qualified as an expert by knowledge, skill, experience, training, or education may be permitted to testify in the form of an opinion if:

- The testimony is based upon sufficient facts
- The testimony is the product of reliable principles and methods
- The expert has applied the principles and methods reliably to the facts of the case

To demonstrate expertise, the witness is expected to:

- Be employed currently or formerly in the specific field about which the witness will testify
- Be an active member of a professional group related to the field

- Be a current or former researcher in the field
- Possess an educational degree directly related to the field or direct experience with the issue, if not employed in the field
- Be a published author or have teaching experience in the subject matter

Private investigators and police investigators can be qualified as experts on sounds, firearms, distances, time, and visibility by years of experience as investigators.

Technical areas, such as firearms, toolmarks, and questioned document examinations, require a combination of specialized training and experience. The same applies to accident reconstruction, computer forensics, and polygraphy.

A PI testifying as an expert witness must enter the courtroom thoroughly prepared, testify in specifics, be truthful, and be prepared to withstand withering cross-examination.

When the defense attorney learns that the prosecuting attorney plans to qualify a police investigator as an expert witness, the PI can be helpful by pointing out flaws that might be used to discredit the police investigator's qualifications.

Conclusion

Criminal defense investigations are conducted, usually by private investigators, in concert with attorneys defending accused persons. The investigative techniques vary little from techniques used by law enforcement investigators.

The big picture functions of the investigator are:

- Conduct a separate, independent investigation.
- Evaluate the police investigation.
- Confer with and advise the defendant's counsel.
- Prepare a written report.
- Testify.

The investigator studies documents that were made available to defense counsel through the discovery process. These would include, for example; charges filed, affidavits, warrants, witness statements, photographs, laboratory examination reports, chain of custody documents, and police reports.

The investigator looks for evidence helpful to the defense, such as violation of the defendant's Miranda rights, improper search and seizure, contamination of physical evidence, and inconsistencies in witness statements.

John J. Fay, *Encyclopedia of Security Management*, second ed., Butterworth-Heinemann, Burlington, MA, 2007, pp. 127–130, 136–138, 153–155, 181–182, and 214–216.

Hans M. Gidion, *Encyclopedia of Security Management*, first ed., Butterworth-Heinemann, Burlington, MA, 2007, pp. 595–597.

Leon C. Mathieu, *Encyclopedia of Security Management*, second ed., Butterworth-Heinemann, Burlington, MA, 2007, pp. 161–167.

Learning Shop USA, Testifying, www.learningshopusa.com

Learning Shop USA, Scientific Analysis of Physical Evidence, www.learningshopusa.com

Learning Shop USA, Criminal Defense Investigation, www.learningshopusa.com

Learning Shop USA, Note Taking, www.learningshopusa.com

Laboratory Services Manual, Federal Bureau of Investigation, Washington, DC, all pages.

CRIMINAL DEFENSE INVESTIGATION SPECIALTIES

Private investigators, like professionals in other fields, tend to gravitate toward a specialty in which the investigator is best suited. Criminal defense investigation is one of such specialties, and within it are a number of functions such as:

- Conduct surveillance
- Analyze and interpret documents
- Examine evidence
- Locate and interview witnesses

- Evaluate the police investigation
- Work with defense attorneys and clients

Specialties are supported by skills. Following are brief comments about the supportive skills.

Conduct Surveillance

For most private investigators, this function is frustrating when it involves long periods of time waiting and watching for the surveillance target to appear and do something. In addition to patience, the work requires skill in using photographic equipment and making notes.

Criminal defense investigators by their nature, the very nature that attracted them to the investigation field in the first place, are action oriented. Sitting in a van, hiding on a rooftop, peeking through a window, or trailing a person on foot or in a vehicle can be unpleasant for some investigators.

Analyze and Interpret Documents

Documents acquired by the investigator or by the discovery process have to be carefully studied and compared against each other. They need to be analyzed as to how they relate to evidence, especially physical evidence. The question "What does this mean?" is key to interpretation.

Documents can conflict with physical evidence and with statements made by witnesses. Facts alleged and judgments made by police investigators and prosecuting attorneys are not always accurate, sometimes not accurate enough to take a case to court or support a plea-bargain offer.

Examine Evidence

Physical evidence is frequently not available for actual examination, but the criminal defense investigator will have the opportunity to look at representations of physical evidence such as photos, videos, sketches,

notes, chain of custody documents, and reports of forensic examinations and conclusions. Other forms of evidence, such as official records, are examined to establish accuracy of and relevance to charges filed against the defendant.

Locate and Interview Witnesses

Witnesses often move to different locations to avoid contact by a criminal defense investigator. Although the defense has a right to interview witnesses that were interviewed by the police and prosecutors, finding the witnesses can be a problem. Also, interviewing presents problems when the witness has:

- A belief that the defendant did in fact commit the crime alleged and that the defendant needs to be punished
- Dislike of the defendant on personal grounds
- A hope that by not being interviewed by the defense, his/her witness testimony will not to be needed at trial
- Fear of reprisal

Success in interviewing is more than being articulate. A combination of other attributes contribute to success. These include appearance, decorum, confidence, and sincerity.

Evaluate the Police Investigation

This function requires skepticism of the police investigation and the conclusions reached from it. Even when the criminal defense investigator holds strong personal beliefs against crime in general, the job requires every effort to give the accused every opportunity to defend against charges. This includes finding holes in the police investigation.

It is well known that police investigators will form a hypothesis without regard to other possibilities, "fudge" on facts that work to the disadvantage of the defendant, and exclude pertinent information. Skepticism extends to information provided by the police to obtain warrants, properly execute warrants, and administer the Miranda warning when the defendant was interrogated.

It is an ugly fact that some police investigators will sometimes conceal exculpatory information and make weak information appear to be very incriminating. Very often, this ugly fact occurs without prejudicial intent. The police investigator may have too many cases to deal with, police supervisors are overly demanding, the investigator is physically exhausted, and unreasonable demands are placed on the investigator when a case has political implications.

Work with the Defense Attorney and Client

The criminal defense investigator is sometimes caught between the client (i.e., the defendant or other party connected to the defense) and the defense attorney. Tact is the answer.

The defense attorney is essentially the boss; the boss tells the investigator what is wanted. The investigator decides how to do what is wanted and does it. A primary task of both the attorney and investigator is to find a defect in the probable cause offered by the police as a reason to identify the defendant as a suspect. Is the probable cause information in conflict with facts that were known at the time a warrant was issued or when the accused was arrested?

Preparation for a case involves working with the defense attorney to decide which pieces of information should be addressed on the witness stand and how to fend off challenges and criticisms made by opposing counsel. Preparation requires multiple conferences with the defense attorney, particularly when a trial is not far off.

Competence and Limitations

Competence is a given necessity in the criminal defense investigation trade. But full,

absolutely full, competence is rare. Some investigators are very good interviewers but not so good in surveillance; some are good at plain old gumshoe work but not so good at writing reports; and some are good on the witness stand but not so good when analyzing case documents. The main reason for the differences is usually a matter of preference. The investigator may enjoy certain activities and seek to perform them in lieu of other activities. That which is pleasing to do is done and done well; that which is not pleasing to do is avoided and, as a consequence, becomes a limitation. It is fortunate when competence overcomes limitations.

The bottom line in criminal defense investigation has two dimensions: discover and develop information that works in favor of the defendant, and dispute information put forth by the opposition.

Lee Dresselhaus

CRIMINAL INTELLIGENCE

In very basic terms, criminal intelligence is collecting, analyzing, and interpreting crime-related data. The interpretations are disseminated to enforcers responsible for dealing directly with the activity. For the most part, the criminal intelligence process has been confined to the law enforcement domain. The process is now migrating to businesses for use by investigators to identify the sources of crime-connected loss. Methods used to generate and collect data include:

- Conducting undercover operations
- Creating "listening posts," e.g., people in positions to see suspicious activity and voluntarily report it
- Using confidential informants
- Giving rewards for information
- Running a "hot line" that guarantees caller anonymity
- Interviewing knowledgeable persons
- Studying internal reports

- Examining the company's control standards, such as a standard that requires two-person approval of payments to vendors
- Creating internal procedures that calculate loss in several dimensions, such as total loss, number of loss incidents, average loss per incident, seasonal loss, loss as a percentage of profit margin, etc.
- Conferring with colleagues employed in similar businesses

Four Steps

The process for creating useable intelligence moves in four steps:

Determination of Requirements. What information is to be collected, for what purpose, by whom, and to whom should it be disseminated? This step is decided at the top and is carried out in a plan.

Collation. In this step, the collected information is organized according to characteristics of the information. In a simplified view, data about "locations" go in one pile, data about "persons" go in a different pile, and data about "movement" go in a third pile. The number of piles can be large, and the nature of them can be complex.

Analysis. The collated information is examined for inter-relevance and in its relationship to information already on file. Analysis is like working on a jigsaw puzzle. The puzzle is rarely solved completely, but with enough data and discovery of connections, a partial image is possible.

Dissemination. Before information (intelligence) leaves the Analysis step, it must be reliable and relevant to the purpose of the plan that was decided in the Determination of Requirements step.

It is helpful to think of the intelligence process as a stand-alone enterprise. The process begins upon receipt of data collected in the field. The process does not collect the data; it processes the data. Useable information produced by the process is released to the field for possible action. The process is not involved in field action. (Note: The word "field" connotes the total environment of the business. Components of the environment can include suppliers, vendors, customers/clients, contractors, business partners, and employees. Users are persons in the field, such as private investigators and corporate security investigators, who hold responsibility for taking action. The action can be as simple as creating or modifying a control standard or as complicated as implementing an undercover operation.)

Direct action by users in the field is not discretionary. Action is decided at the top. The manner of action is decided at the operational level.

Directorate of Intelligence, Federal Bureau of Investigation, http://www.fbi.gov/about-us/intelligence/defined

CRIMINAL INTENT

Criminal intent is a clearly formulated state of mind to do an act that the law specifically prohibits, without regard to the motive that prompts the act and whether or not the offender knows that what he or she is doing is in violation of the law.

It is generally regarded as falling into two categories: general criminal intent and specific criminal intent. General criminal intent is an essential element in all crimes. It means that when the offender acted, or failed to act, contrary to the law, he or she did so voluntarily with determination or foresight of the consequences. For example, general criminal intent is shown in the offense of assault and battery when the offender voluntarily applies unlawful force to another with an awareness of its result. In larceny, general criminal intent (often called larcenous intent) is shown by intent to knowingly take and carry away the goods of another without any claim or pretense of right, with intent wholly to deprive the owner of them or to convert them to personal use.

Specific criminal intent requires a particular mental state in addition to that of general criminal intent. The laws relating to certain crimes may describe an additional, specific mental purpose. For example, the crime of murder has a general criminal intent in that the offender voluntarily applies unlawful force with an awareness of its result. In addition, the crime of murder in a particular jurisdiction may require a showing that the offender acted with premeditation to commit murder.

The term "overt act" is often associated with criminal intent. An overt act is an outward or manifest act from which criminality may be inferred, such as an act done to carry out a criminal intention. In the crime of conspiracy, the overt act is an essential element of proof.

Motive and intent are separate concepts in criminal law. Motive is the desire or inducement that tempts or prompts a person to do a criminal act. Intent is a person's resolve or purpose to commit the act. Motive is the reason that leads the mind to desire a certain result. Intent is the determination to achieve the result.

Motive is an important investigative consideration but is not an essential element of a crime. Intent must be established for a crime to exist. A good motive (as might be represented in a mercy killing) does not keep an act from being a crime, and an evil motive will not necessarily make an act a crime. Furthermore, an accused would not be acquitted simply because a motive could not be discovered.

The basic urge that led the offender's mind to want the result of the forbidden act is immaterial as to guilt. Proof of motive, however, may be relevant and admissible on behalf of either side at trial. Motive can be especially pertinent where the evidence in a case is largely circumstantial. In some statutes, proof of motive may be required.

John J. Fay, *Encyclopedia of Security Management*, second ed., Butterworth-Heinemann, Burlington, MA, 2007, pp. 221–222.

CRIMINAL JUSTICE SYSTEM

The criminal justice system has four parts:

- Police
- Courts
- Prosecution and Defense
- Corrections

Police

The first contact a defendant has with the criminal justice system is usually with the police, who investigate the suspected wrongdoing and make an arrest. When needed, police officers are empowered to use force and other forms of legal coercion and means to maintain public and social order.

The police are mainly concerned with keeping the peace and enforcing criminal law in accordance with a designated mission and jurisdiction. Missions can include: patrolling; responding to burglary and fire alarms; responding to assault and domestic disturbances; responding to major emergencies, such as explosions, floods, and hurricanes; investigating felony crimes, such as manslaughter and murder; and investigating terrorist activities. Individual jurisdictions can be territorial in nature such as law enforcement at city, county, state, and federal levels. Jurisdiction can also be arranged by type of crime, such as kidnapping, drug enforcement, smuggling, illegal entry to the United States, and espionage.

Courts

Courts serve as the venue where justice is administered. There are a number of critical people in a court setting: judge; prosecutor; defense attorney; and an impartial group or person, such as a jury, judge, or panel of judges. A judge, or magistrate, is a person, elected or appointed, who is knowledgeable in the law and whose function is to objectively administer the legal proceedings.

Guilt or nonguilt is decided through an adversarial procedure in which two parties (prosecution and defense) both offer their version of events and argue their version before the court. The case is (or should be) decided in favor of the party who offers the most sound and compelling arguments based on the law, as applied to the facts of the crime.

A court abides by a system of law, the purpose of which is to provide an objective set of rules for maintaining order and governing conduct. Criminal law is concerned with actions that are dangerous or harmful to society as a whole, and prosecution is pursued not by an individual but rather by the state. The purpose of criminal law is to provide a specific definition of what constitutes a crime and to prescribe punishments for committing crime. No criminal law can be valid unless it includes both of these factors: a crime that is defined by law and punishment appropriate to the crime.

Prosecutor and Defense

The prosecutor, or district attorney, is an attorney who brings charges against a person, persons, or corporate entity. It is the prosecutor's duty to explain to the court what crime was committed and to provide in detail a description of the evidence that incriminates the accused. The prosecutor is a servant of the state who makes accusations on behalf of the state in criminal proceedings.

A defense attorney counsels the accused on the legal process, likely outcomes for the accused, and a defense strategy. The accused, not the lawyer, has the right to make final decisions regarding a number of fundamental points, including whether to testify, accept a plea offer, or demand a jury trial (in appropriate cases). It is the defense attorney's duty to represent the interests of the client, raise procedural and evidentiary issues, and hold the prosecution to its burden of proving guilt beyond a reasonable doubt. Defense counsel may challenge evidence presented by the prosecution or present exculpatory evidence on behalf of the defendant. At trial, the defense attorney may offer a rebuttal to the prosecutor's accusations.

In the United States, an accused person is entitled to a government-paid defense attorney if he or she is in jeopardy of losing his or her life and/or liberty. Those who cannot afford a private attorney may be provided one by the state.

The final determination of guilt or innocence is typically made by an unbiased party. This function may be performed by a judge, a panel of judges, or a jury panel. This process varies depending on the laws of the specific jurisdiction. In some places, the panel (judge, judges, or jury) is required to issue a unanimous decision, while in other jurisdictions a majority vote is sufficient. The manner of process depends on the state, level of court, and agreements between the prosecuting and defending parties

A large majority of criminal cases are disposed of without the need for a trial. The rationale is to lessen the case load of courts. If the accused confesses his or her guilt, a shorter process may be employed and a judgment rendered quickly. Plea bargaining allows the accused to plead guilty. The sentence is reduced or eliminated entirely in exchange for a value given to the prosecutor. Such value is often information concerning other criminals and/or trial testimony that is beneficial to the prosecution.

Another method of reducing case load is *nolo contendere*, in which the offender pleads guilty and the prosecution drops or reduces charges. The offender may receive a reduced sentence or be required to complete a designated diversion or rehabilitation program. This usually occurs when the prosecution's case is weak. The advantage to the state is reduction of case load and avoidance of cost to the taxpayer. *Nolo contendere* is sometimes criticized on the ground that it coerces innocent people to plead guilty to avoid harsh punishment.

Corrections

A person convicted of a crime is remanded to the custody of a correctional authority. Punishment (in the form of prison time) may serve a variety of purposes. A concept supporting incarceration is preventing further crime by keeping criminals out of the general population. Another concept is to "correct" unacceptable behavior by schooling and training prisoners so that upon their release they are able to earn a living. Religious studies in prison are aimed at instilling ethics, morality, and respect for other persons.

A person released from prison before completion of sentence is placed on parole. Parole can impose certain restrictions: to live in a halfway house for a designated period of time, remain drug-free, complete a rehabilitation program, obtain a job, perform community service, not carry a weapon, and not consort with criminals. A violation of parole can send an early-released person back to prison to complete his/her sentence and/or be charged with a new crime.

Apart from or in conjunction with incarceration is the administration of monetary fines. Such fines can be paid to the state or to a victim as remuneration for the victim's loss.

A sentence of death is carried out by a corrections authority. The manner of execution varies from state to state. The death penalty is one of the most heavily debated aspects of the criminal justice system.

Joseph A. Senna and Larry J. Siegel, *Introduction to Criminal Justice*, West Publishing, Minneapolis/St. Paul, MN, p. 3.

CRIMINAL LAW

A crime is a legal wrong prosecuted by the state in a formal court proceeding in which a sentence may be imposed. A crime can result from the commission of an illegal act or from the omission of a required legal act.

Felonies and misdemeanors are the two most common classifications of crime in the United States. The decision of whether a crime is a felony or a misdemeanor rests with the individual jurisdiction. The federal government and each state has its own body of criminal law and penalties. The principal distinction between a felony and misdemeanor is the degree of seriousness. In the simplest of terms, a felony is a serious offense and a misdemeanor is a less serious offense. Black's Law Dictionary says, "A felony is a crime of a graver or more atrocious nature than those designated as misdemeanors." Generally, it is an offense punishable by death or imprisonment in a penitentiary. A misdemeanor is lower than a felony and is generally punishable by fine or imprisonment in a place other than a penitentiary.

In proving guilt of a specific crime in a court of law, the prosecution must establish three general facts:

- An injury or loss has taken place.
- The injury or loss resulted from a criminal act.
- The accused committed the act.

To convict, the prosecution must present the evidence of the case without ambiguity. In other words, the prosecution must prove its case beyond a reasonable doubt and to a moral certainty.

Philip P. Purpura, *Encyclopedia of Security Management*, second ed., Butterworth-Heinemann, Burlington, MA, 2007, pp. 224–225.

CRIMINAL PROCEDURE

Introduction

Criminal procedure is that part of the body of law dealing with the investigation of crimes, arrest, charging, trial, and sentencing. The federal government, the 50 states, the military, and U.S. territories have their own sets of criminal procedure. As a result, variation from jurisdiction to jurisdiction is the norm but not to a great degree, however, given the common foundation of common law.

Criminal procedure at the federal level is governed by certain provisions of the U.S. Constitution, especially those contained in the first ten amendments to the Constitution, i.e., the Bill of Rights. The Fourth Amendment (unreasonable search and seizure, and arrest) and the Fifth Amendment (self-incrimination prohibited) have particular application to the work of security officers and private investigators.

Initial Contact

Initial contact is the point at which a person first becomes a subject of interest to a law enforcement agency. Initial contact typically occurs in a police action, such as being arrested or named by a complainant or witness. The documentation of an initial contact is often an incident report, a witness statement, or other record of routine police work.

Investigation

In this stage, facts are obtained and weighed to determine if a crime was committed, to identify persons responsible, and—when done correctly—will satisfy the constitutional requirement called probable cause. The investigation, or at least the start of it, precedes arrest, hence the term "preliminary investigation."

Arrest

Arrest cannot happen without investigation. The investigation may last five seconds or five years, depending on the difficulty of establishing probable cause. In most cases, probable cause is apparent at the outset; in a few cases, probable cause can only be established after long and complex investigations. The determination of probable cause is investigative in nature, thus assuring a 1–2–3 progression: initial contact, investigation, arrest.

If the crime is a felony, the officer can arrest by relying on what he or she personally knows to be true and/or information provided by a credible witness, such as a security officer or private investigator at the scene. If the crime is a misdemeanor, the officer can make an arrest only if he or she personally witnessed the act.

When an arrest is made well after the investigation, the reason is likely to relate to an absence of probable cause at the outset or that the suspect's whereabouts or identification was not immediately known.

Custody

At the moment an arrest is completed, the arrested person is said to be in custody. The police are at liberty to protect themselves, such as by handcuffing the individual and searching for weapons. The arresting officers may also look for crime-related evidence in the immediate control of the individual. The individual is transported to a police station and booked. Booking is the taking of basic information, fingerprinting, and photographing. Any questions asked while a person is in custody, whether at the scene or anyplace else, must be preceded by a Miranda warning.

Charging

A charge is a formal allegation that a certain person committed a certain crime. If the crime is a misdemeanor, the prosecutor may file a charging document with the appropriate court. A misdemeanor charge tends to be settled quickly; for example, with a plea bargain or a plea of no contest called *nolo contendere*.

If the crime is a felony, the prosecutor may submit the charge to either a grand jury or to a judge in a preliminary hearing.

Depending on sufficiency of evidence, seriousness of the crime, and other factors, the prosecutor may decide to not charge the individual. This action is called *nolle prosequi*.

Grand Jury/Preliminary Hearing

Depending on the state, a felony charge is either examined by a grand jury in a closed hearing or by a court in an open hearing called a preliminary hearing. In the grand jury method, the prosecutor presents evidence. If the grand jury agrees that probable cause is present, it issues a bill of indictment. In the preliminary hearing method, the defendant and attorney are allowed to dispute evidence presented by the prosecutor. If the prosecutor prevails, the suspect is ordered to stand trial.

Arraignment

The suspect is brought before a court, informed of the charge, and informed of his or her constitutional rights. At this point, the suspect becomes a defendant. The defendant is allowed to enter a plea (guilty or not guilty). A trial date is set, and the court decides on bail or detention.

If the court is persuaded that the defendant is not a threat to society and will appear at trial, the defendant may be released on personal recognizance. Without that persuasion, a court may set bail (a money bond). If the bond is posted, the defendant may be released pending trial. If the defendant does not appear for trial, the bond is forfeited. If a court determines that the defendant is a societal threat or at risk of fleeing, the court may deny bail and order the defendant held for trial.

Plea Bargaining

Plea bargaining can begin anytime, although usually after arraignment. The usual practice is for the defense to offer a guilty plea in exchange for reducing or dropping one or more of the charges or to obtain a less severe sentence. About nine out of ten felony cases end in a plea bargain.

All criminal law in the United States must conform to the U.S. Constitution. Conflicting criminal law is eventually challenged in the appellate courts and either modified to conform to the Constitution or removed from the legal code by judicial order.

Adversarial Approach

Our legal system is based on common law, which in practice takes an adversarial approach. In the adversarial approach, a verdict results from competition between the prosecution and the defense. Each side presents facts and interprets the law in ways most favorable to its interests. The accused is presumed to be innocent, and the burden of proving guilt belongs to the prosecution.

In this system of justice, judges and juries decide cases. The judge ascertains the applicable law, and the jury determines the facts. The system emphasizes procedural rules designed to ensure that the contest is waged fairly.

Criticisms are made of the adversarial approach: truth is often overcome by the natural urge to win, and disparities between the parties in resources and competencies of the attorneys can affect the outcome.

Criminal Law

The body of law that defines offenses against the state and regulates investigation, prosecution, and punishment is called the criminal law and is different from civil law, which is concerned with relations between private parties. Security officers and private investigators must have a working knowledge of the major criminal law concepts. Without such knowledge, they cannot properly discharge their responsibilities for preventing and investigating crimes committed against their clients, collaborating with law enforcement, and seeking prosecution of offenders.

Defenses to Crime

The law allows many defenses to charges of crime, and it is the right of the accused to use any and all of them.

Capacity Defense. The capacity to commit defense holds that a person should not be held criminally punishable for his conduct unless he is actually responsible for it. Young persons and mentally afflicted persons, for example, may be recognized as not having the capacity to commit crimes because they lack a sufficient degree of responsibility.

Insanity Defense. The insanity defense holds that a person cannot be held liable for his criminal act if he was insane at the time of the act. The defense goes to the heart of the fundamental principle of intent, or guilty mind. If the accused did not understand what he was doing or understand that his actions were wrong, he cannot have criminal intent and, without intent, there is no crime.

Intoxication Defense. The intoxication defense is similar to that of the insanity defense. It argues that the accused could not have a guilty mind due to intoxication. The fact of voluntary intoxication is generally not accepted as a defense. Involuntary intoxication produced by fraud or coercion of another may be a defense, and insanity produced by intoxicants may be acceptable. Intoxication can also be offered as evidence that an accused was incapable of forming the intent to commit a crime, e.g., the accused was too drunk to entertain the idea of breaking and entering into a house at night for the purpose of committing an offense.

Alibi Defense. The alibi defense seeks to prove that because the defendant was elsewhere at the time the offense occurred, the defendant could not have committed the crime.

Compulsion Defense. The compulsion defense argues that a person should not be charged with a crime when the act was committed in response to an imminent, impending, and overwhelmingly coercive influence.

For example, a person who is ordered to drive a getaway car under the threat of immediate death would not be punishable as a principal to the crime.

Immunity Defense. The immunity defense grants protection from prosecution in exchange for cooperation by the accused. The required cooperation might be a full disclosure of all facts and testimony at trial.

Consent Defense. The consent defense may be used when consent of the victim is involved. Where consent is offered as a defense, the consent must have been given by a person legally capable of giving it and it must be voluntary.

Entrapment Defense. The entrapment defense argues that an accused should not be charged if he was induced to commit a crime for the mere purpose of instituting criminal prosecution against him. Generally, where the criminal intent originates in the mind of the accused and the criminal offense is completed, the fact that a law enforcement officer furnished the accused an opportunity for commission does not constitute entrapment. A key point is that when the criminal intent originates in the mind of the officer and the accused is lured into the commission, no conviction may be had.

Withdrawal Defense. The withdrawal defense is sometimes used to defend in a prosecution for conspiracy. A conspirator who withdraws from the conspiracy prior to commission of the requisite overt act may attempt a defense based on withdrawal.

Good Character Defense. The good character defense seeks to offer evidence that the accused is of such good character that it was unlikely he or she committed the act. This is not a defense as a matter of law but an attempt to convince a jury it was improbable for the accused to have committed the crime.

Ignorance Defense. The ignorance defense argues that the accused had no criminal intent. This defense seeks to excuse the accused because he was misled or was not in possession of all facts at the time of the crime. For example, this defense might be used in a case where a homeowner injured someone who he thought was a burglar in his home, but who in fact was the invited guest of another member of the family. This defense is based on the grounds that a defendant did not know certain essential facts, that he could not have been expected to know them, and that there could be no crime without such knowledge. Mistake of law is a rarely allowed defense offered by an accused that he did not know his act was criminal or did not comprehend the consequences of the act.

Statute of Limitations Defense. The statute of limitations defense seeks to prevent prosecution on the grounds that the government failed to bring charges within the period of time fixed by a particular enactment. Not all crimes have time limitations for seeking prosecution, and some crimes, such as murder and other major crimes, have no limits whatsoever.

Irresistible Defense. This is a defense by which an accused seeks to be fully or partially excused from responsibility on the grounds that although he knew the act was wrong, he was compelled to its execution by an impulse he was powerless to control.

Necessity Defense. Necessity is the defense of justifying an otherwise criminal act on the ground that the perpetrator was compelled to commit it because a greater evil would have ensued had he failed to do so. Thus, one could plead necessity if he committed arson to destroy official documents that would otherwise have fallen into the hands of a wartime enemy.

Defense of Life. The defense of life rule is derived from English common law, which authorizes the use of deadly force in self-defense and in order to apprehend persons committing or fleeing from felonies. In many jurisdictions, the rule has been narrowed by statute so that the use of weaponry is limited only to defense of life situations

and to some specific violent felonies, such as murder, rape, aggravated assault, arson, or burglary. This protection against prosecution relies on the premise that every person has a right to defend himself from harm. A person may use, in self-defense, that force which, under all the circumstances of the case, reasonably appears necessary to prevent impending injury.

Diminished Capacity. Diminished capacity is the decreased or less-than-normal ability, temporary or permanent, to distinguish right from wrong or to fully appreciate the consequences of one's act. It is a plea used by the defendant for conviction of a lesser degree of a crime, for a lenient sentence, or for mercy or clemency.

Former Jeopardy Defense. Former jeopardy is a plea founded on the common law principle that a person cannot be brought into danger of his life or limb for the same offense more than once. The former jeopardy defense is founded on the principle that a case once terminated upon its merits should not be tried again. Double jeopardy can only be claimed when the second prosecution is brought by the same government as the first. When the act is a violation of the law as to two or more governments, the accused is regarded as having committed separate offenses.

Related to legal defenses is the bill of particulars. It is a statement by the prosecution filed by order of the court, at the court's own request or that of the defendant, of such particulars as may be necessary to give the defendant and the court reasonable knowledge of the nature and grounds of the crime charged, such as the time and place, means by which it was alleged to have been committed, or more specific information. The concept can also apply to the defendant; for example, a defendant who intends to rely on an alibi defense may be required to furnish the prosecuting officer with a bill of particulars as to the alibi. This bill sets forth in detail the place or places the defendant claims to have been, together with the names and addresses of witnesses upon whom he intends to rely to establish his alibi. The purpose of this procedure is to prevent the sudden and unexpected appearance of alibi witnesses whose testimony in the latter stage of a trial could cast reasonable doubt on the state's case. By compelling advance notice, the prosecutor is afforded time to investigate the alibi, as well as the credibility of the alibi witnesses, and, in so doing, establish a position for refuting the alibi defense.

http://www.uscourts.gov/file/document/rules-criminal-procedure

CRITICAL NATIONAL INFRASTRUCTURE

A primary mission of the Department of Homeland Security is to lead the national effort to protect critical infrastructure from hazards (including terrorist-related hazards) by managing risk and enhancing resilience through collaboration with the critical infrastructure community.

Following are the sectors that comprise the critical national infrastructure. To the right of each sector name is the responsible government agency.

- Chemical: Department of Homeland Security
- Commercial Facilities: Department of Homeland Security
- Communications: Department of Homeland Security
- Critical Manufacturing: Department of Homeland Security
- Dams: Department of Homeland
- Defense Industrial Base: Department of Defense
- Emergency Services: Department of Homeland Security
- Energy: Department of Energy
- Financial Services: Department of Treasury

- Food and Agriculture: Department of Agriculture and the Department of Health and Human Services
- Government Facilities: Department of Homeland Security and the General Services Administration
- Healthcare and Public Health: Department of Health and Human Services
- Information Technology: Department of Homeland Security
- Nuclear Reactors, Materials, and Waste: Department of Homeland Security
- Transportation Systems: Department of Homeland Security and the Department of Transportation
- Water and Wastewater Systems: Environmental Protection Agency

Programs managed by the Department of Homeland Security are designed to unify public and private sector operations in preventing and responding to impacts such as terrorist attacks, natural disasters, and major accidents. Sector stakeholders include facility owners and operators; federal, state, and local government agencies; the law enforcement community; trade associations; and homeland security advisors at the state level.

Although each sector has unique characteristics that require specialized knowledge and security expertise, they share core mission processes, goals, and objectives.

- Align priorities, goals, and strategic planning within the sector and facilitate development and implementation of risk mitigation initiatives.
- Foster education, training, and outreach.
- Conduct security-focused exercises.
- Facilitate risk and security information sharing throughout the sector.
- Identify research and development needs.
- Execute risk management actions designed to prevent, deter, and mitigate threats.

- Support security operations and incident management activities.
- Identify the nation's most critical infrastructure within each respective sector.
- Identify dependencies and interdependencies between sector assets and other critical infrastructure sectors.

Key stakeholders include facility owners and operators; federal, state, and local government agencies; law enforcement personnel; trade associations; state homeland security advisors; and private sector representatives.

US Department of Homeland Security, http://www.dhs.gov/national-infrastructure-protection-plan

John J. Fay, *Encyclopedia of Security Management*, second ed., Butterworth-Heinemann, Burlington, MA, 2007, pp. 516–563.

Learning Shop USA, Homeland Security, Part 1 and Part 2, www.learningshopusa.com

CROSS-EXAMINATION

In a criminal trial, it is the duty of counsel for the defendant, as an officer of the court and as an attorney, to use every legal means to secure the acquittal of the client or obtain the best possible verdict under the circumstances. A defense attorney will attempt to discredit or nullify the testimony of an investigator for the prosecution.

The first appearance of the investigator on the witness stand is called direct examination. The next stage in giving testimony is called cross-examination. During cross-examination, the defense attorney will want to discredit the investigator's testimony by:

- Inferring that the investigator failed to conduct a full and thorough investigation
- Trying to cast doubt on the investigator's competency
- Inferring that the investigator holds a grudge or is biased in some way that operates against the defendant
- Trying to confuse the investigator with misleading questions
- Inferring that the investigator is lying or leaving out facts

When the investigator refers to notes while testifying, defense counsel may try to show that the investigator's recollection of the facts is bad and should be discounted. If the investigator becomes angry or argumentative, the defense attorney will imply that the investigator is personally antagonistic to the defendant.

Kathleen M. Sweet, Encyclopedia of Security Management, second ed., Butterworth-Heinemann, Burlington, MA, 2007, p. 540.

CYBERSTALKING

As the name suggests, cyberstalking is the stalking of a person or group, in this sense, by means of the Internet. Purposes of the cyberstalker are numerous; for example, extortion, theft, defamation, damage to or destruction of data, distortion of facts, and sexual gratification. Like its physical counterpart, the intent of cyberstalking is to control and manipulate the victim through intimidation and inculcation of fear. In some cases, the cyberstalker is known by the victim, and in other cases, the cyberstalker is not known.

Cyberstalking is a crime that often goes unpunished for the simple reason that the offender cannot be identified or sufficient proof cannot be collected to sustain a charge. When a charge is proven and the offender convicted, a criminal penalty can call for imprisonment.

Learning Shop USA, Homeland Security, Part One, www.learningshopusa.com

CYBERTERRORISM

The threat posed by cyberterrorism holds the attention of the public, the mass media, and the information technology (IT) industry. Journalists, politicians, and experts in a variety of fields have popularized a scenario in which sophisticated cyberterrorists electronically break into computers that control dams or air traffic control systems, wreaking havoc and endangering not only millions of lives but national security itself.

Because most critical infrastructure in Western societies is networked through computers, the potential threat from cyberterrorism is alarming. Hackers, although not motivated by the same goals that inspire terrorists, have demonstrated that individuals can gain access to sensitive information and to the operation of crucial services. Terrorists, at least in theory, could thus follow the hackers' lead and then, having broken into government and private computer systems, cripple or at least disable the military, financial, and service sectors of advanced economies. The growing dependence of our societies on information technology has created a new form of vulnerability, giving terrorists the chance to approach targets that would otherwise be utterly unassailable, such as national defense systems and air traffic control systems. The more technologically developed a country is, the more vulnerable it becomes to cyberattacks against its infrastructure.

Concern about the potential danger posed by cyberterrorism is well founded. That does not mean, however, that all the fears that have been voiced in the media, in Congress, and in other public forums are rational and reasonable. Some fears are simply unjustified, while others are highly exaggerated. In addition, the distinction between the potential and the actual damage inflicted by cyberterrorists has too often been ignored, and the relatively benign activities of most hackers have been conflated with the specter of pure cyberterrorism.

The Roots of Cyberterrorism

The roots of cyberterrorism can be traced back to the early 1990s, when the rapid growth in Internet use and the debate on the emerging "information society" sparked several studies on the potential risks faced by the highly networked, high-tech-dependent United States. As early as 1990, the National Academy of Sciences began a report on computer security with the words, "We are at risk. Increasingly, America depends on computers. . . . Tomorrow's terrorist may be able to do more damage with a keyboard than with a bomb." At the same time, the prototypical term "electronic Pearl Harbor" was coined, linking the threat of a computer attack to the historic American trauma.

The Fear of Cyberterrorism

Psychological, political, and economic forces have combined to promote the fear of cyberterrorism. From a psychological perspective, two of the greatest fears of modern time are combined in the term "cyberterrorism." The fear of random, violent victimization blends well with the distrust and outright fear of computer technology. An unknown threat is perceived as more threatening than a known threat. Although cyberterrorism does not entail a direct threat of violence, its psychological impact on anxious societies can be as powerful as the effect of terrorist bombs. Moreover, the most destructive forces working against an understanding of the actual threat of cyberterrorism are a fear of the unknown and a lack of information or, worse, too much misinformation.

After 9/11, the security and terrorism discourse soon featured cyberterrorism prominently. This was understandable, given that more nightmarish attacks were expected and that cyberterrorism seemed to offer opportunities to inflict enormous damage. But there was also a political dimension to the new focus on cyberterrorism. Debates about national security, including the security of cyberspace, always attract political actors with agendas that extend beyond the specific issue at hand.

What Is Cyberterrorism?

There have been stumbling blocks to creating a clear and consistent definition of the term "cyberterrorism." First, much of the discussion of cyberterrorism has been conducted in the popular media, where journalists typically strive for drama and sensation rather than for good, operational definitions of new terms. Second, it has been especially common when dealing with computers to coin new words simply by placing the word "cyber," "computer," or "information" before another word. Thus, an entire arsenal of words—cybercrime, infowar, netwar, cyberterrorism, cyberharassment, virtual warfare, digital terrorism, cybertactics, computer warfare, cyberattack, and cyberbreak-ins— is used to describe what some military and political strategists describe as the "new terrorism" of our times.

It is important to distinguish between cyberterrorism and "hacktivism," a term coined by scholars to describe the marriage of hacking with political activism. ("Hacking" is here understood to mean activities conducted online and covertly that seek to reveal, manipulate, or otherwise exploit vulnerabilities in computer operating systems and other software. Unlike hacktivists, hackers tend *not* to have political agendas.) Hacktivists have four main weapons at their disposal: virtual blockades, e-mail attacks, hacking and computer break-ins, and computer viruses and worms.

A virtual blockade is the virtual version of a physical sit-in or blockade: political activists visit a website and attempt to generate so much traffic toward the site that other users cannot reach it, thereby disrupting normal operations while winning publicity—via media reports—for the protesters' cause. "Swarming" occurs when a large number of individuals simultaneously access a website, causing its collapse. Swarming can also amplify the effects of the hacktivists' second weapon: e-mail bombing campaigns (bombarding targets with thousands of messages at once, also known as "ping attacks").

Many cyberprotesters use the third weapon in the hacktivists' arsenal: web hacking and computer break-ins (hacking into computers to access stored information, communication facilities, financial information, and so forth).

The fourth category of hacktivist weaponry comprises viruses and worms, both of which are forms of malicious code that can infect computers and propagate over computer networks. Their impact can be enormous.

Hacktivism, although politically motivated, does not amount to cyberterrorism. Hacktivists do want to protest and disrupt; they *do not* want to kill or maim or terrify. However, hacktivism does highlight the threat of cyberterrorism, the potential that individuals with no moral restraint may use methods similar to those developed by hackers to wreak havoc. Moreover, the line between cyberterrorism and hacktivism may sometimes blur, especially if terrorist groups are able to recruit or hire computer-savvy hacktivists or if hacktivists decide to escalate their actions by attacking the systems that operate critical elements of the national infrastructure, such as electric power networks and emergency services.

The Appeal of Cyberterrorism for Terrorists

Cyberterrorism is an attractive option for modern terrorists for several reasons.

- First, it is cheaper than traditional terrorist methods. All that the terrorist needs is a personal computer and an online connection. Terrorists do not need to buy weapons such as guns and explosives; instead, they can create and deliver computer viruses through a telephone line, a cable, or a wireless connection.
- Second, cyberterrorism is more anonymous than traditional terrorist methods. Like many Internet surfers, terrorists use online nicknames—"screen names"—or log on to a website as an unidentified "guest user," making it very hard for security agencies and police forces to track down the terrorists' real identity. And in cyberspace there are no physical barriers such as checkpoints to navigate, no borders to cross, and no customs agents to outsmart.
- Third, the variety and number of targets are enormous. The cyberterrorist could target the computers and computer networks of governments, individuals, public utilities, private airlines, and so forth. The sheer number and complexity of potential targets guarantee that terrorists can find weaknesses and vulnerabilities to exploit. Several studies have shown that critical infrastructures, such as electric power grids and emergency services, are vulnerable to a cyberterrorist attack because the infrastructures and the computer systems that run them are highly complex, making it effectively impossible to eliminate all weaknesses.
- Fourth, cyberterrorism can be conducted remotely, a feature that is especially appealing to terrorists. Cyberterrorism requires less physical training, psychological investment, risk of mortality, and travel than conventional forms of terrorism, making it easier for terrorist organizations to recruit and retain followers.
- Fifth, cyberterrorism has the potential to affect directly a larger number of people than traditional terrorist methods, thereby generating greater media coverage, which is ultimately what terrorists want.

U.S. Institute for Peace, 2006, www.usip/org/

D

DATA MINING

Data mining is a type of database analysis used for discovering meaningful patterns or relationships in a large volume of data. The analysis uses advanced statistical methods such as cluster analysis and anomaly detection. A major goal of data mining is to discover previously unknown relationships among the data, especially when the data come from different databases. The overall goal of the data-mining process is to extract information from a data set and transform it into an understandable structure.

Investigators can use the data-mining technique to detect crime and crime patterns or make predictions about future crime. For the most part, the technique is used by companies to gather information of legitimate business interests such as customer preferences and product histories.

John J. Fay

DATABASE SEARCHING

Database searching as we know it today has its roots in the early 1990s. Pioneers in the technology were CDB Infotek, Prentice Hall Online, Merlin Information Services, Information America, Database Technologies, and LocatePlus. In particular, Database Technologies took the database search industry to a new level. As the demand for information grew, prices dropped and the industry remade itself. Mergers, acquisitions, and startups produced over the intervening years a host of new and evolving companies such as ChoicePoint, Lexis-Nexis, Accurint, Thomson Reuters, TLO LLC, and Tracers Information Services.

Generally speaking, a database search company holds or has access to information related to people, assets, and businesses as well as criminal and civil, and asset histories. Each company has its strengths. Some have more data than others or more specialized data. Broken down into smaller segments, the information can be:

- The true names of persons, Social Security numbers, their past and present residences, phone numbers, driver and professional licenses held
- Identification of homes, buildings, land, leases, rights, automobiles, boats, aircraft, and other assets
- The true names of businesses, holding companies, subsidiaries, corporate officers, "doing business as" names, major purchases and sales, and financial information
- Records of arrests, convictions, incarceration, citations, and summonses
- Identification of liens, judgments for and against, evictions, marriage and divorce, settlements, and garnishments

The usual investigative purposes of searching databases are to:

- Locate missing persons for criminal or civil cases
- Locate persons that have absconded with the property of another
- Locate persons that have disguised their personal location to avoid paying debts
- Locate assets to satisfy a legal claims
- Identify personal and corporate liens, judgments, and bankruptcies
- Ascertain prior and current employment of a person
- Ascertain professional licenses and violation history
- Conduct due diligence on companies and potential business partners

State and federal agencies regulate collecting, reporting, and disseminating information obtained through database searching (and other methods). Chief among the regulations is the Fair Credit Reporting Act (FCRA) and the Gramm Leach Bliley Act (GLB).

Greg Roebuck, Criminal Justice Associates, www.cjaexpert.com

DEADLY FORCE

During the twelfth century, the English common law allowed deadly force if needed to capture a felony suspect, regardless of the circumstances. At that time, felonies were not as common as they are now and were usually punishable by death. Also, law officers had a more difficult time capturing suspects because they did not have the technology and weaponry that are present in today's world.

In modern times, the courts have restricted the use of deadly force to certain, dangerous situations. Today's definition of deadly force has been formed by various laws and is usually stated as: an amount of force that is likely to cause either serious bodily injury or death to another person.

Law enforcement officers may use deadly force in specific circumstances when trying to enforce the law. Private citizens, such as private investigators, may use deadly force in certain other circumstances, mainly self-defense and defense of others. The laws governing the use of deadly force by law enforcement officers are different from those for citizens.

For deadly force to be lawful when an arrest is being made, it must be the reasonable choice under all the circumstances at the time. Deadly force is an option to be exercised only when no other option is available. When evaluating a deadly force incident, all circumstances are taken into account: severity of the offense, the seriousness of the threat posed by the offender, and the reasonableness of deadly force.

When deadly force is used by a private investigator, the reasonableness rule does not apply. The citizen must be able to prove that a felony occurred or was being attempted and that the felony threatened death or bodily harm. Mere suspicion of a felony is considered an insufficient ground for a private citizen to use deadly force.

Only in the rarest of circumstances will an investigator need to apply deadly force. Deadly force is justified only when it is believed that the offender has the imminent capacity and the intent to seriously injure or kill you or others. Specifically:

- Imminent means the act is occurring "right now." The threat of harm is not imminent when the offender is running from the scene of a serious crime. The opposite is true if the offender is in the immediate surroundings at that moment in time.
- Capacity means the ability to injure or kill. A person wielding a stick does not have the ability to injure or kill. The opposite is true if the person is wielding a gun or a knife.
- Intent is a clear impression conveyed by the offender of the intention to kill or

injure. "Get out of my way" is less clear than "I am going to kill you if you don't get out of my way."

Example: Robbery

An investigator observes a person committing a robbery in a convenience store. The investigator attempts to intervene. The robber points a gun at the investigator and says, "Get out of my way or I'm going to shoot you."

In this example, the crime is a robbery (a forcible felony); the robber was brandishing a gun right there and then (imminent); the gun gave to the robber the means to kill or injure (capacity); and the robber said, "Get out of my way or I'm going to shoot you" (intent).

In this set of circumstances, the investigator would be justified in resorting to deadly force. But is this the wisest course? Would it be more sensible to stand aside and let the robber escape? What are the chances that the robber will shoot the investigator or bystanders?

Example: Car Theft

An investigator observes a person breaking into a car that is parked in a garage. As the investigator approaches, the offender starts to run away. The investigator yells, "Halt or I'm going to shoot!" or words to that effect. The offender continues to flee. The investigator fires at the offender.

In this example, the offense is not a forcible felony; the imminent factor is not present because the offender is fleeing; the capacity factor is not present because the offender has not shown a weapon; and the intent factor is not present because, by running away, the offender has shown no intent to injure or kill. Therefore, the investigator had no justification for shooting at the offender.

Learning Shop USA, Legal Aspects of Private Investigation, www.learningshopusa.com

DEFENSES TO CRIME

The law allows many defenses to charges of crime, and it is the right of the accused to use any and all of them. The concept of defenses against prosecution may be viewed from two aspects: the basic capacity of the accused to commit the crime charged and the applicability of certain specifically accepted defenses. A very firm understanding of these defenses is essential to the work of criminal defense investigators.

Capacity Defense

The concept called "capacity to commit crime" demands that a person should not be held criminally punishable for his conduct unless he is actually responsible for it. Young persons and mentally afflicted persons, for example, may be recognized as not having the capacity to commit crimes because they lack a sufficient degree of responsibility. The infancy defense holds that children are incapable of committing any crime below a certain age, that at a higher age there is a presumption of incapacity to commit crime, and at an even higher age certain crimes are conclusively presumed to be beyond the capability of a child. For example, it may be presumed that a toddler is incapable of stealing and a five year old is incapable of committing the crime of rape.

Corporation Defense

The corporation defense holds that because a corporation is an artificial creation, it is incapable of forming the requisite criminal intent. This defense has been largely overcome in recent years. Some crimes, such as rape, bigamy, and murder, cannot logically be imputed to a corporation.

Insanity Defense

The insanity defense holds that a person cannot be held liable for his criminal act if he was insane at the time of the act. The defense goes to the heart of the fundamental principle of intent, or guilty mind. If the accused did not understand what he was doing or understand that his actions were wrong, he cannot have criminal intent and, without intent, there is no crime.

Intoxication Defense

The intoxication defense is similar to that of the insanity defense. It argues that the accused could not have a guilty mind due to intoxication. The fact of voluntary intoxication is generally not accepted as a defense. Involuntary intoxication produced by fraud or coercion of another may be a defense, and insanity produced by intoxicants may be acceptable. Intoxication can also be offered as evidence that an accused was incapable of forming the intent to commit a crime, e.g., the accused was too drunk to entertain the idea of breaking and entering into a house at night for the purpose of committing an offense.

Alibi Defense

The alibi defense seeks to prove that because the defendant was elsewhere at the time the offense occurred, the defendant cannot be accused.

Compulsion Defense

The compulsion or necessity defense argues that a person should not be charged with a crime when the act was committed in response to an imminent, impending, and overwhelmingly coercive influence. For example, a banker who is ordered to open a bank vault under threat of immediate death would not be punishable as a principal to the crime.

Condonation Defense

The condonation defense is used in some rare cases where the law allows an accused not to be prosecuted if certain conditions are met. For example, a charge of seduction might be dropped if the parties involved subsequently marry.

Immunity Defense

The immunity defense grants protection from prosecution in exchange for cooperation by the accused. The required cooperation might be a full disclosure of all facts and testimony at trial.

Consent Defense

The consent defense may be used when consent of the victim is involved. Where consent is offered as a defense, the consent must have been given by a person legally capable of giving it, and it must be voluntary.

Entrapment Defense

The entrapment defense argues that an accused should not be charged if he was induced to commit a crime for the mere purpose of instituting criminal prosecution against him. Generally, when the criminal intent originates in the mind of the accused and the criminal offense is completed by him, the fact that a law enforcement officer furnished the accused an opportunity for commission does not constitute entrapment. A key point is that when the criminal intent originates in the mind of the officer and the accused is lured into the commission, no conviction may be had.

Withdrawal Defense

The withdrawal defense may sometimes be used in a prosecution for conspiracy.

A conspirator who withdraws from the conspiracy prior to commission of the requisite overt act may attempt a defense based on withdrawal.

Good Character Defense

The good character defense may seek to offer evidence that the accused is of such good character that it was unlikely he/she committed the act. This is not a defense as a matter of law but an attempt to convince a jury it was improbable for the accused to have committed the crime.

Ignorance or Mistake of Fact Defense

The defense of ignorance or mistake of fact argues that the accused had no criminal intent. This defense seeks to excuse the accused because he was misled or was not in possession of all facts at the time of the crime. For example, this defense might be used in a case where a homeowner injured someone who he thought was a burglar in his home but was actually the invited guest of another member of the family. This defense is based on the grounds that a defendant did not know certain essential facts, that he could not have been expected to know them, and that there could be no crime without such knowledge. Mistake of law is a rarely allowed defense offered by an accused that he did not know his act was criminal or did not comprehend the consequences of the act.

Statute of Limitations Defense

The statute of limitations defense seeks to prevent prosecution on the grounds that the government failed to bring charges within the period of time fixed by a particular enactment. Not all crimes have time limitations for seeking prosecution, and some crimes, such as murder and other major crimes, have no limits whatsoever.

Irresistible Impulse

Irresistible impulse is a legal defense by which an accused seeks to be fully or partially excused from responsibility on the grounds that although he knew the act was wrong, he was compelled to its execution by an impulse he was powerless to control.

Necessity Defense

Necessity is the defense of justification of an otherwise criminal act on the ground that the perpetrator was compelled to commit it because a greater evil would have ensued had he failed to do so. Thus, one could plead necessity if he committed arson to destroy official documents that would otherwise have fallen into the hands of a wartime enemy.

Defense of Life

The self-defense or defense of life rule is derived from English common law, which authorizes the use of deadly force in self-defense and in order to apprehend persons committing or fleeing from felonies. In many jurisdictions, the rule has been narrowed by statute so that the use of weaponry is limited only to defense of life situations and to some specific violent felonies, such as murder, rape, aggravated assault, arson, or burglary. This protection against prosecution relies on the premise that every person has a right to defend himself from harm. A person may use, in self-defense, force that, under all the circumstances of the case, reasonably appears necessary to prevent impending injury.

Diminished Capacity Defense

Diminished capacity is the decreased or less-than-normal ability, temporary or permanent, to distinguish right from wrong or to fully appreciate the consequences of one's act. It is a plea used by the defendant for conviction of a lesser degree of a crime, for a lenient sentence, or for mercy or clemency.

Former Jeopardy Defense

Former jeopardy is a plea founded on the common law principle that a person cannot be brought into danger of his life or limb for the same offense more than once. The former jeopardy defense is founded on the principle that a case once terminated upon its merits should not be tried again. Double jeopardy can only be claimed when the second prosecution is brought by the same government as the first. When the act is a violation of the law as to two or more governments, the accused is regarded as having committed separate offenses.

"But For" Defense

The "but for" rule or the sine qua non rule holds that a defendant's conduct is not the cause of an event if the event would have occurred without it.

John J. Fay, *Encyclopedia of Security Management*, second ed., Butterworth-Heinemann, Burlington, MA, 2007, pp. 214–216.

DEPOSITION

A deposition is a legal proceeding conducted for the purpose of preserving the testimony of a witness for use in court. The deposition is usually held in a reasonably comfortable and private setting, very often the conference room of an attorney's office. The persons present are the witness, a notary public to administer an oath, a court reporter (usually a notary), and lawyers for all parties. The parties themselves or their representatives have a right to attend but seldom choose to do so. The deposition begins by administering an oath to the witness. The lawyers take turns asking the witness questions. A lawyer may skip a turn or take more than one turn. The proceeding is relatively informal, although serious to the outcome of the litigation. The reporter takes down everything said, and the reporter's record will later be typed and bound in a document called a deposition or a transcript. The deposition is essentially a tool for opposing lawyers to discover what a witness's testimony will be at trial. For example, the plaintiff's lawyer in deposing a witness will want to:

- Discover what the witness knows concerning the facts involved in the matter being litigated.
- Discover if the witness knows of any facts that may be damaging to his or her side, e.g., that a party to the matter may have been careless or failed to do something.
- Commit the witness to the statements made under oath at the deposition so that at trial the witness's testimony cannot be changed.
- Discredit the witness's testimony or use the witness's testimony to discredit the testimony of other witnesses. Minor contradictions among witnesses are inevitable, while major contradictions or the appearance of them can be damaging.

Attorneys for both sides may decide that the case for either side will be so formidable that the matter to be litigated will need to be changed. Although a deposition can embarrass or even damage the reputation of a witness, most especially an expert witness, this is not a legitimate purpose of the deposition proceeding. When the anticipated testimony of a witness appears damaging, it is often the result of inadequate preparation, and, of course, preparation can in large part depend on an investigator.

An investigator is often a witness. An investigator who testifies at a disposition, and most importantly at trial, has three fundamental obligations. First is to tell the truth, even if the truth will hurt. This is an obligation that sits above the outcome of the lawsuit. The second is to be fair. This does not mean that the witness has to give equal favor to both sides. The third is to be accurate, and this is where the witness plays a critical part in helping the judge and jurors fulfill their responsibilities in seeing that justice is carried out.

John J. Fay

DIPLOMATIC SECURITY SERVICE

The Diplomatic Security Service (DS) is the agency in the U.S. Department of State that provides law enforcement services domestically and high-threat protection assignments all over the globe.

DS investigations are carried out by numerous field offices and resident agent offices throughout the United States and by Regional Security Offices overseas. The major focus is on passport and visa fraud. DS special agents also investigate international parental kidnapping, assaults on federally protected persons, and fugitives overseas. In addition, DS investigators gather information concerning terrorist plans and activities and neutralize efforts of foreign intelligence services that target Department of State employees, facilities, and diplomatic missions worldwide.

Bureau of Diplomatic Service, U.S. Department of State, http://www.state.gov/m/ds/

DISCOVERY

In American law, discovery is the pretrial phase in a lawsuit in which each party through the law of civil procedure, subpoena or through other discovery devices, such as requests for production of documents and depositions, can request documents and other evidence from other parties and can compel the production of material held by the other side.

Discovery can require the production of interrogatories, motions, or requests for production of documents, requests for admissions, and depositions.

The common or traditional forms of discoverable materials include reports, photos, medical images, drawings, reconstructed video, video and audio tapes, e-mail, fax, archives, and data drawn from a variety of sources.

However, the increased use of technology has produced many new forms of discoverable materials such as that drawn from:

- Servers
- Hard drives
- PCs
- Laptops
- USB flash sticks
- iPods and similar devices
- Any material that appears to have been deleted from a hard drive but can be captured by computer forensic specialists
- Internet sites

Discoverable material that must be disclosed can be placed on one set of equipment, and information that falls under the defendant/client privilege or is of a personal nature can be placed on the other set of devices (*caveat emptor*).

Learning Shop USA, Legal Aspects of Private Investigation, www.learningshopusa.com

DISCRIMINATION

Age Discrimination

The Age Discrimination in Employment Act (ADEA) protects individuals who are 40 years of age or older from employment discrimination based on age. The ADEA's protections apply to both employees and job applicants. Under the ADEA, it is unlawful to discriminate against a person because of his/her age with respect to any term, condition, or privilege of employment, including hiring, firing, promotion, layoff, compensation, benefits, job assignments, and training. It is also unlawful to retaliate against an individual for opposing employment practices that discriminate based on age or for filing an age discrimination charge, testifying, or participating in any way in an investigation, proceeding, or litigation under the ADEA.

The ADEA applies to employers with 20 or more employees, including state and local governments. It also applies to employment agencies and labor organizations, as well as to the federal government.

Apprenticeship Programs. It is generally unlawful for apprenticeship programs, including joint labor-management apprenticeship programs, to discriminate on the basis of an individual's age. Age limitations in apprenticeship programs are valid only if they fall within certain specific exceptions under the ADEA or if the EEOC grants a specific exemption.

Job Notices and Advertisements. The ADEA generally makes it unlawful to include age preferences, limitations, or specifications in job notices or advertisements. A job notice or advertisement may specify an age limit only in the rare circumstances where age is shown to be a "bona fide occupational qualification" (BFOQ) reasonably necessary to the normal operation of the business.

Pre-Employment Inquiries. The ADEA does not specifically prohibit an employer from asking an applicant's age or date of birth. However, because such inquiries may deter older workers from applying for employment or may otherwise indicate possible intent to discriminate based on age, requests for age information will be closely scrutinized to make sure that the inquiry was made for a lawful purpose, rather than for a purpose prohibited by the ADEA.

Benefits. The Older Workers Benefit Protection Act of 1990 (OWBPA) amended the ADEA to specifically prohibit employers from denying benefits to older employees. Congress recognized that the cost of providing certain benefits to older workers is greater than the cost of providing those same benefits to younger workers and that those greater costs would create a disincentive to hire older workers. Therefore, in limited circumstances, an employer may be permitted to reduce benefits based on age, as long as the cost of providing the reduced benefits to older workers is the same as the cost of providing benefits to younger workers.

Waivers of ADEA Rights. An employer may ask an employee to waive his/her rights or claims under the ADEA either in the settlement of an ADEA administrative or court claim or in connection with an exit incentive program or other employment termination program. However, the ADEA, as amended by OWBPA, sets out specific minimum standards that must be met in order for a waiver to be considered knowing and voluntary and, therefore, valid.

Among other requirements, a valid ADEA waiver must:

- Be in writing and be understandable.
- Specifically refer to ADEA rights or claims.
- Not waive rights or claims that may arise in the future; be in exchange for valuable consideration.
- Advise the individual in writing to consult an attorney before signing the waiver.
- Provide the individual at least 21 days to consider the agreement and at least seven days to revoke the agreement after signing it. If an employer requests an ADEA waiver in connection with an exit incentive program or other employment termination program, the minimum requirements for a valid waiver are more extensive.

Disability Discrimination

Title 1 of the Americans with Disabilities Act of 1990 prohibits private employers, state and local governments, employment agencies, and labor unions from discriminating against qualified individuals with disabilities in job application procedures; hiring; firing; advancement; compensation; job training; and other terms, conditions, and privileges of employment.

The ADA covers employers with 15 or more employees, including state and local governments. It also applies to employment agencies and to labor organizations. The ADA's nondiscrimination standards also apply to federal sector employees under section 501 of the Rehabilitation Act, as amended, and its implementing rules. An individual with a disability is a person who:

- Has a physical or mental impairment that substantially limits one or more major life activities
- Has a record of such an impairment
- Is regarded as having such an impairment. A qualified employee or applicant with a disability is an individual who, with or without reasonable accommodation, can perform the essential functions of the job in question. Reasonable accommodation may include, but is not limited to:

  - Making existing facilities used by employees readily accessible to and usable by persons with disabilities
  - Job restructuring, modifying work schedules, reassignment to a vacant position
  - Acquiring or modifying equipment or devices; adjusting or modifying examinations, training materials, or policies; and providing qualified readers or interpreters

An employer is required to make a reasonable accommodation to the known disability of a qualified applicant or employee if it would not impose an "undue hardship" on the operation of the employer's business. Undue hardship is defined as an action requiring significant difficulty or expense when considered in light of factors such as an employer's size, financial resources, and the nature and structure of its operation. An employer is not required to lower quality or production standards to make an accommodation; nor is an employer obligated to provide personal use items such as glasses or hearing aids.

Medical Examinations and Inquiries. Employers may not ask job applicants about the existence, nature, or severity of a disability. Applicants may be asked about their ability to perform specific job functions. A job offer may be conditioned on the results of a medical examination, but only if the examination is required for all entering employees in similar jobs. Medical examinations of employees must be job related and consistent with the employer's business needs.

Drug and Alcohol Abuse. Employees and applicants currently engaging in the illegal use of drugs are not covered by the ADA when an employer acts on the basis of such use. Tests for illegal drugs are not subject to the ADA's restrictions on medical examinations. Employers may hold illegal drug users and alcoholics to the same performance standards as other employees. It is also unlawful to retaliate against an individual for opposing employment practices that discriminate based on disability or for filing a discrimination charge, testifying, or participating in any way in an investigation, proceeding, or litigation under the ADA.

Equal Pay and Compensation Discrimination

The right of employees to be free from discrimination in their compensation is protected under several federal laws, including the following enforced by the U.S. Equal Employment Opportunity Commission (EEOC): the Equal Pay Act, the Civil Rights Act of 1964, the Age Discrimination in Employment Act, and the Americans with Disabilities Act.

The Equal Pay Act requires that men and women be given equal pay for equal work in the same establishment. The jobs need not be identical, but they must be substantially equal. It is job content, not job titles, that determines whether jobs are substantially equal. Specifically, the EPA provides that employers may not pay unequal wages to men and women who perform jobs that require substantially equal skill, effort, and responsibility and that are performed under similar working conditions within the same establishment.

Skill. Skill is measured by factors such as the experience, ability, education, and training required to perform the job. The key issue is what skills are required for the job, not what skills the individual employees may have. For example, two bookkeeping jobs could be considered equal under the EPA even if one of the job holders has a master's degree in physics since that degree would not be required for the job.

Effort. Effort is the amount of physical or mental exertion needed to perform the job. For example, suppose that men and women work side by side on a line assembling machine parts. The person at the end of the line must also lift the assembled product as he or she completes the work and place it on a board. That job requires more effort than the other assembly line jobs if the extra effort of lifting the assembled product off the line is substantial and is a regular part of the job. As a result, it would not be a violation to pay that person more, regardless of whether the job is held by a man or a woman.

Responsibility. Responsibility is the degree of accountability required in performing the job. For example, a salesperson who is delegated the duty of determining whether to accept customers' personal checks has more responsibility than other salespeople. On the other hand, a minor difference in responsibility, such as turning out the lights at the end of the day, would not justify a pay differential.

Working Conditions encompass two factors: physical surroundings like temperature, fumes, and ventilation; and hazards.

Establishment. The prohibition against compensation discrimination under the EPA applies only to jobs within an establishment. An establishment is a distinct physical place of business rather than an entire business or enterprise consisting of several places of business. However, in some circumstances, physically separate places of business should be treated as one establishment. For example, if a central administrative unit hires employees, sets their compensation, and assigns them to work locations, the separate work sites can be considered part of one establishment. Pay differentials are permitted when they are based on seniority, merit, quantity or quality of production, or a factor other than sex. These are known as "affirmative defenses," and it is the employer's burden to prove that they apply. In correcting a pay differential, no employee's pay may be reduced. Instead, the pay of the lower paid employee(s) must be increased.

Title VII, the ADEA, and the ADA prohibit compensation discrimination on the basis of race, color, religion, sex, national origin, age, or disability. Unlike the EPA, there is no requirement under Title VII, the ADEA, or the ADA that the claimant's job be substantially equal to that of a higher paid person outside the claimant's protected class, nor do these statutes require the claimant to work in the same establishment as a comparator. Compensation discrimination under Title VII, the ADEA, or the ADA can occur in a variety of forms. For example:

- An employer pays an employee with a disability less than similarly situated employees without disabilities, and the employer's explanation (if any) does not satisfactorily account for the differential.
- A discriminatory compensation system has been discontinued but still has lingering discriminatory effects on present

salaries. For example, if an employer has a compensation policy or practice that pays Hispanics lower salaries than other employees, the employer must not only adopt a new nondiscriminatory compensation policy, it also must affirmatively eradicate salary disparities that began prior to the adoption of the new policy and make the victims whole.

- An employer sets the compensation for jobs predominately held by, for example, women or African Americans below that suggested by the employer's job evaluation study, while the pay for jobs predominately held by men or whites is consistent with the level suggested by the job evaluation study.

- An employer maintains a neutral compensation policy or practice that has an adverse impact on employees in a protected class and cannot be justified as job related and consistent with business necessity. For example, if an employer provides extra compensation to employees who are the "head of household," i.e., married with dependents and the primary financial contributor to the household, the practice may have an unlawful, disparate impact on women. It is also unlawful to retaliate against an individual for opposing employment practices that discriminate based on compensation or for filing a discrimination charge, testifying, or participating in any way in an investigation, proceeding, or litigation under Title VII, ADEA, ADA, or the Equal Pay Act.

Genetic Discrimination

Genetic information includes information about an individual's genetic tests and the genetic tests of an individual's family members, as well as information about the manifestation of a disease or disorder in an individual's family members (i.e., family

medical history). Family medical history is included in the definition of genetic information because it is often used to determine whether someone has an increased risk of getting a disease, disorder, or condition in the future. Genetic information also includes an individual's request for, or receipt of, genetic services, the participation in clinical research that includes genetic services by the individual or a family member of the individual, the genetic information of a fetus carried by an individual or by a pregnant woman who is a family member of the individual, and the genetic information of any embryo legally held by the individual or family member using an assisted reproductive technology.

The law forbids discrimination on the basis of genetic information when it comes to any aspect of employment, including hiring, firing, pay, job assignments, promotions, layoffs, training, fringe benefits, or any other term or condition of employment. An employer may never use genetic information to make an employment decision because genetic information is not relevant to an individual's current ability to work.

Harassment can include, for example, making offensive or derogatory remarks about an applicant or employee's genetic information, or about the genetic information of a relative of the applicant or employee. Although the law doesn't prohibit simple teasing, offhand comments, or isolated incidents that are not very serious, harassment is illegal when it is so severe or pervasive that it creates a hostile or offensive work environment or when it results in an adverse employment decision (such as the victim being fired or demoted). The harasser can be the victim's supervisor, a supervisor in another area of the workplace, a coworker, or someone who is not an employee such as a client or customer.

It is illegal to fire, demote, harass, or otherwise "retaliate" against an applicant or employee for filing a charge of discrimination, participating in a discrimination proceeding (such as a discrimination investigation or lawsuit), or otherwise opposing discrimination.

It will usually be unlawful for an employer to obtain genetic information. There are six narrow exceptions to this prohibition:

- Inadvertent acquisitions of genetic information do not violate GINA, such as in situations where a manager or supervisor overhears someone talking about a family member's illness.
- Genetic information (such as family medical history) may be obtained as part of health or genetic services, including wellness programs, offered by the employer on a voluntary basis, if certain specific requirements are met.
- Family medical history may be acquired as part of the certification process for FMLA leave (or leave under similar state or local laws or pursuant to an employer policy) when an employee is asking for leave to care for a family member with a serious health condition.
- Genetic information may be acquired through commercially and publicly available documents like newspapers, as long as the employer is not searching those sources with the intent of finding genetic information or accessing sources from which they are likely to acquire genetic information (such as websites and online discussion groups that focus on issues such as genetic testing of individuals and genetic discrimination).
- Genetic information may be acquired through a genetic monitoring program that monitors the biological effects of toxic substances in the workplace where the monitoring is required by law or, under carefully defined conditions, where the program is voluntary.
- Acquisition of genetic information of employees by employers who engage in DNA testing for law enforcement purposes as a forensic lab or for purposes

of human remains identification is permitted, but the genetic information may only be used for analysis of DNA markers for quality control to detect sample contamination.

National Origin Discrimination

National origin discrimination involves treating people (applicants or employees) unfavorably because they are from a particular country or part of the world because of ethnicity or accent or because they appear to be of a certain ethnic background (even if they are not). National origin discrimination also can involve treating people unfavorably because they are married to (or associated with) a person of a certain national origin or because of their connection with an ethnic organization or group. Discrimination can occur when the victim and the person who inflicted the discrimination are the same national origin.

The law forbids discrimination when it comes to any aspect of employment, including hiring, firing, pay, job assignments, promotions, layoff, training, fringe benefits, and any other term or condition of employment.

It is unlawful to harass a person because of his or her national origin. Harassment can include, for example, offensive or derogatory remarks about a person's national origin, accent, or ethnicity.

The law makes it illegal for an employer to use a policy or practice that applies to everyone, regardless of national origin, if it has a negative impact on people of a certain national origin and is not job related or necessary to the operation of the business. An employer can only require an employee to speak fluent English if fluency in English is necessary to perform the job effectively. An "English-only rule," which requires employees to speak only English on the job, is only allowed if it is needed to ensure the safe or efficient operation of the employer's business and is put in place for nondiscriminatory reasons. An employer may not base an employment decision on an employee's foreign accent, unless the accent seriously interferes with the employee's job performance.

Pregnancy Discrimination

The Pregnancy Discrimination Act is an amendment to Title VII of the Civil Rights Act of 1964. Discrimination on the basis of pregnancy, childbirth, or related medical conditions constitutes unlawful sex discrimination under Title VII, which covers employers with 15 or more employees, including state and local governments. Title VII also applies to employment agencies and to labor organizations, as well as to the federal government. Women who are pregnant or affected by related conditions must be treated in the same manner as other applicants or employees with similar abilities or limitations.

Hiring. An employer cannot refuse to hire a pregnant woman because of her pregnancy; because of a pregnancy-related condition; or because of the prejudices of coworkers, clients, or customers.

Pregnancy and Maternity Leave. An employer may not single out pregnancy-related conditions for special procedures to determine an employee's ability to work. However, if an employer requires its employees to submit a doctor's statement concerning their inability to work before granting leave or paying sick benefits, the employer may require employees affected by pregnancy-related conditions to submit such statements. If an employee is temporarily unable to perform her job due to pregnancy, the employer must treat her in the same way as any other temporarily disabled employee. For example, if the employer allows temporarily disabled employees to modify tasks, perform alternative assignments, or take disability leave or leave without pay, the employer also must allow an employee who is temporarily disabled due to pregnancy to do the same. Pregnant employees must

be permitted to work as long as they are able to perform their jobs. If an employee has been absent from work as a result of a pregnancy-related condition and recovers, her employer may not require her to remain on leave until the baby's birth. An employer also may not have a rule that prohibits an employee from returning to work for a predetermined length of time after childbirth. Employers must hold open a job for a pregnancy-related absence the same length of time jobs are held open for employees on sick or disability leave.

Health Insurance. Any health insurance provided by an employer must cover expenses for pregnancy-related conditions on the same basis as costs for other medical conditions. Health insurance for expenses arising from abortion is not required, except where the life of the mother is endangered. Pregnancy-related expenses should be reimbursed exactly as those incurred for other medical conditions, whether payment is on a fixed basis or a percentage of reasonable-and-customary-charge basis. The amounts payable by the insurance provider can be limited only to the same extent as amounts payable for other conditions. No additional, increased, or larger deductible can be imposed. Employers must provide the same level of health benefits for spouses of male employees as they do for spouses of female employees.

Fringe Benefits. Pregnancy-related benefits cannot be limited to married employees. In an all-female workforce or job classification, benefits must be provided for pregnancy-related conditions if benefits are provided for other medical conditions. If an employer provides any benefits to workers on leave, the employer must provide the same benefits for those on leave for pregnancy-related conditions. Employees with pregnancy-related disabilities must be treated the same as other temporarily disabled employees for accrual and crediting of seniority, vacation calculation, pay increases, and temporary disability benefits. It is also unlawful to retaliate against an individual for opposing employment practices that discriminate based on pregnancy or for filing a discrimination charge, testifying, or participating in any way in an investigation, proceeding, or litigation.

Race and Color Discrimination

Title VII of the Civil Rights Act of 1964 protects individuals against employment discrimination on the bases of race and color, as well as national origin, sex, and religion. Title VII applies to employers with 15 or more employees, including state and local governments. It also applies to employment agencies and to labor organizations, as well as to the federal government.

Equal employment opportunity cannot be denied any person because of his/her racial group or perceived racial group, his/her race-linked characteristics (e.g., hair texture, color, facial features), or his/her marriage to or association with someone of a particular race or color. Title VII also prohibits employment decisions based on stereotypes and assumptions about abilities, traits, or the performance of individuals of certain racial groups.

Title VII's prohibitions apply regardless of whether the discrimination is directed at Caucasian; African Americans; Asians; Latinos; Arabs; Native Americans; Native Hawaiians and Pacific Islanders; multiracial individuals; or persons of any other race, color, or ethnicity. It is unlawful to discriminate against any individual in regard to recruiting; hiring and promotion; transfer; work assignments; performance measurements; work environment; job training; discipline and discharge; wages and benefits; or any other term, condition, or privilege of employment.

Title VII prohibits not only intentional discrimination but also neutral job policies that disproportionately affect persons of a certain race or color and that are not related to the job and the needs of the business. Employers should adopt "best practices" to reduce the likelihood of discrimination and to address impediments to equal employment opportunity.

Recruiting, Hiring, and Advancement. Job requirements must be uniformly and consistently applied to persons of all races and colors. Even if a job requirement is applied consistently, if it is not important for job performance or business needs, the requirement may be found unlawful if it excludes persons of a certain racial group or color significantly more than others. Examples of potentially unlawful practices include: soliciting applications only from sources in which all or most potential workers are of the same race or color; requiring applicants to have a certain educational background that is not important for job performance or business needs; and testing applicants for knowledge, skills, or abilities that are not important for job performance or business needs.

Employers may legitimately need information about their employees or applicants race for affirmative action purposes and/or to track applicant flow. One way to obtain racial information and simultaneously guard against discriminatory selection is for employers to use separate forms or otherwise keep the information about an applicant's race separate from the application. In that way, the employer can capture the information it needs but ensure that it is not used in the selection decision. Unless the information is for such a legitimate purpose, pre-employment questions about race can suggest that race will be used as a basis for making selection decisions. If the information is used in the selection decision and members of particular racial groups are excluded from employment, the inquiries can constitute evidence of discrimination.

Harassment/Hostile Work Environment. Title VII prohibits offensive conduct, such as racial or ethnic slurs, racial "jokes," derogatory comments, or other verbal or physical conduct based on an individual's race/color. The conduct has to be unwelcome and offensive and has to be severe or pervasive. Employers are required to take appropriate steps to prevent and correct unlawful harassment. Likewise, employees are responsible for reporting harassment at an early stage to prevent its escalation.

Compensation and Other Employment Terms, Conditions, and Privileges. Title VII prohibits discrimination in compensation and other terms, conditions, and privileges of employment. Thus, race or color discrimination may not be the basis for differences in pay or benefits, work assignments, performance evaluations, training, discipline or discharge, or any other area of employment.

Segregation and Classification of Employees. Title VII is violated where employees who belong to a protected group are segregated by physically isolating them from other employees or from customer contact. In addition, employers may not assign employees according to race or color. For example, Title VII prohibits assigning primarily African Americans to predominantly African American establishments or geographic areas.

It is also illegal to exclude members of one group from particular positions or to group or categorize employees or jobs so that certain jobs are generally held by members of a certain protected group. Coding applications/resumes to designate an applicant's race, by either an employer or employment agency, constitutes evidence of discrimination where people of a certain race or color are excluded from employment or from certain positions.

Religious Discrimination

Title VII of the Civil Rights Act of 1964 prohibits employers from discriminating against individuals because of their religion in hiring, firing, and other terms and conditions of employment. Title VII covers employers with 15 or more employees, including state and local governments. It also applies to employment agencies and to labor organizations, as well as to the federal government. Employers may not treat employees or applicants more or less favorably because of their religious beliefs or practices—except to the extent a religious accommodation is warranted. For example, an employer may not refuse to hire individuals of a certain religion, may not impose stricter promotion requirements for persons of a certain religion, and may not impose more or different work requirements on an employee because of that employee's religious beliefs or practices.

Employees cannot be forced to participate—or not participate—in a religious activity as a condition of employment. Employers must reasonably accommodate employees' sincerely held religious practices unless doing so would impose an undue hardship on the employer. A reasonable religious accommodation is any adjustment to the work environment that will allow the employee to practice his religion. An employer might accommodate an employee's religious beliefs or practices by allowing: flexible scheduling; voluntary substitutions or swaps; job reassignments and lateral transfers; modification of grooming requirements; and other workplace practices, policies, and/or procedures.

An employer is not required to accommodate an employee's religious beliefs and practices if doing so would impose an undue hardship on the employers' legitimate business interests. An employer can show undue hardship if accommodating an employee's religious practices requires more than ordinary administrative costs, diminishes efficiency in other jobs, infringes on other employees' job rights or benefits, impairs workplace safety, causes coworkers to carry the accommodated employee's share of potentially hazardous or burdensome work, or if the proposed accommodation conflicts with another law or regulation.

Employers must permit employees to engage in religious expression, unless the religious expression would impose an undue hardship on the employer. Generally, an employer may not place more restrictions on religious expression than on other forms of expression that have a comparable effect on workplace efficiency. Employers must take steps to prevent religious harassment of their employees. An employer can reduce the chance that employees will engage unlawful religious harassment by implementing an anti harassment policy and having an effective procedure for reporting, investigating, and correcting harassing conduct.

It is also unlawful to retaliate against an individual for opposing employment practices that discriminate based on religion or for filing a discrimination charge, testifying, or participating in an investigation, proceeding, or litigation under Title VII.

Retaliation Discrimination

An employer may not fire, demote, harass, or otherwise "retaliate" against a person for filing a charge of discrimination, participating in a discrimination proceeding, or otherwise opposing discrimination. The same laws that prohibit discrimination based on race, color, sex, religion, national origin, age, and disability, as well as wage differences between men and women performing substantially equal work, also prohibit retaliation against individuals who oppose unlawful discrimination or participate in an employment discrimination proceeding.

In addition to the protections against retaliation that are included in all laws enforced by EEOC, the Americans with Disabilities Act (ADA) also protects individuals from coercion, intimidation, threat, harassment, or interference in their exercise of their own rights or their encouragement of someone else's exercise of rights granted by the ADA.

Retaliation occurs when an employer, employment agency, or labor organization takes an adverse action against a covered individual because he or she engaged in a protected activity. These three terms are described below.

Adverse Action. An adverse action is an action taken to try to keep someone from opposing a discriminatory practice or from participating in an employment discrimination proceeding. Examples of adverse actions include:

- Employment actions such as termination, refusal to hire, and denial of promotion
- Other actions affecting employment such as threats, unjustified negative evaluations, unjustified negative references, or increased surveillance
- Any other action such as an assault or unfounded civil or criminal charges that are likely to deter reasonable people from pursuing their rights

Adverse actions do not include petty slights and annoyances, such as stray negative comments in an otherwise positive or neutral evaluation, "snubbing" a colleague, or negative comments that are justified by an employee's poor work performance or history.

Even if the prior protected activity alleged wrongdoing by a different employer, retaliatory adverse actions are unlawful. For example, it is unlawful for a worker's current employer to retaliate against him for pursuing an EEO charge against a former employer. Of course, employees are not excused from continuing to perform their jobs or follow their company's legitimate workplace rules just because they have filed a complaint with the EEOC or opposed discrimination.

Covered Individuals. Covered individuals are people who have opposed unlawful practices, participated in proceedings, or requested accommodations related to employment discrimination based on race, color, sex, religion, national origin, age, or disability. Individuals who have a close association with someone who has engaged in such protected activity also are covered individuals. For example, it is illegal to terminate an employee because his spouse participated in employment discrimination litigation. Individuals who have brought attention to violations of law other than employment discrimination are NOT covered individuals for purposes of anti-discrimination retaliation laws. For example, "whistleblowers" who raise ethical, financial, or other concerns unrelated to employment discrimination are not protected by the EEOC enforced laws.

Protected Activity. Protected activity includes:

- Opposition to a practice believed to be unlawful discrimination
- Opposition by informing an employer that you believe that he/she is engaging in prohibited discrimination

Opposition is protected from retaliation as long as it is based on a reasonable, good-faith belief that the practice violates anti-discrimination law and the manner of the opposition is reasonable. Examples of protected opposition include:

- Complaining to anyone about alleged discrimination against oneself or others
- Threatening to file a charge of discrimination
- Picketing in opposition to discrimination
- Refusing to obey an order reasonably believed to be discriminatory

Activities that are NOT protected include:

- Actions that interfere with job performance so as to render the employee ineffective
- Unlawful activities such as acts or threats of violence

Participation. Participation means taking part in an employment discrimination proceeding. Participation is a protected activity even if the proceeding involved claims that ultimately were found to be invalid. Examples of participation include:

- Filing a charge of employment discrimination
- Cooperating with an internal investigation of alleged discriminatory practices
- Serving as a witness in an EEO investigation or litigation

A protected activity can also include requesting a reasonable accommodation based on religion or disability.

Sex-Based Discrimination

Title VII of the Civil Rights Act of 1964 protects individuals against employment discrimination on the basis of sex as well as race, color, national origin, and religion. Title VII applies to employers with 15 or more employees, including state and local governments. It also applies to employment agencies and to labor organizations, as well as to the federal government.

It is unlawful to discriminate against any employee or applicant for employment because of his/her sex in regard to hiring; termination; promotion; compensation; job training; or any other term, condition, or privilege of employment.

Title VII also prohibits employment decisions based on stereotypes and assumptions about abilities, traits, or the performance of individuals on the basis of sex. Title VII prohibits both intentional discrimination and neutral job policies that disproportionately exclude individuals on the basis of sex and that are not job related.

Unlike the Equal Pay Act, however, Title VII does not require that the claimant's job be substantially equal to that of a higher paid person of the opposite sex or require the claimant to work in the same establishment. It is also unlawful to retaliate against an individual for opposing employment practices that discriminate based on sex or for filing a discrimination charge, testifying, or participating in any way in an investigation, proceeding, or litigation under Title VII.

Sexual Harassment

Sexual harassment is a form of sex discrimination that violates Title VII of the Civil Rights Act of 1964. Title VII applies to employers with 15 or more employees, including state and local governments. It also applies to employment agencies and to labor organizations, as well as to the federal government. Unwelcome sexual advances, requests for sexual favors, and other verbal or physical conduct of a sexual nature constitute sexual harassment when this conduct explicitly or implicitly affects an individual's employment; unreasonably interferes with an individual's work performance; or creates an intimidating, hostile, or offensive work environment.

Sexual harassment can occur in a variety of circumstances:

- The victim as well as the harasser may be a woman or a man. The victim does not have to be of the opposite sex.
- The harasser can be the victim's supervisor, an agent of the employer, a supervisor in another area, a coworker, or a nonemployee.
- The victim does not have to be the person harassed but could be anyone affected by the offensive conduct. Unlawful sexual harassment may occur without economic injury to or discharge of the victim.
- The harasser's conduct must be unwelcome. It is helpful for the victim to inform the harasser directly that the conduct is unwelcome and must stop. The victim should use any employer complaint mechanism or grievance system available.

When investigating allegations of sexual harassment, EEOC looks at the whole record: the circumstances, such as the nature of the sexual advances, and the context in which the alleged incidents occurred. A determination on the allegations is made from the facts on a case-by-case basis. Prevention is the best tool to eliminate sexual harassment in the workplace.

Employers are encouraged to take steps necessary to prevent sexual harassment from occurring. They should clearly communicate to employees that sexual harassment will not be tolerated. They can do so by providing sexual harassment training to their employees, establishing an effective complaint or grievance process, and taking immediate and appropriate action when an employee complains.

It is also unlawful to retaliate against an individual for opposing employment practices that discriminate based on sex or for filing a discrimination charge, testifying, or participating in any way in an investigation, proceeding, or litigation under Title VII.

U.S. Equal Employment Opportunity Commission, http://www.eeoc.gov/laws/types/

DIVORCE AND CHILD CUSTODY

Divorce is the "breaking" or "undoing" of marriage. Divorce is complicated by laws that differ from state to state and range from simple to extremely complex. A few states do not require involvement by attorneys and allow the spouses to file on their own. However, most states require an attorney for each spouse. Attorney services are especially valuable when child custody and/or a division of assets are involved. In the matter of assets division, a spouse is entitled to a share of assets in accordance with the law of the state. In cases where concealment of assets is alleged, a private investigator might be hired to help prove the truth of the allegation. This investigative function is usually called "assets tracking."

The most painful part of divorce can occur when infidelity is involved and a spouse feels betrayed. In addition to pain from the betrayal is the pain of having to produce proof of infidelity. Intense emotional responses can be followed by actions dangerous to either spouse, to nonspouses who are involved in some way, and to investigators hired to collect evidence for either side. The danger can extend also to family members and close friends. Whenever emotions and money are involved, the investigator must be aware of the potential for violence.

A competent investigator can be of immense help, especially in proving infidelity. The investigator's tasks can be to find love notes, letters, and e-mails; conduct in-place and moving surveillance; take videos and photographs; obtain telephone call records; find and interview witnesses; and communicate with the spouse's attorney. The investigator must stay within the law when gathering evidence in certain ways, such as when photographing private situations, recording private conversations, and attaching a GPS tracker to a vehicle. For example, a law may prohibit GPS tracking when the vehicle is not owned in full or in part by the spouse who retains the investigative service.

In child custody disputes, the investigator must know the laws of the state and the rules of the court that apply. Following are examples of laws and rules that commonly vary from state to state:

- Custody issues may be decided by a judge with or without consideration of facts offered by external parties such as child welfare agencies; child psychologists, psychiatrists, and counselors; persons with knowledge of child abuse; and character witnesses.
- Children, depending on age, may choose the primary custodian.
- A *Guardian Ad Litem* procedure may be in place. In this procedure, a court-appointed attorney or attorneys

gather information from knowledgeable parties who represent the best interests of the children and provide recommendations to the court. The judge deciding the case can choose to accept, not accept, or modify the recommendations. (Author's note: This procedure sometimes results in bad decisions because of views that are in conflict or poorly developed.)

The findings of an investigator can be critical in matters of assets division and child custody.

Joan Earnshaw

DNA ANALYSIS

DNA is the basic genetic material within each living cell that determines a person's individual characteristics. Since the early 1980s, DNA testing has been used in AIDS and genetic disease research, bone marrow transplants, and in anthropological investigations. In forensics, DNA testing is typically used to identify individuals using only small samples of body fluids or tissue—such as blood, semen, or hair—left at a crime scene.

DNA Testing Methodologies

DNA tests investigate and analyze the structure and inheritance patterns of DNA. Many methodologies exist, and new ones are constantly being developed. The particular test used will depend on the quantity and quality of the sample, the objective of the test, and the preferences of the laboratory conducting the procedure. All tests, however, are designed to isolate certain nucleotide sequences—the polymorphic segments of the DNA molecule carrying marked, recurring distinctions—and these variable segments provide the basis for discriminating among individuals' DNA.

In a forensic environment, two common analytical methods used to detect the polymorphic DNA in human samples are the Restriction Fragment Length Polymorphism (RFLP) and Polymerase Chain Reaction (PCR) techniques. The RFLP method identifies fragments of the DNA chain that contain the polymorphic segments, produces a DNA "print" of the fragments, and measures the fragment lengths. The PCR-based methods seek to determine the presence of specific alleles (alternative forms of genes that occur in different individuals), thus indicating specific genetic characteristics.

Restriction Fragment Length Polymorphism (RFLP)

RFLP requires the presence of as little as 50 to 100 nanograms of DNA—an amount of DNA that may be present in a single hair follicle. The distinct stages in developing a DNA print using RFLP will be portrayed here by describing the analysis of a blood sample.

First, white cells containing the DNA are separated from the blood sample by use of a centrifuge, and the cells are ruptured to extract the DNA strands. The DNA strands are then cut, or digested, using restriction endonucleases (REs)—enzymes derived from bacteria that catalyze the cutting process. A particular enzyme will cut the DNA strands at the same nucleotide sequence (restriction site) each time. By cutting a person's DNA in the same place, the several alternate forms (alleles) of a gene are separated from each other. A specific allele will be of the same size and molecular weight as others of its type. The polymorphism, or individuality, of a person will be detected on the basis of differences in DNA fragment lengths.

At this point in the process, all of the DNA fragments are mixed together. Using a technique called electrophoresis, the polymorphic fragments are separated by length. The DNA is placed at one end of a plate containing agarose gel, with a positive electrode placed at the other end. DNA carries a negative electrical charge; therefore, the DNA will move toward the positive electrode. The distance that an individual fragment of DNA travels depends on the amount of its electrical charge, which is determined by its length and molecular weight. Thus, fragments of the same length and weight will travel the same distance while large DNA fragments will move more slowly than smaller fragments. This process sorts the DNA into bands based on length and weight, and these length-dependent bands are the basis for DNA identification.

After electrophoresis, the next step calls for transferring the DNA fragments in the gel to a nylon membrane. In a technique called "Southern blotting," a chemical reagent (such as sodium hydroxide) acts as a transfer solution and a means to separate the double-strand fragments into single-strand fragments.

Using the zipper analogy, the strands are unzipped, exposing the building blocks. The unzipped DNA fragments are now fixed on the nylon membrane, where they are exposed to radioactive DNA probes—laboratory-developed (thus, known sequences), DNA nucleotide fragments which carry a radioactive "marker." The probes seek out the sequence that they match and attach themselves to the complementary split DNA strands.

The probes are made radioactive so that the DNA sequences to which they become attached can be visibly tracked. The nylon membrane is placed against a sheet of X-ray film and exposed for several days. When the film is developed, black bands will appear at the point where the radioactive DNA probes have combined with the sample DNA. The result, called an "autoradiograph" or "autorad" looks much like the bar codes found on items in supermarkets and department stores.

The final step is the band pattern comparison. Genetic differences between individuals will be identified by differences in the location and distribution of the band patterns, which correspond to the length of the DNA fragments present. The actual measurement of the band patterns being compared can be done manually or by machine, but often DNA identification depends upon expert judgment.

Polymerase Chain Reaction (PCR)

PCR is not only an analytical tool but also an amplification technique often used when the available amount of DNA material is insufficient for proper analysis or when the sample is degraded by chemical impurities or damaged by environmental conditions. PCR is an in vitro process that causes a specific sequence to repeatedly duplicate itself, mimicking its natural replication process. Short pieces of purified DNA, called primers, are used to build a foundation upon which the sample DNA can build. The primers must have sequences that complement the DNA that flanks the specific segment to be amplified. The sample DNA is heated to separate the double helix, producing two single strands. By then lowering the temperature, copies of the primers bind to the DNA sample's flanking sequences. A heat-stable DNA polymerase (an enzyme) is then introduced to the DNA sample, causing the primers to synthesize complimentary strands of each of the single strands. This process is repeated for generally 25 cycles, amplifying the original DNA sequence approximately a million times. The amplified DNA can then be analyzed by any one of several methodologies.

Functions of DNA Testing

DNA testing provides a basis for positive identification, but it is not expected to become a suitable technology for validating identification in security settings. DNA analysis would be inappropriate in situations in which a nearly immediate determination must be made as to whether a person

seeking entry to a particular area or seeking to conduct a particular transaction is, in fact, authorized to do so. The chemical analysis required to make a DNA comparison takes weeks, not minutes. DNA testing is increasingly used to determine paternity, and, in forensic settings, it has been most prolifically and successfully used to identify or exonerate a suspect.

Paternity Determinations. In determining paternity, DNA has proven to be extraordinarily useful. Each chromosome contains nucleotides identical to those of each parent, as well as the nucleotides that distinguish the individuality of the person. If samples from the child and from one of the parents are available, the nucleotides of the child that are different from the known parent's DNA must have come from the unknown parent's DNA. If a sample from the suspected, but unknown, parent supplies all the "missing" nucleotides without any superfluous nucleotides, one can conclude that the suspected individual is, in fact, the other parent.

Identification of Suspects. The forensic promise of DNA typing is substantial. Samples of human skin, hair follicles, blood, semen, or saliva containing cells or other tissues found on a crime victim or at a crime scene can be examined to identify the DNA pattern. That pattern can be compared with DNA from a suspect to make a "positive identification" or to exonerate a suspect. DNA examination techniques sometimes permit the use of extraordinarily small samples of human tissues or fluids, such as a few hairs or a single spot of blood. Moreover, DNA is durable and is relatively resistant to adverse environmental conditions such as heat or moisture. DNA degrades slowly in a decomposing body, lasting sometimes for years and allowing samples to be analyzed for some time after the death of an individual. Although some experts debate the percentage of usable tissue and fluid samples that are retrieved from all crime scenes, DNA analysis will have the greatest effect on violent crime cases, such as murder and rape, where hair, blood, semen, or tissue evidence is frequently found.

Bureau of Justice Statistics, U.S. Department of Justice, http://gb1.ojp.usdoj.gov

DNA PROFILING

DNA profiling is a laboratory technique that assists in the identification of individuals by their respective DNA (genetic) profiles. A DNA profile is an encrypted set of numbers that can distinguish one person from another except in the case of identical twins. The technique examines repetitive sequences called variable number tandem repeats (VNTRs) that are so variable that unrelated persons are extremely unlikely to have the same VNTRs.

The profiling process begins with the collection of a sample of an individual's DNA, such as a saliva sample taken from the inside cheek of an individual's mouth. The sample is collected with a buccal swab, a device that reduces the possibility of contamination. DNA profiles can be made also from body fluids or tissue such as blood, semen, and skin. Such samples can be taken from hairbrushes, toothbrushes, shaving razors, and perhaps a postage stamp that has been licked.

In addition to purposes of criminal investigation, DNA analysis is widely applied to determine genetic family relationships such as paternity, maternity, and other kinships. Evidence of a genetic connection can vary from low to high; when testing shows no genetic connection, the evidence is absolutely certain.

Law enforcement officials in the United States are empowered to collect DNA samples without suspects' knowledge and to introduce profiles as evidence at trial. In 2013, the U.S. Supreme Court ruled 5–4 that DNA sampling of prisoners arrested for serious crime is constitutional.

Learning Shop USA, Scientific Analysis of Physical Evidence, www.learningshopusa.com

DOCUMENT EXAMINATION

It is not unusual for an investigator to be called in when a document involving a transaction of value is suspicious in some respect. The nature of the document will determine who will conduct the investigation. If the document is an official government document, the investigator is likely to be an employee of a government department at any level (municipal, county, state, and federal). If the document is not connected to the government, the investigator is likely to be a corporate or private investigator representing the interests of a private sector or nongovernment organization.

Questioned documents can be almost anything: checks, bonds, diplomas, certificates, diaries, notes, letters, memoranda, medical records, work and personal references, and application forms.

At the starting point of the investigation, when a document appears to be spurious, there is suspicion but not probable cause. To move a case to probable cause, the investigator's objectives are to:

- Determine if the suspicious document is in fact a tool of a crime; for example, a forged check is a tool for obtaining funds from the bank account of another person or organization.
- Determine the value of the loss.
- Determine if there were multiple losses and the frequency of losses.
- Determine the time frame in which the losses occurred.
- Identify potential witnesses and suspects.

A very first step, then, is to establish if the document is spurious. This is when a document examiner enters the investigation. The tasks of a document examiner are:

- Establish the genuineness or nongenuineness of the document.
- Discover alterations, deletions, and additions.

- Compare markings (including handwriting) for the purpose of identifying persons that made the markings or wrote upon the document.
- Identify the mechanical device (typewriter, printer, fax machine, etc.) that produced the document or placed markings on it.
- Restore legibility of the document, such as writings that are not visible on charred paper or beneath scratched-out words.
- Identify the writing instrument (pencil, ball point, ink pen, etc.), inks, and paper.
- Provide technical reports and expert witness testimony.

Forged Writings

There are three types of forged writings:

- Traced forgery. In this type, the writer traces over a signature or other writing. Because the writer does not write in his or her natural hand, it is not possible to identify the writer, but it is possible to determine if the writing was produced by tracing.
- Simulated forgery. This is the copying of a signature or other writing by "drawing" it. If the writing contains enough normal characteristics of the writer's true hand, it may be possible to identify the writer. In any case, a determination can be made that the writing itself was produced by simulation.
- Freehand forgery. This writing is made in the natural hand of the writer. No attempt is made at tracing or simulating. In freehand forgery, the identity of the writer may be determined.

In all three types, the document examiner will need to have "true" writing in order to make comparisons.

Torn Paper Examinations

Questioned documents, such as forged checks and official documents with erasures, are not new to private investigators. Torn documents collected during an investigation appear less frequently, and perhaps because of infrequency, investigators make mistakes in submitting these documents to a forensic laboratory. A common mistake is to attempt reconstruction by taping pieces together. The document examiner, no matter how skilled, cannot perfectly disassemble a reconstruction. The result may be a lost opportunity to conclusively determine that torn part A matches perfectly with torn part B. This extra handling at the lab can also damage the document's surface and the writing on it.

Another mistake is to send the document to the lab in an envelope heavily sealed with tape. Tape used in excess makes it difficult for the examiner to open the envelope to remove the torn document without damaging it. Moistened tape, such as brown paper tape drawn through water, can cause moisture to migrate into the envelope, make contact with the torn document, and cause blurring of ink and disappearance of indented impressions.

Other Types of Examinations

A document examiner can make conclusions based on study of:

- Altered or obliterated writing
- Impressions created by a typewriter
- Photocopied material
- Machine-printed material
- Paper (torn edges, water mark, impressions, charring)
- Documents of which the true age is in question
- Inks and writing instruments

It is possible to determine if a particular pen is the source of ink comprising the writing on a questioned document. Ink examinations have only two possible results: significant differences existing between the inks indicate they are different, or no significant difference was found between the two inks by the examination techniques applied. Not finding a difference does not prove that two or more inks are the same.

Ink pens are mass-produced products with class characteristics but virtually no individual characteristics. The only exception to this might be an unlikely situation involving someone creating a very small quantity of ink with a unique formula for one-time use.

A few ink manufacturers have added trace elements to ink formulas to signify the date that the formula was introduced. These "tags" make it possible to determine the earliest possible date that an ink existed for use in producing a questioned writing. Ink examinations are categorized as destructive and nondestructive. Destructive exams involve removing ink samples from documents or pens and analyzing their physical components. Nondestructive exams involve visual and instrumental assessments of the appearance and spectral response characteristics of inks.

When a case goes to trial or to other judicial proceedings, the document examiner can be retained. Document examination is a science. The techniques of examination include electrostatic detection of indentations; infrared reluctance and infrared luminescence to identify writing inks and to make visible writings that are obliterated or charred; and comparison microscopes to match tearing, cutting, and some types of machine shredding. Science is also involved in comparing the handwriting on a spurious (questioned) document against handwriting on a document with known authorship.

A document examination service is not an investigation per se; it is a phase or part of an investigation. Conclusions reached by a document examiner must be supported by other established facts. It is those other facts that fall into the domain of the investigator.

Learning Shop USA, Scientific Analysis of Physical Evidence, www.learningshopusa.com

DRUG ENFORCEMENT ADMINISTRATION (DEA)

The mission of the Drug Enforcement Administration (DEA) is to enforce the controlled substances laws and regulations of the United States and bring to the criminal and civil justice system of the United States, or any other competent jurisdiction, those organizations and principal members of organizations involved in the growing, manufacture, or distribution of controlled substances appearing in or destined for illicit traffic in the United States. The DEA also recommends and supports nonenforcement programs aimed at reducing the availability of illicit controlled substances on the domestic and international markets.

In carrying out its mission as the agency responsible for enforcing the controlled substances laws and regulations of the United States, the DEA's primary responsibilities include:

- Investigation and preparation for the prosecution of major violators of controlled substance laws operating at interstate and international levels
- Investigation and preparation for prosecution of criminals and drug gangs who perpetrate violence in our communities and terrorize citizens through fear and intimidation
- Management of a national drug intelligence program in cooperation with federal, state, local, and foreign officials to collect, analyze, and disseminate strategic and operational drug intelligence information
- Seizure and forfeiture of assets derived from, traceable to, or intended to be used for illicit drug trafficking
- Enforcement of the provisions of the Controlled Substances Act as they pertain to the manufacture, distribution, and dispensing of legally produced controlled substances

- Coordination and cooperation with federal, state, and local law enforcement officials on mutual drug enforcement efforts and enhancement of such efforts through exploitation of potential interstate and international investigations beyond local or limited federal jurisdictions and resources
- Coordination and cooperation with federal, state, and local agencies, and with foreign governments, in programs designed to reduce the availability of illicit abuse-type drugs on the United States market through nonenforcement methods such as crop eradication, crop substitution, and training of foreign officials
- Responsibility, under the policy guidance of the secretary of state and U.S. ambassadors, for all programs associated with drug law enforcement counterparts in foreign countries
- Liaison with the United Nations, Interpol, and other organizations on matters relating to international drug control programs

U.S. Department of Justice, Drug Enforcement Administration, http://www.justice.gov/dea/about/mission.shtml

DRUG INVESTIGATION: CLASSES AND TYPES

Narcotics

Heroin is a highly addictive drug and the most rapidly acting of the opiates. It is processed from morphine, a naturally occurring substance extracted from the seed pod of certain varieties of poppy plants grown in Southeast Asia (Thailand, Laos, and Myanmar [Burma]), Southwest Asia (Afghanistan and Pakistan), Mexico, and Colombia. It comes in several forms, the main one being "black tar" from Mexico (found primarily in the western United States) and white heroin from Colombia (primarily sold on the East Coast).

Hydromorphone belongs to a class of drugs called "opioids," which includes morphine. It has an analgesic potency of two to eight times that of morphine but has a shorter duration of action and greater sedative properties. Hydromorphone is legally manufactured and distributed in the United States. However, abusers can obtain it from forged prescriptions, "doctor-shopping," theft from pharmacies, and from friends and acquaintances.

Methadone is a synthetic (man-made) narcotic that was developed by German scientists during World War II because of a shortage of morphine at that time. Methadone was introduced into the United States in 1947.

Morphine is a nonsynthetic narcotic with a high potential for abuse and is the principal constituent of opium. It is one of the most effective drugs known for the relief of severe pain. In the United States, a small percentage of the morphine obtained from opium is used directly for pharmaceutical products. The remaining morphine is processed into codeine and other derivatives.

Opium is a highly addictive, nonsynthetic narcotic that is extracted from the poppy plant, Papaver somniferum. The opium poppy is the key source for many narcotics, including morphine, codeine, and heroin.

Oxycodone is a semi synthetic narcotic analgesic and historically has been a popular drug of abuse among the narcotic-abusing population. It is synthesized from thebaine, a constituent of the poppy plant.

Stimulants

Stimulants speed up the body's systems. This class includes prescription drugs such as amphetamines; methylphenidate; diet aids; and illicitly produced drugs such as methamphetamine, cocaine, and methcathinone. Stimulants are diverted from legitimate channels and clandestinely manufactured exclusively for the illicit market.

Depressants

Depressants bring about sleep, relieve anxiety and muscle spasms, and prevent seizures. Barbiturates are older forms of drugs. They include butalbital, phenobarbital, Pentothal, Seconal, and Nembutal. Benzodiazepines were developed to replace barbiturates, though they still share many of the undesirable side effects. Some examples are Valium, Xanax, Halcion, Ativan, Klonopin, and Restoril. Rohypnol is a benzodiazepine that is not manufactured or legally marketed in the United States. Other depressants are meprobamate, methaqualone, and an illicit drug called GHB.

Hallucinogens

Hallucinogens are found in plants and fungi, are synthetically produced, and are among the oldest known group of drugs used for their ability to alter human perception and mood. They can be synthetically produced in illicit laboratories or are found in plants.

MDMA acts as both a stimulant and psychedelic, producing an energizing effect, distortions in time and perception, and enhanced enjoyment of tactile experiences. Adolescents and young adults use it to reduce inhibitions and to promote euphoria. MDMA is a synthetic chemical made in labs.

K2 or "Spice" is a mixture of herbs and spices that is typically sprayed with a synthetic compound chemically similar to THC, the psychoactive ingredients in marijuana. Manufacturers of this product are not regulated and are often unknown since these products are purchased via the Internet whether wholesale or retail. Several websites that sell the product are based in China. Some products may contain an herb called damiana, which is native to Central America, Mexico, and the Caribbean.

Ketamine is a dissociative anesthetic that has some hallucinogenic effects. It distorts perceptions of sight and sound and makes the user feel disconnected and not in control. It is an injectable, short-acting anesthetic for use in humans and animals. It is referred to as a "dissociative anesthetic" because it makes patients feel detached from their pain and environment.

LSD is a potent hallucinogen that has a high potential for abuse and currently has no accepted medical use in treatment in the United States. LSD is produced in clandestine laboratories.

Peyote is a small, spineless cactus. The active ingredient in peyote is the hallucinogen mescaline. From earliest recorded time, peyote has been used by natives in northern Mexico and the southwestern United States as a part of their religious rites. Mescaline can be extracted from peyote or produced synthetically.

Psilocybin is a chemical obtained from certain types of fresh or dried mushrooms. Psilocybin mushrooms are found in Mexico, Central America, and the United States.

Anabolic steroids are synthetically produced variants of the naturally occurring male hormone testosterone that are abused in an attempt to promote muscle growth, enhance athletic or other physical performance, and improve physical appearance. Testosterone, nandrolone, stanozolol, methandienone, and boldenone are some of the most frequently abused anabolic steroids.

Inhalants are invisible, volatile substances found in common household products that produce chemical vapors that are inhaled to induce psychoactive or mind-altering effects. There are more than 1,000 products that are very dangerous when inhaled—things like typewriter correction fluid, air conditioning refrigerant, felt-tip markers, spray paint, air freshener, butane, and cooking spray.

U.S. Department of Justice, Drug Enforcement Administration, http://www.deadiversion.usdoj.gov/schedules/index.html

DRUG RECOGNITION

The Drug Recognition Process is a systematic, standardized evaluation. It is systematic in that it is based on a variety of observable signs and symptoms, known to reliably indicate drug impairment. The conclusion is based on the complete analysis, not on any single element of the evaluation. The process is standard in that it is conducted in the same way for every person.

Recognition techniques include the evaluation of specific physical and behavioral symptoms (examination of eyes and vital signs, scrutiny of speech, and coordination) that indicate if a person:

- Is currently under the influence of drugs (substances actively circulating in the blood)
- Has recently used drugs (within the last three days)

The evaluation can also provide information about the category of drug used. The evaluation will not identify the exact drug or drugs a person has used. The process permits the presence of drugs to be narrowed down to certain broad categories (for example, central nervous system stimulants) but not to specific drugs such as cocaine. It can be determined that a person probably used a narcotic analgesic but not whether it was morphine, codeine, heroin, or some other substance.

The evaluation does not substitute for chemical testing of persons who exhibit signs of drug influence or recent use. The process will usually supply accurate grounds for suspecting that a particular category of drugs is present in urine or blood, but sample collection and analysis must still be done if scientific or legal evidence is needed.

The evaluation process can suggest the presence of seven broad categories of drugs, distinguishable from each other by observable signs they generate in users:

- Central nervous system (CNS) stimulants, such as cocaine and amphetamines
- CNS depressants, such as alcohol, barbiturates, and tranquilizers
- Hallucinogens, such as LSD, peyote, and psilocybin but not phencyclidine (PCP)
- Narcotic analgesics, such as Demerol, codeine, heroin, and methadone
- Phencyclidine (PCP) and its analogs
- Cannabis, such as marijuana, hashish, and hash oil
- Inhalants, such as model airplane glue and aerosols

Recognition Techniques

The drug recognition process includes a number of examinations:

Drug History. Ask a structured series of questions concerning prior drug involvement. The drug history may reveal patterns of usage that will be of assistance in the evaluation.

Breath Alcohol Test. With a breath-testing device, it can be determined if alcohol is contributing to the person's observable impairment and whether the concentration is sufficient to be the sole cause of that impairment. An accurate and immediate measurement of blood alcohol determines the person's blood alcohol concentration (BAC). If the BAC is not sufficient to produce the observed level of impairment, the evaluation is continued to detect the presence of other drugs. The BAC is also useful in determining if a person is in need of immediate medical treatment or other special attention.

Preliminary Examination (Prescreen). Ask a structured series of questions, make specific observations, and have the person perform simple tests that provide the first opportunity to examine the person closely and directly. Determine if the person is suffering from an injury or some other condition not necessarily related to drugs. Begin also to systematically assess appearance and behavior for signs of possible drug influence or drug use, as well as screening out persons who do not exhibit signs of drug use. For asymptomatic persons, no further evaluation or drug testing is necessary.

Eye Examination. The inability of the eyes to converge toward the bridge of the nose suggests the presence of certain drugs, such as cannabis. Other categories of drugs can induce horizontal-gaze nystagmus, an involuntary jerking that may occur as the eyes gaze to one side or as they are elevated. CNS depressants (alcohol, barbiturates, or tranquilizers) will typically cause horizontal-gaze nystagmus.

Psychophysical Tests. These include the Rhomberg Balance, the Walk and Turn, One-Leg Stand, and Finger to Nose. Specific errors of omission or commission can point toward specific categories of drugs causing impairment. For example, a person who is under the influence of a CNS stimulant (cocaine or amphetamines) may move very rapidly on the Walk and Turn test but may exhibit a distorted sense of time on the Rhomberg Balance test (such as estimating 15 seconds to be 30).

Dark Room Examination. Make systematic checks of the size of the pupils, the reaction of the pupils to light, and evidence of drugs taken by nose or mouth. Certain categories of drugs affect the eyes, especially the pupils, in predictable ways. For example, a person under the influence of a CNS stimulant or hallucinogen will have dilated (enlarged) pupils. A person under the influence of a narcotic analgesic, such as heroin, will have extremely constricted (small) pupils, which will exhibit little or no response to the presence or absence of light.

Vital Signs. Perform systematic checks of the blood pressure, pulse rate, and temperature. Certain categories of drugs (including stimulants) will elevate blood pressure and pulse rate, raise the body temperature, and cause breathing to become rapid. Other drugs, including narcotic analgesics, have opposite effects.

Muscle Rigidity. Certain categories of drugs, such as PCP, can cause the muscles to become hypertensive and very rigid.

Injection sites. Some users of certain categories of drugs routinely or occasionally inject their drugs. Evidence of hypodermic needle use (scars or "tracks") may be found in veins along the arms, legs, or neck. Injection sites are frequently found on users of narcotic analgesics.

Based on the results of the previous steps, a suspicion can be formed about the category or categories of drugs that may be involved.

Opinion. Based on all the evidence and the observations, it should be possible to reach an informed conclusion about whether the individual is under the influence of drugs or has recently used drugs and, if so, the category or categories of drugs that are the probable cause of the impairment.

Toxicological Examination. Chemical tests provide scientific, admissible evidence to substantiate conclusions. Generally, urinalyses are performed (90 percent of the time); in some cases, blood tests are ordered also.

U.S. Department of Justice, Office of Justice Programs, National Institute of Justice, http://www.nij.gov/searchcenter/pages/results.aspx?k=Drug%20Recognition%20Techniques

DRUG TESTING

Investigators can be employed to monitor the taking of urine specimens from persons in certain work-related situations:

- Screening job applicants
- Random testing of employees working in safety-sensitive environments
- Specific testing of employees involved in on-the-job accidents
- Random and specific testing of professional athletes

Assurance

Before a specimen is sent to a laboratory for testing, there must be assurance that the specimen has been collected according to established procedures. The investigator's part in the collection procedures is to watch for:

- Errors in the identification of persons giving specimens
- Documentation errors, such as failure to obtain prior written consent from the person to be tested
- Deviations from standard collection procedures
- Substituting, switching, and contaminating of collected specimens
- Mislabeling of specimen containers
- Discrepancies in packaging specimens for transport to the testing laboratory
- Chain of custody errors

The Drug Testing Proposition

Drug testing of job applicants and employees has long been used to ensure that workers are able to perform their jobs without risk to themselves or others. Prominent among the various risks is misuse of drugs. In this discussion, note that the terms "drug" and similar terms such as "illicit substance" include alcohol and any other intoxicating substance. The term "misuse" includes the use of legal drugs in a manner not approved by the prescribing physician; use of a legal drug that has been stolen or received as a gift; and legal drugs that have been purchased outside legal channels, such as drugs purchased "on the street."

The drug testing proposition essentially means that when a drug test result conclusively shows that a person is currently misusing a drug, the employer should, for a reason of safety, exclude that person from the employer's premises or other places where the employee is working on behalf of the employer. The proposition means also that the employer must meet stringent standards related to collecting specimens, assuring the accuracy of testing, assuring confidentiality, keeping records, and disseminating information on a "need-to-know" basis.

Error Types

The major assurance of accuracy in testing is a series of checks built into the laboratory's testing system. Two types of errors are of concern. First is the administrative error, which is the consequence of:

- Incorrect transcription of test results
- Incorrect identification of the donor or the donor's specimen
- Failure to maintain chain of custody

Second is the analytical error. It is related to:

- Precision of analysis
- Calibration of equipment
- Qualifications of laboratory personnel
- Interpretation of test results

Techniques of Testing

Urinalysis is the most usual test method. In this method, a specimen is first examined by an immunoassay test. This first examination is called a preliminary or screening test. When a specimen is found to be negative by the immunoassay technique, there is no further testing. When a specimen is found to be positive by the preliminary test, the specimen undergoes a follow-up examination called a confirmatory test. The usual technique in the confirmatory test is gas chromatography/mass spectrometry (GC/MS). When a specimen is found to be negative in the second test, the specimen donor is considered to be drug free. When both techniques are positive, the finding is called "confirmed positive," and the specimen donor is considered to be *not* drug free.

There can be another final test result; it is called a "verified" positive. When the second test is a repeat of the first test or uses a less sensitive technique, it is called a verification test, and a positive result is called a verified positive. Verification falls far short of confirmation.

Medical Review Officer

There is one further step in drug testing programs that are regulated by the federal government. A confirmed positive must be reviewed by a medical review officer (MRO). An MRO is a specially trained medical doctor who evaluates a positive test result in light of further evidence obtained from a physical examination of the individual, an interview of the individual, or a review of the individual's medical history. The MRO seeks to determine if the positive finding could have some other medical explanation, such as the innocent use of a legally prescribed drug.

A specific objective is to identify evidence of drugs or drug metabolites in the urine. Some drug classes, such as the opiates class, can be identified directly by the presence of the drug itself. Other drug classes, such as the cannabinoids (marijuana), are identified indirectly by the presence of metabolites. A metabolite is a compound produced from chemical changes in the body.

False Positives

Certainly a most serious problem is that of false positives. A false positive occurs when a drug or drug metabolite is reported in a urine specimen but is actually not present. False positives can be placed into three groups:

- Chemical False Positive. This is the result of another substance in the sample being mistakenly identified as a drug. Chemical false positives sometimes occur when donors contaminate their specimens at the collection site.
- Administrative False Positive. This is the result of one person's positive test result being attributed to another person. Improper labeling and inaccurate chain of custody documentation are the usual causes.
- Operator Error. This is the result of a mistake by a laboratory technician during an analytical procedure. Inadequate operator training, poor supervision, and failure to follow testing protocols are usually at the root of operator error.

Passive Inhalation

A number of defenses have been put forward to explain positive test results. Passive inhalation or inadvertent exposure to marijuana is frequently cited, but clinical studies show that it is unlikely that a nonsmoking individual can passively inhale sufficient marijuana smoke to result in a high enough concentration for marijuana to be detected by a standard urinalysis method. It is extremely improbable that a person who was not smoking would be exposed to the level of smoke and for the length of time required to produce a positive test result.

An investigator present at the collection site helps insure that precautions are in place. For example, verify that:

- The employer's written policy that authorizes drug testing is available at the collection point for reading by the donor prior to giving a specimen.
- The specimen donor has presented positive personal identification, such as a photo-bearing driving license.
- Written consent is obtained from the donor at the collection point.
- Specimen containers are of the type packaged at the point of manufacture in a protective plastic envelope.
- Nothing (such as a thermometer) is introduced into the specimen or its container.

John J. Fay, The Drug-Free Workplace, Butterworth-Heinemann, Burlington, MA, 2000, pp. 137–138, 540.

DUE DILIGENCE

The term "due diligence" refers to the care a reasonable party would take before entering into an agreement with another party. The inquiry serves to confirm all material facts regarding the agreement under consideration. Very often, due diligence is the method for examining the financial underpinnings of a corporation in a pending investment, merger, or acquisition, with the goal of understanding risks associated with the deal.

For example, in a sell/purchase deal, both parties will want to check out the other party's bona fides. The seller wants assurance that the buyer has the financial ability to meet the sales price, and the buyer wants assurance that the seller's property is worth the price. Due diligence is essentially a way of preventing unnecessary harm to either party.

Issues examined in due diligence are complex. They can involve corporate capitalization, cash flow, loans outstanding, accounts receivable and payable, inventory on hand, ownership of intellectual property, material agreements, public filings, etc.

But even complex issues boil down to simple questions:

- Have any of the corporate officers been indicted or convicted of crime?
- Does the company have a litigation history?
- Is there a lawsuit pending or on the horizon?
- Is the company claiming to possess assets that do not exist?
- Is the company concealing assets?
- Does the company have a hidden agenda?

Learning Shop USA, Background Investigation, www.learningshopusa.com

E

EAVESDROPPING

The first thing that needs to be said about eavesdropping is that investigators, at least those on the right side of the law, do not or should not eavesdrop but should have an understanding of it in order to detect and prevent it.

The investigator will find that the most common victims of eavesdropping are companies with valuable proprietary information, such as research and development information, desired by competitors; criminals looking for sensitive information as a means to commit crimes, such as identity theft; and persons seeking personal information about other persons such as a spouse or a business partner.

The investigator will do well to know the elements of proof in this complicated area.

Generally, the elements are:

- Knowingly and without lawful authority,
- Entering into a private place with intent to listen surreptitiously to private conversations or to observe the conduct of any other person or persons therein, or
- Installing or using outside a private place any device for hearing, recording, amplifying, or broadcasting sounds originating in such place, which sounds would not ordinarily be audible or comprehensible outside, without the consent of the person or persons entitled to privacy therein, or

- Installing or using any device or equipment for the interception of any telephone, telegraph, or other wire communication without the consent of the person in possession or control of the facilities for such wire communication.

The term "eavesdropping" can be misleading. It includes both wiretapping and bugging.

- Eavesdropping by wiretapping is the interception of communication over a wire. It requires physical contact with the communications circuit.
- Eavesdropping by bugging is the interception of communication without penetration of a wire.

A telephone company provides power to move signals along its wires. Power needed to operate the listening device utilizes the telephone company's power. This makes it possible for communications to be sent along the same line without the use of batteries or other sources of power. The destination of the captured communications is usually a recorder concealed in a separate location on or away from the premises.

Methods typically used in eavesdropping by telephone are:

- A wiretap is placed on the telephone wires, such as wires in a telephone junction box or on a telephone pole. This is called a direct physical connection because the wires of the listening device are attached to the wires of the telephone system.

- Another method is called inductive coupling. Voices between parties in a telephone conversation move through the wires in the form of electromagnetic energy. This energy is intercepted, amplified, and converted back to voice.

- A "bug" or tiny microphone is placed in the telephone instrument's handset or other portion of the instrument. The "bug" transmits voices to a recorder secreted nearby.

An advantage of these methods is that the perpetrator can be well away from the crime while it is occurring, thus reducing the chance of being caught. If investigator catches a person in the act of eavesdropping (which is a felony or serious offense), the person may be held for immediate release to law enforcement.

Types of Eavesdropping Devices

The Called Number Recorder is attached to the telephone line and intercepts the pulses and tones from the dial mechanism of the telephone, producing a list of numbers that have been dialed from a particular telephone. A device called a Pen Register records the numbers.

The Harmonica Bug or Infinity Transmitter turns the telephone's mouthpiece into a listening device. The eavesdropper dials the target's telephone number, and the device produces an audio signal that effectively makes the mouthpiece work like a microphone.

The Carbon Microphone is a compression of carbon granules that modulate electric current. The device is usually concealed in a telephone handset. In a wet or humid environment, the granules tend to coagulate, making the microphone ineffective.

The Crystal Microphone and the Dynamic Microphone are self-powered and can be used almost anywhere, but they cannot be used indefinitely because they rely on batteries. Their chief advantage is concealment because they are very small and are capable of being concealed in pens, tie pins, cuff links, wall plugs, lamps, etc. An investigator who has an eavesdropper under surveillance should look for such devices.

Contact Microphones are of two types: the Contact Microphone and the Spike Microphone. The former is attached to the opposite side of a wall, such as a wall in a hotel room immediately adjacent to the target's room. The Contact Microphone is usually of the crystal variety, and it uses the entire wall as a sort of diaphragm that captures many different sounds occurring in the target's room.

The Spike Microphone works like the Contact Microphone, but instead of being attached to a wall, it is inserted through the wall until the tip of it comes into contact with the back side of the wall in the target's room. Again, the wall inside the target's room works like a diaphragm.

The Cardioid Microphone is so named because it is shaped like a heart. It is pointed in one direction only and into a fairly small area. The unidirectional focus of the device avoids extraneous noises.

The Parabolic Microphone is the type you will see on the sidelines of a football game. It is in the shape of a large dish. The dish can capture sounds as far away as 300 feet. The sounds are amplified and sent to a recorder.

The Shotgun Microphone is like the Parabolic except that it is an acoustic tube in the shape of long-barreled shotgun. The "shotgun" is pointed at the target area. The target area could be a conference room in a building across the street or a dining table in a public area such as a food court in a shopping mall. The Shotgun Microphone is considered more effective than the Parabolic.

The Omnidirectional Microphone picks up audio energy from areas around its aiming point. It works well from a concealed location inside a room when the objective is to pick up sounds all around it.

The Condenser Microphone has good fidelity but is fragile. The device uses a series of plates that convert audio energy into vibrations; these vibrations are then converted to electrical impulses capable of being converted to voice.

The Pneumatic Cavity Microphone picks up surface vibrations caused by human speech. This device is technically a component because it is connected to a conventional microphone.

Detection of Eavesdropping Devices

An investigator who is not specially trained in detecting eavesdropping devices must rely on those that are. Investigators who perform eavesdropping services are highly trained technicians who work in a field that is often called Technical Services Countermeasures (TSCM).

The standard method for detecting eavesdropping devices is a three-step process:

- Evaluate the situation and circumstances
- Conduct a visual inspection
- Conduct an electronic inspection

Evaluation is done through interviews with persons knowledgeable about the area and the communication equipment to be inspected. Questions to ask are:

- Have there been previous compromises of sensitive information?
- Where is the information discussed, generated, and stored?
- What equipment is used to transmit sensitive information?
- Who would be the logical suspects if information was stolen?
- What are the current countermeasures in place to prevent eavesdropping, and are they effective?

The visual inspection depends on the experience of the technical services inspector, his knowledge of current eavesdropping devices, and their places of concealment. Most important is knowledge of where to look and how to look. The indicators of concealment are:

- Sawdust that suggests drilling where drilling should not occur
- Popped nails on wood panels and moldings
- Tiny holes on the walls, floor, and ceiling
- Bits of electrical wire and disturbance of dust in plenums
- Mismatched staples on fabric chairs
- Ceiling tiles out of place
- Marks on walls that suggest placement of a ladder
- Loose carpets
- Loose covers on communication equipment
- Loose screw-on covers on telephone mouthpieces

The visual inspection also involves examining telephones, telephone rooms, and telephone wires that lead into and out of the target area and communication equipment such as fax machines, data modems, scramblers, encrypters, and video teleconference equipment.

The electronic inspection takes a multitest approach using some or all of the following devices:

- Nonlinear junction detector
- Spectrum analyzer
- Time domain reflectometer
- Scan and lock receiver
- Tape recorder detector
- Vulnerable path encrypter

The first two steps in the detection process, evaluation and physical inspection, are within the competency of an experienced investigator, but the third step requires skill in operating the equipment named above.

Finally, this defensive approach must be applied periodically, randomly, and with care not to warn eavesdroppers of an imminent inspection. If the eavesdroppers know when an inspection is to be conducted, the eavesdropping devices will be turned off, making the inspection less than fully effective.

Learning Shop USA, Eavesdropping, www.learningshopusa.com

EMBEZZLEMENT

Embezzlement is one of the many forms of internal theft. A common form of embezzlement is financial in nature, such as the attorney who diverts funds from client assets entrusted to the attorney. The act is complete when the funds are used for a purpose not intended by the client/owner.

Embezzlement is not always committed by a single individual. A bookkeeper, for example, might conspire with a supervisor who holds a position that makes the embezzlement undiscoverable.

A common practice is to issue checks to nonexistent vendors or employees. The checks are sent to addresses, such as post office boxes. The embezzler or an accomplice later removes the checks from the box. The accomplice would be someone the embezzler can trust, such as a spouse, family relative, or good friend.

Embezzlement is typically methodical and always done covertly. The embezzler usually holds a position of trust and has been a long-time employee. The act can be carried out over an extended period of time and discovered by accident. Sometimes, the victim will not report the crime to authorities in hope that the stolen money, or a portion of it, can be recovered or that restitution is possible.

Motives of embezzlers vary. The signals include:

- Gambling
- Borrowing
- Living above one's means
- Indebtedness
- Alcohol or drug abuse

The general characteristics of embezzlement are:

- Detection is frequently accidental.
- The crime is frequently reported anonymously.
- The scheme has existed for a long time.
- The embezzler is usually well known, respected, respected, intelligent, and sometimes influential.
- The scheme is sometimes difficult to figure out.
- Evidence tends to "disappear" when the embezzler learns that an investigation has been started.

John J. Fay, *Contemporary Security Management*, second ed., Elsevier, Burlington, MA, 2011, pp. 191–201.

ETHICAL STANDARDS

Ethics are the standards of conduct and judgment in respect to what is perceived as right and wrong. An intrinsic element of ethics is the specification of responsibility for human actions. Ethical standards go beyond merely describing conduct that we habitually accept; they seek to define higher goals and the means for attaining them. An investigator encounters ethics in two dimensions: first, as a person who investigates ethics violations committed by others; and second, as a person obligated to abide by ethical standards.

Mainstream ethicists believe that an act is either intrinsically correct or incorrect and there is a duty to act correctly. However, others argue that the reality of the human condition is that people seek to engage in acts that derive pleasure, and acts that produce the greatest amount of pleasure for the greatest number of people are morally correct.

Code of Ethics

A traditional approach for promoting ethical conduct is the creation of a code of ethics.

But in its creation, disagreements will arise due to questions that ask:

- Who will create the code?
- Who will be affected by it?
- What behavior will the code cover?
- What sanctions will be applied to violators?
- Who will enforce the sanctions?

In attempting to reconcile concerns about a code under development, the drafters may produce an ineffectual document. On the one hand, it may be so watered down as to have no real impact on behavior; on the other hand, it may include unrealistic principles. When moral questions are involved, it is never easy to select between competing and sometimes incompatible interests.

In the business venue, a great difficulty lies in reconciling morality and profit. To the anguish of ethicists, the rule has been that a moral principle is excluded from a code if the principle condemns business activity. The reason for exclusion rests on the reality that business is driven by economic forces. Still, the morality of a business enterprise is influenced by the human values of its leaders, workforce, customers, and the public at large. The practices of an ethical business enterprise will reflect:

- The philosophy of senior management
- The honesty and integrity of employees generally
- Adherence to ethical standards in business practices

Personal Ethics

It is the conduct of people, whether employees, operators, or owners, that reflects the ethical standards of an organization. Boiled down to a simple term, conduct is the measuring stick. The very basic standards, such as honesty and integrity, appear in forms that vary according to practices. The practices of an investigator are rather unique. Following

are a few of the "do nots" common to the field of investigation.

- Do not violate the law.
- Do not disclose confidential information improperly.
- Do not abuse authority.
- Do not accept anything that could affect personal judgment.
- Do not mistreat other persons.
- Do not fail to report "conflict of interest" situations.
- Do not use force unnecessarily.

Learning Shop USA, Ethics, www.learningshopusa.com

EVIDENCE TYPES

Physical Evidence

Evidence is anything that tends to prove or disprove a fact. Within that general definition, physical evidence is any material substance or object, regardless of size or shape. Generally, there are three categories of physical evidence.

- Movable Evidence: items that can be transported or moved, such as weapons, tools, and glass fragments
- Fixed or Immovable Evidence: items that cannot easily be removed, such as walls of a room, trees, and utility poles
- Fragile Evidence: items that are easily destroyed, contaminated, or will easily deteriorate

Evaluating Physical Evidence

In many cases, the success or failure of an investigation depends on the investigator's ability to recognize physical evidence and derive understanding from it. This process of evaluation begins with the initial report of a crime and concludes when the case is adjudicated. Evaluation is usually carried out in concert with laboratory technicians, a prosecuting attorney, other investigators, experts in certain fields, and other persons whose knowledge contributes to a better understanding of physical evidence and its relationship to the many facets of the case.

Identification

Evidence must be marked for identification as soon as it is received, recovered, or discovered. Identification markings help the investigator identify the evidence at a later date. Markings are normally made by placing initials, time, and the date on the items. If it is not practical to mark evidence, it is placed in an appropriate container and sealed. The container is then marked for identification.

Identification markings are supplemented by the use of an evidence tag. An evidence tag is filled out at the time the evidence is acquired. Entries on the tag are made in ink, and the tag accompanies the evidence from the moment it is acquired until it is relinquished. An evidence tag is not a substitute for marking evidence but is an administrative convenience for locating evidence while it is in custody.

Chain of Custody

Chain of custody begins when an item of evidence is received. The number of persons who handle an item of evidence should be kept to a minimum. All persons who handle an item are considered links in the custody chain, and such persons must be given receipt for each item whenever a transfer is made. An investigator in possession of evidence is personally liable for its care and safekeeping. Three factors influence the introduction of evidence at trial:

- The object must be identified.
- Relevancy must exist.
- Continuity or chain of custody must be shown.

Presenting Evidence

The rules for presenting evidence in a criminal investigation are as varied as the types of evidence.

Opinion testimony is a conclusion drawn by a witness, hence the term "opinion testimony." Another form of testimonial information is hearsay evidence. Hearsay is a statement that is made by someone who is not a witness. Hearsay cannot be entered into evidence unless the maker of the statement can be cross-examined.

Privileged communication is confidential information between two persons recognized by law as coming within the so-called privileged relationship rule. The following relationships are generally recognized: a husband and wife, an attorney and client, a physician and patient, and a law enforcement officer and informant.

Character evidence is evidence introduced by either defense or prosecution witnesses to prove the accused's good or bad character. Character evidence is usually introduced only when the defense raises the issue of the accused's character.

Direct evidence is evidence presented by a person who actually witnessed something. Contrast this with circumstantial evidence, which is evidence that proves other facts from which a court may reasonably infer the truth.

Admissibility is a characteristic or condition of evidence. To be admissible, evidence must be material, relevant, and competent. Evidence is material when it plays a significant part in proving a case. Examples of material evidence might be fingerprints of the accused that were found on the murder weapon, an eyewitness account of how the accused committed the crime, or stolen property found in the possession of the accused. Evidence is relevant when it goes directly to the proof or disproof of the crime or of any facts at issue. Examples of relevant evidence might be a death certificate or a medical examiner's report. Evidence is competent when it is shown to be reliable. Examples of competent evidence might be accurate business records or the testimony of an expert fingerprint examiner.

Burden of proof is a rule that holds that no person accused of a crime is required to prove his or her innocence. The prosecution must prove the guilt of a defendant beyond a reasonable doubt. Reasonable doubt means the jury must believe the charges to be true to a "moral certainty." On the other hand, the accused must prove his or her contentions. Such defenses as self-defense, insanity, and alibi are affirmative defenses that must be proved by the accused.

A presumption is a conclusion that the law says must be reached from certain facts. Presumptions are recognized because experience has shown that some facts should be accepted or presumed true until otherwise rebutted. For example, defendants are presumed to be sane at the time the crime was committed, and at the time of trial, in the absence of proof to the contrary. Presumptions are of two classes: conclusive and rebuttable. A conclusive presumption is one that the law demands be made from a set of facts, e.g., a child under seven years of age cannot be charged with a crime. A rebuttable presumption can be overcome by evidence to the contrary, e.g., presumption of death after being unaccounted for and missing for seven years.

Exclusion

In general, exclusion deals with conditions in which evidence will not be accepted. They limit the evidence a witness may present to those things of which he had direct knowledge, i.e., what he saw, smelled, tasted, felt, or heard.

All evidence—direct and circumstantial—if relevant, material, and competent, is admissible provided it is not opinion testimony, hearsay evidence, or privileged communication.

Testimonial Evidence

There are exceptions regarding the admissibility of opinion testimony and hearsay evidence. An exception to the rule against opinion testimony can be made when no other description could be more accurate. For instance, a witness is allowed to testify on such matters as size, distance, time, weight, speed, direction, drunkenness, and similar matters, all of which require the witness to state an opinion. There is no requirement for the witness to be an "expert" when testifying to facts such as these.

Exceptions to the rule against hearsay can be made for the dying declaration and the spontaneous declaration. The admissibility of a dying declaration is limited to homicide cases. Because of the seriousness of homicide, a dying declaration is an exception. A dying declaration is admissible either for or against the accused. The statement must have been made when the victim believed he was about to die and was without hope of recovery. The admissibility of the declaration will not be affected as long as the victim dies; otherwise, the issue would not arise since there would be no charge of homicide.

The spontaneous declaration, a statement made under conditions of shock or excitement, may be admitted as another exception to the hearsay rule. Normally, such a statement is made simultaneously with an event or act, and there is not time or opportunity to fabricate a story. It is generally accepted that the statement will be admitted if it precedes, follows, or is concurrent with the act. The statement cannot have been made in response to a question and must pertain to the act that produced it. The spontaneity of the statement is sufficient guarantee of truthfulness to compensate for the denial of cross-examination.

In prosecutions for sexual offenses, evidence that the victim made a complaint within a short time after the offense occurred (i.e., a fresh complaint) is admissible in certain cases. The fact that the complaint was made is relevant for corroborating the testimony of the victim. The statement may relate only to who and what caused the conditions and merely indicate the credibility of the victim as a witness.

A confession is a statement or complete acknowledgment of guilt. An admission is a statement that does not amount to a complete acknowledgment of guilt but links the maker with a crime. Admissions are forms of hearsay. A court is inclined to apply the same rules of admissibility to admissions as for confessions.

Learning Shop USA, Collection and Preservation of Evidence, www.learningshopusa.com

EXECUTIVE PROTECTION

The Executive Protection Program

Executive protection programs are present in many venues: business, government, entertainment, sports, affluence, royalty, and crime. The protected person can be a prominent businessman, government leader, movie star, sports star, billionaire, or king.

For simplicity, we will use the term "PP" when we refer to the protected person. A PP can be any one of the personalities mentioned above, but again for simplicity, we have chosen business as the venue and the PP as the chief executive officer of the business.

An executive protection program in the business venue can be managed by a corporate security director or corporate investigator. When the business does not have an in-house corporate security/investigative department, the program can be placed under contract to an outside investigator. Whether directly employed by the business or under contract to the business, the term for program manager will be "PM."

Program Elements

Not every organization will provide out-of-the-ordinary protection for the PP. This can be the case because:

- The organization's Board of Directors may see no need for it.
- The PP may refuse to accept it.
- The threat is believed not to exist or is perceived to be at such a low level that an executive protection program is not justified.
- The cost of a program is more than the organization is willing to pay.

A program can be small and simple, large and complex, or somewhere in between. The nature of the threat determines the nature of the program. As the threat level rises, so does the capability of the program.

The protection elements in a small program can consist of guards at the office building and an alarm system in the home. The program enlarges as duress alarms are installed in the executive suite, a security officer is the receptionist at the suite entrance, and secretaries are trained to look for and react to danger.

At the home, exterior lighting is added, and a security patrol passes by several times during hours of darkness.

A comprehensive program can have all of the previous plus a driver and an automobile for local commuting. The driver is skilled in bodyguard tactics, escape driving, use of a firearm, and administration of CPR and first aid. The vehicle is resistant to bullets and explosives and has capabilities for quick acceleration, high speed, and tight cornering. The PP's home has a controlled gate at the entrance to the property and one or a few security officers stationed on the grounds. A communications system allows the PP's driver and other security personnel to communicate among themselves and with a control center.

Protection at the Office and Home

At the office or the home, the protective shield is a combination of physical safeguards and people. The safeguards and people have three main functions:

- Deter threats
- Give warning
- Summon help

Physical safeguards at the home or office can consist of fences, lights, sensors, alarms, and CCTV. When the threat is consistently high, additional safeguards may be appropriate. They include duress alarms, bullet- and explosive-resistant walls, concealed rooms, and escape vehicles.

During routine, nonthreatening conditions, the PP is protected at the office and at home by security officers and specially trained household staff.

Threats

Threats confronting a PP can be categorized as:

- Kidnapping to extort money
- Kidnapping to attain an objective such as release of persons from prison
- Assassination as revenge
- Assassination for an ideological reason
- Kidnapping or assassination to instill fear

Also, experience demonstrates that a PP can be the target of a deranged individual with a motive as strange as the act committed. To use a very basic example, a PP whose decision caused an employee to be disciplined, laid off, or terminated may seek revenge.

A person or group that intends to kidnap or harm the PP may attempt to gain entry to the PP's residence or office through pretext. Examples are posing as a cable repairman, slipping past a guard during shift change, and pretending to be a delivery man.

The group's target can be the PP's child. If kidnapping is the objective, the method may be trickery in effecting release of the child from the custody of a babysitter, child-care center, or school. The target can be the PP's spouse, and the capture may be attempted when he/she is away from the home, such as when shopping, jogging, or socializing.

The best guidance for the protectors and the protected is to anticipate possible scenarios, take preemptive steps, look for the early warning signals, and react quickly.

The organization's security director or retained private investigator evaluates the threat, the weaknesses of the organization to resist the threat, and the range of countermeasures necessary to eliminate the weaknesses.

Kidnap

A program has credibility when it is managed by a professional and anchored in the authority of a clearly stated company policy. The program takes into account specific risks, one of which is kidnap.

A first step in an organization's defense against executive kidnapping is to develop a kidnap policy and an antikidnap plan. Approval of the policy and plan in most cases is made at the Board of Directors level. Consideration is given to kidnap insurance, ransom payments, and a crisis management team (CMT). The policy provides overall direction and authority; the antikidnap plan is the mechanism for carrying out the policy.

Kidnap Insurance

If kidnap insurance is purchased, the carrier will require absolute secrecy with respect to that fact and to any premeditation concerning intent to pay ransom. The carrier may also dictate who is to do the negotiating of ransom payments, require that the organization's response be conducted in accordance with applicable laws of the United States and other nations, and request that prompt and full notification be given to law enforcement. A failure by the organization to meet the carrier's requirements can render the coverage null and void or reduce the carrier's obligations to pay.

Antikidnap Plan

Although the organization's plan for dealing with kidnapping is a highly sensitive matter, it cannot be developed with such great secrecy that it will reflect the thinking of one or a few individuals who may not have all the right answers. An initial planning group consisting of in-house and outside experts can be helpful in touching all the bases. One of the organization's in-house experts will be the security director. A private investigator may very well be one of the outside experts.

Other members of the group can include:

- Agents of the Federal Bureau of Investigation (FBI)
- Counterterrorism experts
- People familiar with the national government of the place where the kidnapped person is held captive
- Kidnap insurance specialist
- Professional hostage negotiator
- Public affairs specialist
- Specialist in receiving, sending, and recording communications
- Human resources specialist

Kidnap Survey

A survey of the PP's home can uncover weaknesses correctible with safeguards such as trimming the shrubs, adding outside lights, and installing an alarm system. In high-risk circumstances, it may become necessary to add watch dogs and security officers.

In the survey, thought is given to the time needed to execute an appropriate response. When an effective or less than timely response is not always certain, protection can be supplemented by creating in the home a concealed room. A concealed room typically features a hidden door that is highly resistive to brute force attack, a panic button, and a telephone. A weapon inside the room is an option.

A survey might call for screening and equipping protective staff. Screening can go beyond routine background checking; equipping can include defensive items such as bullet-resistant vests, firearms, cell phones, and walkie-talkies.

Personal Protection File

An important step is to set up a file on the PP. The file contains details about family members, persons and pets close to him/her, places visited frequently, unique personal characteristics, and proof-of-life information.

People. In the people category are the PP's family, relatives, household help, neighborhood friends, close friends, key working associates, physicians, dentists, and others who play a part in the PP's life.

Places. In the places category are restaurants, lounges, homes of friends and relatives, jogging paths, workout centers, theaters, and other places frequented by the PP.

Unique Characteristics. The unique characteristics category relates exclusively to the PP. It includes descriptions of distinguishing characteristics such as blood type, dental records, eye glasses and contact lenses, hairpiece, prosthetic devices, scars, birth marks, tattoos, and jewelry worn. Also included are hobbies, special interests, and medications. Especially important are handwriting and hand printing samples, fingerprints, and palm prints.

Proof of Life

The proof of life category includes one or a few bits of information that would be known only to the PP. Examples include the name of the PP's first grade teacher, the name of the PP's first dog, or the family nickname of an eccentric aunt. In discussions with kidnappers, proof of life information can be used to verify that the PP is alive.

As much as possible, the PP's file is augmented with photographs, maps, sketches, and the like. In a kidnap situation, information of this type can be extremely helpful in determining where the taking occurred and whether or not the PP is alive.

Training

A private investigator is a good choice for conducting some or all training. A private investigator, more so than a security director and his/her staff, is better skilled at certain protective tasks such as spotting surveillance, conducting surveillance, avoiding road blocks, and serving as a bodyguard.

The PP, his/her immediate family, and protective staff are at the top of the list for training. Below them are house servants and office workers with frequent access to the PP. The training topics address the tactics of kidnappers, the early warning signals of a kidnapping attempt, how to respond, and, if abducted, how to survive.

Avoid Attracting Attention

The PP needs to learn how to avoid attracting attention. Kidnappers are assisted when they possess details of appearance, social activities, local movement, and out-of-town travel. Care has to be taken when talking on the telephone, in restaurants, and in other places where conversations can be overheard. Written information personal to the PP deserves protection and should be shredded when no longer needed.

Avoid Predictable Patterns

Routes to and from work and the vehicles used need to be frequently and randomly changed; the times, dates, and places of out-of-office business meetings should not follow a discernible pattern; and family and social routines should be varied.

Abduction

The value of planning and preparation is immediately evident in the aftermath of abduction. Tasks performed earlier can help in receiving contact from the kidnappers and responding to their demands in a manner that will not place the PP's life at greater risk.

Contact

The kidnappers usually make contact by telephone. In other cases, contact is made by letter or through another party such as a newspaper or radio station. If contact is by telephone, certain protocols are in order:

- Express a willingness to cooperate.
- Ask to speak to the PP.
- Ask for proof-of-life information.

- Record the call.
- If the contact is made in writing, the document and its envelope or outside container are carefully protected in order to not adversely affect forensic analyses such as examinations for fingerprints and saliva on the envelope flap.

Contact by the kidnappers is reported to the FBI immediately. Notifications to law enforcement agencies of other countries that have jurisdiction are also made. An attempt to handle the situation without recourse to government authorities is likely to fail.

By the time the kidnappers have made contact, the crisis management team will have been activated. The CMT leader, to whom considerable decision-making authority has been delegated, is the key person in coordinating major issues with law enforcement and other parties of interest.

The CMT members perform their preplanned tasks, e.g., notifying next of kin, dealing with the news media, setting up a command center, establishing a rumor control function, coordinating with the kidnap insurance carrier, and calling in the professional negotiator.

Ransom

Kidnappers often demand an immediate and large payment but do not expect the demand to be met quickly and entirely. They realize that even if an immediate payment can be effected, it is not likely to be as large as a payment arranged with deliberate speed. Kidnappers focus on "making a big score" and want to believe that the ransom payer has not contacted law enforcement authorities. An expectation of success suppresses their fear of getting caught.

The Reso Case

On April 29, 1992, law enforcement authorities were asked to investigate the disappearance of Exxon executive Sidney J. Reso from his home in Morris Township, New Jersey.

On the morning of that day, Reso's wife discovered her husband's car at the end of the driveway, empty but with the engine running. After calling his office and finding he had not arrived, she called the police.

At first, the Morris County authorities handled it as a missing person case. The next day, however, a caller to the Exxon switchboard claimed to have information about Reso and said that a letter could be found at a nearby shopping mall. Convinced then that a kidnapping had occurred, the Morris County Prosecutor's Office (MCPO) called the FBI.

Within four hours, the Reso home became an FBI command post complete with trap, trace, and recording devices on phone lines. The neighborhood and surrounding wooded areas were thoroughly searched, and 24-hour surveillance and security was set up at the Reso home and at the homes of four children in Texas, Missouri, California, and Washington, DC.

A ransom demand letter was picked up at the mall. The kidnappers instructed that a cell phone be obtained for future calls and that the phone number be published in a classified ad in the Newark Star Ledger. The letter also contained a demand for $18.5 million in hundred-dollar bills.

Exxon provided the ransom money, and the FBI packaged it. A cell phone was obtained, and the waiting for a call began. Specialist teams were gathered and made ready to move on an instant's notice. As they waited, the teams practiced skills that ranged from communication intercepts to sniper firing to SWAT exercises.

The kidnappers made eight calls and sent fourteen letters before attempting to collect the ransom. The attempt occurred on May 3 but went awry when the kidnappers made a mistake in following their own instructions. More calls, letters, and advertisements followed.

On June 16, the kidnappers seemed ready once again to act. They instructed Reso's wife, daughter, and an Exxon executive to deliver the ransom and to take the cell phone with them so they could receive instructions along the way. Two FBI agents posing as Reso's wife and daughter accompanied the Exxon executive. The kidnappers' instructions took them on a rambling journey. Meanwhile, FBI agents in many separate locations watched out of sight. A break came when an agent observed a heavyset white man with blonde hair wearing gloves making a phone call at a shopping mall. The agent also observed this same man remove the gloves when he got into a red Cutlass Ciera, which was traced to a rental car company.

Shortly after that, one of the kidnappers' calls was traced to a pay phone in an area where a surveillance team was in place. The team observed a woman calling from a pay phone, and the time of the call matched the time of one of the kidnappers' calls.

Agents went to the rental car company and waited. Arthur Seale returned the Ciera. His wife Jackie arrived to pick him up. Jackie Seale turned out to be the same woman who had been seen earlier making a call from a pay phone. The Seales were arrested.

Arthur Seale had previously worked as a police officer and a security official at Exxon. He and his wife decided to kidnap and ransom Sidney Reso in order to get out of serious financial difficulty. They began by watching the Reso house and learning Mr. Reso's morning routine. When they felt prepared to act, they went to the house and moved the morning newspaper from one side of the driveway to the other. They knew that he always picked up the newspaper and took it to work with him. To pick up the newspaper where Seale had placed it, Reso would have to get out of his car and walk around the car. When Reso did exactly that, Arthur Seale approached him quickly and at gunpoint forced him into a rental van driven by Jackie Seale. The gun went off, and Reso was shot in the arm. The Seales drove him to a storage facility where, after treating his gunshot wound, they blindfolded him, handcuffed him, gagged him, and placed him in a coffin-like wooden box.

One week after the Seales were arrested, Jackie began cooperating. She said that Reso had died on May 3, just five days after his kidnapping. She and Arthur Seale removed the body from the box at the storage facility and buried it at another location.

The Seales were charged with multiple federal and state offenses. He pled guilty to seven federal counts, including extortion and the use of a weapon in the commission of a crime, and also to a state charge of murder. He was sentenced to 95 years in federal prison to be followed by 70 years' state imprisonment. She was sentenced to 20 years in federal prison for the two counts of extortion.

Event Protection

Kidnapping is but one of several threats confronting a PP. Other threats include assassination, assault, robbery, and nonkidnap threats such as heart attack, sudden illness, or injurious accident. Of these other threats, assassination presents the greatest risk by far.

The PP is most vulnerable when in close proximity to the public. Potential assassins understand this. They know that the protective capability is much reduced and that with little sophistication and a simple weapon the target can be brought down. We know this from experience. In nearly all assassinations of prominent leaders in public places, the assassins were able to get close enough to act, and the weapon was easily obtainable, such as a knife, firearm, or homemade bomb.

PPs are exposed when they appear at a public event. Public events vary, but all of them have one thing in common: the PP is exposed to danger to some degree or other.

Event protection is an activity separate from security provided to the PP in the office, at home, during commuting, and routine out-of-town travel. Routine security requires a lesser number of people; event security can require numerous people, some of whom may be outside contractors such as private investigators.

Team Leader

The person in overall charge of event-related protection can have a number of titles, e.g., mission leader or person-in-charge. We will use "team leader"; for event-related protection activities, we will use "mission."

The team leader will be the organization's security director or a private investigator/ consultant hired to head up a protective mission. The big-picture functions of the team leader are preparing an operational plan and supervising the mission team. The mission team for an event has four groups: advance party, residence party, baggage party, and protective party.

Advance Party

This group travels in advance to the locale of the upcoming mission and:

- Conducts on-site inspections to evaluate probable risks to the PP and proactively sets up countermeasures. Inspections take place at arrival and departure terminals, offices to be visited, conference rooms, restaurants, event venues, and other places on the PP's travel agenda.
- Meets with and initiates working relationships with officials of participating agencies.
- Conducts reconnaissance of local travel routes and makes recommendations to local traffic control officials. Recommendations might include speed, composition, and order of a motorcade.
- Coordinates local ground transportation and arranges for the security of baggage.
- Inspects vehicles to be used for local ground transportation and briefs drivers concerning what to do if a vehicle is involved in an accident or breaks down or if the PP is injured or becomes ill.
- Prepares sketches, maps, photographs, and written reports.

Residence Party and Baggage Party

Residence Party. This group provides around-the-clock protection at the PP's places of stay during travel. Duties can include keeping a log of occurrences, screening incoming telephone calls, checking packages, controlling the access and movements of visitors, and driving the PP from place to place.

Baggage Party. The baggage party provides oversight protection to the PP's baggage. The function begins at the starting point and continues during travel to the visit location. Oversight is discontinued during the time the baggage is in use by the PP. The baggage party resumes oversight at the outset of and during the return trip and concludes when the PP reaches home base. This group does not actually handle baggage but supervises the movement and custody of it.

Protective Party

This group conducts surveillance and provides close-in protection prior to, during, and following the event. The protective party consists entirely of or is complemented by persons from the advance, residence, and baggage parties.

The nuts and bolts of the mission, which are covered in the operational plan, determine the tasks of the protective party. Details of the operational plan are known only by the team leader and members of the protective party. Details can be revealed to outsiders only when knowledge of them is necessary for plan execution. For example, if the team is to be armed, this fact is made known to local law enforcement authorities.

Operational Plan

Information acquired by the advance team is dropped into the planning pot along with information obtained from the PP's staff. Details can include the type and theme of the event, event agenda, names of event speakers, special guests, characteristics of the audience, travel itinerary, persons traveling with the PP, modes of travel to and from the event city, social activities, shopping and sightseeing trips, etc. Also placed into the pot is information about potential threats, especially any threat in the form of a terrorist group. These pot ingredients are a terrorist group's proximity to the event site, its stated intentions, capabilities, resolve, preferred targets, weapons, and tactics. The team leader stirs the pot to see what kind of stew has been cooked.

Based on what has been learned, the team leader begins to put together a plan. The plan will take into consideration:

- The attitude of the PP regarding the protective shield
- Political, religious, and cultural beliefs that pervade or surround the event
- Duration of risk exposure, i.e., the length of time that the PP will be exposed to a potential threat
- Coordination with other agencies, particularly law enforcement
- Ability of the protective force to deflect an attack and react effectively
- Laws that apply such as laws dealing with possession of weapons and the application of deadly force
- Means of communication
- Factors of terrain and geography
- Modes of transportation, both routine and emergency
- Availability of emergency medical treatment
- Selection and training of security personnel
- Dealing with news media

Murphy's Law applies. Even when a plan addresses every possible glitch, the unexpected will happen. It is for this reason that planning has to include a strong flavoring of flexibility.

Overseas Events

The situation changes when the event is to occur overseas. For one thing, the organization sponsoring the event may have to perform administrative tasks normally done by the advance team, such as acquire maps and photographs and identify routes of travel, emergency care facilities, and private security firms. The sponsor can also introduce the advance team to local agencies involved in the event. When the PP's organization has an office near the event site, staff from it can help as well.

Events held overseas present out-of-the-ordinary circumstances, some of which can be problems. Problems decrease the protective capability, which in turn increases risk to the PP. Problems are created when the assisting persons at the overseas site prove to be unreliable. Small details, such as traffic conditions and ground transportation, are certain to be different and therefore problematic. What may work nicely close to home base may not work overseas.

Event Protection Tasks

Event protection is an activity separate from security provided to the PP in the office, at home, during commuting, and routine out-of-town travel. Routine security requires a lesser number of people; event security can require numerous people, some of whom may be outside contractors such as private investigators.

Event protection tasks include:

- Book travel and hotel accommodations in the name of the sponsoring organization. Work through a vetted point of contact (POC). Preferably, the POC will be a senior person in a governmental police or intelligence service.
- Maintain confidentiality of details associated with the PP's travel, accommodations, and attendance. Communicate with the POC and others on a confidential and need-to-know basis.
- Evaluate arrangements made at the location site pertaining to side trips.
- Anticipate potential disruptions, most particularly public demonstrations and actions of unfriendly news media.

- Acquire pertinent maps, sketches, diagrams, photographs, etc. These will depict the layout of the event site, areas surrounding the event site, travel routes to and from the event site, and places where the PP will be stationary. Restrooms are included.
- When the sponsoring organization is company owned or company managed, the POC will be an employee of the sponsoring organization. Make clear to the POC that overall security is the responsibility of the sponsoring organization, subject to approval of the team leader. (Note: bodyguard protection during the event is provided by the team.)
- Confer with and obtain advice of local law enforcement authorities concerning potential security threats, obtain recommendations, and invite participation and use of local resources in carrying out the mission.
- Avoid advance publicity.
- Schedule local ground transportation as tightly as possible. Local ground travel is by a primary vehicle operated or occupied by a team member or a local person vetted, trained in CPR and first aid, and having knowledge of the roadways and emergency medical treatment facilities. The primary vehicle and backup vehicle are equipped with a telephone and cell phone. A primary and an alternate route are selected and tested in advance.
- Confer with security professionals working at hotels to be used. Evaluate security normally provided to PPs at hotels and, where necessary, augment to ensure an adequate level of protection.
- Escort the PP throughout the event and give to him/her a contact telephone number to use in case of an emergency, an unanticipated incident, or a change in schedule.
- Employ local security officers only in exceptional circumstances. Hiring is made through a reputable security company.

- Obtain the services of an antieavesdropping specialist if information security will be an issue at closed meetings of a sensitive nature.

Finally, if the risk is high or local security capabilities are inadequate, advise the PP to cancel or reschedule the event.

In-Depth Defense

This operational concept is used in almost every mission. It consists of one or more layers of protection that an attacker has to penetrate in order to reach the target. For a high-risk mission, the number of layers may be numerous. For example, in a situation where the PP moves through a dense crowd, a tight ring of one to four persons move in unison with him/her, a loose ring of trouble spotters operate 15–25 meters away, and spotters at an elevated location communicate with those down below. In a low-risk situation, the PP may be accompanied by one or two persons and no spotters.

In-depth defense can be likened to an onion. As each layer of the onion is peeled back, another layer is beneath it, and each layer is increasingly difficult to peel.

The whole onion is mobile. As it moves, the PP remains at the center and moves with it. The objective of in-depth defense is to delay an attacker long enough to allow the PP to escape under escort to a safe haven.

After-Action Report

A written report is made for the record at the conclusion of a mission. It is written in narrative style, with emphasis on problems encountered and steps taken to resolve them. The report contains recommendations for improvement of performance in future missions.

Problems described in the after-action report give proof of an irrefutable fact: it is not possible to give absolute personal protection.

The best that can be expected is to reduce the risks as much as possible. Persons assigned to PP protection duties have to understand this basic premise. They also have to know and accept the legal and sociological constraints that are present in every mission.

Buy-In

There can no protective program without the PP's buy-in. A PP may understand risk as a management concept but may not be ready to acknowledge risk in personal terms. PPs have been known to respond with denial, not unlike alcoholics refusing to look at the evidence of addiction. A program will not work until risk is acknowledged.

Buy-in is demonstrated by a commitment to and active involvement in protective arrangements. Involvement has three dimensions: training, interest in the program, and cooperation with the program. The first of the three is problematic. PPs are often busy and do not assign a high priority to training. The security director has to find a way to get past the reluctance. In this case, patience is a virtue; persuasion is a must. Horror stories and cajolery, while not recommended, may help. Fortunately, the key points of training are knowledge-based, i.e., they can be learned without actually getting up from a desk. The exceptions would be firearms and self-defense training. For many companies and many PPs, the use of firearms is not seen as helpful; for some PPs, self-defense is not practical for reasons of age or inclination.

Training of the PP has two learning objectives: know how to keep from being kidnapped or assassinated and how to respond if attacked or taken hostage. As to the first objective, the PP learns to closely control information that an adversary needs to be successful, avoids predictable behavior, and stays within the shell maintained by the protective party at public events. As to response, the PP learns the early warning signals and how to recognize them, actions to take and not take, and, most importantly, how to survive if taken hostage.

Training is a serious and difficult endeavor. It is serious because death or injury can result if the PP makes an incorrect response; it is difficult because the typical PP has little or no familiarity with violence and, without training, is at risk of serious injury or death. Can such things be learned easily? The answer is no. Is this something that has to be learned? The answer is yes.

John J. Fay, *Encyclopedia of Security Management*, second ed., Butterworth-Heinemann, Burlington, MA, 2007, pp. 368–373.

EXPERT WITNESS TESTIMONY

Investigators often testify as "fact witnesses," providing information relevant to civil litigation or a criminal trial. In addition, the professional investigator may also be called upon to testify in another role: as an "expert witness."

As with "fact" testimony, the investigator providing "expert testimony" is *not* an advocate for either side. Advocacy is the role of the attorneys; the role of the investigator is to remain objective and provide honest testimony. There are some important distinctions, however, between expert testimony and fact testimony.

Investigators who testify as expert witnesses will be asked for an *opinion*, not just for a recitation of the evidence collected over the course of an investigation. The investigators are not, however, being paid for that opinion—as a testifying expert, they are compensated for their time in assessing evidence and rendering an objective analysis.

In addition, the content of an expert opinion extends beyond the scope of simple fact testimony. It is likely that the issue about which they are opining may relate to the methods utilized, industry norms, and conclusions drawn by other investigators or some other aspect of a previously conducted investigation. Typical questions to be addressed might include:

- Was the investigation conducted by an appropriately trained and qualified investigator?
- Was the investigation conducted consistent with published (and/or widely accepted) guidelines, standards, or best practices?
- Were the conclusions reached in the investigation supported by the evidence gathered?

Competently addressing these and other questions will require investigative experts to be knowledgeable regarding the relevant investigative issue being considered. Beyond that, however, they should also be prepared to clearly articulate and appropriately support their opinions in a way that is consistent with the relevant court decisions and rules. A testifying investigative expert should be familiar with all relevant, published criteria, but a brief overview follows.

In the United States, several key Supreme Court decisions have influenced the admissibility of scientific expert testimony. For much of the twentieth century, both the Federal Courts and State Courts applied the "Frye test" (*Frye v. United States*, 293 F. 1013 [D.C. Cir. 192]). This is sometimes referenced as the "general acceptance test." In more recent years, the Federal Courts and many of the State Courts have adopted a more rigid standard, often referenced as "Daubert."

This latter standard is actually influenced by a trilogy of Supreme Court decisions:

- *Daubert v. Merrell Dow Pharmaceuticals Inc.*, 509 US 579, 113 S. Ct. 2786 (1993)
- *General Elec. Co. v. Joiner*, 522 US 136, 146 (1997)
- *Kumho Tire Co., Ltd., v. Carmichael*, 526 US 137, 119 S. Ct. 1167 (1999)

In these cases, the Court articulated the "Daubert standard" (guidelines for admitting scientific expert testimony), holding that the 1923 Frye test was superseded by the 1975 Federal Rules of Evidence, specifically Rule 702.

According to Rule 702 (as amended in 2011):

"A witness who is qualified as an expert by knowledge, skill, experience, training, or education may testify in the form of an opinion or otherwise if:

(a) the expert's scientific, technical, or other specialized knowledge will help the trier of fact to understand the evidence or to determine a fact in issue;
(b) the testimony is based on sufficient facts or data;
(c) the testimony is the product of reliable principles and methods; and
(d) the expert has reliably applied the principles and methods to the facts of the case."

Another relevant rule is Rule 26 of the Federal Rules of Civil Procedure (FRCP), which—in part—requires a testifying expert to produce a written report, including:

- Complete statement of all opinions to be expressed and the basis for those opinions
- Facts and data considered by the expert in reaching the opinions
- Exhibits that will summarize or support opinions
- Qualifications of the expert, including a list of publications authored in preceding ten years
- List of all other cases in which the expert has testified (at trial or by deposition) in the preceding four years
- Details regarding the amount of compensation to be paid for the expert's services

Rules governing the expert testimony of an investigator will vary and will be determined largely by both the venue and by decisions of the presiding judge. The retaining client, or another attorney, should be able to provide guidance regarding what criteria will govern testimony in a given case. Though some states have adopted rules similar to Daubert, at the time of this writing there is still variation among different venues. As a result, it is conceivable that an investigator's testimony would be permitted in a "Frye" venue; yet, the exact same testimony would be excluded in a "Daubert" venue.

Regardless of which criteria is applied, the investigator who invests the time and effort into enhancing their professional competency and the scientific accountability of their methodology (e.g., through certifications and continuing education) not only increases the likelihood of successfully clearing the criteria threshold, they also enhance their value in the important role of assisting the trier of fact in rendering an informed decision in a court of law.

John C. Villines, MS, ICPS, CPP

F

FAIR CREDIT REPORTING ACT: ADVERSE ACTION

The Fair Credit Reporting Act regulates the use of information collected and reported by third party agencies when the use pertains to adverse decisions in pre-employment screening, notifications to the job applicant, and other actions incumbent on employers and agents of employers, such as investigators.

Before information can be collected and reported, the job applicant must consent to the inquiry. The findings of the inquiry are included in what is called a consumer report, and the report is provided to the employer. If a consumer report is used as a factor in an adverse hiring decision, the applicant must be presented with a "preadverse action disclosure," a copy of the FCRA summary of rights, and a "notification of adverse action letter." Individuals are entitled to know who collected the information and the source of the information.

A consumer reporting agency (CRA) is a collector and disseminator of information used to evaluate a job applicant's suitability for employment or a loan applicant's trustworthiness. A consumer reporting agency is required to:

- Verify the accuracy of information that has been collected
- Provide a copy to the consumer of collected information about the consumer, upon request of the consumer

Negative information about a consumer must be removed from the CRA files after a period of time set by the FCRA, which for late payments and tax liens is typically seven years from the date of delinquency.

Federal Trade Commission, http://www.ftc.gov/enforcement/rules

FAIR CREDIT REPORTING ACT: CIVIL LIABILITY

Civil Liability for Willful Noncompliance

Any person (or agency, such as a private investigative agency) that willfully fails to comply with any requirement imposed under the Fair Credit Reporting Act with respect to a consumer is liable to that consumer for:

- Any actual damages sustained by the consumer as a result of the failure or damages of not less than $100 and not more than $1,000
- In the case of obtaining a consumer report under false pretenses or knowingly without a permissible purpose, actual damages sustained by the consumer as a result of the failure or $1,000, whichever is greater
- Punitive damages as the court may allow
- Costs of the action together with reasonable attorney's fees as determined by the court

Civil liability for Knowing Noncompliance

Any person or agency that obtains a consumer report from a consumer reporting agency under false pretenses or knowingly without a permissible purpose shall be liable to the consumer reporting agency for:

- Actual damages sustained by the consumer reporting agency or $1,000, whichever is greater
- Attorney's fees

In General

A person or agency that is negligent in failing to comply with any requirement of the FCRA is liable to the consumer for actual damages sustained by the consumer as a result of the failure, plus the costs of the action together with reasonable attorney's fees as determined by the court.

Federal Trade Commission, http://www.ftc.gov/enforcement/rules

FALSE ARREST AND UNLAWFUL DETENTION

False Arrest

False arrest is to take into custody a person without probable cause or without an order issued by a court. The false arrest is often connected to shoplifting, and the persons that make the false arrest are store employees, security personnel, or investigators employed by or under contract to the store.

When an accusation of shoplifting has been dismissed in court, the person arrested is in a good position to sue those who had made the arrest. The usual reason for dismissal of the charge was the absence of probable cause, and without probable cause, the arrest was not legal.

Individual(s) who make or participate in an arrest can become defendants in a civil court. The person who was arrested (the plaintiff) can allege that his or her right of movement was taken away.

Any person may arrest someone suspected of committing a felony as long as the arresting person believes a serious offense had occurred and the person to be arrested committed the crime. A person cannot be arrested on mere suspicion.

Most cases of false arrest involve accusations of shoplifting, and the accusations of shoplifting are made by store employees in the course of their work. A serious mistake is made when the arrest is based on a belief that the arrested person had an intention to shoplift. In such a case, there was no crime and no probable cause. Similarly, there is no probable cause if a shopper has not yet paid for merchandise and is carrying the merchandise inside the store. For there to be a violation of shoplifting, the shopper must attempt to leave, or actually leave, while in possession of store goods for which payment had not been made.

Unlawful Detention

Any form of imprisonment where a person's freedom of movement has been removed meets the definition of detention. Detention, following an arrest based on a reasonable suspicion of shoplifting, becomes unlawful when the arrested person's freedom of movement is withheld beyond a reasonable period of time. What is "reasonable" is a matter for a court to decide. What happens during the period of time can be considered, such as use of force, threat of violence, intimidation (browbeating), search of the person or the person's property, and characteristics of the place of detention.

Learning Shop USA, Laws of Arrest, www.learningshopusa.com

FBI LABORATORY SERVICES

Fingerprints

The FBI's Identification Division contains the largest collection of fingerprint identification data in the world available to law enforcement agencies. Services of the division include furnishing standard forms, such as fingerprint cards, for submitting identification data; searching of fingerprint cards; making name checks to locate identification records; sending fugitive notices to enforcement agencies; making latent print examinations; examining fingers of deceased persons for possible identification; and assisting in the identification of persons killed in major disasters.

Technical Services

The Technical Services Division has capabilities in a wide range of forensic sciences.

Engineering Section

The Engineering Section of the Technical Services Division procures, develops, and deploys many types of technical examinations. This section examines evidence of an electrical or electronic nature, analyzes magnetic recordings, and provides expert testimony.

Authenticity Determination. This analysis is made in cases involving allegations of tape tampering and/or alteration by a defense expert and when the legitimacy of the recording cannot be established through chain of custody and testimony.

Signal Analysis. In this test, various analyses are conducted to identify, compare, and interpret nonvoice sounds on original tape recordings, including telephone dialing, gunshots, and radio transmissions.

Speaker Identification. This test uses the spectrographic (voice-print) technique to compare the recorded voice of an unknown individual to a known recorded voice sample of a suspect. Decisions regarding speaker identification by the spectrographic method are not considered conclusive since there is limited scientific research regarding the reliability of the examination under the varying conditions of recording fidelity, interfering background sounds, sample size, voice disguise, restrictive frequency range, and other

factors commonly encountered in investigative matters.

Sound Recording Comparisons. This is an aural examination to determine if a recovered "bootleg" tape recording contains the same material as a copyrighted commercial tape.

Tape Duplication. This service provides standard format copies of unusual or obsolete tapes or disc recordings.

Tape Enhancement. This is the selective suppression of interfering noise on audio recordings, or the audio track of video recordings, to improve the voice intelligibility. Telephone toll fraud examinations are made to identify:

- "Blue Box" and "Black Box" devices, which receive toll-free long distance telephone calls.
- "Red Box" devices, which allow free pay telephone calls.
- Interception of communications examinations, which includes the identification of:
  - Wiretap devices attached to telephone lines, which monitor, record, or transmit telephone conversations as a radio signal to a remote location.
  - Infinity transmitter devices, which allow a room conversation to be monitored by a remotely activated microphone on a telephone line.
  - Telephones that have been modified to monitor a room conversation when the telephone is not in use.
  - Miniature transmitters, concealed microphones, and recorders designed to surreptitiously intercept oral communications.

Other examinations include identification of devices used to defeat "burglar alarm" systems, FM radio transceivers, scanners and tracking devices, and electronic devices of unknown use or origin believed to have been used in the commission of a crime.

Services in these areas are available to all federal agencies; U.S. attorneys; military tribunals; and state, county, and municipal law enforcement agencies in the United States in connection with official criminal investigative matters only. These services, including the loan of experts if needed as expert witnesses, are rendered free of cost to the contributing agency.

As a general rule, Laboratory Division examinations are not made if the evidence is subjected elsewhere to the same examination for the prosecution. Additionally, in order to more effectively and efficiently utilize its resources, the laboratory will not accept cases from other crime laboratories that have the capability of conducting the requested examination(s).

Because of the nature of the evidence submitted for fingerprint examinations, the previously mentioned Laboratory Division restriction does not apply. Therefore, the Identification Division will examine fingerprint evidence even if it has been or will be subjected to examination by other fingerprint experts.

Blood and Other Body Fluids

Forensic serology involves the identification and characterization of blood and other body fluids on items associated with a crime or crime scene. Evidence from violent crimes, such as murder, rape, robbery, assault, and hit-and-run, usually bear body fluid stains. Blood examinations aid investigations:

- By locating the possible crime scene. Identification of human blood similar in type to that of the victim can assist investigators in identifying the crime scene.
- By discovering a crime. Occasionally, the identification of human blood on a highway, sidewalk, porch, or in a car is the first indication that a crime has occurred.
- By identifying the weapon used. The grouping of human blood found on a club, knife, or hammer can be of considerable probative value.
- By proving or disproving a suspect's alibi. The identification of human blood on an item belonging to a suspect who claims that the blood is of animal origin refutes

an alibi, whereas the identification of animal blood can substantiate the alibi.
- By eliminating suspects. The determination that the human blood on items from the suspect is different in type from that of the victim may exculpate the suspect. Blood similar to that of the suspect can help corroborate a suspect's claim of having a nosebleed or other injury.

Stains. Testing can determine whether visible stains do or do not contain blood. The appearance of blood can vary greatly depending on the age of the stain and the environmental conditions (such as temperature, light, and humidity) to which it was subjected. Chemical and microscopic analyses are necessary to positively identify the presence of blood in a stain and to determine whether blood is of human or nonhuman origin and, if nonhuman, the specific animal family from which it originated.

Blood. Human blood can be classified according to the four groups of the International ABO Blood Grouping System and other blood grouping systems, including red blood cell enzyme and serum protein systems, which are analyzed by electrophoresis. The age of a bloodstain or the race of the person from whom it originated cannot be conclusively determined, and, using conventional serological techniques, it is not possible to identify human blood as having come from a particular person. An investigation can also be aided by the examination of semen, saliva, and urine.

Semen. The identification of semen by chemical and microscopic means on vaginal smears, swabs, or on the victim's clothing may be of value in corroborating the victim's claims. Enzyme typing is possible on semen stains of sufficient size and quality. DNA analysis may allow for positive personal identification of the semen source. If DNA analysis is unsuccessful and the depositor is a secretor, grouping tests may provide information concerning the depositor's ABO blood type.

Saliva. A saliva sample from a known source may be used in conjunction with the liquid blood from the same source to establish the secretor status of the individual. Saliva from a questioned source may provide information as to ABO blood type of the depositor. Known saliva samples should be submitted from both the suspect(s) and victim(s) in sexual assault cases and in cases where a saliva examination may provide probative information (e.g., a cigarette butt found adjacent to a homicide victim's body).

Urine. Urine may be qualitatively identified by chemical testing. Absolute identification of a stain as urine is not possible; however, no routinely reliable forensic techniques are available that provide blood group information from urine.

Secretors. Secretors (which represent approximately 75 percent of the U.S. population) are individuals who have in their nonblood body fluids (e.g., semen, saliva, and vaginal fluid) detectable amounts of substances that are chemically similar to the antigens located on red blood cells, which confer ABO blood type. It is because of this that the ABO blood type of a secretor can often be determined from a nonblood body fluid stain from that individual. Nonsecretors (the remainder of the population) do not exhibit these blood group substances in their nonblood body fluids.

Limitations on Seminal and Saliva Stains. Sometimes semen is mixed with urine or vaginal secretions from the victim. This can make interpretation of grouping tests more difficult inasmuch as the blood group substances from the victim's body fluids could mask the blood group substances in the semen.

To make a meaningful comparison of grouping test results on questioned semen and saliva stains, the investigator will need to obtain known liquid blood and known dried saliva samples from the victim and suspect.

Saliva on cigarette butts are often contaminated with dirt. Saliva on cigar butts cannot be grouped. Ashtrays should not be simply emptied into a container. Rather, individual cigarette butts should be removed from the ash and debris and packaged separately. In view of the difficulties involved in

cigarette-saliva grouping and the circumstantial nature of any successful result, it is often more judicious for the investigator to request latent fingerprint examinations of cigarette butts in lieu of serological examinations.

It is not necessary to submit known semen samples from the suspect in rape cases because the information necessary to make comparative analyses can be gleaned from the suspect's known blood and known saliva samples.

Rape Cases

In light of recent developments in forensic DNA technology, the collection and preservation of serological evidence in a rape case warrants special consideration. The forensic serologist can often provide the investigator with information beyond the fact that "semen is present" on an item if the proper samples are obtained, preserved, and submitted to the laboratory in a timely manner.

Body cavity swabs should be collected from the victim as expeditiously as possible following the assault. Once dried and packaged, these swabs should be frozen until they are submitted to the laboratory.

Toxic Substances

Because of the large number of potentially toxic substances, it is necessary (unless a specific toxic agent is implicated prior to examination) to screen biological samples for classes of poisons. Examples of these classes and the drugs and chemicals that may be found within these classes are as follows:

- Volatile compounds, e.g., ethanol, carbon monoxide, and chloroform
- Heavy metals, e.g., arsenic, mercury, thallium, and lead
- Inorganic ions, e.g., cyanide, azide, chloride, and bromide
- Nonvolatile organic compounds, e.g., most drugs of abuse and other pharmaceuticals as well as pesticides and herbicides

Drug and Pharmaceutical Examinations. The forensic laboratory will determine if materials seized as suspected drugs do in fact contain controlled substances. In addition, the laboratory can examine a wide variety of items, such as boats, aircraft, automobiles, clothing, luggage, and money, for the presence of trace quantities of cocaine, heroin, phencyclidine (PCP), etc. A pharmaceutical examination will identify products for the purpose of matching recovered products with stolen products or for proving that pharmaceuticals were switched.

Arson Examinations. Debris collected at the scene of suspected arson is analyzed using the gas chromatography technique to detect accelerants such as gasoline, kerosene, paint solvent, and other distillate substances.

General Chemical Examinations. Qualitative and quantitative analyses can be made of miscellaneous chemical evidence. Quality analysis is helpful in cases involving theft or contamination of chemical products, malicious destruction, and assault. Analysis of writing inks can match questioned documents with known ink specimens obtained from typewriter ribbons and stamp pads. In consumer product tampering cases, analysis can determine the presence and nature of contaminants, adulterants, and alterations to containers. Chemical examinations can be useful in evaluating tear gas and dyes in bank robber packets, constituents determination in patent fraud cases, and flash and water soluble paper in gambling and spy cases.

Document Examinations

The questioned document field includes examinations of handwriting; hand painting; typewriting; mechanical impressions, such as checkwriter imprints, embossed seals, rubber stamps, and printed matter; photocopies; paper; altered documents; obliterated writing; indented writing; charred documents; and others.

Handwriting and Hand Printing. Writers can be positively and reliably identified with their writings. Other characteristics, such as age, sex, and personality, cannot be determined with certainty from handwriting. A handwriting identification is based upon the characteristics present in normal handwriting. It is not always possible, therefore, to reach a definite conclusion in the examination of handwriting. Some of the reasons for inconclusive results are:

- Limited questioned writing
- Inadequate known samples
- Lack of contemporaneous writing, such as when a long period of time has elapsed between preparation of the questioned writing and the known samples
- Distortion or disguise in either the questioned writing or the known writing; in this situation, the normal handwriting characteristics are not present.
- Lack of sufficient identifying characteristics in spite of ample quantities of both questioned and known writing. Three types of forged writings are commonly examined:

- Traced Forgery. Produced by tracing over a genuine signature, this forgery cannot be identified with the writer. A traced forgery can, however, be associated with the original or master signature from which the forgeries were traced if it is located.
- Simulated Forgery. Produced by attempting to copy a genuine signature, this forgery may or may not be identifiable with the writer, depending on the extent to which normal characteristics remain in the signature. Samples of the victim's genuine signature should also be submitted for examination.
- Freehand Forgery. Produced in the forger's normal handwriting with no attempt to copy another's writing style, this forgery can be identified with the writer.

Typewriting Examinations. Questioned typewriting can be identified with the typewriter that produced it. This identification is based upon individual characteristics that develop on the type face and on other features of the machine during the manufacturing process and through use.

Photocopier Examinations. Photocopies can be identified with the machine producing them provided samples and questioned copies are relatively contemporaneous. Two sets of questioned photocopies can be identified as having been produced on the same machine, and possible brands or manufacturers can be determined by comparison with a reference file maintained at the laboratory.

Mechanical Impression Examination. Questioned printed documents can be compared with genuine printed documents to determine if they are counterfeit. Two or more printed documents can be associated with the same printing, and a printed document can be identified with the source printing paraphernalia such as artwork, negatives, and plates.

A checkwriter impression can be identified with the checkwriter that produced it, and examination of a questioned impression can determine the brand of checkwriter producing it. A rubber stamp impression can be identified with the rubber stamp producing it, and an embosser or seal impression can be identified with the instrument that produced it.

Paper Examinations. Torn edges can be positively matched, the manufacturer can be determined if a watermark is present, and paper can be examined for indented writing impressions. Indentations not visible to the eye can be brought up using appropriate instruments. Some watermarks provide dating information, indicating the date of manufacture of the paper.

Writing Instruments. Chemical analysis can determine if the ink of two or more different writings is the same or different formulation. The same analysis can be conducted with an ink writing and a suspect pen. The examinations do not identify a specific pen, only that the inks are the same formulation.

Ink dating examinations can also show the earliest date a particular ink was produced.

True Age of a Document. The earliest date a document could have been prepared may sometimes be determined by examination of watermarks, indented writing, printing, and typewriting. Chemical analysis of writing ink may determine the earliest date the formulation was available. The laboratory maintains reference files of known standards that can be compared with questioned materials submitted for analysis.

Typewriter Standards. These consist of samples of many styles of both foreign and domestic typewriters; they permit determination of possible brands or manufacturers of typewriters from examination of questioned typewriting.

Watermark Standards. This file is an index of watermarks found in paper; it enables determination of the paper manufacturer.

Safety Paper Standards. These are samples of a variety of safety papers that enable determination of paper manufacturer when used in production of fraudulent documents, such as checks and birth certificates.

Checkwriter Standards. Sample impressions from many checkwriters allow determination of checkwriter brand or manufacturer from examination of questioned impression.

Shoe Print and Tire Tread Standards. A collection of sole and heel designs and tire tread designs helps determine the manufacturer of shoes and tires from prints or impressions left at the crime scene.

Office Copier Standards. A collection of samples from and information about many brands of photocopiers and office duplicating machines assists in determining possible brands and manufacturers of a questioned photocopy.

Explosives Examinations

Explosives examinations are visual and microscopic analyses of bomb remains, commercial explosives, blasting accessories, military explosives, and ordnance items.

Toolmark examinations of bomb components are also possible.

Bomb remains are examined to identify bomb components, such as switches, batteries, blasting caps, tape, wire, and timing mechanisms. Also identified are fabrication techniques, unconsumed explosives, and overall construction of the bomb. Instrumental examination of explosives and explosive residues are carried on in conjunction with bomb component examinations. All bomb components are examined for toolmarks, where possible tools used in constructing the bomb are identified for investigative purposes.

Explosive Reference Files. The laboratory maintains extensive reference files on commercial explosives, blasting accessories, and bomb components. These files contain technical data plus known standards of explosive items and bomb components, including dynamite, water gels, blasting agents, blasting caps, safety fuse, detonating cord, batteries, tape, switches, and radio control systems.

Firearms

Firearms identification is the study by which a bullet, cartridge case, or shotshell casing may be identified as having been fired by a particular weapon to the exclusion of all other weapons. The firearms examiner will provide one of three conclusions:

- That the bullet, cartridge case, or shotshell casing was fired by the weapon
- It was not fired by the weapon
- There are not sufficient microscopic marks to make a positive identification

Bullets. Marks on bullets can be produced by rifling in the barrel of the weapon by a flash suppressor or possibly in loading. When a bullet and/or fragment bearing no microscopic marks of value for identification purposes is encountered, it is often useful to perform a quantitative analysis and compare the results to the similarly analyzed bullets of any recovered suspect ammunition (e.g., cartridges remaining in the suspect firearm, cartridges in suspect's pockets, partial boxes of cartridges in suspect's residence, etc.). When two or more lead samples are determined to be compositionally indistinguishable from one another, a common manufacturer's source of lead is indicated. Lead composition information, in conjunction with other circumstantial information, is often useful in linking a suspect to a shooting. Compositional analysis of shot pellets and rifled slugs can provide similar useful circumstantial information.

Cartridge Cases or Shotshell Casings. Marks on a fired cartridge case or shotshell casing can be produced by breech face, firing pin, chamber, extractor, and ejector with a fired cartridge case. The examiner may be able to determine the specific caliber, type, and, possibly, the make of the weapon that was fired. A fired shotshell casing can reveal gauge and original factory loading. Wadding can indicate gauge and possibly manufacturer. From shot, the examiner can determine size.

Extractor or ejector marks on a fired cartridge or casing that match with a specific weapon mean only that the cartridge or casing had been loaded into and extracted from that specific weapon. To conclude that the cartridge or case was actually fired by the specific weapon, the examiner must rely on a firing pin impression or breech face and chamber marks.

Gunshot Residues. Gunshot residues on clothing may be located, depending on the muzzle-to-garment distance. When a person discharges a firearm, primer residues can be deposited on that person's hands in varying amounts. These amounts are dependent upon the type, caliber, and condition of the firearm and the environmental conditions at the time of the shooting. Residue samples can be collected from a suspect's hands and analyzed for the presence of the chemical elements antimony, barium, and lead, which are components of most primer mixtures. The analytical technique used to analyze these hand samples is dependent upon the type of hand samples collected from the suspect's hands.

Washing the hands and various other activities on the part of the shooter can remove substantial amounts of residue. Therefore, it is imperative to obtain samples as soon after the shooting as possible. Samples obtained more than six hours after a shooting are generally of little value and normally will not be analyzed. Samples obtained from the hands of victims of close-range shootings (within approximately 10 feet) are generally of no value since it is not possible to differentiate between residues deposited on the hands of a shooter and victim of a close-range shooting. Therefore, samples from the hands of victims are not normally accepted for analysis.

Shot Pattern. The distance at which a shotgun was fired can be determined. It is necessary to fire the suspect weapon at various distances using the same type of ammunition involved in the case being investigated.

Hairs and Fibers

Hair and fiber examinations are valuable in person- to-person violence cases, such as rape and murder cases, because they can assist in placing the suspect at the scene of the crime by determining the interchange of hairs or fibers between the victim and suspect. Similarly, these examinations can be helpful in connecting a suspect to surreptitious crimes, such as burglary and auto theft, and in identifying the scene of the crime. Hairs or fibers found on knives, jimmy bars, and the like can identify the weapons or instruments of crime, as well as automobiles involved in hit-and-run cases. Victim and witness testimony can also be corroborated by the discovery of hairs and fibers.

Hairs. Examination of a hair can determine if it is animal or human: if animal, the species from which it originated (dog, cat, deer, etc.), and if human, the race, body area, how removed from the body, damage, and alteration (bleaching or dyeing).

The finding from a hair examination is good circumstantial evidence but not positive evidence. An examination can conclude whether or not a hair could have originated from a particular person based on microscopic characteristics present in the hair. Age cannot be determined, but gender may be determined depending on the condition of the hair's root.

Fibers. Examination of a fiber can identify the type of fiber, such as animal (wool), vegetable (cotton), synthetic (human-made), and mineral (glass). The usual purpose of a fiber examination is to determine whether or not questioned fibers are the same type and/or color and match the microscopic characteristics of fibers in a suspect's garment. Like hairs, fibers are not positive evidence but are good circumstantial evidence.

Fiber examinations can include analyses of fabrics and cordage. A positive identification can be made if a questioned piece of fabric can be fitted to the known material. Composition, construction, color, and diameter of fibers are the points of comparison. Cordage or rope left at the scene of the crime may be compared with similar materials, and in some cases the manufacturer can be identified if the material contains a unique tracer.

The same principles of examination can be applied to botanical specimens, where plant material from a known source is compared with plant material from a questioned locale. Identifications can be made through comparisons of teeth with dental records and X-rays with corresponding bone structures. Examinations may be made to determine if skeletal remains are animal or human. If human, the race, sex, approximate height and stature, and approximate age at death may be determined.

The presence of a suspect at the crime scene can be established from a comparison of wood from the suspect's clothing or vehicle, or possession of wood from the crime scene. The specific wood source can be determined from side or end matching and fracture matching.

Miscellaneous Examinations

Related examinations include button matches, fabric impressions, glove prints, feathers, knots, and identifying the clothing manufacturer through a label search.

Materials Analysis

These examinations entail the use of instrumentation, such as infrared spectroscopy, X-ray diffractrometry, emission spectrometry, and gas chromatography/mass spectrography (GC/MS), for identification or comparison of the chemical compositions of paints, plastics, explosives, cosmetics, tapes, and related materials.

Automobile Paints. It is possible to establish the year and make of an automobile from a paint chip by use of the National Automotive Paint File, which contains paint panels representing paints used on all makes of American cars and many popular imported cars such as Mercedes Benz, Volkswagen, Porsche, Audi, BMW, Renault, Honda, Subaru, Datsun, and Toyota. A very careful search of the accident or crime scene should be made to locate small chips because:

- Paint fragments are often found in the clothing of a hit-and-run victim. Therefore, the victim's clothing should be obtained and submitted to the laboratory whenever possible.
- Paints may be transferred from one car to another, from car to object, or from object to car during an accident or the commission of a crime.

Occasionally it is better to submit an entire component, such as a fender or bumper, if the paint transfer is very minimal.

Nonautomobile Paints. Paint on safes, vaults, windowsills, doorframes, etc. may be transferred to the tools used to open them. Therefore, a comparison can be made between the paint on an object and the paint on a tool.

Cosmetics. Unknown or suspected cosmetics and/or makeup can be compared with a potential source in assault cases, such as rape. The investigator should be alert to the possible transfer of such materials between victim and suspect.

Plastics/Polymers. It is not possible to specifically identify the source, use, or manufacturer of plastic items from composition alone, but comparisons such as the following can be made:

- Trim from automobiles, depending upon the uniqueness of the composition, is compared with plastic remaining on property struck in a hit-and-run case.
- Plastics comprising insulation on wire used in bombings, wiretapping, and other crimes are compared with known or suspected sources of insulated wire.
- Plastic/rubber tapes from crime scenes are compared with suspected possible sources.
- Polymers used in surgical cloth-backed tape are compared with sources.
- Miscellaneous plastic material from crime scenes is compared with possible sources.

Tape. A positive identification can be made with the end of a piece of tape left at the scene of the crime and a roll of suspect tape. If no end match is possible, composition, construction, and color can be compared as in other types of examinations.

Metallurgy

Metals or metallic objects can be examined for comparison purposes and/or information purposes. Determinations to ascertain if two metals or two metallic objects came from the same source or from each other usually require evaluations based on surface characteristics, microstructural characteristics, mechanical properties, and composition.

Surface Characteristics. These are macroscopic and microscopic features exhibited by a metal surface, including fractured areas, accidental marks, or accidentally damaged areas; manufacturing defects; material defects; fabrication marks; and fabrication finish. The fabrication finish reveals part of the mechanical and thermal histories of how the metal was formed, e.g., if it was cast, forged, hot rolled, cold rolled, extruded, drawn, swaged, milled, spun, or pressed.

Microstructural Characteristics. These are the internal structural features of a metal as revealed by optical and electron microscopy. Structural features include the size and shape of grains; the size, shape, and distribution of secondary phases; nonmetallic inclusions; and other heterogeneous conditions. The microstructure is related to the composition of the metal and to the thermal and mechanical treatments that the metal has undergone; it therefore contains information concerning the history of the metal.

Mechanical Properties. These characteristics describe the response of a metal to an applied force or load, e.g., strength, ductility, and hardness.

Composition. This is the chemical element makeup of the metal, including major alloying elements and trace element constituents. Because most commercial metals and alloys are nonhomogeneous materials and may have substantial elemental variation, small metal samples or particles may not be compositionally representative of the bulk metal.

Broken and/or mechanically damaged (deformed) metal pieces or parts can be examined to determine the cause of the failure or damage, i.e., stress exceeding the strength or yield limit of the metal, material defect, manufacturing defect, corrosion cracking, and excessive service usage (fatigue). The magnitude of the force or load that caused the failure can be determined, as well as the possible means by which the force or load was transmitted to the metal and the direction in which it was transmitted.

Burned, heated, or melted metal can be evaluated to determine the temperature to which the metal was exposed, the nature of the heat source that damaged the metal, and

whether the metal was involved in an electrical short-circuit situation.

Rusted or corroded metal can be examined to estimate the length of time the metal has been subjected to the environment that caused the rust or corrosion and the nature of the corrosive environment.

Cut or severed metal can be tested to identify the method by which the metal was severed—sawing, shearing, milling, turning, arc cutting, flame cutting (oxyacetylene torch or "burning bar"), etc.; the length of time to make the cut; and the relative skill of the individual who made the cut.

Metal fragments can be analyzed to reveal the method by which the fragments were formed. If fragments had been formed by high-velocity forces, such as an explosion, it may be possible to determine the magnitude of the detonation velocity. It may also be possible to obtain an identification of the item that was the source of the fragments.

For items unidentified as to use or source, it may be possible to identify the use for which the item was designed, formed, or manufactured, based on the construction and type of metal in the item. The manufacturer and the specific fabricating equipment used to form the item might be revealed, as well as the possible sources of the item if an unusual metal or alloy is involved. Lamp bulbs that are subjected to an impact, such as from vehicles involved in an accident, can be examined to determine whether the lights of a vehicle were incandescent at the time of the accident.

Objects with questioned internal components can be exposed to X-ray radiography to nondestructively reveal the interior construction and the presence or absence of defects, cavities, or foreign material.

Mineralogy

Mineralogy includes materials that are mostly inorganic, crystalline, or mineral in character. Comparisons will, by inference, connect a suspect or object with a crime scene, prove or disprove an alibi, provide investigative leads, or substantiate a theorized chain of events. These materials include glass, building materials, soil, debris, industrial dusts, safe insulation, minerals, abrasives, and gems.

Glass Fractures. Glass, a noncrystalline, rigid material, can be excellent physical evidence. Examination is made of radial cracks and point of penetration. By fitting glass pieces together with microscopic matching of stress lines, the laboratory examiner can positively identify the pieces as originally having been broken from a single pane, bottle, or headlight. If pertinent portions of a bottle, headlight, or taillight can be fitted together, the manufacturer and type may be determined for lead purposes.

When a window breaks, glass particles shower toward the direction of the force 10 feet or more. Particles, therefore, can be found in the hair and on the clothing of the perpetrator. Particles can also become embedded in bullets and/or objects used to break windows. Particles of broken glass from a hit-and-run vehicle are often present on the victim's clothing. Many times, the driver of a hit-and-run vehicle will emerge from the vehicle to determine what was hit or how seriously the victim was injured; consequently, broken glass from the accident may often be found embedded in the driver's shoes.

By microscopic optical and density comparisons, glass particles can be identified or compared with glass from a known source. The laboratory expert cannot identify the source to the exclusion of all other sources; however, it can be stated and demonstrated that it is highly improbable that the particles came from a source other than the matching known source. If two or more different known sources can be matched, the conclusion is greatly enhanced.

Soils, Dust, and Debris. Soil is any finely divided material on the surface of the earth and may contain such human-made material as cinders, shingle, stones, glass particles, paint, and rust. Soil, as a category, includes debris and industrial dusts as well as natural soils.

Soil varies widely from point to point on the surface of the earth and even more with depth. For example, industrial dust specimens or soil near factories are often distinctive, and debris may contain particles characteristic of a specific area. Soil cannot be positively identified as coming from one source to the exclusion of all others, but the laboratory expert can associate questioned soil with a most probable source, conclude that a source cannot be eliminated, or conclude that a point or area could not be the source of the questioned soil. Such conclusions have proven extremely valuable in the proof of criminal cases. Soil specimens will often consist of shoe prints, tire marks, burial sites, or mud taken from an area where a transfer of soil to the suspect is logical.

Safe Insulation and Building Materials. Safe insulation is found between the walls of fire-resistant safes and in vaults and safe cabinets. It is readily transferred to tools and clothing. Samples of insulation collected at the scene can be compared to apparel, shoes, and tools confiscated from the suspect. The same principles apply where unlawful entry through a roof or wall may cause particles to adhere to the suspect or the tools used.

Photographic Examination

Infrared, ultraviolet, and monochromatic photography can be utilized to assist in rendering visible, latent photographic evidence that is not otherwise visible to the unaided human eye. Examples of this type of evidence include alterations and obliteration to documents, invisible laundry marks, and indented writing.

Bank Robbery Film. The laboratory can examine this film to:

- Enhance poor quality photographic exposures and/or prints.
- Compare in detail the unknown subject's clothing as depicted in the film with the clothing obtained from a suspect.
- Determine the individual's height as depicted in the film. Height is determined

preferably from a height chart, but it can also be done mathematically, often to within an inch.

- Compare facial features of the unknown subject in the film with those in a known photograph of a suspect.

Miscellaneous Photographic Examinations. Various other types of photographic examinations can be conducted such as:

- Compare film or prints to determine if they were taken by a specific camera.
- Determine the type and date of Polaroid film, as well as preparing a print from the "throw-away" portion.
- Determine if photographs have been altered. Considerable information can usually be obtained from photographic evidence, using hundreds of various techniques. If photographic materials are in question, they should be forwarded to the laboratory with a clear narrative as to what information or examination is desired.

Reference Files

The laboratory maintains a number of reference files that can be used for comparison purposes in the evaluation of forensic evidence.

National Motor Vehicle Certificate of Title File. Samples of genuine state motor vehicle certificates of title, manufacturer's statement of origin, and vehicle emissions stickers assist in determination of authenticity of questioned certificates. This file contains photographs of fraudulent documents to assist in association of questioned material from different cases with a common source.

National Fraudulent Check File. A computerized file contains images of fraudulent and counterfeit checks, which helps associate fraudulent checks from different cases with a common source and assists in identification of fraudulent check passers.

Anonymous Letter File. A computerized file contains images of kidnapping, extortion,

threatening, and other anonymous communications. This file is matched with questioned documents from different cases with a common source.

Bank Robbery Note File. Images of holdup notes are used to link notes used in various robberies with a common source.

National Stolen Art File. This is a listing of stolen and recovered artwork, mostly paintings, reported by law enforcement agencies. Because artwork does not bear a serial number, entries in the file are based upon a description of the artwork. When available, an image of the artwork is stored, which can be recalled for reference. During a file search, both data and image will appear simultaneously. The minimum value of stolen and recovered artwork for inclusion in the file is $2,000.

National Stolen Coin File. This is a computerized listing of stolen and recovered coins reported by law enforcement agencies. Because coins do not have serial numbers, entries in the file are based upon a description of the coin along with a photograph when available. During a file search, both data and image will appear simultaneously.

Pornographic Materials Files. A collection of evidentiary pornographic materials, printed and video, helps in determining proof of interstate travel of pornographic material and assists in determining production and distribution channels as well as identity of actors.

These consist of materials submitted in connection with investigations of violations of the White Slave Traffic Act, Interstate Transportation of Obscene Materials, and sexual exploitation of children statutes. This computerized file contains over 50,000 records of commercially produced pornographic materials, and the inventory of items is in every medium including video tapes, eight-millimeter movies, books, magazines, and photographs.

These files provide reference materials for laboratory examiners, data searches for investigations (investigative lead information regarding subject, companies, or specific pornographic products), and "charge out" materials for limited courtroom use and undercover operations.

Shoe Print and Tire Tread Evidence

Shoe print and tire tread evidence found at the scene of a crime can provide important evidence for investigation and eventual prosecution of a case. For three-dimensional impressions, casts should always be made immediately following appropriate photography of the impressions. For two-dimensional impressions, the original impression is most valuable and should be retained and preserved whenever possible and practical, such as when the impression is on glass, paper, or some other retrievable surface.

Shoe and tire reference materials are maintained in the laboratory to assist in the determination of the make or manufacturer of a shoe or tire that made a particular impression. This is useful in some cases to help locate suspects or suspects' vehicles.

When known shoes or tires are obtained, comparisons are made between those items and the questioned shoe prints or tire impressions. Comparisons can be made between the physical size, design, manufacturing characteristics, wear characteristics, and random accidental characteristics. If sufficient random characteristics are present, a positive identification can be made.

Toolmark Identification

Using a microscope, the tool mark examiner seeks to determine if a certain tool mark was made by a certain tool. From the examination, a conclusion can be made that:

- The tool produced the tool mark.
- The tool did not produce the tool mark.
- There are not sufficient individual characteristics remaining to determine if the tool did or did not produce the questioned mark.

Several comparisons can be made between a tool and a tool mark. Examination can be made of the tool for foreign deposits, such as paint or metal, for comparison with a marked object, establishment of the presence or nonpresence of consistent class characteristics, and microscopic comparison of a marked object with several test marks or cuts made with the tool. Examination of the tool mark can determine the type of tool used (class characteristics); the size of tool used (class characteristics); unusual features of the tool (class or individual characteristics); the action employed by the tool in its normal operation and/or in its present condition; and, most importantly, if the tool mark is of value for identification purposes.

Fracture Matches. Fracture examinations are conducted to ascertain if a piece of material from an item, such as a metal bolt, plastic automobile trim, knife, screwdriver, wood gunstock, or rubber hose, was or was not broken from a like-damaged item available for comparison. This type of examination may be requested along with a metallurgy examination if questioned items are metallic in composition.

Marks in Wood. This examination is conducted to ascertain whether or not the marks in a wood specimen can be associated with the tool used to cut it, such as pruning shears and auger bits. This examination may be requested along with a wood examination.

Pressure/Contact. Pressure or contact examinations are conducted to ascertain whether or not any two objects were or were not in contact with each other, either momentarily or for a more extended time.

Plastic Replica Casts of Stamped Impressions. Plastic replica casts of stamped numbers in metal, such as altered vehicle identification numbers, can be examined and compared with others, as well as with suspect dies.

Locks and Keys. Lock and key examinations can be conducted to associate locks and keys with each other. Such associations are useful in establishing a conspiracy or link of commonality between or among individuals. It is often possible to illustrate this through their possession of keys that will operate a single lockage instrumentality (e.g., vehicle, safe house, or padlock). Laboratory examination of a lock can determine whether an attempt has been made to open it without the operating key.

Restoration of Obliterated Markings. Obliterated identification markings are often restorable, including markings obliterated by melting of the metal as evidenced by welding marks or "puddling."

Obliterated markings can also be restored on materials other than metal, such as wood, plastics, and fiberglass. Because different metals and alloys often require specific methods for restoration of obliterated markings, the laboratory should be contacted for number restoration procedures for field processing of items too large or heavy for submission.

Conclusion

FBI experts will furnish testimony regarding evidence they have examined. In the interest of economy, however, their testimony should not be requested if it is to be duplicated by another prosecution expert. It is realized that exceptions to this general policy may be required in a given instance.

FBI Laboratory Services, Federal Bureau of Investigation, http://www.fbi.gov/about-us/lab

FEDERAL BUREAU OF INVESTIGATION (FBI)

In the immediate aftermath of 9/11, the FBI's mission changed to meet the threat of terrorism. The change called for a reengineering of structure and operations to closely focus on prevention of terrorist attacks, on countering foreign intelligence operations against the U.S., and on addressing cybercrime-based attacks and other high-technology crimes. However, the FBI continues to maintain its mandate to protect civil rights and combat public corruption, organized crime, white-collar crime, and major acts of violent crime.

Priorities

As both a national security and law enforcement organization, the FBI gathers and uses intelligence to meet its major priorities.

- Terrorism
  - International terrorism
  - Domestic terrorism
  - Weapons of mass destruction
- Counterintelligence
  - Counterespionage
  - Economic espionage
- Cyber crime
  - Computer intrusions
  - Internet fraud
  - Identity theft
- Public corruption
  - Government fraud
  - Election fraud
  - Foreign corrupt practices
- Civil rights
  - Hate crime
  - Human trafficking
  - Color of law
  - Freedom of access to clinics
- Organized crime
  - Italian Mafia/LCN
  - Eurasian
  - Balkan
  - Middle Eastern
  - Asian
  - African
  - Sports bribery
- White-collar crime
  - Antitrust
  - Bankruptcy fraud
  - Corporate fraud
  - Financial institution fraud and failures
  - Health care fraud
  - Insurance fraud

- Mass marketing fraud
- Money laundering
- Mortgage fraud
- Piracy/intellectual property Theft
- Securities and commodities fraud

- Violent crime and major thefts

    - Art theft
    - Bank robbery
    - Cargo theft
    - Gangs
    - Indian country crime
    - Jewelry and gem theft
    - Online predators
    - Retail theft
    - Vehicle theft
    - Violent crimes against children

Federal Bureau of Investigation, http://www.fbi.gov/

FEDERAL EMERGENCY MANAGEMENT AGENCY (FEMA)

The Federal Emergency Management Agency (FEMA) is an agency of the United States Department of Homeland Security. The agency's primary purpose is to coordinate the response to a disaster that has occurred in the United States and that overwhelms the resources of local and state authorities. The governor of the state in which the disaster occurs must declare a state of emergency and formally request from the president that FEMA and the federal government respond to the disaster. FEMA also provides these services for territories of the United States, such as Puerto Rico. The only exception to the state's gubernatorial declaration requirement occurs when an emergency and/or disaster takes place on federal property or to a federal asset, for example, the 1995 bombing of the Alfred P. Murrah Federal Building in Oklahoma City, Oklahoma, or the Space Shuttle Columbia in the 2003 return-flight disaster.

While on-the-ground support of disaster recovery efforts is a major part of FEMA's charter, the agency provides state and local governments with experts in specialized fields and funding for rebuilding efforts and relief funds for infrastructure by directing individuals to access low-interest loans, in conjunction with the Small Business Administration. In addition to this, FEMA provides funds for training of response personnel throughout the United States and its territories as part of the agency's preparedness effort.

Following the September 11, 2001, attacks, Congress passed the Homeland Security Act of 2002, which created the Department of Homeland Security (DHS). FEMA was absorbed into DHS effective March 1, 2003. As a result, FEMA became part of the Emergency Preparedness and Response Directorate of Department of Homeland Security but remained in DHS.

U.S. Department of Homeland Security, Federal Emergency Management Agency, http://www.fema.gov/

FEDERAL OFFENSES

There can be no federal crime unless Congress first makes an act a criminal offense by the passage of a statute, affixes punishment to it, and declares what court will have jurisdiction. This means that all federal crimes are statutory. Although many of the statutes are based on common law, every federal statute is an express enactment of Congress. Nearly all crimes are defined in Title 18 of the U.S. Code.

Generally speaking, federal crimes fall into three large areas: crimes affecting interstate commerce, crimes committed in places beyond the jurisdiction of any state, and crimes that interfere with the activities of the federal government.

Crimes affecting interstate commerce are described in a variety of acts, e.g., the Mann Act, the Dyer Act, the Lindbergh Act, the Fugitive Felon Act, etc. They cover a wide variety of offenses over which Congress has plenary control.

Crimes committed in places beyond the jurisdiction of any state might include, for example, murder on an American ship on the high seas or on a federal enclave such as a military reservation ceded to the United States by a state. It should be noted that when an offense, not covered by a federal statute, is committed on a federal enclave, the case can be tried in a federal court under the laws of the state where the enclave is located. The offense of murder, for example, is not defined in a federal statute. If murder occurs on a military reservation in Texas, the federal government can prosecute the case using the Texas statute covering murder. This procedure is authorized by the Assimilative Crimes Act.

Crimes that interfere with the activities of the federal government include fraudulent use of the mails, robbery of a federal bank, violations of income tax laws, espionage, and many similar offenses. Federal courts have no jurisdiction over crimes against the states, and vice versa. It can happen, however, that an offense will violate both a state law and a federal law, e.g., robbery of a federally insured state bank. In such a case, both the federal and state court will have jurisdiction. Federal death penalty laws include these violations:

- Espionage by a member of the Armed Forces in which information relating to nuclear weaponry, military spacecraft or satellites, early warning systems, war plans, communications intelligence or cryptographic information, or any other major weapons or defense strategy is communicated to a foreign government
- Death resulting from aircraft hijacking
- Murder while a member of the Armed Forces
- Destruction of aircraft, motor vehicles, or related facilities resulting in death
- Retaliatory murder of a member of the immediate family of a law enforcement official
- Murder of a member of Congress, an important executive official, or a Supreme Court justice
- Espionage

- Destruction of government property resulting in death
- First degree murder
- Mailing of injurious articles with the intent to kill or resulting in death
- Assassination or kidnapping resulting in the death of the president or vice president
- Willful wrecking of a train resulting in death
- Murder or kidnapping related to robbery of a bank
- Treason

John J. Fay, *Encyclopedia of Security Management*, second ed., Butterworth-Heinemann, Burlington, MA, 2007, pp. 222–223.

FELONIES AND MISDEMEANORS

Felonies and misdemeanors are titled and defined by category in different ways from jurisdiction to jurisdiction. Examples of titles in the felony category are Class A Felony, or Felony 1 or Felony in the First Degree. In the misdemeanor category, the titles would be Class A Misdemeanor or Misdemeanor 1, and so forth. The titles can be misleading because a Class B Felony in one jurisdiction may be equivalent to a Class C Felony in another jurisdiction.

Also, the crimes in categories can be defined differently than crimes in another jurisdiction. For example, a felony that is named Murder One could be named Premeditated Murder in a different jurisdiction.

But generally speaking, it is understood that a felony is more serious than a misdemeanor; for that reason, a felony is punished more harshly than a misdemeanor. Punishment for the commission of a felony is imprisonment for one year or more. Punishment for the commission of a misdemeanor is imprisonment for less than one year.

Within a title are elements of proof. To prove a crime, the investigator must obtain evidence of the existence of certain facts. These facts are called elements of proof. For example, the felony crime of arson (which might be titled First Degree Arson) has three elements:

- Damage by fire or explosion
- The intentional act or destruction by the defendant knowing that it will damage a protected structure
- Lack of the owner's consent

The elements of proof are further defined. For example, as shown above, the term "protected structures" can be:

- Dwelling houses
- Buildings, vehicles, railroad cars, watercraft, or other structures designed for use as dwellings
- Any structure that is insured against loss or damage by fire or explosive
- Any structure that is damaged with the intent to defeat, prejudice, or defraud the rights of the owner

Seriousness is also a factor. Again, in the case of arson, the most serious form could be called First Degree Arson. Spelled out, a First Degree Arson could relate to damage of a structure under such circumstances in which danger to human life is reasonably foreseeable.

Second Degree Arson would be less serious. It would be limited to structures not designed as dwellings and the damage done without intent to defeat, prejudice, or defraud the rights of the owner.

A person conducting an investigation of arson, or of any crime, must be familiar with categories, titles, and elements of proof.

Learning Shop USA, Felonies and Misdemeanors, www.learningshopusa.com

FIFTH AMENDMENT

The Fifth Amendment protects individuals from being forced to incriminate themselves. Self-incrimination means exposing oneself to an accusation or charge of crime in a criminal prosecution. The Constitutional privilege against compelled self-incrimination is the right of a person to refuse to answer questions or otherwise give testimony against himself or herself.

To "plead the Fifth" is to refuse to answer a question because the implications of the question, in the setting in which it is asked, might be dangerous to the person questioned because the answer could place the questioned person in jeopardy of being charged with a crime.

The Supreme Court has held that "a witness may have a reasonable fear of prosecution and yet be innocent of any wrongdoing. The privilege serves to protect the innocent who otherwise might be ensnared by ambiguous circumstances."

Historically, the English common law protection against self-incrimination was directly related to the question of torture for extracting information and confessions.

Protection against self-incrimination is implicit in the Miranda rights warning, which informs a person of the right to remain silent. The warning varies among jurisdictions. The common version is: "You have the right to remain silent. Anything you say can and will be used against you in a court of law. You have the right to an attorney. If you cannot afford an attorney, one will be provided for you. Do you understand the rights I have just read to you?"

John J. Fay, *Encyclopedia of Security Management*, second ed., Butterworth-Heinemann, Burlington, MA, 2007, pp. 206–207.

FINGERPRINT IDENTIFICATION

Each finger and thumb is unique to an individual, and no two prints have ever been found to be exactly the same from two different people. Also, palm and footprints are unique to each individual and, barring scar-causing injury, will remain the same from birth until well after death.

There are approximately 75 to 200 characteristics on a finger or thumb. The forensic analyst uses a variety of techniques such as carbon powder dusting, superglue and ninhydrin spray techniques, Amido black print visualization, and argon laser analysis to identify and match prints.

Fingerprint Comparison

Fingerprints of unidentified persons may be compared with the fingerprints of known persons or to fingerprints on file. The Federal Bureau of Investigation maintains a fingerprint file on more than 90 million people, which is in addition to fingerprint files maintained by most state law enforcement agencies.

The analysis of fingerprints in a forensic lab is dual purpose: first, to develop the prints to a condition that allows them to be seen; and second, to match the prints with another person such as a suspect, a missing person, or a victim.

Automated Fingerprint Identification System (AFIS)

The most important innovation in fingerprint identification is the Automated Fingerprint Identification System (AFIS). AFIS is a computerized system that stores the fingerprint characteristics of millions of individuals. AFIS makes systematic computer searches of unknown fingerprints by optically scanning a print and comparing it with those on file.

Prior to AFIS, fingerprint searches had to be done manually, making it an impractical, time-consuming process to compare an unknown print to the millions of known prints on file.

Latent and Inked Prints

Latent Print. A latent print is an impression left on a surface that has come into contact with the friction ridge skin located on fingers and palms of the hand and toes and soles of the feet.

The latent print is usually "hidden" or not visible to the human eye. Therefore, latent prints have to be processed by some means to render them visible. A latent print is composed mainly of sweat and foreign material that may be on the skin surface at the time the print is deposited on a surface.

Inked Prints. An inked print is a purposely made recording of the friction ridge skin. This is usually accomplished by placing the fingers and thumb, one at a time, plus all five digits together on a glass platen of a desktop device that looks like a printer/copier. An older method is to roll the five digits from one side of the fingernail to the other on an inked slate and then transfer the ink from the finger in the same manner onto a contrasting colored surface such as a fingerprint card or white sheet of paper. In either method, a permanent record is made of the individualizing details.

FBI Laboratory Services, Federal Bureau of Investigation, http://www.fbi.gov/about-us/lab

FINGERPRINTS: COLLECTING LATENT PRINTS

Friction ridges on the underside of fingers, hands, toes, and soles of the feet form unique patterns that may be found on surfaces of objects touched by a person of interest in a crime investigation. These unique patterns are almost always invisible to the naked eye; for that reason, they are called latent (hidden) prints. Latent prints are made visible by two methods. The first method is to very lightly dust the print. The dust adheres to skin secretions (amino acid). The dusting powder color contrasts with the color of the surface upon which the print rests. Dusting may be done with a brush, lightly applied, that makes the print visible. The next step is to photograph the print.

The second method is to use an aerosol can to very lightly spray the latent print with a chemical, such as ninhydrin, which turns skin secretions purple and therefore makes them visible.

A print collection method that has been reported to be successful in lifting prints from a skin surface uses cyanoacrylate (superglue). The opportunities for use of this method are limited.

After a print is made visible and photographed, it is lifted onto a latent print lift card. A lift card, which comes in a variety of shapes and sizes, consists of a clear plastic tape (think Scotch tape). The tape is adhered to a moderately flexible card. The clear plastic is removed from the card, it is carefully placed on top of the print. The print is then lifted by the clear plastic from the surface it is upon, and the clear plastic is placed on the card. The color of the card will provide a contrasting background to the color of the dust that was used to make the print visible. For example, a print that has been dusted with white powder is placed on a black card. With ninhydrin, which produces a purple color, a good color choice of the card might be white.

Latent print lift cards are transferred (using chain of custody) to a forensic laboratory where they are examined and compared to prints that are on file in a fingerprint identification database. The Automated Fingerprint Identification System (AFIS) is a national database. Many states have separate databases but also send prints to AFIS. A "hit" on a database means that the prints collected at the scene perfectly or closely match fingerprints of a person or persons who may be connected to the crime.

FBI Laboratory Services, Federal Bureau of Investigation, http://www.fbi.gov/about-us/lab

FIREARMS EXAMINATIONS

A firearms examiner studies expended cartridge cases and bullets to determine if they can be linked to a specific firearm. This examination also allows a determination to be made of the type of weapon used. Other examinations can include function and accuracy tests, trigger pull measurement, and measurement of muzzle-to-target distance.

The National Integrated Ballistics Information Network (NIBIN) is a computer-assisted program used to link multiple crimes in multiple jurisdictions. The Bureau of Alcohol, Tax and Firearms (ATF) maintains NIBIN. The core of NIBIN is a vast collection of firearms-related information submitted by federal, state, county and municipal law enforcement agencies.

A fire section examiner relies on two types of characteristics when performing comparisons: class and individual characteristics.

- Class characteristics are common to a group of firearms. They comprise caliber, number of lands and grooves, direction of their twist, and their widths.
- Individual characteristics are the markings that actually allow an examiner to say that a projectile or cartridge case relates to a specific firearm to the exclusion of all other firearms.

Comparisons are conducted using a specialized light microscope that allows the examiner to view both the evidence sample and the test sample at the same time. Comparisons are made of striations imparted to a projectile by lands and grooves on the inner part of the gun barrel, plus firing pin marks and extraction marks on the cartridge. It is also possible to match an expended cartridge, such as one found at a crime scene, with an unexpended cartridge found in the possession of a suspect. Water tanks and bullet traps are typically used for recovering test-fired projectiles.

Several examinations can be performed on evidence involving a shotgun. The hull of the shotgun shell can be matched against the shotgun that fired it. The pellets and wadding can be compared to the expended hull to determine if they are consistent with the type hull submitted, i.e., gauge, shot size, and manufacturer. The firearms examiner will routinely examine an unfired shotshell to determine if it was loaded into and extracted from a weapon based on the presence or absence of extractor marks. The distance at which a shotgun was fired can be determined by test firing the suspect weapon at various distances, using the same type of ammunition that is involved in the case.

FBI Laboratory Services, Federal Bureau of Investigation, http://www.fbi.gov/about-us/lab

FORENSIC PHOTOGRAPHY: A RESOURCE FOR INVESTIGATORS

A vast majority of criminal trials involve the use of photographic evidence. It is the job of both the prosecution and the defense to present evidence in a way that allows the judge and jury to "revisit" the scene. Forensic photography is one of those ways.

Crime scene photographs are often taken by individuals who lack experience and training. Photographs that are dark, blurry, obscure, or faulty in some respect can be the result of little experience and incomplete knowledge on the part of the photographer. Photography is a basic and essential tool for reenacting an event; when that tool is improperly used, the viewer may be unable to understand what actually happened.

A common error in digital photography is to cause a photograph to lose its exactness by overcompression. Compression—even when it is within the boundaries of standard operating procedures—will alter the original image to some degree. An opportunity for challenge is created when compression is not done properly.

Certain types of evidence, such as blood spatters and shoe prints, need to be photographed in the best way possible. When a photograph lacks professional quality, an accurate interpretation is more difficult to be made of the scene or the object depicted in the photograph. A common sense solution is to employ a certified evidence photographer (CEP) to take the photographs, prepare them for presentation, and testify to their accuracy at trial. When a CEP is retained, the CEP's usual practice is to provide a no-cost consultation.

Procedural Questions

Were standard operating procedures followed? SOPs, such as procedures that relate to camera date and time, are critical to producing quality photographs.

Were scales or markers placed correctly to ensure accurate measurements? A set of photographs should be taken before scales or markers are placed and a second set of photographs be taken after placement. Both sets should be taken in exactly the same way. Unfortunately, many investigators skip this step.

Did the photographer use camera equipment designed for infrared or ultraviolet lighting when warranted? These types of lighting can expose evidence that would be invisible to the naked eye. They are also valuable when taking photographs of fingerprints, bruises, tattoos—and, in some cases, an old tattoo under a new tattoo.

What lenses were used? For example, a wide-angle lens may be appropriate for photos taken from a distance, but photographs taken up close can be distorted.

Did the situation call for digital photography? The sheer volume of information stored in a photo's digital file is staggering, yet many individuals do not understand how to access or interpret the information. A CEP can be retained to evaluate the metadata when digital photography file information is overlooked or improperly interpreted.

Did the situation call for High Dynamic Range Photography (HDR)? This technique involves the use of several photo files, taken in succession, with a spectrum of exposures. The information in each image's file can be blended to create a single image that most closely represents reality.

Conclusion

An experienced and well-trained forensic photographer can serve as the eyes for persons who make judgments about the matter investigated. A CEP is expert in the many aspects of photography, from dissecting digital image files to capturing images of skid marks, fingerprints, tread marks, blood spatter, and other forms of hard-to-evaluate evidence.

Keith Rosenthal, CEP

FORENSIC TESTING

The term "forensic" relates to issues of law or the operation of courts and the judiciary. Persons performing forensic tests are trained professionals, the tests are based on scientific principles, test methodologies and equipment are typically state-of-the-art, and the tests are conducted in a laboratory that operates in accordance with standards acceptable to the scientific community and the court system.

The ability of a forensic laboratory to glean every bit of probative value from physical evidence depends in no small part upon the investigator's ability to identify, collect, and preserve the evidence in a manner that facilitates a full scientific examination.

Among all forms of evidence, physical evidence ranks highest in importance to the successful conclusion of an investigation. Physical evidence that has been examined scientifically and concluded to be corroborative is extremely valuable in determining guilt or innocence.

Forensic evidence helps in the solution of a case because it can establish modus operandi, identify suspects, prove or disprove an alibi, connect or eliminate suspects, and provide investigative leads.

Probative Value

Probative means to test for the purpose of proving. The term is also expressed as "substantiating," or establishing by proof of competent evidence. Value is the advantage derived from the test. When a private investigator collects items and materials that have a potential for becoming evidence and submits them to a forensic laboratory, he or she is attempting to establish probative value.

A crime lab examiner is an investigator. He or she applies a skill or knowledge to the analysis of physical evidence. Through the application of scientific principles and equipment, the examiner attempts to glean from the physical evidence every bit of probative value possible.

In a very meaningful sense, the private investigator and the crime lab examiner are partners in a search for truth.

A third party is involved in determining probative value. That party is the legal system. Laws and rules permit or prohibit the admissibility of evidence, and trial courts are required to rule within the framework of laws and rules. A good example is the Exclusionary Rule. Evidence that is collected illegally can be excluded from presentation in court, thus cancelling the probative value of the evidence.

Laboratory Operations

A forensic lab makes determinations as to the properties and composition of samples of materials submitted. Two general types of analyses are conducted: qualitative analysis, which establishes what the sample is, and quantitative analysis, which measures how much.

A sample of a single compound may be analyzed to establish its elemental composition or molecular structure and also its weight or volume. For example, a submitted sample might be a liquid, the properties of which are unknown to the private investigator but are believed to be a poison. A specialist skilled in that area of forensic examination would analyze the sample according its morphological appearance and its molecular structure and arrive at a conclusion as to what the sample really is. The examiner would also determine the quantity of the substance. So in this example, the examination was both qualitative and quantitative.

A sample consisting of more than one element is called a mixed sample. A mixed sample is usually analyzed by separating, detecting, and identifying its components by methods that depend on differences in their properties. Such differences can include volatility, mobility in an electric or gravitational field, and distribution between liquids that do not mix. Also increasingly used are the several types of chromatography, especially with biological and biochemical samples.

A sample that is an object, such as a crowbar or bullet, is not examined in respect to what it is made of but how it was used. In the case of a crowbar, the examiner's objective, as stipulated by the private investigator, is to determine if the size and markings on the crowbar match markings on a jimmied door. In the case of a bullet, the examiner's task is to match the bullet with a particular firearm. In both of these examples, the examination is a visible examination using instrumentation that permits the examiner to see the distinguishing characteristics of the sample and match them against another sample, such as the wood on the jimmied door or the lands and grooves in the barrel of the firearm.

Types of Analyses

The forensic scientist faces uniquely challenging analytical problems. Evidence submitted comes in a wide variety of types, forms, and conditions, thus making standard analytical procedures sometimes difficult to implement.

When a sample is a compound (meaning it is made of different "ingredients"), a different type of analysis might have to be used for each of the ingredients. When such is the case, the forensic specialist will need a sufficient amount of the sample because it is likely to be partially or fully consumed by each analysis. Also, a sample might be altered as a result of the analysis, which makes duplication of a test impossible.

The private investigator that collected the sample should obtain all of what can be obtained or, when the source of the sample is large, obtain enough of it to allow multiple analyses if needed.

Chromatographic Analysis

This method of analysis examines and separates the varying properties of a substance in

a moving stream of gas or liquid. Chromatographic analysis can be done through various methodologies, depending on the substance to be analyzed.

The various methodologies include paper chromatography (PC), thin-layer chromatography (TLC), liquid chromatography (LC), high-performance liquid chromatography (HPLC), gas chromatography (GC), and gas chromatography/mass spectrometry (GC/MS).

The components separated from a substance by chromatography often require further analysis such as by colorimetry, spectrophotometry, mass spectrometry, and measurement of fluorescence. Gas chromatography/mass spectrometry is often used to quantify the concentration of a drug in a urine specimen.

Spectrochemical Analysis

This is a method of chemical analysis complemented with the measurement of the wavelength and intensity of electromagnetic radiation. In more common usage, it usually refers to ultraviolet (UV) and visible emission spectroscopy or to UV, visible, and infrared (IR) absorption spectrophotometry.

Serological Analysis

A major part of a crime lab's work is involved in identifying biological fluids such as blood, semen, tissue, saliva, and sometimes hair samples. Identification includes determining origin: human, deer, dog, cat, and bovine and grouping human blood in the ABO system.

Other forms of analysis can determine the number of red and white blood cells (erythrocytes and leukocytes); red cell volume, sedimentation (settling) rate, and hemoglobin concentration; cell shape and structure; hemoglobin and other protein structure; enzyme activity; and chemistry.

A blood sample is often found as a stain on an object such as a knife, shirt, or bedsheet. The entire object should be collected if it is practical to do so. If not, such as in the case of blood on an immovable object, a piece of the object should be obtained again, if possible. The objective is to allow the forensic specialist to separate the blood from the object. When this is not possible, moisten a cotton swab with one or two drops of distilled water and mop the stain onto the swab. The idea is to get as much of the stain as possible onto the swab so that the stained swab is very concentrated, that is, dark red/brown in appearance.

Another precaution is not to send to the forensic laboratory a blood-stained item while it is wet. Allow the stain to dry at room temperature away from a heating source before it is properly packaged and sent or hand-delivered to the lab.

DNA Analysis

A complete copy of an individual's DNA is found in every nucleated cell in the body. Body surfaces that are normally wet (e.g., surfaces inside the mouth, nose, eyes, and urogenital tract) are lined with epithelial cells that continuously slough off. These cells are easily transferred to objects with which they come into contact; as a result, they can be a good source of material for DNA testing. These sources can include envelopes, stamps, cigarette butts, and chewing gum. Materials very suitable for DNA testing are blood and semen stains, hairs, bone, and teeth. (See DNA Profiling.)

Reference Samples Used in Forensic Testing

Arson Debris. If there is residue at the site of a suspected arson, such as wood that appears to have been soaked with an accelerant such as gasoline, a sample of that residue is collected by the investigator. At a separate location where accelerant residue is not detected, the investigator takes another sample. This second sample is called a reference sample. The sample containing the suspected accelerant is compared against the reference sample. Many such samples are collected to assist the lab technician make a definitive conclusion. (See Arson Investigation.)

Blood. The same approach applies to blood. Assume that blood is found on a bedsheet. The origin of this blood cannot be determined without a reference sample. In this case, a reference sample would be taken from the blood of a suspect. Both are compared to determine if they match. DNA testing is the gold standard for this type of examination.

With recently deceased persons, biological samples are obtained incidental to autopsy. Such samples can be blood, teeth, bones, and tissue. If a blood sample can't be collected, such as would be the case of a badly decomposed or burned person, a tooth can be collected, preferably an unrestored molar. This should be collected only after the teeth have been charted for identification purposes. If teeth are not available, then a segment of rib bone or a segment of the femur can be collected. This segment should be at least one to two inches in length.

Tissue, including partial or complete organs, is collected by a pathologist during an autopsy. These samples are valuable in determining the cause or manner of death, as opposed to identification of the deceased.

Toxicology

Toxicology is the study of poisons and their effects, particularly on living systems. This field of study overlaps with biochemistry, histology, pharmacology, pathology, and other fields.

Forensic toxicologists mostly examine evidence taken in matters involving alcohol and drug ingestion and poisoning. The examinations are often of biological samples, and the objective of the toxicologist is to identify what is in the sample, such as ethyl alcohol, drugs, and other toxins, and determine at what concentration they are present.

Samples are initially tested using an assay. A common assay is the Enzymatic Multiple Immunoassay Test (EMIT). When a sample tests positive for a specific analyte, the sample is retested using specialized instrumentation and procedures such as automated gas chromatography.

When the test is intended to discover if an individual had been using a drug or if the individual's body system contained a drug, testing of urine is the preferred test. If the search is for alcohol, the test is made of a blood sample.

Drug Examinations

Most crime labs perform drug examinations in the serology section or chemistry section. A drug examination is typically of seized illegal drugs. The most common of seized drugs are marihuana, cocaine, methamphetamine, amphetamine, heroin, prescription drugs, and designer drugs.

The examination methods can include use of instrumentation such as gas chromatography/mass spectrometry, Fourier transform infrared spectrophotometry, ultraviolet visible spectrophotometry, and bench chemistry techniques.

Ballistics Examinations

Ballistics examinations are different than firearms examinations. In ballistics, the examination is of the projectile; firearms examinations focus on the weapon used to fire a projectile. The examination draws upon the science of propulsion, flight, and impact of projectiles. The science of ballistics can be divided into several types: internal, external, terminal, and wound.

- Internal ballistics deals with the propulsion of projectiles, such as within the barrel of a gun. A gun converts chemical energy of a propellant into kinetic energy of a projectile.
- External ballistics deals with projectile flight. The trajectory, or path, of a projectile is subject to the forces of gravity, drag, and lift.
- Terminal ballistics deals with the impact of projectiles on a target.
- Wound ballistics deals with the mechanisms and medical implications of trauma caused by bullets and explosively driven fragments such as shrapnel.

Gunshot Residue Examinations

Gunshot residue is material deposited on any part of the body, most particularly the hands, face, and clothing of the shooter, as a result of the discharge of a firearm. The residue can include particles from the primer, gunpowder, the projectile, and the cartridge case. Particles from the primer and gunpowder are most forensically significant.

The presence of gunshot residue on the hands of an individual indicates that the person recently discharged a firearm, handled a firearm or an object with gunshot residue on its surface, or was in close proximity to a firearm when it was discharged.

In a suspected suicide by gunshot, the presence of residue on the victim's hands has little probative value. In those cases where the investigator suspects someone else may have been involved, the analysis of samples from other individuals present at the scene may prove helpful.

Toolmarks

The methodology of tool mark examinations parallels that of firearms examinations: the examiner looks for class characteristics and individual characteristics. By examining impressions on various materials, such as wood, metal and plastics, the examiner is able to identify the class of tool that made the impression; for example, a pry bar or screwdriver. (See Tool Mark Examinations.)

Treadwear Impressions

Marks that appear in soil or on other surfaces that appear to be made by feet, hands, footwear, tire treads, and the like must be photographed before impressions are made. The impressions that are cast from the marks are also photographed. The photographs should be shot from straight overhead, using a good quality 35mm camera, a sturdy tripod, and flash or side lighting that brings out ridge detail. A scale, such as a flat metal ruler, should be included in each photo. Other photos should be made that would indicate movement or direction of travel.

Impressions and/or the photographs of footwear and tire treads can be compared to computer-stored images. In this way, it may be possible to identify the manufacturer of the footwear or tires and to relate a particular tire brand with a particular vehicle model.

Dental stone should be used for casting impressions. Plaster of Paris, modeling plasters, and dental plasters are not sufficiently hard and do not resist abrasion when cleaned.

Glass Examinations

The forensic examination of glass particles can determine if the particles came from the same source. Fracture patterns in glass caused by high-speed projectiles can potentially reveal the direction of impact and angle of penetration. The challenge to the investigator is systematic collection. The forensic examiner will need to know which pieces were forward of and to the rear of the break point, which pieces were found in the hair or on the skin of a victim or suspect, and which pieces were found elsewhere such as embedded in footwear.

Tape Examinations

A forensic examiner can answer two critical questions concerning tape.

- Does either end of a suspect piece of tape match the end of a tape roll found in the suspect's possession?
- Is there a match between the suspect tape and the tape roll in terms of composition, construction, and color?

An examiner can also determine:

- If there is a physical fit between the strip of tape ripped from a roll and the roll itself
- The brand or manufacturer of the tape
- The tape's color, composition, imperfections, thickness, and stains or foreign materials; the number of yarns per square inch; and ingredients of the adhesive, which are usually proprietary and therefore helpful in determining the manufacturer and places where the tape is sold

Duct tape is often used binding, blindfolds, gags, ligatures (strangling), concealing something, and the construction of bombs. The main components of duct tape are a thin outside backing, a reinforcing fabric, and a sticky adhesive on the inside surface of the strip. Duct tape will stick to almost anything, is relatively impervious to chemicals, and will leave little or no physical change to the tape.

Trace Evidence Examinations

Trace evidence is so-called because it is tiny, almost invisible. Trace evidence occurs in myriad types, including fibers, hair, and paint. Most analyses are performed using specialized microscopes or other high-tech instrumentation that allows a comparison of questioned samples to samples of known origin.

There are occasional exceptions, but most examinations do not result in a precise identification of the trace evidence. However, the examination may associate a person, place, or thing with the evidence.

Fibers. Fibers can be very valuable in linking a suspect to a crime scene or other place of interest in an investigation. To illustrate, a woman walking to her car at a shopping mall is confronted by a man carrying a gun. He orders her into the back of his van. He drives to a remote location where he sexually assaults her and then abandons her on the side of a road. She reports the incident to the police. A specialist in sexual assault investigations finds a carpet fiber in the victim's hair. A suspect is later identified. Samples of carpet fiber are removed from a carpet on the back floor of the suspect's van. A forensic examiner studies the fiber found on the victim and the fibers taken from the van. They match. Strong evidence now exists to link the suspect to the crime.

Hair. Like fiber examinations, the objective of the forensic scientist is to match unknown hair with known hair, such as hair collected at a scene to hair collected from a suspect. If hair of unknown origin is on a piece of material that can be easily transported to the lab, such as an item of clothing, leave the hair on the item and send the item to the lab.

A known hair sample, e.g., a sample taken from the body of a suspect, should consist of at least 20 to 25 hairs pulled at random from the area being sampled, such as the head or pubic area. The collected hairs should be folded in clean paper or an envelope with sealed corners. The envelope or package should be clearly marked with the individual's name and the body area sampled.

Paint. Paint fragments and objects containing paint chips and smears, such as those recovered at the scene of a hit-and-run incident, can be collected for comparison purposes.

Paint-related objects vary widely: parts broken from an automobile, clothing worn by a pedestrian-victim, a pry bar used to force open a door, or a sledgehammer used to smash open a safe. Send a suspect object (or a piece cut from the object) to the laboratory.

Also send a comparison sample, such as paint chips removed from a suspect's hit-and-run vehicle or a tool believed to have been used in a forced entry.

Sexual Assault Evidence

The two most common types of evidence recovered in sexual assault crimes are textile fibers and blood. Textile fiber transfer examinations are typically used to link either the suspect with the victim or the location of the offense with any of the body materials testable by DNA.

The key person in the collection of sexual assault case evidence is the investigator. To attain the best possible forensic lab results, provide the forensic lab with information that allows the examiner to know what he or she is looking for.

Following are examples of information to be sent in sexual assault cases (and in almost any other case):

- Provide details as to how you can be contacted.
- Name any other investigators involved.
- Submit a written report.
- Name the place where the incident occurred.
- Name the specific location where the evidence was found such as the bed, car seat, floor, etc.
- Name the date and time the incident occurred.
- Name the date and time the incident was reported.
- Name the date and time the evidence (such as a rape kit) was collected.
- If there was a delay between collection and submission to the lab, explain why.
- Report if the evidence had been laundered.
- Report if there was a prior legitimate contact between the victim and the suspect.
- Report if there are any reliable witnesses who can place the victim and the suspect together and the time.
- Report if there are any reliable witnesses who can place the victim and suspect together at the place of the crime.
- Identify the items of clothing worn by the victim and suspect at the time of the crime.
- Identify any items of clothing being submitted that are NOT believed to be involved.
- Describe or provide conflicting statements by the victim and suspect, such as consent and denial of consent.
- If force is alleged, submit any supporting materials, such as ripped clothing and torn-off buttons.
- If bedding was involved, describe the actual surface where the alleged rape occurred and mark a circle around the places on the bedding that should be carefully examined.
- If bedding was involved, name any other persons who may have been upon it, such as a husband, boyfriend, roommate, etc.

- For specific stains, name the substance that you believe made the stain, such as blood, semen, lubricant, cosmetics, condom residue, etc.
- If a stain was caused by a lubricant, collect the stain with a clean, unused cotton swab and also submit a "blank" swab for use as a control sample. If possible, submit the lubricant container.
- State if the victim has had consensual sex within the last 72 hours.
- Report any possibility that a collected fiber could have been transferred from suspect to victim at a prior time.
- Report if the victim was drugged prior to the alleged rape.
- Submit any other relevant items such as fingerprints, letters, notes, tread marks, tape, rope, soil, and attachments to clothing such as sequins and glitter material.

Chain of Custody

Physical items that are collected for forensic examination must be marked, labeled, and accounted for in a process of documentation called chain of custody.

Chain of custody begins at the moment an item of evidence is first obtained and ends when the item is no longer evidential in nature. Whenever the item changes hands, such as when it is received at a forensic laboratory, an entry is made on an accompanying chain of custody form. Each entry reflects the name and title of the person receiving the item and the purpose of the transfer.

Chain of custody provides assurance that the item examined at a laboratory and later offered into evidence at trial is the same item that was collected by the investigator.

FBI Laboratory Services, Federal Bureau of Investigation, http://www.fbi.gov/about-us/lab

FREEDOM OF INFORMATION ACT (FOIA)

The Freedom of Information Act (FOIA) is a law that allows access to federal government documents. The law provides that any person has a right, enforceable in court, to obtain access to federal agency records, except to the extent that such records (or portions of them) are protected from public disclosure by one of nine exemptions or by one of three special law enforcement record exclusions.

Exemptions

The nine exemptions are:

1. Those documents properly classified as secret in the interest of national defense or foreign policy
2. Related solely to internal personnel rules and practices
3. Specifically exempted by other statutes
4. A trade secret or privileged or confidential commercial or financial information obtained from a person
5. A privileged interagency or intra-agency memorandum or letter
6. A personnel, medical, or similar file, the release of which would constitute a clearly unwarranted invasion of personal privacy
7. Compiled for law enforcement purposes, the release of which:

   a. Could reasonably be expected to interfere with law enforcement proceedings
   b. Would deprive a person of a right to a fair trial or an impartial adjudication
   c. Could reasonably be expected to constitute an unwarranted invasion of personal privacy
   d. Could reasonably be expected to disclose the identity of a confidential source
   e. Would disclose techniques, procedures, or guidelines for investigations or prosecutions
   f. Could reasonably be expected to endanger an individual's life or physical safety

8. Contained in or related to examination, operating, or condition reports about

financial institutions that the SEC regulates or supervises

9. Those documents containing exempt information about gas or oil wells

Exclusions

In particular circumstances, the acknowledgement of the existence of a record, in and of itself, can produce consequences similar to those resulting from disclosure of the record itself. In order to avoid this type of problem, the amendments to the FOIA established three record exclusions. If these records are requested, the agency may respond that there are no dissoluble records responsive to the request.

- Exclusion One authorizes federal law enforcement agencies, under specified circumstances, to shield the very existence of records of ongoing investigations or proceedings by excluding them entirely from FOIA's reach.
- Exclusion Two provides that "whenever informant records maintained by a criminal law enforcement agency under an informant's name or personal identifier are requested by a third party, the agency may treat the records as not subject to the requirements of FOIA unless the informant's status has been officially confirmed."
- Exclusion Three pertains only to certain law enforcement records that are maintained by the Federal Bureau of Investigation.

A FOIA request can be made for any agency record. The request is sent to the federal agency that the requestor believes to be in possession of the record. The request must be in writing and describe in detail the information wanted. The requestor can also ask that the record be in a particular format. The federal agency will not do research, analyze data, answer questions, and create documents or records that are based on records.

The FOIA requires that federal agencies release certain information automatically, without the need for the requestor to make a formal request. Such information is information readily available to the general public.

The time it takes to respond to a request varies, depending on the complexity of the request itself and the backlog of requests already pending at the agency. The standard time limit for a response is one month.

The FOIA pertains to federal agencies only.

U.S. Department of Justice, Freedom of Information Act, www.sec.gov/foia/nfoia.htm

FRUIT OF THE POISONOUS TREE DOCTRINE

The "fruit of the poisonous tree" doctrine is a principle that prohibits at trial the use of secondary evidence that was culled directly from primary evidence obtained from an illegal search and seizure.

The doctrine is an exclusionary rule that mandates that evidence obtained from an illegal arrest, unreasonable search, or coercive interrogation must be excluded from trial. Also excluded is secondary evidence, i.e., evidence obtained from the primary evidence. For example, a notebook is seized during an illegal search. The notebook is primary evidence. Information in the notebook leads to discovery of stolen goods. Because the notebook (primary evidence) was seized illegally, it cannot be introduced at trial. The stolen goods (secondary evidence) are also banned.

The rule was established primarily to deter law enforcement from violating rights against unreasonable searches and seizures. Because the doctrine derives from Fourth Amendment protections, it applies to law enforcement (agents of the government) but not to private citizens such as private investigators.

The name "fruit of the poisonous tree" is a metaphor that means that knowledge (fruit) gained from an illegal search (poisonous tree) is excluded from a criminal trial.

Learning Shop USA, Legal Aspects of Private Investigation, www.learningshopusa.com

G

GLOBAL POSITIONING SYSTEM (GPS)

The Global Positioning System (GPS) is a space-based satellite navigation system that provides location and time information in all weather conditions anywhere on or near the earth where there is an unobstructed line of sight to four or more GPS satellites. GPS has become a widely deployed and useful tool for tracking and surveillance. In this respect, it is a basic tool for investigators. The system provides capabilities to users around the world. It is maintained by the United States government and is freely accessible to anyone with a GPS receiver.

While originally a military project, GPS is considered a *dual-use* technology, meaning it has military and civilian applications. Many civilian applications use one or more of GPS's three basic components: absolute location, relative movement, and time transfer.

Examples of use include tracking vehicles containing cargo that is high-value or sensitive to public safety or national security, locating persons or pets, and signaling when a target leaves or enters a predefined location.

An ordinary use of GPS by investigators is to attach a "beeper" to a vehicle that transports the target.

John J. Fay

GRAMM-LEACH-BLILEY ACT

The Gramm-Leach-Bliley Act requires financial institutions—companies that offer consumers financial products or services like loans, financial, or investment advice or insurance—to explain their information-sharing practices to their customers and to safeguard sensitive data.

The Safeguards Rule

Under the Safeguards Rule, financial institutions must protect the consumer information they collect.

Privacy Notices

Financial institutions are required to explain their privacy practices and tell consumers their rights. An effective privacy notice—one that encourages feedback and is easy to read—is required by the Federal Trade Commission.

Compliance

Financial institutions covered by the Gramm-Leach-Bliley Act must tell their customers about their information-sharing practices and explain to customers their right to "opt out" if they don't want their information shared with certain third parties.

Summary

The Gramm-Leach-Bliley Act requires many companies to give consumers privacy notices that explain the institutions' information-sharing practices. Such notices must give a clear, conspicuous, and accurate statement of the company's practices.

The Safeguards Rule requires financial institutions to secure customer records and information. But the law defines "financial institution" broadly to cover many businesses that might not describe themselves that way.

Federal Trade Commission, Bureau of Consumer Protection, http://www.business.ftc.gov/

H

HIDDEN ASSETS INVESTIGATION

Conducting a hidden asset investigation can be difficult or it can be easy, depending on circumstances. The word "hidden" is misleading because it sometimes happens that the assets being looked for are easily accessible, not hidden. For example, assume that an investigator's client has reason to believe her husband is having an affair. The client intends to file a petition for divorce; she wants to know the extent and location of marital assets. The investigator knows where to look and makes a full discovery. In this hypothetical case, the assets were not actually hidden but in a place difficult for the client to find but not difficult for the investigator to find. The conclusion in this hypothetical case may not be the end point at all because the client's husband may be keeping other assets in other places.

It is safe to say that efforts to hide assets tend to be proportional to the value of them. In other words, a person in control of highly valuable assets may go to great lengths to conceal them, hence the word "hidden." A case cannot be considered complete until the investigator has looked in every nook and cranny.

Divorce and settlement are common reasons to search for shared assets, but there are other reasons as well. A client who wants to collect on a delinquent debt will want to know if the debtor is in fact unable to pay the debt or has sufficient assets to satisfy the debt. In matters called "subrogation," an insurance company will want to know the financial status of an uninsured person who has caused monetary loss to the insurance company's customer. The issue is often a motor vehicle accident. Damages caused by an uninsured driver call for payment by the uninsured driver to the others party's insurance company. It is not unusual for the uninsured to claim insufficient assets. The investigator's objective is to determine if the contention is true or not true.

There is also the matter of a business acquisition, merger, or a limited partnership. An investigator may be retained by an involved party to determine if the other party possesses or does not possess the assets required to formalize an agreement. This type of investigation is called a "due diligence" investigation. The retained investigator may be called upon to verify that assets stated in a preagreement actually exist and are free and clear of debt. Other investigative actions can include conducting a background investigation of the other party to determine credit history, civil suit history, tax payment history, and criminal convictions. In some of these matters, the investigator must be very familiar with restrictions imposed by the Fair Credit and Reporting Act.

Records

A hidden asset investigation starts with collecting and studying known information and then moving, often painstakingly, to discover where the assets are located. A successful outcome depends on the investigator's knowledge of places where relevant information is recorded. Following are such places:

- **District Civil Court Records.** From this source can be found records of divorce, debts, judgments, damages, auto accidents, business disputes, and related cases.
- **County Assumed Name Records.** These records provide information about alias names or "doing business as" (DBA) names.
- **County UCC Financial Records.** Information can be found regarding collateral pledged against loans. A record will show if the debt is still outstanding or if the asset is free and clear and still owned by the subject.
- **County Deed Records.** These records deal with the purchase and sale of property. However, in many jurisdictions, much more information can be found such as gifts received or given and records of garnishments, powers of attorney, liens, judgments, mineral rights, and other pertinent documents. When a record reflects that property changed hands, the investigator may discover that the new owner is a friend hiding the property on behalf of the subject.
- **County Tax Assessor.** Records of the tax assessor's office can identify taxes paid on property not declared by the subject. The nature of taxable property varies, such as real estate and automobiles.
- **County Appraisal District.** In this source, a property is appraised and a value determined. This source can be used to cross-check information in deed records, tax assessor records, mailing address, and property address.
- **Police Department.** It may be possible to obtain a "name survey" through the local police department for at least the past year. The survey might connect the subject to another person or entity having a financial relationship with the subject.
- **State Comptroller.** The records of this office can provide the names of businesses associated with the subject, assets such as mineral and franchise assets, and whether the subject is or was a state employee.
- **Secretary of State.** This office can provide information related to businesses associated with the subject.
- **State Parks and Wildlife.** A check with this office can provide descriptions of watercraft registered to the subject and of hunting and fishing licenses. A license issued at a place outside of the subject's residential and working areas may indicate ownership of property not disclosed by the subject.
- **Federal Civil and Bankruptcy Office.** A review of these records can provide insight into the subject's financial stability. For example, a bankruptcy file can reveal assets, liabilities, and outside interests that produce undeclared income.

Internet

The Internet can be a rich source of information. Here are a few websites worth visiting:

- **www.knowx.com.** This website allows searches to be made of assets held by the subject, such as stocks, real property, boats, and airplanes. This website can also cite bankruptcies, lawsuits, judgments, liens, and much more.
- **www.iqdata.com.** Real property, Social Security numbers, driver's license numbers, motor vehicle licenses, and other information is available on this website.
- **www.dnb.com.** Dunn and Bradstreet, owner of this website, keeps financial and biographical information on companies and their officers.
- **www.searchsystems.net.** This website provides access to property appraisal districts throughout the U.S.

The investigator should recognize that much information on the Internet cannot be verified as absolutely true and cannot be considered the "full story." Internet information must be confirmed or corroborated by a reliable source before being offered as an established fact.

A Technique

A technique for discovering a subject's bank account is to create a fictional company that might be called the XYZ Corporation. A check, perhaps in the amount of $50, is mailed to the subject with an accompanying letter that tells the subject the check is for past services or some other reason. After the subject cashes the check, a copy of it will be returned to the XYZ Corporation. On the back of the check will be information that identifies the bank that accepted the check and the account of the depositor.

Conclusion

Hidden asset investigations are often time consuming but are not always complex. The methods of detection are not much different than in other investigations. The sources of information available to the investigator will vary by jurisdiction. In one place there may not be an office for a particular record, or the record may be incorporated with records in another, larger office. And in some states, such as western states, there will be offices that record livestock brands and mineral leases.

Kelly E. Riddle

HOMELAND SECURITY

Mission

The mission of The Department of Homeland Security (DHS) is to ensure a homeland that is safe, secure, and resilient against terrorism and other hazards. Three key concepts form the foundation of the mission:

• Security
• Resilience
• Customs and Exchange

These mission concepts are not limited to DHS; their associated goals and objectives provide in detail what it means to prevent, protect, respond, recover, and ensure resilience in the face of human-sourced and natural disaster.

The federal government, state, local, tribal, and territorial governments, along with the private sector and other nongovernmental organizations, work together to carry out the mission. These are organizations that regularly interact with each other and the public. Variously, they:

• Provide public safety and security
• Own and operate our nation's critical infrastructures and key resources
• Perform research and develop technology
• Keep watch, prepare for, and respond to emerging threats and disasters

Core Objectives

There are five objectives in the homeland security mission:

• Prevent terrorism and enhance security
• Secure and manage our borders
• Enforce and administer our immigration laws
• Safeguard and secure cyberspace
• Ensure resilience to disasters

Terrorism

The Department of Homeland Security's counterterrorism responsibilities are:

• Prevent terrorist attacks
• Prevent the unauthorized acquisition, importation, movement, or use of chemical, biological, radiological, and nuclear materials and capabilities within the United States
• Reduce the vulnerability of critical infrastructure and key resources, essential leadership, and major events to terrorist attacks and other hazards.

The threat posed by violent extremism is neither constrained by international borders nor limited to any single ideology. Groups and individuals inspired by a range of religious, political, or other ideological beliefs have promoted and used violence against the homeland.

Fusion Centers

State and major urban area fusion centers serve as focal points within the state and local environment for the receipt, analysis, gathering, and sharing of threat-related information between the federal government and state, local, tribal, territorial, and private sector partners.

Located in states and major urban areas throughout the country, fusion centers are uniquely situated to empower front-line law enforcement, public safety, fire service, emergency response, public health, critical infrastructure protection, and private sector security personnel to understand local implications of national intelligence, thus enabling local officials to better protect their communities. Fusion centers provide interdisciplinary expertise and situational awareness to inform decision making at all levels of government. They conduct analysis and facilitate information in preventing, protecting against, and responding to crime and terrorism.

Fusion centers are owned and operated by state and local entities in the form of deployed personnel, training, technical assistance, exercise support, security clearances, connection to federal systems, technology, and grant funding.

The National Network of Fusion Centers empowers front-line law enforcement, public safety, emergency response, and private sector security personnel to gather and share information to identify emerging threats. The idea is to reach beyond the capabilities of the federal government and national intelligence community to identify and warn about impending plots that could impact the homeland, particularly when the individuals responsible for the threats operate within the United States and do not travel or communicate with others overseas.

Fusion centers can gather and share the information necessary to pursue and disrupt activities that may be indicators of, or potential precursors to, terrorist activity. With timely, accurate information on potential terrorist threats, fusion centers can directly contribute to and inform investigations initiated and conducted by federal entities. In short, fusion centers provide a mechanism through which the federal government and the private sector to work together.

National Terrorism Advisory System (NTAS)

NTAS alerts are issued when credible information is available. After reviewing the information, the secretary of Homeland Security makes the decision, in coordination with other federal entities, whether an NTAS Alert should be issued.

The NTAS alerts are based on the nature of the threat: in some cases, alerts are sent directly to law enforcement or affected areas of the private sector, while in other cases, alerts are issued more broadly to the American people through both official and media channels.

These alerts include a clear statement that there is an imminent threat or elevated threat. (An imminent threat warns of a credible, specific, and impending terrorist threat. An elevated threat warns of a credible terrorist threat.)

NTAS has a sunset provision indicating a specific date when the alert expires; there will not be a constant NTAS Alert or blanket warning that there is an overarching threat. If threat information changes for an alert, the secretary of Homeland Security may announce an updated NTAS Alert. All changes, including the announcement that cancels the alert, are distributed the same way as the original alert.

Threats to the Economy

America's economic prosperity depends on the flow of goods and services, people and capital, and information and technology across our borders. The systems that make these flows possible are targeted for exploitation by adversaries, including terrorists and criminals.

DHS plays a role in identifying vulnerabilities to our nation's economic security and collaborating to secure global systems.

DHS works with international partners and the private sector to secure global systems of travel and trade in many ways—including by developing and helping implement global standards for aviation security and container security and by sharing information to help identify potential terrorists before they strike.

Cyberspace

DHS has the lead in the federal government for securing civilian government computer systems. DHS works with industry and state, local, tribal, and territorial governments to secure critical infrastructure and information systems. The tasks for this effort are:

- Analyze and reduce cyber threats and vulnerabilities.
- Distribute threat warnings.
- Coordinate the response to cyber incidents to ensure that our computers, networks, and cyber systems remain safe.

The Secret Service maintains Electronic Crimes Task Forces (ECTFs), which focus on identifying and locating international cyber criminals connected to bank fraud, database breaches, and other computer-related crimes.

Immigration and Customs Enforcement (ICE) maintains a Cyber Crimes Center that looks for and defines fraudulent identity and immigration schemes operating on the Internet. The Center also identifies large-scale producers and distributors of child pornography, as well as individuals who travel abroad for the purpose of engaging in sex with minors.

Human Trafficking

DHS is responsible for investigating human trafficking, arresting traffickers, and protecting victims.

Human trafficking is a form of modern-day slavery and involves the use of force, fraud, or coercion to exploit human beings for some type of labor or commercial sex purpose. Every year, millions of men, women, and children worldwide—including in the United States—are victims of human trafficking. Victims are often lured with false promises of well-paying jobs or are manipulated by people they trust; victims are then forced or coerced into prostitution, domestic servitude, farm or factory labor, or other types of forced labor.

Criminal Threats

Document fraud and benefit fraud pose a severe threat to national security and public safety. They create vulnerabilities that may enable terrorists, criminals, and illegal aliens to gain entry to and remain in the United States. Document and benefit fraud are elements of many immigration-related crimes, such as human smuggling and human trafficking, critical infrastructure protection, worksite enforcement, visa compliance enforcement, and national security investigations.

To combat this type of fraud, U.S. Immigration and Customs Enforcement's Homeland Security Investigations has partnered with federal, state, and local counterparts to create the Document and Benefit Fraud Task Force to target criminal organizations and beneficiaries behind these fraudulent schemes.

The Secret Service's investigative responsibilities include crimes that involve financial institution fraud, computer and telecommunications fraud, false identification documents, access device fraud, advance fee fraud, electronic funds transfers, and money laundering.

Intellectual property rights theft is not a victimless crime. It threatens U.S. businesses and robs hard-working Americans of their jobs, which negatively impacts the economy. It can also pose serious health and safety risks to consumers, and, oftentimes, it fuels global organized crime.

The National Intellectual Property Rights Coordination Center (IPR Center) shares information, develops initiatives, coordinates enforcement actions, and conducts investigations related to intellectual property theft. IPR Center partners employ a strategic approach to combat IP Theft. That approach includes:

- **Investigation.** Identifying, disrupting, prosecuting, and dismantling criminal organizations involved in the manufacture and distribution of counterfeit products.
- **Interdiction.** Using focused targeting and inspections to keep counterfeit and pirated goods out of U.S. supply chains, markets, and streets.
- **Outreach and Training.** Providing training for domestic and international law enforcement to build stronger enforcement capabilities worldwide.

Because DHS has many responsibilities, it is made up of many departments of many sizes. Following are very brief descriptions of some departments.

Homeland Security Information Network (HSIN)

HSIN is a national web-based portal for information sharing and collaboration between federal, state, local, tribal, territorial, private sector, and international partners engaged in the homeland security mission. HSIN is made up of a network of communities called Communities of Interest (COI).

COIs are organized by state organizations; federal organizations; or mission areas such as emergency management, law enforcement, critical sectors, and intelligence.

National Terrorism Advisory System (NTAS)

The NTAS is the nation's primary domestic terrorism alerting resource. This system communicates information about terrorist threats by providing information to the public, government agencies, first responders, airports and other transportation hubs, and the private sector. After reviewing the information, the secretary of Homeland Security decides, in coordination with other federal entities, whether an NTAS Alert should be issued.

Office of Inspector General (DHSOIG)

This office conducts criminal investigations, inspections, and audits into fraud, waste, abuse, mismanagement, theft, or other criminal or noncriminal misconduct related to the funds, programs, or operations of DHS.

United States Coast Guard (USCG)

The USCG has a wide array of surface, air, and specialized assets and capabilities available for multiple levels of response, patrol, and mission-specific tasks.

Deployable Specialized Forces (DSF) include teams such as:

- Maritime Safety and Security Teams
- Port Security Units
- Tactical Law Enforcement Teams
- Maritime Security Response Teams
- National Strike Force Team

The USCG Navigation Center supports maritime transportation by delivering maritime information and Global Position System (GPS) signals that permit high-precision positioning and navigation.

U.S. Customs and Border Protection (CBP)

The CBP is one of the largest and most complex component of DHS. It has a priority mission of keeping terrorists and their weapons out of the United States. It also has a responsibility for securing the border and facilitating lawful international trade and travel while enforcing hundreds of U.S. laws and regulations, including immigration and customs laws.

Domestic Nuclear Detection Office (DNDO)

The DNDO is a jointly staffed office within DHS. It is the primary entity in the U.S. government for implementing domestic nuclear detection efforts for a managed and coordinated response to radiological and nuclear threats.

Federal Emergency Management Agency (FEMA)

FEMA's mission is to support citizens and first responders in preparing for, protecting against, responding to, recovering from, and mitigating hazards.

Federal Law Enforcement Training Centers (FLETC)

The FLETC offers advanced and specialized law enforcement training in a variety of topics to state, local, and tribal law enforcement officers throughout the U.S. and Indian country.

FLETC's training delivery points are located in Artesia, NM; Charleston, SC; Cheltenham, MD; and Glynco, GA.

Office of Health Affairs (OHA)

The OHA serves as DHS's principal authority for medical and health issues. OHA provides medical, public health, and scientific expertise in support of the DHS mission to prepare for, respond to, and recover from threats. OHA serves as the principal advisor to the DHS Secretary and the Federal Emergency Management Agency (FEMA) Administrator on medical and public health issues.

Immigration and Customs Enforcement (ICE)

ICE's primary mission is to promote homeland security and public safety through the criminal and civil enforcement of federal laws governing border control, customs, trade, and immigration.

Office of Intelligence and Analysis (I&A)

The I&A, as a member of the national Intelligence Community (IC), ensures that information related to homeland security threats is collected, analyzed, and disseminated to the full spectrum of homeland security partners.

The I&A is the executive agent for coordinating federal support for state and major urban area fusion centers.

Biometric Identity Management

The Office of Biometric Identity Management (OBIM) provides fingerprint identification services in support of DHS's Automated Biometric Identification System, which contains the fingerprints of over 160 million individuals.

Chemical Security

The Chemical Facility Anti-Terrorism Standards (CFATS) program is the Department's regulatory program focused specifically on security at high-risk chemical facilities not located on navigable waterways.

The program identifies and regulates high-risk chemical facilities to ensure they have security measures in place to reduce the risks associated with dangerous chemicals. DHS chemical security inspectors work in all 50 states to help ensure facilities have security measures in place to meet security risk-based performance standards.

Counter-Improvised Explosive Device (IED) Programs and Resources

This program assists and promotes awareness of IED threats, protective measures for mitigating vulnerabilities, and information on reporting suspicious activity. Awareness topics include information on black powder, black powder substitutes, smokeless powder, hazardous chemicals, peroxide products, suspicious purchasing behavior, suicide bomber/active shooter awareness, suspicious behavior for hotels and lodgings, precursor chemicals, and suspicious purchasing behavior for online retailers.

Federal Protective Service

The Federal Protective Service (FPS) protects federal facilities and their occupants and visitors by providing law enforcement and protective security services, leveraging the intelligence and information resources of federal, state, local, tribal, territorial, and private sector partners. FPS provides security planning, law enforcement and information sharing services, and incident response.

Its Explosive Detector Dog (EDD) program is an element of FPS' comprehensive security measures and supports strategic detection activities to clear identified areas of interest of explosive threats.

Science and Technology (S&T) Directorate

The S&T Directorate's mission is to improve homeland security by providing to customers state-of-the-art technology that helps them achieve their missions. S&T customers include the operating components of the Department and state, local, tribal, and territorial emergency responders and officials.

United States Secret Service (USSS)

The mission of the Secret Service is to safeguard the nation's financial infrastructure and payment systems to preserve the integrity of the economy and to protect national leaders, visiting heads of state and government, designated sites, and National Special Security Events.

Transportation Security Administration (TSA)

The TSA protects freedom of movement for people and the conduct of commerce in the nation's transportation systems. TSA also has a role in protecting the nation's pipeline infrastructure.

US Department of Homeland Security, http://www.dhs.gov/

I

IDENTITY THEFT

Theft of identity occurs when a person, other than the owner of the identity and without permission of the owner, uses the identity to the disadvantage of its owner. In other words, identity theft refers to all types of crime in which someone wrongfully obtains and uses another person's personal data in some way that involves fraud or deception, typically for economic gain.

Personal data includes many things: Social Security number, place and date of birth, current and former addresses, bank account and credit card numbers, telephone and cell phone numbers, driver's license and motor vehicle registration numbers, and military identification number.

A person's identity data are like keys that can be used to unlock places where valuables are stored, such as bank accounts containing money. Identity data can be used to purchase expensive items, borrow money, and even commit crimes in the name of the identity's true owner. A victim's losses can include out-of-pocket financial losses, plus additional costs associated with trying to restore credit reputation.

The methods for stealing identity data include:

- "Shoulder Surfing." The criminal observes the victim making a purchase over the telephone or making a withdrawal at an ATM. The sequence of numbers are memorized or recorded with a small listening device.
- "Dumpster Diving." The criminal sifts through the victim's trash, such as trash left on the sidewalk for pickup by a trash removal service. The criminal is looking for discarded bank statements and similar documents.
- Hacking. The criminal obtains access to the victim's computer system and steals identity data or purchases goods to be delivered elsewhere or makes an EFT transfer of funds from the victim's account to an account controlled by the thief.
- Nigerian Scam. The criminal sends an e-mail to the potential victim, offering a great reward. But to collect the reward, the victim must provide identity data.
- SPAM. The criminal sends an e-mail to the potential victim, such as giving notice that a package cannot be delivered until the victim provides certain information or advising the victim that a payment (fictitious) is overdue.
- Mailed Credit Cards. The criminal intercepts or steals mail containing a credit card that has been newly issued or renewed. The card is activated when the criminal dials a phone number using the victim's phone.

The Internet is a vast repository of data, and within that repository are a multitude of repositories that contain individual financial data owned by millions of persons. An example of such a repository is the electronic filing system of Visa or MasterCard or the records of Experian, a credit rating firm. Another example is a corporation's employee personnel files.

The role of the investigator is two-fold. First is to help prevent the crime by bringing the message to the work force of the organization that employs the investigator and to the public at large. Several modes make this possible: radio and television spots, live presentations (with PowerPoint, for example), bulletin board notices, addenda to e-mails, and in-house training venues. The second part of the investigator's role is to investigate. Because identity theft most often crosses state lines, the principal investigative authority resides within the federal government. This does not mean, however, that nonfederal investigators have no part to play. They can be important contributors to the overall anti-identity theft effort.

Eugene F. Ferraro, *Encyclopedia of Security Management*, second ed., Butterworth-Heinemann, Burlington, MA, 2007, pp. 155–159.

U.S. Immigration and Customs Enforcement, www.ice.gov/

INDUSTRIAL ESPIONAGE

Industrial espionage is the secret collection of proprietary business information. The owner or possessor attaches a value to the information and takes steps to protect it. The term "espionage" most commonly relates to government security and generally has a national security connotation. Industrial or business espionage is associated with economic and marketplace advantages. Although the venues and motives differ markedly, the methods of espionage are fairly standard.

Industrial espionage has flourished in America since the birth of the Industrial Revolution. The founding in 1789 of Slater's Mill in Pawtucket, Rhode Island, is the earliest known example. Samuel Slater had memorized the plans of the layout of an English textile mill where he had worked as an apprentice. Under the then-prevailing English law, the export of factory plans was forbidden as was the emigration of textile workers. Slater nevertheless managed to slip out of the country and find passage to the New World, where he established a textile mill from the plans he had committed to memory.

Espionage has always been a vital tool of politics, diplomacy, and war and, in recent years, a tool of business. Today, nearly every large corporation engages in strategic planning, a function heavily reliant on information about the marketplace and competition. Corporate leaders are undeniably interested in the plans and objectives of their competitors. Despite laws against and public disapproval of industrial espionage, spying practices are routinely carried out. Because industrial espionage is difficult to detect and prove, the law against it is infrequently enforced. Operating a business in today's highly competitive environment places demands on businesses to collect and use large amounts of information, which in turn spawns new technological tools. These same information-handling tools are vulnerable to compromise. Not surprisingly, businesses turn to their CSOs for protection. The duty cannot be taken lightly since survival of the business may be at stake. The clandestine nature of industrial espionage rules out making a reliable identification of those engaged in it.

Industrial espionage is acknowledged as a serious threat to the viability of a business and, in a much larger sense, to entire industries and national economies. As companies, industries, and nations move to dependence on technologically intense products and services, business spying will continue to expand and intensify. Information targeted by industrial spying is usually proprietary in nature, i.e., it is information owned by a company or entrusted to it that has not been disclosed publicly and has value. Trade secrets, patents, business plans, research and development discoveries, and the like are examples. Proprietary information is generally under the owner's protective shield, except when it is also classified government data entitled to protections afforded by the government.

Industrial espionage moves through five stages: decide the information to be collected; collect the targeted information; refine it; and distribute it to the end user, who decides whether or not to use the information.

- Decide the Information to Be Collected. The focus of interest may be long-term and broad, such as to learn and track a competitor's overall research and design capability, or short-term and narrow, such as to learn the details of a new product launch.
- Collect the Targeted Information. In this stage, the espionage apparatus learns where the information is located, how it is protected, and how best to obtain it. The information may be collectable overtly, such as paying attention to newspapers, books, articles, and speeches, or it may be collectable through covert means, such as planting a mole, subverting an employee, or installing electronic listening devices.
- Refine the Collected Information. This step is like working a jigsaw puzzle. Information is organized and evaluated to arrive at an answer to the question initially asked, e.g., is the competitor about to introduce a new product?
- Distribute the Refined Information. The processed information is given to the decision maker and/or the people who can make use of it. To be useful, the information must be timely, accurate, and understandable.
- Ignore or Act on the Information. The users have two choices: ignore the information or act on it. Undesirable consequences may follow when the information happens to be accurate and is ignored, or happens to be faulty and is acted upon.

Cloak and dagger is not a term appropriate for industrial spies. Neither are they of the same ilk. The most effective among espionage spies are professional agents. They operate from various motives.

- Greed
- Financial need
- Revenge
- Ambition
- Political, religious, or cultural ideology
- Belief in a cause

Professional agents (often self-promoted as legitimate consultants) earn hefty fees and are inclined to dismiss greed as a primary motive. Many are former government or military intelligence officers, private investigators, or security consultants. Other types of paid collectors are persons who have been carefully recruited and enticed into cooperation by the promise of reward. Professionals sometimes pose as headhunters to engage in conversation with key employees of the targeted organization. Bogus job interviews can be a rich source of inside information. The more odious tasks performed by hired hands are searching trash, breaking and entering, and blackmailing the vulnerable.

INFORMANTS

The use of informants, paid or unpaid and witting or unwitting, is a standard technique of the professional spy. Informants are often a rival's regular, temporary, or contractor employees; suppliers, vendors, or clients; or wives, children, and friends. Also under the broad heading of informant are infiltrators and undercover operatives who penetrate the rival organization. Their activities can consist of recruiting and directing unsuspecting helpers, copying sensitive documents, intercepting communications, photographing, videotaping, and placing covert listening devices. Following are examples:

- The Set Up. In this technique, a smooth-talking con artist assumes a guise to entrap an innocent or ignorant insider. Using a pretext telephone call, the set-up agent calls an unsuspecting employee and pretends to be a vendor, such as for a company that prints architectural drawings, and elicits sensitive information by asking questions about a nonexistent work order. A variation is the pretext letter. The letterhead bears the logo of a respected professional association. The letter invites the addressee, often a researcher, to submit a professional paper for publication.

- Trespassing. The spy gains access to the facility by breaking and entering or by ruse. In the former, the trespasser enters by stealth and either steals or copies files, documents, computer tapes, etc. In the latter, the trespasser presents false credentials that permit access to the facility and/or to restricted areas within.
- Covert Listening. An eavesdropper uses sophisticated wiretap and bugging devices to capture conversations or simply overhear conversations at employee hangouts.
- Stalking. Surveillance is made of personnel of interest, looking always for the hook—a personal indiscretion, a contact of questionable character, or any shortcoming that may be exploited to extort information.
- Polling. Using phony questionnaires that ask apparently innocuous questions, the pollster obtains information useful in itself or useful in confirming an organization's activities, such as developing a new product or moving into a new market.
- The Finance Ploy. In this approach the spy gains access to a company executive by outlining an enticing proposition. In a one-on-one situation and subsequent telephone calls, the wizard spews attractive numbers that lead the executive to reveal sensitive proprietary information. Once the information is obtained, the wizard calls off the deal. The executive may not even discover he/she had been hoodwinked.
- Blind Advertising. An employment advertisement encourages interested persons to mail their resumes to a post office box. If a resume indicates that the applicant is employed by a company of interest, the spy makes a follow-up telephone call or meets the applicant over lunch or cocktails. During discussion of the job, the spy says that a hiring decision cannot be made in the absence of specific (and sensitive) information about the applicant's job duties.
- Reverse Engineering. The reverse engineer may be the spy or a person employed by the spy. Proprietary information that has been obtained about a product or process is broken down into examinable components. The engineer creates or synthesizes a clone of the product or process.
- Soliciting. A dupe is recruited by deception or by rewarding a desire or satisfying a need. The recruit is connected in some way to the targeted organization: employee, vendor, delivery or repair person, customer, contractor, etc. The solicitor asks for certain types of information and, to the extent the information is delivered, the solicitor satisfies the dupe's desire or need.

Espionage has been romanticized by the mass media but in truth is a dirty game played out of sight. Spying involves recruitment of operatives, encouragement of disloyalty, wiretapping, bugging, electronic and photographic surveillance, bribery, coercion, intimidation, fraud, and plain old stealing.

John J. Fay, *Encyclopedia of Security Management*, second ed., Butterworth-Heinemann, Burlington, MA, 2007, pp. 425–429.

John A. Nolan III, *Encyclopedia of Security Management*, second ed., Butterworth-Heinemann, Burlington, MA, 2007, pp. 111–112.

INFORMATION THEFT

A major concern of businesses, particularly businesses that use and depend on information, are concerned with theft of information assets such as technological discoveries, inventions, trade secrets, copyrights, strategic plans, planned mergers, acquisitions, and many other forms of information critical to the viability of the business. These businesses usually operate in highly competitive industries where information loss can adversely affect their market positions.

Equipment used in the theft of information typically includes:

- Miniaturized cameras and microphones that can be hidden inside telephones, furniture, walls, ceilings, and floors
- Parabolic microphones that can hear conversations from great distances
- Wireless devices that tap into telephone lines
- Devices that record and translate electronic emissions from computers
- Long-distance cameras and video recorders

A specialty in the private investigation industry is prevention and detection of the devices mentioned above. The specialty is often called technical security countermeasures. The first step in TSCM is a physical inspection of areas where sensitive information might be discussed. Such areas could be offices of senior management, conference and briefing rooms, and rooms used for high-level discussions at out-of-office meetings.

One objective of the physical inspection is to "sneak up" on a covert listener. In other words, visually find detection devices without alerting the listener. This is done because certain eavesdropping devices will automatically shut down when the device senses an attempt at detection. In this phase, the inspection phase, the TSCM technician would look above lift-out ceiling tiles, look in and behind air conditioning vents, remove electrical wall plates, remove the mouthpieces of telephones, look at and behind wall pictures, look for small holes (drilled or punctured) in the walls, and hand-examine items that could conceal a listening device. Such items could be a name plate on a desk, photograph frames, or a pen set.

The second phase is an electronic inspection. The technician uses three tools:

- A time-domain reflectometer. This tool examines telecommunications lines entering the protected area.
- The spectrum analyzer. This tool looks for signals generated by eavesdropping devices.
- The nonlinear junction detector. This tool detects hidden recorders and remotely controlled transmitters.

Proprietary information can be the very lifeblood of a business. Investigators that specialize in preventing and detecting eavesdropping are a small but essential resource for information-dependent businesses.

John J. Fay, *Encyclopedia of Security Management*, second ed., Butterworth-Heinemann, Burlington, MA, 2007, pp. 112–117.

Richard J. Heffernan, *Encyclopedia of Security Management*, second ed., Butterworth-Heinemann, Burlington, MA, 2007, pp. 123–125.

INTEGRATED AUTOMATED FINGERPRINT IDENTIFICATION SYSTEM (IAFIS)

The Integrated Automated Fingerprint Identification System (IAFIS) is a national automated fingerprint identification and criminal history system maintained by the Federal Bureau of Investigation. IAFIS provides automated fingerprint search capabilities, latent searching capability, electronic image storage, and electronic exchange of fingerprints and responses. IAFIS is the largest biometric database in the world, housing the fingerprints and criminal histories of 70 million subjects in the criminal master file, 31 million civil prints, and fingerprints from 73,000 known and suspected terrorists processed by the U.S. or by international law enforcement agencies.

Employment background checks and legitimate firearms purchases are permanently recorded in the system. Fingerprints are voluntarily submitted to the FBI by local, state, and federal law enforcement agencies. Fingerprints are acquired through criminal arrests or from noncriminal sources, such as employment background checks. The FBI catalogs the collected fingerprints along with any criminal history linked to the person.

Law enforcement agencies can request a search in IAFIS to identify latent fingerprints obtained during criminal investigations. Civil searches are also performed but the FBI charges a small fee, and the response time is slower.

Federal Bureau of Investigation, http://www.fbi.gov/about-us/cjis/fingerprints_biometrics/iafis/iafis

INTELLECTUAL PROPERTY RIGHTS

Most countries recognize and grant varying degrees of protection to four basic intellectual property rights patents, trademarks, copyrights, and trade secrets.

Patents are grants issued by a national government conferring the right to exclude others from making, using, or selling the invention within that country. Patents may be given for new products or processes. Violations of patent rights are known as infringement or piracy. An example of patent protection is the Process Patent Amendments contained in the Omnibus Trade and Competitiveness Act of 1988. The Act treats unlicensed importers, distributors, retailers, and even consumers of standard products as patent infringers, if an unpatented product was produced by a U.S. patented process. The amendments apply to foreign and domestic manufacture and also to end products that are protected by U.S. process patents.

Trademarks are words, names, symbols, devices, or combinations thereof used by manufacturers or merchants to differentiate their goods and distinguish them from products that are manufactured or sold by others. Counterfeiting and infringement constitute violations of trademark rights.

Copyrights are protections given by a national government to creators of original literary, dramatic, musical, and certain other intellectual works. The owner of a copyright has the exclusive right to reproduce the copyrighted work, prepare derivative works based upon it, distribute copies, and perform or display it publicly. Copyright violations are also known as infringement and piracy.

Trade secrets are information such as formulas, patterns, compilations, programs, devices, methods, techniques, or processes that derive economic value from not being generally known and that cannot be ascertained by unauthorized persons through proper means because they are subject to reasonable efforts to maintain their secrecy. Trade secret violations are known as misappropriation and result from improper acquisition or disclosure. Distinguishing between trade secret safeguards and patent or copyright protection can be difficult. The key elements in a trade secret are the owner's maintenance of confidentiality, limited distribution, and the absence of a patent. A noncompetition or nondisclosure statement is a written agreement that grants protection to an employer from the unauthorized use of the employer's intellectual property by current or former employees.

A noncompetition statement will typically incorporate one or more of three basic conditions:

- Restrictions on competition by departing employees
- Definitions of what constitutes property that the employer can legally protect from use by others
- Requirements that employees are obligated to cooperate with the employer in efforts to protect its intellectual property

Three elements of protection must be in place for the owner to claim violation of intellectual rights:

- The information is not readily accessible to others.

- The information was created by the owner through the expenditure of considerable resources.
- The owner sought to keep the information confidential.

John J. Fay, *Encyclopedia of Security Management*, second ed., Butterworth-Heinemann, Burlington, MA, 2007, pp. 220–221.

INTELLIGENCE COLLECTION

A well-planned intelligence program for the private investigator can be a source of information for use in serving a client's interests. The principal objective of intelligence gathering is the identification of threats such as potential workplace violence, robbery, shoplifting, employee theft, sabotage, fraud, and other loss-producing activities. Inherent to the objective is a warning system that enables anticipation or early detection of undesirable events. However, it needs to be said that an effective intelligence program is not easy to establish and maintain. It requires considerable effort in planning and organizing the program at the outset and directing the program in its operation. Operations involve determining the information desired, determining where the information can be found, exploiting the information sources, analyzing the collected information, and delivering it to the client in a timely and usable configuration. Of great importance is confidentiality.

The primary source of intelligence is open-source information, i.e., information that is publicly available and therefore not difficult to be collected. The news media are excellent open sources. The media publicize many incidents and often present in-depth details on criminal activities, how and where they operate, who they target, and their degree of success. A primary source for clients doing business abroad can be advisories issued by the State Department, as well as on-scene reports made by consultants. Information from people is another valuable source. These can include crime victims, police officers, private investigators, civil servants, workers, and individuals with local or regional knowledge. Liaison is a principal means of collecting information as well as sharing it.

Actions essential in capturing useful information include:

- Identify persons and groups of interest
- Identify leaders and followers
- Identify motivation and intent
- Identify previous successes and failures
- Identify technique and expertise
- Identify capabilities such as possession of tools or weapons

Kathleen M. Sweet, *Encyclopedia of Security Management*, second ed., Butterworth-Heinemann, Burlington, MA, 2007, p. 540.

INTELLIGENCE CYCLE

The intelligence cycle is a process that can be used in multiple venues for various purposes. In the private sector, where investigations are client oriented, the process can be used to detect undesirable activity; identify persons involved; assess past, present, and possible future losses; and suggest preventive actions. In the law enforcement sector, where investigations are society oriented, the end game of the intelligence cycle is to arrest criminals and bring them to justice. In the intelligence community, the focus is on national security.

The process involves collecting and converting raw information into actionable information. The process operates in six steps and is best understood as dynamic and cyclical, i.e., the collected information undergoes change as it moves from step to step, combining and recombining within itself and with other information so that it becomes increasingly intelligible. Movement of information around the cycle is fluid, like the hands of a clock, and when circumstances dictate, the information can be returned to a previous step where it is reprocessed. At any time during the cycle, information that cannot be made intelligible is removed and held for possible future return to the process.

The six steps are:

1. Determine the information needed. For example, information that is needed to protect a client's property, to arrest criminals and seize contraband, or to detect and preempt terrorist intentions.
2. Create and manage a plan for collecting the information needed.
3. Collect the needed information according to the plan. Sources of information can be victims, witnesses, informants, undercover operatives, and counterintelligence agents.
4. Process information so that it can be put into a form usable by analysts. Process is done through a variety of methods translating human and machine languages, decrypting code, searching databases, formatting, and reducing the information to a manageable size.
5. Analyze the collected information. Analysis is made by determining the reliability of the source, such as an informant who has provided information in past instances; validity is assessing the context of collected information (how it fits into the "big picture") and determining if the collected information is relevant to the effort. It is helpful to think of each piece of collected information as a part of a jigsaw puzzle. The picture in the puzzle begins to form as parts of the puzzle are joined together. Disseminate the information once the picture is formed.
6. Disseminate the product to the users, such as owners or operators of business organizations, law enforcement task forces, or national government intelligence agencies. Depending on a user's mission, the product could be used to formulate a plan for direct action, to develop procedures, to formulate a long-range strategy, and to set policy. In some cases, the product is disseminated in its original raw form. Processing then becomes a responsibility of the user.

The term "Intelligence Cycle" is appropriate because when the sixth step is complete, the finished product is channeled into the first step so that there is never-ending movement. The highly finished product of today could be a more highly finished product tomorrow.

Federal Bureau of Investigation, http://www.fbi.gov/about-us/intelligence/intelligence-cycle

INTERNATIONAL CHILD ABDUCTION

Private investigators can help to locate missing children who have been abducted to foreign soil by custodial parents. The cases are complex, and investigators must know the law and the resources available to them.

The Hague Convention on the Civil Aspects of International Child Abduction, established in 1980, is a multilateral treaty that seeks to protect children from the harmful effects of abduction and retention by one parent from another across international boundaries. The Hague Convention provides a procedure in international law to ensure the prompt return of children who have been abducted from their country of habitual residence or wrongfully retained in a contracting state that is not their country of habitual residence.

The primary purpose of the Hague Convention is not to litigate child custody arrangements but rather to preserve the child custody arrangement that existed prior to the alleged wrongful removal or retention. But, unfortunately, the Hague Convention does not apply to all countries, and even those that have signed the treaty do not have their own internal laws; parents must seek assistance from other sources to ensure the safe return of the child.

Considerations for Investigators

Beyond dangerous and unadvised recovery efforts, there are ways private investigators can be of help in these cases. Private investigators can be valuable in locating the abducted children, identifying accomplices, and observing improper support. Also, private investigators can identify and locate people who are helping the abductor retain control of the child. Help by an abductor is usually in the form of money. In this regard, the investigator can be useful to the client and the court in terminating financial and other support being provided by a third party.

The following are considerations for investigators.

Consider If You're the Right Person. No one likes turning down case work, but these are without question the kinds of cases so complex in nature that investigators must consider if they are the right persons for the job. Complex legalities, intense emotional feelings of the left-behind parent, and the physical and emotional safety of the child all play a part in the investigation. The ultimate return of the child hangs in the balance.

Know the Case Inside and Out. Start at the beginning. An investigator should understand the dynamics of the parents, what led to the abduction of the child, and the intent of the left-behind parent. Some cases can be made more complex if there is domestic violence or if the child is simply being used as a pawn in a greater dispute between the parents.

Research and Know the Laws. Not only is a thorough understanding of the Hague Convention in order, but the investigator must also learn the laws of the country where the child is located. The investigator should research the applicable laws and confer with experts to make sure understanding is clear before proceeding with the case.

Learn the lay of the Land. The investigator must become familiar with the geography of the country and the specific area where the child is located. In addition, the investigator should learn the laws, rules, practices, customs, and the general behaviors of people whom the investigator might encounter. Speaking the local language is a very big plus; if not, an interpreter should be hired. An issue of concern is the possibility that the local police will question the surveillance.

Connect with Resources. This is not a one-person job. The left-behind parent will need emotional support and the services of an attorney who specializes in abduction

issues. Working collaboratively with all persons involved can be most effective in achieving a positive outcome.

Conclusion

There is a lot to know before taking an abduction case. The investigator must know the applicable laws, particularly the Hague Convention, and conduct the investigation in a manner that will ensure the physical and emotional safety of the child.

Stacy Jones

INTERROGATION

Interrogation should be conducted out of sight and hearing of other persons, particularly accomplices, and should be conducted on the interrogator's territory. When this is not possible, neutral territory can be used. Very few circumstances permit interrogation on the suspect's territory.

Mental Preparation

Careful mental preparation is absolutely and unequivocally required before interrogating. Mental preparation involves:

- Developing a full knowledge of case facts by, for example, studying the statements of witnesses, notes, sketches, photographs, documents, and forensic findings
- Mentally reconstructing the commission of the incident; anticipating denials
- Preparing a list of logically ordered topics to be covered during the interrogation
- Preparing a list of questions for each topic

Timing

The general rule is to question witnesses first and the suspect last. But you can bend the rule when you think that early questioning will keep the suspect from fabricating an alibi or synchronizing a story with accomplices.

The timing of an interrogation should rely on advantages to be gained. Ask yourself "If I interrogate now, what advantages can I gain?" Potential advantages are discerned from weighing many factors, such as the evidence at hand, your readiness, and the vulnerability of the suspect. Interrogating is like waging a war, and winning the war is often a matter of knowing when to attack.

Evaluate

Generally speaking, physiological changes that occur in a suspect's body are stronger with persons of high intelligence. This does not mean that the indicators of deception are always more visible; the intelligent suspect may possess a well-developed capacity to conceal inner tension. A suspect with low intelligence may not understand or appreciate the full extent of the danger.

A suspect may be emotionally unstable as the result of something entirely separate from the matter under investigation, and it is always difficult to interpret the behavioral signals of an emotionally unstable person. The nonverbal forms of communication exhibited by an unstable person are exactly opposite of a stable person.

Some behavioral signals have cultural or ethnic roots. A gesture might appear to be a deceptive signal when in fact it was a typical, normal expression used by the individual during his interactions with other persons of the same culture or ethnic background.

When a suspect is under the influence of drugs or alcohol, there may be a delay in the response time between stimulus (question) and reaction (deceptive signal). If you believe a suspect is under the influence, terminate the interrogation.

Arrange the Environment

Furniture and seating arrangements should be such as to place the interrogator in a comfortable, psychologically dominant position in relation to the suspect. The physical environment should be interrogator-friendly and provide privacy. It should have clerical assistance, people nearby to serve as observers, and audio/video equipment. An interrogation room is typically plain, but comfortably furnished, and devoid of pictures or items that can distract attention. A room used only for interrogating often will have a built-in two-way mirror. The room must be neither so hot nor so cold as to permit later contentions that information was extracted through physical discomfort. Furniture should consist of three comfortable chairs and a table large enough to write on but not large enough for the suspect to use the table as a psychological barrier. Items that will be needed, such as pens, paper, and forms, should be in place prior to beginning. If the room is equipped with a telephone, it should be disconnected or removed for the purpose of eliminating interruption. Any item in the room that could be used as a weapon must be removed.

Begin Questioning

Interrogation can be time consuming, but this is hardly a reason for hurrying through. A time limit should not be set but neither should the length of the interrogation suggest in any way that the suspect had been denied basic human needs such as rest, food, drink, and toilet use.

The suspect should be seated at the side of a table where you can fully observe body language. If there is a window in the interrogation room, chairs should be arranged so that window light falls on the face of the suspect rather than your face. Chair arrangement should also preclude the suspect from being able to gaze out a window.

Control of the interrogation is in great measure dependent on the initial impression made by you. Because first impressions are important, your appearance must be such that an aura of competence and self-confidence is projected. Your opening remarks should be appropriate in terms of how you evaluate the suspect. For example, a suspect who considers himself or herself superior to you may be addressed by his last name, instructed to sit, instructed not to smoke, and manipulated in ways that quickly establish you as the person in charge.

The degree of success or failure at eliciting information is linked to your ability to estimate the probable guilt of the person to be interrogated. Is the individual a possible suspect or a darn good suspect? The answer to the question may be found in a close look at what you already have, such as witness statements and physical evidence. The answer may also come from your experience as an investigator and what your inner voice is saying.

Also of importance is your ability to select and employ communication approaches that correctly correspond to the suspect's personality and attitude. This ability rests largely on your training, practical experience, psychological insight, and pure native ability. Many investigators refer to these factors as the "key" that allows passage through a door into the heart and mind of the suspect. Finding the correct key and opening the door at the critical moment epitomizes very great skill.

Direct Approach

A direct approach is normally used to interrogate a suspect whose guilt is reasonably certain. A crime that falls into the category of "reasonable certainty" is often opportunistic in nature, involves a single offense, and is committed without an accomplice.

In the direct approach, you assume an air of complete confidence with regard to evidence or witness statements that point to the suspect. You emphasize the strength of the evidence and how it implicates the suspect beyond any doubt. Acting in a brisk and accusatory manner, you state that an admission is not really important because the quantity and quality of evidence already on hand is more than enough to bring the investigation to an end. The purpose of the meeting, according to you, is not to learn if the suspect committed the offense but to learn why. The

meeting is therefore an opportunity for the suspect to tell "the other side of the story."

Indirect Approach

An indirect approach is generally more successful when interrogating a suspect whose guilt is questionable. In the indirect approach, your questioning is designed to establish a detailed account of the suspect's activities prior to, during, and after the offense occurred. Facts that are definitely known should be used in formulating questions to test the suspect's reactions. Guilt is suggested if the suspect lies regarding an established fact.

A problem in carrying out this approach is the possibility that the suspect's involvement is peripheral, i.e., the suspect was a minor actor in the commission of the offense. When this is the situation, you probably possess sketchy facts. Working with inconclusive information is tricky and hazardous to a fruitful interrogation. A large hazard is an appearance that the evidence is weak and you are off track.

Sympathy Tactic

Information-eliciting tactics are limited by laws and ethical standards and, in some cases, the policy of your client. In the latter case, the suspect may be an employee of a large company and your client it's owner. The client may prefer to let the suspect get by than to convey to the workforce an image of a bullying employer.

Before deciding to use a questionable tactic, you would do well to think: "Could this tactic cause an innocent person to admit guilt?" A yes answer rules out use of the tactic.

The sympathy tactic is appropriate when the offense was committed in the heat of passion. Offenses involving violence have emotional overtones that can be exploited by sympathy and understanding. For example, you can describe the offending act as only one of many similar acts committed by lots of people; the act is forgivable, understandable, very human, completely out of character for the suspect, and not likely to ever occur again.

The suspect is described as a clearly rational person, as virtuous as anyone else, and surely sorry for what happened. An explanation by the suspect is encouraged because it may cast the incident in a true light and may help the suspect assuage emotional pain.

Sympathy can be mixed with references to evidence linking the suspect to the offense. Signs of stress and nervous tension can be pointed out to the suspect as indicators of a need to clear the air. Employ euphemisms in place of emotionally charged words like steal, punch, grope, and stab.

A first offender may be amenable to these tactics for the simple reason it is natural for a person to be penitent in the aftermath of an offense, especially when it is a first offense. A suspect who has never been interrogated may perceive you as a newly found friend rather than an adversary. You can show empathy, which in fact may be entirely forthright. Many people, especially youthful offenders, have been turned away from a wrong path by caring investigators.

Reasoning Tactic

In this tactic, the suspect is told that proof of guilt has been or will soon be established, the only sensible option is to confess, and a failure to cooperate is not in the suspect's best interest. Every denial is met with refuting logic and facts. You display or allude to proof of guilt reflected in witness statements, photographs, documents, and similar materials. If the suspect has lied, point that out. Point out other indicators of guilt such as sweating, twitching, crossed arms, dry tongue, eye avoidance, and withdrawal.

Note Taking

Notes should be taken during an interrogation. A skillful interrogator will take notes unobtrusively, i.e., in a manner that does not impede the interrogation, such as causing the suspect to be distracted or fearful. An alternative is note taking by an observer sitting behind or out of sight of the suspect.

If you have a good memory, you can make bullet-point notes as the interrogation progresses, but they may have to be expanded upon in the immediate aftermath of the interrogation, while your memory is still fresh. A variation of this technique is to prepare ahead of time a list of bullet points, leaving sufficient space for notes to be made next to them.

Whatever technique you use, be sure that note taking occurs throughout the entire interrogation, not just when the suspect makes a pertinent disclosure or an incriminating remark.

Notes that you take during an interrogation are called original notes; notes prepared later are not. The distinction is that original notes can be used on the stand while testifying; notes prepared later cannot. A problem might be created if you take nonoriginal notes to the stand. Upon discovering this, opposing counsel might ask that the original notes be produced. Any discrepancy, no matter how small, between the original notes and nonoriginal notes can be used by opposing counsel to discredit your testimony. In light of this possibility, it is better to use an alternate term when referring to notes prepared later; for example, a memorandum or progress report.

Learning Shop USA, Interrogation, www.learningshopusa.com

INTERROGATION: NINE STEPS OF THE REID TECHNIQUE

The Reid Technique is oftentimes just thought of and is frequently referred to as simply an interrogation process—it is much more than that. The Reid Technique is a structured interview and interrogation process that involves three primary stages: Fact Analysis, the Investigative Interview, and, when appropriate, the Interrogation.

An interrogation should only occur when the available investigative information indicates the probable involvement of the subject in the commission of the crime. Generally speaking, a nonaccusatory interview should be conducted before engaging in any accusatory interrogation. During the interview, the investigator, in addition to developing investigative and behavioral information, can gain important insights about the subject's psychological characteristics and possible motives.

In anticipation of a possible interrogation, the investigator's review and analysis of the case facts and evidence should identify what specific details about the crime they can use to corroborate any confession that is made in the case. There are two types of corroborating evidence—dependent, which refers to details about the case that the police know but choose to "hold back"—to conceal from the media and the suspects that they question so they can be used to assess the credibility of a subject's confession. These details may include how the victim was killed, how and where entry was made into the building, where the accelerant was poured, etc.

The second type of corroborating evidence is referred to as independent—this refers to details of the crime that only the offender knows—details that the police do not have, such as where the murder weapon is located, how and where the subject disposed of their bloody clothes, the location of the stolen property, etc.

The purpose of the interrogation is to learn the truth. There are several possible outcomes to a successful interrogation: the subject may be identified as innocent; it may be determined that the subject did not commit the offense under investigation but lied about some aspect of the investigation (motive, alibi, access, relationship with the victim, etc.); the investigator may determine that the subject did not commit the offense under investigation but knows who did; or the subject may be identified as guilty.

Proper Room Setting

Whenever possible, the interview should take place in a quiet, private environment with a minimum of distractions. The room should be set up so that the investigator and subject are facing each other about four to five feet apart, without any physical barriers between them, and the investigator should not block the subject's access to the door. If it is necessary to have a third person in the room, such as a witness, union representative, or human resources representative, that person should be seated off to the side, out of the direct line of the subject's vision as he/she is looking at the investigator, so as to promote the sense of privacy.

Nine Steps of Interrogation

Step One—The Positive Confrontation. Following the interview, the investigator should step out of the room for a short period of time. Upon returning, he should have in his hand a folder containing the results of the investigation. The investigator should stand directly in front of the suspect and, in a confidant manner and tone of voice, confront the suspect with a statement of guilt. The basic confrontation statement should be brief, exact, and unequivocal, such as the following: "Andy, I have in this file the results of our investigation into the missing $10,000 from the vault. The results of our investigation clearly indicate that you are the person who took this missing money." This type of accusation is made only in cases where the suspect's guilt seems very clear.

In those cases where the investigator may prefer to use a statement that is less direct, he may say, "The results of our investigation indicate that you have not told us the complete truth about the missing $10,000."

Following this confrontation, the investigator should pause momentarily to evaluate the suspect's behavioral reaction to the statement. The deceptive suspect will usually drop his eyes, change postures in the chair, and offer a vague denial such as "I don't know what you're talking about." The truthful suspect who has been wrongly accused, on the other hand, will usually lean forward in the chair, maintain direct eye contact with the investigator, appear legitimately shocked or perhaps even angry, and reply in a very direct and spontaneous fashion that the investigator is wrong. "I don't care what your investigation says. I did not steal that money." In either case, however, the investigator should not allow the response to deter him during this initial phase of the interrogation. He should respond by repeating the initial statement of involvement and then, placing the investigation file aside, sit down directly opposite the suspect. "Andy, there isn't any doubt at all that you are the person who took this money. I want to sit down here with you and see if we can't get this thing straightened out." With this statement and the accompanying action of sitting down, the investigator is making the transition to a sympathetic and understanding person.

Step Two—Theme Development. Once the investigator sits down, he should present some type of moral justification for the suspect's act of theft. This presented justification is called a theme. One effective means of presenting this justification to the suspect is to place the moral blame for his actions on some other person or some outside set of circumstances. This procedure is founded on a very basic aspect of human nature—most people tend to minimize their responsibility for their actions by placing blame upon someone or something else.

In employee theft cases, the guilty suspect may place blame for his behavior on such factors as inadequate income, poor security measures by the employer, or someone else who did not do his job (left the money out or left the money drawer unlocked). The suspect may even justify his behavior by pointing out that other employees are engaged in similar activities. In burglary cases, the suspect may justify his theft by blaming unusual family expenses, desperate circumstances (e.g., no job but a family to support), or a friend for suggesting the idea.

As an example of theme development, in an employee theft investigation, the investigator might develop the following theme that places blame on the suspect's inadequate income: "Andy, I know that during your two months here you have done an exceptional

job. You have demonstrated your capabilities time and time again. That is why it becomes so important for us to clear this matter up. I am convinced that what you did here was out of character, and I believe it happened because of the strain all of us are under to pay our bills and take care of our families. The way our economy is going, we just can't keep up. We are falling further and further behind. The cost of everything just keeps going up, but the money we make doesn't always go up as much as it should, so we fall behind. I am convinced most of the people I talk to are good, hard-working people who have simply made a mistake. They have done something against their better judgment because they are under the strain of trying to pay everyday bills on a paycheck that is simply not adequate. I'm convinced, Andy, that if you had gotten the kind of pay you needed to keep up with things, we wouldn't be sitting here today. This wasn't an act of the criminal we read about—this was something you did because you saw no other way to make ends meet."

The investigator should present this moral justification in a sympathetic and understanding way, underscoring his interest in working with the suspect to resolve the problem. He should also present this justification as a monologue, discouraging the suspect from engaging in lengthy discussions until he is at the point of wanting to tell the truth.

Step Three—Handling Denials. During the initial stages of an interrogation, the suspect will very rarely sit quietly and listen to the investigator without making some effort to refute the assertions being made. Almost all suspects, innocent or guilty, will attempt to deny their involvement in the act under investigation. The more often a suspect denies his involvement in an act, the more difficult it becomes for him to eventually tell the truth. Therefore, the investigator should closely observe the suspect to anticipate when he is about to offer a denial.

A guilty suspect will oftentimes introduce his denials by asking permission to speak with such phrases as "May I say something?"

or "If you just let me say one thing. . . ." If the investigator were to allow the suspect to make his full statement, each of these introductory remarks would be followed by the denial, "I didn't do it." Therefore, whenever a suspect asks to speak during this phase of the interrogation, the investigator should respond by saying, "Andy, just hold on for a minute. Let me explain to you exactly what we know." He should then continue with the development of his theme. This exchange may occur on several occasions during the interrogation, but as a general rule, the guilty suspect's denials weaken in time. In many instances, guilty people will change from a defensive position of offering denials to what they perceive as an offensive tactic—offering objections (step 4).

The following is an example of the exchange that may take place as the investigator initially confronts the suspect, begins the development of the theme, and handles the denials presented by the suspect:

Investigator:	[Positive Confrontation Statement] "Joe, the results of our investigation clearly indicate that you are the person who broke into the Village Jewelry Store last week."
Suspect:	[Suspect's Initial Denial] (After pause) "You think I could do something like that?"
Investigator:	[Restatement of Accusation] "Joe, there isn't any doubt about it. What I would like to do now is to sit down with you to see if we can get this thing straightened out. You see, Joe, in situations like this, the important thing for us to understand is the circumstances that led you to this kind of thing." [Theme Development] "Now, I know how tough things have been for
	you since you got laid off last year. The way the. . . ."
Suspect:	[Permission Phrase For Denial] "But sir, may I just explain something?"
Investigator:	[Discouraging Denial] (Interrupting Joe) "Joe, just listen to me for a minute. I want you to know how important this is. Joe, the way today's economy is destroying so many lives with inflated prices and unemployment, we see people like you making mistakes like this all the time." [Returning To Theme] "You see, Joe, I know you would have never done something like this had you not felt that there was no alternative."
Suspect:	[Permission Phrase for Denial] (interrupting the interrogator) "Please, sir, can't I just say one thing?"
Investigator:	[Discouraging Further Denials and Returning to Theme] "Joe, let me finish this because I know the pressure you must have been under to pay your family food bills, the rent, and to buy clothes for your kids." (The suggestions presented during the theme represent the guilty suspect's justifications for his crime. If he did not justify the crime to help out his family, he will not relate to these theme concepts, and the investigator should develop a different theme).
Suspect:	[Permission Phrase for Denial] (interrupting the interrogator) "I understand what you're saying but. . . ."

Investigator:	[*Discouraging Further Denials and Returning to Theme*] (interrupting Joe) "Joe, just hear me out on this. Let me explain everything to you and then I'll listen to you."

The innocent suspect, however, will generally not ask permission to speak when he wants to make a statement. Instead, he will, without any display of etiquette, promptly and unequivocally state that he had absolutely nothing to do with the theft. Innocent denials will strengthen in time, and the suspect will begin to assert control over the interrogation. In the event of such a development, the investigator must begin to modify the intensity of his position and begin a probing search for some other information such as the suspect's suspicions about who may have committed the crime. This will help explain to the suspect why he was questioned. It is very rare for an innocent suspect to move past this denial state. He remains steadfast in the assertion of his innocence. The sincerity with which he presents his case is a clear indication of his truthfulness.

Step Four—Overcoming Objections. When a guilty suspect realizes his attempts to deny any involvement in the incident under investigation are unsuccessful, he will usually try to assert some control over the interrogation by making objections he believes will support his claim of innocence. In a typical employee theft case, the two common objections offered by the guilty are: "I would never to anything like that—I love my job," or "I don't need to do something like that—I have all the money I need in the bank."

The suspect's objections clearly indicate the investigator is making substantial progress in his pursuit of the truth. Generally, the investigator should accept these objections as though they were truthful; indeed, his response should be a statement of agreement. The investigator should then use the objection to his advantage in the further development of his theme.

"Andy, I hope that's true—that you do love your job. That just reinforces my point. Now I know you are basically an honest person, a good hard worker, who just made a mistake. You see, Andy, if you did not love your job, it would be an indication that you very well might be the kind of person who would plan on taking revenge against an employer he did not like—that you were probably looking for the opportunity to do something like this for a long time and that you didn't care who got hurt along the way. But I'm sure you're not that kind of person, Andy. You love working here, and that's why I'm convinced it had to be a severe set of circumstances that would cause someone like you to step off the right track."

Objection statements are feeble arguments supporting innocence, even in those instances where they may be partially true. In any event, the investigator should not argue with the suspect over the statement, nor should there be any indication of surprise or irritation. The investigator should act as though the statement was expected. Such a reaction will have a discouraging effect upon the suspect, who will perceive that he made the wrong statement, or at least an ineffective one. The following illustrates another example of overcoming an objection (in an armed robbery case):

Investigator:	[*Theme Development*] "Joe, I don't think this was your idea or something you planned well in advance. I think that you and some of your buddies went into that liquor store, saw that there weren't any customers around, and one of your buddies told you to go up there and get the money and you just didn't know how to stop it. Then this whole thing happened with the gun and everything else."
Suspect:	"But that's ridiculous."
Investigator:	[*Follow through*] "Why is it ridiculous, Joe?"

Suspect: [*Objection*] "Because I don't even own a gun."

Investigator: [*Overcoming Objection by Agreement and Understanding, and by Pointing Out Negative Aspects of Situation If Objection Was Untruthful*] "I'm glad you mentioned that, Joe, because it tells me that it wasn't your idea to do this—that one of your buddies talked you into this, handed you the gun, and then the whole thing happened. You see, Joe, if you did own a gun and carried it in that night ready to use it, to kill somebody if they got in your way, that's one thing. But if the other guy stuck it in your hand, to use just to scare everybody, that's something else again. . . ."

[*Continuation of Theme Development*]

If the investigator is successful in his efforts to overcome a suspect's objection, oftentimes the suspect will psychologically withdraw and begin to focus his thoughts on what he perceives to be the impending punishment he may have to face. Essentially, he decides to outlast the investigator by tuning out the investigator's statements.

Step Five—Procurement and Retention of Suspect's Attention. At the outset of the discussion in step five, it should be noted that at this stage of the interrogation we are dealing with guilty suspects—the innocent or truthful suspect will not move past step three, denials. He will insist that, irrespective of what the investigator has to say, he did not commit the act in question. An innocent suspect will not offer objections as the guilty usually do but will be adamant in his rejection of any suggestion of guilt.

Following the objection stage, the suspect often becomes pensive, withdrawn, and quiet. Essentially, he is content to allow the investigator to dominate the conversation and simply tunes out the message. It is most important during this phase of the interrogation that the investigator procures the suspect's attention so that he listens to the theme (which reinforces the suspect's justification for his crime) and does not allow the suspect to focus or concentrate his thoughts on punishment (which would only serve to reinforce his resolve to deny the crime).

One of the techniques used to recapture the suspect's attention is to close the physical distance between the investigator and the suspect. Before describing the details of this procedure, it is necessary to briefly review the concept of personal space. Each individual (from the person out forward) has several zones of space around him. The first zone of space, the intimate zone, extends from the person out about 18". This area is reserved for loved ones and close personal friends. If a stranger were to come up to you, face-to-face, less than 18" away, it would present a very uncomfortable situation. The second zone, 18" to 4 1/2", is called the personal zone. It is in the personal zone area where most personal conversations and exchange of personal, private information take place. Following this area is the social zone (4 1/2" to 12 1/2") and the public zone (beyond 12 1/2"). There is very little exchange of personal information in these latter two zones.

At the outset of the interrogation, the investigator generally is seated about 4 1/2" to 5" from the suspect, usually in the social zone area. As the interrogation proceeds, and particularly as the investigator observes the suspect becoming quiet, looking down to the floor, and giving the general appearance of withdrawing from the conversation, it is appropriate for the investigator to lean forward or to unobtrusively pull his chair slightly forward so that he approaches the suspect's intimate zone area. This closer proximity often regains the suspect's attention because, while perhaps not consciously aware of the change in the physical distance, the suspect senses the difference. Usually he will now look at the investigator and by so doing indicate that his thoughts are focused back on what the investigator is doing and saying.

Verbally, in step five, it is important for the investigator to emphasize the essential elements of the selected theme and begin to channel the theme down to the probable alternative components.

Step Six—Handling the Suspect's Passive Mood. Once the investigator has regained the suspect's attention, and as he continues to stress the essential theme elements, he will probably be facing a suspect who is not only listening to what is being said but one who is also feeling a sense of defeat. For the most part now, the suspect realizes the ineffectiveness of his previous efforts to thwart the investigator by making denials or offering objections and has basically resigned himself to the fact that telling the truth seems inevitable.

At this state of the interrogation, the suspect may begin to cry. Rather than leave the room for a few minutes to let the suspect "cry it out," the investigator should commiserate with the suspect and offer encouragement by attempting to relieve his embarrassment. Oftentimes crying is an indication of the suspect's feelings of remorse.

The investigator may say to a crying suspect: "Joe, I know how much you've tried to keep this inside, but I'm glad to see those tears because they tell me you're sorry this thing ever happened—you are sorry you did this, aren't you, Joe?"

During this final phase of the interrogation, many suspects do not cry but express their emotional state by assuming a defeatist posture—slumped head and shoulders, relaxed legs, and a vacant stare. In general, the suspect will appear passive, downcast, and perhaps depressed. In order to facilitate the impending admission of guilt, the investigator should intensify the theme presentation and concentrate on the central reasons he is offering as psychological justification. For example, in an armed robbery case where the general theme development had centered on the suspect's dire circumstances forcing him into a desperate act (versus committing the robbery for drug money), the central justification for the crime may be focused down to just one or two key sentences.

"Joe, I'm sure you were over your head with a thousand different things—the bills, the kids, no job, no light at the end of the tunnel—and this money appeared to solve all your problems; it seemed to be the only way out, the only chance you had to try to take care of your family, to try to catch up and get something going for you—you never saw any other alternative—no other way out of the terrible situation you were in."

As the investigator repeats these central statements, he should continue to display an understanding and sympathetic demeanor in urging the suspect to tell the truth, perhaps even using gestures of sympathy such as a hand on the suspect's shoulder.

Step Seven—Presenting an Alternative Question. The alternative question is one in which the investigator presents to the suspect two incriminatory choices concerning some aspect of the crime. The elements of the alternative are developed as logical extensions from the theme. If the theme focused on contrasting impulsive, spur-of-the-moment behavior with planned, premeditated behavior, the actual alternative question may be: "Did you plan this thing out or did it just happen on the spur of the moment?"—either choice is an admission of guilt. The components of the alternative question contrast a desirable action with an inexcusable, undesirable action (as developed in the theme). For example, in a rape case, the alternative may be: "Is this the first time something like this has happened, or have you done this kind of thing hundreds of times before?" The choice of "the first time" reflects that aspect of the theme development wherein the investigator had suggested that the victim had led the suspect on by her style of dress and behavior and that any man is susceptible to urges in that kind of situation. On the other hand, the choice "hundreds of times" is developed from the concept that if a person "does this kind of thing all the time," it indicates that they simply are out to hurt people no matter what the circumstance, and that kind of person is not worth spending time with to correct the situation.

The alternative question should be based on an assumption of guilt; it should not be something to the effect of "Did you do this or didn't you?" because such phrasing invites a denial. In addition, the alternative question *should not* address possible consequences associated with telling the truth, as illustrated in the following example: "Did you plan this thing out well in advance, where this was first degree premeditated murder, or did it just happen on the spur of the moment, where it was just manslaughter?" This type of alternative question should not be used because it clearly implies that if the suspect accepts the latter choice, his punishment will be less.

The investigator should try to phrase the alternative question so that the suspect's acknowledgement that he did commit the crime can be made in as few words as possible. Therefore, the actual alternative question may be followed by what is referred to as a supporting statement—a statement that encourages the suspect to choose the more understandable side of the alternative. Considering our previous two examples, the alternative questions and accompanying supporting statements would be: "Did you plan this thing out or did it just happen on the spur of the moment? I think it just happened on the spur of the moment, didn't it, Joe?" And, "Is this the first time something like this has happened or have you done this kind of thing hundreds of times before? I think this is the first time, isn't it, Joe?"

By merely requiring a suspect to nod his head or say the word "yes," it is much easier for him to admit his guilt than requiring some type of narrative response. Once the suspect accepts one side of the alternative, he has made his first admission of guilt. The investigator's task now becomes one of developing this admission into a legally acceptable confession.

Step Eight—Having the Suspect Orally Relate Various Details of the Offense. Once the suspect has accepted one side of the Alternative Question (step seven), the investigator should immediately respond with a statement of reinforcement, which is essentially a statement that acknowledges the suspect's admission of guilt. As an illustration of this verbal sequence, consider the following:

Investigator:	[*Alternative Question*] "Jim, is this the first time something like this has happened, or have you done this kind of thing hundreds of times before?" (without waiting for an answer, continue) "I think this is the first time isn't it, Jim?"
Suspect:	"Yeah."
Investigator:	[*Statement of Reinforcement*] "Good Jim, that's what I thought all along."

The statement of reinforcement simply confirms the suspect's admission of guilt. It is essential that the investigator be prepared for the suspect's acceptance of the alternative because any uncertainty or hesitation on his part at this crucial moment may allow the suspect the opportunity to retract his admission. The statement of reinforcement, therefore, should be expressed in an elated tone of voice immediately following the suspect's acceptance of the alternative.

Pursuant to the statement of reinforcement, the investigator's objective is to obtain a brief oral review of the basic sequence of events involved in the commission of the crime while obtaining sufficient detail to corroborate the suspect's guilt. The initial questions asked at this time should be brief, concise, and clear and include questions that only call for a limited verbal response from the suspect. It is premature to ask such an all-encompassing question as, "Well, just tell me everything that happened." The suspect has very probably been quiet and listening to the investigator for some time now and must be gradually allowed to furnish the details of the crime a bit at a time. Furthermore, the questions should be open ended and should not yet contain realistic or emotionally charged terminology. Continuing with our example dialogue (in an arson case in which a factory was set on fire by an ex-employee), the initial questions may be similar to the following:

Investigator:	"Good, Jim, that's what I thought all along. Did you use a match or a lighter?"
Suspect:	"A match."
Investigator:	"What did you light with the match?"
Suspect:	"Some old rags on the dock."
Investigator:	"Did you pour anything on the rags?"
Suspect:	"Not exactly."
Investigator:	"What do you mean, not exactly?"
Suspect:	"Well, there was a can of gasoline on the dock that I kicked over. The gas got on the rags."
Investigator:	"Did you bring the gas can with you?"
Suspect:	"No, it was already there. They used it for the lawn mower they had for outside."
Investigator:	"What part of the dock were the rags on that you started on fire?"
Suspect:	"They were over by the side door by the supervisor's desk."
Investigator:	"What did you do after you started the fire?"
Suspect:	"I didn't do anything. . . . I just watched it for a while and left."
Investigator:	"When you watched the rags burn, did anything else catch on fire?"
Suspect:	"Yeah, some cartons they had all stacked up by the door."
Investigator:	"Anything else?"
Suspect:	"Everything . . . I mean once the boxes started, it spread all over the place—they had a lot of boxes and stuff piled up. It all started to burn."
Investigator:	"Then what did you do?"
Suspect:	"I got scared. I mean, I didn't think it would happen that fast, so I left."
Investigator:	"Jim, did you plan this thing out for a long time?"
Suspect:	"No, I mean when they fired me, I just got ticked off. I didn't think the whole place would burn up like that."

During this initial questioning, it is important to remain in reasonably close proximity to the suspect and maintain eye contact. The questioning should not only focus on what the suspect did at the time of the act, but also information should be developed as to the suspect's activities before and after the commission of the crime. Once a brief verbal statement has been obtained about the overall activities involved, the investigator should initiate a series of detailed questions to develop information that can be corroborated by subsequent investigation. (Caution should be exercised throughout this process about the taking of handwritten notes; doing so may dissuade some suspects from continuing with their verbal statements.)

After this full verbal statement has been completed, it may be necessary to return to the suspect's choice of alternatives, or to some other statement that the suspect has made, to establish his actual purpose and intent at the time of the crime. For example, if in the arson case it was reasonably certain that there was no gasoline can on the dock, and that the suspect actually brought the gas can with him, he should be confronted with that fact.

Investigator: "Jim, you said earlier that the gasoline can was already on the dock—that it was a gas can they used for their lawn mowers. Now, Jim, it is important to get to the whole truth. We know that there was no gas can on the dock. My concern is whether you brought the can with you filled to the top so you could pour it all over, or if it just had a little bit in it. Jim, was the gas can full when you brought it in or did it have just a little bit of gas in it? It probably just had a little in it, didn't it, Jim?"

If the investigator is accurate in his statement that the suspect brought the gas can with him, then, when first confronted with this belief, the suspect will appear uncomfortable, perhaps change posture, and divert his gaze away from the investigator. This deceptive behavior would be a clear indication for the investigator to continue in his effort to seek an acknowledgement that the suspect brought the gas can with him.

Step Nine—Converting an Oral Confession to a Written Confession. When the investigator is satisfied that he has obtained an accurate verbal account of the crime with sufficient supporting detail, it is appropriate to reduce the oral confession to a written document. However, in some instances, the investigator may feel that it would be appropriate to get another person to witness the oral confession before attempting to obtain a written statement. To accomplish this, the investigator should advise the suspect that he is going to step out of the room for a few minutes and, upon doing so, should locate a second person to serve as a witness.

When the investigator and witness return to the room, the witness may be introduced as someone who has been involved in the investigation. Immediately thereafter, the investigator should repeat the essential details of the suspect's confession to the witness, after which the witness should ask a few confirming questions of the suspect. For example, the investigator may say, "Jim, this is Mr. Smith, who has been working with me on this matter. Mr. Smith, Jim explained to me that he did set fire to the ABC Factory last Tuesday night at about 11:00 PM. He said that after he got fired, he was pretty upset and so he broke into the dock area through the side door, poured some gasoline he brought with him on some rags, and set a match to it. He said that the fire spread to the boxes stacked on the dock, that he watched it burn for about 10 minutes and then left." The witness might then ask a number of follow-up questions to allow the suspect to provide spontaneous information to the witness, e.g., "Jim, is that the complete truth?"; "Did anyone help you start this fire?"; "How did you get into the building?"; "What did you do with the gas can?"

When converting an oral confession into a written statement (step nine), there are basically four formats that may be used:

1. A statement written by the suspect
2. A statement written by the investigator that is subsequently read and signed by the suspect
3. A statement taken down by a secretary or stenographer, which is then transcribed into a typed document for the suspect to read and sign
4. A tape-recorded or video-recorded statement

Irrespective of the format utilized, there are several basic guidelines that should be followed in the execution of any written statement. In a custodial setting, even though the Miranda warnings were given and the appropriate waiver obtained before the interrogation, it is advisable to repeat the warnings at the beginning of the documented confession, making reference to the fact that the suspect had received them earlier.

The investigator should keep in mind at all times that the statement must be readable and understandable by someone who is not familiar with what the suspect has done. Leading questions should be avoided, the confessor's own language should be used, and full corroboration should be established.

Certainly any errors, changes, or crossed-out words should be initialed by the suspect, with an "OK" written in the margin by the suspect to acknowledge his awareness of and agreement with the correction or change. The statement should reflect the fact that the subject was treated properly, that there were no threats or promises made, and that the statement was freely given by the suspect.

An investigator should always seek to take as full and complete a confession as reasonably possible. The first page of a confession should include a date and the current time. When the suspect has completed reading the written statement, the investigator should ask the suspect to write down the current time and place his name after it (while pointing to the place for the signature). The investigator should avoid asking the suspect to "sign here" because the word "sign" has a legal stigma attached to it. The suspect should sign each page of the statement in the presence of the investigator and a witness, who should then subsequently sign each page as well.

Core Principals of the Reid Technique. There are a number of basic principles that the investigator should follow when they reach the stage of conducting an interrogation:

- Do not make any promises of leniency.
- Do not threaten the subject with any physical harm or inevitable consequences.
- Do not conduct interrogations for an excessively lengthy period of time.
- Do not deny the subject any of their rights.
- Do not deny the subject the opportunity to satisfy their physical needs.
- Be sure to withhold information about the details of the crime from the subject so that if the subject confesses he can

reveal information that only the guilty would know.
- Exercise special caution when questioning juveniles or individuals with mental or psychological impairments.
- Always act in compliance with the guidelines established by the courts.

The confession is not the end of the investigation—investigate the confession details in an effort to establish the authenticity of the subject's statement.

False Confessions

False confessions are not caused by the application of the Reid Technique; they are usually caused by interrogators engaging in improper behavior that is outside of the parameters of the Reid Technique—using improper interrogation procedures—engaging in behavior that the courts have ruled to be objectionable, such as threatening inevitable consequences; making a promise of leniency in return for the confession; denying a subject their rights; conducting an excessively long interrogation; etc.

As one U.S. Federal Judge stated after hearing testimony from a false confession expert who made a variety of claims that The Reid Technique resulted in false confessions:

"In sum, the proffered expert testimony to the effect that the Reid technique enhanced the risk of an unreliable confession lacked any objective basis for support whatever" (*U.S. v. Jacques*, May 2011, the US District Court of Massachusetts).

Joseph P. Buckley III

INTERROGATION: WRITTEN STATEMENT

Ideally, a written statement comes from the mind of the suspect, is placed on paper by the suspect, and is signed by the suspect. In some circumstances, the suspect may be unable or unwilling to write a statement but may agree to sign a statement prepared by you or an observer. Very important in such a scenario is to ensure that the statement is accurate, complete, and that the wording is that of the suspect. Notes taken during the interrogation may be used to clarify key points. Specific questions can be put to the suspect, with the answers entered on the written statement in the suspect's own words.

The most incriminating type of statement is a full confession, written in the hand of the suspect, in the words of the suspect, sworn to under oath, signed and initialed by the suspect, and witnessed by you and one other person. Although prized, this type of statement is out of the norm; suspects simply will not tell the truth entirely, do not like to write their own confessions, and do not want to sign anything put before them. The best that an investigator may get is a statement typed by the investigator. If the suspect refuses to sign the typed statement, the unsigned statement is at least a record of what the suspect said in your presence and in the presence of a witness.

In constructing a statement, you need to use the words of the suspect. Common sense calls for exclusion of complex words and grammar that do not reflect the suspect's general vocabulary. A statement that reflects your vocabulary level will be regarded skeptically when it bears the signature of a suspect having a sixth-grade education. The opposite is true as well. When the suspect is known to speak with profanity, the typed statement can contain profanity. As much as possible, write words as they have been actually spoken.

Hand the statement to the suspect and ask him/her to read it. Ask for comments that would change the statement or add to it, the purposes being accuracy and completeness. Have the suspect place initials next to changes, additions, corrected cross-outs, and typing errors. Also ask for initials at the bottom and top of each page.

Then ask the suspect to sign the statement. If you get a refusal, ask for a verbal acknowledgement. If the suspect refuses to do even this, you and the observer should so indicate the refusal on the statement and in your notes.

Recordings

Making a record of an interrogation requires retaining and protecting prepared written, aural, and video materials that are incidental to the interrogation. These would include writings, drawings, and sketches that were constructed by the suspect, such as a map of the incident scene, approach and departure routes, a list of items stolen, addresses, phone numbers, etc.

Electronic media, such as audio and video recordings, are ideal for making a record of the interrogation from beginning to end. If there are any breaks during the interrogation, state the time started and ended and ask the suspect to do the same. Capture in the electronic recording the date; time; place of interrogation; the name of the interrogator; the name of the person to be interrogated; and a verbal acknowledgement, certain advisements, and the suspect's responses as to understanding and acknowledging them. Advisements should include making the suspect aware of the matter under investigation and that he/she can terminate the interrogation at any time.

At the beginning, provide your name and the names of other persons present, the time and date, and the purpose of the interrogation. Do not use the word "interrogate" because, for some people, it conjures up images of intimidation and coercion. Instead, use "interview" or "discussion." The same holds true for use of the word "suspect."

Learning Shop USA, Interrogation, www.learningshopusa.com

INTERVIEWING: THE BASICS

The practice of obtaining information useful to an investigation is alternatively identified as "interviewing," "interrogation," or "interviews and interrogation." Although there may be some difference between questioning in a custodial setting (interrogating) and questioning in a noncustodial setting (interviewing), the essential processes and techniques are the same. For the purpose here, the term "interviewing" is used.

Interviews are generally conducted of four categories: victims, witnesses, experts, and suspects. Typically, victims are interviewed first and suspects interviewed last. Collectively, interviewees can be referred to as "sources," and the investigator should be aware that as the investigation proceeds, the sources can switch from one category to another; for example, a person initially identified as a witness might become a suspect and vice versa.

The order in which interviews are conducted is determined by the type and amount of useful information that the source is believed to have. The general rule is to start with sources who appear to be victims or witnesses (i.e., type) and who appear to have the most useful information (i.e., amount). Next in the order of interviewing are nonsuspects who are expected to be uncooperative for whatever reason. Persons in the category of experts can be interviewed whenever expertise is needed: at the outset, during, or at the conclusion. Examples in this category are forensic technicians and pathologists.

The process of interviewing persons who are not suspects is nonconfrontational. The approach begins with questions that encourage the interviewee to respond freely and fully without interruption. The questions start with generalities and move to the specifics. When an interview fails to uncover valuable information, the cause is usually failure to:

- Ask relevant questions
- Ask follow-up questions
- Ask questions clearly
- Ask questions designed to uncover new facts
- Ask questions designed to identify new leads

Suspects are interviewed last. By this time, the investigator will have constructed questions based on the full body of information collected to that point. The interview of a suspect is entirely different; it is adversarial and accusatory. Questions are direct, unambiguous, and probing. The investigator expects and is prepared to respond to lies and evasiveness.

The process of interviewing, whether for suspects or nonsuspects, has five steps:

1. Prepare

   - Study information that is known.
   - Identify existing facts that need to be validated/verified.
   - Identify new issues or points that need to be addressed.
   - Construct questions to be asked during the interview.
   - Arrange the environment in which the interview is to be conducted.

2. Begin the Interview

   - Establish rapport.
   - Assess the interviewee.
   - Determine the questioning approach.

3. Ask the Questions

   - Follow the guidance prepared in the preparation step.
   - Take notes or record the session.
   - Switch from one questioning approach to another as circumstances dictate.

4. Close

   - Make sure that all relevant points have been covered.
   - Have the interviewee acknowledge that nothing has been left out.
   - Clarify points that need to be clarified.
   - Obtain a written statement if needed and if possible to do.
   - Conclude with a comment that a follow-up interview may be necessary. Also inform the interviewee that untruthful information given could cause problems for said interviewee.

5. Review

- Immediately following the interview, type or write a report.
- Compare information obtained during the interview with information already known.

C. Joshua Villines

INTERVIEWING: THE BEHAVIOR ANALYSIS INTERVIEW AND BEHAVIOR SYMPTOM ANALYSIS

Fact Analysis

Before conducting an investigative interview, the investigator must first understand all of the available case information. Factual analysis consists of reviewing the case facts and evidence in an effort to identify the potential scope of suspects, the probability of the offender's characteristics, and what their possible motive may have been.

In the process of analyzing the case facts and evidence, the investigator should develop a description of the crime area and of the crime scene itself; the way in which the crime appears to have been committed and the known details of its commission, i.e., implement used, place of entry or exit, any special knowledge required (such as a safe combination); the presence of any incriminating factors against a particular subject; etc.

Once the investigator has reviewed and analyzed the case facts and evidence, they should prepare an interview strategy, including a list of issues that should be discussed with each subject, and a list of possible questions that need to be asked of each subject, including the victim, any witnesses, and any suspects.

The Behavior Analysis Interview (BAI)

At the outset of the interview, the investigator must be sure to comply with all legal requirements, such as the appropriate advisement of rights. It is imperative that throughout the interview, the investigator maintains an objective, neutral, fact-finding demeanor. The interview should be strictly nonaccusatory as the investigator attempts to develop investigative and behavioral information. The interview is typically conducted in a question and answer format with the subject doing as much as 80 percent of the talking.

The structure of the investigative interview known as the Behavior Analysis Interview (developed by John E. Reid and Associates, Inc., Chicago) consists of three types of questions: questions about the subject's background, questions that are relevant to the specific issue that is under investigation, and behavior-provoking questions.

The background questions generally focus on biographical information about the subject; they may include questions about the subject's employment activities or, if the subject is a student, their school activities, and they may include some casual conversation about a recent event (a news item, a sports event, or a weather situation).

The purpose of spending several minutes on these topics is to establish rapport with the subject, to acclimate the subject to the interview environment, and to establish a behavioral baseline.

The investigative questions will deal with the issue that is under investigation. One of the first things the investigator should do is to ask the subject an open-ended question that invites the subject to tell their story. If he/she is a victim, what happened?

If he/she is a witness, what did the subject see or hear? If he/she is a suspect, what were the subject's activities on the day in question? After the subject relates their initial story or version of events, the investigator will then ask a series of questions to develop additional details to clarify the who, what, when, where, why, and how of the incident under investigation.

During this segment of the interview, the investigator would explore for any precipitators that may have provoked the incident or for any procedural or policy violations that may have contributed to the situation. The investigator should attempt to resolve any inconsistencies or contradictions that may have surfaced from the interviews of other subjects or from the investigative information.

In the book *Criminal Interrogation and Confessions*, 5th edition, 2013, the authors devote several chapters to the topic of investigative questions.

The third type of question that is utilized in the Behavior Analysis Interview is called a behavior-provoking question (BPQ). BPQs are questions that truthful individuals usually answer one way, while deceptive individuals oftentimes answer in a completely different manner. In one study, six reviewers watched 60 real life subjects answer 15 BPQs. Excluding inconclusive opinions, they were 86 percent accurate in identifying truthful suspects and 83 percent accurate in identifying deceptive subjects. It should be pointed out that the evaluators were not provided with any case information or background about the subjects. (See F. Horvath, B. Jayne, and J. Buckley, *Differentiation of Truthful and Deceptive Criminal Suspects in Behavior Analysis Interviews, Forensic Journal of Science* 39, 3 (May 1994): 793–806.)

During the interview, the investigator will present the BPQs as casual inquiries, oftentimes mixed in with the investigative questions. More than 30 BPQs have been developed for potential use in the BAI. For illustrative purposes, four of these questions are presented in a hypothetical investigation into the sale of customers' Social Security numbers from a financial institution to persons who subsequently used them to perpetrate identity theft crimes.

Think. "Jim, have you ever just thought about selling customers' Social Security numbers to persons outside of the bank?"

The think question relies on the guilty suspect's internal need to talk about his crime in a way that relieves anxiety, while at the same time escaping consequences. Everyone knows that thoughts, fantasies, or beliefs cannot be used as evidence in a courtroom. They are, after all, just images in the mind, similar to memories that cannot be captured or reduced to evidence. Because such thoughts or fantasies do not exist in a real sense, deceptive suspects may relieve the anxiety associated with their guilt by acknowledging that they have had such thoughts.

The suspect who readily admits thinking about committing the crime, for example; "Well, sure. I'll bet most of the employees have had thoughts like that from time to time," should be considered more likely to be guilty than the suspect who adamantly denies such thoughts or ideas, particularly on such a serious matter as identity theft. Also, the suspect who qualifies his response to this question, for example, "Not really" or "Not seriously" should be considered more likely to be a deceptive individual.

The typical truthful response to this question unequivocally rejects any possibility of the thought, for example, "Not at all, never." This is so even when the issue under investigation is one that might be considered commonplace for a person to contemplate. The principal involved is that the innocent suspect perceives the question as relating to the present issue under investigation. Under a more casual or informal setting, the innocent subject may discuss with friends or loved ones vague ideas similar to the issue under investigation. However, the level of motivation present during a formal interview with an investigator typically produces an immediate and emphatic rejection from the innocent person.

Punishment. "Jim, what do you think should happen to the person or persons who sold these customers' Social Security numbers?"

Typical responses from an innocent subject are: "He should be prosecuted!" or "I hope they put him in jail!" or "He should be fired (or terminated)."

A guilty subject has a difficult time discussing possible, serious consequences for his crime. Therefore, his response to the punishment question tends to be much more lenient, such as, "Well, I suppose it depends on the circumstances" or "I think he should pay the money back" or "I think the person should be reprimanded." Often, the deceptive suspect will evade offering a punishment of any sort and simply respond, "That's not up to me" or "That will be up to a judge to decide." In this instance, the investigator should ask as a follow-up question: "If it was up to you, what do you think should happen to the person who (committed the crime)?"

Second Chance. "Jim, under any circumstances, do you think a person who sold our customers' Social Security numbers should be given a second chance?"

A subject who knows that someone else committed the crime for which he is being questioned is not going to afford that person a second chance. Therefore, a typical truthful response to this question is: "No way. After what I've gone through, I hope they throw the book at him!" or "Absolutely not, you could never trust a person like that again."

A deceptive suspect is much more likely to agree with the proposed second chance. Often this response will be evasive, such as "That's hard to say. . . ." or contain conditional language, such as "Well, I think it's important to find out all the circumstances that led up to them doing something like that." When a suspect mentions conditions or circumstances within his response, the investigator should ask as a follow-up question: "What circumstances would you consider before giving this person a second chance?" Whatever mitigating circumstances the suspect mentions should be considered as primary theme material during any subsequent interrogation.

Results. "Jim, once we complete our entire investigation, what do you think the results will be with respect to your involvement selling those Social Security numbers?"

Innocent suspects will express confidence in being exonerated. Typical responses from truthful suspects include, "It better show I had nothing to do with this!" "I know I didn't sell those numbers so I'm not worried," or "It will prove that I'm telling the truth about everything I told you."

A guilty subject does not experience the same level of confidence in being cleared. His mind, after all, is focused on avoiding detection. It is, therefore, common for deceptive subjects to answer this question with a sense of uncertainty: "I hope it comes out okay" or "I don't have any idea, I guess we'll see." Some guilty subjects will respond evasively to this question by stating, "Well, I really don't have any control over your investigation, so I don't know." An amazing number of guilty suspects will predict that the investigation will show negative results for them. This will inevitably be coupled with a statement that places blame onto someone or something else, such as "I'm always being blamed for things I didn't do. This will probably be no exception," or "I'm a real nervous-type person and people always think I'm lying when I'm not."

Criminal Interrogation and Confessions discusses numerous behavior-provoking questions that can be asked during the interview.

Behavior Symptom Analysis

Throughout the course of the interview, the investigator should carefully observe the subject's verbal and nonverbal behavior symptoms. Physicians, psychiatrists, psychologists, therapists, and many other professionals have long recognized the value of evaluating a person's behavior to assist in making diagnoses, judging the effectiveness of treatments, and making other assessments. The premise for making these clinical inferences is that there are several levels or channels of communication and that the true meaning of the spoken word is amplified or modified by the other channels, including speech hesitancy, body posture, hand gestures, facial expressions, and other body activities. In other words, a person can say one thing while his body movements, facial expressions, or tone of voice may reveal something entirely different.

Behavior symptom analysis involves the study of inferences made from observing another person's behaviors. This brief discussion addresses behavioral inferences relating to detection of deception, primarily in a clinical, controlled environment. Within the scope of detecting deception, there are two broad inferences that are made through behavioral observations. The first involves inferences of guilt or innocence, that is, "Did this person engage in a particular criminal act?" The second involves inferences of truth or deception, that is, "When this person says such and such, is he telling the truth?" For case-solving purposes, it is important for an investigator to appreciate the distinction between "guilt" and "lying." Consider the following exchange during an interview:

Q: "Have you ever thought about having sexual contact with your stepdaughter?"
A: "Well sure. Anybody in my position would have those thoughts."

This suspect's verbal response to the investigator's question is truthful. Yet, the content of the response infers guilt with respect to sexually abusing his stepdaughter.

Communication occurs at three distinctly different levels:

1. Verbal channel. Word choice and arrangement of words to send a message
2. Paralinguistic channel. Characteristics of speech falling outside the spoken word
3. Nonverbal channel. Posture, arm and leg movements, eye contact, and facial expressions

When evaluating a suspect's behavior for detection of deception purposes, there are five essential principles that must be followed in order to increase the probability that subsequent inferences will be accurate. Failure to recognize any of these principles increases the probability of making erroneous inferences from a suspect's behavior.

There are no unique behaviors associated with truthfulness or deception. The behavioral observations an investigator makes of a suspect do not specifically correlate to truth or deception. Rather, they reflect the subject's internal emotional state, cognitive processes,

and internal physiological arousal experienced during a response. The emotional states most often associated with deception are fear, anger, embarrassment, indignation, or hope (duping). The cognitive processes may reveal concern, helpfulness, and confidence versus offering an unrealistic explanation for the crime, being defensive, or being overly polite. There are also internal physiological responses that cause external behavioral responses such as a dry throat, skin blanching, pupillary dilation, or blushing. Observed in isolation, certainly none of these behaviors should cause an investigator to conclude that a subject is telling the truth or lying.

Evaluate the consistency between all three channels of communication. When a suspect sends behavioral messages that are consistent within all three channels of communication, the investigator can have greater confidence in his assessment of the credibility of the subject's response. However, when inconsistencies exist between the channels, the investigator needs to evaluate possible causes for this inconsistency.

Evaluate paralinguistic and nonverbal behaviors in context with the subject's verbal message. When assessing the probable meaning of a subject's emotional state, the subject's paralinguistic and nonverbal behaviors must always be considered in context with the verbal message. Consider the following two examples:

Question (Q 1): Mike, have you ever been questioned before concerning theft from an employer?
Response (R 1): Well, um, two years ago I worked at a hardware store and they had an inventory shortage so all of the employees were questioned and, in fact, I did take some things from there. [Subject crosses his legs, looks down at the floor, and dusts his shirt sleeve.]

Q 2: Joe, did you steal that missing $2,500?
R 2: No, I did not. [Subject crosses his legs, looks down at the floor, and dusts his shirt sleeve.]

These two subjects displayed identical paralinguistic and nonverbal behaviors during their responses. However, the interpretation of the behaviors is completely different. In the first example, the subject is telling the truth, but he feels embarrassed and possibly even threatened in revealing his prior theft. In the second example, the verbal content of the subject's response does not explain the accompanying nonverbal behaviors, so the investigator should consider these behaviors as reflecting possible fear or conflict—emotional states that would not be considered appropriate from a truthful subject, given the content of the verbal response.

Evaluate the preponderance of behaviors occurring throughout the interview. One of the findings learned through research is the importance of rendering opinions based on evaluating the subject's behavior throughout the course of an entire interview. The confidence of assessing behavior over a five-minute interview will be considerably less than if the behavioral assessments were made over a 30- or 40-minute interview.

Establish the subject's normal behavioral patterns. Certainly there are nondeceptive reasons for a suspect to exhibit poor eye contact, respond to questions quickly or slowly, scratch themselves, yawn, clear their throat, or change their posture. Before any of these behaviors can be considered a criterion of deception, the investigator must first establish what the subject's normal behavioral patterns are. Consequently, as we stated previously, at the outset of each interview the investigator should spend several minutes discussing nonthreatening information (perhaps casual conversation or collecting biographical information) so as to establish a behavioral baseline for the particular subject. Then, as the interview progresses and the subject exhibits behavioral changes when the issue under investigation is discussed, these changes may take on added significance.

Finally, the evaluation of a subject's behavior symptoms should take into consideration the subject's mental capacity, emotional and psychological health, sense of social responsibility, culture, physical condition at the time of the interview, and degree of maturity. No investigative decision should be made solely of the behavior symptoms displayed by a subject during an investigative interview—they should always be evaluated in conjunction with the case facts and evidence.

Behavioral Models

With these cautions in mind, the verbal and nonverbal behavior symptoms displayed by a subject during an interview may provide very valuable and accurate indications of truthfulness and deception.

Attitude. Truthful individuals usually display an attitude that can be characterized as concerned, composed, cooperative, direct, spontaneous, and sincere.

On the other hand, the deceptive individual may appear overly anxious, defensive, evasive, complaining, guarded, or, in some cases, unconcerned.

Posture. In an interview room that meets the criteria described earlier in this chapter, the truthful subject is likely to sit upright in the chair (but not rigid or immobile) and frontally aligned with the investigator. The truthful subject will oftentimes lean forward as a sign of interest and participation; when the subject changes posture, the movement is usually casual and relaxed.

By contrast, the deceptive individual will likely maintain a very rigid and immobile posture throughout the interview. They may lack frontal alignment or slouch in the chair with a closed, barriered posture in which they sit with their arms folded across their chest and their legs crossed. In some cases, the deceptive subject will exhibit very rapid and erratic posture changes.

Significant posture changes are likely to occur when key questions are asked and deceptive answers are given. The deceptive subject's movements are attempts to relieve or reduce the internal anxiety experienced as a result of their deceptive response to a question that poses a psychological threat to their well-being. The truthful person will not usually experience this same level of anxiety and will therefore not exhibit these same pronounced posture changes.

Gestures. In addition to significant posture changes, deceptive subjects also engage in a variety of other tension-relieving activities that include grooming and personal gestures. Examples of grooming gestures include stroking the back of the head, rearranging jewelry or clothing, dusting the pants or lint picking, and adjusting or cleaning glasses. Personal gestures consist of placing the hand over the mouth or eyes when speaking, hiding the hands, and holding their forehead for an extended period of time.

Eye Contact. Deceptive individuals generally do not look directly at the investigator when they answer critical questions—they look down, off to the side, or up to the ceiling. They feel less anxiety if their eyes are focused way from the investigator. Truthful persons, on the other hand, are not defensive and can easily maintain eye contact with the investigator.

Verbal Characteristics. Generally speaking, a truthful person will answer questions in a direct, spontaneous, and sincere manner. The truthful subject will use realistic words, such as steal, embezzle, and forge, while the deceptive person will use euphemisms such as take, borrow, and write. The truthful person will exhibit a reasonable memory, will not qualify their answers, and volunteers helpful information.

On the other hand, the deceptive individual may delay their answer or repeat the question (a stalling tactic) before offering a response. The deceptive subject may also anticipate a question and offer an answer even before the question is completed. The deceptive person will often exhibit a memory of extremes—remembering too much or too little detail. The deceptive individual may preface their answers with qualification phrases such as "To the best of my knowledge. . . ." "As far as I can recall. . . ." "If my memory serves me right. . . ."

At the conclusion of the nonaccusatory interview, the investigator will evaluate the investigative and behavioral information developed during the interview, as well as the information, facts, and evidence developed during the investigation up to this point, and then make one of several possible decisions: the investigator may eliminate the subject from further investigation, he may determine that the investigation of the subject should continue, or he may decide to initiate the interrogation of the subject. Everyone in an investigation may be interviewed, but very few are interrogated.

Joseph P. Buckley

INTERVIEWING: HUMAN FACTORS

Human factors strongly influence interviews. The skilled investigator recognizes this critical truth and strives to understand and deal with the motives, fears, and mental makeup of the interviewee. The line of questions and interview techniques are selected on the basis of an assessment made by the investigator of the interviewee's psychological makeup.

Perception

The average person does not possess strong perceptive skills, and among different people are different skill levels. This point has been illustrated many times in controlled situations where a single event is observed by several persons. As each person recounts his/her observations of the event, we are surprised at how many different versions are offered of the same incident. Why is this so? Psychologists tell us that perception is conditioned by:

- Differing abilities to see, hear, smell, taste, and touch
- The location of the viewer in relation to the incident at the time of occurrence; distance and geographical perspective affect vision
- The amount of time intervening between occurrence and interview

- The number and nature of events that occur during the interval between occurrence and interview

What are the implications of these factors? Well, for one thing, the interviewer should attempt to discover if the person being interviewed has physical disabilities that impair the senses. If it is known, for example, that a witness has a vision problem, the investigator should be careful in accepting at full value statements that are based on what the witness saw. It is far better to discover problems in a witness's perception at the outset than to have such problems exploited at time of trial.

It would be helpful during an interview for the investigator to ask the witness to show on a map the exact place where he or she observed the incident. The position of the witness in relation to other persons and objects can help the investigator evaluate how much the person could have seen, heard, or smelled. This technique also discourages fanciful elaboration.

Memory

Because memory erodes over time, interviews should be conducted as quickly as practical. Memory not only fades; it becomes colored, either consciously or unconsciously, by later events. Remarks made by other witnesses or persons or news media may cause a witness to fill in memory gaps with inaccurate details. A witness may form an opinion of guilt or innocence from details outside the witness's direct knowledge and consequently shape personal testimony at trial. The possibility is reduced when the interview is conducted soon, that is, before the witness has time to form judgments that distort the truth. Prompt interviewing also helps keep a colluding witness, an accomplice, or an as-yet-unidentified suspect to formulate a false alibi or "get the story straight."

Emotion

A person who experienced trauma as a direct result of an incident or who is emotionally affected later is likely to block out details. To illustrate, assume a witness observes a speeding motor vehicle strike a pedestrian in a most gruesome fashion. The witness rushes to the aid of the victim, renders assistance, and calls for help. Two things can happen that will interfere with an accurate recollection: first, the witness is caught up in emotionally charged actions at the scene; second, the witness is subject in memory to ongoing stress.

Prejudice

It is not unreasonable to expect every interviewee to be prejudiced to some degree. The strength and targets of prejudice vary among people. The investigator should be alert to prejudice and deal with it when it surfaces. One way to keep information from being distorted by prejudice is to require detailed, specific answers. If allowed to talk in generalities, a prejudiced person will make statements that are partially accurate and partially misleading. By remaining within a narrow line of discussion aimed at a specific issue, the investigator forces the interviewee to respond with information that is free of bias.

Fear of Self-Involvement

Some people:

- Do not understand the basic process of investigation and are afraid to give a statement.
- Think that crimes that do not happen to them directly are not their business.
- Believe that misfortunes that befall victims are of the victims' own making.
- Are very private, disliking publicity in general.
- Fear reprisal.

Inconvenience

Disruption of lifestyle is not pleasant. We are all pretty much creatures of habit, and we dislike it when the routines of our daily lives are upset because we are kept waiting or inconvenienced by an unexpected event. Some people will actually disclaim knowledge of a matter because they wish to avoid questioning. We are also aware of witnesses waiting several days in courthouse hallways and then not being called to the stand. There is a residue of resentment against a process that penalizes citizens in the name of civic duty.

Resentment

With some people, resentment runs deep and wide. It may manifest itself in a dislike for authority generally, and it can appear as blind loyalty. We are talking here not of the American tradition that pulls for the underdog but of the unreasoning attitude that criminals are victims of a repressive society.

Personality Conflict

Occasionally the witness and the investigator will get along wonderfully well right from the start. More often than not, an interviewing session will begin with mixed feelings, but through the normal give and take of interpersonal communications, a foundation of mutual respect and cooperation will develop. Sometimes, but infrequently, interviewer and interviewee will for one reason or another find it impossible to communicate at all. When this happens, the conflict usually has its roots in the attitudes of the interviewee. A successful interviewer will compensate by demonstrating friendliness, showing respect for the interviewee, and using the right words at the right time. In those cases where the investigator is unable to overcome a basic personality conflict, the best course of action is to voluntarily withdraw in favor of another investigator. This should not be regarded as failure but recognition of a human factor that must be accommodated in the interest of achieving a successful outcome.

Learning Shop USA, Interviewing, www.learningshopusa.com

INVASION OF PRIVACY

An investigator conducting surveillance is at risk of being sued for invasion of privacy. It is the intrusion into the personal life of another, without just cause, that can give the person whose privacy has been invaded a right to bring a lawsuit for damages against the person or entity that intruded. It encompasses investigating, monitoring in the workplace, obtaining personal data on the Internet, collecting private data, and disseminating information, all of which are in the nature of surveillance.

Persons who have voluntarily placed themselves in the public eye have little or no recourse, especially when the information has news value. Celebrities in the entertainment business fall into this category. They can sue on the grounds of libel and slander but not for privacy invasion.

Nonpublic individuals have a right to privacy from:

- Intrusion on one's solitude or into one's private affairs
- Public disclosure of embarrassing private information
- Publicity which puts him/her in a false light to the public
- Appropriation of one's name or picture for personal or commercial advantage

Celebrities are not protected in most situations since they have voluntarily placed themselves already within the public eye, especially when their activities are considered newsworthy.

The United States Supreme Court has ruled that there is a constitutional right of privacy from government surveillance into an area where a person has a "reasonable expectation of privacy." The place of privacy is important. A "reasonable expectation of privacy" is present in:

- A place where a reasonable person would believe that he or she could disrobe in privacy, without being concerned that his or her undressing was being observed, photographed, or filmed by another
- A place where one may reasonably expect to be safe from casual or hostile intrusion or surveillance

The same right of privacy is granted by state laws, which means that nongovernment investigators can be sued as well. Examples of violations include entering private property to view or record or, from outside the boundaries of private property, take photos of activities in bedrooms and bathrooms or other places considered to be "private" places.

The right to privacy extends into matters relating to marriage, procreation, contraception, family relationships, child rearing, and education. However, records held by third parties, such as banks and telephone companies, are generally not protected unless a specific law applies.

Learning Shop USA, Surveillance, www.learningshopusa.com

INVESTIGATIVE CONSUMER REPORT

The Fair Credit Reporting Act (FCRA) gave birth to the term "investigative consumer report." The term means a consumer report or portion thereof in which information on a consumer's character, general reputation, personal characteristics, or mode of living is obtained through personal interviews with neighbors, friends, or associates of the consumer reported on or with others with whom he is acquainted or who may have knowledge concerning any such items of information.

A consumer who is the subject of an Investigative Consumer Report can require the Consumer Reporting Agency (such as a private investigative agency) to disclose the contents of investigative consumer report in writing. The disclosure must be provided to the consumer no later than five business days after receiving the demand. The disclosure must include the nature and substance of all information in the consumer's file at the time the demand was received.

Federal Trade Commission, Bureau of Consumer Protection, http://www.business.ftc.gov/

J

JUSTICE SYSTEM

The system of justice in the United States places a high value on the rights of citizens. investigator's work activities in requesting arrests, collecting evidence, interviewing and interrogating witnesses and suspects, preparing reports, seeking prosecution, and recovering company assets places the investigator within the scrutiny of the justice system. Should the investigator violate a citizen's rights, he or she may be held personally accountable; if the act was performed as a job duty, the investigator's employer may be accountable as well. When the act is a crime, the issue can be decided in a criminal court, and the punishment may be imprisonment and/or a fine; when the act is a civil wrong, the issue may be decided in a civil court, and redress made through monetary awards.

Criminal law deals with crimes against society. The states and the federal government maintain criminal codes that classify and define offenses. Felonies are considered more serious crimes, such as burglary and robbery. Misdemeanors are less serious crimes, such as trespassing and disorderly conduct.

Civil law adjusts conflicts and differences between individuals. Examples of civil law cases in the security field are false arrest, unlawful detention, negligent training of security officers, and inadequate security that results in death or injury. When a plaintiff (i.e., a person who initiates a lawsuit) wins a case against another party, monetary compensation commonly results.

Philip P. Purpura, *Encyclopedia of Security Management*, second ed., Butterworth-Heinemann, Burlington, MA, 2007, pp. 224–225.

K

KICKBACKS

The word "kickback" refers to an illegal payment (in any form such as money, property, goods, service, or favor) made to another person in exchange for an illegal act. A common form of a kickback occurs when a vendor gives an amount of cash to a purchasing agent in exchange for payment of an inflated invoice. For example, a seller of restaurant supplies sends an invoice to the purchasing agent of a restaurant chain. The invoice is false in that the provided supplies were substantially overpriced or that the supplies were provided in a lesser amount than is shown on the invoice. The purchasing agent approves the invoice and sends it to the accounts payable department. A check is sent to the vendor. The vendor kicks back to the purchasing agent a percentage of the overcharge.

A kickback arrangement is sometimes based on a tacit understanding between the two parties. It can begin with a vendor sending a "thank you" gift. Over a period of time, the gift increases in value.

A variation of the scheme can involve an outside party (a kickback broker) who, for a fee, will set up the arrangement; neither of the two parties will directly communicate with each other.

John J. Fay

KINESICS

Kinesics is the study of body language and is based on the behavioral patterns of nonverbal communication. Body language includes any nonreflexive or reflexive movement of a part or all of the body. Such movements can be particularly revealing when a person communicates an emotional message to the outside world. It is not so much what a person says when answering a question; it is the manner of how it is said.

The psychological assumptions underlying kinesics are:

- A person hiding the truth will experience automatic physiological changes when asked questions that challenge the person's withholding of the truth.
- A deceptive person will be aware of physiological changes occurring in the body and may attempt to disguise them.
- A person's fear of detection will intensify at moments when questioning focuses on details having the greatest immediate threat.

Kinesics and Interrogation

A guilty subject will have a general fear of what an investigation will uncover. Fear will intensify during interrogation when questions are directed toward matters that present the greatest threat to exposure of the deception. A guilty person's fear of detection tends to increase as the interrogation proceeds from the general to the specific. The deceptive person will tune in on questions that indicate personal danger ahead.

Body language signals can be understood within context only. Context can be the effect of:

- The nature of the situation under investigation
- The immediate, contemporaneous environment
- Social, cultural, and economic influences

A glance, a smile, and a raised eyebrow are signals but each can have different meanings when they appear in different contexts. A smile in one situation may reflect happiness, pleasure, and satisfaction; in another, it may reflect cynicism or disbelief.

People send signals that reveal their thoughts and feelings. Some signals are deliberate, such as a frown to indicate disapproval of what has been said. Most signals are unconscious, such as a crossing of the arms or a blink of the eyes. Unconscious signals tend to be subtle and indistinguishable to the untrained investigator.

The interrogator cannot always know what questions will produce fear in the guilty subject. As the line of questioning moves closer to the issues having the greatest psychological threat, deceptive signals will likely increase in number and intensity.

Personal Space

Signals that appear in threatening situations can be likened to warnings displayed by territorial animals under attack. Man, being a highly territorial animal, will instinctively attempt to control the immediately surrounding space. The space surrounding the individual can be likened to a bubble within which the individual feels safe. Penetration of the bubble can be threatening. This psychological bubble is the most inviolable of spheres. Threats to penetration of the bubble, whether by physical or psychological intrusion, may be answered with unconscious signals that indicate hostility or a desire to escape or even to submit.

Reactions to invasion of the personal bubble are observable and evaluable. At an intimate distance, two persons cannot help being overwhelmingly aware of each other. In the case of men, it can lead to awkwardness, uneasiness, and violence. Between a man and a woman, such as husband and wife, close physical proximity can be natural and welcome. In addition to context, distance is an important consideration when interpreting reactions.

Whether we know or approve of it, we cannot entirely suppress or conceal our body language. An interrogator who leans in close to the suspect's face (a physical intrusion) or whose question probes close to a hidden truth (a psychological intrusion) may produce a variety of signals ranging from finger and toe tapping, twitching, leg swinging, and body rocking. The signals are saying: "You are getting too near and I don't like it."

Eye Signals

The eyes are rated the most revealing body part; they transmit signals in ways ranging from extreme subtlety to unmistakable clarity. While the eyeball itself reveals little, the muscles around the eyes reveal a great deal. Much can be learned from a raised eyebrow or a squint, provided we understand the context. A very important eye signal is the stare. From a suspect under interrogation, it could mean disbelief, anger, or defiance. From the interrogator to the suspect, a stare could be saying, "I am waiting for your answer and I'm getting impatient."

The stare is a cultural taboo. No one likes being stared at. It is very normal to stare at a painting, a dog, or a sunset, but it is neither normal nor acceptable to stare at a fellow human being. The cultural aspect of the stare confers to it special status.

Physiology

A deceptive person, when immediately facing possible exposure, will experience physiological changes that cannot be controlled, such as a rise in blood pressure and respiration, contraction of the bowels, and release of adrenaline. They can also evoke verbal signals such as "It sure is hot in here" or "I must have eaten something bad this morning." Fear of exposure can magnify the physiological changes and produce new and combining signals such as hunched shoulders and eye avoidance.

Many strong signals are sent through speech. The content of speech can be significant, but a much greater significance can be attached to the manner of speech. An innocent person may express outrage as opposed to fear. Outrage can be shown with verbal signals like "You must be crazy" or "I don't have to tolerate this." A deceptive person may say, "To be perfectly honest" or conclude with "And that's God's truth." Statements like these are made deliberately. They are intended to mislead and/or gain time to think of what to say next.

The deceptive person likely will:

- Be guarded
- Hesitate before answering a question
- Pretend to be unconcerned
- Rationalize
- Be uncooperative
- Be unwilling to talk

By contrast, the truthful person will:

- Be sincere
- Be quick to answer questions
- Be composed
- Be helpful
- Be unyielding in denial
- Give consistent answers

The common behavioral signals of deception are:

- Licking lips
- Swallowing
- Scratching, pinching, and stroking head hair, earlobes, and nose
- Wringing hands
- Drumming fingers
- Bouncing legs
- Tapping toes
- Adjusting clothing, watch, ring, etc.
- Chewing and inspecting nails
- Covering mouth or eyes
- Looking away

A body language signal is like a word in a sentence. The true meaning of the word cannot be established without knowing all of the other words in the sentence. Like words, body language signals are sent in groups, and the sending is a response to a stimulus. Sending the stimulus, observing the response, and understanding the context are the essential elements in making an interpretation.

Kinesics holds that humans everywhere engage in nonverbal communication that is partly instinctive and partly learned. To the untrained eye, body language is largely invisible. For the skilled investigator, body language can be a rich source for determining truth.

Leon C. Mathieu, *Encyclopedia of Security Management*, second ed., Elsevier, Burlington, MA, 2011, pp. 161–167.

L

LAW SOURCES

There are four sources of law in the United States:

- The U.S. and state constitutions
- Legislative or statutory law
- Judicial decisions or case law
- Rules and regulations of governmental agencies or administrative law

Constitutions prevail over statutes, and statutes prevail over common-law principles established in court decisions. Courts will not turn to judicial decisions if a statute is directly applicable. The rules and principles that are applied by courts fall into three groups:

- Laws that have been passed by legislative bodies
- Case law, derived from cases decided by the courts
- Procedural rules, which determine how the law is applied in court, such as rules of evidence

The first two groups are used by the courts to decide controversies. They are often called substantive law. The third group, known as procedural law, provides the machinery whereby substantive law is given effect and applied to resolve controversies.

Substantive law defines rights, whereas procedural law establishes the procedures by which rights are enforced and protected. For example,

Green claims that White should reimburse Green because Green's money was stolen from a safe in the custody of White. The rules that provide for bringing White into court constitute procedural law. Whether White had a duty to protect Green's money against burglary of the safe and whether Green is entitled to damages are matters that fall under the rules of substantive law. Thus in a single matter, two rules may apply: procedural law and substantive law.

Private law pertains to the relationships between individuals. It encompasses the subjects of contracts, torts, and property. The law of torts is a chief source of litigation. A tort is a wrong committed by one person against another or against his property. The law of torts holds that people who injure others or their property should compensate them for their loss.

Constitutional Law

The Constitution of the United States and the constitutions of the various states form the foundation of our legal system. All other laws must be consistent with them. A federal law cannot violate the U.S. Constitution; all state laws must conform to the federal Constitution, as well as with the constitution of the appropriate state.

Statutory Law

Much of law is found in legislation. Legislation is the expression of society's judgment and the product of the political process. Legislative bodies exist at all levels of government. Legislation is created by Congress, state legislatures, and local government bodies. Legislation enacted by Congress or by a state legislature is usually referred to as a statute.

Laws passed by local governments are frequently called ordinances.

Legislation at all levels of government are called codes. For example, city fire codes regulate fire safety; state motor vehicle codes regulate the operation of motor vehicles; and the U.S. Code regulates criminal offenses committed at the federal level.

Case Law

A very substantial part of law is found in cases decided by the courts. This concept of decided cases as a source of law is generally referred to as case law and has been a predominant influence in the evolution of the body of law in the United States. Case law is important because of the great difficulty in establishing law in advance of an issue being raised.

When a case is decided, the court writes an opinion. These written opinions, or precedents, make up the body of case law. The concept of precedent is linked to a doctrine called *stare decisis*, which means "to stand by decisions and not to disturb what is settled." *Stare decisis* holds that once a precedent has been set, it should be followed in later cases involving the same issue. In this way, the law takes on certainty and predictability.

Administrative Law

Administrative law is concerned with the many administrative agencies of the government. This type of law is in the form of rules and regulations promulgated by an administrative agency created by a state legislature or by Congress to carry out a specific statute. For example, in a variety of statutes, Congress gives authority to the U.S. Department of Transportation (DOT) to regulate the nation's transportation systems. DOT rules are in the nature of law to the regulated parties.

The powers and procedures of the administrative agencies do not always correspond exactly to the general intent of the legislature. By its very nature, most legislation is general, and interpretation is necessary to carry out the intent of the legislative body. The rules that implement a legislative act are often the interpretation of a government administrator. Since it is not possible to precisely express legislative intent in words that mean the same thing to everyone, the rules and regulations are often approximations that, when implemented, are quickly challenged by the affected parties.

John J. Fay, *Encyclopedia of Security Management*, second ed., Butterworth-Heinemann, Burlington, MA, 2007, pp. 207–208.

LOCARD'S EXCHANGE PRINCIPLE

The concept known as the "Locard's Exchange Principle" states that every time a person enters an environment, something is added to and removed from the environment. The principle is sometimes stated as "every contact leaves a trace." Investigators are expected to understand that physical evidence of some type is introduced to or left behind at every scene. The amount and nature of the physical evidence is largely dependent on the circumstances of the crime. When such evidence is detected, it will usually fall into the category called fragmentary or trace evidence, such as hair and fibers, which result from contact between two surfaces.

The principle is owed to Dr. Edmond Locard, a pioneer in forensic science.

John J. Fay

LOSS PREVENTION THROUGH DENIAL OF OPPORTUNITY

Loss prevention is an essential goal for business organizations; an investigator who understands loss prevention can provide a valuable loss prevention service. Loss prevention embraces a three-dimensional concept that is often called the Crime Triangle. The dimensions are desire, skill and knowledge, and opportunity.

Desire

For there to be a crime, the criminal must possess a desire or a motivation to commit the crime. Desire is often caused by:

Greed. This is the desire to acquire things of value and is reflected in crimes such as larceny, robbery, embezzlement, and fraud.
Envy. This is the desire to be better than someone else in some particular way. Envy can be expressed in slander and libel.
Jealousy. This is a desire fueled by feelings of inadequacy.
Vengeance. This is the desire to avenge a wrong, genuine or imagined. It can spur murder, assault, and other crimes against a person or organization.
Lust. The crime of rape is in this category. Lust can also be the root of molestation and incest.
Hate. Crimes involving hate can be murder or assault based on sexual orientation, politics, and religion.

Skill and Knowledge

To commit a crime, the person must possess a skill. Skills vary widely: imitating handwriting (forgery), speaking convincingly (fraud), forcing a door open (breaking and entering), and firing a weapon (homicide). Integral to a skill is knowledge. Planned bankruptcy requires knowledge of bankruptcy law, a false workers' compensation claim requires knowledge of how claims are settled, and a store burglary requires knowledge of store hours.

A subtle and sophisticated form of skill and knowledge is the exercise of power. Persons in power positions, such as elected politicians and chief executive officers, are uniquely positioned to accept bribes and kickbacks.

In crimes committed against persons, the same logic prevails. A targeted individual can reduce vulnerability by self-protection, by staying out of social situations that may elevate to violence, and by exercising caution and restraining impulses.

Opportunity

The third dimension of the Crime Triangle is the opportunity to commit the crime. An individual may be greedy and know how to commit a crime, but without opportunity, the individual is powerless to act. If you think of a crime as an object supported by three legs, the object will fall if one of the legs is taken away.

It is interesting to note that desire is in the human psyche, which makes it impossible to eliminate; skill and knowledge are acquired attributes residing in the brain, which make them impossible to eliminate; but opportunity is a factor outside the control of the potential criminal. Who controls opportunity? The potential victim controls opportunity—not the criminal. Following are three actions that deny opportunity:

- Deter the criminal from acting. Examples of direct deterrence are guards, fences, lights, and locks. Examples of indirect deterrence includes termination and prosecution of employees who commit crimes, prosecution of nonemployees who commit crimes against the company, and policy statements and signage that provide warnings and notice of consequences.

- Detect the criminal during the criminal act and launch a response. Detection is possible through sensors installed on a perimeter and in buildings, closed-circuit television cameras and monitors, motion sensors in hallways and rooms, and human observation. A response following detection can be the dispatch of a single guard or members of a response team.
- Delay the criminal long enough for the response to succeed. Delay is possible by use of physical safeguards such as perimeter and on-premises fences, locked exterior and interior doors, locked containers, vaults, and safes.

It is been shown consistently that honest people can succumb to greed when given the opportunity to steal. The rationale tends to be: "If the owner doesn't care enough to protect it, I'm going to take it." This mind-set is particularly powerful when the taker believes he won't get caught.

John J. Fay

M

MIRANDA WARNING

The intent of the Miranda warning is to protect an individual who is in custody and subject to direct questioning by the police. A failure to administer a Miranda warning is a violation of an individual's Fifth Amendment right to not be compelled to make a self-incriminating statement.

The U.S. Supreme Court ruled in the case of *Miranda v. Arizona* that a person suspected of a crime has a Constitutional right to remain silent and a right to legal counsel. The effect of the ruling led to the establishment of a warning. If a suspect voluntarily and knowingly waives the rights to silence and legal counsel, the police may question the suspect concerning the matter under investigation.

Before questioning begins, the police must advise the suspect:

- Of the right to remain silent
- That anything said by the suspect can be used against the suspect in a criminal proceeding
- Of the right to have an attorney present before and during the questioning
- Of the right to obtain the services of an attorney or to have one appointed at public expense for representation before and during the questioning

There is no precise language that must be used in advising a suspect of Miranda rights. The point is that whatever language is used, the substance of the rights outlined above must be communicated to the suspect. The suspect may be advised of rights orally or in writing. An example of a warning is: "You have the right to remain silent. Anything you say can and will be used against you in a court of law. You have the right to an attorney. If you cannot afford an attorney, one will be provided for you. Do you understand the rights I have just read to you?"

Learning Shop USA, Interrogation, www.learningshopusa.com

MISSING AND UNIDENTIFIED PERSONS

Information concerning a missing or unidentified person can be obtained from the National Missing and Unidentified Persons System (NamUs). This system is a national centralized repository and resource center for missing persons and unidentified decedent records. NamUs is a free online system that can be searched by private and government investigators, medical examiners, coroners, law enforcement officials, and the general public.

Missing Persons Database

This database contains information about missing persons that can be entered by anyone; however, before it appears as a case on NamUs, the information is verified. NamUs provides a user with a variety of resources, including the ability to print missing persons posters and receive free biometric collection and testing assistance. Other resources include links to state clearinghouses, medical examiner and coroner offices, law enforcement agencies, victim assistance groups, and pertinent legislation.

Unidentified Persons Database

This database contains information about dead persons who have died and whose bodies have not been identified. The data has been entered by medical examiners and coroners. Anyone can search this database using characteristics such as sex, race, distinct body features, and dental information.

Unclaimed Persons Database

This database contains information about deceased persons who have been identified by name, but for whom no next of kin or family member has been identified or located to claim the body for burial or other disposition. Only medical examiners and corners may enter cases in the UCP database. However, the database is searchable by the public using a missing person's name and year of birth.

When a new missing persons or unidentified decedent case is entered into the National Missing and Unidentified Persons System, the system automatically performs cross-matching comparisons between the databases, searching for matches or similarities between cases.

U.S. Department of Justice, Office of Justice Programs, http://www.namus.gov/

MONEY LAUNDERING

Money laundering generally refers to financial transactions in which criminals, including terrorist organizations, attempt to disguise the proceeds, sources, or nature of their illicit activities. Money laundering facilitates a broad range of serious, underlying criminal offenses and ultimately threatens the integrity of the financial system.

The United States Department of the Treasury holds responsibility for combating money laundering at home and abroad. Money laundering that supports terrorist activities is investigated by the Treasury Department's Office of Terrorism and Financial Intelligence (TFI).

Money laundering occurs in three steps:

- Placement. Introduce cash into the financial system.
- Layering. Camouflage the illegal source.
- Integration. Use the camouflaged funds to acquire wealth.

The techniques of money launderers are:

- Smurfing. Cash is organized into small amounts and deposited in banks. Also, small amounts of cash are used to purchase money orders and similar instruments. This technique circumvents the requirement that cash transactions in excess of $10,000 must be reported.
- Bulk Cash Smuggling. Large quantities of cash are physically transported to a jurisdiction that has no requirement to report deposits, such as deposits made to offshore banks.
- Money Laundering through a Business. Cash is given to a business organization; it is then combined with legitimately derived funds. Such businesses are types that receive cash payments for products that are sold or services provided to the general public.

- Trade Laundering. False invoices and other forms of fraudulent documentation are used to move cash outside the boundaries of mandatory reporting.
- Shell Companies. Cash is moved to an organization located offshore or to a jurisdiction free of reporting requirements. The shell company is a "paper" company that exists only to conceal illegally derived cash.
- Bank Capture. The money launderer will purchase a bank and then move illegally derived cash through legal channels, without scrutiny.
- Casinos. Cash is used to purchase gambling chips. The chips are later redeemed. The redeemed funds are reported as gambling winnings.
- Direct Gambling. Cash is used to gamble. Winnings are reported; losses are not.
- Real Estate: Real estate is purchased with cash (person-to-person). The property is later sold. Proceeds from the sale are reported as legitimate income.
- Black Salaries. A money launderer that employs people pays salaries in cash. A company may have unregistered employees without a written contract and pay them cash salaries.

Money launderers are mostly drug traffickers. Others are embezzlers, corrupt public officials, and criminal syndicates.

U.S. Department of the Treasury, http://www.treasury.gov/resource-center/terrorist-illicit-finance/Pages/Money-Laundering.aspx

N

NATIONAL NAME CHECK PROGRAM

The National Name Check Program (NNCP) disseminates information from FBI files in response to name check requests received from federal agencies, including components within the legislative, judicial, and executive branches of the federal government, for the purpose of protecting the United States from foreign and domestic threats to national security.

The NNCP has its genesis in Executive Order 10450, issued during the Eisenhower administration. This executive order addresses personnel security issues and mandates National Agency Checks (NACs) as part of the preemployment vetting and background investigation process. The FBI is part of the NACs conducted on all U.S. government employees.

Customers of the NNCP seek background information from FBI files before bestowing a privilege, whether that privilege is government employment or an appointment, a security clearance, attendance at a White House function, issuance of immigration benefits, naturalization, or a visa to visit the United States. More than 50 agencies regularly request FBI name checks.

In addition to serving federal government customers, the NNCP conducts numerous name searches in direct support of the counterterrorism, counterintelligence, and homeland security efforts of the FBI.

The NNCP reviews and analyzes potential identifiable documents to determine whether a specific individual has been the subject of or mentioned in any FBI investigation(s) and, if so, what (if any) relevant information may be disseminated to the requesting agency. It is important to note that the FBI does not adjudicate the final outcome; it just reports the results to the requesting agency.

The NNCP conducts manual and electronic searches of the FBI's Central Records System (CRS). The CRS encompasses the centralized records of FBI Headquarters, field offices, and legal attaché offices, as well as all investigative, administrative, personnel, and general files.

The NNCP provides services to more than 50 federal government agencies and entities. Although most name checks are conducted for each agency on a first-come, first-served basis, the contributing agency determines the order of resolution for priority, project, or expedited cases. The major contributing agencies to the NNCP are the U.S. Citizenship and Immigration Services (USCIS), the Office of Personnel Management (OPM), and the Department of State (DOS).

Federal Bureau of Investigation, http://www.fbi.gov/stats-services/name-checks

NATURE OF TERRORISM

Terrorism is commonly defined as violent acts that:

- Are intended to intimidate and create fear
- Meet a religious dictate

- Attain a political goal
- Advance an ideology

Terrorist Groups

The true record of terrorist behavior does not conform to the premise that terrorists are rational actors primarily motivated by achieving political ends. The preponderance of empirical evidence is that terrorists are rational people who use terrorism primarily to develop strong affective ties with fellow terrorists.

Hamas. In 1987, the Arabs living in the territories occupied by Israeli in the Six-Day War began a series of riots and violent confrontations now known as the First Intifada. Soon after, Islamic militants founded the Hamas movement.

Hamas was formed from the Mujama movement, which had been a political party with no military ambitions that was given some encouragement by Israel earlier in the decade, as a means of countering the influence of the Palestine Liberation Organization.

Hamas is an acronym of *Harakat al Mawqawama al Islamiyya* meaning "Islamic Resistance Movement." The word Hamas also means "zeal."

Hezbollah. Hezbollah literally means "Party of God" and is a Shi'a Islamist political and paramilitary organization based in Lebanon. Hezbollah is also a major provider of social services, which operate schools, hospitals, and agricultural services for thousands of Lebanese Shi'a, and plays a significant force in Lebanese politics. It is regarded as a resistance movement throughout much of the Arab and Muslim world.

Hezbollah first emerged in 1982 as a response to the Israeli invasion of Lebanon. Hezbollah leaders call for the destruction of Israel, which they refer to as a "Zionist entity."

The Evolution of Terrorism

Terrorism is hardly new. It has been with civilization at least since the beginning of recorded history.

- In the sixth century BC, Assyrians poisoned enemy wells with rye ergot, a fungus that causes convulsions if ingested.
- The Greek historian Xenophon, in the fifth century BC, wrote of the use and effectiveness of psychological warfare against enemy populations.
- Roman emperors Tiberius and Caligula used banishment, expropriation of property, and execution to discourage opposition to their rule.
- In seventh-century India, cultists called Thuggees (from whom we get the word "thug") ritually strangled travelers as sacrifices to a Hindu deity.
- The Spanish Inquisition used arbitrary arrest, torture, and execution to punish what it viewed as religious heresy.
- The use of terror was openly advocated by Robespierre as a means of encouraging revolutionary virtue during the French Revolution, leading to the period of his political dominance called the Reign of Terror.
- After the end of the American Civil War in 1865, defiant Southerners formed the Ku Klux Klan to intimidate supporters of Reconstruction.
- In the latter half of the nineteenth century, terrorism was adopted by adherents of anarchism in Western Europe, Russia, and the United States. They believed that the best way to effect revolutionary political and social change was to assassinate persons in positions of power.
- From 1865 to 1905, a number of kings, presidents, prime ministers, and other government officials were killed by anarchists' guns or bombs.
- The assassination of Austrian Archduke Franz Ferdinand in 1914 by a Serb extremist touched off World War I.

Events Leading to 9/11

Today's more familiar forms of terrorism, which are often staged for a television audience, first appeared in 1968 when the Popular

Front for the Liberation of Palestine conducted the first terrorist hijacking of a commercial airplane. According to the U.S. State Department, the following terrorist events that foreshadowed the events of 9/11 are:

- In 1983, Hezbollah, an Iranian-backed group of Shiite Islamists, used a suicide bomber to attack the U.S. Marine barracks in Beirut, Lebanon. The bombing killed 242 Americans.
- In 1988, terrorists trained and financed by the Libyan government placed a bomb on board Pan Am flight 103. The aircraft exploded over Lockerbie, Scotland. More than 300 people died.
- The U.S. embassies in Kenya and Tanzania were attacked in 1988 by Al Qaeda suicide bombers, killing 224 people.
- In 1993, Islamist terrorists bombed the World Trade Center, killing six and injuring about 1,000 others.
- Also in 1993, Mir Aimal Kasi killed CIA employees Frank Darling and Lansing Bennett outside CIA headquarters in Langley, Virginia.
- Timothy McVeigh killed 168 people in 1995 by bombing a federal office building in Oklahoma City.
- In 1995, members of Aum Shinrikyo, a Japanese cult, released sarin nerve gas into the Tokyo subway, killing 12 and wounding over 3,500.
- In 1996, a truck bomb exploded outside the Khobar Towers housing complex in Saudi Arabia, killing 19 U.S. military members and wounding 515 people, including 240 U.S. citizen employees.
- In 2000, the USS *Cole*, a destroyer at anchor in the port of Aden, Yemen, was rammed by a small boat carrying explosives. The resulting blast killed 17 sailors and injured 39 others.

Contemporary Events

Some experts claim terrorist attacks increasingly seem to be focused on killing people.

Two reasons are postulated: attacks motivated by religion are free of the restraints of personal conscience; and attacks motivated by organizations initiate enhanced security protections of physical assets, thus making the human asset a substitute. Enhanced protection, frequently called "target hardening," may help explain why many attacks have involved explosives: explosives are not discriminating. They kill people and destroy property alike.

Bombs are relatively easy to assemble and deploy in areas crowded with people, especially when the bomber is willing to be consumed in the blast. Think of the "shoe bomber" from London and his later imitator on a plane to Detroit. They seemed to be acting on their own initiative, certainly in the spirit of terrorism, but apparently not at the specific direction of a terrorist group.

A terrorist act can be seen as:

- Premeditated and planned in advance; not an impulsive act of rage
- Designed to change the existing political order; not violence like that used by common criminals
- Aimed at civilians rather than military targets or combat-ready troops
- Carried out by a subnational group, not by the legitimate army of a country

Political Motives

Groups motivated by political considerations cover a lot of ground. First are terrorists that seek to form a separate state for their own group, which is often an ethnic minority. The group is likely to portray its activist followers as patriots struggling to achieve freedoms unjustly withheld by an oppressive government. Their appeal is to a world audience. They hope to win concessions at home, gain sympathy abroad, and obtain financial and logistical assistance from agreeable supporters.

Nationalistic Motives

Nationalist groups tend to calibrate their violent acts at a level high enough to maintain pressure on the established government but not so high as to alienate the group's members and outside supporters. Among the many nationalist groups that exist or have existed are the:

- Irish Republican Army
- Palestine Liberation Organization
- Basque Fatherland and Liberty
- Kurdistan Workers' Party
- Revolutionary Armed Forces of Columbia
- Armed Forces of Liberation (Colombia)
- National Liberation Front (Algeria)
- Shining Path (Peru)

Also in this arena are state-sponsored terrorist groups that are essentially nameless. They serve as the foreign policy tools of rogue or radical governments. What a rogue state cannot achieve through diplomacy it hopes to achieve by intimidation. Behind the intimidation are violent acts, such as assassinations and bombings, and saber rattling, such as the threatened use of nuclear weapons. Groups in this category operate covertly, often hire mercenaries, and enlist no-cost services of sympathizers. These groups are capable of carrying out large-scale attacks because they can call upon resources of the state: government intelligence and weaponry, diplomatic immunity, documents that permit cross-border travel, and a cloak of legitimacy.

Religious Motives

Religious terrorists use violence to further what they see as divinely commanded purposes. Their playing field is global as opposed to national, and their targets are wide-ranging. Some terrorist groups in this category are small and cult-like, and a few exist on the ultraradical fringe. The larger groups come from major religions and are almost always minorities within them.

One of the difficulties in assessing the intentions of religiously motivated terrorist groups is the vague and irrational statements of their leaders. For example, a leader will

call for a jihad (holy war) but leave followers to use their own imagination in waging it, so leaders in subgroups will interpret the jihad in a variety of ways.

Jihad. *Jihad* is an Islamic term meaning struggle and a religious duty of Muslims. Jihad appears frequently in the Qur'an and common usage as the idiomatic expression "striving in the way of Allah."

A person engaged in jihad is called a *mujahid*; the plural is *mujahideen*. Jihad is an important religious duty for Muslims. A minority among the Sunni scholars sometimes refer to this duty as the sixth pillar of Islam, though it occupies no such official status.

A wide range of opinions exist about the exact meaning of jihad. Muslims use the word in a religious context to refer to three types of struggles: an internal struggle to maintain faith, the struggle to improve the Muslim society, or the struggle in a holy war. Jihad implies warfare. In Western societies, the term jihad is often translated as "holy war."

By contrast, the politically motivated terrorist groups express less amorphous objectives such as removal of a government or establishment of an independent nation. At least with the politically motivated groups, the protectors of peace are able to somewhat more accurately assess the persons and groups with whom they are dealing, their likely targets, and the arenas of operation.

Special Interest Motives in the United States

Terrorist groups in the United States are for the most part special interest groups motivated by opposition to federal taxation and regulation, the United Nations, other international organizations, and the U.S. government generally. Much of the opposition comes from organizations, and, depending on who is doing the estimates, the overall membership of these groups will range from 10,000 to 100,000. Even if the total numbers are high, the extremist core of the militia movement is quite small and often out of sync with the desires of the broad majority. A strategy exercised by the leaders of some groups is to endorse violence but leave the execution of it to hard-core individuals acting on their own. An example of this strategy in action was the bombing by Timothy McVeigh of the Alfred P. Murrah Federal Building in Oklahoma City. The mailing of anthrax letters to government officials is another example.

Some hate groups in the United States terrorize in the name of race or religion, or both. The Ku Klux Klan, which used lynching to terrorize African Americans following the Civil War, was a forerunner of today's neo-Nazis. The neo-Nazis are actually a combination of groups that go by the names Skinheads, Christian Patriots, The Order, and Creativity Movement. They share ideological roots with the National States' Rights Party, founded in 1958 by Edward Reed Fields and J. B. Stoner. Fields and Stoner countered racial integration in the American South with Nazi-inspired publications and iconography. An offshoot of the movement was the American Nazi Party (ANP) founded by George Lincoln Rockwell in 1959. The ANP achieved high-profile coverage in the press through their public demonstrations.

A small minority of American neo-Nazis draw public attention by operating underground so they can recruit, organize, and raise funds without interference or harassment. The American correctional system houses many white supremacist and neo-Nazi prison gangs, and often white prisoners join those gangs for protection while incarcerated.

Aryan Nations. The Aryan Nation group embraces multiple issues: they hate anyone who is not white or is Jewish or is favorably disposed to the U.S. government. A closely related group is the Aryan Brotherhood, which is composed of present and former prison gang members.

Pro-Life Groups. Pro-life zealots have assassinated physicians and bombed abortion clinics, but, because these individuals appear not to be members of an organized group, the FBI has classified their attacks as criminal acts rather than terrorist acts. Eric Robert Rudolph, also known as the Olympic Park Bomber, is best known for his antiabortion terrorist bombings. He was responsible for a series of bombings across the southern United States between 1996 and 1998, which killed two people and injured at least 150 others.

Animal Liberation Front (ALF). ALF encourages individuals to take "direct action" against organizations that commit animal abuse, such as the meat industry's practice of slaughtering cattle or the medical research industry's practice of vivisecting laboratory animals. ALF's call for action is believed to be connected to crimes that include arson, breaking and entering, and theft.

ALF is an underground, leaderless resistance that engages in illegal direct action in pursuit of animal liberation. Activists see themselves as a modern-day Underground Railroad, removing animals from laboratories and farms, destroying facilities, arranging safe houses and veterinary care, and operating sanctuaries where the animals live out the rest of their lives.

ALF cells operate clandestinely, consisting of small groups of friends and sometimes just one person, making their actions difficult for the authorities to monitor. Activists say the movement is nonviolent. However, ALF's code says any act that furthers the cause of animal liberation, where all reasonable precautions are taken not to harm human or non-human life, may be claimed as an ALF action. There has nevertheless been widespread criticism that ALF spokespersons and activists have either failed to condemn acts of violence or have themselves engaged in it, either in the name of ALF or under another banner.

Earth Liberation Front (ELF). ELF is a loosely knit ecoterrorist organization whose primary agenda is protection of the environment. ELF's likely targets are new construction projects, logging sites, petroleum drilling and production facilities, and mining operations. An allied organization with a similar agenda is Earth First.

ELF, also known as "The Elves," is the collective name for autonomous individuals or covert cells who use "economic sabotage and guerrilla warfare to stop the exploitation and destruction of the environment."

Evaluation of Terrorist Groups

People tend to think of terrorism as brutal and senseless. Brutal it is, but senseless it is not. Behind every terrorist act is a motive, if not a calculated strategy. Although the nature of the acts vary widely—from the use of kidnapping and extortion to guns and bombs—they are neither spontaneous nor random. The tactics of terrorists are intended to be spectacular. The greater the spectacle, the greater the fear, the greater the intimidation. In one sense, terrorism is theater.

Terrorist groups can be categorized such as where they are from, where they operate, weapons and tactics they use, and the targets they attack. One categorization label that seems to work well is motivation.

Motivation can spring from many aspirations: promote or live by interpreted tenets of religion, such as destroy all religions but Muslim and establish a world-wide caliphate; destroy or convert political institutions; completely annihilate Israel; and destroy other perceived enemies such as the United States—the Great Satan.

Learning Shop USA, Nature of Terrorism, www.learningshopusa.com

NEGLIGENCE

Negligence is doing something that a reasonably prudent person would not have done or the failure to do something that a reasonably prudent person would have done in like or similar circumstances. It is the failure to exercise that degree of care that reasonably prudent persons would have exercised in similar circumstances.

Degrees of Care

Tort law has attempted to refine the concept of negligence by subdividing it into narrow categories. Degrees of care and degrees of negligence are closely related but are separate approaches in refining negligence. A degree of care is the amount of care that is reasonable for a given situation. It depends on various factors, including the relationship between the parties and the nature and extent of the risk inherent in that situation. For example, transporting school children requires a higher degree of care than hauling watermelons.

Degrees of Negligence

Degrees of negligence embrace the idea that negligence may be classified as slight or gross. This has been a persistent theme in tort law and criminal law. There are statutes in which the term "negligence" is preceded by some adjective, such as "slight" or "gross." In most cases, the statute applies only to a particular situation or activity.

Slight negligence is the failure to exercise great care. It is not a slight departure from ordinary care. Technically, it is the failure to exercise greater care than the circumstances would ordinarily require.

On the other hand, gross negligence is something more than ordinary negligence but only in degree. It is less than recklessness, which is a different kind of conduct showing a conscious disregard for the safety of others. The distinction is important since contributory negligence is not a defense to wanton misconduct, but it is to gross negligence. A finding of reckless misconduct will usually support an award of punitive damages whereas gross negligence will not.

Contributory negligence is an act or omission amounting to want of ordinary care on the part of a complaining party, which, concurring with the defendant's negligence, is the proximate cause of injury. Contributory negligence generally applies to a condition of employment, either express or implied, with which an employee agrees that the dangers of injury are obviously incident to the discharge of required duties. The act or omission will be at the employee's own risk.

Negligent Conduct

Negligent conduct is an element of various tort causes of action. The components of the cause of action for negligence are:

- A duty owed by the defendant to the plaintiff
- A violation of that duty by defendant's failure to conform to the required standard of conduct
- Sufficient causal connection between the negligent conduct and the resulting harm
- Actual loss or damage

The plaintiff's contributory negligence, if any, will reduce or defeat a claim. In many jurisdictions, contributory negligence is a defense to be pleaded and proved by the defendant, but in some jurisdictions the plaintiff must allege and prove his freedom from contributory negligence as a part of his case.

Negligent Hiring

Negligence can be alleged in an employer's hiring practices. The term "negligent hiring" refers to a concept that holds an employer directly liable for an employee's harmful conduct after the employer failed to exercise reasonable care in hiring the employee. Although similar to "respondeat superior," this concept can extend to situations that occur outside of the workplace. For example, assume that during working hours a male supervisor makes a date with a female employee. During the date (off the employer's premises and during nonworking hours) the supervisor rapes the female. If the victim learns that the employer was aware that this same supervisor had assaulted other women whom he had met at work but had hired him anyway without warning her or other female employees, the employer can be charged with failure to exercise reasonable care in the hiring and retention of a dangerous employee.

Reasonable Person

The "reasonable person" concept applies objective standards of reasonableness when judging whether conduct is negligent. The law does not make special allowance for the particular weaknesses of a person acting negligently. Conduct that creates an unreasonable risk of harm is no less dangerous because the actor lacked the capacity to conform to an acceptable level of performance. While it may seem unfair to hold some people to standards they cannot always meet, it would be more unjust to require the innocent victims of substandard conduct to bear the consequences.

The standard is usually stated as reasonable care, ordinary care, or due care and is measured against the hypothetical conduct of a hypothetical person, i.e., the reasonable human of ordinary prudence. Such a person is not the average or typical person but an idealized image. He is a composite of the community's judgment as to how the typical citizen ought to behave in circumstances where there is a potential or actual risk of harm. The reasonable person is not perfect or infallible. He is allowed mistakes of judgment, of perception, and he may even be momentarily distracted. Above all, he is human and prone to errors, but such errors must have been reasonable or excusable under the circumstances.

The law of negligence distinguishes between liability for the consequences of affirmative acts (misfeasance) and liability for merely doing nothing (nonfeasance). Almost any inaction can be characterized as misfeasance. Inaction is substantially the equivalent of active misconduct. For example, the failure to repair defective brakes may be seen as active negligence.

An act not required by duty may be done voluntarily. For example, a person who freely renders aid takes on a duty to act with reasonable care; once the duty is assumed, it may not be abandoned.

John J. Fay, *Encyclopedia of Security Management*, second ed., Butterworth-Heinemann, Burlington, MA, 2007, pp. 209–232.

NOTE TAKING

Purposes of Note Taking

Notes take many forms, such as notes handwritten on paper, notes spoken or "twittered" into a handheld device, or voice-over commentary recorded by an active video device. For the sake of simplicity, this section will discuss note taking in the handwriting mode; the mode can, in fact, be any of the above, and perhaps others.

Taking notes is a routine yet essential task for anyone engaged in investigative work. It is very accurate to say that an investigator's "stock in trade" is information. It is also true that the human memory has limitations. Even the least consequential investigation will generate details well beyond the average human's ability to absorb and retain. This is where note taking has great significance. A method for recording information is essential, and plain old note taking is the principal method.

Anything that can in anyway be of interest to another party at any time should be recorded in notes. Another party can be anyone, such as the investigator's employer or client, prosecutor or defense attorney, judge or jurors, witnesses and complainants, and in fact anyone.

Some items that are entered into notes may never be needed, but there is no way that the investigator can know this. It is much, much better to record something rather than face unpleasant consequences later when the information is needed.

In a nutshell, the purposes of note taking are to:

- Track progress
- Prepare reports
- Recall details
- Aid in giving personal testimony
- Help others understand

Track Progress

At the minimum, notes should contain details concerning the who, what, where, when, how, and why of the matter investigated. Notes include every relevant detail; when a question exists as to whether a detail is relevant or not, it should be written down. If a mistake is made in note taking, the mistake should be on the side of caution, that is to say, taking a note that later proves to be inconsequential is far better than not taking a note in the first place. Only after an investigation has been completed will the investigator be able to distinguish between what is relevant and what is not. Never discard notes no matter how nonrelevant they are.

Notes should reflect what triggered the investigation and all investigative actions that followed. Investigative actions vary widely and, as a consequence, notes will vary; for example, notes taken during surveillance will be written down under conditions different from notes taken during an interview, when at an incident scene, or when receiving physical evidence.

Notes describe environments and conditions at environments; they state times, dates, and places; they describe interactions with persons; they mention things found or not found; and they include just about everything related to the investigation.

Prepare Reports

Notes serve as the primary reference in the preparation of reports. It is correct to say that a report cannot be complete without the use of notes. They can help the investigator visualize and reconstruct important events and, to some extent, provide the words and sentence structure of a report.

For every fact or action expressed in a report, there must be one or more supporting notational entries. It is usual and normal for notes to exceed in number and depth anything that is placed into a report. A report is, after all, a re-creation of notes.

Some investigators do not like to take notes and write reports, even though they may enjoy and be good at interviewing, collecting physical evidence, and analyzing facts. These individuals do not live up to their full potential and will inevitably fall under criticism when a need arises for information that should have been but was not recorded.

Recall Details

Notes jog the memory during and after the investigation. Notes can be reminders of actions that remain to be performed and the results proceeding from the actions. Notes help the investigator recall the details of events and transactions.

More often than not, an extended period of time will elapse between completion of an investigation and adjudication, which may be a hearing, a deposition, a trial, a settlement, a briefing, or other event that requires testimony. Several months or even years can pass during which the investigator has conducted many, many investigations. When informed of the requirement to testify, memory will have eroded, the facts of the case will be fuzzy in the mind, and certainties once held may now seem less certain. It is at this point that case notes are invaluable.

Give Testimony

A legal proceeding will often mark the finality of an investigation. A favorable result, certainly from the point of view of the investigator, will depend to a large extent upon the quality of testimony, and that quality will depend on notes prepared in the course of the investigation.

Notes produced on a witness stand can be taken in hand by opposing counsel and examined in the presence of a judge and/or jury. Notes that are deficient in any way, or made to appear deficient, will damage the investigator's competence and credibility. Opposing counsel will undermine the investigator's testimony by characterizing him or her as incompetent. The investigator's best course of action is to study notes beforehand, keeping in mind that the discovery process will provide to opposing counsel an opportunity to attack testimony. In the absence of preparation enabled by notes, the investigator will be vulnerable on the stand.

All of the effort and cost put into the investigation of a matter can be lost when the failure to take good notes results in weak testimony.

Help Others Understand

Notes are useful to a variety of people for a variety of purposes. These include:

- Informing fellow investigators of an investigative technique that worked or failed to work
- Helping a supervisor revise a practice or procedure that needed revision
- Advising the employer/client to discontinue an investigation or take a different line of investigation
- Helping friendly counsel decide a litigation strategy

Field Notes

Notes prepared outside of the office are called field notes. These can relate to:

- What was seen, heard, touched, smelled, or tasted
- Witness interviews
- Physical evidence collected
- Photographs and video, audio, and digital recordings
- Officials visited
- Record searches made
- Surveillance
- Stakeouts

Shortcuts

Notes often have to be taken "on the run," such as when a witness is talking rapidly or when important activities are occurring simultaneously. To keep up, the investigator abbreviates common words (like bldg for building and sub for subject) and acronyms (like SUV for sport utility vehicle and ASAP for as soon as possible). Selecting relevant details is mostly a matter of separating important facts from information that may be nice to know but not relevant. The fact that the hit-and-run vehicle was a 2014 Ford is relevant. The opinion of the witness concerning the poor attitudes of drivers in general is not relevant.

Another time-gaining step is to leave out connecting words like "I," "a," and "the." Later, under less demanding circumstances, shortened versions are converted to their actual forms. Here is an example: "Met Jones @ Carbo's. Says Brown not in Dec. Skip?" Converted, the abbreviated version becomes: "I met with Jones at Carbo's restaurant. He said that he was unable to spot Brown anywhere in Decatur and that he believes Brown has skipped town."

Shortened versions should not be made so short or so unusual that another person might apply different interpretations. Shortened versions can be kept and used when needed, but they are not a substitute for original notes—which must be retained always.

Office Notes

Actions that occur in the office are recorded on office notes. The items upon which notes are transcribed might be pink-colored slips from a pad next to a telephone, a page on a lined notepad, a pocket notebook, a piece of bond paper, or the reverse side of grocery list. The content of the notes can include information communicated and received by telephone or other communication modes (such as e-mail and fax), significant findings of a forensic report, and discussions with visitors.

Notes need to reflect evidence collected (physical, documentary and testimonial), conclusions reached from evidence examination, and information provided by persons not directly connected to the matter. It is fair to say that case notes should reflect everything related to the case.

Field notes and office notes should be entered in the same notebook, and one notebook should be used for each separate investigation.

Reading File

In some organizations, the substantive content of field and office notes is incorporated into what is often called a reading file or a progress file. A purpose of the reading file is to keep the investigator's superiors informed as to the progress of the investigation. Typically, the reading file is a one-page document that covers investigative activities during the immediately preceding 24-hour period.

The reading file consists of individual entries, each describing an action taken by the investigator, a result achieved, a new development or event related to the case, and other pertinent details. Following is an example of a reading file entry: "10:30 AM: Met with Mr. Harmon at his office and received from him Miss Johnson's time sheet for work she performed on the day of the theft. The time sheet shows that she was in the plant when the theft occurred. Made arrangements to interview Johnson tomorrow."

The reading file is more than an administrative tool for evaluating an investigator's output; it is a tool for bringing together separate pieces of information obtained over a chronological period of time so that they can be analyzed and judgments made (preliminary or otherwise).

The Notebook

The traditional notebook is of a type that fits in the pocket; has lined pages; and is manufactured with a binding that, when examined, will reveal whether or not pages have been torn out. This last feature can be exploited to your disadvantage when opposing counsel alleges that pages torn from a notebook show that you are concealing relevant facts.

The traditional notebook is losing favor. Personal digital assistance (PDA) devices, such as digital pads, tablets, cell phones, video and voice recorders, and cameras, can:

- Speed up the note taking process
- Capture a greater volume of information
- Reduce inaccuracies that would otherwise occur by reason of human failure
- Add realism

Digitized information is downloaded, perhaps printed, and stored in a digital format.

Characteristics of Effective Notes

Notes are regarded as effective when they are:

- Complete. Every relevant piece of information is included. The who, what, where, when, how. and why are covered to the extent they are known.
- Accurate. Notes are free of errors and the product of care. Misspellings and poor grammar cannot always be avoided; they are acceptable so long as they do not distort the facts.
- Specific. Notes are exact, precise, and free of ambiguity. Times, dates, places, names, and other details are right on target.
- Factual. Opinion and unwarranted conclusions do not appear in notes. Theories and hypotheses have no place in notes.
- Clear. Notes work best when they are plain and direct. They are also easier to write when extraneous information is excluded.
- Organized. Notes are regarded as organized when they are methodical, structured, and follow a logical path such as a chronology. They should not jump from one thought to another and then back again.
- Easy to read. Investigative jargon and legalese need to be left out. Words that are big or that have more than one meaning are also taboo.
- Simple. Good notes are conversational and down-to-earth. When read, the reader gets a distinct feel of "being there."

Case File

The case file is a collection of notes, reports, memos, statements, business cards, telephone messages, photographs, recordings—almost anything related to the case.

For tracking purposes, the case file is usually assigned a number, and the investigator is responsible for protecting the file, such as by placing it in a secure container when it is not in use.

The outer folder should be of a nature to prevent spillage of contents or the loss of a document that "slips" out of the file. Folders that meet this requirement are the accordion-type folder and zippered plastic folders.

A general rule says that the original copies of materials in the case file cannot leave the office without permission and must be kept under lock and key when not in use. Copies of items in the case file can be made and taken from the office, usually with permission.

The rationale that requires notes and other case file materials to be protected and treated with confidentiality also applies to the spoken word.

Points to Remember

The quality of an investigative report cannot be better than the quality of notes taken.

- Notes are the building blocks of a report.
- Good notes will reflect dates; times; names of persons; and details of things seen, heard, smelled, and touched.
- Good notes will contain actual quotations. Paraphrasing and restating a quotation are much less effective.
- The investigator's notebook should be bound in such a way that the removal of pages is readily apparent. A notebook of this type will neutralize an opposing attorney's attempt to accuse the investigator of concealing facts.
- The investigator's notebook should be of a size convenient to carry, such as a notebook that fits into a shirt pocket.
- A note made of a pertinent fact, such as the discovery of evidence or a quotation made by a witness, should be written into the notebook by the investigator that personally collected the fact. When circumstances require note taking by an associate investigator present at the scene, the primary investigator should initial the notes.

Learning Shop USA, Note Taking, www.learningshopusa.com

O

OFFICE AND PERSONNEL ADMINISTRATION

Day-to-day administration of an investigation office generally deals with these major tasks:

- Communicate
- Assign tasks
- Monitor and guide
- Keep records
- Control equipment
- Operate within a budget

Communicate

Communication moves up, out, and down. It moves up to directors, managers, and other persons in the "chain of command." It moves out to persons in the criminal justice system, such as police officers and prosecutors, attorneys, and clients. Communication moves down to persons who report directly to the person in charge, such as investigators and support staff.

The modes are face-to-face discussions, briefings, written reports, and information that moves electronically such as by telephone, texting, e-mail, and fax.

Assign Tasks

The person in charge assigns tasks according to functions, e.g., word processing is done by support staff and evidence gathering is done by investigators. Tasks are also assigned according to expertise or experience, e.g., a case that involves theft of data from a computer system is better handled by a person with expertise in that area, rather than an investigator who does not have the expertise. Other factors in choosing the right person for the job include knowledge of a language, ethnicity, stamina, and temperament.

A task is different than a job, a position, a duty, or a function. A task has certain characteristics. A task:

- Is directed toward a specific purpose. Writing reports is a function; writing the final report of investigation of a particular case is a task.
- Has a clear beginning and end. The task begins when pen is put to paper, and it ends when the report is placed on the desk of the person in charge.
- Is visible and measurable. The existence of the report is visible evidence of task completion and the report is measurable in some way, such as the quality of the writing or by finishing the report by a certain date, such as "I want to see it on my desk by tomorrow morning."

Monitor and Guide

These two terms are inseparable in the sense that the nature of guidance cannot be determined until the need for guidance is known. Monitoring identifies the need, and guiding satisfies the need. Need takes several forms: a need to correct a job performance problem, to clarify an issue, or to show how a task can be done better.

Monitoring occurs by observing performance directly, evaluating the product of performance, or simply listening to feedback from the performer or persons close to the performance.

Keep Records

Records mirror the success or failure of an investigation office. Records include everything: reports of investigation; internal, outgoing, and incoming correspondence; memoranda; personnel files; performance reports; overhead budget; accounting for equipment; and many more. In addition to evaluating the completeness of the record-keeping system, questions are asked:

- Are the records accurate?
- Is the recordkeeping system arranged in a manner suitable for easy retrieval of records?
- Are the records stored properly?
- Is confidentiality maintained?

Control Equipment

Control in the sense used here is custody, care, and use. Of all equipment owned by or entrusted to an investigation office, none is more important than vehicles; weapons; photographic and voice recording equipment; and electronic devices such as PCs, cell phones, and tablets.

Control is exercised when every piece of equipment is accounted for by issuance and receipt documents and custodial responsibility is assigned to and accepted by the users and/or supervisors of the users.

Operate within a Budget

A budget is a forecast of expenditures for a specific period of time. It is a basic planning tool because it sets priorities and keeps an eye on ups and downs of costs and expenses. Typically, the person in charge prepares the upcoming budget on the basis of the current budget. The upcoming budget is submitted to a supervisor/manager for approval or review before sending it forward to a financial control unit. Before a budget is approved, it is matched against organizational goals.

Budgeting is a routine, yet essential, function. A budget meets three purposes:

- Estimate the cost of planned activities.
- Provide warning when variances occur during the budget period.
- Exercise uniformity.

Overspending frequently results in a failure to anticipate rises in the cost of "must have" products and services, which is an unwelcome circumstance. Underspending is the opposite and likely to be welcomed. But whether overspending or underspending, the circumstance demonstrates poor planning.

Learning Shop USA, Business Practices, Part 1 and Part 2, www.learningshopusa.com

P

PARTIES TO CRIME

Persons culpably concerned in the commission of a crime, whether they directly commit the act constituting the offense or facilitate, solicit, encourage, aid or attempt to aid, or abet its commission, are called the parties to the crime. In some jurisdictions, the concept is extended to include persons who assist one who has committed a crime to avoid arrest, trial, conviction, or punishment.

The parties to a felony crime fall into four categories:

* Principals in the first degree
* Principals in the second degree
* Accessories before the fact
* Accessories after the fact

Generally, a principal in the first degree is the actual offender who commits the act. If the offender uses an agent to commit the act, the offender is still a principal in the first degree. There may be more than one principal in the first degree for the same offense.

A principal in the second degree is one who, with knowledge of what is afoot, aids and abets the principal in the first degree at the very time the felony is being committed by rendering aid, assistance, or encouragement. A principal in the second degree is typically at the crime scene, nearby, or situated in such a way as to render assistance. Under the concept of "constructive presence," a principal in the second degree could be a considerable distance removed from the crime while it is being committed. An example might be a lookout monitoring police radio communications at a remote location who calls burglar accomplices at the crime scene to alert them of police patrol movements.

An accessory before the fact is a person who, before the time a crime is committed, knows of the particular offense contemplated, assents to or approves of it, and expresses a view of it in a form that operates to encourage the principal to perform the deed. There is a close resemblance between an accessory before the fact and a principal in the second degree. The difference relates to where the accessory was and the nature of the assistance rendered at the time the crime was committed. If a person advises, encourages, and gives aid prior to the act, but is not present at the act and not giving aid at the time of the act, the person would be regarded as an accessory before the fact.

An accessory after the fact is a person who, knowing that another has committed a felony, subsequently aids the felon to escape in any way or prevents arrest and prosecution. The person may help the felon elude justice by concealing, sheltering, or comforting the felon while a fugitive or by supplying the means of escape or by destroying evidence. An accessory after the fact must have an intention to assist the felon and must actually do so. Mere knowledge of the felon's offense and a failure to report it does not make a person an accessory after the fact.

Learning Shop USA, Criminal Law, www. learningshopusa.com

PATRIOT ACT

The Patriot Act is designed to improve the nation's counterterrorism efforts. The Act:

- Allows investigators to use the tools that were already available to investigate organized crime and drug trafficking. Many of the tools the Act provides to law enforcement to fight terrorism have been used for decades to fight organized crime and drug dealers and have been reviewed and approved by the courts.
- Allows law enforcement to use surveillance against more crimes of terror. Before the Patriot Act, courts could permit law enforcement to conduct electronic surveillance to investigate many ordinary, non-terrorist crimes, such as drug crimes, mail fraud, and passport fraud. Agents also could obtain wiretaps to investigate some, but not all, of the crimes that terrorists often commit. The Act enabled investigators to gather information when looking into the full range of terrorism-related crimes, including: chemical-weapons offenses, the use of weapons of mass destruction, killing Americans abroad, and terrorism financing.
- Allows federal agents to follow sophisticated terrorists trained to evade detection. For years, law enforcement has been able to use "roving wiretaps" to investigate ordinary crimes, including drug offenses and racketeering. A roving wiretap can be authorized by a federal judge to apply to a particular suspect, rather than a particular phone or communications device. Because international terrorists are sophisticated and trained to thwart surveillance by rapidly changing locations and communication devices such as cell phones, the Act authorized agents to seek court permission to use the same techniques in national security investigations to track terrorists.
- Allows law enforcement to conduct investigations without tipping off terrorists. In some cases, if criminals are tipped off too early to an investigation, they might flee, destroy evidence, intimidate or kill witnesses, cut off contact with associates, or take other action to evade arrest. Therefore, federal courts in narrow circumstances long have allowed law enforcement to delay for a limited time when the subject is told that a judicially approved search warrant has been executed. Notice is always provided, but the reasonable delay gives law enforcement time to identify the criminal's associates, eliminate immediate threats to our communities, and coordinate the arrests of multiple individuals without tipping them off beforehand. These delayed notification search warrants have been used for decades, have proven crucial in drug and organized crime cases, and have been upheld by courts as fully constitutional.
- Allows federal agents to ask a court for an order to obtain business records in national security terrorism cases. Examining business records often provides the key that investigators are looking for to solve a wide range of crimes. Investigators might seek select records from hardware stores or chemical plants, for example, to find out who bought materials to make a bomb or bank records to see who is sending money to terrorists. Law enforcement authorities have always been able to obtain business records in criminal cases through grand jury subpoenas and continue to do so in national security cases where appropriate.

Under the Patriot Act, the government can now ask a federal court (the Foreign Intelligence Surveillance Court), if needed to aid an investigation, to order production of the same type of records available through grand jury subpoenas. This federal court, however, can issue these orders only after the government demonstrates the records concerned are sought for an authorized investigation to obtain foreign intelligence information not concerning a U.S. person or to protect against international terrorism or clandestine intelligence activities, provided that such investigation of a U.S. person is not conducted solely on the basis of activities protected by the First Amendment.

The Act facilitates information sharing and cooperation among government agencies and removes the major legal barriers that prevent law enforcement, intelligence, and national defense communities from talking and coordinating their work.

The Patriot Act updated the law to reflect new technologies and new threats. The Act brought the law up to date with state-of-the art technology.

Before the Act, law enforcement personnel were required to obtain a search warrant in the district where they intended to conduct a search, a procedure that resulted in delays. But in the current environment, districts and officers can obtain multiple warrants in multiple jurisdictions. The Act provides that warrants can be obtained in any district in which terrorism-related activities have occurred, regardless of where the warrants will be executed. This provision does not change the standards governing the availability of a search warrant, but it streamlines the search-warrant process.

Victims of computer hacking can request law enforcement assistance in monitoring the "trespassers" on their computers. This change made the law technology neutral; it placed electronic trespassers on the same footing as physical trespassers. Now, hacking victims can seek law enforcement assistance to combat hackers, just as burglary victims can invite officers into their homes to catch burglars.

The Patriot Act increases the penalties for those who commit terrorist crimes. In particular, the Act:

- Prohibits the harboring of terrorists
- Provides high penalties for various crimes likely to be committed by terrorists such as arson, destruction of energy facilities, providing material support to terrorists and terrorist organizations, and destruction of national defense materials
- Enhances conspiracy penalties that deal with killings in federal facilities, attacking communications systems, giving material support to terrorists, sabotaging nuclear facilities, and interfering with flight crew members. Under previous law, many terrorism statutes did not specifically prohibit engaging in conspiracies. In such cases, the government could only bring prosecutions under the general federal conspiracy provision.
- Punishes terrorist attacks on mass transit systems
- Punishes bioterrorists
- Eliminates the statutes of limitations for certain terrorism crimes and lengthens them for other terrorist crimes

The Department of Justice has a first priority to prevent future terrorist attacks. Since its passage following the September 11, 2001, attacks, the Patriot Act has played a key part—and often the leading role—in a number of successful preventive operations.

U.S. Department of Justice, USA Patriot Act, http://www.justice.gov/archive/ll/highlights.htm

PHYSICAL EVIDENCE

Physical evidence is anything that tends to prove or disprove a fact. Examples are fingerprints, palm prints, and plantar (foot) prints; biological tissues and fluids; materials displaying bite marks; foot and tire treads; weapons; projectiles; poisons; chemical substances; pieces of metal; dirt; glass fragments; fibers; tools; photographs; video and audio tapes; questioned documents; and much, much more.

Physical evidence can be categorized in several ways. For example, fragile evidence is anything that can be easily lost (e.g., footprints in melting snow), contaminated (bloodstains mixed with dirt), or damaged (fingerprints smudged by rough handling).

Physical evidence that can be picked up and carried away is called moveable or portable evidence, while telephone poles and brick walls are called nonmoveable or fixed evidence. Trace evidence is something very small such as a fiber, a hair, a shard of glass, or a drop of liquid.

Physical evidence can be categorized according to physical properties such as fluids, metals, poisons, glass, plastics, and soil.

An object of evidence can also be categorized according to effect: striations on a bullet are the effect of the bullet passing through a gun barrel. Effect is present in toolmarks on a jimmied door, a signature on a forged document, a stain on a sheet, or a bruise resulting from a blow.

John J. Fay, *Encyclopedia of Security Management*, second ed., Butterworth-Heinemann, Burlington, MA, 2007, pp. 138–140.

PLAIN VIEW DOCTRINE

A law enforcement officer is allowed to seize an item that is in the officer's unobstructed view, provided that the item is contraband (an item that is illegal to possess) or an item that is known by the officer to be connected to a crime. For example, an officer stops a motorist for speeding. The officer asks the motorist to provide a driver's license and vehicle registration. In this process, the officer sees illegal drugs (crime connection). The officer seizes the drugs.

In this example are three requirements that must be met in order for the seizure to be lawful.

- The officer must have a lawful reason to be present at the place of the seizure.
- The item must be plainly seen by the officer.
- The character of the item must be immediately apparent to the officer.

Again, in this example, the seizure would not be lawful if:

- There was no reason for the motorist to be stopped in the first place (lack of probable cause).
- The officer looked in places that were out of his immediate view, such as in the trunk of the vehicle. (If the motorist gives express permission to the officer to look in the trunk, a seizure might be lawful.)
- The officer seized the drugs before knowing that the drugs were illegal to possess.

In this example, the plain view doctrine is connected to the fruit of the poisonous tree doctrine; the fact of an illegal seizure cannot be used as evidence at a trial, and any other evidence discovered as a result of the seizure cannot be used as evidence.

Learning Shop USA, Search and Seizure, www.learningshopusa.com

POLYGRAPH TESTING

The term "polygraph" literally means "many writings." The name refers to the manner in which selected physiological activities are simultaneously recorded. Polygraph examiners may use conventional instruments, sometimes referred to as analog instruments, or computerized polygraph instruments.

A polygraph instrument collects physiological data from at least three systems in the human body. Convoluted rubber tubes that are placed over the examinee's chest and abdominal area record respiratory activity. Two small metal plates, attached to the fingers, record sweat gland activity; a blood pressure cuff or similar device records cardiovascular activity.

A typical polygraph examination will include a period referred to as a pretest, a chart collection phase, and a test data analysis phase. In the pretest, the polygraph examiner completes the required paperwork and talks with the examinee about the test. During this period, the examiner discusses the questions to be asked and familiarizes the examinee with the testing procedure. During the chart collection phase, the examiner administers and collects a number of polygraph charts. Following this, the examiner analyzes the charts and renders an opinion as to the truthfulness of the person taking the test. The examiner, when appropriate, will offer the examinee an opportunity to explain physiological responses in relation to one or more questions asked during the test. It is important to note that a polygraph does not include the analysis of physiology associated with the voice. Instruments that claim to record voice stress are not polygraphs and have not been shown to have scientific support.

Users

Three segments of society conduct polygraph examinations. They are law enforcement agencies, the legal community, and the private sector.

In the law enforcement segment are federal law enforcement agencies, state law enforcement agencies, and local law enforcement agencies such as police and sheriff's departments.

In the legal community are U.S. attorney offices, district attorney offices, public defender offices, defense attorneys, and parole and probation officers.

The private sector is composed of companies and corporations, attorneys in civil litigation, and private citizens in matters not involving the legal or criminal justice system.

Critics

A problem in discussing accuracy figures and the differences between statistics quoted by proponents and opponents of the polygraph technique is the way that figures are calculated. Critics, who often don't understand polygraph testing, classify inconclusive test results as errors. In the real-life setting, an inconclusive result simply means that the examiner is unable to render a definite diagnosis. In such cases, a second examination is usually conducted at a later date.

To illustrate how the inclusion of inconclusive test results can distort accuracy figures, consider the following example: If 10 polygraph examinations are administered and the examiner is correct in seven decisions, is wrong in one, and has two inconclusive test results, we can calculate the accuracy rate as 87.5 percent (eight definitive results, seven of which were correct.)

Critics would calculate the accuracy rate in this example as 70 percent (10 examinations with seven correct decisions.) Since those who use polygraph testing do not consider inconclusive test results as negative, and do not hold them against the examinee, to consider them as errors is clearly misleading.

Positive and False Negative Errors

While the polygraph technique is claimed to be highly accurate, it cannot be infallible, as errors do occur. Polygraph errors may be caused by the examiner's failure to properly prepare the examinee for the examination or by a misreading of the physiological data.

Errors are usually referred to as either false positives or false negatives. A false positive occurs when a truthful examinee is reported as being deceptive; a false negative occurs when a deceptive examinee is reported as truthful. Some research indicates that false negatives occur more frequently than do false positives; other research studies show the opposite conclusion. Since it is recognized that any error is damaging, examiners utilize a variety of procedures to identify the presence of factors that may cause false responses and to ensure an unbiased review. These procedures include:

- Assessment of the examinee's emotional state
- Medical information about the examinee's physical condition
- Specialized tests to identify the overly responsive examinee and to calm the overly nervous
- Control questions to evaluate the examinee's response capabilities
- Actual analysis of the case information
- Pretest interview and detailed review of the questions
- Quality control reviews

Remedies

If an examinee believes that an error has been made, several remedies are available:

- Request a second examination.
- Retain an independent examiner for a second opinion.
- File a complaint with a state licensing board.
- File a complaint with the Department of Labor.

Prohibited Inquiries

Personal and intrusive questions have no place in a properly conducted polygraph examination. Many state licensing laws, the Employee Polygraph Protection Act, and the American Polygraph Association have stated that an examiner may not inquire into any of the following areas during pre-employment or periodic employment examinations:

- Religious beliefs or affiliations
- Beliefs or opinions regarding racial matters

- Political beliefs or affiliations.
- Beliefs, affiliations, or lawful activities regarding unions or labor organizations
- Sexual preferences or activities

In a law enforcement pre-employment polygraph examination, questions can only focus on job related inquiries, such as felony crime, falsification of information, and use of illegal drugs. Test questions are reviewed and discussed with the examinee during a pretest interview. There can be no surprise or trick questions. In a specific-issue polygraph examination, the relevant questions focus on the particular act under investigation.

Results

Polygraph results can be released only to authorized persons. Generally, those individuals who can receive test results are the examinee; anyone specifically designated in writing by the examinee; the person, firm, corporation, or governmental agency that requested the examination; and others as may be required by law.

Employee Polygraph Protection Act (EPPA)

This federal law establishes guidelines for polygraph testing and imposes restrictions on most private employers. The law only affects commercial businesses. Local, state, and federal governmental agencies are not affected by the law, nor are public agencies, such as a school system or correctional institution.

In addition are exemptions for some commercial businesses. These are:

- Businesses under contract with the federal government involving specified activities (e.g., counterintelligence work)
- Businesses whose primary purpose consists of providing armored car personnel, personnel involved in the design, or security personnel in facilities that have a significant impact on the health or safety

of any state. Examples of these facilities would be a nuclear or electric power plant, public water works, or toxic waste disposal.

- Companies that manufacture, distribute, or dispense controlled substances

A business cannot request, suggest, or require a job applicant to take a pre-employment polygraph examination. A business can request a current employee to take a polygraph examination but only when specific conditions have been satisfied. The employer cannot require a current employee to take an examination; if the employee refuses, the employer cannot discipline or discharge the employee based on the refusal alone.

Guidance for the Employer

Employers are encouraged to develop their own forms, use forms that bear their company name, and have the forms approved by legal counsel. When the polygraphist is a private sector person, the employer should demonstrate that the investigation is specific to the loss. In addition, the employer should:

- Show that the investigation is currently in progress.
- Show there is an identifiable economic loss to the employer.
- Abide by the EPPA.
- Provide the employee with a written statement that includes identification of the company and the working location of employee.
- Describe to the employee the incident under investigation.
- Name the location of the loss.
- Name the specific amount of the loss.
- Name the type of loss.
- Determine that the employee had access to the loss. (Access alone is not sufficient grounds for polygraph testing).
- Have a valid reason to suspect the employee.

- Give to the employee a written statement signed by a person authorized to legally bind the employee. The binding statement must be retained by the employer for at least three years following the investigation. Read the statement to the employee. Have the employee acknowledge understanding of the statement. If the employee agrees, the employee should then sign a timed and dated statement in the presence of a witness.
- Notify the employee in writing not less than 48 hours in advance (exclusive of weekends or holidays) as to the time and date of the scheduled polygraph test. If the test is to be conducted at a location other than the place of employment, directions to the location should be provided in writing.
- Conduct a follow-up interview of the employee before an adverse action is taken, during which the employee is told why the adverse action is to be taken.
- Keep all records for at least three years.
- Do nothing to require or otherwise coerce the employee to waive his or her right to refuse taking the polygraph test.

When the investigation is loss related and conducted by a public sector employee, such as a law enforcement or government agent, all of the above apply before conducting a polygraph test.

Guidance for the Polygraph Examiner

- Give to the employer a copy of EPPA guidelines and explain the guidelines in a face-to-face conference.
- Do not participate with the employer in determining if there is reasonable cause to believe a loss has occurred and who should or should not be tested.
- Prior to interviewing or conducting a polygraph exam, obtain from the employer copies of the relevant documents such as the advance notice and explanation of

rights. Also obtain photo identification of the person to be tested.

- At the time and place of a polygraph test, give to the examinee a verbal and written explanation of polygraph test procedures and the examinee's right to refuse to take the test. Obtain from the examinee a written acknowledgment to these effects.
- If the test is to be taped or viewed, such as through a one-way mirror, advise the examinee of these conditions.
- Conduct no more than five polygraph tests in one day.
- Keep a log of the company name, examinee names, and times of polygraph tests conducted in the course of one day.
- Administer a single test for not longer than 90 minutes.
- Give to the examinee a form that identifies the questions to be asked during the test.
- Ask the examinee to answer the questions in writing and sign the form. Retain the original of the form.
- If so required, possess a license issued for use in the state where the test is to be conducted.
- Inform the examinee of test results and allow the examinee to give reasons for the results.
- Inform the examinee in writing of your opinion as to deception or nondeception.
- Base opinion on test results and not behavior. Inform the employer of the opinion but only in the context of the matter under investigation. Do not include extraneous information.
- Keep all documentation for at least three years.
- Provide a copy of charts and questions and an original report to the employee upon request and to the employer (when deception is indicated).
- Provide to the U.S. Department of Labor and other authorized agencies a copy of charts and questions and an original report within 72 hours upon request.
- Carry professional liability coverage.

Qualifications of a Polygraph Examiner

In most jurisdictions, a person is qualified to receive a license as a polygraph examiner when he or she:

- Presents evidence of good moral character
- Has passed an examination to determine competency
- Holds an academic degree at the baccalaureate level from an accredited educational institution
- Has satisfactorily completed six months of study in the detection of deception

American Polygraph Association, http://www.polygraph.org/

John J. Fay, *Encyclopedia of Security Management*, second ed., Butterworth-Heinemann, Burlington, MA, 2007, pp. 170–174

U.S. Department of Labor, Employee Polygraph Protection Act, http://www.dol.gov/ofccp/regs/compliance/posters/pdf/eppac.pdf

POLYGRAPH TESTING LAW

The Equal Employment Protection Act (EPPA) states that an employer cannot request, suggest, or require a job applicant to take a pre-employment polygraph examination. In respect to a current employee, the employer can ask the employee to take a polygraph examination but only when specific conditions have been satisfied. The employer cannot require a current employee to take an examination; if the employee refuses the request, the employer cannot discipline or discharge the employee based on the refusal.

Rules that govern polygraph testing are:

- Demonstrate that a formal investigation has begun and is continuing.

- Establish that an identifiable economic loss to the employer has occurred. The meaning of economic loss is not restricted to physical property; for example, loss or compromise of valuable information, loss of the services of another, and loss of company reputation.

Give to the employee a written document that:

- Identifies the company and work location of the employee
- Describes the loss or reason for the investigation
- Specifies the location where the loss occurred
- Specifies the amount of the loss
- Specifies the type of offense such as theft of property, sabotage, compromise of sensitive data, assault, etc.
- Specifies how the employee was in a position to cause the loss (Note: access alone is not sufficient.)
- Explains why the person to be tested is believed to be involved in the loss

The employee should be given a written notice that sets force the details mentioned above. Receipt of the notice should be acknowledged by the employee, signed, timed, dated, and witnessed.

The examination should not be administered any sooner than 48 hours after the employee has acknowledged receipt of the notice.

The employee should be informed in writing as to the date, time, and location of the polygraph test and the place where the test is to be held.

If adverse action is to follow as a result of the test, the employee should be given notice of the test result, the specifics of the adverse action, and why the adverse action is appropriate. Employees may not waive their rights to any of the protections mentioned above.

All forms provided to the employee should be on company letterhead, and a record of the proceedings must be kept for a minimum of three years.

There is a $10,000 penalty for violation of the EPPA. This underscores the need of the employer to verify the credentials of the polygraph examiner and insure that the examiner is capable of meeting all requirements.

U.S. Equal Employment Opportunity Commission, http://www.eeoc.gov/

U.S. Department of Labor, http://www.dol.gov/oasam/programs/osdbu/eppac.pdf

PRE-EMPLOYMENT SCREENING

The Search

A pre-employment screen is a search for information about a job applicant; the search does not seek to prove or disprove, only to bring relevant information to the surface so that an objective judgment can be made about the suitability of the applicant to perform the job. The private investigator dredges up the relevant information; the PI's client makes the objective judgment.

Private investigators routinely provide pre-employment screening services to businesses. The PI's usual point of contact is the owner or operator of the company or the company's manager of the human resources department. The areas of interest to the client will vary according to the needs of the organization and the preferences of management. For example, a company that operates in a safety-sensitive environment will be interested in a job applicant's accident history, and a retail sales organization will be interested in a job applicant's honesty. A company's chief executive officer (CEO) who by nature is distrustful of people generally may want a job applicant's credentials checked to the nth degree, while a CEO in the same line of business may believe that no one working for him would ever think of doing anything wrong.

Whatever the dictates, the search for information follows the same course: the requested information is gathered and presented to the client, and the client makes the call. An employer can be in the private or public sector, i.e., operate a business or a government organization. When the employer operates a business, the PI and the employer usually have a direct relationship. When the employer is a government organization, the direct relationship usually is between the PI and a group under contract to the government.

Some employers screen applicants using in-house resources; some do not. In the latter category, the employer engages the services of a third party such as a private investigation agency. The employer's rationale in going outside of the company is usually two-fold: less cost and better results. Pre-employment screening done in-house resides in the human resources department most of the time, and the screening work requires one or more dedicated employees, work space, equipment, office supplies, and so forth. The cost of maintaining an in-house pre-employment screening program can be quite high, yet the effectiveness of the program can be quite low. Human resource representatives are simply not skilled at conducting investigations. Hence, the employer turns to investigation professionals.

In essence, a pre-employment screen is a cost-avoidance measure. Applicants that are felons, violence-prone individuals, drug abusers, and safety risks can be filtered out, thus reducing costs associated with theft, injury, accidents, and medical assistance benefits.

Negligence in Hiring

An employer's obligation to maintain a safe and secure workplace can be found in a variety of rules, laws, and legal concepts. These include, for example, safety rules issued by the Occupational Safety and Health Administration, laws enforced by the Environmental Protection Agency, and common law principles such as an employer's duty not to harm others, physically or financially. These include the duty of an employer to:

- Take responsible steps to guard against reasonably foreseeable acts of a harmful nature.
- Prevent wrongful acts that are committed by employees within the course and scope of their employment.
- Prohibit actions of a discriminatory nature.
- Take reasonable steps to determine if the job applicant has a propensity to harm others.
- Maintain a working environment free of danger to employees, others on the premises, and the public at large.

A legal concept called *respondeat superior* roughly means "let the master beware." An employer who assigns or is aware of job performance that harms another can be charged with negligent hiring.

Social Security Number

The Social Security number (SSN) is a nine-digit number that looks like this: 012–34–5678. The first three digits are an area number. Before 1973, the area number corresponded to the state where the individual obtained his or her Social Security card. After that, the first three digits were changed to correspond to the ZIP code of the mailing address shown on the individual's application for the card. The middle two digits are the group number. The last four digits are serial numbers. They represent a straight numerical sequence of digits from 0001–9999 within the group.

A Social Security Number Check can provide the names and addresses associated with a given SSN, and that is all. It only indicates that the number is accurate. To make a check, go to socialsecurity.gov/foia/high-group.htm. A separate file, called the Social Security Death Master list, can be accessed at ntis.gov/products/.

Although originally used to administer Social Security benefits, the SSN has nearly become a national ID number.

Client Preferences

A private investigation agency may provide pre-employment screening services to several clients. In all likelihood, each client will have its own set of pre-employment screening policies and practices; while these guidance documents will be in different words and formats, they must conform to the FCRA and other laws and rules. It is within this one area that the private investigation agency can perform a valuable service, that is, make sure the client does not go astray.

Some clients will want verifications to be made in depth; other clients will not. Some clients will be willing to pay more to make sure they filter out the bad actors; some clients will be willing only to pay the rock-bottom price. Depth refers to how far back in time the client will want to go when looking for misdemeanors as well as felonies. It also means checking out "also-known-as" names and maiden names.

Persons applying for positions of trust and responsibility should be checked out thoroughly. A client may specify that an applicant for the manager of accounting position be screened to a certain level and that the applicant for the chief financial officer be screened at a much higher level. In any of these cases, an applicant's personal credit should be of particular interest.

A client's policy may be to allow appeals that go beyond the FCRA rules, such as to hold formal hearings so that the turned-down applicant can rebut findings or present explanations. If the private investigation agency has done its job properly, there should be no error that could be a foundation for an appeal.

Screening Criteria

A pre-employment screen should address at least three issues:

- The credentials of the applicant. Does the applicant have the skill, knowledge, and attitude demanded by the job sought?

- The identity of the applicant. Is the applicant using a false name, perhaps to conceal a dishonest past?
- The personal history of the applicant. What has the applicant done in the past that could affect his or her job performance if hired?

The first issue is almost always resolved by a human resources specialist or the person that would supervise the applicant if hired. The private investigator has little to do with making these determinations.

The second and third issues, however, are in the purview of the private investigator. The verification process used by the investigator must be able to answer two questions: Is the applicant really the person listed on the employment application? Has the applicant really done the things he or she listed on the application? For example, investigators look at education attainment and job experience.

Although the investigator has no role in judging an applicant's job qualifications, the investigator should understand the nature of the open position and be aware of such matters as visibility of the position, credibility of the incumbent, and industry-specific expectations such as membership in trade associations. Having a handle on these matters can help the investigator craft a meaningful report.

Information Sources

A good deal of pertinent information can be found in the records of a court system. Our nation has two court systems: federal and state/county. The systems are dissimilar in important respects:

- They do not interface; information in one will not be in the other and not be in agreement.
- Each has its own operating rules, filing systems, and procedures that make examination of records difficult.

- One system may be paper dependent and the other electronic.
- One or both of the systems may operate at scattered locations.

Generally, the federal court system is better organized than the state/county system. For example, records of federal offenses are maintained in an electronic file called PACER (Public Access to Court Electronic Records). A PACER search will run an applicant's name looking for federal offenses on file in nearly all federal district courts. (Visit www.pacer.psc.uscourts.gov.)

Criminal history records are the gold standard for private investigators but usually are not easily attainable. Knowing where to look and with whom to speak are keys to finding criminal data.

Civil court records can reveal a lot about an individual, such as why he or she was sued or if the individual has a history of filing frivolous lawsuits. A civil case is a noncriminal action; for example, a complaint was made that a party to an agreement failed to lived up to its obligations, and as a result the complaining party experienced monetary damage. A civil case can involve negligence, such as when an employer failed to reasonably protect employees and patrons against a foreseeable risk.

Proprietary databases are excellent sources. They vary in types of information available but are generally attuned to credit histories in the retail and mortgage sectors and to terminations of employment based on specific behaviors such as identity theft and shoplifting.

A check for incarceration can be made with records of the Federal Bureau of Prisons, state penitentiary records, state and county department of correction records, municipal jail records, and—to some extent—probation and parole records.

Some state agencies maintain sexual offender registries that are accessible over the Internet, and others are accessible through written or face-to-face inquiries.

The National Sex Offender Public Registry (which can be found at www.nsopr. gov), is a cooperative effort between the U.S. Department of Justice and state agencies that maintain sexual offender registries.

Motor vehicle searches usually apply to applicants for jobs that require operation of motor vehicles. Obtaining information from state motor vehicle agencies can be difficult yet rewarding. A state's motor vehicle records typically contain driving violations, fines, and convictions based on use of a motor vehicle. While illuminating in itself, data in a driving record may provide investigative leads.

A main point of interest to the private investigator's client is likely to be credit history. Credit reports can be obtained from different sources yet contain similar data such as the applicant's name, address, current employment, number and types of accounts that are past due or in good standing, accounts turned over to collection agencies, and garnishments.

The federal government maintains Terrorist Watch Lists, and some states and industries maintain lists of individuals and organizations that are barred from employment or for providing services. Some industries require that checks be made before an individual or group can be employed or licensed to work in the industry.

Some states require pre-employment screens and licenses for specific occupations, such as child and elder care. Information along this line can be obtained from state licensing boards and industry associations.

Drug Screening

Industries regulated by the U.S. Department of Transportation (DOT) include trucking, municipal transit, rail, aviation, maritime, and pipeline operations. Rules set by DOT require employers in these industries to operate drug testing programs that focus on safety-sensitive jobs such as airline pilots and drivers of trucks carrying hazardous materials.

Many companies in other industries operate drug testing programs, not by fiat but by common sense and by risk management and cost containment. Drug-influenced employees are more likely to be absent from work, steal to support a drug habit, cause serious accidents, and impose upon the employer higher than necessary health insurance costs related to drug-induced illnesses.

A private investigator should consider these facts when conducting a pre-employment screen. Drug abuse, while not a crime in itself, is sufficient reason for the private investigator to look for indications of abuse and report them to the client.

U.S. Department of Transportation, Office of Drug and Alcohol Policy and Compliance, http://www.dot.gov/odapc
John J. Fay, Encyclopedia of Security Management, second ed., Butterworth-Heinemann, Burlington, MA, 2007, p. 210.
John J. Fay, *The Drug-Free Workplace*, Butterworth-Heinemann, Burlington, MA, 2000, pp. 62–75.
Learning Shop USA, Pre-Employment Screening, www.learningshopusda.com

PRELIMINARY OFFENSES

There are three crimes that are preparatory in nature and serve as part of a larger purpose. Each of them is a means of reaching a criminal end. These so-called preliminary crimes are: solicitation, attempt, and conspiracy.

Solicitation consists of the offender's oral or written efforts to activate another person to commit a criminal offense. The essence of the crime is to incite by counsel, enticement, or inducement. The offense of solicitation is complete if the offender merely urges another to violate the law and otherwise does nothing himself.

Attempt has two elements. First, there must be a specific intent to commit a particular offense; second, there must be a direct, overt act toward its commission. There must be some act moving directly toward the act. Mere preparation, such as obtaining tools or weapons, may be insufficient to establish the crime, especially when made at a distance in time or place.

Conspiracy is the combination of two or more persons working in some concerted action to accomplish some criminal or unlawful purpose or to accomplish some purpose in a criminal or unlawful manner. If there is a common understanding among the participants to achieve a certain purpose or to act in a certain way, a conspiracy exists without regard to whether there is any formal or written statement of purpose or even though there is no actual speaking of words. There may be merely a tacit understanding without any express agreement.

John J. Fay, *Encyclopedia of Security Management*, second ed., Butterworth-Heinemann, Burlington, MA, 2007, pp. 223–224.

PRETEXTING

A pretexter is a person who represents himself as a person having a right to obtain information about another person or entity when no such right exists. Bottom line, pretexting is a practice of collecting information under false pretenses. The pretexter may pretend to be a human resources specialist verifying information on a job application, a banker verifying information on a loan application, or a friend or relative wanting to reconnect.

Pretexting occurs when someone tries to gain access to personal nonpublic information without authority. The act may be done face-to-face, over the phone, by mail or e-mail or fax, and on devices that access the Internet.

A form of pretexting is performed on the Internet and is called "phishing." The person receiving the communication is induced to provide personal information that can be used for various purposes, such as determining a person's spending habits, inducing a payment of some type, or committing identity theft.

Certain types of pretexting are prohibited by the Gramm-Leach-Bliley Act (GLBA). In the matter of pretexting, the main objectives of the GLBA are to take action against information brokering, telemarketing fraud, internet scams, bogus credit card offers, and identity theft. The GLBA does not specifically prohibit pretexting by private investigators who gather information for legitimate purposes, but the private investigator is always at risk of exposure to civil liability under the common law crimes of false pretenses and invasion of privacy.

Pretexting was a valuable investigative technique prior to the computer revolution, but that is not the case today. Databases, easily accessible public records, and even social profiles such as those found on Facebook and Twitter are rich sources of information.

John J. Fay

PSYCHOLOGICAL PROFILING

Psychological profiling is a type of criminal science that is utilized in investigations to find out the reasons why some criminals commit certain types of crimes. Another reason for utilizing psychological profiling in investigations is to make deductions regarding the behavior of an offender and the possible background of the offender. This type of profiling is done in conjunction with other aspects of criminal investigation with a view to moving the investigation in the right direction.

The process of psychological profiling can be either deductive or inductive. The inductive method is done by drawing assumptions based on the belief that people who commit certain types of crimes have backgrounds that are somewhat similar. For instance, when a serial killer targets only a certain class of people, some assumptions can be made regarding the possible background of the

type of person who is likely to commit such an offense. This assumption might increase if the killer exhibits certain characteristics, such a removing something that belongs to the victim or leaving something at the scene of the crime. Such attributes of a crime might allow some deductions to be made regarding the group to which the criminal likely belongs.

Investigators often profile certain types of individuals who are more likely to perpetrate crimes. Many of these suspects are profiled because of activities observed by police officers. For example, if someone who is obviously poor is frequently seen in a more affluent neighborhood, such a person may be profiled as someone with possible criminal intent. Similarly, if an individual living in an obviously poor neighborhood has in his or her possession several expensive items, that person may be profiled as someone involved in crime, such as drugs or theft. Although this type of profiling is not always considered fair, law enforcement officers consider it necessary to identify possible criminal activity before it occurs and causes injury to others.

Wayne W. Bennett and Karen M. Hess, Criminal Investigation, Wadsworth Publishing, Belmont, CA, 1998, pp. 242–245, and 345–347.

John J. Fay, *Security Dictionary*, American Society for Industrial Security, Alexandria, VA, 2000, pp. 201–202.

PUBLIC ACCESS TO COURT ELECTRONIC RECORDS (PACER)

Public Access to Court Electronic Records (PACER) is an electronic, public access, centralized service that allows users (such as investigators) to obtain case and docket information from federal appellate, district, and bankruptcy courts. PACER's Case Locator is accessed from the Internet.

Case Locator is a national index for U.S. District, Bankruptcy, and Appellate courts. A small subset of information from each case is transferred to the PACER Case Locator server each night. The system serves as a locator index for PACER. Investigators are allowed to conduct nationwide searches to determine whether or not a party is involved in federal litigation.

PACER users are typically investigators, attorneys, pro se filers, government agencies, trustees, data collectors, researchers, educational and financial institutions, commercial enterprises, and the media.

An online registration process establishes an account for the user. Each court maintains its case information locally. A court's records can be searched directly if the name of the district or circuit court is known to the user.

Case and docket records are available immediately after they have been electronically filed. However, in order to protect private information, personal identifiers are removed or redacted before the records become public. These identifiers include the first five digits of a Social Security number, financial account numbers, the name of a minor, a person's date of birth, and home addresses in a criminal case.

United States Courts, Public Access to Court Electronic Records, http://www.pacer.gov/

R

RACKETEER INFLUENCED AND CORRUPT ORGANIZATIONS (RICO)

The Racketeer Influenced and Corrupt Organizations Statute is commonly referred to as the "RICO" statute. The purpose of the RICO statute is "the elimination of the infiltration of organized crime and racketeering into legitimate organizations operating in interstate commerce."

Generally, RICO crimes fall into one or more of these categories:

- Syndicated gambling
- Loansharking
- Violent crimes in aid of racketeering

A decision to institute a federal criminal falls within the purview of the U.S. Attorney General. Investigation and prosecution involves balancing society's interest in law enforcement against consequences for the accused. Enforcement of the RICO statute requires particularly careful and reasoned application because the statute incorporates certain state crimes. One purpose of these guidelines is to reemphasize the principle that the primary responsibility for enforcing state laws rests with the state concerned. "Imaginative" investigations and prosecution will not be approved by the Attorney General.

A RICO investigation is not intended to duplicate the elements of proof for traditional crimes that are investigated by other investigation agencies. Examples of traditional crimes are mail fraud, gambling, and some drug cases. Only in exceptional circumstances will approval be granted when RICO is sought merely to serve some evidentiary purpose.

The usual procedure to initiate a RICO crime is to seek approval of a government attorney. Approval is usually granted when one or more of the following requirements is present:

- RICO is necessary to ensure that the indictment adequately reflects the nature and extent of the criminal conduct involved in a way that prosecution only on the underlying charges would not.
- A RICO prosecution would provide the basis for an appropriate sentence under all the circumstances of the case in a way that prosecution only on the underlying charges would not.
- A RICO charge could combine related offenses that would otherwise have to be prosecuted separately in different jurisdictions.
- RICO is necessary for a successful prosecution of the government's case against the defendant or a codefendant.
- Use of RICO would provide a reasonable expectation of forfeiture that is proportionate to the underlying criminal conduct.

- The case consists of violations of state law, but local law enforcement officials are unlikely or unable to successfully prosecute the case, in which the federal government has a significant interest.
- The case consists of violations of state law but involves prosecution of significant or government individuals, which may pose special problems for the local prosecutor.
- The last two requirements reflect the principle that the prosecution of state crimes is primarily the responsibility of state authorities. RICO should be used to prosecute what are essentially violations of state law only if there is a compelling reason to do so.

However, a RICO charge can be approved when:

- Local law enforcement officials are unlikely to investigate and prosecute otherwise meritorious cases in which the federal government has significant interest.
- Significant organized crime involvement exists.
- The prosecution of significant political or governmental individuals may pose special problems for local prosecutors.

U.S. Department of Justice, RICO pdf, http://www.justice.gov/usao/eousa/foia_reading_room/usam/title9/rico.pdf

RAPE

Rape as defined by the FBI is:

"Penetration, no matter how slight, of the vagina or anus with any body part or object, or oral penetration by a sex organ of another person, without the consent of the victim is rape. This definition includes any gender of victim or perpetrator. Sexual penetration means the penetration, no matter how slight, of the vagina or anus with any body part or object, or oral penetration by a sex organ of another person. This definition also includes instances in which the victim is incapable of giving consent because of temporary or permanent mental or physical incapacity (including due to the influence of drugs or alcohol) or because of age. Physical resistance is not required on the part of the victim to demonstrate lack of consent."

The revised definition:

- Includes either male or female victims or offenders
- Includes instances in which the victim is incapable of giving consent because of temporary or permanent mental or physical incapacity, (e.g., due to the influence of drugs or alcohol or because of age)
- Reflects the various forms of sexual penetration understood to be rape

Rape is a particularly odious form of assault. It is generally accepted that rape is first and foremost a crime of force. The rapist uses or threatens to use violence in what is essentially an exercise of power. The primary motive of the rapist is not to attain sexual pleasure but to feel a sense of superiority by dominating the victim.

Rape has no boundaries. Males have been victims as well as females. Anyone, regardless of age, race, economic status, and physical appearance, can be victimized. Victims have included infants, mentally retarded persons, and the elderly.

Rape is also unlimited as to time and place of occurrence. It is not something that happens mainly at night or in high-crime areas. Rapes occur at all times of the day in the poorest and wealthiest sections of cities, suburbs, and rural areas all around the world. Many rapes take place in the victim's home, and frequently the rapist is there by invitation. This is so because the rapist is likely to be a friend, relative, or work associate. In some cases, he is an estranged husband or lover and, in about nine of every ten reported cases, is of the same race as the victim. Violence is an element of the act, and only about three of ten incidents will involve the use of a weapon.

Only very infrequently will a rape end in murder. This is not to suggest that the crime is any less serious, but it does point to the high probability that the victim will survive. There has never been any truth to the notion that rape is an invited crime, meaning that the victim invited rape because of the way she talked, dressed, or behaved. The idea that the rapist was provoked by the victim's sexual advances reflects a dishonored and mistaken view that rape is motivated by sexual desire. There is also little evidence to support the proposition that women use accusations of rape as a means of obtaining revenge. On the contrary, there is evidence to show that women accusers often suffer further harm by being stigmatized in their communities and abandoned by friends and loved ones.

Another disturbing reality is that a rapist will usually continue to rape until caught and removed from society. The only effective remedy is for the victim to report the crime and assist in the investigation and prosecution. This can be difficult and unpleasant for the victim but is essential in preventing repeat occurrences of the crime.

The rapist, like most criminals, will prefer the "easy target," that is to say, a woman who has the appearance of vulnerability. If the rapist can be made to believe that a particular woman would be difficult to overcome, he will look elsewhere for easier prey.

Interviewing the Victim

Interviews of rape victims can provide valuable information for investigators. The most valuable information will be found in three broad areas:

- Initial approach of the rapist
- Control of the victim
- The rapist's sexual behavior

Approach. Was the approach physical, such as mugging, grabbing or throwing the victim to the ground? Was it launched from a place of concealment, such as from behind a wall, a tree, or bushes? Was the victim gagged or blindfolded? Did the rapist attack while the victim was unaware, such as when sleeping in bed? Was the approach friendly, charming, and verbal in nature? Did the rapist use a prop to hide intention, such as showing the victim a puppy or a bouquet of flowers? Did the rapist approach on foot, by bicycle, or by motor vehicle?

Control. Was the victim controlled by verbal threats such as "I will kill you"? Was it physical, such as slapping, hitting, kicking, beating with fists, or striking with an object? Did the rapist display a gun or a knife and promise to use it if the victim resisted? Was the rapist's demeanor so threatening that the victim dared not resist?

The Rapist's Behavior. Did the rapist become excited in response to the victim's fear, pain, or suffering? Did the rapist torture the victim, such as by use of a broomstick inserted into the vagina or pliers clamped on nipples? Was the rapist's overall behavior motivated by domination, infliction of pain, or sexual gratification? Did intercourse actually occur?

The investigator will want to obtain information beyond the standard descriptors of height, weight, etc. The investigator should ask the victim about items in the rapist's possession, such as a cane, walking stick, or briefcase. What was the rapist's verbal behavior? Was there a theme, perhaps exemplified by statements such as "You really want this" or "I'll make you pay"? Did the rapist reveal anything personal, utter obscenities, or make racial epithets? Did the rapist take photos or voice recordings, take something that belonged to the victim, or deliberately leave behind something personal?

Also of value is information about attempts of the rapist to conceal his identity, such as by wearing a ski mask, telling the victim to look away, or by disguising his voice with a fake accent.

The outcome of the investigation will in large part be attributed to the investigator's skill in obtaining details in three broad areas: the rapist's approach to the victim, methods used to control the victim, and the rapist's behaviors during commission of the crime.

John J. Fay

REPORT TYPES

Investigative reports vary between one agency and another. Differences often relate to the types of investigations that are routine to an agency: variations in processing, storing, and retrieving information; requirements of other agencies (such as a legal department); and preferences of the people in charge. Despite differences, four types of reports stand out, and each has a distinctive purpose.

The Initial Report

An initial report describes the nature of the matter, what was done, and what was learned at the very outset of the investigation. The initial report also identifies investigative work that remains to be done, such as interviewing witnesses and obtaining public domain documents. Because of management's interest in the details of a new case, the initial report is usually submitted within 48 hours and certainly not more than five days after the investigation begins.

Very often, the matter to be investigated will not be fresh. Many cases will have been investigated in part by one agency and referred to another agency as the result of jurisdiction issues, an imperative to bring the matter to full resolution quickly and when certain investigative expertise is needed but is not possessed by the referring agency. Referred investigations are problematic because:

- Evidence that could have been acquired at the outset of the case is no longer acquirable.
- Physical evidence could have been lost, contaminated, or deteriorated since first being collected.
- Witnesses might have disappeared or their recollection of events might have been dimmed by the passage of time.

The initial report often begins with a brief opening statement. This statement should identify:

- Persons known to be connected to the matter
- Contact information for these persons
- Time and date of initial notification
- Time and date of the event
- Place of the event
- How the event occurred and why, if known
- Statements made by witnesses
- Property involved in the matter
- Injuries sustained
- Reports made by first responders

The initial report may also identify investigative leads to be followed and investigative actions remaining to be performed. A lead might be the discovery of an eyewitness who had not been interviewed, and a pending action might be to take photographs of the scene.

The Progress Report

This type of report picks up where the initial report ends. Progress reports are usually prepared on a scheduled basis, such as every 30 days, or on an as-needed basis, such as when an important development needs to be disseminated.

If the initial report or a prior progress report mentions a lead to be followed or an action to be taken, the current progress report should reflect the attempt made and results achieved, even when minor in importance.

A progress report is different from and much more important than internal records that also track "progress." Records called the Daily Progress Report, Reading File, or Log of Investigative Activities are records made for in-house use and intended to keep the management informed of the day-to-day activities of the investigative staff.

The Final Report

A final report is prepared when the investigation has ended, such as when a definite conclusion has been reached or all investigative avenues have been exhausted. The final report should state the basic facts, which can be quite long, often several pages in length. Some agencies may want the opening paragraph of the final report to describe how the agency first became involved and the central circumstances of the incident.

The final report incorporates everything mentioned in the initial and progress reports but not necessarily with the same detail or words used. The final report is a stand-alone document that brings all the facts together and presents them in context.

Substantiation is an essential part of a final report. Substantiate means to verify, corroborate, validate, or support conclusions made in the final report. Substantiation is often a recitation of facts. Considered together, facts show proof of findings. Substantiation can be drawn from a variety of sources: statements obtained from the suspect, victim, complainant, and witnesses; notes, sketches, diagrams, and photographs; physical evidence collected; reports of analyses made by forensic experts; and official records.

A final report typically ends with one or more conclusions reached by the investigator. An investigator's conclusion is not the same as an opinion. A conclusion is a reasoned judgment made from a combination of facts. The substantiation part of the final report states those facts. From these facts, the investigator states his or her conclusion.

The final report should be stored in a secure, fire-resistant container under the control of two agency persons, such as the agency head and second-in-command.

The Supplemental Report

The supplemental report covers new issues that arise after the filing of a final report. These issues often relate to the outcome of a trial or hearing, punishment and penalties imposed, persons confined or released, punitive and compensatory awards, restitution, recovery of property, and out-of-court settlements.

It sometimes happens that new evidence will come to light concerning a previously closed investigation. A supplemental report is filed and, if desired by management, the investigation can be reopened.

However, if new information comes to light before the final report is submitted, the new information should be reported in a progress report.

General Rules

The first mention of a person should include the proper form of address (e.g., Mr., Mrs., Ms., Sergeant, Attorney, etc.) and, if appropriate, the person's organization (e.g., Hillsdale Police Department or Smith County District Attorney's Office). Later mention of the person can appear as last name only. For example, Sergeant Milton T. Stone can be referred to as STONE. This procedure is intended to aid the reader by making names stand out.

Attached to or included with the final report of investigation will be case documentation such as copies of written statements, laboratory reports, sketches and diagrams, questioned documents, official records, maps, photographs, estimates of loss or damage, a list of persons connected to the case, and descriptions of physical evidence and where evidence is stored.

Originals of documentary materials and physical evidence are not attached to a final report. They are retained until needed for adjudication or other official purpose.

The investigator's notes are seldom attached to a final report. They are retained in the case file along with telephone message slips, business cards, newspaper clippings, and like items.

Learning Shop USA, Report Writing, www.learningshopusa.com

REPORT WRITING

One of the most important tasks of the investigator is report writing. Some investigators do not like to write reports because they find the task tedious, some investigators lack writing skills, and some investigators undervalue the importance of the task. By nature, investigators are action-driven and do not like to be tied to a desk. Although report writing is found in the curricula of training programs, some persons enter training without writing skills, and the deficiency becomes apparent during performance on the job. Because report writing can be regarded as an "after-the-action" endeavor, it is sometimes seen to be not all that important. An accurate and well-written report can highlight the probative value of evidence, it can inform people who need to be informed (such as decision makers and prosecutors), and it is a permanent record that may be critical to the understanding of a future issue.

The formats of reports vary according to the goals or mission of the organization. Investigators in the private sector, public sector, and government sector organizations operate differently from each other. Private investigators, for the most part, work for individuals and business organizations and are oriented toward the civil law; law enforcement investigators in the public sector operate within legal jurisdictions and work for the public at large and are oriented toward the criminal law; and government agencies enforce federal laws and gather criminal intelligence.

Generally, a report of investigation (ROI) answers three questions: What initiated the investigation? What investigative actions were taken as a result? What were the findings of the investigation? In this sense, an ROI moves chronologically. The blocks or sections of an ROI tend to follow a traditional approach, i.e., introduction, body, and conclusion. A fully rounded report will make clear "who did what to whom, where, when, how, and why, if known."

ROIs are of three general types: the initial report, progress reports, and the final report. In some cases, all three or combinations of the three are incorporated into one report that covers why the investigation was launched, what the investigator did, and what the conclusions were. An ROI will have an identifier or code that makes it distinct from other cases. The code, for example, might be FO3–2014–56. In this example, the FO3 could be Field Office Three, followed by 2014 (the year in which the case was opened), and followed by 56 (the 56th case opened in 2014).

The ROI will have attachments, sometimes called exhibits; they are numbered or lettered, such as Exhibit 1 or Exhibit A. Exhibits are attachable to an ROI; they are documents, such as written statements and forensic lab reports, or photographs of a scene, property, or people. They are not evidence; they support the investigator's conclusions and make reference to evidence. A pry bar used in a burglary is physical evidence. One or more exhibits will make reference to the pry bar—explaining its relationship to the case—such as a photograph of it and a statement as to its use and ownership.

An exhibit is a copy of an original. Exhibits include:

- Probable cause affidavit
- Inventory of seized items

- Police incident report
- Victim and complainant statement
- Witness statements
- Investigator statements
- Confessions and admissions
- List of persons connected to the case
- Maps, layouts, diagrams, sketches
- Photographs
- Lab reports
- Medical report
- Statement of loss or value

The composition of an ROI is one matter; writing it is another matter. Notes have extremely high value in the writing of a report. It is possible that a report, most especially a final report, will not be written until the investigation is finalized, which may be months or years after the investigation was initiated. Case details are found in notes that were taken at the moment of occurrence.

Depending on the nature of the investigative work and the preferences of those who manage the work, the format of the ROI will vary. The form upon which the report is written may or may not have blocks, such as blocks for names, dates, times, locations, and nature of the incident. But in almost every instance, the ROI form will have a space for a written narrative. The narrative brings together facts that were determined by the investigator. In the initial report, the facts will be few; in the progress report(s), the facts build; and in the final report, all facts are presented.

The narrative takes a chronological path, i.e., it starts at the time the investigation started and ends when the investigation ended.

Following are tips on writing the narrative:

- Use notes and study them beforehand.
- Start paragraphs with a sentence that tells the time, date, location, person, and action, for example: "At 11:30 PM, December 8, 2014, at the offices of Excelsior Marketing, Inc., located at 4056 Polk Street, San Francisco, CA, a person or persons used a pry bar to force open the door marked 406, entered, and stole a computer printout titled Client Database." Another example: "At 2:30 AM, December 9, 2014, at my office I interviewed Oscar Darwin, manager of operations, Excelsior Marketing, Inc., who stated that . . ."
- Use one paragraph for one idea.
- Do not use legalese, such as "heretofore," or jargon, such as "the perp."
- Do not use "the undersigned investigator" or "this investigator." The correct term is "I."
- Review and rewrite as many times as needed.

A written report reflects the competency of the person who wrote it. A written report is useful to the extent it is understood by the persons who read it. A written report has an indefinite lifetime.

J. "Tripp" Mitchell

RESTRAINING ORDER

A restraining order is an order issued by a court in order to provide relief to a complainant (victim). The person (abuser) receiving the order is required by the order to do or not do certain acts that have been alleged by the complainant. If the receiver fails to comply with the order, the receiver can face criminal or civil charges. Refusal to comply with the order can result in arrest and possible imprisonment.

Domestic violence, estrangement, harassment, and stalking are the common bases for issuing restraining orders. An order can stipulate "stay away from," "no contact," "cease abuse," "provide support," and "make restitution" requirements.

A restraining order can include provisions that require the abuser to relinquish firearms, undergo treatment and counseling programs, and take alcohol or drug tests.

John J. Fay

RETAIL THEFT PREVENTION

Arguably, most theft from retail businesses involves employees. To remove the potential argument from "arguably," we may safely say that a great deal of retail theft is attributable to employees. It is easy, by comparison, to protect retail goods from the public. That is simply a matter of where to "draw the line." How much investment in security is cost-effective? How suspicious of customers may we appear to be, without driving customers into a competitor's store? How zealous can security personnel be without generating lawsuits over errors made? How much surveillance technology and high-value-item protection technology are cost-effective, considering that the cost is not only in the choosing, acquisition, and maintenance of the technology but also in the personnel hours involved in utilizing the technology?

On the other hand, guarding against theft of property by employees is a more complex matter. Employees who perceive that they receive just compensation for their time and labor, and who perceive that they are treated justly, are generally reliable and protective of the interests of the employer.

Good employees can become righteously indignant when the employer seems to be groundlessly suspicious of them. It helps when the employer can say, "We use outside private investigators, and they follow their own procedures." The outside PI agency can serve as a buffer against the possibility of turning good employees into bad ones.

It is possible that a socially oriented employer will knowingly hire a person with a criminal record. That is the employer's choice. In contrast, a business-centered employer will decide otherwise, with the decision predicated on the findings of a background investigation conducted by a private investigator or private investigative agency.

Depending on the nature of the business enterprise in question, a pre-employment polygraph screening may be in order. An applicant who has lied on his employment application may simply remove himself as a candidate when faced with the polygraph screening. The polygraph screening may catch not only application lies but also patterns of criminal activity that are not a matter of official record. (Please note that the Employee Polygraph Protection Act restricts testing of certain persons in certain situations and places certain requirements on the employer.)

Another possibility is the "mystery shopper" service. An investigator looks for deviations from loss-prevention procedures while pretending to shop. In high-dollar retail operations, an undercover operation may be appropriate.

Private investigation services should always be founded on a well-understood written agreement between the employer and the investigative agency.

Weeden Rockwell Nichols

RISK ANALYSIS

Risk is associated with virtually every activity one can think of, but in the present context it is limited to the uncertainty of financial loss, the variations between actual and expected results, and the probability that a loss has occurred or will occur. In the insurance industry, the term "risk" is also used to mean "the thing insured," for example, the XYZ Company is the risk. Risk is also the possible occurrence of an undesirable event.

Risk should not be confused with perils, which are the causes of risk and are things such as fire, flood, and earthquake. Nor should risk be confused with hazard, which is a contributing factor to perils. Almost anything can be a hazard: a loaded gun, a bottle of caustic acid, a bunch of oily rags, or a warehouse used for storing paper products. The end result of risk is loss or a decrease in value.

Risks are generally classified as "speculative" (the difference between loss or gain, for example, the risk in gambling) and "pure risk," a loss or no-loss situation, to which insurance generally applies. The divisions of risk are limited to three common categories:

- Personal (having to do with people assets)
- Property (having to do with material assets)
- Liability (having to do with legalities that could affect both of the previous categories, such as errors and omissions liability)

What Is Risk Analysis?

Risk analysis is a management tool, the standard that is determined by whatever management decides it wants to accept in terms of actual loss. In order to proceed in a logical manner to perform a risk analysis, it is first necessary to accomplish some basic tasks:

- Identify the assets in need of being protected (money, manufactured product, and industrial processes to name a few).
- Identify the kinds of risks that may affect the assets involved (internal theft, external theft, fire, or earthquake).
- Determine the probability of risk occurrence. Here one must keep in mind that such a determination is not a science but an art—the art of projecting probabilities.
- Determine the impact or effect, in dollar values if possible, if given loss does occur.

A risk assessment analysis is a rational and orderly approach as well as a comprehensive solution to problem identification and probability determination. It is also a method for estimating the anticipated or expected loss from the occurrence of some adverse event. The key word here is *estimating*, because risk analysis will never be an exact science. Nevertheless, the answer to most, if not all, questions regarding one's security exposures can be determined by risk analysis.

Risk analysis is not a task to be accomplished once and for all time. It must be performed periodically in order to stay abreast of changes in mission, facilities, and equipment. Since security measures designed at the inception of a system have generally proved to be more effective than those superimposed later, risk analysis should have a place in the design phase of every system. Unfortunately, this is seldom the case.

The major resource required for a risk analysis is human power. For this reason, the first analysis will be the most expensive as subsequent ones can be based in part on previous work, and the time required will decrease to some extent as experience is gained. The time allowed to accomplish the risk analysis should be compatible with its objectives. Large facilities with complex, multishift operations and many files of data will require more time than the single-shift, limited-production locations. If meaningful results are expected, management must be willing to commit the resources necessary to accomplish this undertaking.

The Role of Management in Risk Analysis

The success of any risk analysis undertaking will be strongly contingent on the role top management takes in the project. Management must support the project and express this support to all levels of the organization. Management must delineate the purpose and scope of risk analysis. It must select a qualified team and formally delegate authority, and management must review the team's findings.

Personnel who are not directly involved in the analysis process must be prepared to provide information and assistance to those who are conducting the analysis and, in addition, to abide by any procedures and limitations of activity that may ensue. Management should leave no doubt that it intends to rely on the final product and base its security decisions on the findings of the risk analysis team. The scope of the project should be defined, and the statement of scope should specifically spell out the limitations of the analysis. It is oftentimes equally important to state specifically what the analysis is not designed to accomplish or cover. This will serve to eliminate any misunderstandings at the start rather than at the conclusion of the exercise.

At this point, it may be well to define and explain two other terms that are sometimes used interchangeably with risk. They are "threats," which include anything that could adversely affect the enterprise or the assets, and "vulnerability," which includes weaknesses, flaws, holes, or anything that may conceivably be exploited by a threat. Threats are most easily identified by placing them in one of three classifications or categories: natural hazards, accidents, or intentional acts. Vulnerabilities are most easily identified by collecting information from interviewing persons employed in the facility, by field observation and inspection, by document review, and, in the case of hardware or electronics, by conducting tests designed to highlight vulnerability and expose weaknesses or flaws in the design of the system.

Threat occurrence rates/probabilities are best developed from reports of occurrence or incident reports whenever this historical data exist. Where the data do not exist, it may be necessary to reconstruct them by conducting interviews with knowledgeable persons.

Risk Exposure Assessment

Before any corrective action can be considered, it is necessary to make a thorough assessment of one's identifiable risk exposure. In order to accomplish this, it is essential that three factors be identified and evaluated in quantitative terms.

The first is to determine the types of loss or risk that can affect the assets involved. Here examples would be fire, burglary, robbery, or kidnapping. If one of these were to occur, what effect would the resulting disruption of operations have on the company? If the

chief executive officer, on an overseas trip, were to be kidnapped by a terrorist group, who would make the day-to-day operating decisions in his absence? What about the unauthorized disclosure of trade secrets and other proprietary data? After the risk exposure potentials are identified, one must then proceed to evaluate those threats that, should they occur, would produce losses in quantitative terms.

To do this, we proceed to the second factor: estimate the probability of occurrence. What are the chances that the identified risks may become actual events? For some risks, estimating probabilities can be relatively easy. This is especially true when we have documented historical data dealing with identifiable problems. For example, how many internal and external theft cases have been investigated over the past year? Other risks are more difficult to predict. Sabotage, industrial espionage, kidnapping, and civil disorder may never occur or may occur only on a one-time basis.

The third factor is quantifying loss potential. This is measuring the impact or severity of the risk, if in fact a loss does occur or the risk becomes an actual event. This exercise does not become final until one develops dollar values for the assets previously identified. This part of the survey is necessary to set the stage for classification evaluation and analysis of the comparisons necessary to the establishment of countermeasure priorities.

Some events or kinds of risk with which business and industry are most commonly concerned are as follows:

- Natural catastrophe (tornado, hurricane, earthquake, volcanic eruption, and flood)
- Industrial disaster (explosion, chemical spill, structural collapse, and fire)
- Civil disturbance (sabotage, labor violence, and bomb threats)
- Criminality (robbery, burglary, pilferage, embezzlement, fraud, industrial espionage, internal theft, and hijacking)

- Conflict of interest (kickbacks, trading on inside information, and unethical practices)
- Miscellaneous risks, threats, or loss factors (bookkeeping errors, unaccounted-for inventory losses, traffic accidents, alcohol and drug abuse, absenteeism, gambling, and improper leave or time clocking)

Admittedly, some of the listed events are unlikely to occur. Also, some are less critical to an enterprise than others. Nevertheless, all are possibilities and are thus deserving of consideration.

James F. Broder

ROBBERY

The crime of robbery is a serious offense capable of being carried out by a variety of means. Crime statistics show that robbers are not always men and come from a wide range of age, racial, social, economic, and occupational groups. The robber's principle motive is usually to obtain money or property that is easily converted to cash. Robbery is also a crime that is sometimes committed in conjunction with another crime, such as murder or rape, and because robbery is a form of larceny that uses violence as its means, the investigative techniques used in larceny and assault cases have application to robbery cases.

Types of Robberies

Mugging. Mugging is a type of robbery committed by the muffling of the victim's mouth (or by choking) while forcibly taking property from the victim's possession. The amateur or inexperienced mugger will usually act on the earliest opportunity to victimize a lone person. He will act on the spur of the moment, usually with little or no preparation, and is acting in response to some urgent need for money, such as the drug addict in early withdrawal who needs money to buy his next fix. At the other extreme is the experienced mugger who usually selects his target carefully and formulates a plan that includes a concealed location and an unobstructed escape route. His victims are chosen on the basis of the valuables they are expected to be carrying. The experienced mugger looks for high return at low risk. When a particular mugging method proves successful over a period of time, the experienced mugger will establish a modus operandi or pattern of activity.

A common example of a mugger's operandi is the yoking technique. The largest of a group of two or three muggers subdues the victim from behind by a stranglehold on the neck. If there are three or more muggers, the victim's arms are pinned while the last mugger, usually the smallest, searches the victim's pockets and removes valuables. Other similarities in the mugger's method of operation might include use of the same or similar locations such as parking lots or stairwells; weapons used, if any; the manner of approach; opening statement to the victim or other conversation leading up to the incident; and the use of violence inflicted in certain ways upon the victim. A particularly dangerous type of mugger is the sadist-flagellant robber whose primary motive is sexual gratification through inflicting injury on his victim. The theft aspect of the crime is a secondary consideration.

Robberies of Places. Banks, stores, and residences are common robbery targets. As is the case with mugging, this type of robbery can be committed by amateurs or professionals. The amateur robber is capable of traveling to and from the place of robbery in his own car or with a leased car, sometimes leased in his own name, or may travel on foot or even by bicycle. Because the inexperienced robber is certain to be nervous during the commission of the crime, he is apt to use violence unnecessarily. The experienced robber is likely to retain his composure and is comforted by the preparation and planning that has preceded the act. He knows what he is doing, is operating on a schedule, and realizes the risk of causing injury. He will usually use a stolen car, which he later abandons, or he might rent a car in a false name and use stolen plates.

Vehicle Robberies. The target of the crime is frequently a commercial-type vehicle carrying cash or high-value cargo. Vehicle robberies are more likely to be committed by experienced, professional robbers because of the requirements to obtain "inside" information concerning the valuables being transported, the schedule of the vehicle, and its defense capability. A vehicle robber needs also to stop his target, extricate the valuables, and safely get away.

Investigative Techniques. Robberies that are committed on the spur of the moment by amateurs or robberies that are committed by professionals only after long and intricate planning have at least one thing in common: they are both difficult to solve. Many robberies are committed during hours of darkness or under conditions that make it difficult for the robber's features to be seen by the victim. Adding to this is the fact that the attention of the victim is frequently focused on the weapon, thereby making it difficult for the victim to provide a good description of the suspect.

A robbery is usually reported fairly soon after it has happened. The investigator who is called to the scene of the robbery should follow the basic steps of crime scene processing. The crime scene is usually larger than the normal crime scene because it covers that territory where a robber may have lain in wait for his victim, the approach routes of the suspect and victim, the place of the robbery, and the escape route of the suspect. Persons who were present immediately before, during, and after the incident are potential witnesses. The investigator should question witnesses, as well as the victim, to determine the following:

- A description of the robber to include words used, voice peculiarities, gestures, mannerisms, and clothing
- The direction and type of approach used by the suspect
- A description of valuables taken
- The victim's action prior to the robbery
- The direction traveled by the robber when he left the scene and the method of travel

After the victim has had time to recover and the investigator has had an opportunity to make a careful examination of the crime scene, a second interview should be conducted. The victim may remember details after he has settled himself emotionally, and the investigator may have to ask specific questions to clarify details or develop leads on the basis of evidence discovered. The second interview can also be used as an opportunity to prepare a composite likeness of the suspect.

If an automobile is involved in the robbery, the investigator should obtain a detailed description of it from as many persons as possible. In addition to making a routine stolen vehicle check, the investigator should contact car rental agencies. When a rental automobile is used in the commission of a robbery, it is possible that a description will be obtained from the clerk who handled the rental transaction. If and when an abandoned vehicle used in a robbery is located, latent fingerprints and items recovered from it will provide valuable leads. Items of clothing found in the car or close to it should be checked for laundry marks or other peculiarities that may provide leads to the identity of the suspect. Footprints at the scene of an abandoned stolen vehicle should not be ignored. Valuable leads can also be developed from discarded items such as newspapers, matchbooks, and cigarette butts that are inside or around the vehicle. When a robbery has occurred indoors, there should be an intensive search for latent fingerprints.

Furniture, counter tops, and anything else that could have been touched by the robber should be processed for latent prints. Notes handed to a teller, discarded deposit slips, or counter checks not only provide opportunities to obtain fingerprints but can also link the robber to the crime through handwriting analysis.

Some robbers feel a need to restrain their victims using such items as rope or adhesive tape. When rope has been used and to the extent that it is possible to do so, the investigator should obtain the rope with any knots still intact. The type of knot used by the robber may provide a link to him and to other crimes he may have committed. It may also be possible to trace the type of rope to a particular dealer. Adhesive tape has an especially high potential as evidence because it may be possible to obtain fingerprints from either side of it. It may also be possible to match the torn edge of the tape to the end of a roll of tape found in the possession of the suspect.

When interviewing witnesses or victims, the investigator should concentrate on determining the exact words used by the robber. The use of particular words or groups of words is valuable in matching the crime against previous robberies. The speech, gestures, and mannerisms of the robber are sometimes the only leads an investigator may be able to develop. Any discussion of robbery is not complete without mention of the critical importance that informants can play in the identification and arrest of robbery suspects. While there is no replacement for hard work in developing physical evidence and testimony from people having knowledge of a robbery, there is tremendous value in obtaining the right piece of information from a confidential source that is in a position to know or acquire information beyond the influence of the investigator.

Learning Shop USA, Felonies and Misdemeanors, www.learningshopusa.com

ROLE OF LAW ENFORCEMENT
Introduction

Essential to the correct performance of private investigative functions is an understanding of public law enforcement, especially in the area of criminal investigations. Police detectives and private detectives often perform identical activities, and that reality alone is sufficient reason for private investigators to have a solid understanding of their counterparts in the public sector.

Early English Customs

Law enforcement in the United States today has roots in early English customs. The word "shire" means a geographic area. The United States version of a shire is a county. Men called shire-reeves governed early English shires. A sheriff in the United States is a police official at the county (shire) level.

The shire-reeve was a freeman appointed by a nobleman or the king. The shire-reeve had the power to enforce the law. Helping him keep good order were constables. In time of war, the shire-reeve was also tasked with raising and maintaining an army. The military style of police organizations in the United States was inherited from the early English tradition.

As England began changing from a society mainly based on farms in rural areas to a society based on manufacture of industrial goods in urban areas, the shire-reeve system began to break down. In 1748, Henry Fielding, a magistrate in the Bow Street section of London, formed the Bow Street Horse and Foot Patrol. The patrol covered the interior of the city and the roads leading into it.

Fielding called upon citizens to assist the patrol by watching for, chasing after, and capturing criminals. Citizens who performed these voluntary duties came to be called the Bow Street Runners.

In 1829, Sir Robert Peel established a police force called the Metropolitan Police of London. A primary purpose of this police force was crime prevention. Peel hired men in good physical condition who possessed above-average intelligence and high moral character. Police officers in modern-day England are called "bobbies" in honor of Sir Robert Peel.

Policing in America

English colonists brought to America the traditions of English policing. Sheriffs and constables enforced the law. During the hours of darkness, watchmen patrolled. A watchman's chief duty was to raise a hue and cry when he spotted a criminal act in progress. In New York City, night watchmen carried wooden rattles to announce their presence. This practice, called the rattle watch, was intended to scare away lawbreakers.

In the early 1800s, policing began a transition from voluntary or obligatory service to paid service administered by elected government. At this point, politics entered the picture. People with political power determined who would be placed in charge of a police department, who would be hired as police officers, who would be promoted, and, in some cases, who among the lawbreakers would be immune from enforcement. Near the end of the 1800s, pressure from the public forced political reform that brought about changes in police activities. Reforms continue to be made to this day.

In the 1920s, policing in the United States began to shift away from an emphasis on social services to an emphasis on enforcing the law and fighting crime. Practices that had been successfully applied in business and industry were introduced to policing. Among these were setting policies and strategies that target specific violators (e.g., bootleggers, Mafia members, and drug traffickers), improving human performance through education and training of police officers, and tapping into new technology.

Starting in the 1960s and continuing to the present moment, police leaders have learned the value of working with community leaders on a variety of mutual concerns.

Jurisdictions

Law enforcement agencies can exist at several levels of government: municipal, county, state, and federal. Jurisdiction defines a law enforcement agency. Jurisdiction can refer to the geographical area in which the agency operates and has authority, and it can refer to the type of law or crime that the agency is responsible for enforcing or investigating. For example, the jurisdiction of a state highway patrol agency is limited to roadways within the borders of the state and is responsible for enforcing motor vehicle laws of the state. The Drug Enforcement Agency (DEA) has authority nationwide and is responsible for enforcing federal drug laws and related crimes such as money laundering.

Most law enforcement agencies in the United States operate in the military style. Police officers wear uniforms that look like military uniforms, they hold military-sounding titles like sergeant and lieutenant, they follow a chain of command, and many policing actions involve tactics and equipment used in the military.

Patrol

Under patrol are the functions of deterring crime, responding to calls, maintaining order, arresting offenders, resolving conflict, giving assistance to injured persons or persons in danger, and securing crime scenes.

Foot patrol. This policing method that goes back to Biblical times and earlier. Police departments in today's large cities commonly use the "watchman" and the "walking the beat" styles of policing that found favor in early England and moved to these shores with settlers. Foot patrol is consistently effective as a deterrent to crime, especially crimes that rely on opportunity such as burglary, armed robbery, and mugging. Studies have shown that foot patrol can reduce fears that citizens have about crime in their neighborhoods. The visibility of the patrol officer on the street can give to citizens a feeling of protection, which in turn gives to the police an opportunity to enlist community support in keeping criminals off the street.

The effectiveness of foot patrol can be very high even though the patrol officer is limited in the amount of territory that can be covered in a single tour of duty.

Fixed Post Patrol. A variation is the fixed post patrol in which the officer remains at one location, usually for a specific purpose such as assisting tourists and visitors, controlling entrances and exits, and observing large crowds.

Moving Patrol. The type of patrol that occurs with the use of an automobile generally is called mobile patrol, and the automobile is called a cruiser. The typical cruiser is a late-model, four-door sedan marked on the exterior with distinctive insignia and colors. It is equipped with a radio and computer, communications, a rifle and/or shotgun, rescue tools, first aid kit, oxygen tank, defibrillator, and personal protective items such as latex gloves and surgical masks. In addition, the officer usually will carry a sidearm and a handheld radio.

Many people in the upper ranks of the police field believe there is a definite relationship between aggressive mobile patrol and crime prevention. Their logic is that police officers patrolling in vehicles are in good position to discover crimes in progress, get quickly to the scenes of reported crime, and apprehend criminals before they can flee. And, since many crimes are committed with the aid of a motor vehicle, officers in patrol vehicles are able to spot suspect vehicles, give chase, and make arrests.

Helicopters, fixed-wing aircraft, boats, motorcycles, bicycles, golf carts, and horses are other forms of mobile patrol.

Traffic Control

Traffic control operations are at the core of safety. The intended and underlying purpose of traffic enforcement is prevention of death and injury to drivers, passengers, pedestrians, and others whose safety can be imperiled by improper operation of motor vehicles.

Selective Enforcement. A technique often used to achieve the safety purpose is selective enforcement. The technique can take several forms, such as watching for and ticketing speeders on particular roadways at particular times; monitoring pedestrian crossing points to identify drivers who fail to yield the right of way; and setting up checkpoints to identify persons driving under the influence, driving without a valid license, and operating a motor vehicle without insurance coverage.

In small police departments, the patrol division usually performs traffic control along with its other duties. Large departments, such as a state patrol agency or the police department of a major city, typically form special units for controlling traffic and investigating serious traffic accidents. The training and equipment essential to special units can be unaffordable to small departments.

Accident Investigation. The tasks performed in accident investigations differ very little from tasks performed in criminal investigations. A scene is photographed and searched, evidence collected and analyzed forensically, notes and sketches made, a final report prepared, and testimony delivered.

Criminal Investigation

Criminal investigation is a systematic process of collecting evidence related to a crime and applying to that evidence a combination of human reasoning and scientific procedures so that the nature of the crime and the identity of the criminal can be determined. In this definition, evidence includes all manner of tangible objects plus the testimony of witnesses and experts. Human reasoning refers specifically to inductive and deductive reasoning, and scientific procedures refer to forensic examinations of evidence.

Evidence. Evidence can be categorized by type. For example:

- Physical evidence consists of fingerprints, palm prints, and plantar (foot) prints; biological tissues and fluids; materials displaying bite marks, foot and tire treads, weapons; projectiles; poisons; chemical substances; pieces of metal; dirt; glass fragments; fibers; tools; photographs; video and audio tapes; and much, much more.
- Documentary evidence is in the form of documents such as official records, files, reports, and logs.
- Testimonial evidence consists of oral and written statements of persons having knowledge of the crime. These persons can be the responding officers, investigators, attending physicians, complainants, victims, suspects, eyewitnesses, reluctant witnesses, and expert witnesses.

Inductive Reasoning. The thinking process that brings together separate observations drawn from objects, occurrences, and pieces of information is called inductive reasoning. Considered together, the observations or facts lead to a conclusion or a theory. To illustrate, Smith is found dead in his apartment. The coroner concluded that Smith died of a gunshot wound to the head. A projectile removed from Smith's body was identified as a .38 caliber bullet. A witness heard a gunshot come from inside Smith's apartment. Seconds later, another witness saw Jones running from Smith's apartment. A third witness saw Jones throw a gun into a trash barrel. The gun, a .38 caliber revolver, was recovered. Lands and grooves inside the gun barrel matched striations on the bullet. Each fact by itself is insufficient to form a conclusion, but taken together they form a reasonable conclusion.

Deductive Reasoning. This thinking process tests facts against one another. In the above scenario, the investigator observed that the entry point of the projectile was at the back of the head and that the wound was covered with a heavy concentration of gunpowder residue. Comparing these two facts, the investigator concluded that the killer was behind the victim and that the muzzle of the gun was close to the victim's skin.

Police Investigation Objectives. Many of the techniques used by police detectives and private detectives are similar, if not identical. Yet, in spite of the similarities, very important differences exist. In police investigations, the objectives are to:

- Determine that a crime has been committed
- Collect information and evidence concerning the crime
- Identify the person who committed the crime
- Recover stolen property
- Assist in the prosecution of the defendant

Private Investigation Objectives. In private investigations, the objectives can be to:

- Disprove or cast doubt on the methods and findings of police detectives
- Collect information and evidence that point to the innocence of the suspect or defendant
- Assist in the defense of the defendant, who is usually the private detective's client

Special Units

Many law enforcement departments form special units to target particular crimes or deal with particular issues. Typically, a special unit is staffed with two to 10 officers who work in support of a larger segment of the department. For example, an accident investigation team, antigang team, antimugging team, and special weapons and tactics team (SWAT) support the patrol division; the narcotics squad, vice squad, and polygraph section support the criminal investigation division; and the crime prevention team and community relations team support the department as a whole. A large department will have an internal affairs section to investigate allegations of police misconduct and will create and disband various task forces from time to time as needed. Task forces tend to be formed in response to public concern, such as during a rise in juvenile delinquency or white-collar crime.

Forensics

The term "forensics" has various meanings. Here, it refers to the analysis of evidence by technical specialists using scientific methods in an accredited crime laboratory. A crime lab, like a special unit, is a support function. For the most part, a crime lab supports the criminal investigation division. Because a crime lab is expensive to create and maintain, often it will be funded by several sources and committed to serve several agencies.

Crime lab scientists examine physical evidence using many technologies, e.g., gas chromatography, mass spectrometry, DNA, and microscopy. Conclusions reached through scientific analysis provide investigative leads and aid in the prosecution of criminals.

Police Culture

The meaning of the term "police culture" is fuzzy at best. According to some researchers, the police culture is made up of beliefs generally held by police officers. For example, researchers have declared that police officers believe:

- They are different from all other people in our society.
- They are the only crime fighters. The only barrier standing between the forces of evil and the defenseless are police officers.

- No one understands the work they do.
- Loyalty to fellow police officers is absolutely essential.
- Criminals have too many rights. Bending the rules to convict criminals is okay.

People outside the police profession hold a different set of beliefs about police officers. The prominence of law enforcement in society at large causes people to form views of police officers as persons. At least three of these are false.

- Police officers are perfect people who enforce the law exactly and without bias in any way.
- Police officers enforce the law according to their personal racial, sexual, religious, and political views.
- Police officers are drawn to law enforcement because they have aggressive or authoritarian tendencies.

The only certainty about the police culture is that it exists. Trying to define it with any degree of precision seems to be very difficult, if not impossible.

Learning Shop USA, Role of Law Enforcement, www.learningshopusa.com

Joseph A. Senna and Larry J. Siegel, *Introduction to Criminal Justice*, West Publishing, Minneapolis/St. Paul, MN, pp. 211–218.

RULES OF EVIDENCE

Physical Evidence

Physical evidence is any material, substance, or object, regardless of size or shape. There are three categories of physical evidence:

- Moveable Evidence. Items that can be transported or moved, such as weapons, tools, and glass fragments.
- Fixed Evidence. Items that cannot easily be transported or moved, such as walls, rooms, and utility poles.

- **Fragile Evidence.** Items that deteriorate or are easily contaminated or destroyed, such as shoe and tire prints, blood, semen, and fingerprints.

Testimonial Evidence

Testimonial evidence is evidence presented by a witness under oath.

Direct Evidence

Direct evidence is evidence that shows the existence of a fact without requiring proof of any other fact. A birth certificate is direct evidence of a birth, a fingerprint is direct evidence of a person's identification, and a bank statement is direct evidence of an account balance as of a certain date.

Circumstantial Evidence

Also called indirect evidence, circumstantial evidence is a fact that can be inferred either alone or from collateral facts. In cases where the prosecution relies wholly on circumstantial evidence, the facts must be of such a nature that they exclude to a moral certainty every other hypothesis except that of the defendant's guilt.

Admissibility

Admissibility is a characteristic or condition of evidence. To be admissible, evidence must be material, relevant, and competent. Evidence is material when it plays a significant part in proving a case. Examples of material evidence might be fingerprints of the accused that were found on the murder weapon, an eyewitness account of how the accused committed the crime, or stolen property found in the possession of the accused. Evidence is relevant when it goes directly to the proof or disproof of the crime or of any facts at issue. Examples of relevant evidence might be a death certificate or a medical examiner's report. Evidence is competent when it is

shown to be reliable. Examples of competent evidence might be accurate business records or the testimony of an expert fingerprint examiner.

Opinion Testimony and Hearsay

Opinion testimony is a conclusion or judgment made by a witness, hence the term "opinion testimony." Another form of testimonial information is hearsay evidence. Hearsay is testimony given by one person as to what another person said. Hearsay cannot be entered into evidence unless the maker of the statement can be cross-examined.

All evidence, if relevant, material, and competent, is admissible provided it is not opinion testimony, hearsay evidence, or privileged communication. There are exceptions regarding the admissibility of opinion testimony and hearsay evidence. An exception to the rule against opinion testimony can be made when no other description could be more accurate. For instance, a witness is allowed to testify on such matters as size, distance, time, weight, speed, direction, drunkenness, and similar matters, all of which require the witness to state an opinion. There is no requirement for the witness to be an "expert" when testifying to facts such as these.

Exceptions to the rule against hearsay can be made for the dying declaration and the spontaneous declaration. The admissibility of a dying declaration is limited to homicide cases. Because of the seriousness of homicide, a dying declaration is an exception. A dying declaration is admissible either for or against the accused. The statement must have been made when the victim believed he was about to die and was without hope of recovery. The admissibility of the declaration will not be affected as long as the victim dies; otherwise, the issue would not arise since there would be no charge of homicide.

The spontaneous declaration, a statement made under conditions of shock or excitement, may be admitted as another exception to the hearsay rule. Normally, such a statement is made simultaneously with an event or act and there is not time or opportunity to fabricate a story. It is generally accepted that the statement will be admitted if it precedes, follows, or is concurrent with the act. The statement cannot have been made in response to a question and must pertain to the act that produced it. The spontaneity of the statement is sufficient guarantee of truthfulness to compensate for the denial of cross-examination.

Exclusionary Rule

In general, a witness is excluded from presenting testimony other than those things of which he had direct knowledge, i.e., what he saw, smelled, tasted, felt, or heard.

Privileged Communication

Privileged communication is confidential information between two persons recognized by law as coming within the so-called privileged relationship rule. The following relationships are generally recognized: a husband and wife, an attorney and client, a physician and patient, and a law enforcement officer and informant.

Character Evidence

A defendant's good or bad character can be introduced by either side. Usually, the defense will raise the issue of good character, which than makes it possible for the prosecution to introduce evidence to the contrary.

Burden of Proof

The U.S. Constitution provides that a person accused of a crime cannot be required to prove innocence. The burden of proof of guilt is on the prosecution. For the proof to be met, the jury must believe the charges to be true to a "moral certainty."

Fresh Complaint

In prosecutions for sexual offenses, evidence that the victim made a complaint within a short time after the offense occurred is admissible in certain cases. The fact that the complaint was freshly made is relevant for corroborating the testimony of the victim. The statement may relate only to who and what caused the conditions and merely indicate the credibility of the victim as a witness.

Confessions and Admissions

A confession is a statement or complete acknowledgment of guilt. A confession alone, uncorroborated by any other evidence, cannot sustain a conviction. To make a confession admissible, it must have been made voluntarily, without being induced by another by the slightest hope of benefit or remotest fear of injury.

An admission is a statement that does not amount to a complete acknowledgment of guilt but links the maker with a crime. A court is inclined to apply the same rules of admissibility to admissions as for confessions.

Acquiescence or silence, when the circumstances require an answer, a denial, or other conduct, may amount to an admission. Admissions obtained by constraint, by fraud, or the use of compromise are inadmissible.

Fruit of the Poisonous Tree

The "fruit of the poisonous tree" is a legal concept holding that evidence may be suppressed at trial if it is tainted by prior illegal conduct on the part of the person collecting the evidence. For example, drug trafficking information obtained with the use of an illegal wiretap can be suppressed, as well as any drugs confiscated as a result of the information.

Good Faith Exception

The "good faith exception" is a legal concept holding that unlawfully acquired evidence may be admissible if the person who acquired the evidence had acted in good faith when acquiring the evidence.

Reasonable Doubt

Proof beyond a reasonable doubt is a requirement in criminal proceedings. The prosecutor shows without ambiguity that the defendant committed the crime charged. Reasonable doubt is any uncertainty in the minds of jurors that would cause them to believe the defendant is innocent.

Preponderance of Evidence

A preponderance of evidence is evidence that produces an impression stronger than opposing evidence. In a civil suit, a preponderance of evidence must be shown by the plaintiff to win.

Learning Shop USA, Rules of Evidence, www. learningshopusa.com

S

SEARCH AND SEIZURE: FOURTH AMENDMENT RIGHTS

The Fourth Amendment to the Constitution of the United States guarantees the right of the people to be secure against unreasonable searches and seizures. The Amendment specifically provides:

The right of the people to be secure in their persons, houses, papers, and effects against unreasonable searches and seizures shall not be violated, and no warrants shall issue, but upon probable cause, supported by oath or affirmation, and particularly describing the place to be searched, and the persons or things to be seized.

Federal and state laws provide to agents of the government (e.g., police officers) very limited authority to conduct searches and seizures and make arrests. The Amendment does not extend that authority to nongovernmental agents such as private investigators. This means that in the course of private employment, a private investigator cannot receive and carry out a search warrant. They can, however, submit an affidavit to a magistrate and request that a warrant be issued directing the police to make the search and seizure. Then, with permission of the magistrate and/or police official, the private investigator can be present as an observer.

Search

To "search" means to examine a certain person, place, or thing for the purpose of discovering and seizing certain specified items. For an examination to be properly called a "search," the person conducting the examination must be duly empowered by law to make searches and possess a specific authority or permission, such as a warrant or the consent of the person to be searched.

Search Warrant

A search warrant directs that a search be conducted, names the agency to conduct the search, names who or what is to be searched, describes the items to be looked for, and sets a time frame in which the search is to be conducted.

The word "warrant" itself means an order. Although the person or agency carrying out the warrant was the requester of the warrant in the first place, it is the issuing judge who gives the order for a search to be conducted. A warrant is not simply a permit granted to someone to conduct a search; it is an order to do so and is very specific in what must be done. The warrant will name a person or small number of persons who will carry out the warrant. The warrant will name the person, place, or property to be searched. Knowing the details of the area to be searched is sometimes of great importance to the requester of a warrant. For example, it might be very important to know that the building to be searched has a separate shed. Unless the shed is included in the warrant, it cannot be lawfully searched. It might be that the items to be looked for are in the shed. A little advance knowledge on the part of the searcher is important in getting a properly worded warrant.

Along the same line, it is important that the warrant include mention of all items that are useful as evidence. If the case involves a search for an automatic rifle, the person requesting the warrant would want to include mention of ammunition, ammunition clips, magazines, or parts pertaining to the type of automatic rifle involved. If the warrant simply names the rifle as the item to be looked for, the searcher cannot technically seize anything except the rifle and misses the chance of getting other pieces of evidence related to the same crime. Advance preparation in the wording of a warrant is therefore important.

Seizure

Seizure is the taking of contraband, fruits of a crime, tools of a crime, or incriminating evidence. The person taking the items must be empowered to make the seizure, and the items seized must be protected until disposed of in some proper fashion. If, for example, the item seized is a stolen ring, the ring will be safeguarded as evidence until the trial is completed. When the judicial action against the offender ends, the ring will be returned to the owner. For some kinds of seized items, final disposition might be destruction. Narcotics, certain kinds of weapons, and illegal whiskey are examples of items that are usually destroyed after court action has ended.

The warrant to search may specify that any seized property be taken to a designated place or agency. Seized items are sometimes regarded as property of the court until such time as the items are properly disposed of, with disposition instructions normally issued by the court in writing. The proper safeguarding of seized property requires that the property be inventoried at the time it is seized. The inventory is placed into writing, usually on a receipt type of form that identifies all items taken. The copy of the receipt is given, with the search warrant, to the person from whom the items were taken. If no such person is available, the receipt and search warrant are left at the place of seizure. The original copy of the receipt remains with the seized items and is used to account for the property from the time of seizure until the time of final disposition.

Affidavit

An affidavit is a written document that supports the issuance of a search warrant. An affidavit is nothing more than a written statement made under oath. It sets forth details that provide the issuing judge with enough information to conclude that a crime was committed and that a search of a certain place will probably reveal the presence of some evidence pertaining to that crime. The affidavit therefore provides a type of information called "probable cause."

Reasonable

The term "reasonable" is sometimes used to describe the nature of a search conducted with authority of a search warrant. Since probable cause has to be present for a search warrant to be issued, it can be said that the search was reasonable. The term "reasonable" then becomes almost identical with words like "constitutional," "lawful," or "legal." The term "unreasonable" is therefore just the opposite of "reasonable" in meaning. "Unreasonable" has often been used to describe searches that were conducted without benefit of a search warrant. An example of an "unreasonable search" would be an examination of a place for the purpose of finding any kind of evidence that might possibly be used against a person. This type of search is unreasonable because it is exploratory in nature.

Contraband

Contraband is any item that, by itself, is a crime to have. Bootleg whiskey is contraband because possession of it is against the law. The same holds true for certain types of firearms, explosives, illegal narcotics, and counterfeit money.

Fruits of the Crime

This term refers to the advantage derived by the criminal by committing the crime. Shoplifted items and money obtained through fraud are examples of fruits of crime.

Tools of the Crime

In the commission of a burglary, a tool could be a crow bar, lock pick, or bolt cutter. In fraud, a tool could be a false document or worthless check.

Search Incidental to Arrest

Searches can be made without a warrant under some circumstances. Most common of these circumstances is a search made during an arrest. A check of a person's possessions at the moment of arrest is mainly intended to discover the presence of weapons that can be used against the arresting person. The arresting person has a right to protect against attack by a weapon concealed on the body of the arrested person. A second consideration is to see if the offender is in possession of evidence connected to the reason for the arrest.

Property in the possession of the arrested person can also be searched. This would include packages, briefcases, and the like. The place under immediate control of the arrested person can be searched for evidence connected to the crime. Thus, when a person is arrested in his private office, the unlocked areas of the office can be legally searched. If the arrest is made in a building lobby, the lobby cannot be searched because it is not under immediate control of the suspect at the time of arrest. Vehicles driven by an arrested person can be searched but only those areas of the vehicle that are controlled by the suspect. The trunk of a vehicle is not considered to be under control of the suspect at the time of arrest. If it is felt that a search of the trunk will probably yield evidence connected to a crime, a search warrant can be requested. If the arrested person is a woman and the arresting official is a man, the search can include only the purse, coat, parcels, baggage, or other articles not worn.

Emergency Search

Another type of lawful search and seizure is the looking for and taking of criminal goods before the goods can be hidden, removed, destroyed, or used. An emergency search is justified when facts show that a crime was committed, the criminal goods are probably in the possession of the suspect, the suspect is leaving with the goods, and there is no time to obtain a search warrant.

Search with Consent

Consent to search must be voluntarily and knowingly given. Threats, trickery, or other method of inducing consent without voluntariness and intelligence are prohibited. Consent is not valid when given by a person who is too young, intoxicated, sick, cognitively impaired, or insane. Submission or giving in to a request for consent is not the same as giving a free consent. In order to demonstrate that consent to search was freely and intelligently given, the consent should be in writing. The writing itself, the words used, and the physical act of writing help to demonstrate that the consent was properly obtained.

Also, consent must come from a person who has the right to give the consent. A hotel manager cannot give consent to search a paying guest's hotel room. A person sharing an apartment cannot give consent to a search of another person's property within the apartment.

Plain View Doctrine

The plain view doctrine holds that no warrant is required to confiscate contraband that is in the plain view of a law enforcement officer who has a lawful right to be at the place where the items are open to view. Plain view exists when an officer who has justification for being at a certain place in the course of official duties inadvertently comes into contact with contraband in open view and who, prior to the discovery, was unaware of the existence of the contraband before coming upon it. An example would be an officer who is called to the scene of an assault and observes cocaine on a coffee table. The officer is legally on the premises and can seize the cocaine. The plain view doctrine would not apply if an officer was observing through an open window, not in connection with official police business.

Criminal Liability

At the federal level, Title 18 of the United States Code provides fines and imprisonment for persons found guilty of conducting unlawful searches. Most states have tended to model their search and seizure laws in conformance with the federal law. Where differences might exist between a particular state and the overall guiding federal law, the difference is more likely to be a matter of semantics rather than spirit or intent of the law.

Civil Liability

In addition to possible criminal prosecution, the offending person is likely to be charged in a civil suit. A defense is possible if it can be shown that the searcher was acting in good faith, according to an official duty. A person who uses bad judgment and conducts an illegal search has an excuse, but when the search is conducted illegally by intent, or not in connection with official duties, the person can be charged.

Learning Shop USA, Search and Seize, www.learningshopusa.com

SHOPLIFTING

Shoplifting is the act of knowingly taking goods from a mercantile establishment without paying for them. The goods taken are typically on display and accessible and the methods of taking are various:

- Concealing goods on the body or in a container such as a purse or briefcase
- Transferring goods to an accomplice before leaving the store
- Using an accomplice to divert the attention of store personnel so that the taker is better able to conceal the goods and leave the store without detection
- Switching price tags from expensive goods to less expensive goods
- Using a store employee-accomplice to facilitate the taking, such as by a cashier not ringing up the sale or not charging the full price

Shoplifting includes theft by employees who steal goods when the goods arrive at the delivery point, when the goods are in a storage area not under observation, when the goods leave the store through an unmonitored exit, and when goods pass a register with help of an accomplice such as a cashier.

Most shoplifters are nonprofessional opportunists, they are unsophisticated in technique; the items stolen are for personal use, and they steal when they believe they will not be caught. Professional shoplifters are skilled; they have a backup story to keep from being detained, and they convert the stolen goods to cash by selling them to another party such as a fence.

Shoplifting is made easier when the customer is allowed to carry goods and move around the store. At a propitious time and place, the shoplifter will conceal the property. A variation is to partially conceal the property in the shopping cart or bag and, at the point of sale, attempt to leave the store without paying. If questioned by the cashier, the shoplifter will claim to have forgotten to return the property to the place where it was on display.

Prevention

Methods to prevent shoplifting fall into three general categories: prevention by policy, detection by equipment, and prevention/detection by human observation.

Prevention by policy:

- Acknowledges that shoplifting is a significant source of loss, which justifies a loss-prevention program
- Trains employees how to see and recognize shoplifting when it occurs
- Trains employees how to respond when shoplifting is observed
- Designates certain employees, especially supervisors, to take control of the response to a shoplifting incident
- Educates responders as to probable cause, unlawful detention, false arrest, improper questioning and accusing, and privacy invasion
- Displays high-value items so that customer access can be only through an employee
- Arranges merchandise neatly and orderly. This will help an employee see if anything is missing.
- Checks large items to see if smaller items are inside at the point of sale
- Applies price tags that are not easily switched or altered
- Gives to each purchaser a sales receipt and requires that it be presented if the item is returned
- Vigorously prosecutes offenders

Detection by equipment uses:

- Closed-circuit television. Monitoring by CCTV both discourages shoplifting and detects shoplifting as it occurs.

- Electronic article surveillance. An EAS system alerts store employees when a person leaves without paying for a relatively expensive item. When payment for the item is not made, an electronic tag or badge will sound an alarm when the item passes through an exit.
- Radio-frequency identification. When an alarm is triggered, RFID will identify the specific item that caused the activation. Thus, EAS is augmented by RFID. Another use of RFID is to keep a running inventory of stock that is both on the shelf and in storage waiting to be put on the shelf. A shortage is immediately detected.
- Bottom-of-basket mirrors. BOBs are commonly used in grocery stores where checkout lanes are close enough to help cashiers and bagging persons see if the bottom of the basket contains items not rung up by a cashier.
- Locks. Combination, key, and pad locks are used to remove customer accessibility to high-value items.
- Dummy case. A dummy case is an empty box that the customer takes from a shelf and carries to a register. The item is rung up, and the content of the box (such as a mini-computer) is delivered to the customer at the register or the purchaser is given a chit that can be carried to a place in the store where the chit is exchanged for the item.

Detection and prevention by human observation includes:

- Loss prevention practitioners. These persons may be employees or contract persons who are trained in shoplifting detection. They do not wear uniforms, patrol the store inconspicuously, and sometimes look for suspicious activity using a CCTV monitor.
- Uniformed guards. These persons usually observe from a particular location, such as an exit or a place where high-value items are sold.

- Employees.
- Test or mystery shoppers. Persons who appear to be shoppers rove the store and alert store employees of a shoplifting in progress. Another strategy is to test a cashier. For example, the test shopper hands the cashier a $20 bill before the sale can be rung up on the register; the test shopper dashes out the door before receiving one dollar in change; and at the end of the cashier's shift, the cash register tape is examined to see if the sale had been rung up. If not, there is a suspicion of theft.

False Arrest

False arrest is to take into custody a person without probable cause or without an order issued by a court. The false arrest is often connected to shoplifting, and the persons that make the false arrest are store employees, security personnel, or investigators employed by or under contract to the store.

When an accusation of shoplifting has been dismissed in court, the person arrested is in a good position to sue those who had made the arrest. The usual reason for dismissal of the charge was the absence of probable cause; without probable cause, the arrest was not legal.

Individual(s) who make or participate in an arrest can become defendants in a civil court. The person who was arrested (the plaintiff) can allege that his or her right of movement was taken away.

Any person may arrest someone suspected of committing a felony as long as the arresting person believes a serious offense had occurred and the person to be arrested committed the crime. A person cannot be arrested on mere suspicion.

Most cases of false arrest involve accusations of shoplifting, and the accusations of shoplifting are made by store employees in the course of their work. A serious mistake is made when the arrest is based on a belief that the arrested person had an intention to shoplift. In such a case, there was no crime and no probable cause. Similarly, there is no probable cause if a shopper has not yet paid for merchandise and is carrying the merchandise inside the store. For there to be a violation of shoplifting, the shopper must attempt to leave, or actually leave, while in possession of store goods for which payment had not been made.

Unlawful Detention

Any form of imprisonment in which a person's freedom of movement has been removed meets the definition of detention. Detention, following an arrest based on a reasonable suspicion of shoplifting, becomes unlawful when the arrested person's freedom of movement is withheld beyond a reasonable period of time. What is "reasonable" is a matter for a court to decide. What happens during the period of time can be considered, such as use of force, threat of violence, intimidation (browbeating), search of the person or the person's property, and characteristics of the place of detention.

Here is an example to illustrate the concept: Jones leaves a store without having paid for an item; in the parking lot, a store employee stops Jones and asks Jones to return to the store; Jones agrees; the store employee escorts Jones to a room in the back of the store; Jones gives consent to the store employee to look in a shopping bag in Jones's possession; the store employee finds in the bag an item for which payment had not been made; Jones cannot explain why; the police are called; Jones is arrested, booked, and released; when the case comes before a court, the judge dismisses the charge of shoplifting; Jones files a suit against the store employee.

The judge's decision as to unlawful detention might have been made after receiving answers to these questions:

- Was Jones told that he or she was arrested?
- Did Jones agree to return to the store?

- When were the police called?
- How long did it take for the police to arrive?
- In total, how long was Jones detained?

The judge might have considered contributing facts such as:

- Touching
- Force or threat of force
- Intimidating language
- The nature of the room: visible to others, uncomfortable, locked

Conclusion

False arrest and unlawful detention are two different things but are very often present in a single situation—often a shoplifting situation.

Fred E. Inbau, Bernard J. Farber, and Donald W. Arnold, *Protective Security Law*, second ed., Butterworth-Heinemann, Newton, MA, 1996, pp. 173–176.
John J. Fay, *Security Dictionary*, American Society for Industrial Security, Alexandria, VA, 2000, p. 102.
Learning Shop USA, Criminal Procedure, www.learningshopusa.com

SKIP TRACING

Skip tracing is the investigative research done to locate a person. This term is coined from the phrase "skipping out" or "skipped town" and typically refers to a person who is alive and deliberately hiding or has innocently moved to a new unknown location due to circumstance.

Many occupations employ skip trace methods not only to locate persons but perform due diligence for the purpose of verifying that information provided by a person is truthful and accurate.

Resident screening and employment background searches are standard in today's business practices and are performed with signed releases. Many of the same methods are used in asset searches related to court rulings and validation of ownership of bequeathed property.

"Permissible purpose" is a general, legal right granted to persons whose occupations require the use of skip trace methods. To help guard against illegal skip trace methods, some states have enacted laws that more narrowly define permissible purpose. A simple example is Florida law that requires a collection agency that performs skip tracing to employ a private investigator licensed in that state.

Collection agencies and finance companies have access to credit bureau information, but such information is not accessible to private investigators and process servers. Privatized databases acquire information from credit bureaus and then sell it to persons/companies that possess the permissible purpose right.

Privatized databases buy information from sources other than credit bureaus. These can include addresses related to pizza and food deliveries, magazine subscriptions, insurance policies, utility connections, memberships in professional and social organizations, and a myriad of other service-related businesses that sell customer data.

A basic step in skip tracing is to search private and subscription databases. Searching by Social Security number will provide every name and address combination of every person who has used that Social Security number. Searching by an address without a name will give results of every person associated with that address, in some cases including personal identifiers such as the Social Security number itself and the subject's date of birth.

Cross-referencing database results can create a big picture of where the subject has lived and the identities of persons who may know the subject's present location. Public databases are maintained in city, county, and state governments. Court records; UCC filings; corporation and LLC filings; property tax records; civil lawsuits; and personal records, such as federal tax liens, are examples. Public databases are a starting point when attempting to locate real property.

When a subject is hiding, there may be more than one reason for the subject to be hiding. Studying criminal records in jurisdictions where the subject has lived or worked may reveal other reasons for evasion; for example, an outstanding arrest warrant. A refined list of skip trace actions with brief explanations of how to utilize the results in other types of searches is shown below:

- Run the Social Security number through all databases and assimilate the results.
- Search every known previous address without identifiers (names, dates of birth, or Social Security numbers) to reveal every person connected with each address and possible dates.
- Information related to family members and friends is helpful when a person not wanting to be found moves in with family or friends.
- When a phone number is known, use Internet search engines to tap into databases maintained by White Pages and similar services. Subscription-based databases provide similar or more expanded information on a fee basis.
- Voter registration online searches are available for most counties and states. People who register to vote provide home addresses.
- Court appearances are usually recorded online. Appearances may relate to traffic offenses, worthless checks, and similar offenses. A record is also made of failure to appear.
- Driver's license and motor vehicle registration records are very good sources. Knowing a license plate number is valuable when making a visual search, such as in a certain neighborhood.
- Carfax and similar companies maintain records of motor vehicle accidents. With a license plate number or vehicle identification number (VIN), Carfax can retrieve in-house records that could reflect an as-yet-unknown address. The data may also name companies that did repair and warranty work. Those companies will have repair orders and sales slips that contain an address.
- County governments keep marriage and divorce records. The county and contiguous counties where the subject is believed to have been married and/or divorced will contain information. Marriage information is accessible online and at the county courthouse, but divorce information is available at the courthouse only.
- Civil lawsuits filed by or against the subject may reveal the identities of persons not revealed previously. These persons may possess useful information. Limitations may apply when the lawsuit involves family matters.
- Judgments recorded in district and small claims courts can include names of creditors, collection agencies, and business associates.
- Housing authority offices, also known as Section 8 offices, are rent assistance programs that keep information on persons residing in rent-assisted houses.
- Doing business as (DBA) listings are kept by cities and counties. The DBA list will reveal names and addresses of persons associated with the business.
- Secretary of State LLC and corporation filings include the names and addresses of corporate officers and investors. Also named is the person designated to accept service.
- Landlord and property management agreements may provide current contact information on persons making payments or using the property. Eviction filings may be available from a process server or constable.
- A letter mailed to the subject's address, and marked ADDRESS SERVICE REQUESTED, may result in USPS sending back a post card with the last known forwarding address of the subject.

- State driver's license searches in private databases may allow a search by address of licensed drivers and drivers whose licenses have expired. Access varies from state to state.
- Permit and licensing offices have open records. Employees holding positions that affect public safety, health, trust, and responsibility are usually licensed by the state. Many occupational licenses require that a bond be filed with the state; existence of the bond is public information. The bond company will also have in its files related documents.
- Property tax records and deed filings show a mailing address for purchasers and sellers, taxes levied and paid, and ownership history. Property that has passed from ownership of the subject to ownership by a family member or a friend is a good indication of unlawful concealment when the matter under investigation involves property subject to a court order or settlement agreement.
- Social media Internet sites may show friend and family member connections that lead back to the subject.
- Workers' compensation claims are in the public domain. The public agency holding the records is the state's board of insurance. Workers' compensation claims are important in pre-employment screening and background investigations.
- Traffic citation and warrant searches in the city, county, and statewide can be sometimes found online and are also available over the phone. Violations, fine amounts, missed court dates, and future court dates can lead to discovery of the subject's current location. Contact with a bonding company can help also.
- Criminal record searches may show details on convictions, parole, and probation. Arrest records held by a court or other public agency cannot be accessed, but many private databases have arrest records that were compiled from daily arrest reports made public by the arresting agency.
- Criminal charges pending disposition in some situations may be learned by calling the office of criminal courts at the county level.
- Directory assistance for listed and unlisted phone numbers is an information source. The directory assistance operator will likely refuse to provide the phone subscriber's address. If an address is already known to the investigator but needs verification, the operator may agree to say that the address is incorrect; if that happens to be the case, the investigator has eliminated that address from further consideration.
- A credit report inquiry shows that the subject may have applied for credit to purchase a product or service. In addition to the credit application form, there may be a variety of supporting documents, any or all of which may provide information useful to finding the subject. Obtaining this type of information usually requires a subpoena.
- A loan application made by the subject to a bank for home improvement, purchase of a vehicle, or other purpose will contain useful information (and requires a subpoena to obtain), but the investigator must first know that such an account exists and at what bank. A starting point is to identify all banks within a given radius. To narrow the search even further, the investigator should attempt to learn if the subject has a friend at a bank or has a positive personal history with a bank, which would increase the chances that the loan account is at that bank.
- The Freedom of Information Act makes it possible for a citizen to obtain information held by the federal government. A request for information under the Act is made by written communication.

Valerie McGilvery

SMART PHONE: THE INVESTIGATOR'S TOOL BOX

The smart phone, a device small enough to fit in a pocket, can be used to send and receive phone calls, e-mails, and text messages and take photos and videos. For the investigator, a smart phone is an indispensable tool box, and "tool box" is the appropriate term because the smart phone can perform the tasks mentioned above, plus a large number of other tasks that are not generally known or understood in the field of investigation.

Software applications (apps) are like keys that open many doors, and behind those doors are many, many features of considerable value to investigators. Here are five of the many apps that can be loaded into a smart phone.

Camera+. This camera is fully automatic, much like the popular "point and shoot" digital camera. Camera+ allows users to overcome problems that typically confuse automatic cameras.

Using two fingers on the screen, a user can control both the focus and, where the exposure should be calculated, make a correction that will eliminate the "dark shadow" problem.

Additionally, users can shoot bursts of photos like a motor-driven camera or use the timer to allow the photographer to get into the shot. This feature can block out the orange and blue hues that accompany unnatural lighting.

Zoom can be controlled with a numbered sliding scale. With the iPhone, a wide angle shot is taken if the zoom has not been adjusted. While a wide angle lens is appropriate for some photos, the majority of evidence photography should be shot with a normal lens. This keeps perspective equivalent to what is visible to the human eye.

With a smart phone, a zoom setting of 1.5 is approximately equal to a normal lens. A numbered scale allows users to more effectively select a "normal" setting, which is the preferred setting for most evidence photographs.

Turbo Scan. This feature allows the investigator to scan documents, even when documents are smudged or bear faint type and handwriting. Turbo Scan will autocorrect a scan that was taken at an angle; images can be viewed in color, black and white, and with photo quality.

Best results are achieved with a steady hand and an evenly lighted area. Even when lighting conditions are poor, Turbo Scan will produce quality images. Another advantage of Turbo Scan is SureScan 3x, a feature that has a high dynamic range setting. This feature will take three successive images and blend them together to compensate for trouble spots in the document.

Theodolite. Theodolite is an app with an incredible twist. A theodolite is a surveyor's tool. Photos and videos taken with this app can accurately document date, time, GPS coordinates, altitude, compass heading for direction of view, camera angle, and horizon elevation.

Evernote. Evernote is a powerful organizational tool. It allows users to place a variety of multimedia files into a "note" or a "notebook," such as files that contain photos, scanned documents, notes, audio recordings, text messages, e-mails, web pages, and GPS data, all pertaining to a single case. Also, the files can be organized in the field.

When the investigator returns to the office, the entire collection of files can be uploaded to the office computer. The app can be set to wirelessly synchronize and efficiently deliver a large collection of data in moments.

Google Translate. Not only does a smart phone offer a great camera and an impressive array of office and organizational tools, it serves as an efficient translator for dozens of languages. The app gives investigators the ability to communicate with and understand people or text in a number of languages.

Users select a language and speak into the device's microphone or type the words; the app will translate then provide a phrase or sentence in text or dialogue that corresponds to the language of interest. Witnesses that speak in a language that is not understood by the investigator can be interviewed without the need for a translator or a cumbersome foreign language dictionary.

Conclusion

To be taken seriously as a photographic tool, the smart phone camera should have at least 8 megapixels, which are found in the iPhone 4s and 5 models and in several Android products. Storage capacity is another important consideration; more is better.

An Internet connection is essential for the smart phone to deliver many of the services already mentioned. More importantly, a smart phone cannot exceed the knowledge and skill of the user. A significant amount of time is necessary to become an expert with apps and features. A powerful step to learning how to use the camera is to take screenshots as many times as needed to become competent. The process is simple; point the smart phone's eye lens at the image to be captured, with steady hand movements place the image into the field of view, and press a button.

Keith Rosenthal, CEP

SOCIAL MEDIA INVESTIGATIONS AND CYBERVETTING

Social media investigation is the gathering of personal and proprietary information residing on social media websites. A majority of persons and companies that have posted information on social media websites are not aware that information about them can be freely collected and used for a wide range of purposes. No court order or special permission is required to look at information posted on the Internet. An enormous amount and wide range of information can be easily

seen and downloaded from websites such as Facebook and Twitter and search engines such as Google, Yahoo, and Bing. Invasion of privacy and identity theft are common results.

In addition to the authorized collection of information is the posting of damaging information, such as intimate details and photographs acquired during romantic relationships, and false descriptions and reviews of a company's products or services.

Cybervetting is another form of social media investigation. It is often used for pre-employment screening purposes and as a tool to examine and acquire (quite legally) information that appears on websites and search engines. It has been reported that 82 percent of exploitation incidents involve human resource departments that are seeking information about job applicants. A human resources department is likely to innocently explain that the Internet is an open source and that an employer has a right to use Internet-collected information to validate representations made on a job application or acquired during a job interview. The categories of information generally sought by a human resource department are social media postings made by the applicant on Facebook, Twitter, LinkedIn, and other personal and business social media websites. All provisions of the Fair Credit and Reporting Act and the Equal Opportunity Commission are to be followed when cybervetting for pre-employment purposes. Some law enforcement agencies, to protect sensitive information and the agency's reputation, ask their officers to carefully review what they post or have posted on Facebook, Twitter, and similar sites.

Another use of cybervetting is to gather information about an employee under consideration for a promotion or transfer to a high position of responsibility.

Investigators, whether in the private or public sectors, need to be familiar with these practices. An information technology revolution is taking place today that is not very much different from database searching that began in the early 1990s.

Greg Roebuck

SOURCES OF LAW

Law acts as an instrument of social control and change. Many of the laws that regulate the private investigation industry, for example, have evolved in response to societal demands. In responding to the will of society, the law is in a constant state of flow, ebbing and rising in relation to pressures from many different sources. Law can have a profound impact on the decisions of persons working in all levels of private investigation. An overall view of law has two perspectives: broad and purposeful. Law is broad because it expresses concepts that generally ascribe to the notion that for civilization to be functional there must be a body of rules enforced by the government for the good of the people. Law is purposeful because it focuses on functional purposes, such as prevention and investigation of crime, recovery of property, and identification of violators. Law is not just a statement of rules of conduct; it is also the mechanism for dealing with violations and affording remedies.

American law has four sources:

- U.S. and state constitutions
- Legislation or statutory law
- Judicial decisions or case law
- Rules and regulations of governmental agencies or administrative law

The general priority among the various sources of law is that constitutions prevail over statutes, and statutes prevail over common-law principles established in court decisions. Courts will not turn to judicial decisions for law if a statute is directly applicable.

The rules and principles that are applied by the courts fall into three groups:

- Laws that have been passed by legislative bodies
- Case law, derived from cases decided by the courts
- Procedural rules, which determine how lawsuits are handled in the courts and include matters such as the rules of evidence

The first two groups are used by the courts to decide controversies. They are often called substantive law. The third group, known as procedural law, provides the machinery for resolving controversies. Procedural law establishes the procedures by which rights are enforced and protected.

Constitutional Law

The Constitution of the United States and the constitutions of the various states form the foundation of our legal system. All other laws must be consistent with them. A federal law cannot violate the U.S. Constitution; all state laws must conform to the federal Constitution, as well as with the constitution of the appropriate state.

Statutory Law

Much of law is found in legislation. Legislation is the expression of society's judgment and the product of the political process. Legislative bodies exist at all levels of government. Legislation is created by Congress, state legislatures, and local government bodies. Legislation enacted by Congress or by a state legislature is usually referred to as a statute. Laws passed by local governments are frequently called ordinances. Compilations of legislation at all levels of government are called codes. For example, at the municipal level are fire codes, at the state level are motor vehicle regulations, and at the federal level are codes consisting of statutes that regulate general conduct.

Substantial differences in the law exist among the various states simply because each state has its own constitution, statutes, and body of case law. Because of these differences, private and public investigators of crimes and offenses must understand law as it applies to their work.

Case Law

A very substantial part of law is found in cases decided by the courts. This concept of decided cases as a source of law is generally referred to as case law and has been a predominant influence in the evolution of the body of law in the United States. Case law is important because of the great difficulty in establishing law in advance of an issue being raised. When a case is decided, the court writes an opinion. Written opinions, or precedents, make up the body of case law.

Administrative Law

Administrative law is concerned with the many administrative agencies of the government. This type of law is in the form of rules and regulations promulgated by an administrative agency created by a state legislature or by Congress to carry out a specific statute. For example, Congress has given authority to the Federal Trade Commission (FTC) to enforce The Fair Credit Reporting Act (FCRA). Rules established by the FTC are in the nature of law to the regulated parties, e.g., private investigators, lenders, and employers.

Learning Shop USA, Criminal Law, www.learningshopusa.com

STATE COURTS: PRACTICES AND PROCEDURES

Prosecutors

A chief prosecutor is the attorney who advocates for the public in felony cases, as well as in a variety of other cases. A prosecutor's responsibilities are limited geographically. A prosecutorial district follows county lines and typically consists of a single county but may include two or more. Many prosecutors hold the title of either district attorney or county attorney. A chief prosecutor may have a staff of "assistant prosecutors" who do much of the actual case work.

The prosecutor usually does not know of a felony matter until a law enforcement agency makes an arrest. Because 95 percent of prosecutors receive felony cases from three or more arresting agencies, an opportunity exists for considerable variation in the time between arrest and notification of the prosecutor's office. About 73 percent of law enforcement agencies in the United States are state or local police departments, and 18 percent are county sheriff's departments; the rest are special agencies such as transit police or campus police.

Some prosecutors are notified only after the arresting agency has filed papers in a special or "lower" court. This court conducts necessary pretrial events, such as informing the accused person of the charges, setting bail, and assigning defense counsel.

When a staff attorney handles all phases of a criminal case, the processing is known as "vertical" case assignment. A career-criminal unit is an example of a vertical case assignment in which certain assistant prosecutors handle repeat offenders from the targeting stage onward. "Horizontal" assignment means that different assistants specialize in different phases—drafting complaints, conducting trials, or doing appellate work.

Indigent Defendants

The U.S. Constitution guarantees rights to citizens as they relate to the federal government and federal criminal prosecutions. Such rights are not automatically applicable to state governments and state criminal prosecutions. In lawsuits concerning specific rights, the U.S. Supreme Court decides the applicability of such rights to the states.

The Sixth Amendment to the U.S. Constitution establishes the right of a criminal defendant to have assistance of counsel for his or her defense. The Supreme Court has ruled that counsel must be available to any defendant who is at risk of a federal or state sentence of incarceration. This right extends to indigent defendants unable to pay a lawyer. If an indigent defendant who faces a penalty of incarceration wants a lawyer, the state must either provide a lawyer or seek a lesser penalty.

Filing

After a document charging a person with a crime is submitted to the felony court, an event known as a case "filing," the court takes control of the case. Most felony cases begin with the filing of an indictment issued by a grand jury. In most other felony cases, the charging document is an "information" filed by the prosecutor. Either type of document states who the accused person is and what illegal acts were committed. To proceed on the basis of an information rather than an indictment, the prosecutor normally must present the case in a preliminary hearing, which in some places occurs in a lower court. In a preliminary hearing, the judge reviews the facts and circumstances of the case to determine whether there are reasonable grounds ("probable cause") to believe the accused person committed the crime for which he or she is being charged. The accused person may waive any right to have the matter reviewed by grand jury. Such waivers often occur, particularly when the accused decides to plead guilty early in the case.

The Fifth Amendment to the Constitution establishes that a citizen accused of a felony has the right to have a grand jury, rather than the prosecutor, decide whether he or she shall be prosecuted. Except in cases that could involve a death sentence, the accused may waive this right. The grand jury right does not apply to prosecutions in state courts. About half of the states, however, have laws allowing or requiring the use of grand juries in felony cases.

Where grand juries are used, an indictment takes precedence over the prosecutor's view of whether probable cause exists in a case. The court rather than the prosecutor convenes grand juries. In districts with grand juries, however, judges of a lower court or a felony court often screen cases for probable cause, providing for greater grand jury efficiency.

Criminal History Data

When a person is arrested or brought before a court on a criminal charge, usually a government agency keeps a permanent official record of the event. These records enable prosecutors to find out about a person's "criminal history." That knowledge can help prosecutors make proper decisions.

Plea Negotiation

In a vast majority of felony convictions, the defendant pleads guilty rather than requesting a trial. The high percentage of guilty pleas is a key factor in minimizing case backlogs. Guilty pleas often result from negotiations: the defendant agrees to plead guilty to a lesser charge or to a charge for which the prosecutor recommends a reduced sentence. The court may impose deadlines on negotiations when responding to requests for extensions of time or continuances. Requests for more time to negotiate a plea agreement are sometimes made on the day of trial, even when witnesses, juries, and court personnel have already assembled.

Speedy Trial

The Sixth Amendment of the U.S. Constitution guarantees to the accused in a criminal trial, whether federal or state, the right to a speedy trial. In recent years, legislatures and courts have established limits on the time following an arrest that a prosecutor has to bring the case to trial. Such speedy trial requirements often apply when a defendant is held in custody but do not apply when the defendant has been granted pretrial release.

Jury Trial

The Sixth Amendment to the U.S. Constitution gives state and federal felony defendants the right to trial by jury. This right may be waived in favor of trial by judge. An estimated 4 percent of all felony convictions are the result of a judge trial. In some jurisdictions, the prosecutor also has the right to have a case tried by a jury. In such jurisdictions, the jury may be used even if the defendant prefers a judge trial, although how the proceedings are carried out is decided by the trial judge. The prosecutor may exercise this right to a jury trial for many reasons, including belief that:

- A jury is more likely than a particular judge to convict.
- A jury is likely to impose or recommend a desired sentence.
- A jury trial will attract more public attention to a defendant's heinous conduct.

Policies and Practices after Trial

A convicted defendant remains under the court's jurisdiction until sentencing. Between conviction and sentencing, information is often gathered to enable the judge to impose an appropriate sentence. In most districts, the judge requests a presentence report containing information about the defendant, family and employment circumstances, mental or physical health problems, and history of drug or alcohol abuse. This information may have an important bearing on the choice between a sentence of confinement and a sentence of probation.

A convicted defendant may appeal to a higher court, asking it to review any defect in the proceedings of the original trial. Only certain major issues, such as the sentence or what trial evidence was admitted or excluded, will serve as a basis for the appeals court accepting the appeal. Under some circumstances, the prosecutor may also appeal. The special conditions for a prosecutorial appeal usually do not include the prosecutor's view of the determination of guilt in a particular case.

An appeal involves two main activities: preparing the written document (brief) that explains both the case and the defects, and presenting this material verbally to the appeals judges (oral argument).

U.S. Department of Justice, Offices of the United States Attorneys, http://www.justice.gov/usao/justice101/federalcourts.html

STALKING

Stalking is obsessive attention given by a person to another person. Stalking behaviors often take the form of harassment, intimidation, and threat; in some jurisdictions, stalking is a criminal offense. A stalker can be an estranged husband, rejected lover, jealous competitor, or—in extreme situations—a mentally disturbed person who cannot understand or resist his or her stalking behavior.

Seen as a crime, stalking is a series of unwanted actions that occur over a period of time, during which the victim experiences emotional distress such as loathing and fear.

It is not stalking when an unwanted action is contacting a person to gather information or sell a product or service; sending advertisements by direct mail, telephone, e-mail, text, or fax; and sending nonharmful gifts. When such actions are frequently repeated against the express wishes of the recipient, stalking may be the operative word and defined as illegal.

The Stalker's Psychology

A person characterized as a stalker may have a mistaken belief that another person is in love with him/her or needs to be rescued from an imaginary situation. The stalker may make demands or threats of violence, vandalize the victim's property, commit trespass, or create events that constitute disorderly conduct. The stalker usually craves attention and usually does not commit sexual assault.

Generally, stalkers fall into two main groups: psychotics and nonpsychotics. The psychotic stalker may have a preexisting disorder such as delusion, schizophrenia, or paranoia. Common among psychotics are neuroses such as major depression, inability to adjust, antisocial behavior, narcissism, dependence on others, obsession, compulsion, and substance abuse.

The nonpsychotic stalker is influenced by anger, hostility, projection of blame, minimization, rationalization, denial, and jealousy. The nonpsychotic stalker can simply operate from a longing that cannot be satisfied by reason of personality deficiencies or an inability to meet the demands of society.

Types of Stalkers

Within the main groups, stalkers can be characterized by mindset:

- Incompetence. The stalker feels inadequate, usually in connection with establishing or retaining an intimate relationship.
- Predation. The stalker feels compelled to hunt the victim in preparation for an attack, which can be actual or imagined.
- Revenge. The stalker wants to avenge for a reason, often any reason at all.
- Ideology. The stalker may act from a religious or political conviction. Terrorism based on religion or antigovernment beliefs are examples.
- Delusion. The stalker believes a situation exists, when it does not, and wants to correct it.
- Rejection. The stalker wants to undo or correct a rejection such as a divorce or separation.

- Resentment. The stalker has a grievance, often because of a slight.

Victim Responses

The victim may obtain a restraining order, which, if violated, can result in the arrest of the stalker. Disruptions in the daily life of the victim can make it necessary to move to another location, take another job, and change telephone numbers and e-mail/text addresses.

According to scientific research, women often target other women, whereas men generally stalk women only. A separate study has found that men are stalked by women and other men to a significant degree.

In a good number of cases, the victim does not know the stalker personally.

U.S. Department of Justice, Stalking, http://www.ovw.usdoj.gov/aboutstalking.htm

SURVEILLANCE

The principal purpose of surveillance is to document activities, such as the activities of:

- An adulterous spouse
- A person suspected of making a false insurance claim
- A person or persons planning to commit a crime
- A person under protection, such as a celebrity
- A person in control of a very valuable asset such as a nanny or a jewel cutter

Surveillance has many uses and can be a valuable method for obtaining information meaningful to the work at hand. Surveillance is a function appropriate for many issues. Among them are:

- Documenting the activities of a spouse in a divorce or child custody action. In many cases, the surveillance will consist of monitoring the movements of a spouse to confirm infidelity or to document other activities that will support a client's case in court.

- Observing the activities of persons suspected of making false workers' compensation claims and medical insurance claims. The typical surveillance here is to discover if a claimant is or is not demonstrating the symptoms of the disability for which a claim has been made. For example, an employee may claim that an on-the-job accident has injured his leg to the extent he can barely walk. Through photographic surveillance, the investigator may create a visual record of the claimant playing basketball once a week at the local YMCA.

- Providing early warning of an anticipated crime. In this case, the investigator receives from a client or other source certain information indicating that a crime is being planned. For example, the client owns a warehouse. A reliable employee has told the owner that other employees have obtained a key to the warehouse and intend to enter the warehouse after working hours for the purpose of stealing certain valuable property. The investigator is engaged to verify the report of the employee-informant and, if appropriate, coordinate with law enforcement a stakeout form of surveillance at the warehouse.

- Gathering information to plan a protective services operation. An example here is an upcoming business trip to be made by the chief executive officer of a large corporation involved in the manufacture of fur products. Threats by the Animal Liberation Front have been made against the CEO and the corporation. A private sector investigative agency has been engaged to conduct surveillances of the places to be visited, the primary and alternate routes to be taken by the vehicles transporting the CEO, and identifying positions of opportunity from which

the CEO can be targeted with weaponry. Information developed by the agency is used to develop a plan designed to protect the CEO during the course of the visit.

- Monitoring a public event to spot trouble brewing. Concerts, football games, and other crowded public events are sometimes disrupted deliberately by persons who object to the event for one reason or another. More often, disruption occurs when attendees get into arguments and fight with one another. The task of the private sector investigator is to move among the crowd or take up an elevated position and look for the early warning signals of a disruption. Early notification to event security personnel is made so that preemptive action can be initiated.

- Identifying criminal activity. A client may engage an investigator to determine if his personal or business property has been targeted by a criminal enterprise or if his business processes have been corrupted by crime or are being used to carry out criminal activity. For example, a company with operations in South America may recognize the possibility that cocaine can be smuggled into the United States aboard aircraft owned by or contracted to the company. Surveillance of aircraft operations and the movements of aircrew members can uncover the indications of drug trafficking.

Fixed Surveillance

Also known as a stakeout or static surveillance, this method is used when the persons or activities of interest are stationary. The number and positioning of investigators depends on the number of persons to be observed, the nature of their activities, and the size and layout of the area.

When conducting surveillance at separate locations simultaneously, a means of secure communication is essential both for the success of the operation and the safety of the investigators.

It is not unusual for a fixed surveillance to switch suddenly to a moving surveillance and then back again to the fixed mode. For this reason, the planning of the surveillance has to allow for alternate forms of transportation, well-understood procedures, and coordination among members of the surveillance team.

It is very typical of surveillance that the unexpected will occur. When the surveillance is strictly covert, the general rule is to abort the operation when there is a chance that the surveillance has been detected. In less critical operations, snap decisions are often made by the leader of the surveillance team.

Fixed surveillance from a parked vehicle, such as an inconspicuous van, is a common technique. Documenting the target's activity is by the human eye, still camera, motion camera, and, in some cases, voice recorder. A written log reflects time started and ended and the events that occurred within the time frame.

Loose Surveillance

Loose surveillance is in the nature of spot checks made randomly. A common technique is to watch the target for a period of time and then cut it off. The surveillance is resumed later at the start of the previous cut-off time. The process is repeated until the target's full routine has been recorded.

Loose surveillance is a good choice when the surveillance has to continue over a long period. If absolute secrecy is required, the investigator who conducts the surveillance should not be the same person every time.

Close Surveillance

Among the various forms of surveillance, close surveillance is the most difficult to work and the most likely to be discovered.

In close surveillance, several investigators are required; they must be good at what they do; and they must work in teams so that if surveillance is lost or broken off, a backup team is already in place and ready to take over. Close surveillance:

- Requires extensive human and equipment resources
- Requires much planning and preparation
- Requires skilled and dedicated investigators
- Presents challenges not associated with less demanding forms of surveillance
- Is not a good choice when surveillance is to occur over an extended period
- Is often a choice of last resort

Whatever the form of surveillance, the investigator has not necessarily been "burned" when the target looks at the investigator. Looking is not the same as understanding.

Learning Shop USA, Surveillance, www.learningshopusa.com

SURVEILLANCE OPERATIONS

Surveillance is an essential investigative tool that can often make or break a case. The evidence acquired during a surveillance operation can provide undeniable proof to support a claim or catch a suspect in the commission of an unlawful or unauthorized act. However, the success of a surveillance detail depends on many factors starting from the objective of the surveillance assignment; the quality of the subject data provided by the client; and ultimately to the quality, training, and implementation of the field investigator. The information provided herein is based on the writer's 40,000 plus hours of extensive covert video surveillance experience and conducting thousands of surveillance assignments in a plethora of situations.

The Objective

It is essential that the field investigator clearly understand the objective of the assignment and the specific information the client is expecting to receive as a result of the surveillance. The client should provide recommendations as to the most likely productive days, times, and any restrictions associated with the surveillance request. If the client is expecting to view evidence acquired during the surveillance, is a verbal report enough or does the client prefer covert video, photographs, or both? A detailed client interview by the investigator will certainly help to avoid any misunderstandings about the surveillance assignment and confirm most, if not all, of the client's expectations.

If surveillance is being conducted for an insurance-related matter, the investigator must be informed of the alleged claimant injury so special attention can be made to observing and acquiring video targeting the movements of the specific alleged body parts in question.

The objective of a matrimonial investigative surveillance is usually simply to confirm the client's suspicions of infidelity. However, the client will normally expect proof in the form of video and photographs, especially to help identify the paramour and provide the client the opportunity and confirmation to see the cheating spouse displaying affection to another person.

The field investigator needs to be completely informed and updated with the latest client provided data as soon as it arrives no matter the type of surveillance assignment being requested.

The Budget

The success of nearly every surveillance operation is determined by the client-allocated financial budget. The surveillance budget determines the number of hours and days and the number of investigators that can be assigned to the surveillance operation.

Unfortunately, the client budget for a majority of surveillance assignments is usually limited to only one investigator, yet the client expects tremendous results even under the most trying conditions. However, clients are often more inclined to increase the budget and man power if it can be justified, such as conducting mobile surveillance in a major city. All it takes is one red traffic light or traffic congestion to lose a subject. Therefore, the success of a surveillance operation depends on having the right number of investigators, especially when it simply makes sense, such as when operating in heavily populated urban areas with an abundance of traffic signals or even in extremely rural areas. The budget also determines the number of hours the client is willing to allocate for the investigator to acquire the desired evidence. It is very common for clients to want to spend the least amount of money yet expect maximum results in the least amount of time. So, educate the client as best as you can, provide options, and let the client understand the potential consequences of their ultimate budget decision.

Subject Information

This is an area that causes investigators much grief as it is very common for the client to provide investigators with incorrect or minimal information. Often there are no subject pictures or they are of very poor quality. In addition, the subject description is usually lacking or wrong, yet the client expects the investigator to pick the subject in a crowd with less than accurate descriptions. It is essential that the subject description be as compete as possible and preferably relayed by someone who has actually seen the subject. Investigators often follow the wrong person, especially out of multiple family dwellings, simply because of an incomplete description. It is also not uncommon for the investigator to following a similar-looking relative. Therefore, a photograph of the subject should always be requested and provided. A search of social media, such as Facebook, can often provide the investigator with a subject photo, but you must be sure the social profile belongs to the target subject.

At the very least, the investigator needs to know the subject's age, height, weight, race, hair color and length, and vehicle description to include make, model, color, and plate number.

Verify Subject Data

The investigator must always verify the information the client has provided, especially confirming the subject residence address. It is very common for the subject address supplied by the client to be incorrect or not current. A quick database search should either confirm or reveal a new address. The last thing you want to do is spend a full day of surveillance sitting at the wrong location. A simple rule I have always followed is to expect the client information provided to be wrong and that it must always be verified.

Presurveillance

In the most ideal situations, it would be extremely beneficial to do a drive-by and personally check out the target surveillance location *prior* to the actual surveillance. This presurveillance drive-by can provide the investigator with valuable information that can reveal advantageous surveillance positions(s), as well as identify potential problems pertaining to the neighborhood, lack of visual vantage points, and issues with street layout or direction such a one-way streets. It is also a good idea to check the target area out in the early morning or during the anticipated hours of surveillance.

Google Street View

In the event that a drive-by is not local or logistically possible, a search of Google Maps satellite and street view can provide the investigator with a preliminary scouting report. Knowing the house location and description as well as potential issues such as one-way streets, cul-de-sacs, an area school or bus stop, a park, a playground, or heavy commercial traffic all help to prepare for the surveillance. Web technology allows investigators to know what situations they might be dealing with well before ever leaving the office. The presurveillance mapping also allows for the investigator do determine the more direct and likely direction of subject travel once moving surveillance commences. This also allows the investigator the opportunity to map out directions to the surveillance site to ensure a timely arrival. Many a surveillance has been ruined because the investigator arrived too late to the subject residence.

Dealing with the Police

There is always a strong likelihood that a nosey neighbor will find your presence suspicious and you can expect a visit from the local police patrol. It is common for many investigators to call the police and provide them with a courtesy call announcing their presence in a particular area. In most cases, the police dispatcher will request the investigators go to police headquarters in person to present their identification. This is often not practical, especially if you are in the process of following a subject throughout several towns. One would never expect the investigator to break surveillance to "check-in" with the police when it is not a mandated requirement. Experienced investigators rarely check in with the police as they have learned to truly blend in with their environment and maintain a nonthreatening presence. The choice to "check-in" is ultimately up to the investigator or the investigative agency policy.

Avoiding Detection

Vehicle positioning is crucial when conducting surveillance. Hiding in the back of a minivan provides protection from nosey neighbors. Not sitting in the driver's seat is a must when logistically possible. Neighbors and vehicles driving by will notice a person sitting in the driver's seat for long periods of time, causing alarm and more than likely a visit from the police. The surveillance investigator should also refrain from smoking and listening to the car radio as this will also attract attention. A vehicle running to operate the heating or air conditioning system will also attract attention. Many surveillance vehicles are equipped with a portable heater, usually propane, but the vehicle must be equipped to allow for fresh air ventilation. Portable air conditioners that operate with ice and battery power are also very popular in extreme warm weather areas. Also, commencing surveillance in the early morning hours prevents neighbors from seeing the surveillance vehicle arrive and noticing that no one has exited the vehicle.

Anticipate the Unexpected

The one word most successful investigators focus on is "anticipate." From the moment you arrive on location, you need to start anticipating everything, such as:

- Which door will the subject most likely egress from?
- Which direction will the subject most likely take when exiting the driveway?
- Where will the subject likely to travel to?

The investigator must also anticipate getting the video or photographic shot. For example, there is no reason why the investigator should be zooming in or out to get a shot. The investigator should have already zoomed the camera lens in to the appropriate focal setting while not in the record mode. Anticipating the shot throughout the surveillance will also help to minimize zooming while in record mode. Also make sure you have plenty of battery power, spare batteries, recording media, and a method to record notes during the surveillance.

Surveillance Tools

Vehicles. The number one rule of surveillance is to avoid being detected by the subject, neighbors, and law enforcement. Covertness is essential in order to maintain surveillance of the subject at the subject residence without attracting attention. Utilizing a vehicle such as a minivan allows the investigator to remain hidden from the subject and nosey neighbors. Sitting in the front seat of any vehicle will immediately arouse suspicion and generate unnecessary attention. Investigators normally commence surveillance in the early morning hours and are tucked away in the rear of the surveillance vehicle behind tinted windows and curtains before most people are awake. The surveillance vehicle should also be parked on the street on the borderline of two houses as compared to being directly in front of someone's house. It is human nature for people to take personal ownership of the parking area directly in front of their home. By parking on the border of two houses, the homeowner might assume the occupants of the vehicle are visiting a neighbor.

Surveillance minivans also provide more room to make the investigator comfortable during long periods of surveillance. A portable camping toilet is essential to avoid breaking surveillance to find a restroom. Murphy's Law is always in effect during surveillance. The moment you leave the surveillance site to find a bathroom or food, you can always anticipate that will be the exact moment the subject becomes active and departs the residence or target location. Therefore, always have food, liquids, and a handy P-bottle or toilet to accommodate your physical needs.

Video and Photographs. Most investigators shoot video on surveillance and acquire still images from the video. This requires using a high definition video camera, ideally with an image stabilizer and the ability to display time and date on the screen while recording. Using a tripod or a monopod will also help to eliminate camera shake when taking video for extended periods of time. The Camera-Clamp and the Joe-Mount allow the video camera to be clamped to the steering wheel, the dash, or any of the vehicle windows to facilitate steady video. Investigators should always have a back-up video camera, extra batteries, and recording media and should anticipate that the chance for equipment failure is always a possibility.

Covert Video Equipment. There was a time in history when a person raising their hand in courtroom and swearing to tell the truth was sufficient. Unfortunately, we have become all too accustomed to seeing criminal acts caught on video. Therefore, the "show me the video" attitude has become more of the norm and puts more pressure on investigators to acquire video of the subject, no matter where they may be when in public. Getting video using a camcorder may work when in a surveillance vehicle but not when inside a bar, restaurant, grocery store, strip club, or a health club. There are a myriad of body-worn video cameras and digital video recorders (DVRs) investigators can now use to capture complete, covert high-definition video.

The basic equipment needed to acquire high quality covert video usually consists of a very small DVR connected to a covert video camera. The Lawmate HD pocket DVR (PGPV500EVO2) can accept up to a 32GB SD card allowing for covert video recording up to seven hours with the optional extended battery. You can then plug a variety of covert cameras into the DVR such as the button cam, video glasses, tie cam, hat cam, ear bud camera, etc. These cameras, when used with the DVR, can capture high quality HD video, especially in very little light. There are also covert video camera/DVRs that can be attached to your smartphone to record video

while your phone is lying flat on a table pointed at the subject.

The main benefit of using covert video devices is the investigator's ability to acquire video anywhere the subject may go. Again, the investigator must always anticipate what the subject may do and where the subject may go and be able to record the activity for the client.

GPS Trackers. The advancement of GPS technology now allows investigators the ability to electronically follow subjects without leaving their offices. Laws and permitted use vary by state, and investigators must be completely familiar with the legal and permissible restrictions for their state. In many cases, it is best to have the client lease or purchase the GPS tracker directly and have them also install the tracker.

GPS trackers can either be passive/recorded (where were you?) or live (where are you now?). Passive trackers are placed on the target vehicle and removed as much as three to four weeks after having recorded the vehicle activity. Therefore, passive trackers record past activity and do not require any fees for usage.

Live trackers provide the investigator with 24/7 live tracking, with updates as frequent as every 10 seconds. The tracker location can be monitored on any smartphone, computer, or portable device connected to the Internet. Live trackers require a small activation fee and a monthly service fee. Fortunately, there are many live trackers such as the PGMICRO or the PGPTX5 that do not require any minimum annual usage contracts, allowing the tracker to be turned off when not being used.

Trackers can be placed inside the vehicle under a passenger seat or under the dash by the glove compartment. When access to the inside of the vehicle is not possible, investigators can affix the GPS tracker to the rear bumper area using a waterproof magnetic case. It is always important for the investigator to inquire as to the battery life of the tracker being used and consider using an optional extended battery, which can extend tracking life to as much as 130 hours of motion tracking.

Surveillance Reports

The final product the client usually receives after hiring a private investigator is an investigative report detailing the subject activities observed along with photos, videos, and a summary narrative of the surveillance. That's why it's very important that the surveillance investigator take detailed notes and save those notes for preparation of a final report, as well as saving them in case testimony needs to be provided. It is essential the surveillance report contain nothing but factual content and focus on the results of the initial client request.

Jimmie Mesis

SURVEILLANCE TECHNIQUES

The art of surveillance is a technique that relies on instinct and experience. Instinct comes into play as the investigator "sizes up" the situation, and experience is a factor in choosing the surveillance mode and using the correct surveillance equipment. The objective of surveillance is to observe and record without being noticed. When the surveillance is noticed by the subject, two negative consequences can follow: compromise of the entire investigation and physical harm to the investigator.

The common mistakes are:

- Not having the right equipment to do the job
- Not knowing how to use the equipment
- Not choosing the correct vantage point

The worst mistake is not to analyze how a mistake happened and what needs to be done to keep it from happening again. Mistakes occur when the investigator has not been trained, is inexperienced, or is overly confident. Once the causes are understood, corrective actions can be taken.

Planning

A surveillance plan answers these questions:

- Who, among all investigators, is the best choice for the job?
- Is the subject easy-going, flighty, unpredictable, or aggressive?
- What should the investigator do if the nature of the surveillance needs to be changed, such as switching from static surveillance to moving surveillance?
- What can the investigator expect if the surveillance is blown, and what should the investigator do if it happens?
- Is the surveillance location the best location? Does it offer concealment? Is it free from prying eyes?
- What equipment will be needed? Include type of vehicle, binoculars, cameras and lenses, laptop or tablet, listening and lighting devices, the investigator's clothing, food and water, toilet accommodations, and more.
- What will be the method of communication between the investigator and home base? How often will the investigator call the home base to give a status report?
- What is the back-up plan if something should go wrong?

Plan Execution

The quality of surveillance can never exceed the quality of planning. Not much more than that needs to be said.

A failure in execution is not a total loss because there are lessons that can be learned. Mistakes in surveillance are inevitable at some time or another, and they can be powerful motivators to improving quality.

Learning Shop USA, Surveillance, www.learningshopusa.com

T

TACTICS OF TERRORISTS

Knowledge held by the U.S. general public, which is not the same as knowledge held by the U.S. intelligence community, is that all of the below listed tactics have been used somewhere except for the last two shown, i.e., chemical and biological weapons and nuclear weapons.

- Bombings
- Suicide attacks
- Rocket and mortar attacks
- Vehicle-based attacks
- Aircraft attacks and hijackings
- Conventional firearms
- Chemical and biological weapons
- Nuclear weapons

Bombings

The relative ease of access to the chemicals used to make explosives and the relative simplicity of bomb construction has made improvised bombs increasingly prominent. This has the dual effect of increasing the available firepower of terrorists who are generally far weaker than their targets as well as assuring the publicity necessary to attract sympathizers to their cause. These may be implanted in automobiles, planted on the roadside to detonate near target vehicles, or strapped to the bodies of individuals. Vehicle-borne

bombs act as their own delivery mechanisms and can carry a relatively large amount of explosives. A suicide vest has a much smaller payload but allows the wearer access to congregated places.

Suicide Attacks

A suicide attack is an attack upon a target in which an attacker intends to kill others and/or cause great damage, knowing that he or she will certainly or most likely die in the process. Two main motives behind suicide attacks are to draw attention (propagandize) and bring about political change.

Rocket and Mortar Attacks

The primary advantage of rocket and mortar attacks is distance from the attackers and the persons being attacked. Rocket and mortar attacks have been widely used by political entities to attack cities and settlements. The number of attacks using projectiles is seen by experts as more effective than suicide or "in close" attacks.

A disadvantage from the user's perspective is the relatively short range of projectiles.

Vehicle-Based Attacks

A Vehicle Borne Improvised Explosive Device (VBIED) is an improvised bomb that is placed in a vehicle; the vehicle is then driven to the target and detonated. A VBIED is its own delivery mechanism. It can carry a large amount of explosives without attracting suspicion. When the VBIED is left at the target area, it may be triggered to detonate, such as by opening a door or starting the ignition.

Aircraft Attacks and Hijackings

On December 21, 1988, Pan Am Flight 103 was heading from London's Heathrow International Airport to New York Kennedy International Airport when it exploded en route over Lockerbie, Scotland. The flight originated in Frankfurt, Germany, where explosives—packed into passenger luggage—were placed onto the flight after being ferried to Frankfurt on a flight from Malta. The explosion killed all 259 of the passengers and crew, as well as 11 residents of Lockerbie.

The event known as 9/11 is an example of simultaneous aircraft attack and hijacking. On the morning of September 11, 2001, four airliners were hijacked. Two of them were deliberately flown into the Twin Towers of the World Trade Center in New York City. Another airliner crashed into the Pentagon, and another crashed into a field in Pennsylvania after passengers revolted.

In December 2009, Richard Reid attempted to detonate explosives hidden in his sneakers on an American Airlines flight from Paris to Miami. Passengers thwarted his plan, and the plane landed safely in Boston.

Conventional Firearms

Availability and lower cost make conventional firearms preferred weapons of terrorists. The numbers of conventional firearms are too great to list here, but the reader will understand what they are, how they are used, and where.

Learning Shop USA, Tactics of Terrorists, www.learningshopusa.com

TECHNICAL SURVEILLANCE COUNTERMEASURES

Intense competition and rapidly evolving markets are just a few of the external forces that are changing the ways we do business. Upper managers are pushing decision situations down the corporate ladder to operational managers, the operational managers are spread across large expanses of geography, and the decisions they make are based on great amounts of detail pulled from many centers of expertise. Businesses are working hard to generate meaningful information, to open the information to greater numbers of key players, and to maintain a working dialogue with affected groups in widely separated places.

Business information, including the most sensitive possessed by an organization, is valuable to the extent it is put to work. Although an investigator or agency head would like sensitive information to be constantly kept under lock and key, the reality is that information exists to be used. Further, in a fast-track environment, many types of information will have a relatively short life span, meaning that it must be put to advantage fairly quickly in order to wring value from it.

Valuable information is most vulnerable to compromise when it is in use. Loss that results from compromise can be many hundreds of times greater than the utilitarian value of the information during its moment of use. This is the problem and the challenge.

When is sensitive information at greatest risk? Experience tells us that those who are determined to acquire someone else's secrets will focus on two opportunities: when secrets are brought into the open for discussion, such as at a conference, and when they are transmitted from one place to another, such as messages across an electronic network. In short, sensitive information is at risk when it is being communicated.

The risk is considerably heightened when the business sphere is global. The dollar stakes are higher, and political aims are often intertwined. We see, for example, the extraordinary ambitions of Eastern Bloc countries and former Soviet republics to establish business ties with the non-Communist world. The newcomers to Western-style democracy are discovering that capitalism is fueled by technology, and until they develop a technological base and become producers and suppliers instead of consumers, they will be junior partners in the economic alliances they wish to forge.

A picture can be drawn that the American business sector, situated as a major repository of technology, is a natural target for those who desperately need technology to become competitive but lack the time and the resources to develop it on their own. An era of industrial espionage on a global scale is being ushered in, and the United States is among the few who have the greatest to lose.

The communications networks that support international commerce are notoriously vulnerable to surreptitious attack, and although efforts have been undertaken by governments to establish some modicum of secure transmissions, the principal protection must come from the network users. Self-protection has even more validity with respect to sensitive information disclosed at conferences and meetings. The owner of the information is the exclusive protector.

This section discusses a form of self-protection called the TSCM inspection, that is, making an organized search for technical surveillance devices. The places of search are typically at corporate offices and off-site meeting places. They include, at the corporate offices, the chief executive officer's suite, executive conference and dining rooms, the telecommunications center, and the telephone switching room. Off site, the search activity might be of the facilities at a resort hotel where a senior management meeting has been scheduled. Findings from the inspection become the basis for taking steps to counter actual or potential surveillance attempts.

A handful of major corporations retain on staff one or a few technicians whose primary duties involve making TSCM inspections. The technicians are usually highly trained and are supplied with an array of electronic sensing equipment. Most companies, however, choose to obtain the inspection service from a TSCM provider. The guidance here is applicable to either situation, although written for the investigator or agency head who engages a provider. The first contact made by the agency to the TSCM provider should be via a communications medium separate from the site that is to be inspected. The idea is not to disclose details that could compromise the inspection. If the agency is in fact under electronic surveillance, communication between the agency and the TSCM provider should be protected, such as by using a secure line or talking face to face. The TSCM provider will want certain details in advance of the inspection. For example:

- The number of phones, identity of manufacturer, and model numbers
- The number and size of rooms
- The location of rooms relative to each other
- The number of floors and buildings involved
- The type of ceiling, such as fixed or moveable
- The types of audiovisual and communications devices, computers, and other special electronic equipment on site
- The forms of electronic communications and networks in use at the place to be inspected, including local area networks, microwave links, and satellite teleconferencing facilities

The user of the service should expect the TSCM provider to supply all equipment required to carry out a comprehensive inspection. The equipment used should be the products of manufacturers that are recognized by TSCM professionals. The following described pieces of equipment should be expected of any TSCM provider selected for consideration:

- Time domain reflectometer capable of evaluating telephone systems cables, terminals, and equipment utilized by the telecommunications system to be examined
- Tuneable receiver or spectrum analyzer with sufficient sensitivity to be capable of detecting extremely low-powered devices and continuous coverage from 10 kilohertz to 21 gigahertz and a capability to analyze power lines and provide a panoramic visual display of any video signal present, with a capability to extend frequency coverage as may be required by circumstances. Older equipment with frequency coverage that does not extend coverage to five gigahertz and above is obsolete to address current and evolving threats.
- Nonlinear junction detector for detecting hidden tape recorders, nonoperating transmitters, and remotely controlled transmitters. This instrument can also aid in detecting devices that use transmission techniques that go beyond the frequency range of countermeasures receivers.

Thermal imaging equipment for thermal signature spectrum analysis is used for locating operating video and audio transmitters though ceiling tiles and Sheetrock walls by detecting their thermal (heat) signature. Additionally, this methodology can help detect differences in ceiling and wall construction with the potential to indicate current or previous placement of pinhole cameras, microphones, etc. Thermal imaging equipment can also help evaluate AV system components to ensure system components are not powered up when the system is deactivated. Thermal imaging equipment utilized must have sufficient sensitivity to resolve thermal signatures of eavesdropping devices through standard Sheetrock walls.

TSCM technicians must be thoroughly grounded in countermeasures work, be current in their knowledge of state-of-the-art equipment, and be schooled and experienced in telephone systems to be examined. All detected signals must be identified as either legitimate or suspect. The source of a legitimate signal might, for example, be an FM broadcast station. A suspect signal would be one that is found to emanate from the area being inspected and cannot be attributed to a legitimate source.

Electronic emissions from computers, communications equipment, and teleconferencing facilities should be evaluated to determine their vulnerability to interception. The TSCM provider must be sufficiently competent to both detect readable emissions and formulate sensible, cost-effective recommendations to prevent exposure of sensitive data to unauthorized parties.

Telephones and telephone lines within the area under inspection should be examined with a time domain reflectometer, a TSCM audio-amplifier, and other specialized analyzers as required. These instruments check for compromises to telephone cables and terminals as well as devices that allow listening of conversations over the telephone and within the office or area nearby, even when the phone is not in use. Telephone satellite terminals and frame rooms, as well as station and distribution cables in the areas of concern, should be inspected. Telephone systems should be evaluated for potential programming problems.

A thorough physical search should be made, with particular attention to areas adjoining rooms where sensitive communications occur. The walls between the rooms require careful inspection, and exiting wires need to be examined including, in some cases, electrical testing of wires for audio signals. Ceilings, radiators, ducts, electrical outlets and switches, picture frames, furniture, lamp fixtures, and plants all deserve the TSCM technician's attention.

All walls and ceilings and furniture need to be evaluated with thermal imaging equipment to detect heat signatures from operating eavesdropping devices as well as differences in wall or ceiling density that may indicate current or previous pinhole camera, microphone, or other device placement. All AV equipment needs to be evaluated to ensure that powered-down systems do not have components that have been compromised to remain on, picking up room conversations that may be routed out of the area of concern.

Selected objects, such as desks, tables, chairs, and sofas, can be examined with a nonlinear junction detector. This instrument uses a low-power microwave beam to detect energy reflected from electronic components such as diodes, transistors, and integrated circuits. These components are integral to radio transmitters, tape recorders, and other eavesdropping devices. Also, microwave transmitters, remotely activated transmitters, and transmitters that operate on infrared and ultrasonic principles can be spotted with a nonlinear junction detector.

At the conclusion of the inspection, the TSCM provider should meet with the user to verbally discuss the work performed, the findings, and the recommendations. A fully detailed written report should be submitted within ten days.

Safeguarding proprietary information is a concern for all companies of substance. TSCM inspections is one tool for reducing the organization's exposure to loss or compromise of valuable information as well as providing assurance to management, customers, partners, and regulators concerning their information protection efforts.

Richard J. Heffernan

TERRORISM: CHEMICAL AND BIOLOGICAL WEAPONS

Chemical Weapons

By definition, a chemical warfare agent is any chemical substance, whether gaseous, liquid, or solid, that might be employed because of its direct toxic effects on man, animals, and plants. A toxic chemical can kill, injure, or incapacitate any living process. Included within the definition of a chemical warfare agent are dispersal mechanisms such as ammunition, projectiles, and aerosolizing devices.

Toxins. Thousands of toxic substances exist, but only a few are amenable to chemical warfare. This is because a number of rigorous demands must be met before a toxic substance can be used as a chemical warfare agent. Mainly, these are:

- The agent cannot be so toxic as to affect the persons preparing to use it.
- The agent must be capable of being stored for a long period without degradation and without corroding the packaging material.
- The agent must be relatively resistant to atmospheric water and oxygen so that it does not lose effect when dispersed.
- The agent must withstand heat that is generated during dispersal.

Chemical warfare agents, at least the way they are produced today, are liquids or solids of which a certain amount is in a volatile form. Both solid and liquid substances can be dispersed in the air in an aerosolized form. As such, they enter the human body through the respiratory organs. Some chemical warfare agents can also penetrate the skin. The penetration of a solid substance is slow except when it is mixed with a penetrating solvent.

To achieve good ground coverage when dispersed from a high altitude, a chemical warfare agent must be in the form of droplets sufficiently large to ensure they fall within the target area. This can be achieved by making the agent viscous by the addition of polymers. In this form, the chemical warfare agent lasts longer and complicates decontamination.

Nerve Agents. Nerve agents are so called because they affect the transmission of nerve impulses in the nervous system. Nerve agents are stable and easily dispersed, highly toxic, and have rapid effects both when absorbed through the skin and inhaled into the lungs. Nerve agents can be manufactured by means of fairly simple chemical techniques. The raw materials are inexpensive and generally readily available.

In 1936, Dr. Gerhard Schrader, a chemist at IG Farben, developed a phosphorus compound for use as an insecticide. Named tabun, the compound was later adapted for use as a nerve agent. In 1938, Schrader produced a second nerve agent called sarin and, in 1944, a third agent called soman. These three compounds are known as G agents.

In 1958, discovery was made of an even more effective nerve agent known by its U.S. Army code name VX. This is a persistent substance that can remain on material, equipment, and terrain for long periods. Penetration is mainly through the skin but also through inhalation when dispersed as a gas or aerosol.

Mustard Agent. Mustard agent is often called a "blistering agent" because the wounds it causes resemble burns and blisters. It also causes severe damage to the eyes, respiratory system, and internal organs.

Mustard agent was produced in 1822, but its harmful effects were not discovered until 1860. It was first used as a chemical warfare agent during the latter part of the First World War and caused lung and eye injuries to a very large number of soldiers.

During the war between Iran and Iraq in 1979–1988, Iraq used large quantities of chemical agents. About 5,000 Iranian soldiers were reportedly killed, 10–20 percent of them by mustard agent, plus 40,000 to 50,000 injured.

Hydrogen Cyanide. Hydrogen cyanide is usually included among the chemical warfare agents, but there is no solid proof it has been used in chemical warfare. Iraq is suspected, however, of using hydrogen cyanide in its war against Iran and against Kurds in

northern Iraq. During World War II, a form of hydrogen cyanide (Zyklon B) was used in Nazi gas chambers.

Chlorine. Chlorine is widely used in industry and found in some household products. As a gas, it can be converted to liquid form by pressurizing and cooling. In liquid form, it can be shipped and stored. When liquid chlorine is released, it quickly turns into a gas that is heavier than air. In this form, it stays close to the ground and spreads rapidly. Chlorine is recognizable by its pungent, irritating odor, which is like the odor of bleach. The strong smell may provide warning to people that have been exposed.

Phosgene is an industrial chemical similar to chlorine. Both are transported in multiton shipments by road and rail. Rupturing a transport container can easily disseminate these gases over a fairly wide area. For this reason, these gases, while in transit, can have particular appeal to terrorists because the transport vehicle is a weapon in itself.

Biological Weapons

Discussion of the possible use of bioweapons by terrorists began even earlier than September 11, 2001, during the breakup of the Soviet Union. The specter of Russia's biological agents covertly migrating into the weapons inventory of terrorist groups moved the issue from discussion to prevention and response.

Biological weapons are mysterious, unfamiliar, indiscriminate, uncontrollable, inequitable, and invisible—all characteristics associated with heightened fear. To the extent terrorists believe that a bioattack would help their cause, the greater the likelihood of it.

A case can be made for anticipating the use of a bioweapon. At some point, the magnitude of terrorist attacks using conventional weapons will plateau. The next logical step in escalation will be the use of chemical and bioweapons. Unlike conventional weapons, biological agents would be effective in destroying crops, poisoning foods, or contaminating pharmaceutical products. Terrorists might use biological agents to attack corporations perceived to be national icons such as Coca-Cola and Gerber. In addition to the fear factor, such an act would place enormous demands on the medical system, require large clean-up expenditures, and damage the economy.

On the other side of the coin, a terrorist group contemplating use of a bioweapon will face several problems:

- Formidable political risk and loss of private support
- Acquisition or construction of a dispersal device
- The ability to deliver or disperse the agent covertly
- The risk of infection to themselves and to others they do not wish to infect

Biological agents with a potential for use by terrorists can be placed into three groups and their subgroups:

- Bacteria
  - Anthrax
  - Plague
- Viruses
  - Smallpox
  - Viral Hemorrhagic Fevers
- Toxins
  - Botulism
  - Ricin

Bacterial Agents

Bacterial agent is a general term. In the current context, it means any bacteria that has been or can be used by terrorists to kill people. Lethal bacteria are numerous. In this section, we will address those that are amenable to use as a weapon of mass destruction.

Anthrax. Anthrax is an acute, specific, infectious, febrile disease of animals, including humans, and is caused by an organism that under certain conditions will form highly resistant spores capable of persisting and retaining their virulence in contaminated soil or other material for many years. The anthrax bacterium is often found naturally in the soil of rural Texas and Oklahoma and in areas near the Mississippi River. It is also produced in research laboratories—but not easily. Significant scientific training is needed.

Probably because so little is known about anthrax, opinions of it as a terrorist weapon vary widely. On the one hand, it is touted as the terrorist's preferred biological warfare agent because a single gram of anthrax material is believed capable of producing 100 million lethal doses, and a single dose is 100,000 times deadlier than the deadliest chemical warfare agent. It is also considered a silent, invisible killer because the symptoms of infection mimic nonlethal ailments. This view also holds that the barriers to production of anthrax are minimal because production costs are low; large quantities can be produced and stockpiled without great difficulty; and production knowhow, although technical, is in the public domain. There is also little agreement on the extent of damage to human health if anthrax was introduced; for example, into an office building's ventilation system, a crowded bus, or a football stadium filled to capacity.

Among the experts is a shared belief that anthrax can be weaponized. Because anthrax is stable, it can be stored almost indefinitely as a dry powder. When freeze-dried, it can be loaded into munitions and, with limited technology, can be disseminated as an aerosol. With a little more expertise, the spores can be made smaller so they're easier to inhale and made lighter so they float in the air longer. Also, it is possible to alter the genetic makeup of the spore so that it is resistant to medical treatment.

Smallpox. The most common and deadly form of smallpox is *variola major*. Smallpox is ancient; descriptions of the disease have been found dating from as far back as the fourth century AD in China.

Smallpox was eradicated in 1979, and samples of it are kept only in the United States and Russia.

Viral Hemorrhagic Fever (VHF). The term "viral hemorrhagic fever" refers to a group of illnesses that are caused by several distinct families of viruses. In general, the term describes a severe syndrome that impairs the body's ability to regulate itself. These symptoms are often accompanied by hemorrhage or bleeding. With a few noteworthy exceptions, there is no cure or established drug treatment for VHFs. Some viruses that cause hemorrhagic fever can spread from one person to another, once an initial person has become infected. Ebola, Marburg, Lassa, and Crimean-Congo hemorrhagic fever viruses are examples.

Compared to anthrax and smallpox, VHFs are less stable; more vulnerable to heat, light, and disinfectants; and, once released into the air, have shorter life spans than either anthrax or smallpox. Some experts, with good evidence, argue that terrorists would sooner turn to anthrax or smallpox than VHFs.

Toxins

Toxins are unusual because they are both chemical and biological agents.

Rapid development of gene technology during the 1970s stirred interest in creating bioweapons using toxins, both natural and synthetic. Later research in cancer treatment discovered a way to target toxins to different body organs. Still, toxins are considered to be less suitable as a bioweapon because they cannot be dispersed on a large scale; however, they could be used for sabotage of a specific location or assassination of specific persons.

Botulism. The botulinum nerve toxin is the single most toxic substance known to science. Its extraordinary potency has made

it one of the most widely researched bioweapons. If a lethal dose were administered to each person individually, a single gram of botulinum toxin would theoretically be enough to kill more than a million people.

Botulinum toxin is the first biological toxin to be approved for medical treatment. It is used to treat neuromuscular disorders, lower back pain, and cerebral palsy. It is also an ingredient in Botox, a product that temporarily eliminates wrinkles by paralyzing the facial muscles.

Ricin. This toxin is found in the mash-like waste left over from the processing of castor beans, which are used to make castor oil. The ricin in the waste can be made into the form of a powder, pellet, or mist, and it can be dissolved in water or a weak acid. Ricin is only minimally affected by extreme temperature conditions and is stable in aerosolized form.

Ricin is produced easily and inexpensively, is highly toxic, and has no treatment or vaccine. When compared to some of the other biological agents that could be used to produce the desired effect of a weapon of mass destruction, ricin ranks relatively low. For example, to achieve the same damaging effect produced by one kilogram of anthrax would require four metric tons of ricin.

U.S. Department of Health and Human Services, Centers for Disease Control and Prevention, http://www.cdc.gov/about/organization/cio.htm

TERRORISM: EXPLOSIVE AND RADIOLOGICAL WEAPONS

Explosive Weapons

The most frequently used terrorist weapon is the explosive bomb. The materials for constructing a bomb are not difficult to obtain, and the knowhow of construction is relatively simple. For the totally uninformed potential bomber, do-it-yourself information is available on the Internet and in bookstores.

Explosion Dynamics. An explosion is an extremely rapid release of energy in the form of light, heat, sound, and a shock wave. The shock wave consists of highly compressed air that travels outward from the source at supersonic velocities. When the shock wave encounters a surface that is in line-of-sight of the explosion, the wave is reflected, resulting in a tremendous amplification of pressure.

Late in the explosive event, the shock wave is followed by a partial vacuum, which creates suction behind the shock wave. Immediately following the vacuum, air rushes in, creating a powerful wind or drag pressure. This wind picks up and carries flying debris in the vicinity of the detonation. In an external explosion, a portion of the energy is also imparted to the ground, creating a crater and generating a ground shock wave analogous to a high-intensity, short-duration earthquake.

Explosives are categorized as high and low. The primary distinguishing characteristic is the pressure wave. A high explosive detonation can produce a pressure wave ranging from 50,000 to 4 million pounds per square inch (psi), while a low explosive detonation will produce a pressure wave under 50,000 pounds psi.

Among the high explosives are military compositions 3, 4, B, TNT, nitroglycerin, dynamite, RDX, semtex, amatol, ednatol, picric acid, pentolite, and tetrytol. The low explosives are fewer in number: black powder, ammonium nitrate, and the pyrotechnics.

Although not accurate technically, incendiaries are often considered explosives. An incendiary is any device used to start a fire; it is generally man-made, handheld, and thrown or propelled a short distance. The Molotov Cocktail is an incendiary device, typically a glass bottle filled with gasoline. At the mouth of the bottle is a piece of gasoline-soaked cloth. The tip of the cloth is ignited, and the bottle is thrown. The bottle breaks upon impact; the gasoline is dispersed and ignited by the flaming cloth.

It is difficult to quantify the risk of terrorist-style bombings. However, qualitatively it may be stated that the chance of a large-scale terrorist attack occurring is extremely low. A smaller explosive attack is far more likely.

Radiological Weapons

A radiological dispersion device (RDD), commonly known as a dirty bomb, is a device that combines a radioactive material and a conventional explosive. The explosive is used to disperse the radiological material. The area of dispersal is conditioned by the type and amount of explosive; the nature of the container; the detonation height; and weather/wind factors such as rain, wind velocity, and air currents.

The harmful effects of an RDD include radiation burns, acute poisoning, and contamination of the environment. The tasks of first responders are complex and very much different in an RDD incident than a conventional bomb incident.

The radiological material in an RDD is not weapons-grade fissionable material such as that contained in a nuclear weapon. The more likely terrorist attack involving radiological material is by use of the RDD rather than a nuclear weapon. This is the case because construction of a nuclear weapon is enormously difficult, whereas the RDD can be constructed simply and with types of radiological material that are routinely used in health care, research, metal structure evaluation, and a variety of industrial applications. These materials include cobalt, cesium, strontium, and others.

U.S. Department of Homeland Security, Federal Emergency Management Agency, http://www.fema.gov/

TERRORIST GROUP MOTIVES

Terrorist groups can be categorized in several ways, e.g., where they are from, where they operate, weapons and tactics they use, and the targets they attack. One categorization label that seems to work well is motivation. Terrorist groups can be seen to operate from one or any combination of politics, religion, and special interests.

Politics

Terrorist groups motivated by political considerations cover a lot of ground. First are terrorists that seek to form a separate state for their own group, which is often an ethnic minority. The group is likely to portray its activist followers as patriots struggling to achieve freedoms unjustly withheld by an oppressive government. Their appeal is to a world audience. They hope to win concessions at home, gain sympathy abroad, and obtain financial and logistical assistance from outside supporters.

Nationalist groups tend to calibrate their violent acts at a level high enough to maintain pressure on the established government but not so high as to alienate the group's members and outside supporters.

Religion

One of the difficulties in assessing the intentions of religiously motivated groups is the vague and irrational statements of their leaders. For example, a leader will call for a jihad (holy war) but leave followers to use their own imagination in waging it, or leaders in subgroups will interpret the jihad in a variety of ways. By contrast, the politically motivated terrorist groups express less amorphous objectives: removal of a government or establishment of an independent nation. At least with the politically motivated groups, the protectors are able to somewhat more accurately assess the persons and groups they are dealing with, their likely targets, and the arenas of operation.

Special Interest

What the United States lacks in the way of political and religious terrorism, it makes up for in special interest terrorism. Many of the special interest groups are motivated by opposition to federal taxation and regulation, the United Nations, other international organizations, and the U.S. government generally. Much of the opposition comes from right-wing militia organizations, and, depending on who's doing the estimates, the overall membership of these groups will range from 10,000 to 100,000. Even if the total numbers are high, the extremist core of the militia movement is quite small and often out of sync with the desires of the broad majority. A strategy exercised by the leaders of some groups is to endorse violence but leave the execution of it to hard-core individuals acting on their own. An example of this strategy in action was the bombing by Timothy McVeigh of the Alfred P. Murrah Federal Building in Oklahoma City. The mailing of anthrax letters to government officials may be another.

Then there are the hate groups that terrorize in the name of race or religion or both. The Ku Klux Klan, which used lynching to terrorize African Americans following the Civil War, was a forerunner of today's neo-Nazis, Skinheads, and so-called Christian Patriots. The Aryan Nation group embraces multiple issues: they hate anyone who is not white, is Jewish, or is favorably disposed to the U.S. government. A similar group is the Aryan Brotherhood, which is composed of present and former prison gang members.

Pro-life believers have assassinated physicians and bombed abortion clinics, but because these individuals appear not to be members of an organized group, the FBI has classified their attacks as criminal events rather than terrorist events.

The Animal Liberation Front (ALF) encourages individuals to take "direct action" against organizations that commit animal abuse, such as the meat industry's practice of slaughtering cattle or the medical research industry's practice of vivisecting laboratory animals. ALF's call for action is believed to be connected to crimes that include arson, breaking and entering, and theft.

The Earth Liberation Front (ELF) is a loosely knit ecoterrorist organization whose primary agenda is protection of the environment. ELF's likely targets are new construction projects, logging sites, petroleum drilling and production facilities, and mining operations. An allied organization with a similar agenda is Earth First.

It is most probably correct to believe that only a very few animal-rights and environmental activists would resort to activities that kill and maim. The troubling part of the belief is that the "very few" are alive and well and that law enforcement authorities have no way of knowing who they are before they act. Even more troubling is the reality that one person, a Timothy McVeigh for example, can bring about hundreds of deaths and injuries in a single act.

Policing Priorities

A consequence of terrorism has been a nationwide shift in policing priorities. Police departments, especially those in major cities, are devoting increased resources to prevent and mitigate terrorist attacks, the effect of which is to reduce other law enforcement services. And then there is the cost of gearing up to meet extreme circumstances. Because police officers are almost always first to arrive at the scene of a disaster and first to begin rendering aid, they have to be specially trained and adequately equipped.

The shift in law enforcement priorities varies according to a community's perception of threat, its vulnerabilities, and resources available to law enforcement. Even where great variance exists, law enforcement departments in general have:

- Created new working relationships with other first-responder agencies, such as fire departments and agencies responsible for delivering emergency medical treatment and hazardous materials containment

- Acquired new communication equipment and revised their methods for communicating within and outside of the department
- Refined their training programs and emergency response plans to address terrorist threats, including attacks with weapons of mass destruction
- Given more patrol attention to potential target sites such as government buildings, ports of entry, transportation hubs, nuclear power plants, chemical plants, and other facilities of a symbolic or critical nature
- Increased their presence at major public events
- Reorganized and reassigned officers to perform counterterrorism duties; major city departments have joined with federal agencies to form Joint Terrorism Task Forces
- Employed new technologies in metal detection, X-ray scanning, and sensors for detecting the signals of chemical, biological, and radiological attacks

Conclusion

Extraordinary antiterror measures have been taken both in the government and private sectors. The government's efforts have moved along two tracks: destroy terrorism wherever it exists and prevent further terrorist attacks on U.S. soil. The private sector has taken a serious look at its vulnerabilities to terrorism and in substantial measure has turned to chief security officers for help.

Arising out of these efforts is a growing recognition that the public and private sectors must form a partnership and pool their separate resources and expertise. More than ever before, community leaders in law enforcement, firefighting, and emergency management are sitting down with chief security officers and chief executive officers of local businesses. Vulnerability assessments are being made, new and comprehensive emergency plans developed, mutual aid agreements signed, and likely scenarios rehearsed. Federal government funding for the purchase of emergency equipment and supplies is flowing to areas where public and private sector leaders have rationally assessed and reached agreement on actual needs. It is in this context that the chief security officer can be an important participant in the war against terrorism.

Learning Shop USA, Tactics of Terrorists, www.learningshopusa.com

TERRORIST METHODS

Historically, the prevailing view has been that terrorists stage their attacks to derive maximum propaganda value. Their attacks are deliberate and calculated to achieve goals: recruit new followers, obtain financial and in-kind support, influence public opinion, force political decisions, undermine a government, and demonstrate a capacity and resolve to act. Their targets are often symbolic and intended to deliver a message, usually political or religious.

The 9/11 attacks conformed to the prevailing view. They were staged, deliberate, and calculated; they influenced public opinion and demonstrated a capacity and resolve; they targeted symbols and delivered a message. Billions of people around the globe saw on television screens an impression that the United States was vulnerable.

But given the inhumanity of the 9/11 attacks, the prevailing view seems to have shifted: the primary objective, certainly of religion-based terrorist groups, may no longer be the attainment of propaganda value but the infliction of casualties.

Exploitation of the Media

There can be no doubt that terrorists use television, radio, newspapers, and websites to deliver their messages. Neither can there be doubt that the media give to violent acts a high level of coverage, a circumstance that often encourages further violence. Benefits accrue to the terrorists, who want publicity, and to the media, which thrive on sensational events. A further observation of news reporting organizations is that they are nearly always motivated by profits and rarely motivated by a sense of public service.

Not all experts agree, however. They point out that media reporting of a particularly horrendous act can alienate supporters, turn away sympathizers, and close off the flow of essential outside financing. Of equal or greater importance can be a garbling of the terrorist message. Instead of the act defining the cause, it can make the public see only the brutality of the act.

In extortive acts, such as kidnapping or the taking of hostages, media coverage can protect lives by building sympathy for the victims and antipathy for the captors. Conversely, the victims can suffer when the media report resistance to the extortion, the effect of which can induce the captors to carry out their threats because they do not want to be seen as weak or compromising.

Another negative effect of media reporting can be the pressure placed on the government (or corporation) to make a quick response when caution is the better course. To round out the negatives, the media have a knack for ferreting out and exploiting inside sources that, with assurances of anonymity, may reveal an intended response such as a rescue attempt.

Kidnap and Assassination

Kidnapping can be labeled as political and criminal. In the former, the kidnappers' adversary is a government or a prominent government figure. The kidnapping victim may be one person, e.g., a prominent government figure or other noted government official, a diplomat of another nation, and sometimes a nongovernment celebrity revered by the governed. The kidnappers may choose to take several hostages, who may or may not be linked to the government or have celebrity status.

The typical motive behind a political kidnapping is to attain a specific objective, such as amnesty or release of prisoners. Money is not a common demand. The kidnappers communicate to the government through the news media and often use videotapes of the victims to elicit public sympathy and sow discord in the government. Because the government has no direct communication channel to the kidnappers, it must reply through the media. From a propaganda standpoint, the kidnappers benefit greatly.

If the kidnappers' demands are not met, the hostages are assassinated singly, in combinations, or all at once. Videos of the murders are sent to the news media and over the Internet. (Note: Technically, an assassination is the murder of a politically important person or otherwise prominent individual. In recent days, the term is being applied to the murder of people, prominent or not, when the purpose is to advance a cause or extort money.)

The criminal form of kidnapping is motivated by criminal greed or by a terrorist group's need to procure operational funds. The target is usually a profitable business or wealthy family, the demand is for money, the kidnap victim is a sole figure, selection of the victim is made on the basis of economic value and vulnerability, and communications between the kidnappers and the business or family is direct and sometimes kept secret from the media and law enforcement.

Suicide Attack

Suicide terror has been around a long time. When the killing weapon was a knife, assassins of public figures rarely escaped with their own lives. The same held true for later assassins firing pistols at close range or throwing makeshift bombs. Today's suicide terrorists use explosive-laden trucks and themselves. While suicide terror has remained constant, the killing methods have kept pace with weapons technology.

A knife, a gun, or a thrown bomb has a limit to the number of casualties, but this is not so with vehicle-laden bombs or biological, chemical, and radiological bombs. A single terrorist with a single weapon can cause mass casualties not ever known before. At the same time that weapons technology has evolved, the sophistication of terrorists has evolved. They are now at a level that enables them to construct rudimentary, but nonetheless effective, weapons of mass destruction. If the objective of the terrorist is to strike fear through the infliction of death and injury, the tools are at hand.

Suicide terrorism as we know it today began in 1983 when the Hezbollah blew up the marine barracks in Lebanon. It has since been picked up by Hamas and other Palestinian groups in their attacks upon Israel. Al Qaeda used it effectively in attacks upon U.S. Embassies in Kenya and Tanzania and U.S. military living quarters in Saudi Arabia. We have seen the same in Afghanistan and Iraq.

The notion that suicide terrorists are insane is simply too simple and not at all conducive to coming to grips with the threat. Suicide terrorists see themselves as martyrs to be glorified and rewarded in the hereafter. This is not to suggest that we should empathize but to know who and what we are dealing with.

Early on, Middle East suicide terrorists tended to be male, young, uneducated, and impoverished. But like the change in weapons technology, so have the users changed. They are not always male or young or uneducated or impoverished. This was seen in the events of 9/11. The terrorists were mature, intelligent, at least moderately affluent, and knew they were going to die. Terrorist bombers in Israel have been young women and mothers, as was the case with Chechen terrorists.

A suicide terrorist rarely acts without encouragement and support from a larger organization. The decision to use this tactic, as well as to select the target, the time, and the place, rests not with the individual but with functionaries of the terrorist group. Moreover, the individual is often recruited, psychologically prepared, and trained well in advance. The idea that suicide terrorism is an individual act of uncontrolled rage is false. If the objective of the larger organization is to achieve dramatic results with minimum expenditure of resources, suicide terrorism is a good choice.

A question worth asking is whether or not suicide terrorism can be prevented. The answer can be a yes—but only when preventive measures are in place. At a minimum, these would include a well-conducted vulnerability assessment followed by implementation of countermeasures designed to keep the suicide terrorist out of range of the target.

Vehicle Bomb Attack

Compared with other weapons, vehicle bombs are inexpensive, simple to assemble, and easy to use. The number of vehicle bomb attacks around the world supports the view that vehicle bombs are the weapon of choice. In the United States, where vehicles of all types are commonplace everywhere, it is extremely difficult, if not impossible, to differentiate between vehicles that are innocent and those that are lethal.

The challenge is to establish procedures for keeping vehicles outside the blast zone of the protected facility. The blast zone is the area within which a high-explosive bomb will inflict death and serious injury. The size of the area is determined by the type of explosive and the carrying capacity of the vehicle.

High Explosive versus Low Explosive. An explosion is the conversion of a solid or liquid into a gas. The rate of conversion for a bomb constructed with high explosives is much higher than the rate of conversion for a low-explosive bomb. Rapid conversion creates a blast or shockwave. With a high explosive, the blast or shockwave can travel through air up to 27,000 feet per second; the shockwave of a low explosive moves at about 3,000 feet per second. Because blast or shockwave causes death, injury, and serious physical damage, the high- explosive bomb is the better choice for terrorists.

Types of high explosives:

* Military C-4
* PETN (pentaerythritol tetranitrate)
* TNT (trinitrotoluene)
* Dynamite
* Nitroglycerine
* ANFO (ammonium nitrate and fuel oil)

The high explosive very often used by terrorists is ANFO, ammonium nitrate laced with diesel fuel. The ANFO-type bomb is inexpensive, easy to construct, and very effective. A terrorist-controlled aircraft with a near-full gas tank is a type of vehicle bomb, as we saw on 9/11. The same can be true of other transport vehicles such as buses, trains, and ships.

An organization owning or contracting for vehicles ought to consider making background checks of operators; using a global positioning system; and placing within easy reach of the operator a duress alarm that annunciates at a monitoring station, security control center, or a dispatcher's office when a vehicle is in jeopardy such as a hijacking. Another step would be an engine kill switch for land-based vehicles.

Direct Action Attack

Direct action refers to any effort that seeks to achieve an end directly and by the most immediately effective means. Public demonstrations, boycotts, and labor strikes are nonviolent forms. In terrorism, direct action typically takes the form of armed assault in which a group, as opposed to an individual, seeks to attain a well-defined objective. The objectives tend to be assassination of opposition leaders, armed assault of government buildings, and storming prisons to obtain release of group members.

An example of direct action occurred in Munich, Germany, on September 5, 1972, when five Black September terrorists wearing sweat suits and carrying gym bags climbed over a fence surrounding the Olympic Village. Inside the gym bags were assault rifles. Three more terrorists already inside the village joined them. They went to the dormitory housing Israeli athletes and knocked on the door of a room occupied by the wrestling team. Two Israelis who resisted were shot and killed. Nine other Israeli athletes were taken captive to be used as bargaining chips in negotiating the release of Arab terrorists held in Israel and safe passage of the terrorists and their captives from Germany to Cairo, Egypt. The German government provided helicopters to transport the terrorists and their hostages to an airfield where German marksmen were in position. A fierce gunfight, followed by a second gunfight, ended with the deaths of all nine Israel athletes, one policeman, five terrorists, and capture of three terrorists.

Preparation of Terrorists

An Al Qaeda training manual obtained in 2000 by United Kingdom authorities provides insights to terrorist preparation in targeted countries. The manual suggests that up to 80 percent of information useful to a terrorist group can be collected from public sources.

Information Gathering. Much of the collected information is downloaded from:

- The target's website, where it may be possible to obtain the names of senior persons, their photographs, and biographies; physical addresses and photos of site locations and processes; phone numbers; and announcements of upcoming conferences and stockholder meetings
- Government websites that contain public records
- Fact sheets and images discovered by Internet search engines
- Chat rooms and bulletin boards

Other open sources that are available and of possible interest to terrorists include:

- Records available to the public at federal, state, and county agencies, with particular interest given to technical facts such as those that can be derived from maps, as-built plans, blue prints, and engineering schematics
- Public libraries
- News media
- People knowledgeable about the target site such as employees, ex-employees, contractors, and vendors; and pretext interviews conducted on the phone and in person
- The target's trash bins

Surveillance. Operatives will reconnoiter the areas around the target site and travel routes to and from the site. They will look for police patrols to determine:

- Frequency and pattern
- The number of officers in a patrol unit
- The distance and time between the target site and the nearest police station

Operatives will stake out the target site from several vantage points at various times: day and night, workdays and weekends, holidays, shift changes, and morning and afternoon rush hours. They will take photographs and make notes, sketches, and maps. Operatives will look for vulnerabilities, such as poor or nonexistent fencing and lighting;

unlocked gates; and a guard service that may be stretched thin, poorly trained, or inadequately equipped.

Opportunities for surveillance are presented when the target site is open to the public such as during an open house or a seasonal party when access control measures are relaxed. The operatives will pay attention to sign-in procedures, security posts and patrols, security communications, access control devices, intrusion detection sensors, CCTV cameras, elevators, hallways, restrooms, and similar places where bombs can be planted. Also of interest will be the physical aspects of the interior plus the parking area and its proximity to people and on-site operations.

Photographs are highly prized by the planning cadre of the terrorist group. Operatives will be trained in photography and provided with cover identification such as a college student ID card or tourist visa.

Testing of Security. Operatives will want to determine the effectiveness of security at the target site. They may test security officers by attempting to gain entry using innocuous appearing ruses. They may rattle perimeter fences to determine if they are alarmed, measure response times to alarms, or break out security lights to see how long it will take for them to be replaced.

Acquisition of Needed Materials. The individuals that do the preattack preparation may or may not be the same individuals who carry out the attack. In either case, the attack party will acquire necessary materials; for example, firearms and ammunition, explosives and detonators, night vision equipment, vehicles, communications gear, camouflaged clothing, counterfeit identification, and funds for escape. The attack party will make several dry runs in order to identify and correct flaws in the attack plan.

Learning Shop USA, Nature of Terrorism, Tactics of Terrorism, Homeland Security, Part and Part 2, www.learningshopusa.com

TESTIFYING

Testifying is the last and most critical stage of an investigation. All work done earlier can be wasted work if the investigator's testimony is faulty.

Good testimony relies on:

- The quality and completeness of notes prepared during the course of the investigation and other documents generated such as formal reports, status and progress reports, memoranda, and letters to the client
- Preparation made immediately before the legal proceeding such as reinterviewing witnesses to refresh their memories, studying notes and documentation, reading statements, admissions and confessions, reviewing photographs and laboratory reports, and examining physical evidence
- Contribution made in the pretrial conference such as informing friendly counsel of key events during the investigation, reviewing evidence, discussing the strengths and weaknesses of the case, and discussing the probable lines of questioning by both sides
- Quality of the investigator's deposition given prior to trial
- The investigator's:
  - Understanding of how a trial is conducted
  - Knowledge of direct and cross-examination
  - Ability to withstand intense cross-examination
  - Behavior in the presence of the judge and jury
  - Personal appearance, tact, and demeanor

All of the above factors add up to one essential quality: believability. In addition, the investigator should be careful:

- Not to discuss the case in public or any-place where his or her conversation may be overheard
- Not to discuss in public personal likes and dislikes, biases, or any controversial subjects that could in any way come to the attention of a judge or juror
- Not to arrive late to give testimony
- Not to contact or agree to be contacted by opposing counsel or witnesses for the opposing side

Preparation

Effective testimony is founded on preparation, which is often made difficult when there has been an extended passage of time between the time of investigation and the start of the legal proceeding.

Case files are essential study material in preparing to testify. These files can contain a wide variety of documents such as formal reports, memorandums, notes, voice and video recordings, sketches, diagrams, and photographs. If any of these materials find their way into testimony, their meaning and relevance to the case must be shown in the testimony. For example, if a case photograph is introduced while testifying, the investigator must be prepared to say who took the photograph and why, how it was taken, where and when it was taken, and the relationship of the photograph to the case.

Memory can be helped by visualizing and mentally reconstructing what led up to the incident, what occurred in the incident itself, and what happened later. For the investigator, this may be a daunting task when the investigation is complex and extended over a long period of time.

Memory tends to work best when thoughts are organized in an orderly chain of events. Also, the trier of fact (the judge or the judge and jurors) will frequently find testimony interesting and convincing when it is recalled in this manner. While memory is important,

pure memorization can make testimony flat and emotionless.

Preparation also means knowing the opposition. Much can be learned by actually watching opposing counsel in action in other cases. When this is not possible, friendly counsel can provide clues as to what the investigator can expect while testifying, such as techniques to discredit testimony and cast doubt on the investigator's competency.

Pretrial Conference

Prior to testifying, the investigator will very likely meet with the client and the client's attorney at what is called a pretrial conference.

To avoid unwelcome surprises, the client's attorney will want to hear the investigator state key details, and the investigator will want to ensure that the attorney knows all the facts, whether favorable or unfavorable. The attorney may be very interested in some facts and less interested in others.

The client's attorney will explain strategy and predict the types and sequence of questions expected to be asked. Ethically, the attorney cannot tell the investigator to stray from the truth.

In addition to being clear on details, the investigator will want to understand how evidence can and cannot be presented. This will help avoid mistakes that can lead to the exclusion of testimony and physical evidence.

Other witnesses are often asked to participate in the pretrial conference. The investigator needs to pay attention to what other witnesses are prepared to say at trial. Small differences in the separate testimony of witnesses can be damaging to the case.

Knowledge of the Case

As the time of trial draws near, the investigator should make a complete review of the case and refresh his memory of the facts by carefully reading through all notes and reports. He should also examine physical evidence that has been collected, in the event that it has to be identified or referred to in court. Then he should put his thoughts together so he can visualize the whole case in the sequence in which it happened.

An investigator may be allowed to refresh his memory on the witness stand by referring to his notes or reports. However, if he does, the defense counsel has a right to examine these notes and question him about them. Therefore, the investigator should discuss with the prosecuting attorney the advisability of taking notes to the witness stand.

Also, the prosecuting attorney may want to confer with the investigator about the facts of the case at a pretrial session. At this session, the prosecuting attorney may try to reawaken the investigator's senses to recall parts of the investigation that he deems essential to the case and to go over the investigator's testimony. This is entirely proper and, at this time, the investigator should make sure that the prosecuting attorney knows all the facts of the case, whether favorable or unfavorable to the defendant. The prosecuting attorney may not, however, tell the investigator what to say or influence the investigator to deviate from the truth in any way.

Knowledge of the Rules of Evidence

Besides knowledge of the case being tried, the investigator testifying in court should have a basic knowledge of the rules of evidence. This knowledge will help him to better understand the proceedings and enable him to testify more intelligently, removing the opportunities for delay and confusion that can occur in the mind of the investigator when placed under pressure in the courtroom.

Appearance and Attitude

When an investigator appears in court, he must observe the highest standards of conduct. The minute he walks to the witness stand, he becomes the focal point of interest and observation by the public.

The key thing for an investigator to impress in his mind when testifying in court is that he is engaged in a very solemn and serious matter. He should look and act accordingly. While waiting to testify, the investigator should not linger outside the door of the courtroom smoking, gossiping, joking, laughing, or engaging in other similar conduct. This distracts attention from the proceedings and shows little regard for the serious nature of the occasion. Rather, the investigator should be seated quietly in the courtroom while awaiting his turn to take the stand, unless he is directed to wait in the witness room.

An investigator's appearance while testifying should be neat and well-groomed. He should wear a clean suit, tie, and shined shoes. Neither should he wear dark glasses, smoke, chew gum, or generally fidget around while on the witness stand. A favorable impression is created if the investigator sits erect but at ease in the witness chair and appears confident, alert, and interested in the proceedings.

Testimony during Trial

Our system of securing information from a witness at a trial is by the question and answer method. The questioning by attorneys on direct examination serves merely to guide the witness in his testimony and to indicate the information that is required. After direct examination, the witness may be subject to cross-examination by the opposing counsel. The questions on cross examination will have the opposite purpose of those asked on direct examination. Cross-examination questions may be devious, deceptive, or innocent in appearance, masking the opposing counsel's real objective, which is to discredit or minimize, to as great an extent as possible, the effect of the witness's testimony. The investigator is usually a witness for the state. Direct examination is by the prosecuting attorney, with cross-examination by counsel for the defense.

There are no definite rules for testifying effectively in court because each case has its own peculiarities. However, there are general guidelines for answering questions that should be followed in most cases and some specific suggestions designed to aid the witness on cross examination.

Answering Questions on the Witness Stand

When taking the oath, the investigator should be serious and stand upright, facing the officer administering the oath. He should say "I do" clearly and positively and then be seated to wait for further questioning.

The investigator should listen carefully to the questions asked and make sure he understands each question before answering. If he does not understand, he should say so and ask to have the question repeated. He should then pause after the question long enough to form an intelligent answer and to allow the attorneys and judge time to make objections.

Answers to questions should be given in a confident, straightforward, and sincere manner. The investigator should speak clearly, loudly, and slowly enough so that all in the courtroom can hear, and he should avoid mumbling or covering his mouth with his hand while talking. He should look at the attorney asking the questions but direct his answers toward the jury. Simple conversational English should be used, and all slang and unnecessary technical terms should be avoided. Most importantly, the investigator should be respectful and courteous at all times despite his feelings toward the people involved in the case. He should address the judge as "Your Honor," the attorney as "Sir," and the defendant as "the Defendant."

The essential rule to be observed above and beyond all others is to always tell the truth, even if it is favorable to the defendant. Facts should not be distorted or exaggerated to try and aid a conviction, nor should details be added to cover up personal mistakes. Once it has been shown that an investigator has not truthfully testified as to one portion of his investigation, no matter how small and inconsequential, the jury may reject the truthfulness of all other testimony that he may offer. On the other hand, an investigator's testimony will appear strong if it is a truthful recital of what he did and observed, even though it reveals human error on his part and favors the defendant in some parts.

Answers to questions should go no further than what the questions ask for. The investigator should not volunteer any information not asked for. If a question requests a "yes" or "no" answer and the investigator feels it cannot properly be answered in this manner, he should ask to have the question explained or reworded or request the right to explain his answer. He may state that he cannot answer the question by "yes" or "no." This should alert the prosecuting attorney to come to his assistance.

Answers to questions should be given as specifically as possible. However, figures for time, distance, size, etc. should be approximated only, unless they were exactly measured by the investigator.

When an investigator is referring to a map or plan in his testimony, he should identify the point on the map as clearly as possible so it becomes part of the trial record. For example, he should say "the northwest corner of the room" rather than just point to the spot and say "here" or "there." If the investigator does not understand the map or plan that is to be used at trial, he should tell the prosecuting attorney before trial and go over it with the person who prepared it.

If a wrong or ambiguous answer is given, it should be clarified immediately. It is far better for an investigator to correct his own mistakes than to have them pointed out to the jury by the defense attorney or a subsequent witness.

If a judge interrupts or an attorney objects to an investigator's testimony, the investigator should stop talking instantly. However, he should not anticipate an objection when a difficult question is asked but should only pause long enough to form an intelligent answer.

Rarely will it help an investigator to memorize testimony. Memorized testimony tends to sound less than truthful. Instead, the investigator should have a thorough knowledge of the facts of the case and organize them in his mind so that he can recite them as a narrative. If a particular fact or circumstance becomes hazy or is forgotten, the investigator may be allowed to refresh his memory from his notes as long as this does not become a habit. It is worth noting that if an investigator does refer to notes, they may be examined by the opposing counsel. If for any reason the judge criticizes an investigator's conduct in court, the investigator should not allow it to disturb his composure. The best policy is to ask the court's pardon for the error committed and proceed as though nothing had occurred.

Jurors

Great care is taken to select a jury. The usual selection procedures are:

- Obtain background information from every potential juror to ensure the person is eligible to testify.
- Narrow the list of potential jurors to a manageable number.
- Subject each juror to a series of questions, called *voir dire*, that are designed to determine if the juror is not predisposed in support of either party. The prosecutor and defense may dismiss potential jurors for reasons unfavorable to their respective sides.
- The judge may also dismiss potential jurors.

A verdict of guilty accomplishes little if an investigator has testified so poorly that he affords the accused good grounds for a new trial or for a reversal on appeal.

Learning Shop USA, Testifying, www.learningshopusa.com

THREAT ELEMENTS IN LOSS PREVENTION

A threat is the potential for harm, and a threat event is the occurrence of the harm. In terms of loss prevention, the objective is to neutralize the threat before it can occur or, when it has occurred, to keep it from happening again. There is a science, if you will, that will allow an investigator to evaluate a threat and estimate the consequences should the threat event materialize.

The concept of threat is not isolated to a single context. The sources of threat (or threat elements) are many and various. Elements in the category of crime include thieves, burglars, robbers, muggers, embezzlers, fraudsters, thugs, kidnappers, terrorists, saboteurs, rapists, and others. In the category of human-caused loss incidents are fire, explosions, hazardous materials releases, traffic crashes, and human injuries and deaths. A third category of threat elements includes so-called Acts of God such as earthquakes, hurricanes, tornadoes, and floods.

A threat of loss has two dimensions. The first is past experience, and the second is predictive experience. Examples can be found in an organization's history of loss. For example:

- If thefts have been on the rise during the past five years, there can be a prediction that the rise will continue until intervened.
- If damage was done to property five years ago as the result of a severe flood, there can be a prediction that damage will be repeated unless something is done now to mitigate effects of the next flood.
- If five years ago a civil court found a company negligent for failing to protect

an employee, there is a prediction that another lawsuit will occur if the source of negligence is not removed.

A business organization faces risk from persons inside and outside the organization. Inside are employees, contractors, service providers, and others who have access to the organization's assets. The common motives of insiders are greed, revenge, and disgruntlement; the acts that follow motivation are common as well: theft, violence, and sabotage.

Human threat elements outside the organization run the gamut from unskilled to professional criminals, ideologues of all stripes, avengers, and punishers. Following are thumbnail descriptions.

The Insider

The insider threat is typically manifested in theft, destruction, damage, and disruption. A combination of physical and procedural safeguards is valuable in thwarting the inside threat. Access controls that regulate movement of people into and inside physical premises will not significantly impede the insider. The insider can be expected to have access to protected areas and enjoy freedom from restraint and suspicion.

The Outside Opportunist

The opportunist is typically a petty, common criminal lacking in sophistication, intelligence, and skill. He or she is constantly on the lookout for easily convertible assets such as cash, jewelry, small appliances, and desktop computer equipment. Some opportunists are oriented to sexual assault crimes; they prey upon the unprotected.

The Professional

The professional has a particular target in mind, possesses technical knowledge of protective measures and how to defeat them, has a plan of action, has resources for carrying out the plan, and has an escape plan if the attempt goes awry. The professional is often patient, is willing to abort, and has a plausible story if caught in the act.

The Ideologue

The ideologue seldom operates alone and is usually supported morally or materially by a sponsoring group. Ideologies spring from many sources: religion, nationalism, human rights, animal rights, environmental protection, etc. Each group will have a support base and a set of targets. Material greed and unmet psychological needs for power/sexual satisfaction are not motivators for ideological groups, although groups have a history of resorting to robbery and kidnapping to acquire operating revenue. Group tactics can range from highly terroristic acts, such as bombings and assassination, to purely symbolic acts, such as splashing blood on walls or burning a flag on an organization's front steps.

The ideologue may or may not be skilled, is likely to be intelligent, very likely to be strongly committed and dedicated, and willing to take chances and suffer the consequences of being caught.

The Avenger

Workplace violence is often an act of vengeance. When robbery-related shootings are factored in, workplace killings are a leading cause of on-the-job deaths. The typical workplace homicide is committed by an unstable worker who has been disciplined, laid off, or terminated; the worker returns with a gun and kills supervisors and others who get in the way and concludes by committing suicide.

Employees who are likely to release frustration through acts of violence are also likely to have a history of violence and likely to indicate growing frustration by changes in behavior at work. The implication is that background checks can be helpful in identifying applicants who bring a potential for violence into the workplace and that supervisors during periods of layoffs and terminations be alert to radical changes in employee attitudes and performance.

John J. Fay

TOOLMARK EXAMINATION

Toolmarks fall into two general categories: marks made with a class of tools, such as a screwdriver, knife, or pry bar, and marks made with a particular tool, such as a tool found in the possession of a suspect.

In the class-of-tool examination, the examiner might conclude that the mark was made by a screwdriver with a blade and the tip of the blade is 2/8 inches in length and 1/8 inches in width. The examiner might also conclude that the features of the blade suggest it is a Craftsman product.

The examination of a mark made by a particular tool compares the characteristics of the certain tool with a certain mark, typically a mark on the surface of wood, metal, or plastic. When the tool matches the mark and the origin of the tool is known, such as a tool confiscated from a suspect, the examiner's conclusion has evidential value. The basic fundamental of toolmark examination rests on the fact that when two objects come in contact, the harder object disturbs the softer object.

Toolmark examination is almost entirely a microscopic examination. An examination can potentially reveal:

- Foreign deposits, such as paint or metal flakes, on either the tool or the mark made by the tool
- Dimensions of the tool
- Significant features of the tool, such as a crooked shaft on a pry bar or striations on the blade of a screwdriver

- Direction and strength of force
- Movements of the tool when it was in contact with the softer surface
- Fracture of the tool, such as a chip made to the blade of a chisel or a wood screw snapped in two
- Serial numbers that have been altered or made invisible to the human eye

Tools and objects that bear tool marks should be submitted to the laboratory whole. When the object is too large or immovable, a piece can be cut from the object and submitted. An example would be a cut around a jimmied section of a doorframe. The investigator must be careful to keep a tool or object out of physical contact with each other or anything else. Photographs should be made before anything is touched.

Learning Shop USA, Scientific Analysis of Physical Evidence, www.learningshopusa.com

TORTS

A crime is a public wrong, and a tort is a private wrong. A public wrong is remedied in a criminal proceeding, and a private wrong is remedied in a civil proceeding. A single act in some instances will constitute both a crime and a tort. For example, if a person commits an assault and battery upon another, he commits a crime (a public wrong) and a tort (a private wrong). The law will seek to remedy both wrongs, but it will do so in different ways.

The state will move on its own authority to do justice by bringing a criminal action against the offender. The victim is also entitled to bring action against the offender in a civil suit. Tort law gives the victim a cause of action for damages in order that he may obtain sufficient satisfaction. The victim, however, pursues a civil remedy at his own discretion and in his own name. Whether the victim wins his lawsuit or not, the judgment will not prevent prosecution of the offender by the state.

The civil injuries involved in tort cases usually arise from acts of negligence. The fact that by his own negligence the victim contributed to the harm done may afford the offender a defense in a civil action of tort, but it does not constitute a defense to the offender in a criminal prosecution.

The single characteristic that differentiates criminal law from civil law is punishment. Generally, in a civil suit the basic questions are:

- How much, if at all, has the defendant injured the plaintiff?
- What remedies, if any, are appropriate to compensate the plaintiff for his loss?

In a criminal case, the questions are:

- To what extent has the defendant injured society?
- What sentence is appropriate to punish the defendant?

Tort Law Purposes

Tort law has three main purposes:

- To compensate persons who sustain a loss as a result of another's conduct
- To place the cost of that compensation on those responsible for the loss
- To prevent future harms and losses

Compensation is predicated on the idea that losses, both tangible and intangible, can be measured in money.

If a loss-producing event is a matter of pure chance, the fairest way to relieve the victim of the burden is insurance or governmental compensation. Where a particular person can be identified as responsible for the creation of the risk, it becomes more just to impose the loss on the responsible person (tortfeasor) than to allow it to remain on the victim or the community at large.

The third major purpose of tort law is to prevent future torts by regulating human behavior. In concept, the tortfeasor held liable for damages will be more careful in the future, and the general threat of tort liability serves as an incentive to all persons to regulate their conduct appropriately. In this way, tort law supplements criminal law.

Damages: Compensatory and Punitive

When one person's tortious act injures another's person or property, the remedy for the injured party is to collect damages. The common law rules of damages for physical harm contain three fundamental ideas:

- Justice requires that the plaintiff be restored to his preinjury condition, so far as it is possible to do so with money. He should be reimbursed not only for economic losses but also for loss of physical and mental well-being.
- Most economic losses are translatable into dollars.
- When the plaintiff sues for an injury, he must recover all of his damages arising from that injury, past and future, in a lump sum and in a single lawsuit.

If the defendant's wrongful conduct is sufficiently serious, the law permits the trier of fact to impose a civil fine as punishment to deter him and others from similar conduct in the future. Punitive damages (also called exemplary or vindictive damages) are not really damages at all since the plaintiff has been made whole by the compensatory damages awarded in the same action. Punitive damages are justified as:

- An incentive for bringing the defendant to justice
- Punishment for offenses that often escape or are beyond the reach of criminal law
- Compensation for damages not normally compensable, such as hurt feelings, attorneys' fees, and expenses of litigation

- The only effective means to force conscienceless defendants to cease practices known to be dangerous and which they would otherwise continue in the absence of an effective deterrent

The Intentional Tort of Intrusion

Interference with the right to be "let alone" can be grouped into four categories: intrusion, appropriation of one's name or likeness, giving unreasonable publicity to private facts, and placing a person in a false light in the public eye. The latter three of these are founded upon improper publicity, usually in the public press or electronic media. They are beyond the scope of this concept and will not be discussed.

Intrusion is an intentional tort closely related to infliction of emotional distress. Both torts protect a person's interest in his mental tranquility or peace of mind. A person has a basic right to choose when and to what extent he will permit others to know his personal affairs. Essentially, intrusion is an intentional, improper, unreasonable, and offensive interference with the solitude, seclusion, or private life of another. It embraces a broad spectrum of activities. It may consist of an unauthorized entry; an illegal search or seizure; or an unauthorized eavesdropping, with or without electronic aids.

The tort is complete when the intrusion occurs. No publication or publicity of the information obtained is required. It is, of course, essential that the intrusion be into that which is, and is entitled to remain, private. Additionally, the harm must be substantial. The intrusion must be seriously objectionable, not simply bothersome or inconvenient.

Philip P. Purpura, *Encyclopedia of Security Management*, second ed., Butterworth-Heinemann, Burlington, MA, 2007, pp. 248–250.

John J. Fay, *Encyclopedia of Security Management*, second ed., Butterworth-Heinemann, Burlington, MA, 2007, pp. 250–251.

TRIAL EVIDENCE

Testimonial evidence is the statements or spoken words given by a victim or witness. A form of testimonial evidence is opinion testimony, which is a conclusion drawn by a witness, hence the term "opinion."

Hearsay evidence is a statement made by a person other than a witness. Hearsay cannot be entered into evidence unless the maker of the statement (i.e., the actual witness) can be cross-examined.

Privileged communication is confidential information between two persons recognized by law as coming within the so-called privileged relationship rule. The following relationships are generally recognized: a husband and wife, an attorney and client, a physician and patient, and a law enforcement officer and informant.

Direct evidence is evidence that, if believed, proves the existence of the fact in issue without inference, presumption, or the intervention of another fact. Examples of direct evidence are:

- Body fluids such as blood, semen, or saliva
- Fibers
- Paint chips
- Glass and glass fragments
- Soil and vegetation
- Accelerants
- Fingerprints
- Hair
- Tread marks such as impressions of shoes or tire tracks
- Toolmarks such as those made by a crowbar or file
- Marks on a firearm or knife such as striations on a projectile or a broken knife tip
- Rip or tear marks on paper, fabrics, and tape
- Natural occurring drugs and synthetic drugs

Circumstantial evidence is evidence that infers truth based on other facts. It is evidence that relates to a series of facts other than the particular fact sought to be proved. The party offering circumstantial evidence argues that a series of facts, by reason and experience, is so closely associated with the fact to be proved that the fact to be proved may be inferred simply from the existence of the circumstantial evidence.

Admissibility is a characteristic or condition of evidence. To be admissible, evidence must be material, relevant, and competent. Evidence is material when it plays a significant part in proving a case. Examples of material evidence are the fingerprints of the accused that were found on the murder weapon, an eyewitness account of how the accused committed the crime, or when property (such as stolen property) is found in the possession of the accused. Evidence is relevant when it goes directly to the proof or disproof of the crime or of any facts at issue. Examples of relevant evidence might be a death certificate or a medical examiner's report. Evidence is competent when it is shown to be reliable. Examples of competent evidence might be accurate business records or the testimony of an expert fingerprint examiner.

Burden of proof means that the prosecution must prove the guilt of a defendant beyond a reasonable doubt.

Reasonable doubt means a jury must believe the charges to be true to a "moral certainty." On the other hand, the accused must prove his or her contentions. Such defenses as self-defense, insanity, and alibi are affirmative defenses that must be proved by the accused.

A presumption is a conclusion that must be reached from certain facts. Presumptions argue that some facts are irrefutable or presumed true until otherwise rebutted. For example, defendants are presumed to be sane at the time the crime was committed. Presumptions are of two classes: conclusive and rebuttable. A conclusive presumption is one that the law accepts from a set of facts, e.g., a child under ten years of age cannot be charged with a crime. A rebuttable presumption is based on evidence to the contrary, e.g., death can be presumed when a person has been missing or unaccounted for after a certain period of time, such as seven years.

John J. Fay

U

U.S. AIR FORCE OFFICE OF SPECIAL INVESTIGATIONS (AFOSI)

The mission of the Air Force Office of Special Investigations (AFOSI) is to identify, exploit, and neutralize criminal, terrorist, and intelligence threats to the U.S. Air Force, U.S. Department of Defense, and U.S. Government.

AFOSI investigates a wide variety of serious offenses:

- Espionage
- Terrorism
- Crimes against property
- Violence against people
- Larceny
- Computer hacking
- Acquisition fraud
- Drug use and distribution
- Financial misdeeds
- Military desertion
- Corruption of the contracting process
- Other illegal activity that undermines the mission of the U.S. Air Force or the Department of Defense

AFOSI units are stationed at many U.S. Air Force bases worldwide.

U.S. Air Force Office of Special Investigations, http://www.osi.af.mil/

U.S. ARMY CRIMINAL INVESTIGATION DIVISION (CID)

The U.S. Army Criminal Investigation Command is responsible for investigating felony crimes of army interest. The headquarters is located at Quantico, Virginia.

The army established CID as a major command on September 17, 1971. The acronym CID retains the "D" as a historical reminder of the first Criminal Investigation Division formed in 1918 by General John J. Pershing during World War I.

This worldwide command is comprised of approximately 2,000 soldiers and civilians and is organized into five subordinate organizations.

As the army's primary criminal investigative organization and the Department of Defense's premier investigative organization, CID is responsible for conducting criminal investigations in which the army is, or may be, a party of interest.

Special agents conduct criminal investigations on and off military reservations and, when appropriate, in conjunction with local, state, and federal investigative agencies.

CID operates a certified forensic laboratory at its headquarters in Quantico, Virginia. Special units provide services in personal protection, computer crime detection, polygraph testing, criminal intelligence collection and analysis, and a variety of other services normally associated with law enforcement activities.

CID's mission is the same in both the installation and battlefield environments; however, traditional roles are expanded once deployed to the battlefield or to a contingency operation. Advanced theater operations include recovering and analyzing forensic and biometric evidence, collecting criminal intelligence, and mentoring and training the national police to perform standard law enforcement procedures.

On the battlefield, CID engages in force protection operations, investigates war crimes and crimes against coalition forces and host nation personnel, and operates preventive and reactive anti terrorist programs.

U.S. Army Criminal Investigation Command, http://www.cid.army.mil/

U.S. BUREAU OF ALCOHOL, TOBACCO, FIREARMS, AND EXPLOSIVES (ATF)

ATF is part of the U.S. Department of Justice. ATF investigates crimes of violence, criminal organizations, use and trafficking of firearms, use and storage of explosives, acts of arson and bombings, acts of terrorism, and the diversion of alcohol and tobacco products.

ATF:

- Enforces provisions of the Safe Explosives Act, which restricts the use/possession of explosives without a federal license. ATF is considered the leading federal agency in most bombings that occur within the United States.
- Provides investigative support through the National Integrated Ballistic Information Network (NIBIN), a system that allows federal, state, and local law enforcement agencies to image and compare crime gun evidence

- Collects federal tax revenue derived from the illegal production of tobacco and alcohol products and the regulatory function related to protecting the public in issues related to the production of alcohol

Bureau of Alcohol, Tobacco, and Firearms, https://www.atf.gov/content/About

U.S. DEPARTMENT OF DEFENSE CRIMINAL INVESTIGATIVE SERVICE

The U.S. Department of Defense Criminal Investigative Service (DCIS) is the criminal investigative arm of the Office of the Inspector General, U.S. Department of Defense. Within the Department of Defense, DCIS investigates fraud; bribery; corruption; and the illegal transfer of sensitive defense technologies and companies that use defective, substandard, or counterfeit parts in weapons systems and equipment utilized by the military. DCIS also investigates cybercrimes and computer intrusions.

The mission of the Department of Defense Inspector General is to initiate, conduct, and supervise investigations in the Department of Defense, including the military departments.

U.S. Department of Defense Criminal Investigative Service, http://www.dodig.mil/INV_DCIS/index.cfm

U.S. DEPARTMENT OF HOMELAND SECURITY: INVESTIGATIONS

The U.S. Department of Homeland Security (DHS) was created following attacks made by terrorists on the World Trade Center on September 11, 2001. DHS has primary responsibilities of protecting the United States by preventing and responding to terrorist attacks, man-made accidents, and natural disasters that occur within national borders.

A major organizational step occurred on March 1, 2003, when DHS absorbed the

Immigration and Naturalization Service. DHS split INS, creating two new agencies: Immigration and Customs Enforcement (ICE) and Citizenship and Immigration Services. The investigative divisions and intelligence gathering units of the former INS were merged, forming Homeland Security Investigations. Also, border enforcement functions of the former INS were consolidated into a new agency and named the U.S. Customs and Border Protection.

The group called Homeland Security Investigations investigates a wide range of crimes:

- Human trafficking and smuggling
- Arms trafficking and drug smuggling
- Possession of weapons of mass destruction
- Financial crimes
- Computer crimes
- Intellectual property crimes
- Crimes against the critical national infrastructure

A subcomponent of HSI is the Office of Intelligence where gathered intelligence is analyzed and disseminated for use by the operational elements of ICE and DHS.

U.S. Department of Homeland Security, http:// www.ice.gov/about/offices/homeland-security- investigations/

U.S. IMMIGRATION AND CUSTOMS ENFORCEMENT (ICE)

The U.S. Immigration and Customs Enforcement (ICE) agency operates under the Department of Homeland Security (DHS). ICE is responsible for identifying, investigating, and dismantling vulnerabilities regarding the nation's border, economic, transportation, and infrastructure security. ICE has two primary components: Homeland Security Investigations (HSI) and Enforcement and Removal Operations (ERO).

Homeland Security Investigations

Homeland Security Investigations deals with a wide range of issues such as arms and drug smuggling, smuggling or possessing CBRNE weapons (chemical, biological, radioactive, nuclear, and explosive), cybercrimes, and threats against the critical national infrastructure and key resources.

Enforcement and Removal Operations

The ERO unit is responsible for enforcing the nation's immigration laws and ensuring the departure of removable aliens from the United States. ERO agents arrest and remove aliens who violate U.S. immigration law. Agents locate, apprehend, and remove aliens who have absconded from immigration proceedings and remain in the United States with an outstanding Warrant of Deportation. Other duties include transportation and detention of illegal immigrants as well as presentation of evidence in the prosecution of illegal immigrants.

ERO also identifies removable and criminal aliens located in jails and prisons. Identification is assisted by examination of fingerprints acquired during the normal booking process. Examination is done by both the Integrated Automatic Fingerprint Identification System (IAFIS) of the FBI's Criminal Justice Information Services and the Automated Biometric Identification System (IDENT) of the Department of Homeland Security.

Immigration and Customs Enforcement, https://www.ice.gov/

U.S. MARSHALS SERVICE

Having been formed in 1789, the U.S. Marshals Service is the nation's oldest federal law enforcement agency. The Marshals Service supports the federal courts system by apprehending fugitives, protecting the federal judiciary, transporting and housing prisoners, managing and selling assets confiscated from criminals, seizing contraband (such as illegal weapons and drugs), and operating the Witness Protection Program.

The Marshals Service operates a Threat Management Center that detects and responds to threats, especially threats posed against the federal court system.

U.S. Marshals are members of various task forces. Other members of task forces are assigned from federal, state, and local law enforcement agencies. In addition, the Service operates overseas to find and apprehend fugitives from the United States and assist foreign agencies in doing the same in this country.

U.S. Department of Justice, U.S. Marshals Service, http://www.justice.gov/marshals/

U.S. NAVY CRIMINAL INVESTIGATION SERVICE (NCIS)

The NCIS mission is to investigate and defeat criminal, terrorist, and foreign intelligence threats to the United States Navy and Marine Corps—ashore, afloat, and in cyberspace.

Counterintelligence

Counterintelligence activities are authorized by Presidential Executive Order 12333, which defines counterintelligence as "information gathered and activities conducted to identify, deceive, exploit, disrupt or protect against espionage, other intelligence activities, sabotage or assassinations conducted for or on behalf of foreign powers, organizations or persons, or their agents or other international terrorist organizations or activities."

Within the Department of the Navy, NCIS has exclusive investigative jurisdiction into actual, potential, or suspected acts of espionage, sabotage, assassination, and defection.

NCIS works to neutralize foreign intelligence services and foreign commercial activities seeking information about critical naval programs and research, development, test, and evaluation facilities. To prevent the compromise of military technology, NCIS pursues a robust Research and Technology Protection program, which works to safeguard the nation's vital defense technology.

Cyber Protection

NCIS has computer investigations and operations agents assigned throughout the world focusing on hackers, criminal groups, foreign intelligence services, terrorists, and insiders.

U.S. Navy Criminal Investigation Service, http://www.ncis.navy.mil/Pages/publicdefault.aspx

U.S. POSTAL INSPECTION SERVICE (USPIS)

The USPIS is the law enforcement arm of the United States Postal Service. Its jurisdiction is defined as "crimes that adversely affect the U.S. Mail, the postal system and postal employees." The mission of the U.S. Postal Inspection Service is to support and protect the U.S. Postal Service, its employees, infrastructure, and customers by enforcing the laws that defend the nation's mail system from illegal or dangerous use.

The USPIS has approximately 4,000 employees, 1,200 criminal investigators, an armed uniformed division, forensic laboratories, a communications system, and 1,000 technical and administrative support personnel.

U.S. Postal Inspection Service, https://postalinspectors.uspis.gov/

U.S. SECRET SERVICE (USSS)

The United States Secret Service (USSS) was established as a law enforcement agency in 1865. While most people associate the Secret Service with presidential protection, its original mandate was to investigate the counterfeiting of U.S. currency, a mission the Secret Service is still mandated to carry out.

The Secret Service's initial responsibility was to investigate counterfeiting of U.S. currency, which was rampant following the Civil War. The agency then evolved into the United States' first domestic intelligence and counterintelligence agency. Many of the agency's missions were later taken over by subsequent agencies such as the Federal Bureau of Investigation (FBI), Bureau of Alcohol, Tobacco, Firearms, and Explosives (ATF), U.S. Immigration and Customs Enforcement (ICE), and Internal Revenue Service (IRS). Prior to March 2003, the USSS was part of the Department of the Treasury. Today it is part of the Department of Homeland Security.

The USSS has two distinct areas of responsibility:

- Prevention and investigation of counterfeiting of U.S. currency and U.S. treasury securities, and investigation of major fraud
- Protection of current and former national leaders and their families, such as the president, past presidents, vice presidents, presidential candidates, visiting heads of state, and foreign embassies

Investigative Mission

The agency's primary investigative mission is to safeguard the payment and financial systems of the United States. This has been historically accomplished through the enforcement of counterfeiting statutes to preserve the integrity of the United States' currency, coin, and financial obligations.

Over a period of time, the Secret Service's investigative responsibilities expanded to include crimes that involve financial institution fraud, computer and telecommunications fraud, false identification documents, access device fraud, advance fee fraud, electronic funds transfers, and money laundering

as it relates to the agency's core violations. The Secret Service derives its authority to investigate specified criminal violations from Title 18 of the United States Code, Section 3056.

Crimes commonly investigated by the Secret Service include counterfeiting of U.S. currency (to include coins), U.S. Treasury checks, Department of Agriculture food coupons, and U.S. postage stamps. The counterfeiting of money is one of the oldest crimes in history. At some periods in early history, it was considered treasonous and was punishable by death. During the American Revolution, the British counterfeited U.S. currency in such large amounts that the Continental currency soon became worthless. "Not worth a Continental" became a popular expression of the era. During the Civil War, one-third to one-half of the currency in circulation was counterfeit. At that time, approximately 1,600 state banks designed and printed their own bills. Each bill carried a different design, making it difficult to detect counterfeit bills from the 7,000 varieties of real bills.

Today, new forms of counterfeiting are on the rise. One reason for this is the ease and speed with which large quantities of counterfeit currency can be produced using modern photographic, printing, and computer equipment.

Financial Crimes

The Secret Service exercises broad investigative jurisdiction over a variety of financial crimes. As the original guardian of the nation's financial payment systems, the Secret Service has a long history of protecting American consumers and industries from financial fraud. In addition to its original mandate of combating the counterfeiting of U.S. currency, the passage of federal laws in 1982 and 1984 gave the Secret Service primary authority for the investigation of access device fraud, including credit and debit card fraud, and parallel authority with other federal law enforcement agencies in identity crime cases. The Secret Service also was given primary authority for the investigation of fraud as it relates to computers.

In the early 1990s, the Secret Service's investigative mission expanded to include concurrent jurisdiction with the United States Department of Justice regarding Financial Institution Fraud. Also during this time, the Internet and use of personal computers became commonplace and expanded worldwide. The combination of the information revolution and the effects of globalization caused the investigative mission of the Secret Service to expand dramatically. As a result, the Secret Service has evolved into an agency that is recognized worldwide for its investigative expertise and its aggressive and innovative approach to the detection, investigation, and prevention of financial crimes.

On October 26, 2001, President George W. Bush signed into law H.R. 3162, the USA PATRIOT Act. The USSS was mandated by this legislation to establish a nationwide network of Electronic Crimes Task Forces (ECTFs). The concept of the ECTF network is to bring together not only federal, state, and local law enforcement but also prosecutors, private industry, and academia. The common purpose is the prevention, detection, mitigation, and aggressive investigation of attacks on the nation's financial and critical infrastructures.

Identity Crimes

Identity crimes are defined as the misuse of personal or financial identifiers in order to gain something of value and/or facilitate other criminal activity. The Secret Service is the primary federal agency tasked with investigating identity theft/fraud and its related activities under Title 18, United States Code, Section 1028. Identity crimes are some of the fastest growing and most serious economic crimes in the United States for both financial institutions and persons whose identifying

information has been illegally used. The Secret Service records criminal complaints; assists victims in contacting other relevant investigative and consumer protection agencies; and works with other federal, state, and local law enforcement and reporting agencies to identify perpetrators.

Identity crimes investigated by the Secret Service include:

- Credit card/access device fraud (skimming)
- Check fraud
- Bank fraud
- False identification fraud
- Passport/visa fraud

Fraudulent Identification

The Secret Service enforces laws involving fraudulent identification, which means a crime where someone knowingly and without lawful authority produces, transfers, or possesses a false identification document to defraud the U.S. Government. The use of desktop publishing software/hardware to counterfeit and produce different forms of identification used to obtain funds illegally remains one of the Secret Service's core violations.

Access Device Fraud

Financial industry sources estimate annual losses associated with credit card fraud to be in the billions of dollars. The Secret Service is the primary federal agency tasked with investigating access device fraud and its related activities under Title 18, United States Code, Section 1029. Although it is commonly called the credit card statute, this law also applies to other crimes involving access devices including debit cards, automated teller machine (ATM) cards, computer passwords, personal identification numbers, credit card or debit card account numbers, long-distance access codes, and the

Subscriber Identity Module (SIM) contained within cellular telephones that assign billing.

Computer Fraud

Title 18 of the United States Code, Section 1030 authorizes the Secret Service to investigate computer crimes. Violations enforced under this statute include unauthorized access to protected computers, theft of data such as personal identification used to commit identity theft, denial of service attacks used for extortion or disruption of e-commerce, and malware (malicious software) distribution to include viruses intended for financial gain.

The proliferation of the Internet has allowed the transition of traditional street crimes to flourish in the anonymity of cyberspace. The borders of a state or a country are no longer boundaries for cyber criminals to reach their victims. As a result of advancements in technology, the Secret Service established the Electronic Crimes Special Agent Program (ECSAP) and the network of ECTFs (mentioned previously).

Forgery

Hundreds of millions of government checks and bonds are issued by the United States each year. This large number attracts criminals who specialize in stealing and forging checks or bonds from mailboxes in apartment complexes and private homes. During a fraudulent transaction, a check or bond thief usually forges the payee's signature and presents false identification.

Money Laundering

The Money Laundering Control Act makes it a crime to launder proceeds of certain criminal offenses, called "specified unlawful activities," which are defined in Title 18, United States Code, Sections 1956 & 1957, as well as Title 18, United States Code, Section 1961 (Racketeer Influenced and Corrupt Organizations Act). The Secret Service monitors money laundering activities through other financial crimes such as financial institution fraud, access device fraud, food stamp fraud, and counterfeiting of U.S. currency.

Electronic Benefits Transfer Fraud

Congress enacted the Food Stamp Act of 1977 to provide nutritional food to low-income families. It further directed the Secret Service to aggressively pursue fraud in the food stamp program. The possession or use of food stamp coupons, "Authorization to Participate" cards, or Electronic Benefit Transfer cards by unauthorized persons compromises the integrity of the Food Stamp Program and is a criminal violation of the Food Stamp Act.

Asset Forfeiture

The seizing and forfeiture of assets is a byproduct of the Secret Service's criminal investigations. As a result, the Secret Service, through its asset forfeiture program, provides assistance to investigative offices by supplying direction, expertise, and temporary support personnel, as needed, in criminal investigations seizure and during the seizure and the forfeiture of assets.

Advance Fee Fraud

The perpetrators of advance fee fraud, known internationally as "4–1–9 fraud" (after the section of the Nigerian penal code which addresses these schemes), are often very creative. A large number of victims are enticed into believing they have been singled out from the masses to share in multimillion-dollar-windfall profits.

Forensic Services

The U.S. Secret Service is home to an advanced forensic laboratory, which includes the world's largest ink library. Secret Service forensic analysts examine evidence, develop investigative leads, and provide expert courtroom testimony. Forensic examiners analyze questioned documents, fingerprints, false identification documents, credit cards, and other related forensic science areas. Examiners also are responsible for coordinating photographic and graphic production, as well as video, audio, and image enhancement services.

As part of the 1994 Crime Bill, Congress mandated the U.S. Secret Service to provide forensic/technical assistance in matters involving missing and exploited children. The Secret Service offers this assistance to federal, state, and local law enforcement agencies and the National Center for Missing and Exploited Children. On April 30, 2003, President George W. Bush signed the PROTECT Act of 2003, known as the "Amber Alert Bill," which gave full authorization to the U.S. Secret Service in this area.

U.S. Secret Service, http://www.secretservice.gov/mission.shtml

UNDERCOVER OPERATIONS

The use of an undercover operative should only be a consideration when serious criminal activity is affecting an organization, when the details of the activity are unknown, and when proof is needed to bring it to an end.

The operative must be reliable, experienced, and have a personal background free of prior crime or other questionable behavior. The organization that employs the operative should possess authority to conduct the operation and be clear as to objectives.

Managing the Operation

An undercover operation is essentially a project that requires a high degree of management. Its infrastructure consists of:

- Preplanning
- Setting targets

- Determining the nature and extent of evidence to be gathered
- Determining resources required
- Establishing a cover story
- Selecting the operative
- Selecting the handler
- Assigning responsibility and delegating authority to the handler
- Starting the operation
- Safety of the operative
- Gathering evidence
- Closing down the operation

Preplanning

The person who manages the operation will need to meet with persons who discovered the activity, have knowledge of the activity, and are authorized to make preplanning decisions.

Preplanning sessions should take place as many times needed to assure that both parties are in agreement that:

- The operation is necessary.
- The operation will be legal.
- The operation will be carried out in a mutually satisfactory manner.
- The objectives of the operation are clearly understood.

In logistical and manpower respects, preplanning should include agreement as to who will pay the costs, the projected amount of costs, and who will provide what and when.

In order to reach a sound agreement, certain questions need to be answered:

- What is the nature of the property being stolen, compromised, damaged, or destroyed?
- What safeguards are currently in effect to protect the property?
- What makes it possible for the activity to be done?
- Where is the activity occurring, and what is the nature of that environment?
- What are the names and positions of persons believed to be involved in the activity?

- What are the names and positions of supervisors/managers responsible for protecting the property?

Preplanning is exactly what the term suggests. It is an activity that occurs before anything is done. Preplanning is not action in itself; it is a description of action that is designed and intended to meet specific expectations. All persons charged with managing the operation should be a member of the preplanning team.

Setting Targets

It should be agreed among all parties that certain targets are intended to be achieved. A target typically will include a statement of who is responsible for achievement, what is to be achieved, a time table for achievement, the conditions under which the target is to be worked, and the identification of demonstrable achievements.

Targets are specific, measurable, relevant, and time related. Although firm when formulated, they can be amended and supplemented throughout the period of the operation. Although targets will consistently correspond with results, they can vary according to the type of work to be performed by the operative.

To the uninitiated, target setting may appear to be more trouble than it's worth. Targets can be difficult to formulate and sometimes impossible to agree upon. They cause problems when the targets are irrelevant or overly demanding.

The manager of the operation, speaking from experience, might reject suggestions that are inflexible or laden with the risk of failure. Posing questions such as the following may be helpful in formulating mutually agreeable targets:

- Does the target make good sense? Is it important to achieving a successful outcome?

- Does it mesh with the goal of the operation?
- Does it carry risks operationally? Financially?
- Will the target withstand Monday-morning scrutiny?
- Is the undercover operative capable of meeting target objectives?
- Can attainment of the target be verified in a measurable way?

Targets assigned to the operative should be as few as possible because some or all of the targets will change or evolve as the operative's work progresses. Targets will sometimes be contingent upon factors beyond the ability to control, such as availability of funds or equipment, or dependent upon approval by persons who are unaware of the operation.

In determining targets, it is useful to focus on the action steps required for achievement. A single target can incorporate several action steps. If the target is to "Establish a cover story," the action steps could include having a third person ready to affirm that the story is legitimate or leaving an item for the criminals to see, such as a fake letter from a person mentioned in the cover story. Time frames or deadline dates can be established for each action step and can be programmed to occur in a particular sequence. However, like the decisions reached in preplanning, the time factor should be flexible.

Undercover operatives are almost always in the game for personal reasons, which is very often money. A bonus can be available if the undercover operative is successful beyond the established target. For example, if the target is to identify where the stolen goods are taken, a plus would be an identification of the individual(s) receiving the stolen goods or fencing them. Once targets are set, they need to be put into writing, and any later changes should be written down and acknowledged by the head of the affected organization and the persons managing the operation.

Determining the Nature and Extent of Evidence Required

From an evidential point of view, photographs, video tapes, and other forms of imagery are very, very good but difficult to acquire. An operative seen taking photos can be placed in great danger. A fairly effective method of showing the thieves in action is to install a fiber optic lens that sends images to a photographic recording device that has a time and date generator. A fiber optic lens is easy to conceal, such as in a fire alarm sound box or inserted in a plasterboard wall. The downside is that the area of view can be less than desirable.

Of great importance is the identification of places where stolen goods are hidden before being removed from the premises. When the operation comes to a conclusion, the hidden stolen goods can be seized and held as evidence. Typically, a warrant would be issued before a search and seizure occurs.

The appearance of entrapment can be a serious problem. If there is any indication the police played a part in the operation, there is a risk that the criminal group will escape prosecution. There is also the possibility that the criminal group will show or attempt to show that the operative helped plan the criminal activity, participated in it, and the activity would not have occurred if it were not for the operative.

Establishing the Cover Story

A cover story should be in agreement with the nature of the criminal activity. For example, a cover story that portrays the operative as a thief is much better than a cover story that portrays the operative as a Las Vegas card cheat.

A cover story should not be complicated. Every detail in a cover story presents a possibility that the cover story will be compromised. Also, too many details may be difficult for the operative to remember and be able to accurately state the details repetitively.

If the operative, the controller of the operative, or the manager of the operation believes the cover story has been "blown," the operative should be extracted at once using a contrived story that will not confirm the criminals' belief the operative is a "plant." The main reason for taking this action is protection of the operative from harm. A second reason is to discourage the criminals from destroying evidence.

When a cover story appears to be blown, a judgment call needs to be made to either pull the operative or continue the operation. The judgment should be reached after a thorough analysis of facts and agreement from the operative to continue.

Selecting the Operative

It is often believed that the operative must have undercover experience. If this belief were literally true, there would be no operatives from which to choose. However, it is a fact that some investigators have a knack for and experience in effecting pretensions.

There is also a belief that an investigator is a better choice than a person not skilled as an investigator. This belief is true. It is also true that persons skilled in acting can be effective.

Cost of an operative's services is also a matter for consideration. Higher-priced operatives are not always the best operatives.

Selecting the Operative's Handler or Controller

The person directly controlling the operative should be an experienced investigator. Experience in this sense would include skill and knowledge in:

- Inspiring confidence in the operative
- Relieving the operative of undeserved anxieties
- Staying informed of activities that are relevant to the case but are occurring outside the operative's realm of knowledge
- Informing the operative of external details that could influence the operative's activities

- Directing the operative
- Managing communications daily, if possible. The method of communication should be amenable to the operative's situation. Many methods are available: telephone voice-to-voice, telephone voice to recorder, e-mail, Twitter, fax, drop site, mail, delivery service, or face-to-face meeting. The operative should not retain notes in any form.

Starting the Operation

A possible method for inserting the operative is to:

- Create a job position, complete with job description
- Advertise the job opening
- Interview applicants
- Hire the operative from among the applicants
- Provide to the operative a regular paycheck and the same benefits afforded to employees of equal grade
- Treat the operative in the same way all other employees of equal grade are treated

Knowledge of the insertion should be limited to as few people as possible.

It will help if the operative has the skill and know-how to perform the tasks of the job, or the job can be made so simple that skill and know-how are not necessary. Preferably, the operative would be placed as a coworker within the criminal group or in a job affording a view of the activity.

Safety of the Operative

Common infiltration techniques are to make friends with a member of the criminal group or pose as a thief interested in becoming a member of the group.

If the operative is in danger, such as his or her cover being blown or about to be blown, the operative must be extracted in a manner that does not raise or confirm suspicions

of the criminal group. Examples would be transferring the operative to a different location for a business reason or terminating the operative's employment for cause or for manpower reduction. The objective is to protect the operative first and investigate the criminal activity second. After a reasonable period of time, a second operative can be inserted.

Gathering Evidence

A main target in the operative's game plan is determine the nature of the activity, i.e., the what, where, how, and who. In other words, find out what is being stolen or compromised, where the activity is occurring, how the activity is being carried out, and the identities of the persons involved.

A form of evidence is testimonial evidence. The operative is a witness who can testify as to the names of those involved. A related form of evidence is photographic evidence. For photographs of the individuals, preferably in the process of committing the crime, there must be testimony to verify the accuracy and truthfulness of the photographs.

Better still is physical evidence, such as the property stolen. Material collected by the operative must be identifiable as to date obtained and how obtained. In other words, details are necessary, and documentation for the record should be made by the handler.

Closing Down the Operation

The typical procedure for closing down a successful operation is for the police or prosecuting agency to obtain warrants for search, seizure, and arrest. The principals in the operation (such as the operative, handler, or operation manager) would provide affidavits in support of the request for warrants.

To reduce the chance of retaliation, the operative is arrested along with the criminals, separated from them after booking, and then released. Retaliation is a serious matter because if any of the criminals are released on bail, the operative is a natural target, not necessarily out of spite, because he or she will be a key witness at trial.

Eugene F. Ferraro, Encyclopedia of Security Management, second ed., Butterworth-Heinemann, Burlington, MA, 2007, pp. 189–194.

UNIFORM CRIME REPORTING

The FBI's Uniform Crime Report is available to law enforcement executives, students of criminal justice, researchers, members of the media, and the public at large. The idea for crime reporting was conceived in 1929 by the International Association of Chiefs of Police to meet the need for reliable uniform crime statistics for the nation. In 1930, the FBI was tasked with collecting, publishing, and archiving those statistics.

Crime in the United States is an annual publication in which the FBI compiles the volume and rate of violent and property crime offenses for the nation and by state. Individual law enforcement agency data are also published and given to the providers of data. The publication includes arrest, clearance, and law enforcement employee data. This publication is the most comprehensive analysis of violent crime and property crime in the nation.

The National Incident-Based Reporting System, or NIBRS, was created in 1991 to improve the quantity and quality of crime data collected by law enforcement by capturing more detailed information on each single crime occurrence.

Other FBI reports and publications address:

- Bank crime
- Campus crime
- Financial crime
- Financial institution fraud
- Internet crime
- Mass marketing fraud
- Mortgage fraud
- National drug crime
- National gang crime
- Terrorism

Federal Bureau of Investigation, http://www.fbi.gov/about-us/cjis/ucr/ucr

UNPAID FEES

A reality of the private investigation business is that clients do not always pay what is owed. A failure by the agency head to vigorously seek collection can be seen as an exploitable weakness, and some practices can be harmful to the attempt to collect a debt. Following are examples of what not to do:

- Do not call a debtor at work.
- Do not violate a debtor's privacy, such as by mentioning the debt to another person.
- Do not tell the debtor that he/she is at risk unless payment is made.
- Don't mention debt when you are trying to track down a debtor.
- Do not publicly announce a debt.
- Do not call a debtor at home between the hours of 9 PM and 8 AM the following day.
- Do not use deceptive tactics to collect a debt, such as by pretexting to obtain financial information about the debtor.
- Do not send the debtor faked documents, such as a phony subpoena or a letter that appears to be from someone else.
- Do not threaten the debtor unless you mean to carry it out. Don't say, "I'm going to sue you" if you have no intention to do so.
- Do not hesitate to take legal action.

If an attempt is made by sending a letter to a debtor, the outer envelope should be marked "Personal and Confidential." The idea is not to inform a third party of the debt. Also, a letter can be physical evidence of a complaint that alleges harassment.

Learning Shop USA, Business Practices, Part 1 and Part 2, www.learningshopusa.com

V

VOICE STRESS ANALYSIS

The products, manufacturers, and organizations discussed in this section are presented for informational purposes only and do not constitute product approval or endorsement by the U.S. Department of Justice.

Law enforcement agencies across the country have invested millions of dollars in voice stress analysis (VSA) software programs; visit http://www.nij.gov/journals/259/Pages/voice-stress-analysis.aspx. One crucial question, however, remains unanswered:

Does VSA Actually Work?

According to a recent study funded by the National Institute of Justice (NIJ), two of the most popular VSA programs in use by police departments across the country are no better than flipping a coin when it comes to detecting deception regarding recent drug use. The study's findings also noted, however, that the mere presence of a VSA program during an interrogation may deter a respondent from giving a false answer.

VSA manufacturers tout the technology as a way for law enforcers to accurately, cheaply, and efficiently determine whether a person is lying by analyzing changes in their voice patterns. Indeed, according to one manufacturer, more than 1,400 law enforcement agencies in the United States use its product. But few studies have been conducted on the effectiveness of VSA software in general, and until now, none of these tested VSA in the field—that is, in a real-world environment such as a jail. Therefore, to help determine whether VSA is a reliable technology, NIJ funded a field evaluation of two programs: Computer Voice Stress Analyzer (CVSA) and Layered Voice Analysis (LVA).

Researchers with the Oklahoma Department of Mental Health and Substance Abuse Services (including this author) used these VSA programs while questioning more than 300 arrestees about their recent drug use. The results of the VSA output—which ostensibly indicated whether the arrestees were lying or telling the truth—were then compared to their urine drug test results. The findings of our study revealed:

- Deceptive respondents. Fifteen percent who said they had not used drugs—but who, according to their urine tests, had—were correctly identified by the VSA programs as being deceptive.
- Nondeceptive respondents. Eight and a half percent who were telling the truth—that is, their urine tests were consistent with their statements that they had or had not used drugs—were incorrectly classified by the VSA programs as being deceptive.

Using these percentages to determine the overall accuracy rates of the two VSA programs, we found that their ability to accurately detect deception about recent drug use was about 50 percent.

Based solely on these statistics, it seems reasonable to conclude that these VSA programs were not able to detect deception about drug use, at least to a degree that law enforcement professionals would require—particularly when weighed against the financial investment. We did find, however, that arrestees who were questioned using the VSA instruments were less likely to lie about illicit drug use compared to arrestees whose responses were recorded by the interviewer with pen and paper.

So perhaps the answer to the question "Does VSA work?" is . . . it depends on the definition of "work."

What Is VSA?

VSA software programs are designed to measure changes in voice patterns caused by the stress, or the physical effort, of trying to hide deceptive responses. VSA programs interpret changes in vocal patterns and indicate on a graph whether the subject is being "deceptive" or "truthful."

Most VSA developers and manufacturers do not claim that their devices detect lies; rather, they claim that VSA detects microtremors, which are caused by the stress of trying to conceal or deceive.

VSA proponents often compare the technology to polygraph testing, which attempts to measure changes in respiration, heart rate, and galvanic skin response.

Even advocates of polygraph testing, however, acknowledge its limitations, including that it is inadmissible as evidence in a court of law; requires a large investment of resources; and takes several hours to perform, with the subject connected to a machine. Furthermore, a polygraph cannot test audio or video recordings or statements made either over a telephone or in a remote setting (that is, away from a formal interrogation room), such as

at an airport ticket counter. Such limitations of the polygraph—along with technological advances—prompted the development of VSA software.

Although some research studies have shown that several features of speech pattern differ under stress, it is unclear whether VSA can detect deception-related stress. In those studies that found that this stress may be detectable, the deception was relatively minor and no "jeopardy" was involved—that is, the subjects had nothing to lose by lying (or by telling the truth, for that matter). This led some researchers to suggest that if there is no jeopardy, there is no stress—and that if there is no stress, the VSA technology may not have been tested.

The NIJ-funded study was designed to address these criticisms by testing VSA in a setting where police interviews commonly occur (a jail) and asking arrestees about relevant criminal behavior (drug use) that they would likely hide.

Our research team interviewed a random sample of 319 recent arrestees in the Oklahoma County Jail. The interviews were conducted in a relatively private room adjacent to the booking facility with male arrestees who had been in the detention facility for less than 24 hours. During separate testing periods, data were collected using CVSA and LVA.

The arrestees were asked to respond to questions about marijuana use during the previous 30 days and cocaine, heroin, methamphetamine, and PCP use within the previous 72 hours. The questions and test formats were approved by officials from CVSA and LVA. The VSA data were independently interpreted by the research team and by certified examiners from both companies.

Following each interview, the arrestee provided a urine sample that was later tested for the presence of the five drugs. The results of the urinalysis were compared to the responses about recent drug use to determine whether the arrestee was being truthful or deceptive.

This determination was then compared to the VSA output results to see whether the VSA gave the same result of truthfulness or deceptiveness.

Can VSA Accurately Detect Deception?

Our findings suggest that these VSA software programs were no better in determining deception about recent drug use among arrestees than flipping a coin.

To arrive at this conclusion, we first calculated two percentage rates:

- Sensitivity rate. The percentage of deceptive arrestees correctly identified by the VSA devices as deceptive.
- Specificity rate. The percentage of nondeceptive arrestees correctly classified by the VSA as nondeceptive.

Both VSA programs had a low sensitivity rate, identifying an average of 15 percent of the responses by arrestees who lied (based on the urine test) about recent drug use for all five drugs. LVA correctly identified 21 percent of the deceptive responses as deceptive; CVSA identified 8 percent.

The specificity rates—the percentage of nondeceptive respondents who, based on their urine tests, were correctly classified as nondeceptive—were much higher, with an average of 91.5-percent accuracy for the five drugs. Again, LVA performed better, correctly identifying 95 percent of the nondeceptive respondents; CVSA correctly identified 90 percent of the nondeceptive respondents.

We then used a plotting algorithm, comparing the sensitivity and specificity rates, to calculate each VSA program's overall "accuracy rate" in detecting deception about drug use. We found that the average accuracy rate for all five drugs was approximately 50 percent.

Does VSA Deter People from Lying?

Although the two VSA programs we tested had about a 50-percent accuracy rate in

determining deception about recent drug use, might their very presence during an interrogation compel a person to be more truthful?

This phenomenon—that people will answer more honestly if they believe that their responses can be tested for accuracy—is called the "bogus pipeline" effect. Previous research has established that it is often present in studies that examine substance use.

To determine whether a bogus pipeline effect existed in our study, we compared the percentage of deceptive answers to data from the Oklahoma City Arrestee Drug Abuse Monitoring (ADAM) study (1998–2004), which was conducted by the same VSA researchers in the same jail using the same protocols. The only differences—apart from the different groups of arrestees—were that the ADAM survey was longer (a 20-minute survey compared with the VSA study's five-minute survey) and did not involve the use of VSA technology.

In both studies, arrestees were told that they would be asked to submit a urine sample after answering questions about their recent drug use. In the VSA study, arrestees were told that a computer program was being used that would detect deceptive answers.

Arrestees in the VSA study were much less deceptive than ADAM arrestees, based on responses and results of the urine test (that is, not considering the VSA data). Only 14 percent of the VSA study arrestees were deceptive about recent drug use compared to 40 percent of the ADAM arrestees. This suggests that the arrestees in the VSA study who thought their interviewers were using a form of "lie detection" (i.e., the VSA technology) were much less likely to be deceptive when reporting recent drug use.

The Bottom Line: To Use or Not Use VSA

It is important to look at both "hard" and "hidden" costs when deciding whether to purchase or maintain a VSA program. The monetary costs are substantial: it can cost up to $20,000 to purchase LVA. The average cost of CVSA training and equipment is $11,500. Calculating the current investment nationwide—more than 1,400 police departments currently use CVSA, according to the manufacturer—the total cost is more than $16 million not including the manpower expense to use it.

The hidden costs are, of course, more difficult to quantify. As VSA programs come under greater scrutiny—due, in part, to reports of false confessions during investigations that used VSA—the overall value of the technology continues to be questioned.

Therefore, it is not a simple task to answer the question: does VSA work? As our findings revealed, the two VSA programs that we tested had approximately a 50-percent accuracy rate in detecting deception about drug use in a field (i.e., jail) environment; however, the mere presence of a VSA program during an interrogation may deter a respondent from answering falsely. Clearly, law enforcement administrators and policymakers should weigh all the factors when deciding to purchase or use VSA technology.

Kelly Damphousse, National Institute of Justice Journal No. 259, March 2008.

VULNERABILITY ASSESSMENT IN LOSS PREVENTION

Background

Vulnerability assessment (VA) is an advanced version of the traditional loss prevention inspection. VA has the same purpose as the crime prevention inspection but goes about it in a much more detailed way. Both methods are alike because they look for weaknesses in the scheme of protection for assets.

Investigators, whether in the government, public, or private sectors, are loss prevention practitioners—whether they know it or not. An informal, off-hand comment by an investigator, such as "It would be a good idea to lock that up," is in the nature of loss prevention guidance. In a formal, written report

made on the basis of a VA, an investigator would say the same thing but in detail.

In another context, investigators are loss prevention practitioners when, in the final report of investigation, they state how the crime occurred. The "how" explains the circumstances that made the crime possible. In some investigation units, the "how" is a formal, required element of the final report. Usually, at the end of the report, there will be a statement such as "This crime could have been prevented by. . . ." The loss prevention connect is apparent.

In this section, terms such as "asset" and "target" mean the same thing. An asset can be anything of value: a diamond ring, a race horse, or a biological agent. Each has a value, but the values have different sources: the ring might be a family heirloom, the race horse might be loved by the owner, and the value of a biological agent is the value of freedom from illness.

In general usage, asset value is expressed in dollars because dollars are a common denominator. Material assets, if stolen, can be assigned a value according to replacement price; if material assets are damaged, value is determined by repair cost. Injury to or death of a human asset also can be measured in dollars. The variables would include the nature of the injury (loss of a limb, for example), age of the victim at time of death, number of years the person would have been able to work, projected income during that period, pain and suffering, loss of conjugal relations, and other variables.

The VA Model

The VA is a logical, systematic approach that proceeds step-by-step. The steps are:

- Select the investigator
- State the objectives
- Identify critical assets
- Characterize threat
- Identify current capabilities
- Identify missing capabilities

- Recommend corrective measures
- Implement the measures

Select the Investigator

In most instances, one investigator can conduct the VA. When the VA is expected to be complicated or lengthy, more than one investigator should be assigned.

The decision to hire an investigator to conduct a VA is made by the owner/operator of the business or organization. Organizations of all types and sizes conduct VA and for different reasons. The usual reasons are a need to protect against theft of high-value items, damage to property, and injury/death of people.

The VA can begin ahead of time. Descriptive and explanatory documents given to the investigator in advance can provide a "running start" and reduce the length of the learning curve. Much time can be saved if the investigator begins VA with some understanding of the organization to be assessed.

State the Objectives

The owner or operator tells the investigator:

- The dates the investigator is to start and end VA
- To confirm (or refute) what the owner/operator believes to be critical assets
- To identify weaknesses in the protection of the critical assets
- Make recommendations to eliminate the weaknesses
- Make recommendations to implement new protections
- Provide a written report at the conclusion of VA

Identify Critical Assets

Let's define assets from bottom to top. At the bottom level are nonessential assets such as office supplies and furniture. At the mid-level are essential assets such as tools, machinery, and computer equipment. Assets at the top level are:

- People, especially people essential to operations and to business continuity
- Those things that, if stolen, damaged, or destroyed, would shut the enterprise down and, in the worst case scenario, produce extremely consequential damage to outside people or entities
- Lethal materials, such as chemical agents
- Materials that have high monetary value, such as cash and gold

In short, top-level assets are critical assets.

How does the investigator get to the point where judgments can be made as to what, and what is not, a critical asset? The process is not unlike conducting a criminal investigation. For example:

- **Interview the owner/operator.** The person in charge of operations will know what is critical. But don't bet on it.
- **Interview knowledgeable persons.** Interviewees can be employees, contractors, vendors, and people working in external support agencies such as police, fire, and emergency medical service. An excellent source can be janitors and maintenance personnel who work during evening hours.
- **Look at the site from the outside.** Enter the site during normal and nonworking hours, at night and early in the morning, and during one or more weekends. Determine the potential criminal's route to, from, in, and away from the site.
- **Acquire relevant documents.** Relevant documents identify and describe critical assets. Such documents can be organizational charts, policies, plans, procedures, schematics, interview statements, maps, notes, sketches, photos, video recordings, and agreements with outside parties

such as law enforcement and emergency responders.

Characterize Threat

This section addresses crime, although VA has application to other human-related events, such as accidents and mistakes in judgment as well as nature-related events, such as hurricanes and earthquakes. The focus here is on crime and using the VA as a tool to prevent it.

A threat is an event that has a potential to cause theft of or damage to an asset. Specific naming and characterization of potential crime is a murky endeavor at best. Names of criminals and criminal methods become known after the fact; what is potential becomes real and recognizable. Arrests, mug shots, fingerprints, and DNA are characteristics on file with law enforcement. Examination of files can reveal the cause (the criminal) and effect (the loss).

Four factors can be used to characterize criminal threat:

- **Existence.** Does the threat actually exist? Is there evidence to pinpoint the "who" involved in criminal activity? What has the threat done in the recent past? Where and how many times? When did the most recent event occur, where, and against what target?
- **Territory and Time.** Where is the "home base" located? Is there a particular area where the crimes occur? Do the crimes occur at particular times or within a particular span of time?
- **Capability.** What does the criminal threat possess? Tools? Weapons? Manpower? Skill? Knowledge? Resolve? Determination? What tactics were used and to what degree of success?
- **Target.** Does the criminal focus on specific assets such as money, jewelry, boats, automobiles, or merchandise?

Identify Current Protective Capabilities

The next step in VA is to evaluate resistance of the facility to crime. For example, the potential criminal may be planning to steal, damage, or destroy a critical asset. The essential question to be asked is, "Does the facility currently have all the capabilities needed to prevent a successful attack?" If the answer is no, a vulnerability has been identified.

A missing capability is vulnerability, and vulnerability is a weakness that can be exploited by the criminal. A simple way to identify missing capabilities is to compare current capabilities against required capabilities.

Identify Current Capabilities

In this step, the investigator evaluates protective measures already in place. These measures can include:

- **Guards.** Weaknesses in this protective measure would be no guard or not enough guards, untrained guards, poorly supervised guards, and procedures that do not exist or are not followed.
- **Perimeter fencing.** A fence may not exist when it is needed; the fence may be non-resistant to penetration or in need of repair.
- **Security lighting.** Outdoor lights may not exist where they are needed, the strength of illumination may not be adequate, placement of the lights may not be adequate, or lights may be in need of repair.
- **CCTV.** Weaknesses here could be insufficient illumination to permit adequate viewing, defective monitors, lack of someone to watch the monitors, or cameras that are in need of repair or replacement.
- **Detection sensors.** Sensors, if used, should work in all conditions (bad weather, extreme temperature, loud noise, etc.),

activate when intrusion occurs, and connect to a place and person trained to respond.

- **Access control.** High-value items are usually located indoors. The movement of persons entering indoor locations and moving within should be checked for access authority.
- **Use of locks.** The investigator should physically examine locks to evaluate resistance to attack, guarantee that issuance of keys to locks are limited on a "right to possess" basis, ensure that keys to locks are not duplicated without permission, and make sure that locks are consistently accounted for.

The above capabilities (or lack thereof) are suggested; they are not necessarily the only capabilities. It is possible that an organization will have different or varying capabilities.

Identify Missing Capabilities

Now is the moment for comparison. The investigator has determined what is needed to protect the asset; has determined what is not in use; and, from a comparison of the two, has identified what is needed.

Recommend Corrective Measures

Corrective measures are submitted in a written report. The format of the report is chosen by the investigator or specified by the owner/operator. Attached to the report should be pertinent documents, i.e., those that describe the assets to be protected; the criminal threat; protective measures needed; protective measures not in place;

and recommendations, that if implemented, will eliminate or reduce risk of loss. (Among examples of pertinent documents are written policies, plans, and procedures; diagrammatic layouts of the facility and systems; and photographs, video recordings, and maps. Documents not attached to the written report are placed in a case file. The case file belongs to the owner/operator.)

Recommendations should:

- **Be concise.** Concise means avoiding unnecessary comments.
- **Be realistic.** Realistic means staying within the boundaries of what is possible.
- **Be logical.** Logical means linking corrective measures so that one recommendation will lay the foundation for the next measure.
- **Be written in the past tense.** Do not use first tense, such as "I noticed."
- **Present a timetable.** Show the number of days required to implement a recommendation and the order of implementation.
- **Show availability and cost.** If the owner/operator desires, the investigator can provide the names of companies that sell physical safeguards and the costs of the safeguards.

Implement the Measures

Technically, this step is not a step of the VA process. It is a step taken by the owner/operator. The investigator should not expect that the recommended measures will be implemented in whole or in part.

John J. Fay

W

WARRANTLESS BEEPER

Connected to a device called a "beeper," the Global Positioning System (GPS) can be used to track the movement of people and things. Movement of the beeper is displayed as dots on a map-like screen.

In general application, people can be children, persons suffering from amnesia and dementia, and nannies caring for babies; things can be cash, bonds and jewelry, valuable cargo in transit, expensive vehicles, watercraft and aircraft, and many, many other things that merit protection.

In private investigation, a beeper is typically attached to an item carried by a person of interest or to a motor vehicle in which the person is riding. A person of interest could be a spouse suspected of cheating, a person suspected of having filed a false workers' compensation claim, or an employee using the employer's vehicle for a nonbusiness purpose.

A common type of beeper is a magnetic device that can be quickly and surreptitiously attached to the undercarriage of a motor vehicle that transports the suspect. In this mode, the beeper is a surveillance tool.

When the word "warrantless" appears before the word "beeper" there is a connotation that criminal activity is the reason for use of the beeper and that the users are public law enforcement officers. Even when a warrant authorizes use of a beeper, there can a question about the rights of the person being tracked. In 2012, the U.S. Supreme Court ruled that use of a GPS tracking device is a search and is therefore subject to provisions of the Fourth Amendment to the Constitution. In the case ruled upon, a drug trafficking case, the police obtained a beeper warrant for the purpose of obtaining information, but in the manner of carrying out the warrant, the police violated the suspect's reasonable expectation of privacy.

There is a message here: private investigators that use beepers can be accused of trespass and invasion of privacy violations.

John J. Fay

WARRANTLESS SEARCHES

A search without a warrant can be considered reasonable if it is conducted in certain situations.

Search Incidental to Arrest

There being insufficient time to obtain a search warrant when a person is arrested, a search of the person may be done. The search can be made of the person and of items in the possession of the person or in the immediate surroundings. The search is intended to discover the presence of weapons or items that can harm the arresting person or other persons. A search at the time of arrest is mainly directed toward this consideration. A secondary consideration is to see if the arrestee possesses material connected to a crime.

Emergency Search

When reasonable cause exists to believe that material subject to seizure is located at a certain place and it is believed that the material will be taken from that place to an unknown place before a warrant can be obtained, a search can be conducted. Material subject to seizure varies and includes: drugs, explosives, and weapons that are illegal; stolen property; and goods that can be destroyed, consumed, or hidden.

An emergency search is proper when a crime has been committed and the material seized is directly related to the crime.

Search with Consent

Consent to search is proper when it is freely and intelligently given. Consent cannot be obtained through the use of threats or trickery. The person giving permission to the search must be able to recognize the potential consequences of the search. A person who is too young, too old, too drunk, mentally handicapped, ill, or insane cannot intelligently give consent. Also, mere submission or giving in to a request for consent is not the same as giving a free consent. In order to demonstrate that consent to search was freely and intelligently given, the investigator should obtain the consent in writing. The writing itself, the words used, and the physical act of writing help to demonstrate that the consent was properly obtained.

Consent is proper when it is obtained from a person who has a right to give consent. For example, a hotel manager cannot give consent to search a paying guest's hotel room, and a person sharing an apartment cannot give consent to a search of another person's property within the apartment.

Learning Shop USA, Search and Seizure, www.learningshopusa.com

WEAPONS SAFETY AND NOMENCLATURE

The National Rifle Association (NRA) provides the following rules with respect to weapons safety.

The Target and Beyond

The shooter must be absolutely sure the target is identified beyond any doubt. Equally important is an awareness of the area beyond the target. This means observing the prospective area of fire before shooting. Never fire in a direction in which there are people or any other potential for mishap. Think first. Shoot second.

Operation

The person handling a gun must know how it operates, such as knowing its basic parts, how to safely open and close the action, and how to remove any ammunition from the gun or magazine. A gun's mechanical safety device is never foolproof. Nothing can ever replace safe gun handling.

Maintenance

Just like other tools, guns need regular maintenance to remain operable. Regular cleaning and proper storage are a part of the gun's general upkeep. If there is any question concerning a gun's ability to function, a knowledgeable gunsmith should look at it.

Correct Ammunition

Only BBs, pellets, cartridges, or shells designed for a particular gun can be fired safely in that gun. Most guns have the ammunition type stamped on the barrel. Ammunition can be identified by information printed on the box and sometimes stamped on the cartridge.

Eye and Ear Protection

Guns are loud, and the noise can cause hearing damage. They can also emit debris and hot gas that could cause eye injury. For these reasons, shooting glasses and hearing protectors should be worn by shooters and spectators.

Alcohol or Other Drugs

Any substance likely to impair normal mental or physical bodily functions must not be used before or while handling or shooting guns.

Unauthorized Persons

Many factors must be considered when deciding where and how to store guns. A person's particular situation will be a major part of the consideration. Dozens of gun storage devices, as well as locking devices that attach directly to the gun, are available. However, mechanical locking devices, like the mechanical safeties built into guns, can fail and should not be used as a substitute for safe gun handling and the observance of all gun safety rules.

Cleaning

Regular cleaning is important in order for a gun to operate correctly and safely. A gun should be cleaned following every time it has been fired. A gun brought out of prolonged storage should also be cleaned before shooting. Accumulated moisture and dirt, or solidified grease and oil, can prevent the gun from operating properly.

Locks

Gun safety for situations where firearms are not in use is intended to prevent access to and subsequent discharge of a firearm. Preventing access to firearms can serve a double purpose in that it can also protect the firearm from theft. Access to a functioning firearm can be prevented by keeping the firearm disassembled and the parts stored at separate locations. Ammunition may also be stored away from the firearm. Sometimes this rule is codified in law.

There are several types of locks that serve to make it difficult to discharge a firearm. Such locks are commonly designed so they cannot be forcibly removed without permanently disabling the firearm. Locks are considered less effective than keeping firearms stored in a lockable safe since locks are more easily defeated than approved safes. In addition, while gun locks may prevent a stolen firearm from being discharged, they cannot prevent the theft itself.

Trigger Locks. Trigger locks prevent motion of the trigger. However, a trigger lock does not guarantee that the firearm cannot be discharged. Some trigger locks are integrated into the design of the weapon, requiring no external parts besides the key.

Chamber Locks. Chamber locks aim to block ammunition from being chambered since most firearms typically cannot be discharged unless the ammunition is in the correct position.

Cable Locks. Cable locks are a popular type of chamber lock that usually threads through the breech and ejection port of repeating-action firearms; they generally prevent full cycling of the action, especially preventing a return to "battery," with the breech fully closed. In many designs of pistol and rifle, they also prevent the proper insertion of a magazine.

Misfires

Though firearms and their ammunition are made to exacting specifications and tolerances and designed to function reliably, malfunctions of firearms and ammunition do happen. Malfunctions of the primer and/or powder within a cartridge are colloquially known as "misfires" and include failures to discharge (duds), delayed discharge (hang-fires), and incomplete or insufficient discharge (squibs).

Mechanical malfunctions of the firearm are generally referred to as "jams" and include failures to feed, extract, or eject a cartridge; failure to fully cycle after firing; and failure of a recoil- or gas-operated firearm to lock back when empty (largely a procedural hazard, as "slide lock" is a visual cue that the firearm is empty). In the extreme, an overloaded round, blocked barrel, poor design, and/or severely weakened breech can result in an explosive failure of the receiver, barrel, or other parts of the firearm.

When a misfire or jam occurs, gun safety dictates that the handler should exercise extreme caution, as a cartridge whose primer has been struck in a misfire or deformed in a jam can discharge unexpectedly. The handler should wait two minutes with the firearm pointed in a safe direction, then carefully remove the magazine, extract any misfed or misfired cartridge, and, with the breech open, carefully check to ensure there is not a bullet or other obstruction lodged in the barrel. If there is, and a subsequent round is fired, the firearm can fail explosively, resulting in serious injury.

Accidental Discharge

Accidental discharge is the event of a firearm discharging (firing) at a time not intended by the user. Perhaps most commonly, accidental discharges (sometimes called ADs by military and police personnel and referred to as negligent discharges by several armies) occur when the trigger of the firearm is deliberately pulled for a purpose other than shooting—dry-fire practice, demonstration, or function testing—but ammunition is mistakenly left in the chamber. Unintentionally leaving a firearm loaded is more likely to occur when the individual handling the gun is poorly trained and perhaps also with removable-magazine-fed firearms (the magazine may be removed, giving an unloaded appearance even when a round remains chambered—see discussion of magazine safeties below).

A second common cause of accidental discharges is when the gun handler places his finger on the trigger before he has decided to shoot. With the finger so positioned, many activities may cause the finger to compress the trigger unintentionally. For example, if one attempts to holster the firearm with finger on trigger, the holster edge will drive the finger onto the trigger, and discharge is likely. If one stumbles or struggles (with an adversary) with finger on trigger, the grasping motion of both hands will likely cause the trigger finger to compress the trigger.

On occasion, an accidental discharge can occur by means other than the finger pulling the trigger, such as dropping a loaded weapon. Because of this possibility, most currently produced pistols are designed with a "drop-safety" or firing pin block, a mechanism inhibiting or isolating the firing pin, preventing accidental discharge if the firearm is dropped. However, most long guns do not have drop safeties.

Prevention of dropped long guns therefore depends on the user being familiar with the precautions needed for that particular gun: it is standard practice for all long-gun users to unload the firearm's chamber before any activity that might result in a dropped firearm (e.g., climbing a fence while hunting) and before placing the firearm in a vehicle (where sudden deceleration may cause the firearm to act as if dropped).

Accidental discharges not involving trigger pull can also occur if the firearm is mechanically unsound: poor maintenance, abuse, inept "gunsmithing," or the use of substandard materials or defective ammunition in the gun may all lead to breakage.

A relevant discussion attends the use of magazine safeties in semiautomatic pistols. Such safeties prevent the pistol from firing if there is a round in the chamber, but the magazine is removed. Some self-defense experts dislike this feature, as it may allow the pistol to be "disabled" unexpectedly during a struggle, causing the pistol to fail when needed. Others feel that it may improve user safety and prevent some accidental discharges. Both semiautomatic pistol designs, with and without magazine safeties, are currently manufactured.

One last form of accidental discharge, known as cooking off, occurs when a weapon becomes overheated; the firing chamber becomes hot enough to ignite the propellant charge in the ammunition round, causing the cartridge to fire.

"Cooking off" is typically encountered only in fully automatic weapons, such as machine guns, when they are fired for long periods of time without allowing the barrel and chamber of the weapon to cool down to safe temperatures. For this reason, modern crew-served machine guns are equipped with spare barrels to allow a machine gun crew to replace an overheated barrel with a cool one, thus restoring the weapon to action while the overheated barrel is allowed to cool. Also, the majority of machine guns fire from an open bolt, so the round is chambered only after pressing the trigger, just before firing.

Safeties

Safeties can generally be divided into subtypes, such as internal safeties, that do not receive input from the user and external safeties that allow the user to give input, such as toggling a lever from "on" to "off" or something similar. Sometimes these are called "passive" and "active" safeties or "automatic" and "manual" safeties.

Integral Safety. Some firearms manufactured after the late 1990s include mandatory integral locking mechanisms that must be deactivated by a unique key before the gun can be fired. These integral locking mechanisms are intended as child-safety devices during unattended storage of the firearm—not as safety mechanisms while carrying. Other devices in this category are trigger locks, bore locks, and gun safes.

Switch Safety. The most common form of safety mechanism is a switch that, when set to the "safe" position, prevents a pull of the trigger from firing the firearm. Designs of such safeties are as varied as the designs of firearms themselves, but the two most common mechanisms are a block or latch that prevents the trigger and/or firing mechanism from moving and a device that disconnects the trigger from the firing mechanism of the firearm. These are the oldest forms of "active" safety mechanism and are widely used; however, many "double-action" firearms such as revolvers do not have manual safeties as the longer, harder trigger pull to cock and fire double-action firearms provides adequate trigger safety, while keeping the firearm in a more ready state.

Grip Safety. A grip safety is a lever or other device situated on the grip of a firearm that must be actuated by the operator's hand, as a natural consequence of holding the firearm in a firing position, in order for the firearm to fire. It is usually similar to a manual safety in its function but is momentary; the safety is deactivated only while the shooter maintains their hold on the grip and is reactivated immediately once the shooter releases it.

Decocker. Semiautomatic pistols are designed to be carried with the hammer down (uncocked) on a chambered round, with or without a manual safety engaged. The pistol is considered safe in this state as the "double-action" pull that both cocks and fires the firearm is both longer and heavier than the "single-action" pull that simply releases the cocked hammer. However, the act of "cycling" the action on such a firearm (as a natural consequence of discharging the firearm or to chamber the first round) will leave the hammer cocked. To return the pistol to its safe state, it is necessary to "decock" the hammer; this is traditionally done by holding the hammer spur, pulling the trigger, and then slowly lowering the hammer. This process is dangerous if done carelessly or in adverse conditions, and it violates the third rule of gun safety: "Keep your finger off the trigger until you wish to fire."

A decocker or manual decocking lever allows the hammer to be dropped on a live cartridge without risk of discharging it, usually by blocking the hammer or retracting or covering the firing pin before releasing the sear. This eliminates the need to control the fall of the hammer, although since all mechanisms can fail, it is still necessary to keep the muzzle of the gun pointed in a safe direction while operating the decocker.

Drop Safety. A drop safety, as the name implies, is designed to reduce the chance of a firearm accidentally discharging when it is dropped or roughly handled. Such safeties generally provide an obstacle to proper operation of the firing mechanism that is only removed when the trigger is pulled, meaning any other possible cause of the firearm discharging is generally prevented.

Safety Notch. The safety notch is a relief cut made in the tumbler that is connected mechanically to the hammer that allows the sear to catch and hold the hammer a short distance from the pin or cartridge primer in a "half-cocked" position. The safety notch works first by allowing the handler to retract the hammer a short distance from the firing pin or primer, such that dropping the firearm on its hammer will not result in an energy transfer to the pin or spur, which could then discharge a chambered cartridge.

A second purpose is to allow the sear to "catch" a hammer that is falling when the trigger has not been pulled, such as in cases where a drop jarred the sear loose or when the hammer was not fully cocked before being released. However, a safety notch used to "half-cock" a firearm is an active feature that must be engaged, and a safety notch does not positively prevent accidental discharges in all cases. A certain amount of manual dexterity and familiarity with a firearm is also required to "half-cock" a firearm; unfamiliarity with how to engage the "half-cock" position can result in accidental discharges.

Firing-Pin Block. A firing pin block is a mechanical block used in semiautomatic firearms and some revolvers that, when at rest, obstructs forward travel of the firing pin but is linked to the trigger mechanism and clears the obstruction to the pin just before the hammer or striker is released. This prevents the firing pin from striking a chambered cartridge unless the trigger is pulled, even if the hammer is released due to a faulty sear or the pin is dropped or struck by another object.

Hammer Block. A hammer block is similar to a firing pin block. It is a latch, block, or other obstruction built into the action and normally positioned to prevent the hammer contacting the cartridge primer or firing pin when at rest. Similar to the firing pin block, the obstruction to the hammer's travel is removed as a consequence of pulling the trigger. This allows the hammer to contact the primer or firing pin only when the trigger is pulled.

Transfer Bar. A transfer bar is also used in revolvers but works the opposite way from a hammer block. The transfer bar, in a firearm so equipped, features the spur that would otherwise be found on the hammer or encloses a firing pin similar to autoloading designs. The hammer itself cannot contact a loaded cartridge; it must instead strike the transfer bar, which then contacts the cartridge primer with the spur or pin. The transfer bar is normally positioned out of line with the hammer's travel but is moved into place by the normal action of the trigger, providing similar "drop safety" to a firing pin block.

Bolt Interlock and Trigger Disconnect. Popular on bolt, pump, and lever-action firearms such as shotguns and rifles, a bolt interlock disengages or blocks the trigger if, for any reason, the bolt/breech is not in its fully closed, ready position. A variation is the trigger disconnect, which prevents the gun from firing until the gun has not only been fully and completely cycled but the trigger is released and squeezed again. This defines the behavior of semiautomatic firearms that require a separate trigger pull to fire each successive cartridge and ready the next, and this is the preferred mechanism of disengaging the trigger on repeating-action firearms.

Magazine Disconnect. A magazine disconnect is an internal mechanism that engages a mechanical safety such as a block or trigger disconnect when the firearm's magazine is removed.

Integrated Trigger Safety. These safeties, similar to grip safeties, are deactivated as a natural consequence of the shooter firing the firearm but are engaged in most other circumstances. The trigger is composed of two interdependent parts, and the shooter, in firing the firearm, manipulates both parts of the trigger. Conversely, unintentional pressure or a strike against the trigger is unlikely to do so, and such an action will not fire the firearm.

Other designs include a spring-loaded pad that forms the upper portion of the trigger face and manipulates a similar lock. This design has more moving parts but is advantageous in that accidental pressure on the lock release has reduced leverage, thus requiring more force to pull the main trigger, where force against the lower portion does not release the lock and will not move the trigger.

Single-Action Revolver Safety. Single-action revolvers have no external safeties, and they usually have no internal safeties, such as a hammer block or transfer bar, to render them drop-safe. Most single action revolvers have a half-cock "safety" notch on the hammer, but many of these are not drop-proof. Real antiques are in this category; modern replicas may have internal hammer blocks. Therefore, carrying them with a loaded chamber under the hammer is not safe. When they are carried (concealed or openly), the hammer should be left down on an empty chamber.

However, some single-action revolvers have relief cuts in between cylinder bores that allow the hammer to be laid to rest directly upon the cylinder with no chance of interacting with loaded cartridges or primers. These are also known colloquially as "safety notches." They are usually found on black powder revolvers, but there are cartridge-firing revolvers that utilize safety notches as well.

Double-Action Revolver Safety. On almost all double-action revolvers, there are no external safety devices; a trigger pull will always result in firing. In general, the heavy trigger pull required to cock and fire prevents accidental discharges from dropping or mishandling the gun. In addition to that fact, most modern double-action revolvers do have an internal safety, either a hammer block or a transfer bar, that prevents firing not originating from a trigger pull (e.g., gun is dropped). The only double-action revolvers with external safeties are unusual cases available only on special order or modified through aftermarket conversions.

Shotgun Safeties. Common manual safeties for shotguns include button safeties located near or in front of the trigger guard and tang safeties located at the top rear (or "tang") of the receiver. Button safeties are either left- or right-handed, but tang safeties are ambidextrous.

Shotguns

A shotgun (also known as a scattergun and peppergun, or historically as a fowling piece) is a firearm that is usually designed to be fired from the shoulder, which uses the energy of a fixed shell to fire a number of small spherical pellets called shot or a solid projectile called a slug. Shotguns come in a wide variety of sizes, ranging from .2 inch bore up to 2 inch bore.

A shotgun is generally a smoothbore firearm, which means that the inside of the barrel is not rifled.

Shotguns are widely used as support weapons. One of the rationales for issuing shotguns is that, even without much training, a person will probably be able to hit targets at close to intermediate range due to the "spreading" effect of buckshot. This is mainly a myth due to the fact that the spread of buckshot at 25 feet averages eight inches, being very capable of missing a target.

Shotgun Pellets

The shot pellets from a shotgun spread upon leaving the barrel, and the power of the burning charge is divided among the pellets, which means that the energy of any one ball of shot is fairly low. In an enforcement context, the large number of projectiles makes the shotgun useful as a defensive weapon.

The disadvantages of shot are limited range and limited penetration, which is why shotguns are used at short ranges and typically against smaller targets. Larger shot size, up to the extreme case of the single-projectile slug load, results in increased penetration but at the expense of fewer projectiles and lower probability of hitting the target.

Aside from the most common use against small, fast moving targets, the shotgun has several advantages when used against still targets. First, it has enormous stopping power at short range, more than nearly all handguns and many rifles. Though many believe the shotgun is a great firearm for inexperienced shooters, the truth is, at close range, the spread of shot is not very large at all, and competency in aiming is still required. A typical self-defense load of buckshot contains 8–27 large lead pellets, resulting in many wound tracks in the target. Also, unlike a fully jacketed rifle bullet, each pellet of shot is less likely to penetrate walls and hit bystanders. It is favored for its low penetration and high stopping power.

On the other hand, the hit potential of a defensive shotgun is often overstated. The typical defensive shot is taken at very close ranges, at which the shot charge expands no more than a few centimeters. This means the shotgun must still be aimed at the target with some care. Balancing this is the fact that shot spreads further upon entering the target, and the multiple wound channels of a defensive load are far more likely to produce a disabling wound than a rifle or handgun.

Compared to handguns, shotguns are heavier, larger, and not as maneuverable in close quarter, but they do have these advantages:

- They are generally much more powerful.
- The average shooter can engage multiple targets faster than with a handgun.
- They are generally perceived as more intimidating.

On average, a quality pump-action shotgun is generally less expensive than a quality handgun (self-loading shotguns are generally more expensive than their pump-action counterparts).

Shotguns are, in general, not as heavily regulated by legislation as handguns.

When loaded with smaller shot, a shotgun will not penetrate walls as readily as rifle and pistol rounds, making it safer for noncombatants when fired in or around populated structures. This comes at a price, however, as smaller shot may not penetrate deeply enough to cause an immediately incapacitating wound; those who recommend birdshot for minimizing wall penetration also suggest backing it up with a larger buckshot if the first shot fails to stop the threat.

Types of Shotguns

Riot Gun. The riot gun has long been a synonym for a shotgun, especially a short-barrel shotgun. The wide spray of the shot ensures more wounds than fatalities. The introduction of rubber bullets and bean bag rounds ended the practice of using shot for the most part, but riot shotguns are still used to fire a variety of less lethal rounds.

Sawed-Off Shotgun. A sawed-off shotgun refers to a shotgun whose barrel has been shortened, leaving it more maneuverable, easier to use at short range. and more readily concealed.

Coach Gun. Coach guns are similar to sawed-off shotguns, except they are manufactured with an 18" barrel and are often used for hunting in bush, scrub, or marshland where a longer barrel would be unwieldy or impractical.

Backpacker Shotgun. A backpacker shotgun has a short barrel and either a full-size stock or pistol grip. The overall length of these weapons is frequently less than 36 inches, with some measuring 25 inches. Backpacker shotguns are popular for "home defense" purposes and as "survival" weapons.

Shotgun Pattern and Choke

Pattern. As shot leaves the barrel, it begins to disperse in the air. The resulting cloud of pellets is known as the shot pattern. The ideal pattern would be a circle with an even distribution of shot throughout, with a density sufficient to ensure enough pellets will intersect the target to achieve the desired result.

Choke. A constriction in the end of the barrel known as the choke is used to tailor the pattern for different purposes. Chokes may either be formed as part of the barrel at the time of manufacture by squeezing the end of the bore down or by threading the barrel and screwing in an interchangeable choke tube. The choke typically consists of a conical section that smoothly tapers from the bore diameter down to the choke diameter, followed by a cylindrical section of the choke diameter.

Shotgun Barrel Length

Shotguns generally have longer barrels than modern rifles. Unlike rifles, however, the long shotgun barrel is not for ballistic purposes; shotgun shells use small powder charges in large diameter bores, and this leads to very low muzzle pressures and very little velocity change with increasing barrel length.

Shotguns made for close ranges, where the angular speed of the target is great, tend to have shorter barrels, around 24 to 28 inches. Shotguns for longer range shooting, where angular speeds are less, tend to have longer barrels, 28 to 34 inches. The longer barrels swing more slowly but more steadily. The short barrels swing faster but are less steady.

Shotshells

Shotshells are the most commonly used projectiles, filled with lead or lead substitute pellets. Of this general class, the most common subset is birdshot, which uses a large number (from dozens to hundreds) of small pellets, meant to create a wide "kill spread." Shotshells are described by the size and number of the pellets within and numbered in reverse order (the smaller the number, the bigger the pellet size).

Buckshot

Buckshot is similar to but larger than birdshot and was originally designed for hunting larger game, such as deer (hence the name). Buckshot is still the most common choice for police, military, and home defense uses.

A typical round for defensive use would be a 12-gauge buck shell, which contains nine pellets roughly .33 inch in diameter, comparable to a .38 Special bullet in damage potential. New "tactical" buckshot rounds, designed specifically for defensive use, use slightly less shot at lower velocity to reduce recoil and increase controllability of the shotgun. There are some shotgun rounds designed specifically for police use that shoot effectively from 50 yards with a 20" diameter grouping of the balls.

Slug Round

Slug rounds are rounds that fire a single, solid slug. They are used in certain military and law enforcement applications. Modern slugs are moderately accurate, especially when fired from specially rifled slug barrels.

Sabots

Sabots are a common type of slug round. While some slugs are exactly that—a 12-gauge metal projectile in a cartridge—a sabot is a smaller but a more aerodynamic projectile surrounded by a "shoe" of some other material. This jacket seals the barrel, increasing pressure and acceleration, while also inducing spin on the projectile in a rifled barrel. Once the projectile clears the barrel, the sabot material falls away, leaving an unmarked, aerodynamic bullet to continue toward the target. The advantages over a traditional slug are increased shot power, increased bullet velocity due to the lighter-mass bullet, and increased accuracy due to the velocity and the reduction in deformation of the slug itself.

Less Lethal Rounds

Flexible Baton Round. Flexible baton rounds, commonly called bean bags, fire a fabric bag filled with birdshot or a similar loose, dense substance. The 'punch' effect of the bag is useful for knocking down targets; the rounds are used to subdue violent suspects. The bean bag round is by far the most common less lethal round used. Due to the large surface area of these rounds, they lose velocity rapidly and must be used at fairly short ranges to be effective, though use at extremely short ranges, under 10 feet, can result in broken bones or other serious or lethal injuries. The rounds can also fly in a Frisbee-like fashion and cut the person being fired upon. For this reason, these types of rounds are referred to as "less lethal," as opposed to less-than-lethal.

Gas Shell. Gas shells spray a cone of gas for several meters. These are primarily used by riot police. They normally contain pepper gas or tear gas. Other variations launch a gas-grenade-like projectile.

Rock Salt Shell. Rock salt shells are hand loaded with rock salt, replacing the standard lead or steel shot. Rock salt shells are the forerunners of modern less lethal rounds.

Rubber Slug. Rubber slugs or rubber buckshot are similar in principle to the bean bag rounds. Composed of flexible rubber or plastic and fired at low velocities, these rounds are probably the most common choice for riot control. Shapes range from full bore diameter cylinders to round balls of varying sizes.

Breaching Round. Breaching rounds, often called Disintegrator or Hatton rounds, are designed to destroy door-locking mechanisms without risking lives.

Bird Bomb. Bird bombs are low-powered rounds that fire a firecracker that is fused to explode a short time after firing. They are designed to scare.

Screecher. Screechers fire a whistle that emits a loud whistling sound for the duration of its flight. These are also used to scare.

Blank Shell. Blank shells contain a small amount of powder and no actual load. When fired, the blanks provide the sound and flash of a real load but with no projectile. These are used for simulation of gunfire.

Stinger. Stinger is a type of shotgun shell that contains balls made of a soft material and is designed as a nonlethal ammunition ideally used in small spaces.

Shotshell Sizes

Shotgun shells are generally measured by gauge or bore. Rifles and handguns are almost always measured in caliber, which is simply a measurement of the internal diameter of the barrel measured in inches and, consequently, is approximately equal to the diameter of the projectile that is fired.

The term "gauge" is the weight, in fractions of a pound, of a pure lead round ball that is the same diameter as the internal diameter of the shotgun barrel. Because gauge vs. weight is expressed inversely, a 10-gauge shotgun has a larger-diameter barrel than a 12-gauge shotgun. The most popular shotgun gauge by far is the 12-gauge.

Shotgun Stocks

Wood. Traditionally, stocks are made from a durable hardwood such as walnut. A growing option is the laminated wood stock, consisting of many thin layers of wood bonded together at high pressures with epoxy, resulting in a dense, stable composite.

Composite. Folding, collapsible, or removable stocks tend to be made from a mix of steel or alloy, for strength and locking mechanisms, and wood or plastics for shape.

Injection-Molded Synthetic. Injection molding produces stocks that are virtually identical in dimension to the wood stock. The downsides are a lack of rigidity and thermal stability, which are side effects of the thermoplastic materials used for injection molding.

Hand-Laid Composite Stock. Hand-laid composite stock is made from materials such as fiberglass, kevlar, and/or graphite cloth, saturated in an appropriate binder and placed in a mold. The resulting stock is stronger and more stable than an injection-molded stock. It can also be as little as half the weight of an injection-molded stock.

Laminated Wood. Laminated wood consists of two or more layers of wood impregnated with glue and attached permanently to each other. The combination of the pieces of wood results in moderating the effects of changes in temperature and humidity.

Metal. Some firearms make use of metal stocks in order to have a strong, thin stock that can be folded away in order to make the weapon more compact. It should be noted that even a skeletal steel stock is often heavier than the equivalent wooden fixed stock.

Speedloaders

Revolver Speedloader. This device is used to load a revolver with loose ammunition very quickly. A speedloader can load all chambers of a revolver simultaneously.

Modern Revolver Speedloader. This device holds a full cylinder complement of cartridges in a secure fashion, spaced in a circular configuration so as to allow the cartridges to drop simultaneously into the cylinder easily. A mechanism is provided that allows the cartridges to be released from the speedloader

when loaded so that when it is removed, the cartridges remain in the cylinder.

Shotgun Speedloader. Shotgun speedloaders are slightly more complex, since shotgun magazines load from the breech. Shotgun speedloaders generally have a special bracket mounted near the magazine loading port; many models mount by replacing existing pins that hold the trigger group in the receiver, so they can be installed easily without permanent modification of the gun. This bracket serves to hold the end of the speedloader tube in the correct position to feed the rounds out of the speedloader and into the magazine.

Pistol Speedloader. The speedloader for a pistol is simply a replacement magazine. The empty magazine can be ejected automatically or manually by pressing a button or lever. The full magazine is inserted in place of the ejected magazine. The location of the magazine is a hollow space inside the pistol grip.

National Rifle Association, http://home.nra.org/

WHITE-COLLAR CRIME

The term "white-collar crime" is a general descriptor that relates broadly to a wide variety of specific crimes. It may take the form of consumer fraud, illegal competition, deceptive practices, check and credit card fraud, tax evasion, bankruptcy fraud, bribes, kickbacks, pay-offs, computer-related crime, pilferage, insurance fraud, fencing stolen property, securities fraud, and many similar offenses. Nearly all offenses are in the larceny category.

The white-collar criminal can be a bank executive who embezzles or a shipping clerk who pilfers. However, the essential characteristic of white-collar crime has more to do with the nature of the offense rather than the status of the offender. It is a nonviolent crime that involves deceit, corruption, or breach of trust. The offense frequently involves lying, cheating, or stealing through misrepresentation. It can be committed against private individuals, business corporations, nonprofit organizations, and government units.

A problem in detecting white-collar crime is the absence of reliable measures for determining if criminal activity is present and to what extent. One difficulty in detecting its presence is the fact that a victim is not aware that he is being victimized; when discovery is made, it may be too late to recover assets stolen and obtain conclusive evidence. This is because the criminal often becomes aware that an investigation is underway and destroys evidence before it can be seized. In a sense, white-collar crime is an invisible crime.

The Nature of White-Collar Crime

In most crimes there is a "crime scene," but with white-collar crime the scene of the theft can be anyplace and ongoing. The usual investigative approach, after there is reason to believe an offense has occurred or is occurring, is to identify the principals by working backward from what is known. This approach is often called following an audit trail.

The general characteristics of white-collar offenses are:

- Detection is frequently accidental.
- Offenses are frequently reported anonymously.
- There is usually no complainant.
- The scheme has been in existence over a long period of time.
- The crime tends to cover a large geographical area, often spanning several prosecutorial jurisdictions.
- The scheme tends to involve several specific violations of law.
- The principals are usually well known, respected, intelligent, and, in some cases, influential.
- The scheme is sometimes difficult to decipher.

- Evidence tends to get "lost or destroyed" when the principal learns that an investigation is in progress.

Types of White-Collar Crime

White-collar crime comes in many shapes and sizes. By name only, these include:

- Advanced fee
- Bid-rigging
- Business opportunity
- Chain referral
- Charity fraud
- Check kiting
- Commercial bribery
- Computer-related fraud
- Corruption of office
- Credit card fraud
- Debt consolidation fraud
- False claims
- False merchandising
- Food stamp fraud
- Fraud against the elderly
- Fraud by claim adjusters
- Fraud by insurance agents
- Fraud by insurance policy holders
- Fraud by organized rings and syndicates
- Home improvement fraud
- Identity theft
- Land sale misrepresentation
- Medical fraud
- Mortgage loan frauds
- Planned bankruptcy
- Ponzi fraud
- Pyramid fraud
- Service and repair fraud
- Welfare fraud

John J. Fay, *Encyclopedia of Security Management*, second ed., Butterworth-Heinemann, Burlington, MA, 2007, pp. 74, 194–199.

WORKERS' COMPENSATION FRAUD

Workers' compensation laws are designed to ensure that employees who are injured or disabled on the job are provided with fixed monetary awards, thereby eliminating the need for litigation. These laws also provide benefits for dependents of those workers who are killed because of work-related accidents or illnesses. Some laws also protect employers and fellow workers by limiting the amount an injured employee can recover from an employer and by eliminating the liability of coworkers in most accidents.

Workers' compensation statutes at the state level establish a framework for most employment. Federal statutes are limited to federal employees or those workers employed in some significant aspect of interstate commerce.

Fraudulent workers' compensation claims are frequent and costly. The victims are employers that purchase workers' compensation insurance and insurance carriers that write the policies. The typical workers' compensation fraud is a faked on-the-job injury. For example, an employee stages an accident or reports an injury-producing event that did not occur, the employee seeks treatment from a medical provider known to have issued suspicious treatment reports on previous occasions or the medical provider validates the alleged injury by relying solely on the employee's representations, and the employee remains out of work while drawing pay.

On occasion, a genuine injury-producing accident will become a scam when the injury is deliberately exaggerated or the recuperation period unnecessarily extended. Less occasionally, the alleged accident will involve multiple claimants. Suspicion is raised when multiple claimants:

- Report similar injuries
- Receive treatment from the same medical provider
- Have similar prognoses
- Are socially connected outside of the workplace
- Hire the same attorney

The medical provider angle can be explored by visiting the place where treatment was provided. The investigator takes note of the sign-in sheet to see if it reflects more entries than customers, if office literature says that rewards can be obtained by referring injured workers, and if the provider has the type of medical equipment necessary to perform the tests for which results are reported.

Liability

Care must be taken not to step over the line when investigating a suspicious claim. Entering onto the property of a claimant to take photographs, for example, may seem like a good idea but at the same time may be trespassing. A claimant has an expectation of privacy that cannot be violated.

Stalking laws can place the investigator in legal hot water. As a general rule of thumb, an investigator gets into trouble in this area when the person being watched is placed in reasonable fear of bodily injury or is caused substantial emotional distress.

Learning Shop USA, Insurance Fraud, www.learningshopusa.com

WORKPLACE VIOLENCE

Workplace violence touches everyone. It affects the way people think, feel, and behave. The threat of workplace violence affects the emotional stability and productivity of employees, and ultimately profitability. Although the incidence of actual physical violence at work is relatively low, workplace violence affects the lives of thousands of innocent Americans each year. These unfortunate and often preventable crimes can destroy people, families, and businesses. Even when the act of aggression is only psychological, it can be painful and costly.

More locks, cameras, and guards are not the answer, however. Employers need strong policies, effective security protocols, and a well-conceived strategy to confront the potentially violent employee and prevent workplace violence.

Employers have a moral duty to provide a safe workplace for their employees. They also have statutory obligations under federal and state law to provide and promote a safe and violence-free work environment. Illustrative of these responsibilities are the requirements under the Occupational Safety and Health Act (OSHA) and state workers' compensation laws. Employers also have responsibilities to the public. Either vicariously or directly, employers may be liable for the harm brought to others by workplace violence. Moreover, employers have additional legal obligations to job applicants.

This intricate web of statutes, standards, rules, and regulations creates a legal minefield for supervisors and managers. Wading through that minefield is precarious at best; employers must protect those employees and other parties without infringing on anyone's rights. Rarely has the challenge for employers been greater. Fortunately, there are solutions.

The Profile of an Aggressor

Research shows that workplace aggressors follow a typical sequence of behavior, called a progression, that in many cases ultimately leads to violence. They usually suffer a traumatic, insoluble (or so they believe) experience, and they project the blame for that experience on others. Egocentric by nature, they believe that everyone is against them and the world is out to get them. Unable to resolve personal, interpersonal, and work-related problems, these individuals typically resort to violence.

Progressions can be detected, though predicting an aggressor's behavior is a considerable challenge. Experts agree that without careful evaluation and analysis it is reckless, if not dangerous, to predict an individual's future behavior. Without the help of an experienced clinician or other qualified professional, it is impossible for the typical supervisor or manager to psychologically assess an emotionally troubled employee and determine his or her fitness for duty. However, many workplace aggressors share certain characteristics. They often relate poorly to people, have difficulty getting along with others, strongly believe they have been wronged, have recently been adversely influenced by something or someone outside of their control, and *have a history of violence* (domestic, public, or workplace).

Though no two aggressors are alike, they share some common characteristics and behaviors:

- Most often male
- Withdrawn and considered a loner
- Owns or is familiar with weapons
- Has few interests outside work
- Self-esteem depends heavily on job
- Strong sense of injustice to self or beliefs
- Externalizes blame, projects
- Poor people skills, difficulty getting along with others
- Has served in the military (or so claims)
- Has a history of substance or alcohol abuse
- History of violence (domestic, public, and work)
- Functions in a "toxic or dysfunctional work environment"

Motivation behind Violence

We are a culture steeped in violence and a society burdened with enormous economic pressures. The threat of a corporate downsizing, restructuring, or layoff looms over many of us. As a result, many have rid themselves of traditional values and chosen to accept less personal responsibility while expecting more from their employers and government. People are afraid and angry. Truly, the sanctity of the workplace is being challenged.

Research reveals that perpetrators of workplace violence generally fall into six motivational categories or typologies. They include:

- Economic. The aggressor believes the target is responsible for undesirable economic conditions affecting him, his family, or a particular group.
- Ideological. The aggressor believes that the target is imperiling principles the attacker considers extremely important.
- Personal. The aggressor possesses distorted feelings of rage, hate, revenge, jealousy, or love.
- Psychological. The aggressor is mentally deranged or clinically psychotic, a condition often exacerbated by drugs or alcohol.
- Revolutionary. The aggressor obsessively desires to further political beliefs at any costs.
- Mercenary. The aggressor is motivated by opportunity for financial gain.

Behavior Changes

However, those who commit workplace violence don't simply snap without warning. Research has shown that aggressors tend to exhibit inappropriate and disruptive behavior prior to committing an act of violence. To the observant supervisor or manager, this behavior serves as a warning sign and allows time for preventative action. Listed below are characteristics and behavior that might signal a potentially violent employee:

- Inappropriate emotional outbursts
- Intense mood swings
- Overreaction to criticism
- Unusual paranoia
- Inappropriate statements or comments
- Rambling, incoherent speech
- Isolation from others
- Volatile, sociopathic personality

- Uncontrollable romantic obsession
- Distorted values
- Devaluation of other people
- Reckless impulsiveness/destructiveness
- Obsessive-compulsive personality
- Exaggerated self-importance and value to the organization

Aggressors generally exhibit several of these behaviors over a period of time. The aggressor tends to display a progression toward violent outburst, with his or her behavior becoming increasingly inappropriate. This incremental escalation, or "ramping up," is typical and should serve as a warning to the supervisor or manager. During progression, the aggressor generally passes through three phases, each one more destructive than the previous:

Phase One

- Refusal to cooperate with supervisor
- Spreads rumors to harm others or cause disruptions
- Is argumentative or resists compromise
- Seems to enjoy being disruptive
- Acts belligerent toward customers and/or clients
- Often uses inappropriate language
- Makes inappropriate comments and/or gestures

Phase Two

- Increasingly argues with others
- Refuses to obey policies/procedures
- Repeatedly probes boundaries
- Engages in subversive and/or manipulative behavior
- Sends inappropriate messages to coworkers or management
- Expresses repeated claims of victimization or mistreatment
- Articulates desire to harm others or self
- Communicates nonverbal and veiled threats

Phase Three

- Sabotages equipment and steals property for revenge
- Threatens suicide and makes references to the afterlife
- Vandalizes private property
- Intentionally destroys company property
- Is physically aggressive or abusive
- Threatens physical violence
- Becomes physically assaultive
- Commits a violent crime

Once set in motion, rarely does a progression reverse without intervention. Supervisors and managers must recognize inappropriate and disruptive behaviors and interrupt the progression before it is too late.

Recognizing and Overcoming Denial

Supervisors, managers, and even companies engage in denial. Supervisors and managers may deny that an employee has a problem, even in the face of irrefutable proof. They may refuse to admit that someone for whom they are responsible could be violent or dangerous to others. They deny the existence of a problem by excusing or overlooking the employee's inappropriate behavior. But by denying the existence of a problem, they are also denying the employee help.

Companies engage in denial by failing to create sound policies, by failing to enforce the policies they have, and by failing to respond to incidents suggesting the potential for violence when they occur. Denial is not only destructive, it is cruel. Out of fear and unwillingness to confront the truth, employers deny the troubled employee the help they need. In so doing, they not only participate in the progression toward violence but also incur what may be immeasurable liability.

Recognizing danger, supervisors and managers must act appropriately and quickly. That action is called intervention.

Redefining Boundaries

Intervention is the process of returning the employee to a structured work environment and helping him regain control of his or her life. To successfully intervene, management must have the will to redefine boundaries and overcome the aggressor's base of power. The intervention process must be well planned and executed. Nothing should be left to chance.

Upon recognizing inappropriate or disruptive behavior, management must act immediately and put the employee on notice. If a progression is identified early enough, the first warning is usually oral. Verbal warnings often suffice to cause behavior changes and halt further aggression. When such warnings are not enough, written warnings should follow. If the progression continues after written warnings are issued, the aggressor may be referred to the company's employee assistance program (EAP) or an outside resource for counseling. Monitoring performance and addressing behaviors is called performance-based management. It provides structure to the work environment while at the same time offering the employee choices.

In extreme cases, progressive discipline and professional counseling may not be enough. Under these circumstances, termination, temporary restraining orders, hospitalization, or prosecution may be the only solutions available.

Threat Management

Intervention is not possible without a well-conceived plan. That plan or strategy is developed and implemented by what is often called the threat (or incident) management team. Depending upon circumstances, the threat management team will consist of professionals from the following areas or disciplines:

- Executive management
- Human resources

- Security/executive protection
- Employment/labor law
- Public law enforcement
- Clinical psychology/psychiatry
- Private investigation
- Incident/crisis management

Though each member of the team has an important role, that of the clinician is probably the most critical. The clinician will typically be a licensed psychological or psychiatric professional, preferably at a PhD or MD level. He or she will have experience in dealing with the criminally insane, conducting hostage negotiations, and handling trauma management. He or she will also be familiar with local and state employment and labor law.

Each team member will be carefully selected. Each should have the necessary skills and experience to make difficult decisions quickly. Once the members are identified, the team will meet and decide on preliminary objectives based on available information. However, the safety of the intended target (if known) always come first. Protection of property, inventory, and equipment is secondary.

Lacking adequate information, the team is often unable to make decisions. When this situation occurs, one or more team members will be assigned to collect the necessary information. That process may involve discreetly interviewing the target, witnesses, coworkers, supervisors, former employers, or family members.

A professional background investigation of the aggressor may also be in order. The typical background investigation includes the detailed examination of the following records:

- Criminal history
- Driving history
- Civil indices
- Notices of default
- Judgments

- Tax liens
- Bankruptcies
- Ownership or registration of weapons

Additionally, the aggressor's personnel file (if available) will be reviewed. Treating physicians, law enforcement officials, and other professionals can also be contacted for additional information whenever possible. As in all employment situations, however, the privacy of all parties should be respected. To ensure that the balance between need and privacy is adequately struck, the team attorney will be consulted during the entire information gathering process.

The assignment of such tasks and the overall coordination of the intervention process is usually the responsibility of human resources. The senior level human resources professional assigned as the coordinator must have the experience and leadership skills necessary to steer the incident management team and facilitate the decision-making process.

After gathering all reasonably available information, the incident management team will review it and make an assessment. That assessment will form the basis for a strategy to deal with the aggressor. With the information available, the team will determine the seriousness of the threat, an appropriate course of action, and possible outcomes. Predicting the future behavior of the aggressor is another matter. As discussed earlier, this complicated task is usually left to experts.

If termination, hospitalization, or prosecution is appropriate, the team will strategize and do all that is practicable to achieve that result without provoking a violent response. Even if management intends to work with the troubled employee, the threat management team must still create a workable strategy. That strategy should redefine performance and behavior boundaries for the aggressor and tolerance thresholds for management.

In summary, the threat management team will, whenever possible:

- Conduct a thorough and comprehensive investigation of the aggressor and the allegations.
- Have the aggressor professionally assessed and determine the potential for violence.
- Decide best course of action with the information available. Options include a variety of disciplinary and/or corrective action, management referral to EAP, discharge, hospitalization, or prosecution.
- Implement all appropriate safety and security precautions, making sure to protect people before property.
- Coordinate with local law enforcement and access all available outside resources.
- Review, rehearse, and refine the plan.
- Review legal implications and potential liability.
- Make contingency plans and communicate with the intended target.
- Meet face-to-face with the aggressor and disclose actions intended by management.
- Determine future safety and security needs.
- Notify law enforcement of outcome.
- Take appropriate legal action (e.g., obtain a restraining order).
- Debrief target and tie up loose ends.
- Provide professional counseling to those in need.
- Hold employee communication sessions. Be frank but respectful of the rights of the target and the aggressor.

The Five-Step Safety Plan

Employees can help protect themselves and their coworkers by exercising the following simple steps:

- Plan head and prepare for the unexpected.
- Treat coworkers with respect and dignity.
- Respect clients and customers.

- Be aware of strangers and surroundings.
- Report inappropriate behaviors and activities.

Prevention

Though an employer cannot be expected to provide an impenetrable island of safety for its employees, supervisors and managers are expected to do as much as possible to promote safety and prevent workplace violence. Employees can de escalate tense situations and avoid conflict. When confronted by a potential aggressor:

- Remain calm.
- Slow down and speak clearly.
- Lower voice.
- Avoid arguing or making threats.
- Don't use hands.
- Use a barrier and create space.
- Get help immediately.
- Report to management or security.

Supervisors and managers must also enforce company policies fairly and consistently and allow employee complaints and grievances to be heard. As mentioned earlier, aggressors follow a typical sequence of behavior. They usually suffer a traumatic, insoluble (or so perceived) experience. They then project the blame for that experience on others. Unable to resolve personal, interpersonal, and work-related problems, these individuals often conclude that their only recourse is violence. Consequently, supervisors and managers must provide employees the opportunity to resolve problems without resorting to violence.

Training and education are also important in creating a safe and violence-free workplace. Employees must understand what is expected of them to create a violence-free work environment. Every employee must also understand that violence or the threat of violence will not be tolerated and that policy violations may result in immediate termination and/or prosecution.

In a nutshell, supervisors and managers should:

- Treat others with respect.
- Observe and document behavior changes.
- Keep human resources informed.
- De escalate tense situations.
- Retreat to safety when necessary.
- Never hesitate to call for help.

Conclusion

According to the Bureau of Labor Statistics report, homicide accounts for 17 percent of all occupational fatalities. More alarming, the report indicates that homicide is the leading cause of occupational fatality for women, accounting for 40 percent of all female deaths in the workplace. And of course, murder is only the tip of the iceberg. Incidents of workplace assault, rape, and psychological abuse occur by the thousands every year.

In conclusion, supervisors and managers must:

- Treat all people with respect and dignity.
- Listen to those who come and seek help.
- Recognize and document inappropriate behaviors.
- Properly enforce company policies.
- Hold subordinates accountable.
- Document performance.
- Keep management and human resources informed.

Eugene F. Ferraro, *Encyclopedia of Security Management*, second ed., Butterworth-Heinemann, Burlington, MA, 2007, pp. 404–408.

Bureau of Alcohol, Tobacco, Firearms, and Explosives

Atlanta Field Division
2600 Century Parkway, Suite 300
Atlanta, GA 30345
Voice: (404) 417-2600
Fax: (404) 417-2601

Baltimore Field Division
31 Hopkins Plaza, 5th Floor
Baltimore, MD 21201
Voice: (443) 965-2000
Fax: (443) 965-2001

Boston Field Division
10 Causeway Street, Suite 791
Boston, MA 02222
Voice: (617) 557-1200
Fax: (617) 557-1201

Charlotte Field Division
6701 Carmel Road, Suite 200
Charlotte, NC 28226
Voice: (704) 716-1800
Fax: (704) 716-1801

Chicago Field Division
525 West Van Buren Street, Suite 600
Chicago, IL 60607
Voice: (312) 846-7200
Fax: (312) 846-7201

Columbus Field Division
230 West Street, Suite 400
Columbus, OH 43215

Voice: (614) 827-8400
Fax: (614) 827-8401

Dallas Field Division
1114 Commerce Street, Room 303
Dallas, TX 75242
Voice: (469) 227-4300
Fax: (469) 227-4330

Denver Field Division
950 17th Street, Suite 1800
Denver, CO 80202
Voice: (303) 575-7600
Fax: (303) 575-7601

Detroit Field Division
1155 Brewery Park Boulevard,
Suite 300
Detroit, MI 48207
Voice: (313) 202-3400
Fax: (313) 202-3445

Houston Field Division
5825 N. Sam Houston Parkway, Suite 300
Houston, TX 77086
Voice: (281) 716-8200
Fax: (281) 716-8219

Kansas City Field Division
2600 Grand Avenue, Suite 200
Kansas City, MO 64108
Voice: (816) 559-0700
Fax: (816) 559-0701

Los Angeles Field Division
550 North Brand Boulevard Suite 800
Glendale, CA 91203
Voice: (818) 265-2500
Fax: (818) 265-2501

Louisville Field Division
600 Dr. Martin Luther King Jr. Place,
Suite 322
Louisville, KY 40202
Voice: (502) 753-3400
Fax: (502) 753-3401

Miami Field Division
11410 NW 20 Street, Suite 201
Miami, FL 33172
Voice: (305) 597-4800
Fax: (305) 597-4801

Nashville Field Division
5300 Maryland Way, Suite 200
Brentwood, TN 37027
Voice: (615) 565-1400
Fax: (615) 565-1401

Newark Field Division
1 Garret Mountain Plaza, Suite 400
Woodland Park, NJ 07424
Voice: (973) 413-1179
Fax: (973) 413-1190

New Orleans Field Division
One Galleria Boulevard, Suite 1700
Metairie, LA 70001
Voice: (504) 841-7000
Fax: (504) 841-7039

New York Field Division
Financial Square
32 Old Slip, Suite 3500
New York, NY 10005
Voice: (646) 335-9000
Fax: (646) 335-9001

Philadelphia Field Division
601 Walnut Street, Suite 1000E
Philadelphia, PA 19106
Voice: (215) 446-7800
Fax: (215) 446-7811

Phoenix Field Division
201 E. Washington Street, Suite 940
Phoenix, AZ 85004
Voice: (602) 776-5400
Fax: (602) 776-5429

San Francisco Field Division
5601 Arnold Road, Suite 400
Dublin, CA 94568
Voice: (925) 557-2800
Fax: (925) 557-2805

Seattle Field Division
915 2nd Avenue, Room 790
Seattle, WA 98174
Voice: (206) 204-3205
Fax: (206) 204-3252

St. Paul Field Division
30 East Seventh Street, Suite 1900
St. Paul, MN 55101
Voice: (651) 726-0200
Fax: (651) 726-0201

Tampa Field Division
400 North Tampa Street, Suite 2100
Tampa, FL 33602
Voice: (813) 202-7300
Fax: (813) 202-7301

Washington, DC Field Division
1401 H. Street NW, Suite 900
Washington, DC 20226
Voice: (202) 648-8010
Fax: (202) 648-8001

Department of Veterans Affairs Criminal Investigation Division

Headquarters
(202) 461-4702

Newark
(973) 297-3338

New York
(212) 951-6850

Massachusetts
(781) 687-3157

New Hampshire
(603) 222-5866

Buffalo
(716) 857-5012

Washington DC
(202) 530-9193

Columbia
(803) 695-6707

Fayetteville
(910) 482-5133

Pittsburgh
(412) 482-6301

St. Petersburg
(727) 319-1215

Atlanta
(404) 929-5950

Nashville
(615) 695-6373

Tallahassee
(850) 656-1145

Chicago
(708) 202-2676

Kansas City
(816) 997-6976

Denver
(303) 331-7674

Cleveland
(216) 522-7606

Dallas
(214) 253-3360

Houston
(713) 383-2793

Little Rock
(501) 257-3446

Jackson
(601) 364-7041

New Orleans
(504) 566-8413

Los Angeles
(310) 268-4269

Phoenix
(602) 627-3257

Las Vegas
(702) 791-9108

San Diego
(858) 404-8332

San Francisco
(510) 637-6360

Seattle
(206) 220-6637

Spokane
(509) 353-0637

Sacramento
(916) 923-4952

Drug Enforcement Administration Offices

Atlanta Division
75 Spring Street, SW, Room 800
Atlanta, GA 30303
Diversion Number: (404) 893-7165
Diversion Fax: (404) 893-7095
Diversion Program Manager Fax: (404)
893-7110
Jurisdiction: Georgia

Savannah Resident Office
56 Park of Commerce Blvd, Suite A
Savannah, GA 31405
Diversion Number: (912) 447-4427
Diversion Fax: (912) 652-4081
Jurisdiction: Eastern Georgia

Dallas Division
10160 Technology Boulevard, East
Dallas, TX 75220
Diversion Number: (214) 366-6900
Diversion Fax: (214) 366-6984
DPM Fax: (214) 366-6902
Jurisdiction: Northern Texas and Oklahoma

Ft. Worth Resident Office
801 Cherry Street, Suite 700
Ft. Worth, TX 76102
Diversion Number: (817) 639-2000
Diversion Fax: (817) 288-1007
Jurisdiction: Northern Texas

Tyler Resident Office
909 East SE Loop 323, Suite 280

Tyler, TX 75701-9665
Diversion Number: (903) 579-2400
Diversion Fax: (903) 579-2415
Jurisdiction: East Texas

Oklahoma City District Office
9900 Broadway Extension
Oklahoma City, OK 73114-6323
Diversion Number: (405) 475-7500
Diversion Fax: (405) 475-7574
Jurisdiction: Oklahoma

Tulsa Resident Office
Three Memorial Place
7615 E. 63rd Place, Suite 250
Tulsa, OK 74133
Diversion Number: (918) 459-9600
Diversion Fax: (918) 459-2570
Jurisdiction: Northeastern Oklahoma

Denver Division
12154 E. Easter Avenue
Centennial, CO 80112-6740
Diversion Number: (720) 895-4231
Diversion Fax: (720) 895-4386
Assistant Special Agent in Charge—David
Schiller
Jurisdiction: Colorado

Billings Resident Office
2970 King Avenue West
Billings, MT 59102
Diversion Number: (406) 655-2900

Diversion Fax: (406) 651-1600
Jurisdiction: Montana

Salt Lake City Resident Office
348 East South Temple
Salt Lake City, UT 84111
Diversion Number: (801) 524-4156
Diversion Fax: (801) 524-6961
Registration Number: (801) 524-4389
Registration Fax: (810) 524-6961
Jurisdiction: Montana, Utah, and Wyoming

Greensboro Resident Office
1801 Stanley Road, Suite 201
Greensboro, NC 27407
Diversion Number: (336) 547-4219
Diversion Fax: (336) 547-4209
Jurisdiction: North Carolina

Columbia District Office
1835 Assembly Street, Suite 1229
Columbia, SC 29201
Diversion Number: (803) 253-3441
Diversion Fax: (803) 253-3163
Jurisdiction: South Carolina

Knoxville Resident Office
1721 Midpark Drive, 3rd Floor
Knoxville, TN 37921
Diversion Number: (865) 584-9364
Diversion Fax: (856) 584-8763
Jurisdiction: Eastern Tennessee

Nashville Resident Office
801 Broadway, Suite 500
Nashville, TN 37203
Diversion Number: (615) 736-2559
Diversion Fax: (615) 736-2558
Jurisdiction: Central and Western Tennessee

Detroit Division
211 W. Fort Street, Suite 610
Detroit, MI 48226
Diversion Number: (313) 226-9876 (Group 12A) or (313) 226-9874 (Group 12B)
Diversion Fax: (313) 226-7545 or (313) 226-7542

Diversion Program Manager Fax: (313) 226-7541
Jurisdiction: Michigan and Northwest Counties in Ohio

Cincinnati Resident Office
36 East 7th Street, Suite 1900
Cincinnati, OH 45202
Diversion Number: (513) 684-3671
Diversion Fax: (513) 684-3080
Jurisdiction: Southern Ohio

Cleveland Resident Office
Courthouse Square
1375 East 9th Street, Suite 700
Cleveland, OH 44114
Diversion Number: (216) 274-3600
Diversion Fax: (216) 664-1307
Jurisdiction: Northern Ohio

Columbus Resident Office
500 South Front Street, Suite 612
Columbus, OH 43215
Diversion Number: (614) 255-4200
Diversion Fax: (614) 469-5788
Jurisdiction: Central and Southern Ohio

London (KY) Resident Office
150 Hal Rogers Drive
London, KY 40744
Diversion Number: (606) 862-4500
Diversion Fax: (606) 862-8296
Jurisdiction: Eastern Counties in Kentucky

Louisville District Office
1006 Federal Building
600 Martin Luther King, Jr. Place
Louisville, KY 40202
Diversion Number: (502) 582-5905
Diversion Fax: (502) 582-6360
Jurisdiction: Western Counties in Kentucky

Houston Division
1433 West Loop South, Suite 600
Houston, TX 77027-9506
Diversion Number: (713) 693-3670
Diversion Fax: (713) 693-3661

Diversion Program Manager Fax: (713) 693-3388
Jurisdiction: Eastern and Southern Texas

Beaumont Resident Office
350 Magnolia Avenue, Suite 290
Beaumont, TX 77701
Diversion Number: (409) 981-7407
Diversion Fax: (409) 839-2551
Jurisdiction: San Augustine, Sabine, Tyler, Jasper, Newton, Liberty, Hardin, Orange, and Jefferson Counties

Mcallen District Office
1200 N. Commerce Center
McAllen, TX 78501
Diversion Number: (956) 992-8400
Diversion Fax: (956) 992-8478
Jurisdiction: Starr, Hildago, Willacy, Cameron, Lavaca, Jackson, Dewitt, Victoria, Calhoun, Goliad, Refugio, Aransas, Bee, San Patricio, Live Oak, Duval, Jim Wells, Nueces, Kleberg, Brooks, and Kennedy Counties

San Antonio District Office
10127 Morocco, Suite 200
San Antonio, TX 78216
Diversion Number: (210) 442-5678
Diversion Fax: (210) 442-5679
Jurisdiction: Central and Western Texas

New England Division
JFK Federal Building
15 New Sudbury Street, Room E-400
Boston, MA 02203
Diversion Number: (617) 557-2191
Diversion Fax: (617) 557-2126
Diversion Program Manager Fax: (617) 557-2279
Jurisdiction: Maine, Massachusetts, Rhode Island, New Hampshire

Hartford Resident Office
716 Brook Street
Rocky Hill, CT 06067
Diversion Number: (860) 257-2601

Diversion Fax: (860) 257-2615
Jurisdiction: Connecticut, Western Massachusetts, and Vermont

Manchester Resident Office
324 South River Road
Bedford, NH 03110
Diversion Number: (603) 628-7411
Diversion Fax: (603) 628-7488
Jurisdiction: Maine and New Hampshire

Providence Resident Office
2 International Way
Warwick, RI 02886
Diversion Number: (401) 732-2550
Diversion Fax: (401) 732-3310
Jurisdiction: Rhode Island

Burlington Resident Office
55 Community Drive, Suite 101
South Burlington, VT 05403
Diversion Number: (802) 951-2900
Diversion Fax: (802) 951-2970
Jurisdiction: Vermont

New York Division
99 Tenth Avenue
New York, NY 10011
Diversion Number: (212) 337-3900
Diversion Program Manager Fax: (212) 337-1536
Jurisdiction: New York (except Albany, Buffalo, and Long Island)

Albany District Office
10 Hastings Drive
Latham, NY 12110
Diversion Number: (518) 782-2000
Diversion Fax: (518) 782-2068
Jurisdiction: Albany, Broome, Chenango, Clinton, Columbia, Cortland, Delaware, Dutchess, Essex, Franklin, Fulton, Greene, Hamilton, Herkimer, Jefferson, Lewis, Madison, Montgomery, Oneida, Onodaga, Oswego, Otsego, Rensselaer, Saratoga, Schenectady, Schoharie, St. Lawrence, Tioga, Ulster, Warren, and Washington Counties

Buffalo Resident Office
535 Washington Street, Suite 500
Buffalo, NY 14203
Diversion Number: (716) 846-6030
Diversion Fax: (716) 843-2154
Jurisdiction: Allegany, Cattaragus,
Chautaqua, Chemung, Erie, Genesee,
Livingston, Monroe, Niagara, Ontario,
Orleans, Schuyler, Seneca, Steuben, Wayne,
Wyoming, and Yates Counties

Long Island District Office
400 Federal Plaza
Central Islip, NY 11722
Diversion Number: (631) 420-4540
Diversion Fax: (631) 420-4551
Jurisdiction: Long Island, NY

Chicago Division
Kluczynski Federal Building
230 South Dearborn Street, Suite 1200
Chicago, IL 60604
Diversion Number: (312) 353-7875
Diversion Fax: (312) 353-1235
Diversion Program Manager Fax: (312)
353-1476
Jurisdiction: Central and Northern Illinois

Springfield Resident Office
2875 Via Verde Street
Springfield, IL 62703
Diversion Number: (217) 585-2751
Diversion Fax: (217) 585-2753
Jurisdiction: Central Illinois

Indianapolis District Office
575 N. Pennsylvania, Room 408
Indianapolis, IN 46204
Diversion Number: (317) 226-7977
Diversion Fax: (317) 226-7703
Registration Number: (317) 610-3152
Registration Fax: (317) 610-3151
Jurisdiction: Indiana

Merrillville Resident Office
1571 East 85th Avenue, Suite 200
Merrillville, IN 46410

Diversion Number: (219) 681-7000
Diversion Fax: (219) 681-7022
Jurisdiction: Northern Indiana

Minneapolis/St. Paul District Office
100 Washington Avenue South, Suite 800
Minneapolis, MN 55401
Diversion Number: (612) 344-4143
Diversion Fax: (612) 348-1968
Registration Number: (612) 344-4136 or
(800) 251-1472
Jurisdiction: Minnesota and North
Dakota

Milwaukee District Office
4725 West Electric Ave
West Milwaukee, WI 53219-1627
Diversion Number: (414) 336-7370
Diversion Fax: (414) 727-5454
Jurisdiction: Wisconsin

El Paso Division
El Paso Federal Justice Center
660 South Mesa Hills Drive, Suite 2000
El Paso, TX 79912
Diversion Number: (915) 231-4300
(Interpretive Services Available)
Diversion Fax: (915) 587-9502
Assistant Special Agent in
Charge—Mark Payne
Jurisdiction: Western Texas and New
Mexico

Albuquerque District Office
2660 Fritts Crossing SE
Albuquerque, NM 87106
Diversion Number: (505) 452-4500
Diversion Fax: (505) 873-9925
Jurisdiction: New Mexico

Los Angeles Field Division
255 East Temple Street, 20th Floor
Los Angeles, CA 90012
Diversion Number: (213) 621-6942
Diversion Fax: (213) 894-3946
Diversion Program Manager Fax: (213)
894-5924

Jurisdiction: South Central California
(Counties of Los Angeles, Ventura, Santa
Barbara, and San Luis Obispo)

Riverside District Office
4470 Olivewood Avenue
Riverside, CA 92501-4155
Diversion Number: (951) 328-6200
Diversion Fax: (951) 328-6210
Jurisdiction: South Central California
(Counties of Orange, Riverside, and San
Bernardino)

Honolulu District Office
P.O. Box 50163
300 Ala Moana, Room 3-147
Honolulu, HI 96850
Diversion Number: (808) 541-1930
Diversion Fax: (808) 541-3048
Jurisdiction: Guam, Hawaii, and
Saipan

Las Vegas District Office
550 S. Main Street, Suite A
Las Vegas, NV 89101
Diversion Number: (702) 759-8110
Diversion Fax: (702) 759-8119
Jurisdiction: Nevada

Miami Field Division
2100 N Commerce Pkwy
Weston, FL 33326
Diversion Number: (954) 306-4650
Diversion Fax: (954) 306-5351
Diversion Program Manager Fax: (954)
306-5352
Jurisdiction: Broward, Miami-Dade, and
Monroe

Ft. Lauderdale District Office
1475 W Cypress Creek Road, Suite 301
Ft. Lauderdale, FL 33309
Diversion Number: (954) 489-1789
Diversion Fax: (954) 489-1903
Jurisdiction: Highland, Indian River,
Martin, Okeechobee, Palm Beach, and
St. Lucie Counties

Jacksonville District Office
4077 Woodcock Drive, Suite 210
Jacksonville, FL 32207
Diversion Number: (904) 348-7415
Diversion Fax: (904) 348-7433
Jurisdiction: Northeast Florida

Orlando District Office
Heathrow Business Center
300 International Parkway, Suite 424
Heathrow, FL 32746
Diversion Number: (407) 333-7046
Diversion Fax: (407) 333-7056
Jurisdiction: Orlando and Gainesville

Tallahassee Resident Office
1510 Commonwealth Business Drive
Tallahassee, FL 32303-3170
Diversion Number: (850) 350-7350
Diversion Fax: (850) 575-0724
Jurisdiction: Northern Florida

Tampa District Office
4950 W. Kennedy Blvd, Suite 400
Tampa, FL 33609
Diversion Number: (813) 287-5160
Diversion Fax: (813) 287-4766
Jurisdiction: West Central Florida

New Jersey Division
80 Mulberry Street, 2nd Floor
Newark, NJ 07102
Diversion Number: (973) 776-1172
Diversion Fax: (973) 776-1166
Jurisdiction: Northern and Central New
Jersey

Atlantic City Resident Office
2111 New Road, Suite 203
Northfield, NJ 08225
Diversion Number: (609) 383-3322
Diversion Fax: (609) 383-0884
Jurisdiction: Atlantic City Area and
Southwestern New Jersey

Camden Resident Office
211 Boulevard Avenue

Maple Shade, NJ 08052
Diversion Number: (856) 321-2439
Diversion Fax: (856) 321-2437
Jurisdiction: Southern New Jersey

New Orleans Division
3838 N Causeway Blvd, Suite 1800
Lakeway III
Metairie, LA 70002
Diversion Number: (504) 840-1100
Diversion Fax: (504) 840-1076
Assistant Special Agent in Charge—Joseph
Shepherd
Jurisdiction: Louisiana and Mississippi

Birmingham Resident Office
920 18th Street North
Birmingham, AL 35203
Diversion Number: (205) 321-8600
Diversion Fax: (205) 321-8599
Jurisdiction: Northern Alabama

Mobile Resident Office
900 Western America Circle, Suite 501
Mobile, AL 36609
Diversion Number: (251) 441-6370
Diversion Fax: (251) 441-5877
Jurisdiction: Southern Alabama

Little Rock District Office
10825 Financial Parkway, Suite 200
Little Rock, AR 72211-3557
Diversion Number: (501) 217-6500
Diversion Fax: (501) 217-6597
Jurisdiction: Arkansas

Gulfport Resident Office
2909 13th Street, Suite 500
Gulfport, MS 39501
Diversion Number: (228) 863-2992
Diversion Fax: (228) 868-3112
Jurisdiction: Mississippi

Jackson District Office
100 W. Capitol Street, Suite 1213
Jackson, MS 39269
Diversion Number: (601) 965-4400

Diversion Fax: (601) 965-4401
Jurisdiction: Mississippi

Philadelphia Division
William J. Green Federal Building
600 Arch Street, Room 10224
Philadelphia, PA 19106
Diversion Number: (215) 238-5160
Diversion Fax: (215) 238-5170
Jurisdiction: Eastern Pennsylvania and
Delaware

Pittsburgh District Office
1781 McKees Rocks Road
Pittsburgh, PA 15136
Diversion and Registration Number: (412)
777-1870
Diversion and Registration Fax: (412)
777-1880
Jurisdiction: Western Pennsylvania (ZIP
codes 150 to 168)

Scranton Resident Office
235 N. Washington Avenue, Room 205
Scranton, PA 18503
Mailing Address:
DEA Scranton RO
P.O. Box 751
Scranton, PA 18501-0751
Diversion Number: (570) 496-1020
Diversion Fax: (570) 496-1025
Jurisdiction: Northeastern Pennsylvania

Phoenix Division
3010 N. 2nd Street, Suite 100
Phoenix, AZ 85012
Diversion Number: (602) 664-5600
Diversion Fax: (602) 664-5820
Assistant Special Agent in Charge—Chris Feistl
Jurisdiction: Northern and Central Arizona

Tucson District Office
6970 S. Palo Verde Road
Tucson, AZ 85756
Diversion Number: (520) 573-5500
Diversion Fax: (520) 573-5632
Jurisdiction: Southern Arizona

St. Louis division
317 South 16th Street
St. Louis, MO 63103
Main Number: (314) 538-4600
Diversion Fax: (314) 538-4622
Jurisdiction: Eastern Missouri and Southern Illinois

Des Moines Resident Office
Federal Building, Room 937
210 Walnut Street
Des Moines, IA 50309
Diversion Number: (515) 284-4709
Diversion Fax: (515) 323-2656
Jurisdiction: Iowa, South Dakota, Moline and Rock Island, Illinois

Kansas City District Office
7600 College Boulevard, Suite 100
Overland Park, KS 66210
Diversion Number: (913) 951-4100
Diversion Fax: (913) 951-3684
Jurisdiction: Kansas, Nebraska, and Western Missouri

San Diego Division
4560 Viewridge Avenue
San Diego, CA 92123-1637
Diversion Number: (858) 616-4100
Diversion Fax: (858) 616-4084
Assistant Special Agent in Charge—Stephan Tomaski
Jurisdiction: San Diego and Imperial Counties

San Francisco Division
450 Golden Gate Avenue, 14th Floor
P.O. Box 36035
San Francisco, CA 94102

San Jose Resident Office
150 Almaden Boulevard, Suite 500
San Jose, CA 95113
Diversion Number: (408) 282-3477
Diversion Fax: (408) 282-3482
Jurisdiction: San Francisco County; Santa Clara County; San Benito County; Santa

Cruz County; San Mateo County; and Monterey County, including the cities of San Francisco and San Jose

Fresno Resident Office
2444 Main Street, Suite 240
Fresno, CA 93721
Diversion Number: (559) 487-5406
Diversion Fax: (559) 487-5428
Jurisdiction: Central California

Oakland Resident Office
1301 Clay Street, Suite 460N
Oakland, CA 94612
Diversion Number: (510) 637-5665
Diversion Fax: (510) 637-5655
Jurisdiction: Alameda, Contra Costa, Del Norte, Humboldt, Mendocino, Sonoma, Marin, Napa, and Lake Counties

Sacramento District Office
4328 Watt Avenue
Sacramento, CA 95821
Diversion Number: (916) 480-7250
Diversion Fax: (916) 480-7248
Jurisdiction: Northern California

Seattle Division
300 5th Avenue, Suite 1300
Seattle, WA 98104
Diversion Number: (206) 553-5990
Diversion Fax: (206) 553-7757
Assistant Special Agent in Charge—Randal Devine
Jurisdiction: Washington

Anchorage District Office
1630 East Tudor Road
Anchorage, AK 99507
Diversion Number: (907) 271-5033
Diversion Fax: (907) 271-3097
Jurisdiction: Alaska

Boise Resident Office
607 North 8th Street, Suite 400
Boise, ID 83702-5518
Diversion Number: (208) 386-2100

Diversion Fax: (208) 334-9253
Jurisdiction: Idaho

Portland District Office
100 SW Main, Suite 500
Portland, OR 97204
Diversion Number: (503) 721-6660
Diversion Fax: (503) 721-6605
Jurisdiction: Oregon

Washington Division
Techworld Plaza
800 K Street, NW, Suite 500
Washington, DC 20001
Diversion Number: (410) 244-3587
Diversion Fax: (202) 305-8355
Assistant Special Agent in Charge—Scott
Masumoto
Jurisdiction: Washington, DC, Southern
Maryland, and Northern Virginia

Baltimore District Office
200 St. Paul Place, Suite 2222
Baltimore, MD 21202-2004
Diversion Number: (410) 244-3581
Diversion Fax: (410) 244-3590
Jurisdiction: Maryland (except Washington,
DC suburbs)

Charleston Resident Office
Union Square
2 Monongalia Street, Suite 300
Charleston, WV 25302
Diversion Number: (304) 347-5209
Diversion Fax: (304) 347-5212
Jurisdiction: West Virginia

Richmond District Office
111 Greencourt Road

Richmond, VA 23228
Diversion Number: (804) 627-6300
Diversion Fax: (804) 627-6352
Jurisdiction: Central and Southern
Virginia

Roanoke Resident Office
105 W. Franklin Road, Suite 3
Roanoke, VA 24011
Diversion Number: (540) 857-2555
Diversion Fax: (540) 857-2569
Jurisdiction: Western Virginia

Caribbean Division
Mailing Address:
P.O. Box 2167
San Juan, PR 00922-2167
Physical Address:
Metro Office Park, Millennium Park Plaza
Building 15 2nd Street, Suite 710
San Juan, PR 00968
Diversion Number: (787) 277-4940
Diversion Fax: (787) 277-6092
Jurisdiction: Northeastern Puerto Rico and
U.S. Virgin Islands

Ponce Resident Office
Mailing Address:
P.O. Box 7449
Ponce, PR 00732-7449
Physical Address:
La Rambla Plaza Tower
606 Tito Castro Avenue, Suite 301
Ponce, PR 00716-0210
Diversion Number: (787) 284-3902 or
284-3905
Diversion Fax: (787) 812-2111
Jurisdiction: Southwestern Puerto Rico

Federal Bureau of Investigation Field Offices

Alabama
FBI Birmingham
1000 18th Street North
Birmingham, AL 35203
(205) 326-6166
FBI Mobile
200 N. Royal Street
Mobile, AL 36602
(251) 438-3674

Alaska
FBI Anchorage
101 East Sixth Avenue
Anchorage, AK 99501-2524
(907) 276-4441

Arizona
FBI Phoenix
21711 N. 7th Street
Phoenix, AZ 85024-5118
(623) 466-1999

Arkansas
FBI Little Rock
24 Shackleford West Boulevard
Little Rock, AR 72211-3755
(501) 221-9100

California
FBI Los Angeles
Suite 1700, FOB
11000 Wilshire Boulevard
Los Angeles, CA 90024-3672

(310) 477-6565
FBI Sacramento
4500 Orange Grove Avenue
Sacramento, CA 95841-4205
(916) 481-9110
FBI San Diego
10385 Vista Sorrento Parkway
San Diego, CA 92121
(858) 320-1800
FBI San Francisco
450 Golden Gate Avenue, 13th Floor
San Francisco, CA 94102-9523
(415) 553-7400

Colorado
FBI Denver
8000 East 36th Avenue
Denver, CO 80238
(303) 629-7171

Connecticut
FBI New Haven
600 State Street
New Haven, CT 06511-6505
(203) 777-6311

District of Columbia
FBI Washington
Washington Metropolitan Field Office
601 4th Street, NW
Washington, D.C. 20535-0002
(202) 278-2000

Florida

FBI Jacksonville
6061 Gate Parkway
Jacksonville, FL 32256
(904) 248-7000
FBI North Miami Beach
16320 Northwest Second Avenue
North Miami Beach, FL 33169-6508
(305) 944-9101
FBI Tampa
5525 West Gray Street
Tampa, FL 33609
(813) 253-1000

Georgia

FBI Atlanta
Suite 400
2635 Century Parkway, NE
Atlanta, GA 30345-3112
(404) 679-9000

Hawaii

FBI Honolulu
91-1300 Enterprise Street
Kapolei, HI 96707
(808) 566-4300

Illinois

FBI Chicago
2111 West Roosevelt Road
Chicago, IL 60608-1128
(312) 421-6700
FBI Springfield
900 East Linton Avenue
Springfield, IL 62703
(217) 522-9675

Indiana

FBI Indianapolis
8825 Nelson B Klein Parkway
Indianapolis, IN 46250
(317) 595-4000

Kentucky

FBI Louisville
12401 Sycamore Station Place
Louisville, KY 40299-6198
(502) 263-6000

Louisiana

FBI New Orleans
2901 Leon C. Simon Drive
New Orleans, LA 70126
(504) 816-3000

Maryland

FBI Baltimore
2600 Lord Baltimore Drive
Baltimore, MD 21244
(410) 265-8080

Massachusetts

FBI Boston
Suite 600
One Center Plaza
Boston, MA 02108
(617) 742-5533

Michigan

FBI Detroit
26th Floor, P. V. McNamara FOB
477 Michigan Avenue
Detroit, MI 48226
(313) 965-2323

Mississippi

FBI Jackson
1220 Echelon Parkway
Jackson, MS 39213
(601) 948-5000

Missouri

FBI Kansas City
1300 Summit
Kansas City, MO 64105-1362
(816) 512-8200

Nebraska

FBI Omaha
4411 South 121st Court
Omaha, NE 68137-2112
(402) 493-8688

Nevada
FBI Las Vegas
John Lawrence Bailey Building
1787 West Lake Mead Boulevard
Las Vegas, NV 89106-2135
(702) 385-1281

New Jersey
FBI Newark
11 Centre Place
Newark, NJ 07102-9889
(973) 792-3000

New Mexico
FBI Albuquerque
4200 Luecking Park Avenue NE
Albuquerque, NM 87107
(505) 889-1300

New York
FBI Albany
200 McCarty Avenue
Albany, NY 12209
(518) 465-7551
FBI New York
26 Federal Plaza, 23rd Floor
New York, NY 10278-0004
(212) 384-1000

North Carolina
FBI Charlotte
7915 Microsoft Way
Charlotte, NC 28273
(704) 672-6100

Ohio
FBI Cincinnati
2012 Ronald Reagan Drive
Cincinnati, OH 45236
(513) 421-4310

Oklahoma
FBI Oklahoma City
3301 West Memorial Drive
Oklahoma City, OK 73134
(405) 290-7770

Oregon
FBI Portland
9109 NE Cascades Parkway
Portland, OR 97220
(503) 224-4181

Pennsylvania
FBI Philadelphia
8th Floor
William J. Green Jr. FOB
600 Arch Street
Philadelphia, PA 19106
(215) 418-4000

Puerto Rico
FBI San Juan
Room 526, U.S. Federal Building
150 Carlos Chardon Avenue
Hato Rey
San Juan, PR 00918-1716
(787) 754-6000

South Carolina
FBI Columbia
151 Westpark Boulevard
Columbia, SC 29210-3857
(803) 551-4200

Tennessee
FBI Knoxville
1501 Dowell Springs Boulevard
Knoxville, TN 37909
(865) 544-0751

Texas
FBI Dallas
One Justice Way
Dallas, Texas 75220
(972) 559-5000
FBI Houston
1 Justice Park Drive
Houston, TX 77092
(713) 693-5000

Utah
FBI Salt Lake City
5425 West Amelia Earhart Drive

Salt Lake City, UT 84116
(801) 579-1400

Virginia
FBI Norfolk
509 Resource Row
Chesapeake, VA 23320
(757) 455-0100

Washington
FBI Seattle

1110 Third Avenue
Seattle, WA 98101-2904
(206) 622-0460

Wisconsin
FBI Milwaukee
Suite 600
330 East Kilbourn Avenue
Milwaukee, WI 53202-6627
(414) 276-4684

Federal Investigative Agencies

Bureau of Alcohol, Tobacco, Firearms, and Explosives

"A unique law enforcement agency in the United States Department of Justice that protects our communities from violent criminals, criminal organization, the illegal use and trafficking of firearms, the illegal use and storage of explosives, acts of arson and bombings, acts of terrorism, and the illegal diversion of alcohol and tobacco products. . . ."

Department of Veterans Affairs (Criminal Investigations Division, Office of the Inspector General)

"The Criminal Investigations Division conducts investigations of criminal activities affecting the programs and operations of VA in an independent and objective manner, and assists the Department in detecting and preventing fraud and other criminal violations. . . ."

Drug Enforcement Administration

"The mission of the Drug Enforcement Agency (DEA) is to enforce the controlled substances laws and regulations of the United States and bring to the criminal and civil justice systems of the United States, or any other competent jurisdiction, those organizations, and principal members of organizations, involved in the growing, manufacture, or distribution of controlled substances appearing in or destined for illicit traffic in the United States. . . ."

Environmental Protection Agency (Office of Inspector General)

"The Office of Inspector General is an independent office within EPA that helps the agency protect the environment in a more efficient and cost effective manner. We perform audits, evaluations, and inspections of EPA and its contractors, to promote economy and efficiency, and to prevent and detect fraud, waste, and abuse. . . ."

Federal Bureau of Investigation

"As a threat-based and intelligence-driven national security organization, the mission of the FBI is to protect and defend the United States against terrorist and foreign intelligence threats, to uphold and enforce the criminal laws of the United States, and to provide leadership and criminal justice services to federal, state, municipal, and international agencies and partners."

Fish and Wildlife Service (Office of Law Enforcement)

"The Office of Law Enforcement investigates wildlife crimes, regulates wildlife trade, helps

Americans understand and obey wildlife protection laws, and works in partnership with international, state, and tribal counterparts to conserve wildlife resources. . . ."

Health and Human Services (Office of Inspector General)

"The mission of the Office of Inspector General (OIG) is to protect the integrity of Department of Health and Human Services (HHS) programs, as well as the health and welfare of the beneficiaries of those programs. The OIG's duties are carried out through a nationwide network of audits, investigations, inspections and other mission-related functions performed by OIG components. . . ."

Immigration and Customs Enforcement

"Immigration and Customs Enforcement is the principle investigative arm of the U.S. Department of Homeland Security (DHS) and the second largest investigative agency in the federal government. . . ."

Internal Revenue Service (Criminal Investigation Division)

"Criminal Investigation (CI) Division serves the American public by investigating potential criminal violations of the Internal Revenue Code and related financial crimes."

U.S. Marshals Service

"The U.S. Marshals Service is the nation's oldest and most versatile federal law enforcement agency. Among their many duties, they apprehend federal fugitives, protect the federal judiciary, operate the Witness Security Program, transport federal prisoners and seize property acquired by criminals through illegal activities. . . ."

U.S. Postal Inspection Service

"The mission of the U.S. Postal Inspection Service is to support and protect the U.S. Postal Service and its employees, infrastructure, and customers; enforce the laws that defend the nation's mail system from illegal or dangerous use. . . ."

U.S. Secret Service

"The mission of the United States Secret Service is to safeguard the nation's financial infrastructure and payment systems to preserve the integrity of the economy, and to protect national leaders, visiting heads of state and government, designated sites and National Special Security Events. . . ."

Immigration and Customs Enforcement Offices

Atlanta Field Office
Area of Responsibility: Georgia, North Carolina, South Carolina
180 Spring Street SW, Suite 522
Atlanta, GA 30303
Phone: (404) 893-1210

Baltimore Field Office
Area of Responsibility: Maryland
31 Hopkins Plaza, 7th Floor
Baltimore, MD 21201
Phone: (410) 637-4000

Boston Field Office
Area of Responsibility: Connecticut, Maine, Massachusetts, New Hampshire, Rhode Island, Vermont
10 New England Executive Park
Burlington, MA 01803
Phone: (781) 359-7500

Buffalo Field Office
Area of Responsibility: Upstate New York
130 Delaware Avenue
Buffalo, NY 14202
Phone: (716) 843-7600

Chicago Field Office
Area of Responsibility: Illinois, Indiana, Wisconsin, Missouri, Kentucky, Kansas
101 West Congress Parkway, 4th Floor
Chicago, Illinois 60605
Phone: (312) 347-2400

Dallas Field Office
Area of Responsibility: North Texas, Oklahoma
8101 N. Stemmons Freeway
Dallas, TX 75247
Phone: (214) 424-7800

Denver Field Office
Area of Responsibility: Colorado, Wyoming
12445 E. Caley Avenue
Centennial, CO 80111
Phone: (720) 873-2899

Detroit Field Office
Area of Responsibility: Michigan, Ohio
333 Mt. Elliott Street
Detroit, MI 48207
Phone: (313) 568-6049

El Paso Field Office
Area of Responsibility: West Texas, New Mexico
1545 Hawkins Boulevard
El Paso, TX 79925
Phone: (915) 225-1901/1941

Houston Field Office
Area of Responsibility: Southeast Texas
126 Northpoint Drive
Houston, TX 77060

Los Angeles Field Office
Area of Responsibility: Los Angeles Metropolitan Area (Counties of Los Angeles,

Orange, Riverside, and San Bernardino) and
Central Coast (Counties of Ventura, Santa
Barbara, and San Luis Obispo)
300 North Los Angeles Street, Room 7631A
Los Angeles, CA 90012

Miami Field Office
Area of Responsibility: Florida, Puerto
Rico, U.S. Virgin Islands
865 SW 78th Avenue, Suite 101
Plantation, FL 33324
Phone: (954) 236-4900

Newark Field Office
Area of Responsibility: New Jersey
614 Frelinghuysen Avenue, 3rd Floor
Newark, NJ 07112
Phone: (973) 645-3666

New Orleans Field Office
Area of Responsibility: Alabama, Arkansas,
Louisiana, Mississippi, Tennessee
1250 Poydras Suite 325
New Orleans, LA 70113
Phone: (504) 599-7800

New York Field Office
Area of Responsibility: The five boroughs
(counties of NYC) and the following
counties: Duchess, Nassau, Putnam, Suffolk,
Sullivan, Orange, Rockland, Ulster, and
Westchester
26 Federal Plaza
9th Floor, Suite 9-110
New York, NY 10278
Phone: (212) 264-4213

Philadelphia Field Office
Area of Responsibility: Delaware,
Pennsylvania, West Virginia
1600 Callowhill Street, 6th Floor
Philadelphia, PA 19130
Phone: (215) 656-7164

Phoenix Field Office
Area of Responsibility: Arizona
2035 N. Central Avenue
Phoenix, AZ 85004
Phone: (602) 766-7030

Salt Lake City Field Office
Area of Responsibility: Utah, Idaho,
Montana, Nevada
2975 Decker Lake Drive, Suite 100
W. Valley City, UT 84119-6096
Phone: (801) 886-7400

San Antonio Field Office
Area of Responsibility: Central
South Texas
1777 NE Loop 410, Suite 1500
San Antonio, TX 78217
Phone: (210) 967-7012

San Diego Field Office
Area of Responsibility: San Diego and
Imperial County
880 Front Street, Suite 2232
San Diego, CA 92101
Phone: (619) 557-6343

San Francisco Field Office
Area of Responsibility: Northern California,
Hawaii, Guam
630 Sansome Street, Rm 590
San Francisco, CA 94111
Phone: (415) 844-5512

Seattle Field Office
Area of Responsibility: Alaska, Oregon,
Washington
12500 Tukwila International Boulevard
Seattle, WA 98168
Phone: (206) 835-0650

St Paul Field Office
Area of Responsibility: Iowa,
Minnesota, Nebraska, North Dakota,
South Dakota
2901 Metro Drive., Suite 100
Bloomington, MN 55425
Phone: (952) 853-2550

Washington, DC Field Office
Area of Responsibility: District of Columbia
and Virginia
2675 Prosperity Avenue, 3rd Floor
Fairfax, VA 20598-5216
Phone: (703) 285-6200

Private Investigator State Licensing Boards

Alabama
License not required.

Alaska
License not required.

Arizona
Dept. of Public Safety, Licensing Division
P.O. Box 6328
Phoenix, AZ 85005
(602) 223-2361

Arkansas
Arkansas Board of Private Investigators and
Private Security Agencies
1 State Police Plaza Drive
Little Rock, Arkansas 72209
(501) 618-8600

California
Licensing Division, Bureau of Security and
Investigative Services
400 R Street
Sacramento, CA 95814
(800) 952-5210

Colorado
The Office of Private Investigator Voluntary
Licensure
Colorado Department of Regulatory
Agencies
1560 Broadway, Suite 1550
Denver, CO 80202
(303) 894-7855

Connecticut
Department of Public Safety, Division of
State Police
294 Colony Street
Meriden, CT 06450-2098

Delaware
Detective Licensing, Delaware State Police
P.O. Box 430
Dover, DE 19903
(302) 672-5304

District of Columbia
Security Officers Management Branch,
Metro Police Security, Unit 2000 14th
Street NW
Washington, DC 20009
(202) 671-0500

Florida
Florida Department of Agriculture and
Consumer Services
Division of Licensing, Bureau of License
Issuance
P.O. Box 6687
Tallahassee, FL 32314-6687
(850) 488-5381

Georgia
State Board of Private Security
Agencies
237 Coliseum Drive
Macon, GA 31217-3858
(478) 207-1460

Hawaii
Board of Private Detectives and Guards
DCCA, PVL, Licensing Branch
1010 Richards Street
P.O. Box 3469
Honolulu, HI 96801
(808) 586-3000 or (808) 586-2701

Idaho
License not required.

Illinois
Illinois Department of Professional
Regulation
320 West Washington Street, 3rd Floor
Springfield, IL 62786

Indiana
Private Detective Licensing Board
100 N. Senate Avenue, Room 1021
Indiana Government Center North
Indianapolis, IN 46204-2246
(317) 232-2980

Iowa
Administrative Services Division, Iowa
Department of Public Safety
Wallace State Office Bldg.
Des Moines, IA 50319
(515) 725-6230

Kansas
Office of Kansas Attorney General, Private
Detective Licensing Unit
1620 SW 10th Avenue
Topeka, KS 66612
(785) 296-4240

Kentucky
Kentucky Board of Licensure for Private
Investigators
PO Box 1360
Frankfort, KY 40602

Louisiana
LSBPIE

2051 Silverside Drive, Suite 190
Baton Rouge, LA 70808

Maine
State Police Licensing Division
State House Station, #164
Augusta, ME 04333
(207) 624-7216

Maryland
Maryland State Police, PI Licensing Division
Jessup, MD
(410) 653-4500

Massachusetts
Massachusetts State Police
Special Licensing Unit
485 Maple Street
Danvers, MA 01923
(978) 538-6128
Fax: (978) 538-6021

Michigan
Department of Consumer and Industry
Services
P.O. Box 30018
Lansing, Michigan 48909
(517) 241-5645

Minnesota
Department of Public Safety
Private Detective and Protective Agent
Services Board
445 Minnesota
St. Paul, MN 55101
(651) 793-2666

Mississippi
License not required.

Missouri
Missouri Board of Private Investigator
Examiners
P.O. Box 1335
Jefferson City, MO 65102
(573) 522-7744

Montana

Board of Private Security Patrol Officers
and Investigators
301 S Park, Room 430
PO Box 200513
Helena, MT 59620-0513
(406) 841-2387
Fax: (406) 841-2309

Nebraska

Secretary of State
State Capitol, Suite 2300
Lincoln, NE 68509
(402) 471-2554

Nevada

Private Investigator's Licensing Board
3476 Executive Pointe Way, Suite 14
Carson City, NV 89706
(775) 687-3223

New Hampshire

New Hampshire State Police
Division of Licenses and Permits
Hazen Drive
Concord, NH 03305
(603) 271-3575

New Jersey

New Jersey State Police
Department of Law and Public Safety
Private Detective Unit
P.O. Box 7068
W. Trenton, NJ 08688-0068
(609) 633-9352

New Mexico

Bureau of Private Investigators
P.O. Box 25101
Santa Fe, NM 87504
(505) 476-7080

New York

Department of State
Division of Licensing Services
84 Holland Avenue
Albany, NY 12208-3490

North Carolina

Private Protective Services Board
1631 Midtown Place, Suite 104
Raleigh, NC 27609
(919) 875-3611
Fax: (919) 875-3609

North Dakota

Private Investigative and Security Board
P.O. Box 7026
Bismarck, ND 58505
(701) 222-3063

Ohio

Divison of Homeland Security/PI/SG Unit
1970 W. Broad Street
Columbus, OH 43223
(614) 466-4130
Fax: (614) 752-6380

Oklahoma

Council on Law Enforcement Education
and Training
Private Security Division
P.O. Box 11476, Cimarron Station
Oklahoma City, OK 73136-0476
(405) 239-5110

Oregon

Department of Public Safety Standards and
Training
4190 Aumsville Hwy SE
Salem, Oregon 97317
(503) 378-8531
Fax: (503) 378-4600

Pennsylvania

Information not available.

Puerto Rico

Policia De Puerto Rico
GPO Box 70166
San Juan, PR 00936
(787) 793-1234

Rhode Island

License not required.

South Carolina
State Law Enforcement Division
Regulatory Services
P.O. Box 21398
Columbia, SC 29221-1398
(803) 896-7015
Fax: (803) 896-7041

South Dakota
License not required.

Tennessee
Department of Commerce and Insurance
Private Protective Services Division
500 James Robertson Parkway
Nashville, TN 37243-1158
(615) 741-6382

Texas
Texas Commission on Private Security
4930 S. Congress, Suite C-305
Austin, TX 78745
P.O. Box 13509
Austin, TX 78711
(512) 463-5545
Fax: (512) 452-2307

Utah
Department of Public Safety and Law
Enforcement Services
Bureau of Regulatory Licensing
4501 South 2700 West
Salt Lake City, UT 84119
(801) 965-4544

Vermont
Board of Private Investigative and Armed
Security Services
Office of Professional Regulation
109 State Street
Montpelier, VT 05609-1101
(802) 828-2837

Virginia
Department of Criminal Justice Services
Private Security Section
P.O. Box 10110
Richmond, Virginia 23240-9998
(804) 786-4700

Washington
Department of Licensing, Public
Protection Unit
405 Black Lake Boulevard
P.O. Box 9649
Olympia, WA 98507-9649

West Virginia
Secretary of State
Licensing Division
Private Investigator Licensing
Charleston, WV 25301

Wisconsin
Department of Regulation and Licensing
P.O. Box 8935
Madison, WI 53708
(608) 266-0829

Wyoming
Regulated by jurisdictions.

U.S. Fish and Wildlife Service Law Enforcement Offices

Region 1
P.O. Box 9
Sherwood, OR 97140-0009
(503) 521-5300
Oregon, Washington, Idaho, Nevada,
California, Hawai'i, Guam, American
Samoa, Northern Mariana Islands

Region 2
P.O. Box 329,
Albuquerque, NM 87103
(505) 248-7889
Arizona, New Mexico, Oklahoma,
and Texas

Region 3
Bishop Henry Whipple Federal Building
P.O. Box 45
Fort Snelling, MN 55111-4056
(612) 713-5320
Illinois, Indiana, Iowa, Minnesota,
Missouri, Ohio, Michigan, and Wisconsin

Region 4
P.O. Box 49226
Atlanta, GA 30359
(404) 679-7057
Alabama, Arkansas, Florida, Georgia,
Kentucky, Louisiana, Mississippi,
North Carolina, South Carolina,
Tennessee, Puerto Rico, and the Virgin
Islands

Region 5
300 Westgate Center Drive
Hadley, MA 01035-0779
(413) 253-8274
Connecticut, Delaware, District
of Columbia, Maine, Maryland,
Massachusetts, New Hampshire, New
Jersey, New York, Pennsylvania, Rhode
Island, Vermont, Virginia, and West Virginia

Region 6
P.O. Box 25486-DFC
Denver, CO 80225
(303) 236-7540
Colorado, Kansas, Montana, Nebraska, North
Dakota, South Dakota, Utah, and Wyoming

Region 7
P.O. Box 92597
Anchorage, AK 99509-2597
(907) 786-3311
Alaska

Region 8
The law enforcement offices located in the
Pacific Southwest region are overseen by the
special agent in charge in Sherwood, Oregon.

Region 9
4401 North Fairfax Drive Central Office
Arlington, VA 22203-3247
(703) 358-1949

U.S. Marshals Service

Northern District of Alabama (N/AL)
1729 N. 5th Avenue, Room 240
Birmingham, AL 35203
(205) 776-6200

Middle District of Alabama (M/AL)
Frank M. Johnson Federal Building
15 Lee Street, Room 224
Montgomery, AL 36104
(334) 223-7401

Southern District of Alabama (S/AL)
U.S. Courthouse
113 St. Joseph Street, Room 413
Mobile, AL 36602
(251) 690-2841

District of Alaska (D/AK)
U.S. Courthouse
222 W. 7th Avenue, Room 189
Anchorage, AK 99513
(907) 271-5154

District of Arizona (D/AZ)
U.S. Courthouse
401 W. Washington Street, SPC 64,
Suite 270
Phoenix, AZ 85003-2159
(602) 382-8768

Eastern District of Arkansas (E/AR)
U.S. Courthouse
600 W. Capitol Avenue, Room A328

Little Rock, AR 72201
(501) 324-6256

Western District of Arkansas (W/AR)
Judge Isaac C. Parker Federal Building
30 S. 6th Street, Room 243
Fort Smith, AR 72901
(479) 424-5000

Northern District of California (N/CA)
U.S. Courthouse/Phillip Burton Building
450 Golden Gate Avenue, Room 20-6888
San Francisco, CA 94102
(415) 436-7677

Eastern District of California (E/CA)
U.S. Courthouse
501 I Street
Sacramento, CA 95814
(916) 930-2030

Central District of California (C/CA)
U.S. Courthouse
312 N. Spring Street, Room G-23
Los Angeles, CA 90012
(213) 894-6820

Southern District of California (S/CA)
U.S. Courthouse Annex
333 W. Broadway, Suite 100 (Plaza)
San Diego, CA 92101
(619) 557-6620

District of Colorado (D/CO)
U.S. Courthouse
901 19th Street, 3rd Floor
Denver, CO 80294
(303) 335-3400

District of Connecticut (D/CT)
U.S. Courthouse
141 Church Street, Room 323
New Haven, CT 06510
(203) 773-2107

U.S. Courthouse
3rd and Constitution Avenue, NW,
Room 1103
Washington, DC 20001
(202) 353-0600

District of Columbia (Superior Court)
H. Carl Moultrie Courthouse
500 Indiana Avenue, NW, Room C-250
Washington, DC 20001
(202) 616-8600

District of Delaware (D/DE)
U.S. Courthouse
844 King Street, Room 4311
Wilmington, DE 19801
(302) 573-6176

Northern District of Florida (N/FL)
U.S. Courthouse
111 N. Adams Street, Room 277
Tallahassee, FL 32301
(850) 942-8400

Middle District of Florida (M/FL)
U.S. Courthouse
801 N. Florida Avenue, 4th Floor
Tampa, FL 33602-4519
(813) 483-4200

Southern District of Florida (S/FL)
Federal Courthouse Square
400 N. Miami Avenue, 6th Floor
Miami, FL 33128
(786) 433-6340

Northern District of Georgia (N/GA)
Federal Building
75 Spring Street, SW, Room 1669
Atlanta, GA 30303
(404) 331-6833

Middle District of Georgia (M/GA)
U.S. Courthouse
3rd and Mulberry Street, Room 101
Macon, GA 31201
(478) 752-8280

Southern District of Georgia (S/GA)
U.S. Courthouse
125 Bull Street, Room 333
Savannah, GA 31401
(912) 652-4212

District of Guam (D/GU)
344 U.S. Courthouse
520 West Soledad Avenue
Hagatna, Guam 96910
011-671-477-7827

District of Hawaii (D/HI)
U.S. Courthouse
300 Ala Moana Boulevard,
Room C-103
Honolulu, HI 96850
(808) 541-3000

District of Idaho (D/ID)
U.S. Courthouse
550 W. Fort Street, MSC-10, Room 777
Boise, ID 83724
(208) 334-1298

Northern District of Illinois (N/IL)
219 S. Dearborn Street, Room 2444
Chicago, IL 60604
(312) 353-5290

Central District of Illinois (C/IL)
600 E. Monroe Street, Room 333
Springfield, IL 62701
(217) 492-4430

Southern District of Illinois (S/IL)
U.S. Courthouse
750 Missouri Avenue, Room 127
East St. Louis, IL 62201
(618) 482-9336

Northern District of Indiana (N/IN)
Federal Building
204 S. Main Street, Room 233
South Bend, IN 46601
(574) 236-8291

Southern District of Indiana (S/IN)
U.S. Courthouse
46 E. Ohio Street, Room 179
Indianapolis, IN 46204
(317) 226-6566

Northern District of Iowa (N/IA)
111 7th Avenue, SE Box 7
Cedar Rapids, IA 52401
(319) 362-4411

Southern District of Iowa (S/IA)
U.S. Courthouse
123 E. Walnut Street, Room 208
Des Moines, IA 50309
(515) 284-6240

District of Kansas (D/KS)
Robert Dole Federal Courthouse
500 State Avenue, Suite G-22
Kansas City, KS 66101
(913) 551-6727

Eastern District of Kentucky (E/KY)
Federal Building
Barr and Limestone Streets, Room 162
Lexington, KY 40507
(859) 233-2513

Western District of Kentucky (W/KY)
U.S. Courthouse
601 W. Broadway, Room 162
Louisville, KY 40202
(502) 588-8000

Eastern District of Louisiana (E/LA)
U.S. Courthouse
500 Camp Street, Room C-600
New Orleans, LA 70130
(504) 589-6079

Middle District of Louisiana (M/LA)
U.S. Courthouse
777 Florida Street, Room G-48
Baton Rouge, LA 70801
(225) 389-0364

Western District of Louisiana (W/LA)
U.S. Courthouse
300 Fannin Street, Suite 1202
Shreveport, LA 71101
(318) 676-4200

District of Maine (D/ME)
156 Federal Street, 1st Floor
Portland, ME 04101
(207) 780-3355

District of Maryland (D/MD)
U.S. Courthouse
101 W. Lombard Street, Room 605
Baltimore, MD 21201
(410) 962-2220

District of Massachusetts (D/MA)
John Joseph Moakley Courthouse
1 Courthouse Way, Suite 1-500
Boston, MA 02210
(617) 748-2500

Eastern District of Michigan (E/MI)
U.S. Courthouse
231 W. Lafayette Street, Suite 300
Detroit, MI 48226
(313) 234-5600

Western District of Michigan (W/MI)
744 Federal Building
110 Michigan Street NW
Grand Rapids, MI 49503
(616) 456-2438

District of Minnesota (D/MN)
U.S. Courthouse
300 South Fourth Street
Minneapolis, MN 55415
(612) 664-5900

Northern District of Mississippi (N/MS)
Federal Building
911 Jackson Avenue, Room 348
Oxford, MS 38655
(662) 234-6661

Southern District of Mississippi (S/MS)
Jackson Federal Courthouse
501 E. Court Street, Suite 1.150
Jackson, MS 39201
(601) 608-6800

Eastern District of Missouri (E/MO)
Thomas Eagleton Courthouse
111 S. 10th Street, Room 2.319
St. Louis, MO 63102-1116
(314) 539-2212

Western District of Missouri (W/MO)
U.S. Courthouse
400 E. 9th St., Room 3740
Kansas City, MO 64106
(816) 512-2000

District of Montana (D/MT)
2601 2nd Avenue North, Suite 2300
Billings, MT 59101
(406) 247-7030

District of Nebraska (D/NE)
Roman L. Hruska—United States
Courthouse
111 South 18th Plaza, Suite B06
Omaha, NE 68102
(402) 221-4781

District of Nevada (D/NV)
U.S. Courthouse
300 Las Vegas Boulevard S., Room 448
Las Vegas, NV 89101
(702) 388-6355

District of New Hampshire (D/NH)
Federal Building
55 Pleasant Street, Room 409
Concord, NH 03301
(603) 225-1632

District of New Jersey (D/NJ)
U.S. Courthouse
50 Walnut Street
Newark, NJ 07102
(973) 645-2404

District of New Mexico (D/NM)
U.S. Courthouse
333 Lomas Boulevard, NW, Suite 180
Albuquerque, NM 87101
(505) 346-6400

Northern District of New York (N/NY)
100 S. Clinton Street
Syracuse, NY 13261
(315) 473-7601

Eastern District of New York (E/NY)
U.S. Courthouse
225 Cadman Plaza
Brooklyn, NY 11201
(718) 260-0400

Southern District of New York (S/NY)
500 Pearl Street
Suite 400
New York, NY 10007
(212) 331-7200

Western District of New York (W/NY)
2 Niagara Square
Buffalo, NY 14202
(716) 348-5300

Eastern District of North Carolina (E/NC)
Federal Building
310 New Bern Avenue, Room 744
Raleigh, NC 27611
(919) 856-4153

Middle District of North Carolina (M/NC)
U.S. Courthouse
324 W. Market Street, Room 234
Greensboro, NC 27401
(336) 332-8700

Western District of North Carolina (W/NC)
401 West Trade Street
Charlotte, NC 28202
(704) 350-8000

District of North Dakota (D/ND)
Old Federal Building
655 1st Avenue N., Room 317
Fargo, ND 58108
(701) 297-7300

District of the Northern Mariana Islands (D/NMI)
U.S. Courthouse—Horiguchi Federal Building
P.O. Box 500570, Garapan Village
Beach Road
Saipan, MP 96950
(670) 236-2954

Northern District of Ohio (N/OH)
U.S. Courthouse
801 West Superior Avenue, Suite 1200
Cleveland, OH 44113
(216) 522-2150

Southern District of Ohio (S/OH)
U.S. Courthouse
85 Marconi Boulevard, Room 460
Columbus, OH 43215
(614) 469-5540

Northern District of Oklahoma (N/OK)
U.S. Courthouse
333 W. 4th Street, Room 4557
Tulsa, OK 74103
(918) 581-7738

Eastern District of Oklahoma (E/OK)
U.S. Courthouse
111 N. 5th Street, Room 136

Muskogee, OK 74401
(918) 687-2523

Western District of Oklahoma (W/OK)
U.S. Courthouse
200 N.W. 4th Street, Room 2418
Oklahoma City, OK 73102
(405) 231-4206

District of Oregon (D/OR)
Mark O. Hatfield U.S. Courthouse
1000 S.W. 3rd Avenue, Room 401
Portland, OR 97204
(503) 326-2209

Eastern District of Pennsylvania (E/PA)
U.S. Courthouse
601 Market Street, Room 2110
Philadelphia, PA 19106
(215) 597-7273

Middle District of Pennsylvania (M/PA)
Federal Building
Washington Avenue and Linden Street, Room 231
Scranton, PA 18501
(570) 346-7277

Western District of Pennsylvania (W/PA)
U.S. Courthouse
700 Grant Street, Suite 2360
Pittsburgh, PA 15219
(412) 644-3351

District of Puerto Rico (D/PR)
Federal Building
150 Carlos Chardon Avenue, Room 200
Hato Rey, PR 00918
(787) 766-6000

District of Rhode Island (D/RI)
2 Exchange Terrace
Providence, RI 02903
(401) 528-5300

District of South Carolina (D/SC)
U.S. Courthouse

901 Richland Street, Suite 1300
Columbia, SC 29201
(803) 765-5821

District of South Dakota (D/SD)
Federal Building
400 S. Phillips Avenue
Room 216
Sioux Falls, SD 57104
(605) 330-4351

Eastern District of Tennessee (E/TN)
Eastern District of Tennessee
Federal Building
800 Market Street, Suite 2-3107
Knoxville, TN 37902
(865) 545-4182

Middle District of Tennessee (M/TN)
Estes Kefauver Federal Building
110 9th Avenue S., Room A750
Nashville, TN 37203
(615) 736-5417

Western District of Tennessee (W/TN)
Federal Building
167 N. Main Street, Room 1029
Memphis, TN 38103
(901) 544-3304

Northern District of Texas (N/TX)
Federal Building
1100 Commerce Street, Room 16F47
Dallas, TX 75242
(214) 767-0836

Eastern District of Texas (E/TX)
U.S. Court House
211 West Ferguson St.
Tyler, TX 75702
(903) 590-1370

Southern District of Texas (S/TX)
U.S. Courthouse
515 Rusk Avenue, Room 10130
Houston, TX 77002
(713) 718-4800

Western District of Texas (W/TX)
U.S. Courthouse
655 E. Durango Boulevard, Room 235
San Antonio, TX 78206
(210) 472-6540

District of Utah (D/UT)
U.S. Post Office & Courthouse
350 S. Main Street, Room B-20
Salt Lake City, UT 84101
(801) 524-5693

District of Vermont (D/VT)
11 Elmwood Avenue, Suite 601
Burlington, VT 05401
(802) 951-6271

District of the Virgin Islands (D/VI)
U.S. Courthouse
Veteran's Drive, Room 371
St. Thomas, VI 00801
(340) 774-2743

Eastern District of Virginia (E/VA)
CDUSM: John O. Bolen
401 Courthouse Square
Alexandria, VA 22314
(703) 837-5500

Western District of Virginia (W/VA)
247 Federal Building
210 Franklin Road SW
Roanoke, VA 24009
(540) 857-2230

Eastern District of Washington (E/WA)
U.S. Courthouse
920 W. Riverside Avenue, Room 888
Spokane, WA 99201
(509) 368-3600

Western District of Washington (W/WA)
700 Stewart Street, Suite 9000
Seattle, WA 98101-1271
(206) 370-8600

Northern District of West Virginia (N/WV)
U.S. Courthouse
500 W. Pike Street
P.O. Box 2807
Clarksburg, WV 26302
(304) 623-0486

Southern District of West Virginia (S/WV)
300 Virginia Street East, Suite 3602
Charleston, WV 25301
(304) 347-5136

Eastern District of Wisconsin (E/WI)
U.S. Courthouse
517 E. Wisconsin Avenue, Suite 38

Milwaukee, WI 53202
(414) 297-3707

Western District of Wisconsin (W/WI)
U.S. Courthouse
120 N. Henry Street, Room 440
Madison, WI 53703
(608) 661-8300

District of Wyoming (D/WY)
Joseph C. O'Mahoney Federal Center
2120 Capitol Avenue, Room 2124
Cheyenne, WY 82001
(307) 772-2196

U.S. Secret Service Offices

Alabama
Birmingham (205) 731-1144
Mobile (251) 441-5851
Montgomery (334) 223-7601

Alaska
Anchorage (907) 271-5148

Arizona
Phoenix (602) 640-5580
Tucson (520) 622-6822

Arkansas
Little Rock (501) 324-6241

California
Fresno (559) 487-5204
Los Angeles (213) 894-4830
Riverside (951) 276-6781
Sacramento (916) 325-5481
San Diego (619) 557-5640
San Francisco (415) 576-1210
San Jose (408) 535-5288
Santa Ana (714) 246-8257
Ventura (805) 383-5745

Colorado
Denver (303) 850-2700

Connecticut
New Haven (203) 865-2449

Delaware
Wilmington (302) 573-6188

District of Columbia
Washington, DC (202) 406-8000

Florida
Fort Myers (239) 334-0660
Jacksonville (904) 296-0133
Miami (305) 863-5000
Orlando (407) 648-6333
Tallahassee (850) 942-9523
Tampa (813) 228-2636
West Palm Beach 561) 659-0184

Georgia
Albany (229) 430-8442
Atlanta (404) 331-6111
Savannah (912) 652-4401

Guam
Hagatna (671) 472-7395

Hawaii
Honolulu (808) 541-1912

Idaho
Boise (208) 334-1403

Illinois
Chicago (312) 353-5431
Springfield (217) 726-8453

Indiana
Indianapolis (317) 635-6420

Iowa
Des Moines (515) 284-4565

Kansas
Wichita (316) 267-1452

Kentucky
Lexington (859) 223-2358
Louisville (502) 582-5171

Louisiana
Baton Rouge (225) 925-5436
New Orleans (504) 841-3260

Maine
Portland (207) 780-3493

Maryland
Baltimore (443) 263-1000

Massachusetts
Boston (617) 565-5640

Michigan
Detroit (313) 226-6400
Grand Rapids (616) 454-4671
Saginaw (989) 497-0580

Minnesota
Minneapolis (612) 348-1800

Mississippi
Jackson (601) 965-4436

Missouri
Kansas City (816) 460-0600
Springfield (417) 864-8340
St. Louis (314) 539-2238

Montana
Billings (406) 245-8585

Nebraska
Omaha (402) 965-9670

Nevada
Las Vegas (702) 868-3000
Reno (775) 784-5354

New Hampshire
Manchester (603) 626-7026

New Jersey
Atlantic City (609) 383-8687
Newark (973) 971-3100
Trenton (609) 989-2008

New Mexico
Albuquerque (505) 248-5290

New York
Albany (518) 436-9600
Buffalo (716) 551-4401
JFK (718) 553-0911
Melville (631) 293-4028
New York City (718) 840-1000
Rochester (585) 232-4160
Syracuse (315) 448-0304
White Plains (914) 682-6300

North Carolina
Charlotte (704) 442-8370
Greensboro (336) 547-4180
Raleigh (919) 790-2834
Wilmington (910) 313-3043

North Dakota
Fargo (701) 239-5070

Ohio
Cincinnati (513) 684-3585
Cleveland (216) 706-4365
Columbus (614) 469-7370
Dayton (937) 222-2013
Toledo (419) 259-6434

Oklahoma
Oklahoma City (405) 272-0630
Tulsa (918) 581-7272

Oregon
Portland (503) 326-2162

Pennsylvania
Harrisburg (717) 234-0214
Philadelphia (215) 861-3300
Pittsburgh 412) 281-7825
Scranton (570) 346-5781

Puerto Rico
San Juan (787) 277-1515

Rhode Island
Providence (401) 331-6456

South Carolina
Charleston (843) 388-0305
Columbia (803) 772-4015
Greenville (864) 233-1490

South Dakota
Sioux Falls (605) 330-4565

Tennessee
Chattanooga (423) 752-5125
Knoxville (865) 545-4627
Memphis (901) 544-0333
Nashville (615) 736-5841

Texas
Austin (512) 916-5103
Dallas (972) 868-3200
El Paso (915) 532-2144
Houston (713) 868-2299
Lubbock (806) 472-7347
McAllen (956) 994-0151
San Antonio (210) 308-6220
Tyler (903) 534-2933
Waco (254) 741-0576

Utah
Salt Lake City (801) 524-5910

Vermont
Burlington (802) 651-4091

Virginia
Norfolk (757) 441-3200
Richmond (804) 592-3086
Roanoke (540) 857-2208

Washington
Seattle (206) 553-1922
Spokane (509) 353-2532

West Virginia
Charleston (304) 347-5188

Wisconsin
Madison (608) 264-5191
Milwaukee (414) 297-3587

Wyoming
Cheyenne (307) 772-2380

Overseas Offices: Listed by Country
Brazil (Brasilia) 011-55-613-312-7523
Bulgaria (Sofia) 011-359-2-939-5646
Canada

Montreal 1-514-939-8400 x2092
Ottawa 1-613-688-5460
Toronto 1-416-640-8661
Vancouver 1-604-689-3011

Colombia (Bogota) 011-571-315-1318
China (Hong Kong) 011-852-2841-2524
France (Paris) 011-331-4312-7100
France (Interpol/Lyon) 011-334-7244-7198
Germany (Frankfurt) 011-49-697-535-3763
Italy Rome 011-390-64-674-2736
Mexico (Mexico City) 011-52-55-5080-2212
Netherlands (Europol/The Hague) 011-3170-353-1533
Romania (Bucharest) 011-40-21-200-3462
Russia (Moscow) 011-7495-728-5093
South Africa (Pretoria) 011-2-712-342-3380
Spain (Madrid) 011-34-91-587-2202
Thailand (Bangkok) 011-662-255-1959
United Kingdom (London) 011-44-20-7894-0846

PEFC Certified

This product is
from sustainably
managed forests
and controlled
sources

www.pefc.org

PEFC/16-33-415

This book is made of chain-of-custody materials; FSC materials for the cover and PEFC materials for the text pages.

#0041 - 190516 - C0 - 235/187/23 - PB - 9780323296120